PC Hardware FAI FAQs

OTHER BOOKS BY STEPHEN J. BIGELOW

Troubleshooting, Maintaining, and Repairing Personal Computers: A Technician's Guide

Troubleshooting and Repairing Computer Monitors, 2d ed.

Troubleshooting and Repairing Computer Printers, 2d ed.

Bigelow's Computer Repair Toolkit

You can find or order any of these books through your local bookstore, or order directly from McGraw-Hill at 800-722-4726. Find McGraw-Hill on the web at: **www.mcgraw-hill.com**

PC Hardware FAT FAQs

Troubleshooting, Upgrading, Maintaining, and Repairing

Stephen J. Bigelow

McGraw-Hill

New York • San Francisco • Washington, D.C. • Auckland • Bogotá
Caracas • Lisbon • London • Madrid • Mexico City • Milan
Montreal • New Delhi • San Juan • Singapore
Sydney • Tokyo • Toronto

McGraw-Hill

*A Division of The **McGraw·Hill** Companies*

1 2 3 4 5 6 7 8 9 0   DOC/DOC   9 0 2 1 0 9 8 7

ISBN 0-07-036939-9

The sponsoring editor for this book was Scott Grillo, the editing supervisor was Scott Amerman, and the production supervisor was Sherri Souffrance. It was set in Sabon by Maya Riddick, freelance designer.

Printed and bound by R.R. Donnelley & Sons Company.

McGraw-Hill books are available at special quantity discounts to use as premiums and sales promotions, or for use in corporate training programs. For more information, please write to Director of Special Sales, McGraw-Hill, 11 West 19th Street, New York, NY 10011. Or contact your local bookstore.

 This book is printed on recycled, acid-free paper containing a minimum of 50% recycled de-inked fiber.

Disclaimer and Cautions

It is IMPORTANT that you read and understand the following information. Please read it carefully!

PERSONAL RISK AND LIMITS OF LIABILITY:

The repair of personal computers and their peripherals involves some amount of personal risk. Use **extreme** caution when working with AC and high-voltage power sources. Every reasonable effort has been made to identify and reduce areas of personal risk. You are instructed to read this book carefully *before* attempting the advice or procedures discussed. If you are uncomfortable following the advice or procedures that are outlined in this book, do NOT attempt them—refer your service to qualified service personnel.

Contents

Preface

Your Questions Answered

No matter how many classes you take, or how many books you read, it always seems like there are questions unanswered. Ever since I started writing, I've been answering questions about all aspects of the personal computer. Folks have asked me to explain just about everything from the inner workings of a CPU to how to solve the toughest troubleshooting nightmares. In all that time, one thing has become clear: there is *no* end of questions when it comes to PCs. As the computer industry continues to evolve by leaps and bounds, there are ever-more questions that need answering.

This book has allowed me to share many of those questions and answers with you. As you read, you'll notice that many answers are up-to-the-minute, and a few can date back several years, but *all* address the most important recurring problems and issues that you've had to grapple with. So whether you fix PCs for a living or just like to tinker in your spare time, you're bound to find a wealth of useful information in the following chapters. So, you have a question of your own? Good. Send it to me:

Stephen J. Bigelow
P.O. Box 282,
Jefferson, MA 01522 USA
sbigelow@cerfnet.com

Or visit me on the web at: **www.dlspubs.com**

Introduction

Going Farther

Before you get started with the book, there are two things I need to cover. First, I've compiled a list of "computing rules" that you should follow. You might call these "computing commandments"; if you follow these rules, your experiences with personal computers should be a lot less stressful. Second, you're going to have many more questions of your own (it's inevitable). Today, the Internet offers a number of useful forums for computer-related questions, so I've also put together a list of news groups (Table I-1) that deal with all manner of PC topics.

BIGELOW'S TIPS FOR TROUBLE-FREE COMPUTING

Drivers are important. Driver problems account for many problems when a PC is upgraded or optimized. Many of the drives, video boards, and other devices in our PCs are *heavily* dependant on drivers, which are relatively small programs that simply tell the operating system how to talk to hardware that is not supported by BIOS. The driver must be the latest version. It must be the proper mode for your operating system (real mode for DOS and Windows 3.1x; protected mode for Windows 95); it must be installed correctly; and it must not conflict with other device drivers loaded in the system.

Go easy on your power supply. Every device and circuit in your PC consumes power, and that power is provided by the power supply. If your PC is demanding more from the supply than it can provide, you may see erratic system behavior or crashes. You may even damage the power supply itself. For small desktop systems with a hard drive, floppy drive, and CD-ROM, a 200 W supply is adequate. Larger desktop and mini-tower systems with several hard drives, one or more CD-ROMs, and other drives like tape drives will typically run 250 W or more. Large tower systems with many drives, lots of memory, and a number of expansion boards will often use 300-W supplies or larger.

Careful with your cabling. It is common for drive cabling to be "unkeyed." This allows for cables to be inserted backward (actually upside-down). While rarely harmful to the drive, it can be a real nuisance during upgrades or repairs. When inserting cable connectors, always look for the faint red or blue stripe along one side of the cable; this always designates the location of pin 1. Make sure that the "pin 1" side of your cable is aligned with pin 1 on your signal connectors.

Check your BIOS versions. Sooner or later you're going to need to know your BIOS version. In many cases, this is because you want to perform a BIOS upgrade, and you need to know the current version first. In other cases, you'll find that your BIOS is buggy or won't support some "latest and greatest" device, and you'll need the BIOS version to identify whether your system is afflicted. You can find the current BIOS version in your display during the first few moments after the system powers up. That's not much time, but it should be enough to jot down the version number. Remember, *never ever* update your BIOS with a version that is not intended for your specific motherboard!

Record your CMOS setup. The CMOS is often the most misunderstood and neglected part of a PC, yet the CMOS RAM contains information that is absolutely vital to the proper startup and operation of your system. Make it a point to record the contents of your CMOS setup. You can do this simply by entering your CMOS Setup routine and taking <PrintScreen> captures of each setup page and printing them out to any local printer. This creates a "hard copy" of your CMOS Setup that you can refer to in the event that your CMOS RAM contents are lost. Remember to keep those screen captures with your system documentation, and take new <PrintScreen> captures whenever you make changes to the CMOS Setup.

Check for viruses. Computer viruses are a fact of life, and with expansive online resources like the Internet, it is easier than ever for viruses to proliferate. Run your virus checker regularly, keep the virus-checking utility current, and always remember to scan newly downloaded programs before running them for the first time.

Keep your boot disk current. We never realize just how much we rely on a hard drive until it fails. When a hard drive goes down, you still must boot the system to have any hope at all of recovering your data; the only way to accomplish this is with a working boot disk. Not only should the boot disk just start the PC, but it should also contain all of the real-mode drivers needed to configure your system for DOS (namely your CD-ROM). Keep a boot disk handy, and update it whenever you add or upgrade system hardware.

Backup, Backup, Backup. It is said that "an ounce of prevention is worth a pound of cure," and this wisdom is certainly not lost on the PC. File recovery techniques are notoriously limited, and only a complete and current copy of your work may save the day if your hard drive fails totally. It doesn't really matter whether you use a tape drive, large removable media drive (like an Iomega Jaz drive), or second hard drive as a backup, so long as you *have* a backup. Remember to keep your backup current.

Invest in Storage. RAM and hard drive space are two resources that we never seem to have enough of. When you're planning a new system purchase, or considering an upgrade, get as much of both as you can afford—the investment will always pay you dividends later on.

TABLE I.1 PC NEWS GROUPS

For Questions on	Post the Message to
Acer users and support	alt.sys.pc-clone.acer
CD-ROM drives	comp.sys.ibm.pc.hardware.cd-rom
Chips, RAM and cache	comp.sys.ibm.pc.hardware.chips
Dell users and support	alt.sys.pc-clone.dell
Gateway users and support	alt.sys.pc-clone.gateway2000
Hardware for sale	misc.forsale.computers.discussion
Home-built PCs	alt.comp.hardware.pc-homebuilt
Laptops and notebooks	comp.sys.laptops
Magnetic drives	comp.sys.ibm.pc.hardware.storage
Memory for sale	misc.forsale.computers.memory
Micron users and support	alt.sys.pc-clone.micron
Modems	comp.sys.ibm.pc.hardware.comm
	comp.dcom.modems

TABLE I.1 PC NEWS GROUPS (CONTINUED)

For Questions on	Post the Message to
Monitors and video cards	comp.sys.ibm.pc.hardware.video
Networking, hardware	comp.sys.ibm.pc.hardware.net-working
Networking, networks	comp.os.netware.* (where * is, announce, connectivity, misc, or security)
	comp.dcom.lans.* (where * is, ethernet, fddi, misc, or token-ring)
	comp.protocols.tcp-ip.ibmpc
	comp.os.os2.networking.misc
	comp.os.os2.networking.tcp-ip
	comp.os.ms-windows.networking.* (where * equals misc, ras, tcp-ip, or windows)
Networking, NSF-based	comp.protocols.nfs
Networking, SMB-based	comp.protocols.smb
Palmtops	comp.sys.palmtops
PCMCIA devices	alt.periphs.pcmcia
PC-specific for sale	misc.forsale.computers.pc-specific.* (where * equals audio, cards.misc, cards.video, misc, motherboards, portables, software, or systems)
Printers	comp.periphs.printers
SCSI devices	comp.periphs.scsi
Servers	comp.dcom.servers
Sound card topics	comp.sys.ibm.pc.soundcard.tech
	comp.sys.ibm.pc.soundcard.advocacy
	comp.sys.ibm.pc.soundcard.games
	comp.sys.ibm.pc.soundcard.music
	comp.sys.ibm.pc.soundcard.misc

TABLE I.1 PC NEWS GROUPS (CONTINUED)

For Questions on	Post the Message to
Other for sale	misc.forsale.computers.other.* (where * equals misc, software, or systems)
Other hardware questions	comp.sys.ibm.pc.hardware.misc
Other peripherals	comp.periphs
Vendors and specific systems	comp.sys.ibm.pc.hardware.systems
Zenith users and support	comp.sys.zenith
Zeos users and support	alt.sys.pc-clone.zeos

System Questions

System questions represent a huge range of
possible topics and information, but this chapter will focus on just a few key areas. The
chapter starts with basic terminology definitions, explores system problems indigenous to
drive controllers, and looks at some system
troubleshooting issues (i.e., system crashes).
This chapter also explores power supply and
battery backup questions. The last part of this
chapter examines a comprehensive selection of
SCSI questions.

Terminology and General Topics

UNDERSTANDING JUMPERS

Q1.   *What is a jumper and how do I use it?*

A.   A *jumper* (Fig. 1.1) has the same function as a switch—it turns
       something on or off. For example, a jumper may determine
       whether or not a color monitor is attached to the system or if a
       hard drive is a master or a slave. If you have to set a jumper, refer
       to your user's manual for the settings—Do *not* change a jumper
       unless you know the correct setting for that jumper.

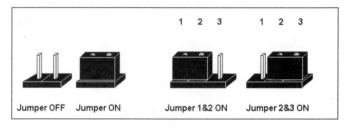

Figure 1.1 Typical jumper configurations

COMPUTER MAKES A SQUEALING NOISE

Q2.   *I get a squealing noise from my computer when I turn it on. Why?*

A.   Squealing sounds are usually caused by mechanical problems—
       things are rubbing together. In most cases, you'll find that a fan
       is failing. Check to be sure that the squealing is *not* being gener-
       ated from your sound board. Once that's out of the way, take a
       look at your CPU fan and power supply fan(s). Make sure all the
       fans are spinning, and see that there is no excess of dust built up
       on the fan blades. If you find the source of the squealing noise,
       replace it.

UNDERSTANDING BIOS

Q3. *I've just started learning about computers, and I'm already con-fused by most of the jargon. I've seen the word BIOS used all over the place, but nothing seems to describe what it is. Can you clarify things?*

A. BIOS stands for basic input/output system. It is a set of *very* important software routines that have been tailored to your spe-cific motherboard and encoded on a permanent memory chip (called a ROM chip) which is mounted on your computer's motherboard. Whenever an operating system (like DOS) or an application program needs to interact with your computer's hard-ware (i.e., saving or recalling a file from your hard drive), it works through an appropriate BIOS routine to accomplish that task. As far as the PC user is concerned, the BIOS is completely transparent—you're not even supposed to know it's there. In addition, the BIOS provides the test routines that check your computer each time it boots up. In fact, a BIOS is *so* important to a computer that if the BIOS is damaged or altered in any unexpected way, your computer may not even start up until the BIOS is replaced.

Traditionally, BIOS instructions on ROM were unchangeable, so to upgrade a BIOS, the physical IC had to be replaced with a new one. Today, BIOS is stored in a sophisticated type of repro-grammable memory chip called flash ROM, and this allows a BIOS to be reprogrammed (or flashed) by downloading and exe-cuting a BIOS update file obtained from the motherboard or computer maker.

THE NEED FOR BIOS UPGRADES

Q4. *I've been working with my Pentium 100 for a while now (and been pretty satisfied with it too), but my cousin told me that I should upgrade my flash BIOS. I've heard of this, but what real-ly is flash BIOS? Should I even worry about upgrading? How much does it cost? How do I use flash BIOS?*

A.   That's a great question—let's start with the basics. Every PC has a BIOS (basic input/output system) which contains the instructions needed to operate most your computer's hardware. For XT, 286, 386, and most 486 systems, the BIOS is permanently recorded onto Read Only Memory (ROM) ICs so that the instructions would be maintained every time PC power was turned off. If you need to change those BIOS ROM ICs, you will literally have to purchase ICs containing updated BIOS programming and then replace the physical BIOS IC on the motherboard. To avoid the problems associated with hands-on BIOS replacement, designers started using a new generation of reprogrammable memory ICs called *flash* ROM. The idea is that you can reprogram your existing BIOS without ever having to replace the physical BIOS IC itself. Flash BIOS has some major advantages over traditional BIOS ROM: Flash BIOS files can be distributed freely over the Internet (so there are no costs for a new IC or shipping), and there are no replacement problems like bent IC pins or system damage from accidental static discharge.

There are two reasons *why* you'd want to upgrade your BIOS: bug fixes and new features. Bug fixes are intended to correct errors somewhere in the BIOS that might crash your PC under the right circumstances. If you're upgrading for new features, that might include support for huge hard drives or support for a non-Intel CPU. Regardless of your reasons, upgrading your BIOS is usually a good thing, but it's not something to be undertaken lightly. Unless you have a clear reason *why* you need an upgrade, it's best to just leave your current BIOS alone. If you do decide to upgrade, make sure that you download the BIOS file that is intended for your *exact* motherboard or system model.

Before you can flash your BIOS, you need to have the updated BIOS file (downloaded from your motherboard or system manufacturer), and you need to know the location of the write-protect jumper on your motherboard. Start by copying the new BIOS files to a bootable floppy disk. Turn the PC off and disable the write protect jumper for your flash BIOS. Boot the system again with that floppy disk in the drive, and allow the flash program to start (if your particular flash program gives you an opportunity to save your current BIOS to a file on the disk, *do it*). Select the option to flash your BIOS, and allow the process to proceed all the way through to completion. It is *critical* that you don't reboot the PC or lose power in the middle of a flash process. This can corrupt your BIOS and render the whole system unbootable until the BIOS IC is replaced.

In most cases, the flash process should finish painlessly, and you'll probably hear several beeps to tell you the flash is finished. You should then shut down the PC, reenable the write-protect jumper, remove the flash disk from the floppy drive, and restart the PC. Flashing the BIOS is really not that hard, but you should *always* refer to the manual for your motherboard or PC for more specific directions or precautions.

FINDING SUPPORT FROM ZEOS

Q5.   *Do you know whatever happened to Zeos? I have a monitor under warranty from them that is now nonfunctional. It seems I recall seeing mention on a mailing list somewhere that Zeos has gone out of business. Would you know if someone else took over their warranty work? Any information would be appreciated.*

A.   Zeos and Micron merged last year, but Zeos operations were shut down shortly after the merger. You can contact remaining Zeos technical support at 800-228-5390, or send an e-mail to *support@zeos.com*. Also, all of the files that were part of the Zeos Web site are now residing at the Micron Web site: *http://www.mei.micron.com.*

DISPOSING OF OLD PCS

Q6.   *I often find myself inheriting old (286 and 386) systems from colleagues and friends who upgrade to newer systems. The problem is that I don't know what to do with this hardware, and I don't have the heart to just toss it all in the dumpster. What can I do with this equipment?*

A.   There is really no limit to the uses of older PCs. Your local church or church group is probably in desperate need of PCs for mailing lists and basic word processing. Schools and vocational institutes are another major consumer of used PCs for computer classes of all sorts. Amateur radio groups and computer users groups often scramble for used equipment. You might also try to sell off working equipment through yard sales and flea markets.

Defining SCSI and ATAPI

Q7.   *Can you tell me what SCSI and ATAPI stand for?*

A.   SCSI means small computer system interface. It is an efficient means of connecting numerous different devices (i.e., hard drives, CD-ROMs, tape drives, and so on) to the same 50- or 68-pin bus so that they can be run by the same controller. This is much easier than driving all kinds of different devices from their own proprietary controllers. SCSI also provides excellent data throughput for good overall performance—particularly in true multitasking systems such as file servers. ATAPI means AT attachment packet interface. This is a specification that defines the device characteristics for an IDE peripheral such as a CD-ROM or tape drive. Basically, any non-hard-drive IDE device must conform to the ATAPI specification in order to operate over the IDE port. ATAPI is roughly the IDE equivalent of SCSI.

SX vs. DX Designations

Q8.   *I'm new to computers, and I've been studying a lot on my own while using a 486 system. I've seen a lot of references to SX and DX can you tell me what these mean? Why aren't those references used with Pentium CPUs? What is DX2 and DX4?*

A.   Prior to the release of the 486 CPU, the CPU and math coprocessor were provided as two different devices. The 486SX (in addition to some other simplifications) also used a separate math coprocessor. The 486DX was the first Intel CPU to incorporate the math coprocessor into the CPU. *All* the 486 designations after that (i.e., 486DX2/50, 486DX4/100, and so on) incorporate an internal math coprocessor. The reason that Pentiums no longer carry that designation is that *all* Pentiums carry math coprocessors, so there is no reason to distinguish the two.

The DX2 and DX4 designations also refer to math coprocessors, but the 2 refers to a clock-doubling CPU, while the 4 refers to a clock-tripling (yes, tripling) CPU. For example, if the motherboard clock frequency is 25 MHz, a 486DX2 would run internally at 50 MHz. If the motherboard clock frequency is 33 MHz, a 486DX4 would run internally at 99 MHz (~100 MHz), and so on.

CHIPSETS AND CODE NAMES

Q9. *Sorry if this is a dumb question, but I am a bit confused, and I am sure that someone can help. Who exactly is Triton? I have seen a vast number of references to the Intel Triton chipset, apparently referring to the Intel 430 (FX, HX, VX) chipsets, but who exactly is Triton?*

A. Once upon a time, Intel used code names to identify their CPU chipsets. Intel's 430FX chipset was often called Triton, the 430HX chipset was called Triton II, and I believe that the 430FX chipset was dubbed *Natoma*. In all cases, the chipsets are indeed manufactured by Intel. However, Intel has adopted a naming policy which abandons the use of names in conjunction with their chipsets— choosing instead to use the designations FX, HX, VX, and so on.

CPU NAME CONFUSION

Q10. *I have some questions, and hope that they do not sound too crazy. First, what is the difference between a 5x86 and a Pentium? Second, what is the difference between a 6x86 and a Pentium? I currently have a 486DX4/100 that I built and want to upgrade it to a new CPU, but I want to get as close to a Pentium as I can.*

A.   With so many CPU versions in the market today, I'm not surprised that you're confused. A 5x86 (both AMD and Cyrix make
CPUs using this name) is basically a souped-up version of a 486
processor that is designed to be pin-compatible with a 486. This
way it can be used on a 486 motherboard—although sometimes
the BIOS needs to be upgraded first. By comparison, a 6x86
(made by IBM and Cyrix) and the AMD K5 CPUs are Pentium-
compatible chips. These are pin-compatible with the Pentium and
must be used in a Pentium-class motherboard (and also may need
a BIOS upgrade).

Given your current system, your least expensive and most trouble-free upgrade would probably be to use a 5x86 so that you
can continue to use your current motherboard. Check with your
motherboard or system manufacturer and determine if a BIOS
upgrade is necessary in order to support the 5x86. If you decide
that you really want a Pentium or K5 CPU—which will yield a
dramatic performance improvement—you'll need to upgrade
your entire motherboard and CPU.

GETTING THE MOST FROM DRIVESPACE

Q11.   *I'm a little unsure about how safe DriveSpace is. I have talked to
a few technicians, and some of them say that it is fine, while the
others say that it is as bad (unreliable) as DoubleSpace. I've
worked on a computer with DriveSpace and it is working well (it
has been for almost 6 months). Any recommendations?*

A.   Generally speaking, drive compression programs are some of the
most reliable and well-tested software ever developed. But compression software does make some unusual demands on a system.
By understanding these demands, you can improve compression's
reliability:

■   If possible, compress a drive with nothing on it except the
files required to make it boot and the files required to support compression. This makes the compression installation
much faster.

■ ScanDisk the drive often. Eventually, sectors of the drive media will fail. If compression software attempts to use these faulty areas, problems will occur. So keep defective sectors checked and marked.

■ Never hit the reset button while the hard drive is reading or writing. If you often lose power, consider a fast battery backup or a UPS.

■ Defragment your drives on a regular basis to keep your compressed volume file contiguous.

■ Check your compression ratios often and adjust them as required.

■ Always leave 5 to 10 percent of your compressed drive empty. Problems can occur if you exhaust the compressed volume.

UNDERSTANDING INTERRUPT PRIORITIES

Q12. *Aren't IRQs prioritized, with IRQ1 being the highest ("sysclk," I think) down to IRQ16 being at the end of the queue for attention? That wouldn't have much of an impact on the mouse I suppose, but wouldn't it be important for other things?*

A.   Yes, interrupts are prioritized with IRQ0 being the *most* important and IRQ15 being the *least* important. (IRQs are numbered 0 to 15.) As you deduced, mission-critical functions (like the system clock) must have access to a high-priority IRQ. Theoretically, the less important devices should utilize higher IRQs. In actual practice, however, almost no devices utilize IRQs for critical timing— they just access the CPU as needed. The result is that you almost *never* notice device performance problems because of poor interrupt choices (after all, we rely on our hard drives, but the primary EIDE channel is assigned to IRQ14). So you're right technically, but it makes little difference in today's PCs because of the noncritical nature of our add-on devices.

INTERMEDIATE

IRQ2 AND AVAILABLE SYSTEM INTERRUPTS

Q13.   *I've heard that I can't use IRQ2 when configuring PC hardware. Is this true?*

A.   Technically, IRQ2 is used to cascade the second programmable interrupt controller (PIC) on AT machines. The IRQ2 line on the old XT bus has been renamed to IRQ9. This has one and only one side effect (from a software point of view): IRQ2 and IRQ9 are perceived as the same interrupt. You can freely use IRQ2 on any hardware device—provided you are not already using IRQ9. Your associated software drivers can be set to IRQ2 or IRQ9, whichever the drivers happen to prefer. Note that many old video cards have an IRQ2 enable jumper. For *very* old backward-compatibility reasons, you should disable this jumper before attempting to use the IRQ for something else.

RUNNING OUT OF IRQs

Q14.   *Is there a relatively inexpensive way to add a video capture board when you have maxed out your IRQs? I have a Pentium PC with CD-ROM drive, printer, external modem, EIDE hard drive, and so on. When I attempt to add a Miro video capture card, my computer says "no way." Is there an alternative other than replacing my IDE CD-ROM and hard drive with SCSI versions?*

A.   Well, no. Once you're out of IRQs, you can't add any new hardware. Your only option is to use a parallel port capture tool like GrabIt from Aims *(www.aimslab.com)*. You *could* go SCSI, but it would probably be much cheaper to take back the Miro and go with a parallel port device.

EKING OUT ANOTHER INTERRUPT

Q15.   *It's a battle to squeeze out another usable IRQ. I have a SuperMicro CMS motherboard with a Western Digital 1.6GB HDD and a Creative Labs 4X IDE CD-ROM drive. I recently installed an SCSI adapter card, so I had to disable my second*

LPT port to free the IRQ. The CD-ROM drive is currently con-nected to my Sound Blaster 16 card. The sound board and its IDE interface are each using an IRQ. Can the CD-ROM drive run as slave to the HDD? Note that the hard drive is set to PIO mode 4.

A.   So you're trying to shut down the sound card's IDE interface. You *might* be able to run the HDD and CD-ROM drives togeth-er on the same channel, but I believe you will have trouble. The data transfer rate for the HDD is so much faster than the CD-ROM, I suspect that the CD-ROM will not be detected properly during system initialization or may cause the HDD to malfunc-tion in PIO mode 4 (forcing you to use PIO mode 3 or an even slower data transfer rate). The only way to avoid that is to install a PIO mode 4-aware CD-ROM drive, but this will mean replac-ing your existing CD-ROM.

Instead, your motherboard probably has a secondary IDE port right on the motherboard (right next to the primary EIDE port). If this port is still active, you would have better luck leaving your fast hard drive where it is and placing the CD-ROM drive on the secondary IDE channel. You can then disable the sound card's IDE interface and free an IRQ for other uses.

UNDERSTANDING THE MEMORY HOLE

Q16.   *I'm configuring a newly built system, and the CMOS Setup makes reference to something called a* memory hole. *What is a memory hole? Should I enable or disable it?*

A.   A memory hole provides performance improvement by reserving certain parts of memory for use by ISA cards. The ISA cards can then be mapped into memory—but they must be mapped some-where under 16MB. The "hole" starts at 16MB minus the hole size, and you can generally select different hole sizes (i.e., 1, 2, or 4MB) through CMOS Setup (Fig. 1.2). The memory hole is usu-ally disabled because there are few ISA cards today that need to be mapped. If you have an ISA card that refuses to function properly in a PC with more than 16MB of RAM, you should enable the memory hole. Start with a 1MB hole and use larger sizes only if the card continues to encounter problems.

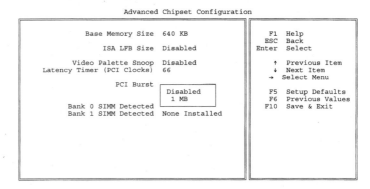

Figure 1.2 Configuring a "memory hole" in the CMOS Setup

486 CACHE SIZES

Q17.   *Can you tell me how big the internal cache of a 486 is?*

A.   *Almost all Intel i486 CPUs use an 8KB internal (or L1) cache. The Intel i486DX4 series uses a 16KB L1 cache.*

486 OPERATING VOLTAGES

Q18.   *I'm working to upgrade a friend's 486 PC, and I'm curious about voltages. Were all of the 486s designed to run at 5V?*

A.   Intel provided both 5- and 3.3-V versions of their i486. The CPU packages that plug into a ZIF socket are typically 5 V versions. The CPU packages that soldered directly to the motherboard are usually 3.3 V versions. The i486DX4 is a bit of a wrinkle since available in both 5- and 3.3-V socketed versions. Generally speaking, you cannot use a 5-V CPU in a 3.3-V socket (because there is no way to boost the voltage to operate the CPU). But you can use a 3.3-V CPU in a 5-V socket *if* you use a voltage regulator to cut down the extra voltage.

Understanding ATX

Q19.   *What is the ATX form factor and how will I know if an ATX motherboard will fit in my current case?*

A.   One of the traditional problems with building and upgrading PCs has been finding a motherboard to fit properly in a case—especially with all the ports and connectors typically found on a motherboard. The ATX form factor is basically a specification that outlines "what goes where" in the PC. This way, you know that an ATX motherboard and power supply will fit in an ATX case. The ATX specification also places requirements for mounting, cooling, and peripheral connections. The ATX specification is available on the Intel Web site at *http://www.intel.com/design/motherbd/atx.htm.* You can find additional ATX information at *http://www.teleport.com/~atx.* As to whether an ATX motherboard will fit in your case, that depends on the case. If your case follows the ATX specifications, an ATX motherboard should fit. Otherwise, don't bet on it.

ATX versus AT Form Factors

Q20.   *My company is getting ready to make a large purchase of PCs, and we are trying to decide whether to go with ATX form factor or AT motherboards. Our trouble is that the only recent information we can find is from the manufacturers like Intel. We would like an unbiased perspective to go on. Can you help?*

A.   The ATX form factor was developed as a way to avoid the confusion of fitting everything together when selecting motherboards, power supplies, and cases. By designing everything to fit the ATX form factor, manufacturers (and PC users) can upgrade a motherboard, power supply, or case and know that everything will fit physically. ATX is a *physical* specification and really has no bearing on just how *well* things work—for example, an ATX motherboard won't necessarily perform better than a Baby AT motherboard. The bottom line here is that if you're looking to upgrade PCs down the road with new motherboards, I'd seriously suggest that you consider ATX form factor systems. If you won't be touching those new systems after they're installed (or would just be replacing the entire systems outright), the choice is really moot.

ATX AND MOTHERBOARD CLOCK LIMITS

Q21.   *I've been researching the ATX motherboard and it seems to have a lot of great qualities—particularly the ability to upgrade and expand, as well as a more sane placement of the "bulky" items in relation to the card slots. However, one thing I read that bothers me is the opinion that because it's a four-layer printed circuit board it will not reliably go past 66 MHz. Is that true?*

A.   I think you're mistaking an ATX motherboard for the ATX form factor. The ATX approach really only defines the physical layout and characteristics of cases and motherboards (and power supplies to a lesser extent), which helps to ensure that ATX components will all fit together properly. However, the ATX specification has no impact on the electrical design of a motherboard—that is up to individual manufacturers. So it is entirely possible that the ATX motherboards you saw were limited to 66 MHz. Many are because 66 MHz is a high speed for the motherboard (remember that you can employ clock multipliers to operate a CPU at 2, 2.5, or 3 times the clock speed. But after you check some other motherboard makers, you'll notice that there are ATX motherboards available that can operate at 75 MHz and a bit higher.

MATCHING NEW MOTHERBOARD DIMENSIONS

Q22.   *I am hoping to upgrade my 486DX 25 MHz to an entry-level Pentium motherboard. The current board appears to be 8.5x12 inches. Several of the new motherboards I am looking at are 8.5x10.5 inches. Is there any way of determining what the dimensions are for the screw and standoff holes on a new motherboard so that I can check it against the current case?*

A. This is probably the most frequent question that I get asked by folks looking to upgrade their motherboard—"how can I tell if the new motherboard will fit"? The answer to your question is It's not easy.

With the development of standard dimensioning like the ATX specification, you know that any ATX motherboard, case, or power supply should all fit together. For older motherboards and cases, however, the choices are not so clean cut.

I usually recommend one of two tactics when choosing a new motherboard. Take the original motherboard with you to the store and compare the boards one on one (just remember to keep the old motherboard in antistatic packaging). A less-risky (but more time-consuming) alternative would be to outline the original motherboard on a large piece of paper, mark the position of each mounting hole, and then take the drawing to the store with you as a template.

As a rule, you should be able to line up a few metal and nylon standoffs. If you find that there are metal standoffs without corresponding holes on the new motherboard, you're going to need to remove the metal standoffs (with luck they'll unscrew from the chassis) or insulate the motherboard from them. As an extra measure of caution, add a thin nonconductive washer between each metal standoff and the motherboard. If you find that nylon standoffs don't line up, you can always snip the tips off the nylon standoffs.

INTERMEDIATE

PROTECTING LAPTOPS FROM THEFT

Q23. *There has been a recent rash of laptop thefts from my company. I also have a laptop of my own that I use at work. How can I protect my laptop PC from theft?*

A. Unfortunately, PCs were never designed with security in mind. In the days of desktop PCs, this was never an issue—it's not hard to spot a guy walking out the door with a desktop PC under his arm. Laptop, notebook, and subnotebook computers are another matter. They are small, light, and easily concealed in such things as brief cases and small shipping boxes. This makes small computers prime targets for unscrupulous people or disgruntled employees.

The easiest way to protect your laptop is to keep it locked up in your desk during lunch, breaks, meetings, or whenever you're not around—this is a habit that takes effort to form, but it's well worth it. If you want to protect the data on your system, there are several options available to you. First, employ the BIOS password on your system. While experienced thieves may know how to defeat the BIOS password, it does throw up a roadblock to most people and will make the laptop very difficult for a thief to resell. If you need even more security, you can purchase file encryption utilities which can encrypt your disk before shutting the system down. Without the proper password, the files cannot be unlocked. Now a thief can still repartition and reformat the disk, but this will wipe out your files and keep your secrets secure. Make sure to have the model and serial number of the laptop in your records so you can pass that information along to law enforcement authorities if necessary.

There are two more notes to consider. First, always keep a current backup of your laptop contents, and store that backup in another physical location. If your PC does disappear, you can at least restore your important data to another system and keep working. Second, few companies will reimburse an employee for personal property lost or stolen from work. If you're using your own PC in the workplace, check to see if the company will cover your loss (get it in writing)—if not, you might demand that the company acquire a PC for you.

TROUBLE OPENING A LAPTOP

Q24. *I'm trying to install a replacement floppy drive in my laptop PC, but I cannot get the bottom cover off. I know that all the screws are out, but the bottom is not loosening. Any ideas?*

A. First, use *patience*—notebooks use "cheap" plastic shells and are pretty unforgiving if they get scratched or gouged—we don't want that. Second, you probably missed a screw or two. Try checking under any labels or "snap-in" compartments. Finally, if you're *absolutely* sure that all the screws are out, but the bottom cover just won't budge, it may be held in place with molded plastic snaps located at intervals around the perimeter of the enclosure. You'll need to take a thin, flexible metal blade (like a ruler) and gently proceed around the perimeter, "unhinging" the bottom cover. Honestly, my money says you missed some screws, so take a careful second look.

MAXIMIZING LAPTOP BATTERY LIFE

Q25.   *I would like to hear your strategies for maximizing laptop battery life. For example, do you keep the laptop plugged in all weekend, nights, and so on? I do not initially plan on buying a spare battery.*

A.   The rule for laptop batteries is generally to run down the battery as much as possible before completing a full recharge, but once recharged, there's no problem with leaving the laptop plugged in to "trickle charge" the battery. The most troublesome aspect of nickel cadmium (or NiCd) batteries is the tendency to step discharge where the battery is regularly discharged to some level and then fully recharged. After a while, the NiCd battery will only be able to provide current down to that "regular" discharge point and no more. This is sometimes referred to as the *memory effect* and can often be cleared by deeply discharging the battery and then recharging it completely (you may have to repeat this through several full cycles). Note that lithium and nickel-metal hydride batteries don't seem to suffer from step discharge effects—at least not to the extent that NiCd batteries do.

COMMENTS ON CPU OVERCLOCKING

Q26.   *I've been reading some news groups and mailing lists recently, and it sounds like I could overclock my CPU for added speed. Before I did that though, I figured I'd check in and see if you had any comments about CPU overclocking.*

A.   Simply stated, overclocking is the practice of running a CPU at a higher clock frequency than it was intended for. Since CPUs are speed-rated in batches, it is possible that some CPUs can tolerate the additional speed and perform a bit faster. But other CPUs will not handle the extra speed. In short, overclocking is a gamble—you're wagering your CPU in exchange for a bit more speed. A side effect of higher clock frequencies is added heat generated by the overclocked CPU. In some cases, the added heat can diminish the CPU's working life. An overclocked/overheated CPU can also suffer from glitches and stalls that can corrupt your data or even crash your system. Although there are many PC users who claim to overclock their CPUs very successfully, it is generally regarded as an unwise practice.

AN OVERVIEW OF OVERCLOCKING

Q27.   *I've recently heard of CPU overclocking—which amounts to changing the clock frequency supplied to the CPU by the motherboard. This is done by changing an oscillator module or jumpers on the motherboard. Any comments about overclocking?*

A.   Yes, I have a comment—don't do it. While it's true that most designs are built with a certain amount of tolerance, there can be some serious consequences for the CPU. The heat generated by a CPU is proportional to its clock speed—overclocking the CPU will overheat its internal connections and shorten its life span. There may also be errors during initialization or operation. For example, a colleague recently tried overclocking, setting a 75 MHz CPU to 100, 120, and 133 MHz. The PC booted at 100 and 120 MHz but wouldn't boot at 133 MHz. He ran it for a while at 100 MHz with no apparent errors—until he saw some incorrect output. Even if an overclocked PC boots up, there is no guarantee that it will run reliably, and the performance increase realized from overclocking is typically marginal (only a few percent).

OVERCLOCKING CAN RESULT IN SYSTEM ERRORS

Q28. *I recently put a new motherboard in my PC—complete with an AMD 5x86 chip. The supplier had set it up to run overclocked at 166 MHz (the chip normally runs at 133 MHz), and I've been experiencing some problems such as Fatal Exception errors, assorted crashes, and so on in Windows 95. I notice that the problems are more frequent after the PC has been on for a while and wonder if you know whether this could be due to the chip becoming too hot. I haven't tried configuring the motherboard for 133 MHz yet since I was made to understand that many overclocking PCs run perfectly.*

A. CPU overclocking continues to be an important topic, and excessive heat from overclocking may *certainly* be at the root of your trouble. Basically, CPUs are rated in terms of batches, so a CPU that runs at 140, 143, 150 MHz, and so on, will usually be marked 133 MHz. A CPU that runs at 170, 175, or 180 MHz, or in that range, will likely be marked as 166 MHz, and so it goes. The problem is that there is no way to tell if your particular 133 MHz CPU will run as high as 166 MHz or not—it might only run up to 135 or 140 or 143 MHz (you get the idea). I doubt your supplier has any way of knowing either. Try setting the clock speed back to 133 MHz. If your problems disappear, you will have found the cause. You should also tell the supplier that if they intentionally clocked that CPU at 166 MHz, they should guarantee that the computer will run reliably at 166 MHz, and give it a warranty for a reasonable period.

INTERMEDIATE

UNDERSTANDING THE DIFFERENT DX4 OVERDRIVES

Q29. *I've been doing some research into 486DX4 OverDrive processors so that I can update my old 486DX PC. I suppose that I could use a Pentium OverDrive, but I really don't want to spend the extra money. It seems like there are two different types of DX4 OverDrives. Is this true? If so, what is the difference between the two?*

A.   You're right—there are two commercial versions of the Intel 486DX4 OverDrive. The two types are designed to upgrade the two different classes of 486-based systems. Parts marked "BOXDX4ODPR" have 168 pins and are designed to upgrade i486DX systems. In most cases, the i486DX processor is simply removed and replaced with the OverDrive chip. These parts use the same jumper settings as the i486DX processor. By comparison, parts marked "BOXDX4ODP" have 169 pins and are designed to upgrade i486SX systems. The majority of such SX systems include a keyed upgrade socket with one extra pinhole to ensure correct orientation of the OverDrive processor. In many cases, this socket may be a separate, empty socket which the OverDrive is installed into, or it may be the same as the i486SX socket. The ODP parts use jumper settings specific to the OverDrive processors and the old i487SX math coprocessors. Both OverDrive variations are available in 75- and 100-MHz versions, and they are designed to upgrade 25- and 33-MHz i486 processors, respectively.

The Intel DX4 OverDrive processors have been discontinued and are no longer available from Intel. Availability is now limited only to existing stock at local dealers, on the Internet, or by mail order.

Note

DIFFERENCES BETWEEN THE PENTIUM 120 AND 133 CPUs

Q30.   *Can you tell me if there is a major difference between an Intel Pentium 120 and an Intel Pentium 133 (besides the obvious 13 MHz difference in clock speed)?*

A.   Generally speaking, you can expect noticeably better performance from a 133-MHz Pentium CPU. Aside from the additional 13 MHz of clock speed, the P120 uses a 60-MHz bus speed, while the P133 uses a 66-MHz bus speed. The PCI bus also jumps from 30 MHz with the P120 to 33 MHz with the P133. Taken together, this can make a significant improvement in the system. The rule of thumb suggests a 10 percent improvement. However, the added performance may not warrant the added cost of the Pentium 133 upgrade.

UNDERSTANDING SIMD

Q31. *I was looking over some MMX documents the other day, and I came across a reference to something called* SIMD. *What is SIMD?*

A. SIMD stands for single instruction, multiple data and it refers to the way in which a CPU operates on data. Traditionally, data is handled serially—one piece at a time. With MMX architecture, the CPU can work on multiple pieces of data at the same time using the 64-bit registers in a Pentium MMX. Typical data sizes that will fill a 64-bit register are defined as eight 8-bit bytes, four 16-bit words, two 32-bit double words, or one 64-bit quad word.

MMX AND OLDER WINDOWS

Q32. *I know that MMX processors are being developed mostly for Windows 95 and NT environments, but will MMX CPUs still work with older Windows versions like 3.1 or 3.11?*

A. Yes, MMX technology is compatible with older versions of Windows, so it should work with no problems. However, few (if any) MMX applications will be written for Windows 3.1x, so if you hope to take full advantage of MMX processors, you should upgrade to a more popular operating system (such as Windows 95), which will have MMX-specific applications available.

TAKING ADVANTAGE OF MMX

Q33. *I've been hearing that you need a new motherboard to handle MMX CPUs, but that's not right—I just installed an MMX CPU in place of my 166-MHz Pentium. The MMX processor just uses extra processor extensions that the chipsets could not care less about, right?*

A. I don't think you know the whole story about MMX. Yes there are 57 or so new instructions for the MMX processors—and these new instructions are independent of the chipset. It is this independence that makes Pentium MMX OverDrive processors possible. The new CPU which you installed *had* to be an OverDrive processor because "true" MMX CPUs also incorporate a number of internal features and enhancements that go far beyond instructions. As a result, you *do* need a new chipset such as the Intel 82430TX in order to take full advantage of a true MMX processor.

Detecting FAT32 and FAT16

Q34.   *I work on a lot of PCs, and I've been starting to see machines with FAT32 coming in for service. Is there a simple way of finding out what FAT an HDD is formatted in (i.e., FAT32 or FAT16)?*

A.   A utility package like Norton Utilities will tell you, but another quick and easy method of checking is to go to DOS, type the command CHKDSK, and press <Enter>. The CHKDSK utility will present a whole suite of information about the hard drive, but look for the number of bytes in each allocation unit. If you see an entry such as;

```
4,096 bytes in each allocation unit
```

the disk is either formatted FAT32 or is a very small hard disk. If the value is anything other than 4096, the disk is formatted FAT16. As an alternative, you can also use FDISK. Go to a DOS prompt and type FDISK and then go to the option called Display Partition Information. One of the parameters will show which FAT the disk has been partitioned with.

BIOS and Alternative Processors

Q35.   *I heard that you need a new BIOS before you can use an AMD or Cyrix CPU. Is this true? Why?*

A.   You probably only heard half of the truth. Most BIOS is written around Intel CPUs because Intel is the world's leading maker of CPUs, and their CPUs typically lead the PC industry in speed and performance. Companies such as AMD and Cyrix often cannot release compatible products simultaneously, and sometimes, there are subtle differences (such as CPU IDs) between Intel, AMD, and Cyrix CPUs that must be accounted for in BIOS. As a result, there are some BIOS versions that were released before competitive CPUs were available, and therefore they do not support similar AMD or Cyrix CPUs without a BIOS upgrade. Before selecting a non-Intel CPU, check with your motherboard or system manufacturer to see if there are any later BIOS revisions necessary to accommodate AMD or Cyrix.

DUAL CPU VOLTAGES

Q36.   *What is dual I/O and CORE voltage? Don't CPUs require one voltage?*

A.   You're probably referring to the new generation of Intel Pentium processors with MMX support. These CPUs use two different voltages. The main logic parts of the CPU use 2.8 V, while the I/O parts of the CPU (the circuits that allow the CPU to exchange signals with the motherboard) continue to use 3.3 V. The lower core voltage reduces the CPU's power demands and allows it to run cooler. Your motherboard must be capable of providing this "split plane" voltage to the CPU, or you will need a specially designed voltage regulator socket between the CPU and motherboard.

DROPPING IN THE K6

Q37.   *I've heard that I can just drop a new K6 CPU into my Pentium MMX motherboard, and according to AMD, the motherboard should still work even if the motherboard doesn't know that it is a K6 chip in there. Why doesn't that sound right?*

ADVANCED

A.   Well I can't speak for AMD, but it's been my experience that CPUs never work in a vacuum—the motherboard *must* know which CPU is in the system. That's why we have things like motherboard jumpers to identify different CPUs. More current BIOS versions can interrogate the CPU and extract a CPU ID to identify the CPU and configure the system accordingly. Still, history has shown us that many motherboards needed a BIOS upgrade to operate with the AMD 5x86 and K5 (even though these processors have proven to be as good as Intel's). Ideally, the K6 should be a drop-in replacement for comparable MMX CPUs, but I strongly suspect that there will still be BIOS problems and upgrades needed as the K6 takes its place in the industry.

MOTHERBOARD CONNECTORS VERSUS RIBBON CABLE CONNECTORS

Q38.   *I was wondering about the merits of motherboards that have the mouse, keyboard, and serial ports on the motherboard itself compared to the motherboards that require you to connect a ribbon cable to the connections and then connect them to the back of the case. Any comments?*

A.   Both approaches are perfectly workable, but motherboards with the main ports already installed are easier to install in the case and stand less of a chance of user error during system assembly or upgrade. Since the actual connectors on the motherboard take up about as much space as corresponding ribbon cable headers, most motherboard manufacturers are incorporating the full connectors right on the motherboard. Today, it would be reasonably rare to find a motherboard that still uses ribbon cable headers.

UNDERSTANDING PLUG-AND-PLAY

Q39.   *I've heard the term* plug-and-play *used a lot over the last few years, but I never thought much about it because I'm using an older PC. Now that I'm planning to buy a new PC (a Pentium MMX system), I need to know just what plug-and-play is and how to use it.*

A.   Plug-and-play (PnP) is a technology developed for the PC by
      Microsoft and Intel, and it is designed to make PC configuring
      and upgrades easier for average users. Normally, you need to set
      jumpers for IRQ, DMA, and I/O settings when installing a new
      device in a PC. You then have to install the driver software man-
      ually. Not only is this a chore, but it presents the possibility of
      conflicts if you set the device's jumpers incorrectly. PnP is
      designed to detect the new device automatically, assign proper
      resources (IRQs, DMAs, and I/Os) automatically, and call for the
      proper driver(s). Ideally, you just need to install the device, turn
      on the power, and away you go.

      In actual practice, PnP is not quite so elegant. You need three ele-
      ments to support PnP: a PnP BIOS, a PnP operating system, and
      PnP devices. Windows 95 and most BIOS versions today support
      PnP. Many devices are also PnP-compliant, but a large number
      are not. If you plan to use older (or "legacy") adapter boards
      from your existing system, they will not be PnP-compliant, so
      you will still have to set the resources and inform Windows 95 of
      the device manually through the Add New Hardware wizard.
      Similarly, traditional devices often allowed you to disable differ-
      ent features by setting jumpers. PnP may try to automatically
      enable all of the features that it detects—whether you want them
      enabled or not. Finally, PnP is not supported in DOS. So if you
      have a PnP device (i.e., a PnP sound board), it will not run in
      DOS without a special DOS PnP driver.

Pentiums and Floating-Point Problems

Q40.   *What is the floating-point (FDIV) problem I've been hearing
       about with the Pentium? How do I know if my Pentium CPU
       has the problem?*

A.   Under certain circumstances, the Pentium's mantissa bit 13 and
      beyond can be incorrectly calculated during a floating-point divi-
      sion—and can possibly cause a system crash. This problem affects
      several different functions of the math coprocessor when used in
      single, double, and extended precision modes. In actual practice,
      this is a rare condition, but many programs and operating systems

promptly employed software patches to work around the problem. If you purchased your Pentium in 1994 or earlier (Pentium 60, 66, and possibly 75), chances are near 100 percent that it has the FDIV problem. You can use the $cpuid.exe program (from Intel's FTP site at *ftp.intel.com:/pub/IAL/pentium/$cpuid.exe*) to identify whether or not your Pentium has the problem. Keep in mind that if your Pentium *does* suffer from an FDIV fault, you probably don't need to replace it unless you plan to run high-precision scientific software.

GOING TO DUAL PROCESSORS

Q41.   *I'm looking to upgrade to a dual processor system, but I have some questions. What effect does the second CPU have on clock speed? What is required to handle multiprocessing? Will the new K6 from AMD support multiprocessing?*

A.   First, you need to understand that multiprocessing has no effect on clock speed—each CPU continues to run at its original clock speed (i.e., 166 or 200 MHz). Two 200-MHz CPUs do *not* make a 400-MHz system. As far as requirements go, you need several critical elements: a multiprocessing motherboard (with supporting chipset and BIOS), the CPUs, and an operating system capable of handling symmetric multiprocessing (SMP) such as Windows NT—Windows 95 does *not* support SMP.

You can typically use Pentium or Pentium Pro CPUs in multiprocessing motherboards. In fact, choose a motherboard that will allow you to run with *one* processor if you wish and then add the second CPU later (such as the Tyan Tomcat III motherboard). Another myth is that the CPUs have to be "matched" and tested at the factory—that's nonsense, although the CPUs must be of the same type and clock speed. One final note is that the AMD K6 (while expected to be a fine processor) does *not* support multiprocessing, so it looks like you're going with Intel.

PCI-to-PCI Bridge

Q42. *I've been studying the specifications for different motherboards in preparation for an eventual upgrade. Most of them I understand, but PCI-to-PCI bridge has me confused. What does this mean?*

A. A PCI-to-PCI bridge is a means of extending the number of PCI bus slots on a motherboard. Normally, a PCI bus can only support a limited number of slots (I think about two). When motherboard designers want to add more PCI slots, they use a PCI-to-PCI bridge chip which creates a "new" PCI bus which can support more slots. A PCI-to-PCI bridge also allows designers to incorporate a PCI bus onto an actual adapter card. In actual practice, a motherboard with more than two PCI bus slots is probably using a PCI-to-PCI bridge chip.

Pipeline Transfer Enhancements

Q43. *I was looking over the specifications for my new drive adapter board, and I saw the phrase "pipelined transfer counter for scatter/gather operations." What in the world is this, and how does it affect my drive performance?*

A. These are performance improvements. When large blocks of data are transferred to or from memory, the data is often broken up in memory into smaller blocks, or pages. These pages are typically scattered around in system memory. A host adapter capable of scatter/gather operations can improve data transfer performance by handling the gathering of these pages into large blocks and then managing the transfer of large data blocks without host CPU intervention.

Data transfer performance can be further enhanced by *pipelining* those pages. Pipelining allows multiple pages to be transferred during a single PCI bus access. So, once the drive adapter takes control of the PC bus, it can gather up all of the pages in memory and then send all of those pages to the drive at the same time rather than sending one page at a time—and having to request control of the bus each time.

ADVANCED

UPDATING OLD HARD DRIVE TYPES

Q44.   *I'm trying to change the disk in an old portable Toshiba 2000SX,*
        originally a 386SX system with a 40MB hard disk. The BIOS only
        has data for a few old disk types ranging from 20 to 60MB. Today,
        I only find 500MB disks which can be fitted to portables. The
        BIOS has no "user definable" disk type. I've read the BIOS (a 40-
        pin EPROM), found the disk data area (16 bytes/disk), taken the
        first entry and changed it to 1023 cyl/16 heads/63 sects per track
        (the geometry of the new disk), adjusted the BIOS checksum, and
        then programmed a new BIOS EPROM. The system boots from
        floppy, but BIOS still doesn't recognize the new disk.

A.   You are playing some *very* advanced games with your BIOS—this
        process is certainly *not* for general-purpose PC users. While your
        overall procedure seems sound, I suspect there are one of two
        problems. First, when you powered up the PC, you should have
        started CMOS and made sure that the updated drive type was
        indeed selected. Second, I'm not sure your drive geometry is cor-
        rect, so check the documentation for your new drive and see if
        there are any preferred translation geometries that should be used
        instead. If problems persist, there may be other "simplifications"
        in your BIOS code that prevent the drive from being recognized.
        In that case, you have little chance of ever using the large drive.

Start-up and Performance

UNDERSTANDING THE P-RATING

Q45.   *It seems like everybody is using P numbers on their CPUs today.*
        What is this P-rating system? Is this a new way of expressing
        clock speed?

A.   The P-rating system was jointly developed by Cyrix, IBM
        Microelectronics, SGS-Thomson Microelectronics, and Advanced
        Micro Devices (all competitors of Intel). In theory, the P-rating
        system allows end users to purchase new CPUs based on relative

PC performance levels rather than just the clock speed (MHz). The P-rating relates the results of industry-standard benchmarks to the performance achieved by an Intel Pentium processor at a given speed. For example, a processor with a PR150 rating would have performance comparable to a 150-MHz Pentium processor (even though the CPU's actual clock frequency might be quite different).

UNDERSTANDING POST AND POST CODES

Q46.   *What is POST? What are the POST codes?*

A.   POST stands for power-on self-test—it is the traditional name for the tests which BIOS performs when power is first applied to the system. Over time, the meaning has grown to include anything the BIOS does before an operating system is started (such as initializing chipsets). Each of these routines is assigned a POST code, a unique number which is sent to I/O port 080h before the routine is executed. If the computer hangs up during POST, a computer technician can locate the problem by finding the last value written to I/O port 080h. The list of POST codes and associated POST test or initialization routines for your BIOS are typically available in your motherboard manual or from the system maker, but you can see an example of AMI BIOS POST codes in Table 1.1.

TABLE 1.1 POST CODES FOR AMI BIOS VERSION 2.2x

POST code	Description
00	Flag test (the CPU is being tested)
03	Register test
06	System hardware initialization
09	Test BIOS ROM checksum
0C	Page register test
0F	8254 timer test

TABLE 1.1 POST CODES FOR AMI BIOS VERSION 2.2x (CONTINUED)

POST code	Description
12	Memory refresh initialization
15	8237 DMA controller test
18	8237 DMA controller initialization
1B	8259 PIC initialization
1E	8259 PIC test
21	Memory refresh test
24	Base 64KB address test
27	Base 64KB memory test
2A	8742 keyboard test
2D	MC146818 CMOS IC test
30	Start the protected mode test
33	Start the memory sizing test
36	First protected mode test passed
39	First protected mode test failed
3C	CPU speed calculation
3F	Reading the 8742 hardware switches
42	Initializing the interrupt vector area
45	Verifying the CMOS configuration
48	Testing and initializing the video system
4B	Testing unexpected interrupts
4E	Starting secong protected mode test
51	Verifying the LDT instruction
54	Verifying the TR instruction
57	Verifying the LSL instruction
5A	Verifying the LAR instruction
5D	Verifying the VERR instruction
60	Address line A20 test
63	Testing unexpected exceptions

TABLE 1.1 POST CODES FOR AMI BIOS VERSION 2.2x (CONTINUED)

POST code	Description
66	Starting the third protected mode test
69	Address line test
6A	Scan DDNIL bits for null pattern
6C	System memory test
6F	Shadow memory test
72	Extended memory test
75	Verify the memory configuration
78	Display configuration error messages
7B	Copy system BIOS to shadow memory
7E	8254 clock test
81	MC46818 real-time clock test
84	Keyboard test
87	Determining the keyboard type
8A	Stuck key test
8D	Initializing hardware interrupt vectors
90	Testing the math coprocessor
93	Finding available COM ports
96	Finding available LPT ports
99	Initializing the BIOS data area
9C	Fixed/floppy disk controller test
9F	Floppy disk test
A2	Fixed disk test
A5	Check for external ROMs
A8	System key lock test
AE	F1 error message test
AE	System boot initialization
B1	Call Int 19 boot loader

Cyrix Floating-Point Performance

Q47.   *I am considering a Cyrix 6x86 P200+ processor, which is sup-*
posed to run even faster than the 200-MHz Pentium. My teenage
son says he read that earlier versions of the Cyrix 6x86 run only
at the 486 level with certain games. Is this true? And if so, would
the P200+ have the same slowdown problems?

A.   First, I'd have to say that Cyrix 6x86 chips running at 486
speeds is a gross exaggeration. I think what your son is referring
to is the fact that the Cyrix chips do not perform as well as the
Intel versions concerning floating-point calculations. Since many
games make extraordinary use of floating-point functions (Quake
being a prime example), the games may run slower with the
Cyrix chips than the Intel equivalents. Therefore, a Pentium 200
will theoretically run Quake faster than a Cyrix P200+. For other
applications which do not rely so heavily on floating-point calculations, the Cyrix 6x86. series is easily comparable to the
Pentiums.

PCs and Thermal Cycling

Q48.   *For the longest time, I've heard people say that it is better to*
leave your computer turned on all the time, but lately, it seems to
be just the opposite. What's the latest strategy?

A.   This an old question, but one that remains timely. You have to
understand that the idea of turning a PC off versus leaving it on
comes from the days of the PC/XT and PC/AT when a motherboard could contain well over 150 ICs and countless discrete
components. When such a classic, power-hungry PC runs, it can
generate substantial amounts of heat as each component rises to
some working temperature. When the machine was turned off, the
components fell to room temperature. This constant cycling
between room and working temperature could loosen solder joints
and connections as well as accelerate the thermal breakdown of
older ICs. The strategy, then, was to leave the PC on full time and
allow the unit to remain at a stable working temperature.

By comparison, today's PC motherboard can be built with 8 to 10 ICs. Except for the CPU and math co-processor, those ICs produce relatively little heat, but even such hot components now have effective cooling devices. This makes the problem of thermal cycling far less of an issue. When coupled with the idea of "green" PCs and concerns over the environment, it makes little sense to leave PCs turned on all the time. Even hard disks are smaller and lighter, so there is less inertia to stress the motor and bearings. In most circumstances, the general rule should be this: Turn your PC on when you need it (or at the start of your work day). If you are going to be away from the PC for more than a few hours (i.e., for a meeting or to go home for the evening), turn the PC off.

UNDERSTANDING SYSTEM BURN-IN

Q49.   *I recently built a new system—a Pentium motherboard, CPU, and EDO RAM. But I was wondering about the issue of burn-in. I burned mine in by simply leaving it on and using the system normally. I did not turn the machine off for 2 days and had about 5 hours of genuine use during that time. There were no troubles at all. Am I going to have troubles later because of this improper burn-in? Everything seems to be running properly.*

A.   The purpose of burn-in is to "stress" a new system in order to weed out any premature failures of major components while the system is still under warranty. The rule in electronics is that anything which doesn't fail quickly is likely to last a long time. No system will fail for *not* performing a burn-in; it is simply a quality control step. If you use the system regularly and everything seems to be working, chances are that a prolonged burn-in would buy you very little—don't lose any sleep over it. However, if you're building systems for customers, you should use a good burn-in utility which will stress the system for 24 hours or so and generate a printed report that things are working normally.

INTERMEDIATE

SYSTEM BURN-IN ADVICE

Q50.   *I'm building a new system, but I'm not sure at what point I should use a burn-in utility. Should I build up the entire system first and install the operating system before running the burn-in, or should I just install the bare necessities and run the burn-in before completing the assembly and installing the operating system? Also, how long should I run the burn-in test?*

A.   Build up all of your hardware, perform an initial check to see that things appear to be working, and then install DOS (or Windows 95 with DOS 7.0) before running your burn-in utility. If you do install Windows 95, be sure to shut down the computer to the DOS mode before invoking the burn-in utility. As for time, the conventional wisdom is 24 hours of continuous testing. According to reports that I have seen, however, an aggressive 4- to 6-h burn-in test seems to provide just as much assurance as a 24-h test. But more time certainly won't hurt—especially if you're building the PC for someone else.

SWITCHING MONITORS DURING BURN-IN

Q51.   *I am going to run a 24-h burn-in test on my newly assembled PC, but since I only have one monitor and no A/B switch, it will be necessary to unplug the monitor from my $200 Matrox Millennium video board (not to mention my new motherboard) once I have set up and initialized the burn-in program. A little voice keeps saying "don't do this," but I'm asking anyway.*

A.   What you are describing is not forbidden, but it does carry a little risk. You can leave the PC running; be sure to turn off and unplug the monitor before removing the video cable. When reconnecting the monitor later, plug it in and connect the video cable before turning the monitor back on. Those video cables were not meant to be disconnected and reconnected repeatedly. Another issue to consider is that once your monitor is disconnected, you won't see any warnings or error messages that might be generated by the burn-in program unless you bring the monitor back to the machine under test.

PENTIUM OVERDRIVES AND PERFORMANCE

Q52.   *Here's one that I just don't understand. I installed one of those Pentium OverDrive CPUs in my system, but after running a benchmark, I don't see any performance improvement. I'm very dissatisfied right now, but can you tell me if there's anything I missed?*

A.   Changing a CPU alone will rarely make a *drastic* difference in PC performance—but it *should* have some effect. First, check the installation of your OverDrive CPU and make sure that you've made any necessary changes to your clock speed, and other motherboard settings. If the question persists, I might suspect a problem with your particular benchmarking program. Many benchmark programs rely on frequent data transfer into and out of RAM from various peripherals (more of an I/O test). The performance of such data transfers is accomplished by the motherboard and the peripherals—not the processor. Other measurements such as system boot time or software load time are also I/O-intensive operations and are not greatly enhanced by the addition of an OverDrive processor. The bottom line here is to try a different benchmark (or even an assortment of benchmarks) and then compare your results to the original program. If all else fails, you can always return the OverDrive for a refund.

INTERMEDIATE

CAPTURING START-UP MESSAGES

Q53.   *I configure a lot of different systems, but the new PCs are so fast that I can't see the CONFIG.SYS and AUTOEXEC.BAT messages that are generated during initialization. Is there any way to capture the messages generated during power-up?*

A.   This has become an all-too-common complaint in today's PC service community. Fortunately, there are several ways to get around it. If you're using DOS 6.2x, one of the easiest methods of reviewing screen output during initialization is to press <F8> when the system says "Starting MS-DOS...." The <F8> key takes you step by step through each CONFIG.SYS and AUTOEXEC.BAT statement and asks if you wish to process that particular step. Not only does this allow you to view any messages that are produced by that step, but you can skip steps—a handy feature when troubleshooting or modifying a system's configuration.

If you're using Windows 95, you can press the <F8> key when the system says "Starting Windows 95...." This will produce a start-up menu which allows you to select a system start-up mode. You can choose the LOG option which will create a start-up log file. You can review the log file afterward to help pinpoint any problems. You can also select a step-by-step start-up to review the individual start-up points in real time.

PERFORMANCE PENALTY SEEN WITH AN OVERDRIVE

Q54.   *Help! I installed an Intel OverDrive CPU on my older Pentium motherboard, but instead of better performance, I'm seeing worse performance—the PC actually seems to boot and run more slowly. What's the deal?*

A.   I suspect that your cache is disabled. Start your CMOS Setup routine and check the status of your L1 (internal) and L2 (external) cache settings. Chances are that your L1 or L2 cache (perhaps both) are disabled. The most probable culprit is your new CPU's L1 cache. Try reenabling the cache and then save your changes and reboot the system.

COOLING A WARM CPU

Q55.   *I have a 3-in fan blowing air into my midtower case. Yet this fan alone does not provide an adequate amount of air, and the CPU is warm to the touch—sometimes it is hot (depending on the amount of usage I am giving the system). I have no additional mounting points for another fan so how should I keep the CPU cooler?*

A.   You don't mention what CPU you're using or the clock speed that it's operating at, but from your symptoms, I'd say you've got an older i486 CPU (probably 25 or 33 MHz). Fast 486s and essentially all Pentiums run so hot that they demand a heat sink/fan. If your CPU is as old as I think it is, you would probably do well to use a basic heat sink. Attach the heat sink to the CPU with a thin layer of thermal grease to aid heat transfer. If you are actually using a later model CPU, get a heat sink/fan instead. The heat sink does exactly the same job, but the fan assembly dramatically improves the cooling efficiency.

Handling CPU Heat in a Laptop

Q56.   *I've been considering investing in a Pentium laptop system—probably a Toshiba. However, I'm very concerned with the heating problems that I have heard of with Pentium CPUs. How do they keep Pentiums cool in a notebook when PC makers have trouble keeping the CPUs cool in a tower? Should I be worried about this?*

A.   Well, heating is always a valid concern—it affects the longevity of the notebook (and your investment). Fortunately, Intel has come a long way with their Pentium heat management techniques. The trick behind heat management is to draw as much heat as possible away from the IC chip (or die). New IC fabrication techniques place the die on heat-conductive plastics and solder mounts which aid heat transfer. So Pentiums are running cooler because they are packaged better. Pentiums manufactured today are designed for 3.3 V operation (rather than 5 V), so they are cooler because there is less power to be dissipated. The newest generation of MMX CPUs uses 2.8 V for core logic operations, so power dissipation is even less. Laptops also employ passive liquid cooling devices which act similarly to heat sinks. Ultimately, you should not be overly concerned with excessive heating, but check your warranty carefully and make sure you have plenty of time to bring it back if something *does* go wrong.

FASTER MOTHERBOARD BOOTING

Q57.   *I have heard that it is possible to make a motherboard boot faster by making a change to the system's CMOS Setup. Is this true? If so, what changes need to be made?*

A.   For some motherboards and BIOS versions, if only a single device is connected to either the primary EIDE channel or to the secondary IDE channel, the BIOS may wait for a nonexistent slave device to be initialized. When this happens, the BIOS will wait until it determines that the nonexistent slave device is not responding and then will proceed with the initialization. This can often be avoided by marking any entries for slave devices as Disabled in CMOS Setup (remember to save any changes to CMOS before exiting and rebooting the system).

Note   *This principle is not universal, and not all motherboard designs and BIOS revisions will suffer such a delay. Therefore, do not be surprised if you see no significant improvement in boot speed after changing your CMOS Setup.*

WHY SO LONG TO BOOT?

Q58.   *I'm perfectly happy with my system, and it's not giving me any trouble, but I'm wondering if you can tell me why it takes up to 30 seconds for the system to boot? It just seems slow for today's fast PCs.*

A.   Booting is a very important part of the PC's normal operation. All the hardware must be identified and tested before the system can be used. Add-on cards (like video boards and SCSI adapters) must be located and their BIOS found. PCI card slots must be configured. PnP devices must be isolated (and assigned resources). Then the operating system must be loaded. Ultimately, booting is a complex and demanding operation, so a lot is going on in a very short period of time. As you might expect, the more hardware you have in a PC, the longer booting can take. You may be able to shorten the boot cycle by disabling entries in the CMOS Setup that correspond to unused IDE devices (remember to save your changes to CMOS before rebooting the system).

ADVANCED

OVERCOMING BOOT DELAY PROBLEMS

Q59. *I inherited a Gateway 2000 i486DX2/50 system fitted with a Maxtor 340 SCSI HDD and an Adaptec 1542 SCSI adapter. During a cold boot, the system checks memory and then waits idle for about 2 minutes before finally checking the floppy disks and continuing to boot from the SCSI drive. Once the PC boots, I have no problems—warm boots (<CTRL>+<ALT>+<DEL>) do not suffer that delay problem. Any ideas?*

A. Since your system apparently works once initialization is complete, I have to suspect that perhaps there is an entry in your CMOS Setup that should not be there. Since your PC is SCSI-based, there should be no drive entries in the CMOS Setup (hard drives should be set to "none" or "not installed"). If there is a drive indicated in the setup, the PC will take time attempting to locate the specified drive—which is not there. Also, check all of the jumpers on both your SCSI adapter and drive to see if there is any sort of peripheral delay jumper that may be enabled. Some systems support this as a means of allowing slower peripherals to initialize before the system checks them—if such a jumper exists, try disabling it.

COMPARING SCSI AND IDE PERFORMANCE

Q60. *I've been hearing a lot about SCSI versus IDE lately—from what I understand, both run at about the same speed. If so, what's that advantage of SCSI? I've also seen many references to Enhanced IDE (EIDE). Is that the same thing? What's going on?*

A. I'm not surprised that you're confused. You're not alone either—this has been an incredibly active topic. In actual practice, each standard is designed around a slightly different transfer rate as shown in Table 1.2. As you can see, IDE is a midrange standard. EIDE is a relatively recent enhancement designed to support more than two hard drives and facilitate faster data transfer. Table 1.3 lists the number of devices that each interface can support.

ADVANCED

TABLE 1.2 INTERFACE DATA TRANSFER RATES

Interface	Data rate (MB/second)
SCSI-1	5
Fast SCSI-2	10
IDE	10
EIDE	13.3
Fast/Wide SCSI-2	20

TABLE 1.3 INTERFACE DEVICE SUPPORT

Interface	Supported devices
SCSI-1	8
Fast SCSI-2	8
IDE	2
EIDE	4 (two sets of two drives)
Fast/Wide SCSI-2	16

Unfortunately, specifications don't tell the whole story. While EIDE appears faster than Fast SCSI-2, it is actually Fast SCSI-2 which outperforms EIDE because of the SCSI ability to use bus mastering—a technique whereby the bus controller has enough intelligence to communicate on the bus (or master it) without intervention from the main system CPU. EIDE does not (and cannot) use bus mastering because the actual drive electronics are built into the hard drive (or CD-ROM drive) itself (hence the term *integrated drive electronics*. Since the drive electronics are built into each device, it would be extremely difficult to allow any one device to take command of the bus. So, EIDE needs constant intervention from the main system CPU to act as a mediator.

Since the SCSI controller manages its own independent bus, it has a completely clear highway all its own and doesn't need the main system CPU. Also, since each SCSI bus controller runs its own bus and has its own unique SCSI ID (7 for 8-bit SCSI and 15 for 16-bit SCSI), it's very common to gang multiple SCSI bus controllers

ADVANCED

in the same system. For example, a Quad SCSI board (with four SCSI busses) can accommodate 28 physical devices. (32 devices minus 4 controller IDs). This can't be done with EIDE.

Ultimately, IDE and EIDE provide a simple and inexpensive drive interface solution for small personal systems. But high-end systems and file servers will benefit much more from SCSI flexibility than from sheer speed.

SYSTEM WON'T RECOGNIZE THE OVERDRIVE

Q61.   *I've been struggling with an upgrade for a few days now, and maybe you can help me. I replaced my CPU with a Pentium OverDrive, and my system starts (so I guess it's not a critical problem), but the system doesn't recognize the CPU speed correctly. Why would that be?*

A.   CPU identification and speed information are gathered by routines in your BIOS which are executed during the POST. If your BIOS was created before the OverDrive became available, the BIOS has no way of dealing with unknown CPUs, so it reports incorrect information—be thankful that your system even starts. If the incorrect speed is causing your PC to malfunction, you should investigate a possible BIOS upgrade from the motherboard or system manufacturer. If the error is not affecting your system's performance, chances are that you can just ignore it.

BOOTING FROM DIFFERENT HARD DRIVES

Q62.   *I installed Windows 95 on one hard drive even though I boot from another, but after the installation, the system wants to boot from the Windows 95 hard drive. Why is this, and how can I change it?*

A.   The Windows 95 setup program checks all the hard disks in your computer to make sure that only one contains 0x80h in the DriveNumber field of the boot sector. Setup makes this change so that Windows 95 can always find the boot disk when you start the computer and can recognize the other drives. You can use either of the following methods to correct the DriveNumber field:

ADVANCED

- Use the FDISK program that is included with Windows 95 to set the primary active partition.

- Use another disk editor to change a disk's DriveNumber field, allowing you to boot from that hard disk.

INTERPRETING BEEPS

Q63.   *I have a fairly new Intel motherboard. Every time I turn the PC on, I get a strange beeping sound, and the PC refuses to work. Can you tell me what the problem is?*

A.   Every time your PC boots, its BIOS performs a comprehensive series of tests to make sure that everything is working as expected. If a serious failure occurs before the PC's video system can be started, the error message is expressed as a series of beeps—the specific beep pattern represents the failure. The BIOS itself is also very important since different BIOS makers can use radically different beep codes. It just so happens that many of the more recent Intel motherboards use AMI BIOS. Since you didn't tell me exactly what the beeping pattern *is*, I've given you the whole beep code table for AMI BIOS in Table 1.4.

TABLE 1.4 TYPICAL AMI BEEP CODES

Beeps	Error Message	Description
1 long	No video card found	Applies only to motherboards with no on-board video.
2 short 1 long	No monitor connected	Applies only to motherboards with on-board video present.
3 short 1 long	Video related failure	Other video beep codes may exist and are tied to specific video BIOS implementations.

TABLE 1.4 TYPICAL AMI BEEP CODES (CONTINUED)

Beeps	Error Message	Description
1 short	Refresh failure	The memory refresh circuitry on the base-board is faulty.
2 short	Parity error	Parity is not supported on this product and will not occur.
3 short	64KB memory failure	Memory failure in first 64KB of RAM.
4 short	Timer not operational	Timer 1 on motherboard is not functioning.
5 short	Processor error	The CPU on the motherboard generated an error.
6 short	8042-gate A20 failure	BIOS cannot switch to protected mode. Keyboard controller (8042) may be bad.
7 short	Processor exception	The CPU generated an exception interrupt.
8 short	Display R/W error	The video adapter is either missing or its memory is faulty.
9 short	ROM checksum error	ROM checksum does not match the value encoded in BIOS.
10 short	CMOS shutdown register	The shutdown register for CMOS RAM failed.
11 short	Cache error	The external cache is faulty.

ADVANCED

44   *Chapter 1*

Controller Issues

BEGINNER

STAND-ALONE OR INTEGRATED DRIVE CONTROLLERS

Q64.   *My motherboard is fitted with both a hard drive and floppy drive
controller. I'm wondering if these are the best types of drive controllers and if I should install an expansion drive controller.*

A.   First, there's no reason that you *have* to upgrade your motherboard's drive controllers unless the motherboard controllers fail
or you can get better performance or more features from a stand-
alone model. In general, a motherboard drive controller is no
better or worse than an expansion drive controller.

MOTHERBOARD CONTROLLERS VERSUS STAND-ALONE CONTROLLERS

Q65.   *Since my old computer died, I am looking at the specifications for
some new computers. Micron told me that their newest system
has the floppy and EIDE controller (supporting up to four
devices, excluding the floppies) all on the motherboard instead of
on plug-in controller boards. New systems are expensive, and I'd
hate to waste my money—is there any disadvantage to that setup?*

A.   It is common for motherboards to integrate such functions as
floppy drive, hard drive, and video controller circuitry. This often
results in an efficient design which requires an absolute minimum
of expansion boards (while still being very competitively priced).
If you do choose to upgrade the motherboard's controllers later,
you can usually disable the motherboard circuitry with one or
two jumpers (or through the CMOS Setup) before installing the
new controller boards. If you're worried about future upgrades,
make sure that you can disable the motherboard controllers completely before committing to the new motherboard.

CLEARING UP DRIVE ADVERTISING ERRORS

Q66.   *I finally decided to upgrade my old hard drive. I currently have a 170MB IDE drive, and I figure that an 850MB or 1.2GB drive ought to do. I've come up with about $169 to $199 for Western Digital drives, but sources sometimes list these as IDE or EIDE. I know my drive controller supports EIDE, so I'm wondering (1) what is the real difference between the two and (2) are the prices about right?*

A.   Both IDE and EIDE use the same 40-pin interface scheme, but EIDE ports (in conjunction with BIOS) support large hard drives over 528MB, as well as fast data transfers, automatic drive identification, and other performance features. An IDE drive will work in an EIDE port, although data transfer modes will be slower. The prices you quoted are about right, but for $250 or less, you can get a 2.1GB EIDE drive.

SORTING OUT DRIVE CONTROLLERS

Q67.   *I have a full-featured DTC I/O card which I'm planning to add to my system, and I'm wondering if I should use it for the floppies, hard drives, and CD-ROM (since I can put them all on that card), or should I use a separate controller card for the CD-ROM?*

A.   If your motherboard already offers drive support (or already uses a drive controller card), you'd be just as well off to disable those ports on the I/O card and leave your drives configured as they are. It is unlikely that you'll get better drive performance out of an I/O controller than you would out of motherboard or standalone PCI drive controllers. If the CD-ROM uses a proprietary interface, you'll need to use a proprietary controller. If the CD-ROM uses an IDE interface, you should usually install the CD by itself on a secondary IDE channel.

TRICKS TO INSTALLING A NEW DRIVE CONTROLLER

Q68.   *I am trying to use a new floppy and hard disk controller card to replace a defective floppy controller embedded on the motherboard. On CMOS Setup (BIOS is Phoenix 4.4), the floppy controller setting was disabled. The floppy LED lights during boot-up, but when I try accessing the floppy, the system gives a "Drive not ready, Retry/Abort/Fail" message. The controller card is working well on another system. Is there anything else that needs to be done besides disabling the controller from BIOS.*

A.   When installing a new drive controller, you first have to disable the corresponding ports on your motherboard. For example, if you're only using the floppy controller function of your new controller, you'll have to disable the motherboard's floppy controller and *also* disable any unused controllers on the new board. If you're using the floppy *and* hard drive controllers of the new board, you'll need to disable both the motherboard's floppy and hard drive controllers. Floppy and hard drive interfaces are typically disabled using a motherboard jumper, so check the motherboard documentation for any important jumper arrangements.

If your motherboard is jumperless, you will need to disable the motherboard's floppy controller through the CMOS Setup, but you must still enter the drive parameters in CMOS. So, if you cleared the floppy drive references from your CMOS Setup, your system will not recognize the floppy drive(s)—no matter *which* controller you use. In many cases, you would leave the floppy drive entries alone in the CMOS main page but disable the motherboard's floppy controller in a page marked Advanced Chipset Setup or some similar designation. That should enable the new floppy controller to work. Double-check the floppy signal and power cables.

USING AN EIDE DRIVE ON AN IDE CONTROLLER

Q69.   *A friend of mine is going to replace her hard drive soon. The question is, can you buy an Enhanced IDE drive and use it with a normal IDE controller (her controller is built into the motherboard)?*

A.   Yes, you could use the EIDE drive on a standard IDE controller,
       but you cannot access over 1024 cylinders or make use of higher
       data transfer modes. In effect, your fast 2GB drive may end up
       appearing just like a standard 504MB drive. Your friend has
       three means of getting around this problem: She can upgrade the
       motherboard BIOS to support EIDE, disable the motherboard
       drive controller and install a stand-alone EIDE drive controller
       with its own BIOS, or use the drive overlay software (such as
       Disk Manager or EZ-Drive) that accompanies the drive. Drive
       overlay software is the most convenient option since it minimizes
       hardware upgrading and typically comes free with new drives.

SUPPORTING PIO MODE 4

Q70.   *I'm looking at new HDDs, some of which claim to use PIO
       mode 4. My drive controller card supports Fast ATA-2 PIO
       mode 3. The card's manufacturer says it cannot be upgraded by
       software to support PIO mode 4. Am I out of luck, or will mode
       4 still work (as I plan to partition to <530MB)? Also, my new
       motherboard has a built-in drive controller. Being a motherboard
       with VL bus, does the on-board controller work as a VL bus
       controller, or would it act as an ISA controller?*

A.   Data transfer modes are a function of the drive controller *and*
       EIDE interface on the drive. *Both* must function in PIO mode 4
       in order to support such data transfer rates. Otherwise, you'll
       probably wind up using PIO mode 3. If you really want PIO
       Mode 4 performance, chances are you'd need to disable the
       motherboard controller and use a VL bus EIDE controller capa-
       ble of PIO mode 4 operation (although I think they'd be hard to
       find). As far as whether your controller would act as an ISA or
       VLB, the answer is *neither*. Since the controller is on the mother-
       board, you don't need to worry about ISA or VL bus bottlenecks.

INTERMEDIATE

MAKING THE MOST OF EIDE TRANSFER MODES

Q71. *I have a question relating to the EIDE controller. My controller can handle four drives. I currently have two drives (one EIDE and one standard IDE) hooked up to the same channel. I had to disable the PIO mode 3 support because the IDE drive can't operate at that speed. If I move the IDE drive to the secondary channel and make it the master of that channel (instead of the slave of the channel it is on), will I be able to use PIO mode 3 with my EIDE drive?*

A. Perfect—you're on the right track. If you pull your IDE drive off the primary channel, rejumper the drive as a master drive, and then connect it to the secondary channel, you should be able to increase the data transfer mode of your primary channel and increase the performance of your EIDE drive. When you shift your drives around, remember to update your drive entries in CMOS Setup accordingly.

INTERMEDIATE

ADDITIONAL HDD SUPPORT WITH AN EIDE ADAPTER

Q72. *Can an Enhanced IDE card without an on-board BIOS support four hard disks? My understanding is that to support four hard disks either the motherboard BIOS or the EIDE card BIOS needs to handle EIDE extensions (or LBA). I am trying to get the EIDE card to support another two hard disks since my motherboard already handles two hard disks.*

A. EIDE support refers to addressing large hard drives (over 528MB) at high data transfer rates. If your motherboard BIOS and controller board do *not* support both LBA, you'll need to use overlay software such as Ontrack's Disk Manager or EZ-Drive in order to fully access large hard drives. The actual number of drives is another matter (EIDE does not influence the number of drives supported in a system). If your motherboard supplies an IDE port, that port can handle two hard drives. If you install a controller board, you'll need to disable the board's primary port to prevent it from conflicting with the motherboard's primary IDE port (depending on whether your BIOS will automatically disable the motherboard IDE port if an add-on controller is detected). If you can reconfigure the controller's primary channel as a tertiary channel, you may be able to support up to six IDE devices in your system, two from the motherboard's primary channel, two on the adapter board's secondary channel, and two on the adapter board's tertiary channel.

REARRANGING EIDE AND SCSI DEVICES

Q73.   *I built a computer using a Tyan Titan III motherboard. The motherboard has an on-board EIDE controller that supports four hard drives (through a primary and secondary channel). I currently have two hard drives and a 6X internal CD-ROM connected to the primary and secondary ports. If I choose to switch to SCSI hard drives and install an SCSI controller, will I still be able to keep my IDE CD-ROM connected to the on-board IDE controller?*

A.   Yes, you should be able to leave your CD-ROM drive by itself on the secondary channel. Just remember to enter your CMOS Setup and remove the entries for your EIDE hard drives after you remove them from the primary EIDE channel. Make sure you enter none or not installed. The SCSI drives that you install do not need CMOS entries, and since there are no EIDE boot devices, the SCSI BIOS will allow your first SCSI hard drive (ID0) to be bootable. The most you might need to do with your CD-ROM drive would be to change its drive letter in MSCDEX (depending on how you partition the SCSI drives).

NEW VL DRIVE CONTROLLER PROBLEMS

Q74.   *I have tried four different I/O cards (including a new one) in a VL bus system, all with the same result—HDD controller failure. I have switched cables and slots all to no avail. What am I missing?*

A.   Always start by checking your CMOS Setup to verify that the proper hard drive parameters are entered (Fig. 1.3). Also check that your cabling between the drives and controller is secure. Try an ISA controller—if the problem goes away, make sure that the clock frequency on the VL bus is 33 MHz or less.

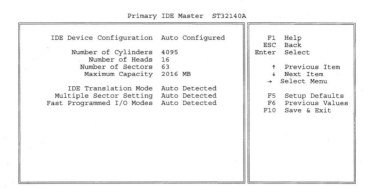

Primary IDE Master   ST32140A

IDE Device Configuration Auto Configured	F1 Help
	ESC Back
Number of Cylinders 4095	Enter Select
Number of Heads 16	
Number of Sectors 63	↑ Previous Item
Maximum Capacity 2016 MB	↓ Next Item
	→ Select Menu
IDE Translation Mode Auto Detected	
Multiple Sector Setting Auto Detected	F5 Setup Defaults
Fast Programmed I/O Modes Auto Detected	F6 Previous Values
	F10 Save & Exit

Figure 1.3 Configuring a hard drive in the CMOS Setup

NEW HARD DRIVE CONTROLLER CAUSES FLOPPY PROBLEMS

Q75.   *I just installed a Seagate ST3283 HDD using a BOCA drive controller board. When the machine boots up, drive A: spins with a
weird sound and then drive B: spins with a weird sound. I then
see an FDD DRIVE CONTROLLER FAILURE. Press <F1>
error message. After I press <F1>, the machine boots, but I cannot get reliable access to my floppy drives.*

A.   The BOCA controller board should work well with the Seagate
HDD, but it is odd that your floppy drives should make such
strange noises. Check the jumper settings on your BOCA board.
There may be a hardware conflict between floppy circuitry on
the BOCA board and floppy circuitry (if any) on your motherboard or any other expansion board you may have with floppy
drive capability. Disable any floppy circuitry *not* driving your
floppies. Double-check your floppy drive cable. Make sure it is
secure and connected properly to your drives. Replace the cable
if necessary. Try a different drive controller board (BOCA or otherwise). There may be a fault in the floppy controller section of
the BOCA board which developed during your hard drive installation. If a different board clears the problem, the controller
board was at fault.

REPREPARING DRIVES AFTER AN EIDE CONTROLLER UPGRADE

Q76. *I'm upgrading an on-board IDE controller to EIDE in order to add a third HDD. The new controller card (a VL board) requires that I reformat my existing 1GB HDDs, which are presently software driven using Ontrack software. Do I really have to go through the trouble of reformatting and restoring my drives?*

A. I'm not so sure that a reformat is absolutely necessary, but be sure to perform a *complete* system backup to tape before proceeding. Once you've upgraded the drive controller and attached the drives to your new controller, boot to your CMOS Setup and try autoidentifying the drives. The new controller may simply recognize the existing Ontrack partitions, and you can continue on without losing any data. However, if the Ontrack partition prevents your drives from being read by the new controller, you will need to repartition and reformat the drives.

BOOTING PAST A NO ROM BASIC ERROR

Q77. *I have a MicroStar 4144 motherboard with the SiS chipset and an AMI BIOS. After the board runs through its boot sequence and begins to look for an operating system, the screen goes blank and I get a NO ROM BASIC SYSTEM HALTED error. I already know that the on-board floppy controller is bad—should I just assume that the whole controller board is bad?*

A. Your No ROM BASIC error is occurring because the BIOS cannot find any valid boot device (i.e., no bootable floppy disks, no hard drives, no SCSI systems, and so on). As a last resort, the BIOS attempts to load a version of BASIC. Unfortunately, ROM BASIC hasn't been incorporated into systems for years, so you simply get an error message, and the system halts. In order to correct this issue, you need a drive that the PC can boot from. Replace your drive controller and install a working floppy drive. The system should start from a bootable floppy disk. You should also consider adding a hard drive to the system.

DEALING WITH A SUDDEN DRIVE CONTROLLER FAILURE

Q78.   *As part of a modest upgrade, I put in a VL-Bus Promise 2300+*
controller card with the external BIOS and a 1.08GB Western
Digital EIDE drive in my 486/33 home computer. Today, I boot-
ed the system and got a double beep with an HDD Controller
failure. Press (F1) to continue message. Rebooting brought same
message. I haven't opened the case to see if everything is connect-
ed properly—which is my intent when I get home tonight.
However, is it likely that the controller card has failed, or are
there other reasons for failure?

A.   As I understand it, you installed a new drive and controller card,
and the system worked, but now you have a drive controller failure that seems to have appeared out of nowhere. Unfortunately,
controller errors are not always that precise, so there are a few
things to check. Take a look at your drive controller board first
and make sure it is installed into its VL bus slot completely. You
may try removing it from the slot and then reinstalling it completely. Also check the drive cables to see that they are attached
properly at both ends. Open your CMOS Setup routine and verify
that the CMOS geometry for your drive is entered correctly (or
set to a general-purpose entry like auto-detect). Check the drive
jumper again—it should be set as the primary (or master) drive. If
all else fails, then try replacing your drive controller board.

PC STALLS AFTER MEMORY CHECK

Q79.   *My computer is a Dell DX2/66 with 32MB of RAM. It is almost*
3 years old. I am getting an error message about one in ten times
when I boot up. It hangs up after checking memory and says
there is a controller error. I reboot and it has always gone
through the second time with no problem. I am running
Windows 95. I ran the Dell test which showed that the controller
card is OK. What can I do?

A.   Before you start getting really worried, I suggest you turn off and
unplug the system, open the case, and check the signal cable
between the controller and drive. Make sure the cable is attached
completely at both ends—you may even want to reseat the cable

at each end. Also make sure that the controller is seated properly in its expansion slot. If there is a major accumulation of dust on the controller, gently blow the dust out.

EIDE CONTROLLER CAUSES NON-SYSTEM DISK ERRORS

Q80. *I'm helping a neighbor with his EIDE upgrade. He installed a new EIDE controller, but now the drive returns a Non-System Disk or Missing Operating System Error. What's going on here?*

A. Boot to a floppy disk and try to access the C: drive. If the C: drive is accessible, run FDISK /MBR to rewrite the master boot sector, and run SYS C: to transfer system files to the hard drive. If the C: drive is not accessible, check the partition information by running FDISK. Choose option 4—there should be a Primary (DOS) partition set as Active. If not, you may have to repartition the drive correctly. A disk drive overlay (DDO) such as Disk Manager may have been used originally to partition the drive. Some LBA BIOS may be incompatible with the DDO. Remove the DDO before continuing. Finally, try disabling some of the advanced drive features in CMOS Setup (like IDE Block Mode and 32-bit transfers). If problems persist, try replacing the hard drive.

DTC IDE CONTROLLER CAUSING ERRORS

Q81. *After loading the DTC DOS driver and rebooting the system, my system locks up and reports; Bad Command or Missing COM-MAND.COM.*

A. This situation will occur mainly because the DTC controller is transferring data too fast for the IDE drive. When the DTC driver loads, it obtains information from the IDE drive, including drive speed. Sometimes the drive reports that it can support PIO modes 4 or 3 when in actuality it cannot. The solution is to slow down the transfer rate. Edit CONFIG.SYS and add the following to the DTC driver line:

```
DEVICE=DOSEIDE.SYS /V /D0:P0
```

ADVANCED

Reboot the system and see if the problem is corrected. If it is corrected, you can increase the value of P by 1 until the failure occurs again. Then you will know what drive speed your drive works at.

EIDE Controller's On-Board BIOS Doesn't Load

Q82.   *I installed a Promise EIDEMax controller, but I can't get the card's on-board BIOS to load. Any ideas?*

A.   There is actually a whole protocol of points to try if the on-board BIOS refuses to load:

- Try out a different BIOS address other than the default address of D000h. BIOS addresses are typically set through a jumper.

- Double-check that the EIDEMax BIOS is enabled (also handled through a jumper on the controller card).

- Ensure that the controller card seats evenly and firmly in its slot. Do the same for the BIOS on the card.

- Check other cards installed on the system for a resource conflict such as network cards, sound cards, etc. Certain models of sound cards have an IDE port that may be using the same IRQ or port address of the EIDEMax IDE port. disable the sound card's IDE port.

- Use the HDD autodetect feature of the motherboard BIOS. If BIOS does not detect the drive, double-check cable connections, jumpers, drive settings, and so on. Once the BIOS detects the drive, proceed with the installation.

- Disable LBA, IDE Block Mode (and on some systems, 32-bit Transfer) in the CMOS Setup.

- Disable the controller's BIOS to determine if the card's BIOS is defective. The EIDEMax BIOS may be defective or the card itself is defective. Try replacing the controller card.

Crash and Lock-up Troubleshooting Issues

COOING FAN CAUSING DRIVE ERRORS

Q83. *I just put a P166 Asus P55T2P4 together with a 230-W power supply. I wanted to experiment with adding a 4-in case fan. When I connected the fan power leads in parallel with power going to the hard drive or the floppy, the hard drive and the floppy gave errors. I have it now powered on a separate power cable (the only one left), and things seem OK. Would the fan be causing electrical noise to interfere with the other peripherals? Maybe the power supply is not filtered enough. Any thoughts on this?*

A. According to your description of the problem, the fan was certainly responsible for your drive errors. When a fan is placed in parallel with other devices, the current demanded by a fan (as well as its electrical noise) can interrupt the operation of other power-hungry devices such as hard drives and floppy drives. By placing the fan on its own power cable, you eased the current drain and reduced the noise being passed back to the power supply. If things are running properly now, you may be able to leave the fan in place. Still, you may think about upgrading the power supply to a larger model now.

USING THE RACER II BOARD FOR TROUBLESHOOTING

Q84. *I have a RACER II card for troubleshooting and diagnosing PC motherboards. Can you tell me if I can use it in IBM, Compaq, NEC, Zenith, Dell, Toshiba, and Packard Bell systems?*

A. After speaking with technical support at UltraX (408-988-4721), the RACER II card is definitely compatible with IBM, Compaq, Dell, and Packard Bell systems. As for the other three systems, RACER II should be compatible (as well as with any 100 percent IBM-compatible motherboard). You can also contact UltraX by fax at 408-988-4849. Their mailing address is P.O. Box 730010, San Jose, CA 95173-0010.

BEGINNER

POST Readings Suggest Motherboard Problems

Q85. *I have a 386DX/33 from my sister that is giving me a headache. The fan comes on during power up, but nothing else happens— no beeps, no drive action, nothing. The power supply to the board is fine. I bought a POST reader, and it displays a POST code of 00 (but there is no code 00 in the enclosed manual for the AMI BIOS). I am pushing my sister to invest in a new motherboard, but do you have any ideas first?*

A. You've got a serious failure on that motherboard. A POST code of 00 basically means that the motherboard isn't processing anything at all. This usually indicates a failure in the CPU or elsewhere in the main processing elements of the motherboard (such as the system clock or BIOS). Given the age of your sister's system, I would highly recommend upgrading the motherboard, CPU, and RAM for at least a fast 486 or entry-level Pentium. You can still use the same drives, sound board, and video board if you wish, although your sister may choose to upgrade those devices later on.

CD-ROM Trouble After Acer Suspend Modes

Q86. *I don't understand what's going on with my AcerNote 970CX. I put down the display lid which places the notebook into a Suspend mode. Later, I resume the system, but the CD-ROM "eject" function doesn't work. Do I need a BIOS upgrade, or is there some other problem?*

A. After returning from the suspend mode, you need to wait about 10 to 15 seconds for the CD-ROM to reinitialize and then eject the CD using the eject button or the hot key (<Fn>+<F9>) or by right-clicking on the CD-ROM drive icon in My Computer and then selecting the Eject option. Note that closing the display lid enters a 0-V suspend mode, which saves more power than the 5-V suspend mode which is entered using hot keys (<Fn>+<Esc>).

Floppy LED Stays On and PC Won't Boot

Q87. *I just built my second computer; a 5x86 133 MHz system. When I try to start it up, all I get is the grinding sound of the 3.5-in floppy (and maybe the hard drive). The PC won't boot—there is no display and no beeps, but the floppy LED stays on. What could I have done wrong?*

A. From your description of the problem, you reversed pin 1 at one end of the floppy drive cable. This is a very common mistake which happens a lot during new constructions like yours. When the floppy is connected in this fashion, most PCs often just lock up and refuse to boot. Shut down the PC and check your floppy system. Make sure to align pin 1 correctly at the drive and floppy controller.

Intermittent System Lock-ups with Keyboard and Mouse

Q88. *I'm working on a Dell 486DX2/66. It has 1MB of video RAM onboard, and is an all-ISA system. This machine has an intermittent lock-up problem where the keyboard and the mouse freeze. I already switched the HDD and removed all the optional cards (modem, sound board, and CD-ROM interface). It still locks up whether in DOS or Windows. I guess I know that I have to change the motherboard, but can you tell me what part of the board is causing this problem?*

A. The term *lock-up* is generic at best, so it is extremely difficult to say with any certainty where such a problem might be located. However, we can suggest some of the areas it is *not*; Since you removed a great deal of hardware (and haven't added anything new), it is probably not a hardware conflict. Since the lock-ups occur under both DOS and Windows, it is probably not a driver or operating system issue. As a result, your trouble is (as you suspect) somewhere on the motherboard. Still, before you change the motherboard, try the following: (1) check the installation of your CPU and make sure that any heat sink/fan is affixed to the CPU properly and (2) reseat all of your SIMMs (clean the contacts if necessary). Also check the metal standoffs beneath the motherboard for possible shorts against any printed circuit traces. Try insulating the metal standoffs with thin, nonconductive washers.

System Configuration Causing Hang-ups

Q89.   *I am having problems with my Aptiva A90. It hangs up a lot and has done so since I first got it. I have tried the help line at IBM, and I've also reformatted my hard drive and still encounter the same problems intermittently. I should also mention that I have disabled the Automatic Power Manager (APM) and I have not been able to use my other features (wake up and communications center). I would like to install an Adaptec AHA2940U SCSI PCI Controller card so that I can hook up my Iomega Jaz External SCSI drive. My second question is could I use the AHA2940UW SCSI card which has a 69-pin external connection? The 2940U has a 50-pin external connector that I will need to hook up my cable for the Jaz drive. Am I able to use the 68-pin (AHA2940UW) and use an adapter or whatever to hook up my Jaz drive? Any suggestions on what options I have?*

A.   You've got a couple of *very* important questions going on here, so let me try to answer each one. First, do *not* attempt to add new hardware without correcting your lock-up problem first. Check for hardware conflicts. Two or more devices in the system may be using the same IRQs, DMA channels, or I/O port addresses. Check for buggy drivers. Your system may be using an older or buggy driver (i.e., video driver). Make sure that all the drivers are installed correctly and are up to date. Check for loose connections. Make sure that all the cables and connections in the PC are installed correctly and completely. If you're running Windows 95, open the Device Manager and look for any yellow icons that may indicate a resource conflict (or red icons that indicate an inoperative device). Once you have your lock-up problems under control, you can think about installing the SCSI adapter. The 68-pin SCSI bus is not the same as the 50-pin SCSI bus.

PC Hangs Up After the Operating System Starts

Q90.   *Why does my computer hang after the operating system (Windows 95) starts?*

A. I'm assuming that the system is turned on, and you see all the normal POST messages, there are no errors reported during POST, the speaker beeps once, and the system dies as it tries to access the hard disk while loading Windows 95. If this is the case, there are three distinct possibilities to consider:

■ The hard disk information stored in CMOS may be corrupted. Run the CMOS Setup program and confirm that the hard disk configuration is correct. If it is not, reenter the correct values. You may have to call the hard disk manufacturer for the proper values (the number of cylinders, number of heads, and number of sectors per track). Some hard disk manufacturers print this information on the label attached to the top of the disk. Enter this information in Setup, save your values, and restart the computer.

■ The operating system is corrupted. If your CMOS hard disk values are correct and the system still does not boot, try reinstalling the operating system from the disks that came with your computer. Your operating system manuals will describe the process.

■ Your hard disk may have crashed. If you have confirmed that the hard disk parameters in CMOS Setup are correct, and you are not successful in installing the operating system, it may be necessary to replace the hard drive.

Handling PnP BIOS Resource Conflicts

Q91. *Why does the error message; System Resource Conflict appear on my AMI BIOS POST screen? Aren't system resources assigned by Windows 95?*

A. This is a plug-and-play-related message. Although Windows 95 does assign some resources dynamically, the actual PnP system starts with a PnP BIOS. While initializing the system, your AMI PnP BIOS detected a resource conflict (i.e., IRQ, DMA, or I/O address conflicts) between two or more devices and was unable to assign unique resources to all the devices that were detected. You may try to force the PnP BIOS to reconfigure the conflicting resource by pressing <Insert> during POST instead of pressing <Delete>.

INTERMEDIATE

DEALING WITH AN INTERNAL STACK OVERFLOW PROBLEM

Q92. *I have been having trouble with an internal stack overflow problem, and I have not been able to determine if the trouble is hardware or software related. The system is a 486SX/25 laptop running Windows for Workgroups. It also has a 260MB HDD and 8MB of RAM. The unit may have to be booted two or three times before it finally runs—but when it runs, it runs error-free. The unit has already been sent back several times to the manufacturer, who finally put in a new motherboard. However, a new motherboard did not resolve the problem. Any ideas?*

A. When an interrupt occurs in a PC, the CPU must drop whatever it was doing in order to attend to the interrupt. This usually involves jumping to a routine used to deal with the interrupt (an interrupt handler routine). Before a CPU can deal with an interrupt, it must save (or *push*) its state (the contents of its registers) to a small area of memory referred to as the stack. When the interrupt is handled, the CPU can return to the point it left off by *popping* its previous state off the stack. However, the stack is only just so big. If the CPU is overloaded with interrupts and tasks, it is possible to exceed the available stack space and a "stack overflow" message is produced. Since a new motherboard has been installed, you have pretty much ruled out the possibility of a hardware problem.

Windows generally requires much more stack space than DOS. That is why the statement stacks=9256 is added to the CONFIG.SYS file when Windows is installed. Check your CONFIG.SYS file and be sure that line is included. You should also consider the possibility of drivers or TSRs affecting your system's stability. Check your CONFIG.SYS and AUTOEXEC.BAT files and disable any drivers or TSRs that are unneeded. You should also make sure that any remaining drivers are using the correct command line switches. If you can't clear the problem, check your SYSTEM.INI file for any obsolete entries that you can disable (such as drivers being loaded that are no longer needed). Always remember to make backup copies of your start-up and .INI files before you begin editing them.

PREVENTING PREMATURE CPU FAILURES

Q93. *I had a case where a nine-month old Pentium133 machine died prematurely. The CPU is confirmed dead. It sat on a cheap no-name motherboard—no overclocking, no overvoltage. Replacing the chip is not difficult, but the reason behind the CPU's failure concerns me. Is the socket supplying proper voltage to the CPU? Is there a simple test for that? I don't want the motherboard to keep frying CPUs.*

A. There are several issues that can affect the longevity of a CPU. As you suspect, you should be sure to check the CPU voltage regulator first—there is no direct test, but review your motherboard's documentation and locate the jumper(s) used to set CPU voltage. Make sure that jumper is set to the right position. Another important factor to consider is CPU cooling. All Pentium CPUs should be fitted with a good-quality heat sink/fan (you don't mention whether your 133-MHz system had a heat sink/fan or not). Frankly, I wouldn't suspect CPU voltage or cooling in this case—your system worked for nine months. A voltage or cooling problem would have certainly destroyed the CPU before now.

It is possible that the CPU just died spontaneously—it's rare, but it does happen. Try replacing the CPU and return the system to service. If you encounter subsequent CPU failures, I'd suspect the power supply (or your ac power source). Power problems can send spurious signals through the power supply and into the motherboard. Serious or regular power problems may have shortened the life of the CPU. The reason I did not mention this problem earlier is that power problems often crash or hang up the PC. Since you don't mention a history of erratic system behavior, I believe that the power supply is working properly.

INTERMEDIATE

ISOLATING A PAGE FAULT ERROR

Q94. *Do you know what might cause a Page Fault error? The system belongs to my boss at work, and it uses IBM's Cougar 486SLC/66 motherboard, DOS 4.1, and 4MB of RAM. The sys-*

tem is also the server on an old Alloy network. It sounds like a memory issue—I replaced all the SIMMs and the problem went away for about a week. Could it be cache or video memory?

A.   Expanded memory is typically divided into *pages*, and a Page Fault error means that DOS had a problem moving a page around between expanded and conventional memory. However, there are several reasons why this can occur. Start by checking for computer viruses—some viruses load into memory and cause havoc with hardware operations. If the system checks clean for viruses, investigate your power supply. Spikes and surges on the ac line are notorious for interrupting memory (sometimes even killing it). Try a good-quality surge and spike suppresser between the ac wall outlet and computer. Get one with a small neon light that will go out if the suppresser is tripped. You might want to check that no heavy equipment has been installed on the same ac line that the server is on.

Next, consider your network environment—any new applications or changes to the hardware/software configuration can cause problems (i.e., new drivers or memory managers). You might try to temporarily disable any such alterations and see if the problems disappear. Finally, you may still have a problem with your physical memory. Even though you replaced all the SIMMs, a motherboard of the 486SLC vintage often incorporates 1 or 2MB directly on the motherboard. It may be that some of your non-SIMM RAM may be marginal. Try a good commercial diagnostic program and set up a long-term stress test for memory (perhaps even with the SIMMs removed). If you see Page Fault errors (or the diagnostic reports memory errors) with SIMMs removed, your motherboard RAM may be defective. In that case, you might consider replacing or upgrading the motherboard.

Can't Make a Working Boot Disk

Q95.   *I have tried several times to create a workable boot disk by following the instructions furnished in the computer manual. Each time I format and copy AUTOEXEC.BAT files and so on, I then boot up in drive A:\. The computer will then load to the C:*

prompt and run with no noticeable program changes of any kind. According to the instruction book, my computer should load to the A:\ prompt. If this is true, what am I doing wrong?

A. The problem is that you haven't edited your start-up files to point to the boot disk. For example, if you boot from the A: disk and CONFIG.SYS runs and finds:

```
device=c:\cdd\cd1234.sys /a20
```

the boot disk will still go to the C: drive, open the \cdd directory, and run the CD1234.SYS file just as if the C: drive were booting. You should have copied the CD1234.SYS file to the boot floppy and edited the entry in CONFIG.SYS to read:

```
device=a:\cd1234.sys /a20
```

You need to do this for all the files referenced in your start-up files. Once you update your start-up files, the system should boot entirely from the floppy disk.

The file CD1234.SYS is a bogus file name and is used merely for example purposes.

Note

LONG BEEP INDICATES SYSTEM FAILURE

Q96. *I'm working on a computer that refuses to boot. It makes one long beep, but it continues to repeat it every few seconds. It has an AMI BIOS. Any idea what this means? Before it failed completely, it lost CMOS and would sometimes boot with a short double beep. It has the Dallas RTC 12887A with the battery in it. It's only a couple of years old, so would this battery be likely to fail? Any ideas on what might be wrong with this thing?*

A. I'm not inclined to suspect the CMOS at this point because lost contents would usually result in a CMOS Mismatch error. The fact that your PC isn't even booting suggests that you have a catastrophic failure somewhere in the system. First, check all of your SIMMs, expansion boards, and cables. Make sure that everything is installed properly and securely. For example, make sure your video board didn't fall out of its expansion slot. If the problem continues, check your power supply. All the cables should be secure. Finally, check the motherboard for any metal or standoffs that might be shorting the motherboard out. If you're really stuck at this point, replace your motherboard.

BEEPS INDICATE FAILING MEMORY

Q97.   *I had been piecing together a PC from all kinds of spare parts, but recently I got a 5x86 motherboard with an AMI BIOS. Then I bought a Cirrus Logic 5436, 64-bit, 2MB video card for it. When I turn on the PC, I get one long beep and three short beeps from the BIOS. What's wrong?*

A.   According to our notes, a 1l-3s beep sequence from an AMI BIOS indicates a memory test failure, which would suggest that the memory residing on your motherboard has failed. Before you focus on your RAM, take another look at your video board. Make sure the video board is installed correctly and completely. Try reinstalling the video board, or try a different video board in the system. If the problem persists, consider replacing your RAM. If RAM is all in the form of SIMMs, you can try replacing the memory outright—usually one SIMM at a time. If not, you will have to replace that new motherboard (otherwise you'd have to unsolder the existing RAM and solder in new RAM—a tricky proposition even for experienced technicians).

SYSTEM DOESN'T POWER UP RELIABLY

Q98.   *Six years ago, I bought a 386 40-MHz computer in a full tower case. Later on I upgraded it with a generic 486 VLB motherboard with an Intel 486/33 CPU and OPTI chipset. I have 16MB of RAM, a DTC VL bus EIDE drive controller, a Caviar hard drive, and an STB VLB Lightspeed graphics accelerator. The original 300W switched power supply, front switches, and display are all that are left of the original system. Now sometimes when I turn on the computer, it doesn't power up (no lights come on, the fan doesn't start, and so on). This has gradually gotten worse and is becoming quite a nuisance. When the system does come on, everything works, but if I turn it off, it usually won't come on again right away. Is this a case of the power supply overheating? I have never had it stop working once it is on. Should I replace the power supply or is there something else that could cause my problem.*

A.   It certainly sounds like your power supply is giving you trouble, but check all the connections between your power supply and you motherboard (as well as to the drives). Also check your ac cord to see that it's secure in the power supply (I've seen loose power connections shut down more than one network server). If the problems persist, you should try another power supply.

PC Occasionally Fails During First Boot

Q99.   *On rare occasions (maybe once a month), I hit the power button to start up my PC and it immediately starts beeping loudly. It continues beeping until I power it off and then on again. Then the system starts and boots normally. Nothing shows on the monitor when this happens—just a blank screen. The PC uses a Tomcat motherboard with a Cyrix P150+, Award 4.51PG BIOS, Enlite case, and runs Windows 95. There are no other problems with configuration or hardware conflicts.*

A.   Occasional intermittent behavior such as yours is extremely difficult to track down, but there are some points to check. I have seen this type of problem caused by loose SIMMs, so my first suggestion would be to remount your SIMMs in their holders. You might also check to see that the contact metal on each SIMM is clean and is the same metal as your SIMM holders (i.e., gold to gold or tin to tin). Dissimilar metals can cause contact problems. The second thing to check is your video board. It should be seated evenly and completely in its bus slot, and secured to the chassis with a single screw. Try the video board in a different slot if you wish. Finally, keyboard problems can cause some BIOS versions to generate large numbers of beeps. Check your keyboard connection, and perhaps try a different keyboard.

ADVANCED

PC Upgrade Causes Looping Memory Count

Q100. *I've got a clone 486DX/33 VL bus system with 8MB of RAM, Maxtor 125MB HDD, Genoa VLB video card, and a 32-bit drive controller card. The system is running Windows 3.1. I upgraded the system with 4MB of RAM (giving a total of 8MB), and added a 3.5-in floppy disk. Now every time I boot up, I get the normal AMI BIOS count through the RAM; it shows the drives, cache, and CPU details. BIOS then hits the A20 gate, and just before it's about to hit the hard drive, it jumps back to count the RAM—the system loops like this continuously. I've turned off external cache and internal cache and still the problem persists. The only change I made to BIOS was an update to specify the 3.5-in floppy disk.*

A. If the system loops back before you see "Starting MS-DOS," there may be a problem with your new memory. Try removing the new memory and test the system again. You may have installed incompatible SIMM sizes or SIMMs of a different type or speed. Check your motherboard manual and verify that you have installed the recommended SIMMs in the correct memory banks. If the problem persists, you may have a problem with the A20 line. The A20 gate feature is controlled by the keyboard controller IC on your motherboard. Try replacing the keyboard controller (or replace the motherboard). If you *do* see the Starting MS-DOS message, you may be able to correct the problem by adding a command line switch to your HIMEM.SYS entry in the CONFIG.SYS file such as:

```
device=himem.sys /a20control:off
```

Computer Boot Problems Cause CMOS Concerns

Q101. *I'm working on a computer that refuses to boot. It makes one long beep, but it continues to repeat it every few seconds. It has an AMI BIOS—any idea what this means? Before the system failed completely, it lost its CMOS settings and would sometimes boot with a short double beep. It has the Dallas RTC 12887A with the battery inside it. The system is only a couple of years old, so would this battery be likely to fail? Any ideas on what might be wrong with this thing?*

A.   The Dallas unit can fail after a few years because the battery is simply not that large, but I'm not inclined to suspect the CMOS at this point because lost contents would usually result in a CMOS Mismatch error. The fact that your PC isn't even booting suggests that you have a catastrophic failure somewhere in the system. First, check all of your SIMMs, expansion boards, and cables. Make sure that everything is installed properly and securely. For example, make sure your video board didn't fall out of its expansion slot. If the problem continues, check your power supply. All the cables should be secure, and each output (+5 V, −5 V, +12 V, and −12 V) should be correct—you should measure each of these outputs with a multimeter. If you find an output (particularly the +5 V output) which is low or absent, you should replace the power supply. Finally, check the motherboard for any metal or standoffs that might be shorting the motherboard out.

Poor Connections Causing System Problems

Q102.   *I have a 486DX/33 AST computer. The system has 16MB of RAM, two 120MB hard drives, a 3.5-in floppy drive, a Sony 8X CD-ROM with controller, and a 16-bit sound card. When I boot up the machine, the hard drive light stays on and the keyboard lights flash. It stays this way until you lightly tap on the case. Sometimes it boots without the flashing lights, but after the memory count, it says the hard drive adapter is defective. It acts normally after you go into the CMOS and resave the settings.*

A.   Start by focusing on your CMOS Setup routine. If your CMOS RAM refuses to hold its settings after power is turned off, you should check the CMOS backup battery. Make sure the battery is installed securely and is in the right orientation. Try replacing the battery. If you can get CMOS to hold its settings and the system stabilizes, you'll need to check your hardware for loose connections. Examine the motherboard for any metal filings, staples, or other metal items that might be causing intermittent short circuits. Also check the metal standoffs to see that none of them are shorting out printed traces on the motherboard. Take a look at your CPU, BIOS IC, and SIMMs to see that they are all secure. Every expansion board (i.e., your video board, drive controller, modem, and so on) should be seated firmly and completely. Check all of your drive cables—especially your floppy and hard drive cables—for proper installation.

SYSTEMS CRASHES MAY BE DUE TO FAULTY MEMORY

Q103.   *I am experiencing periodic system crashes (about once a day) while doing innocuous things like scrolling in Explorer on my Windows 95 machine and have heard suggestions that it might be due to bad memory chips. Since I recently installed some bargain memory from CompUSA, this might make sense. Does this make any sense to you? And is there any program you know of that performs a more exhaustive memory test on a PC?*

A.   Yes, the fault you describe is consistent with intermittent memory operation. I suggest you check the SIMM installation again and see that your SIMMs are installed securely. Also see that the contact metals on the SIMM match the contact metals on the sockets. For example, tin SIMM sockets should use SIMMs with tin contacts, while gold SIMM sockets should use SIMMs with gold contacts. If you want a good diagnostic to stress test your memory, try TuffTest; *http://www.tufftest.com.*

PC REBOOTS FOR NO OBVIOUS REASON

Q104.   *I have a 486 PC that's running Windows 95, and the PC reboots for no apparent reason. I can be in a word processor, spreadsheet, Windows Explorer, or other application when it reboots. There doesn't seem to be a common element from a software standpoint, so now I'm tackling the hardware for a resolution. I've replaced the motherboard and CPU, but it still reboots. I've considered replacing memory and the hard drive, but first I thought I'd check in with you for ideas.*

A.   There are many reasons that your PC might be rebooting, and I suspect that you're right that the problem is hardware related. Still, before you go any farther, try starting Windows 95 in the

ADVANCED

Safe Mode and see if the system stabilizes. If it does, you may have a driver problem after all. You might also try booting the system to DOS and running it there for a while. Once again, if the system runs OK in DOS, you may have a registry problem or a driver issue in SYSTEM.INI or another .INI file. If the system continues to crash, you've taken another step toward confirming a hardware problem. Here are the hardware points that you should examine:

- Check your system for computer viruses. I think this is a rather unlikely problem given your symptoms, but it never hurts to run a current virus checking utility just to be safe.

- New hardware can always be a problem. If your trouble started after adding a new expansion board or other device, there may be a hardware conflict between it and another device in the system (IRQ conflicts are especially notorious for causing crashes and reboots).

- Check the ac power cord. I've seen ac cords that looked OK at the wall outlet but were loose at the PC power supply. Make sure the ac cord is tight.

- Check the other power connectors. Double-check your motherboard and drive power connectors and see that everything is inserted tightly.

- Your power supply may be failing. Noisy electrical lines and faulty power supplies can certainly cause the PC to crash. Try the PC on a different ac circuit that is free of heavy electrical loads like coffee makers and motors. If the problem continues, try a different power supply.

- If you're running your PC from a UPS, the backup may be overloaded. Try running JUST the PC from the backup outlet.

- Motherboard shorts can easily cause spontaneous system crashes. Even though you replaced the motherboard, there may still be a metal standoff or other metal object causing your reboots.

REVIVING A PS/2 MODEL 80

Q105. *I have an IBM PS/2 Model 80 386 PC and it is dead. I have no documentation. When booting, it beeps twice and displays the RAM count, then 162 on first line and 163 on next line. That's it. I have no experience with the IBM PS/2 line.*

A. For the PS/2-class systems, 16x errors are usually related to system configuration problems—the contents of your system's CMOS are probably corrupted or lost. Replace the CMOS backup battery and use the IBM setup disk to reload your system configuration. You can obtain a PS/2 setup disk (or reference disk as IBM often refers to them) from the IBM FTP site at; *ftp.pc.ibm.com*. Once you prepare the reference disk, boot the system with that disk, and correct your setup errors.

REVIVING A DEAD 486DX/33

Q106. *I have a 486DX/33 system that is dead—all I get is the fan noise. There are no beeps, and nothing is on the screen. When I take out all the adapter cards, the same condition persists. And there is no change when I insert a 486DX/33 CPU from a working system. Please tell me an easy systematic way of finding out where the problem lies. Fortunately I have a similar working 486DX/33 system with which I can swap out parts.*

A. The protocol for troubleshooting a dead PC is really pretty straightforward. Always check the power connections first. If the power supply is not connected to the motherboard properly, the system will appear totally dead. There are typically two power cables that attach to the motherboard. You should also measure each power supply output (+5 V, −5 V, +12 V, −12 V) and make sure each output is at the level it should be. If any output is low or absent, it could indicate a faulty power supply (and the supply should be replaced). Check each of your expansion cards plugged into your bus slots. The cards should be inserted evenly and completely. Any card inserted improperly may be shorting metal "fingers," causing power or signal shorts that can disable the PC.

Next, check the motherboard to ensure that no printed circuit traces are shorted to the case or any of the metal standoffs mounting the motherboard. Since you replaced the CPU (and the CPU is obviously OK), that is not the problem. If the problem persists, try clearing the CMOS (this is rare, but some motherboards can lock up if there is trouble with CMOS contents). Finally, you should replace the motherboard outright.

PC Won't Boot After Move

Q107. *I moved my computer to another room last night, and now it will not boot at all. It will not even load the BIOS. My hard drive light comes on for a second, but the screen stays blank. Any suggestions? It's an Intel P120 Triton II motherboard.*

A. You'd be amazed how often I hear this one. In *every* case, something has come loose during the move. Start by checking your video board. For some reason, video boards seem to have a habit of leaping out of their bus slots at the first opportunity—and without a video board, the system will invariably freeze. After you reseat the video board (and check the monitor cable), check all the other expansion boards for proper installation, as well as every SIMM and cable in the PC. Pay particular attention to the power cables which attach to the motherboard. One of those is bound to be the culprit.

System Won't Boot After New Motherboard Installation

Q108. *I got a used 486DX2/66 motherboard for Christmas (well, my son did). I'm putting it into a box that held a 386DX/44, but when I put the motherboard in, I get no video. It beeps twice, pauses, beeps eight times, pauses, then beeps twice more. I immediately shut it off. The CPU is a 3-V AMD Am486 chip. It says to set the jumper for 3-V operation. I saw the computer; it was in running properly, so I guess the jumper is already set for 3 V (no manual available). It has an AMI BIOS. Could this be a voltage problem? Do I need a different power supply?*

ADVANCED

A.   I haven't been able to find any 2-8-2 beep codes for AMI BIOS—
the closest I could come is two beeps for a memory parity error
and eight beeps for a video memory error. As it happens, memory
and video problems are the two most common issues when replacing a motherboard. Check the installation of your SIMMs. If these
are new SIMMs (installed from the original motherboard), make
sure that they match the memory type and speed of any other
memory in the system. You may need to add wait states in CMOS
or disable parity checking. Also make sure that a complete bank is
filled. Next, check your video board to see that it is seated properly in its expansion slot. Try reseating the video board.

DEAD PC SEEMS TO HAVE POWER

Q109.   *I've got a dead computer that seems to have adequate power
(i.e., the hard drive spins, CPU fan spins, and so on) but that's
it—nothing appears on the screen, the keyboard doesn't light up,
and there are no beeps. It's a Biostar 486 PCI motherboard that
doesn't appear to have a CMOS backup battery. Should I check
the power supply? Does it sound like a battery problem?*

A.   I doubt that you've got a battery problem—at worse, that would
cause a CMOS configuration error or other type of message.
From your description of the problem, I'd say you have a power
problem, short circuit, or motherboard failure. As you suspected,
make it a point to check your power levels first. Make sure that
the power connectors are securely attached to your motherboard.
Also check that your memory, video board, and other expansion
boards are installed evenly and secured in their bus slots. Check
the motherboard to see that no metal standoffs are shorting any
of the motherboard's printed traces. Use a voltmeter and measure
the voltages feeding your motherboard. The red wires should
measure +5 V, the blue wires should measure –12 V, the yellow
wires should read +12 V, and the white wires should be –5 V.
The orange "power good" signal should be about +5 V. If any of
those voltages are low or absent, your power supply is probably
defective and should be replaced. If the voltages are good, you
have a defective CPU or another major fault on the motherboard,
and the motherboard should probably be replaced.

ADVANCED

Power Supplies and Backups

Y Cable Problems

Q110. *I've heard that some Y cable adapters can actually damage a drive. Is this true? If so, how does it happen?*

A. The Y cable is little more than a splitter which gives you two power connections from one. However, there have recently been some poorly made Y cables on the market that carelessly reverse several of the power lines. If you attach a drive to the end of such a poorly made Y cable, you stand a very good chance of damaging the drive permanently. To check the Y cable for incorrect wiring, examine both female connectors. Make certain that both of the female connectors are lined up with the two chamfered (rounded) corners facing up and both of the squared corners facing down. The four wires attached to the female connectors should now be in the following order from left to right; Yellow (12 V), Black (ground), Black (ground), Red (5 V). If this order is reversed on one or both of the connectors, your Y cable is faulty and should not be used.

Power Supply Fan Voltages

Q111. *What's the voltage of those 4-in square fans that are sold as auxiliary exhaust fans? Is it the same as the fan in a power supply?*

A. Supplemental fans which plug into the system bus on a fan card typically use +12 V. Fans inside the power supply itself also typically use +12 V, although some power supply designs employ 120-V ac fans that run directly from the main power switch.

SHORT LAPTOP BATTERY LIFETIME

Q112. *My laptop battery is giving me problems. Most of the time, my laptop is on my desk and plugged into its ac adapter. In that case, the laptop works properly. But when I try to "go mobile," I can only get 60 to 90 min from a charge (it should be at least 2 h). Should I be replacing the battery pack?*

A.   You have not told me how old your system is or if the battery pack has ever worked properly, so here are some ideas to try. First, I seriously recommend getting a second battery pack—they're not that expensive, and we always seem to need the battery most just as it goes dead. A second pack is good insurance. Now that you've got a second battery pack, let's see what the problem is with your original pack. Try running the system on your new battery pack (be sure it's fully charged first).

If you do *not* get a full 2-h plus charge from the new pack, the original pack is probably good, and you should inspect your system configuration closely. Mobile computers make extensive use of power conservation features such as shutting down the hard drive after some minutes without file activity, or shutting down the LCD backlight after some minutes without mouse or keyboard activity. Power conservation settings can usually be enabled, disabled, and adjusted from a DOS utility or system CMOS Setup routine. Locate and check these settings. If your power conservation modes are disabled, you may be unable to get the full life from an average battery charge.

If you *do* get a full charge from the new pack, the original pack may indeed be defective, but before you toss it out, let's try a few experiments. First, do you leave the laptop plugged into its ac adapter all the time? This type of continuous charging may eventually weaken a battery pack. Also, frequent partial discharges can cause nickel-cadmium (NiCd) cells to succumb to a discharge effect which leaves the cells unable to provide substantial power once that regular point of discharge is reached. In either case, try cycling the battery through several complete discharges and full recharges. If the problem persists, you can probably discard the original battery pack.

MONITOR POWER PROTECTION

Q113. *My friend told me that I shouldn't have my monitor plugged into my UPS (along with my PC). Is that true? I know that takes more backup power, but what else can I do?*

A.   The traditional wisdom of UPS and battery backup systems is that you place only essential equipment on the backup outlets, and all nonessential equipment is placed on surge-protected outlets. It is perfectly acceptable to place a monitor on a backup outlet, but you do reduce your backup time because monitors take a significant amount of power. If you're always working at the PC, and you need to shut down quickly in the event of an emergency, leave the monitor on a backup outlet. You may want to upgrade the size of the battery backup to support more running time with the added load of your monitor. On the other hand, if you're running a file server, or some other system which may need to continue running for a while after power is lost, keep the monitor on a surge-protected outlet only—this affords you the maximum running time. Also, if you use a UPS system with backup utilities that can automatically proceed with a safe system shutdown when a power loss is detected, there's little need to keep the monitor backed up as well, so let it cut out, and the PC will take care of itself. Keep in mind that other peripherals (such as printers and scanners) are almost never backed up by a UPS. Instead, invest in a good-quality surge protection power strip.

SUPPLYING AMPLE POWER TO YOUR DRIVES

Q114. *I know that most motherboards now will take four hard drives. But in real terms, how many drives can an average 220-W power supply handle?*

A.   That's not always an easy question to answer because it depends on the vintage of your particular drives. Today, hard drives need about 10 to 12 W to operate (with a bit more on initial start-up). This means your power supply will need to provide as much as 50 W to support four drives. Here's the rule I use for power estimates: 150 W for the motherboard, CPU, RAM, and cache, 12 W per drive (such as HDDs, FDDs, CD-ROMs, tape drives, and so on), and 12W per expansion board (i.e., video, drive, and SCSI adapters). So if you've got a system with a video board, modem, HDD, FDD, and CD-ROM drive, you should plan on using a power supply of at least 210 W (150 + 12 + 12 + 12 + 12 + 12)—a 220 W unit would probably be the nearest commercial match. If you added a drive controller and two more hard drives to the system, you should plan on a 246 W supply (210 + 12 + 12 + 12) with 250 W being the nearest match. If you had been using a 220-W supply previously, you will need to upgrade the power supply. Also keep in mind that it's perfectly acceptable to overrate the supply. For example, you could buy a 250-W supply in place of a 220-W supply or a 300-W supply instead of a 250-W supply.

KNOWING THE LIMITS OF YOUR POWER SUPPLY

Q115.   *How many drives (floppy drives, hard drives, CD-ROM drives, and so on) could a 250-W supply handle? I just bought a case with 10 expansion bays, and it has a 250-W power supply. Did I get taken? I only plan on having about five bays filled (at the most).*

A.   I usually use the 150 plus 12 rule where I plan on 150 W for the motherboard, CPU, RAM, and cache, and 12 W for every drive and expansion board. Assuming you have a motherboard and 10 drives (we'll figure the motherboard provides video and drive adapters), you'd need about 270 W [150 + (12 * 10)]. For that many drives, you'd probably need a SCSI adapter, so the total would probably be closer to 282 W (270 + 12). A 300-W supply would probably be in order for a full-blown system. Since you're only planning on up to five drives and probably a 3-D video adapter, modem, and sound board, I'd say you need more like 246 W (150 + 12 + 12 + 12 + 12 + 12 + 12 + 12 + 12). Since your system has a 250-W supply, I think you'll be OK. Keep in mind that if you add more expansion boards or drives, you probably *will* need a power supply upgrade.

Power Supplies and System Cooling

Q116. *I'm thinking about the PC cooling system. If you purchase a sep-arate power supply for your case, will it have less cooling power than one that's been integrated to the case?*

A.   Whether a power supply is purchased as a separate component or sold as an integrated part of the case, the supply is *still* sealed in its own metal housing for the sake of electrical safety. As a result, I believe you'll find that the fan inside a power supply is intended primarily to cool the power supply (not the inside of the case). If there are vents in the supply housing, there may be some added air flow in the case—but not much. Similarly, the fan(s) that blow air through the case area will have almost no effect on power supply cooling. The bottom line is that there's very little "mutual cooling" between the power supply and case regardless of whether the supply is integrated into the case or not.

Selecting Separate or Integrated Power Supplies

Q117. *I'm planning to rebuild my PC, and I was surfing the Web look-ing for a new chassis and power supply. I was wondering if it's better to purchase a separate power supply or buy one that is already mated to a case. How would that affect the performance of the overall system and its design?*

A.   The question of power supplies is always a touchy one. Some folks swear by purchasing a matched power supply and case, while others will opt for the separate supply and case. The advantage of a matched set of course is convenience. But there are two problems with convenience—you don't really have any say over the power supply quality (which can have a profound impact on your system stability), and if the power supply should ever fail, you may find yourself having to replace it *and* case. This forces you into a massive rebuild that will take much longer than simply replacing the failed power supply. In my opinion, get the separate power supply and case if you can.

The Consequences of an Overloaded Power Supply

Q118.   *I want to upgrade my PC with some new drives, but I'm worried
about my power supply. My system only has a 200-W supply in
it, and I'm just not sure it'll be enough power. What will happen
if my 200-W power supply is not enough to power all of my
peripherals? Will the power supply fail? Is it dangerous to the
other components in my system?*

A.   This is a great question and one that pops up regularly.
Insufficient power can have a wide variety of effects depending
on the quality of your power supply and the severity of the overload. If a power supply is overloaded just a little, a good one
might be able to compensate for the extra load—it will just run a
bit hotter. This is actually the most dangerous mode for the
power supply, because you're likely to run the overloaded system
for weeks (if not months) before the additional heat can cause a
premature failure. If the power supply can't compensate for the
extra load, the loss of power can result in intermittent system
operation. You may see sporadic system crashes where you never
saw them before (and incorrectly attribute them to the new hardware you installed). An underpowered drive may also corrupt or
lose files. If the overload is a bit more serious, there may not be
enough power to drive the computer's logic correctly. This can
cause more severe crashes and reboots—the system may occasionally fail to start or may freeze at different points in the POST
process. Finally, a substantial overload will almost certainly prevent the system from even starting up. In all cases, it is extremely
unlikely that an overload would cause a sudden power supply
failure—unless the power supply is of questionable quality to
begin with.

UPS Systems versus Battery Backups

Q119.   *What's the difference between a UPS and a battery backup unit?*

A.   Simply, the difference is in how the battery is used. For a battery
backup, the battery power is switched in only when main ac
power is lost. For the UPS, the battery provides the primary
power source which is constantly kept charged by the main ac

source. The UPS is generally regarded as the preferred option because the battery source is free of ac anomalies like surges, spikes, and brownouts, and there is no switching time which might allow some PC power supplies to glitch and reboot the PC.

SYSTEM DAMAGE FROM A UPS

Q120. *I just got an uninterruptible power supply for my dad's office. Reading its manual, I see: "CAUTION: The output of this unit is a sine approximation suitable for use with modern computer power supplies. Other loads may malfunction or damage the UPS. In particular, FERRORESONANT type regulating trans- formers are not recommended...." Now, the problem is, my dad's machine has a 110-V monitor that requires a transformer (our mains are 220 V) to work. Does the above CAUTION tell me that I cannot use the UPS with the monitor?*

A. UPS systems do not produce *pure* sine waves but rather a digital representation that looks rather like an up/down staircase. For most power supplies, this approximated sine wave will work. Some more specialized switching power supplies, however, may not respond properly to the harmonics generated by the approxi- mated wave. If you need to connect a 110-V monitor to the 220- V UPS, simply try connecting the transformer and then measure the output. If the output measures 110 V as expected, chances are that the monitor and transformer will work properly. If the output appears far too high or far too low, the transformer may be distorting the sine wave at the secondary (output) windings. My guess is that an ordinary step-down transformer will work since it is typically not ferroresonant and does not have any effect on the monitor's power supply regulation.

INTERMEDIATE

POWER CONTROLS CAUSING INTERMITTENT MONITOR

Q121. *I have a very intermittent problem with my monitor. I control all the power to my PC and monitor with a surge protector outlet strip, so I turn the strip on and off rather than the PC and moni- tor. Most of the time everything turns on properly but about 10 percent of the time, the monitor stays dark while the PC seems to be booting. When I reboot the system again, the monitor comes to life and all appears to run normally. I have reproduced this effect using a different monitor, and I have also tried various energy-saving video settings in the BIOS (which I have completely disabled). I have a Matrox Mystique graphics card. What could be the source of this problem?*

A.   When you power up the system, the monitor should begin displaying a video signal as soon as valid video data is being generated by the video board. Check for power at your monitor outlet. If your power indicator LEDs on the monitor always come on, the video board may not be firing up properly (you may want to check the video board's installation). If you notice that the monitor's power LEDs do not come on, you've got trouble with the surge suppresser socket or ac power cable. Should you determine that the video board itself is acting up, you should consider upgrading or replacing the video card.

POWER SUPPLY NOISE

Q122.   *Over the last two weeks, I have noticed that my power supply makes a distinct sound. In the past, I may have heard the sound of the fan if I put my ear towards the case, but now the power supply emits a very low humming sound. My current power supply is a 230 V unit that powers a CPU fan, two hard drives, an internal tape backup drive, a floppy drive, and an internal CD-ROM. How long does the typical power supply last?*

A.   Ideally, a power supply should last indefinitely, but in practical terms, it will eventually fail from regular use or damage due to overloading or power anomalies (i.e., lightning strikes). A low humming sound may indicate an imminent failure. Take a voltmeter and check each voltage output—if any of the outputs are low (especially the +5- or +12-V outputs), consider replacing the power supply before the situation degrades any further. Another type of low hum may occur from the fan itself. Dust buildup on the fan blades can affect the fan's balance, and worn motor bearings can cause vibration—both of which can easily result in a hum. Try cleaning the fan blades, and drop a bit of light lubricant into the fan bearings (if possible).

BUZZING SOUND MAY INDICATE BAD POWER SUPPLY

Q123.   *Can you help me regarding my power supply unit? Last night my
PC wouldn't power up. There is a small buzzing sound coming
from the power supply. Is there any way of fixing it, or would it
be better to just replace it? The power supply is about three years
old.*

A.   A buzzing sound does not necessarily dictate a bad power supply.
Check the installation of all adapter boards on the motherboard
(make sure they are all seated properly). Next, use a voltmeter to
measure each voltage output from the power supply. You will
find several wire colors: black (ground), white (–5 V), yellow
(+12 V), red (+5 V), and blue (–12 V). If one or more of the voltages are low or absent, the power supply is probably defective. If
you have some serious electrical troubleshooting experience, you
could troubleshoot the power supply (buzzing often suggests
transformer or filter failures), but it is often faster and easier to
just replace it outright. Be sure that your new power supply is
compatible with the existing mounting points in your chassis,
and see that there are enough drive power cables to run all your
drives properly.

BEEPS CAN INDICATE A SERIOUS POWER PROBLEM

Q124.   *I'm trying to build a system with a used AMD 486DX2/66
motherboard. When I apply power, I get an odd beep code (a
total of 12 beeps) and no video. I got a better (165 W) power
supply and hooked it up again—and nothing happened. The fan
on the power supply moved about an $1/8$ inch and stopped. The
fan on the CPU also moved just a hair and stopped. I know this
motherboard functioned when it was removed from the original
computer. Any thoughts?*

A.   I don't know what kind of BIOS you're using, but in the literature I've been able to scrape up for AMI, 12 beeps refers to a
power supply failure. Check all of your power supply connections and verify that none of the voltage outputs are shorted.
Examine the motherboard and see that no standoffs or other
metal parts are shorting the motherboard's printed traces.
Another issue is your power supply rating itself. I feel that a

ADVANCED

165-W power supply is far too small for a modern motherboard, fans, drives, and (probably) expansion boards. The way to find out is to place a voltmeter across your +5- or +12-V outputs. If the supply outputs measure properly when the system is turned off, but drop terribly when the system is turned on, you're definitely overloading the power supply. Try a 230- to 250-W power supply and see if the problem persists.

DEALING WITH A FAILED POWER SUPPLY COOLING FAN

Q125. *Recently, I've noticed that my computer has been getting pretty hot. When I checked a little closer, I found that the power supply fan is not turning. The PC works, so I know that the power supply must be working. Should I replace the fan, or would it be easier to replace the entire power supply?*

A. Heat is probably the worst enemy of electronic circuitry. Fans (especially in high heat areas such as the power supply) create air flow which carries away an amazing amount of heat. When the fan stopped, air flow stopped as well—the power supply enclosure is probably not ventilated properly for convection (hot air rising) cooling. As a result, the heat builds up inside the supply. If the load on the power supply is not too severe, it may continue to work for an extended period, but its life span will undoubtedly be shortened.

First, you need to find if the fan has failed or not. If the power supply is welded or riveted shut, it may be faster and easier to replace it outright. Many computer superstores offer replacement power supplies, and you can now find a wealth of PC parts distributors on the Internet—you only need to know the approximate wattage of the original one. Select a replacement power supply that provides at least as much power (and at least as many drive power cables) as the original. It is appropriate to select a power supply with a higher wattage capacity as long as it will fit into the available space of the PC.

If you have a power supply that is accessible (bolted together rather than welded), you can open it and use a voltmeter to check the voltage level operating the fan. Some fans are ac and some fans are dc. Use *extreme* caution when accessing a power supply. The ac voltages available in the power supply can cause serious shocks—even death. If you do not get a reading, a portion of the power supply circuit has probably failed. You can troubleshoot the power supply if you have the skill and test instruments to do so, but your best course is often to replace it outright. If there is power reaching the fan, and it is not turning, the fan is probably defective. You can replace the fan if you can find a replacement with the proper mounting holes and air flow capacity (in cubic feet per minute or CFM). Many full-featured electronics stores and distributors carry a selection of fans. If you cannot find an appropriate replacement fan, replace the power supply outright. A company such as PC Power and Cooling (619-723-9513) can often help you find replacement fans or power supply assemblies.

No Power Good Signal from the Power Supply

Q126.   *In an attempt to build my first PC, I have gutted an old 286 case and hope to use it along with the remaining power supply. However, the voltage readings are puzzling to me. With P8 and P9 (the power connectors) attached to the new motherboard, my voltage reading on P8's power good wire (the first orange wire) measures 0.14 V although the blue wire reads –12 V, yellow reads +12 V, white reads –5 V, and red reads +5 V. It seems that the power good pin should be about +5 V since the other voltages are OK. Is this power supply usable? If not, is there something I can do to repair it, or should I spring for $40 and start fresh with a new one?*

A.   You are correct—the power good signal should normally be about +5 V when all voltages are correct. In its current state, it is keeping the motherboard in a reset state and will not allow it to boot. This suggests that the power supply has failed for some reason. Before you do anything else, double-check your voltage readings—especially the power good signal. Also examine each of the metal standoffs mounting your motherboard and make sure that none of them are shorting any printed traces on the motherboard. If you can verify that all the voltage outputs are correct, but the power good signal has failed, you should be able to dis-

connect the orange power good wire, and the system should boot
right up. It is then up to your discretion whether or not to
replace the power supply outright. For the sake of safety, I would
recommend that you *do* replace the power supply eventually—
sooner rather than later.

SCSI Terminology and General Topics

MANY DEVICES ARE SUPPORTED BY SCSI

Q127. *I'm just getting into computers, and I have a question about
SCSI. I know that an SCSI adapter will support SCSI hard
drives, but what other devices will SCSI support? Do you need
an SCSI adapter for every device?*

A.   SCSI is a versatile bus which allows the connection of many different types of devices—all daisy chained to the same ribbon
cable. Hard drives are certainly the most common SCSI devices,
but you can also attach SCSI CD-ROM drives, SCSI tape drives,
SCSI zip drives, SCSI scanners, and really any other device that
uses the SCSI interface. Typically, one SCSI adapter will support
up to seven SCSI devices (each with its own SCSI ID number 0 to
6). The only time an SCSI device may demand its own SCSI
adapter is when you are working in some network environments
(such as a network tape backup for NetWare).

FAST AND WIDE SCSI

Q128. *I've heard the terms Fast SCSI and Wide SCSI used quite frequently, but I can't find any definitions for them. What are they,
and how are they different—or are they different?*

A.   Fast and Wide SCSI are quite different, but they are both variations
of the same SCSI interface. Fast SCSI is a speed-enhanced version of
the SCSI interface, and it can transfer 8-bit data at 10MB/s, or 16-
bit data at 20MB/s. Wide SCSI refers to the 16-bit (68-pin) SCSI
bus, whose speed is below fast SCSI. As a result, a fast *and* wide
SCSI interface will give you the best data throughput.

FINDING INFORMATION FOR DTK SCSI ADAPTERS

Q129. *I'm trying to use an old DTK PTI-222 SCSI Host Adapter. I have no technical information on the card. Can you share this information with me or direct me to some DTK tech support site?*

A. DTK manages an extensive Web site for technical support of their products at *http://www.dtk.com/sp.html*. They also have an FTP site for manuals and BIOS at *ftp://www.dtk.com/pub/dtk/*.

SCSI CONNECTORS

Q130. *What types of connectors do SCSI hard drives use?*

A. Basically, SCSI hard drives can employ any of three connector types, depending on the drive's capabilities. A 50-pin SCSI connector can be a Centronics or IDC-style connector (known as an A-style connector). Fifty-pin connectors can transfer data in 8-bit (narrow) mode only. A 68-pin SCSI connector almost always uses an IDC-style connector, which is called the P-style connector. It can transfer data in 8-bit (narrow) and 16-bit (wide) modes. Both single-ended and differential SCSI interface versions are supported with 68-pin connections. Figure 1.4 illustrates the difference between 50- and 68-pin SCSI connectors. Finally, the 80-pin SCSI connector uses a Single Connector Attachment (SCA-2) connector, which is designed for backplane connections. It can also transfer data in 8-bit (narrow) and 16-bit (wide) modes.

50-pin IDC SCSI Connector

68-pin IDC SCSI Connector

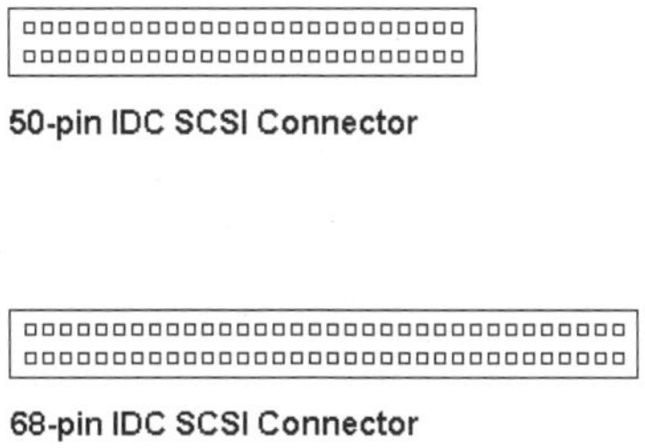

Figure 1.4 Comparing 50 and 68-pin SCSI connectors

Motherboard Requirements for Installing SCSI

Q131.   *When installing an internal SCSI hard drive, do I have to have a motherboard that is exclusively SCSI?*

A.   Absolutely *not*! Most motherboards have an EIDE interface built in and a few have an SCSI interface on board, but even if the motherboard has no SCSI features by itself, you can easily add SCSI devices (such as hard drives, scanners, CD-ROM drives, tape drives, and so on) by first installing an SCSI adapter card in an expansion slot. You will then need to install a driver to access the SCSI controller, as well as a unique driver for every SCSI device (except for hard drives which are typically handled by the SCSI adapter's BIOS).

Connecting SCSI Devices to the Motherboard

Q132.   *Is it possible to connect a second (but external) SCSI drive directly to the motherboard without the use of an SCSI card?*

A.   If the motherboard has an on-board SCSI interface and BIOS support, I suspect that you can connect any suitable SCSI device. However, there may be some difficulty in converting the internal SCSI cable to an external SCSI cable. If there is no native SCSI support on the motherboard, you will need to add a stand-alone SCSI adapter.

SCSI Devices and Cable Lengths

Q133.   *What are the cable length specs for SCSI?*

A.   That's a great question because so many SCSI installations are fouled up by cabling problems. SCSI cables and terminations are *very* particular, and Table 1.5 lists the preferred cable lengths for major SCSI types.

TABLE 1.5 SCSI CABLE LENGTHS AND DEVICE SUPPORT

SCSI TYPE	Maximum Bus Length [1] (Meters—single-ended)	Maximum Devices
SCSI-1	6	8
Fast SCSI	3	8
Fast Wide SCSI	3	16
Ultra SCSI	1.5	8
Wide Ultra SCSI	-	16
Wide Ultra SCSI	1.5	8
Wide Ultra SCSI	3	4
Ultra2 SCSI[2]		8
Wide Ultra2 SCSI[2]		16

Notes

[1] This parameter may be exceeded in point-to-point and engineered applications.

[2] Single-ended and high-power differential are not defined at Ultra2 speeds.

SCSI BIOS Space

Q134. *How much memory space does an SCSI BIOS require? How will that affect other real-mode drivers loaded in RAM?*

A. Most SCSI BIOS takes up 16 or 32KB depending on the sophistication of the particular SCSI controller. When installed, the SCSI BIOS occupies space in the upper memory area (UMA)—that 384KB space between 640 and 1024KB where other BIOSes such as the motherboard BIOS and the video BIOS reside. When you add SCSI BIOS, it reduces the amount of UMA available for loading real-mode drivers (if you use the DOS DEVICEHIGH or LOADHIGH commands). If your current UMA is already filled with drivers, adding the SCSI controller may force you to move some of those drivers back to conventional memory (below 640KB). The relocation of those drivers (previously loaded high) may prevent some large DOS applications from loading or running correctly.

Finding SCSI Diagnostics

Q135.   *I do a lot of SCSI installations at my site, and I'm always looking for diagnostics to help me check and repair SCSI systems, but it doesn't seem like many diagnostic makers go into SCSI. Is there anything out there?*

A.   The reason many commercial diagnostics do not incorporate SCSI testing is that each SCSI host adapter is designed differently, so they each need dedicated programming—thus, the diagnostic maker would have to write code for each SCSI adapter—a formidable task. Only now are the SCSI adapters (under the SCSI-2 standard) using a common command set (CCS) that can work with many SCSI peripherals, but the SCSI host drivers are still often radically different. There are two notable diagnostic makers who have taken the plunge into SCSI diagnostics. However, you may wish to call first and check compatibility against the SCSI controllers you intend to use; they are SCSIDiag (American Megatrends 404-263-8181) and PC-Technician (Windsor Technologies 415-456-2200).

SCSI IDs versus EIDE IDs

Q136.   *I know that EIDE drives are identified as primary (master) or secondary (slave) devices, but how are SCSI devices identified?*

A.   While an EIDE port can only support up to two devices, an SCSI port can support up to eight devices. As a result, the master and slave designations are replaced with SCSI IDs (i.e., ID0 through ID7). Typically, the SCSI adapter itself is given ID7, and the first and second SCSI hard drives are assigned ID0 and ID1, respectively. Other SCSI devices (such as scanners and CD-ROMs) are assigned to the remaining IDs. SCSI IDs are selected through jumpers on each SCSI device. Unlike EIDE devices, most SCSI devices will also require a device driver in order for the hardware to be recognized.

UNDERSTANDING SCSI TERMINATION

Q137. *I've been reading up on SCSI, and I've seen a lot about termination. What is termination and why is it necessary with SCSI when it is not necessary with other devices?*

A.   When electronic signals operate at very high frequencies, they become very sensitive to issues like line length, impedance, and signal reflection. In simple terms, all this means that the SCSI signal line impedance has to be matched—this is accomplished by placing the proper resistance at the ends of each SCSI bus cable (usually on the devices at each end of the chain). Note that improper termination will not damage anything (although it may corrupt data), but your SCSI system will not work. Other cable-related systems such as floppy drives and hard drives are *also* terminated, but their termination is internal and less critical to overall operation than SCSI.

SOME GOOD RULES FOR SCSI TERMINATION

Q138. *I'm having a real problem with my new SCSI equipment. I just don't understand how to accomplish the SCSI terminations.*

A.   Termination is certainly a troublesome aspect of SCSI installations, but if you follow a few basic rules, you should be able to master termination with no problems. Remember that a poorly terminated SCSI system is potentially unreliable, so you really should *fix* any termination that's incomplete or incorrect.

- ■ The SCSI bus needs exactly *two* terminators, never more, never less.

- ■ Devices on the SCSI bus should form a single chain that can be traced from the device at one end to the device at the other. No T's are allowed—cable lengths should be kept as short as possible.

INTERMEDIATE

■ The device at each end of the (physical) SCSI bus must be terminated; all other devices must be unterminated.

■ All unused connectors must be placed between the two terminated devices.

■ The host adapter (controller) is treated as an SCSI device.

■ Host adapters may have both an internal and external connector; these are tied together internally and should be thought of as an in and out (although direction has no real meaning in SCSI). If you have only internal or external devices, the host adapter is terminated; otherwise it is not.

■ SCSI ID's are logical assignments and have nothing to do with where they go on the SCSI bus or if they should be terminated.

USING A MOTHERBOARD SCSI ADAPTER

Q139.   *I want to add an SCSI drive to my PC, and my motherboard already has a 50-pin SCSI adapter built into it. But I was told that I would need an SCSI host adapter board anyway. Is this just a blatant attempt to get me to buy more stuff, or do I really need another adapter? There are no other SCSI devices currently connected to my motherboard.*

A.   The answer to your question is maybe—that's because a 50-pin SCSI interface offers only 8 bits. Some SCSI devices use the 68-pin 16-bit interface, which yields much better performance. If the SCSI device you plan to buy uses a 50-pin interface (and you don't plan to add any other SCSI devices in the foreseeable future), you should be able to use your existing motherboard interface. But, if the device you plan to buy uses a 68-pin interface, you should disable the motherboard SCSI interface and install a new SCSI host adapter in your PC. Critics might say that there are 50-to-68 pin SCSI adapters, but your performance will suffer. The new adapter will offer much better performance, which may be *vital* for many devices such as hard drives—the added cost is well worth the result. Now, if you do connect a 50-pin device to the 50-pin motherboard interface, and you can't get the SCSI device to work, you may still need to upgrade to a stand-alone SCSI host adapter.

Booting from SCSI

Q140. *I have both EIDE and SCSI hard drives in my PC, and I want to boot from my SCSI hard drive. I heard that this was impossible, but I thought you might be able to shed some light on this.*

A. Traditionally, SCSI drives would not boot if there were IDE/EIDE drives in the system as well. However, some of the newer SCSI adapters use SCSI BIOS that will allow an SCSI drive to boot. You will need to make your SCSI hard drive bootable (if it is not already) and configure your suitable SCSI for booting (refer to the documentation for your particular adapter). Late model SCSI adapters not only allow the SCSI drive to boot but will allow you to boot from SCSI IDs other than ID0.

Flatbed Scanner Interface Considerations

Q141. *I'm interested in purchasing a flatbed color scanner. Since they're pretty cheap right now, it seems like the best time to buy. But I just realized most of the scanners have an SCSI-2 interface, and I just purchased a Tyan motherboard which only has an EIDE controller. It looks like most scanners come with an SCSI interface card (which I think is all I need), but my brain keeps telling me that I need some other kind of controller card. How would having this SCSI controller alongside my EIDE controller on the motherboard affect performance? Could I possibly use the SCSI interface card that comes with these scanners for other devices such as a CD-ROM drive?*

A. Those are very good questions because EIDE and SCSI are both very popular interface schemes. First, SCSI and EIDE interfaces can coexist since both use completely different IRQs and other resources. This means you can install the SCSI adapter and scanner, and then just install the SCSI drivers and scanning software; there will be no impact on your EIDE hard drives or IDE CD-ROM. In general, system performance will not be affected at all by the addition of an SCSI scanner. You would need no other controller besides the one that comes with your scanner. If your system had an SCSI adapter *already*, you could probably install the scanner to your existing adapter instead of using the new

ADVANCED

one. If you do choose to add more SCSI devices in the future (like an SCSI CD-ROM drive), chances are excellent that you can use the scanner's SCSI adapter as the host.

SCSI Won't Boot with Some BIOS Versions

Q142. *I can't get my SCSI hard drive to boot on my system. I've tried both the SCSI adapter and hard drive in other PCs, and they work properly, so I know the problem is related to my specific motherboard. I'm using an Award BIOS.*

A. This is a rare question and is almost certainly due to your particular BIOS version. According to my sources at Award, SCSI hard drives cannot boot if your Award BIOS release date falls from September 23, 1996, to September 27, 1996, *and* supports the CD-ROM boot function. To work around this problem, first find out whether your BIOS supports the CD-ROM boot function. Enter CMOS Setup. Move the cursor to BIOS Features Setup and press the <Enter> key. Move the cursor to the Boot Sequence field, and toggle through the available values by pressing the <Page Up> or <Page Down> or the <+> or <–> keys. If you see CD-ROM listed as an available entry, this BIOS supports the CD-ROM boot function (and you should consider a BIOS upgrade). If CD-ROM does not appear as an option, your BIOS does not support the CD-ROM boot function, and you may have a hardware issue with your particular motherboard.

Using Multiple SCSI Adapters

Q143. *I have an Adaptec SCSI adapter in my PC, but the SCSI bus is filled (six devices plus the adapter). Can I add another SCSI adapter to my system? I was told that the different SCSI BIOS versions would conflict.*

A.   You can have more than one SCSI adapter in your system, but there are some rules. As you probably expect, the adapter's resources (i.e., IRQ, DMA, I/O) cannot conflict with the original SCSI adapter or any other device in the system. Also, the BIOS versions will not conflict as such, but you should make sure that the BIOS address ranges for both SCSI BIOS versions do not overlap. Finally, you will need to add an SCSI driver for your new host adapter.

MIXING AND MATCHING SCSI ADAPTERS

Q144.   *I am thinking of buying an HP ScanJet 4C. It comes with a dedicated SCSI adapter (which I assume is a card). The computer that I plan to use it with is running a Creative Labs Sound Blaster 16 ASP SCSI-2, with my NEC CDR-510 connected to it. I'm running Windows 95, and the following files are loaded at boot-up:*

```
SCSI\ASPI2DOS.SYS /D /Z
SCSI\ASPICD.SYS /D:ASPICD0
```

Will there be a conflict if I use multiple SCSI cards, or will one have to be disabled?

A.   Your question is not quite so simple because SCSI offers a number of twists and turns. In theory, you should be able to connect your new scanner to the existing SCSI controller as long as the SCSI chain is terminated properly and the correct SCSI IDs are assigned. But I've seen cases where certain SCSI devices don't interact correctly with some controllers. As an alternative, you could add the second SCSI controller, which should coexist with the original controller as long as the new controller uses unique IRQ, I/O address, and BIOS address settings. Still, you'll need to add even more drivers to your system (and Windows 95 platform). If the HP scanner uses an SCSI-2 interface, you can try it on your existing controller, and you should just need to add the Windows 95 drivers to make it run. If you cannot get the scanner to work, you can add the SCSI controller that accompanies the scanner.

ADVANCED

SCSI Controllers and Drive Formatting

Q145. *Help! Can you tell me if it's possible to format and verify an SCSI disk through an NCR controller? Also, after performing this operation, could the disk then be read by an Adaptec controller? I have heard of incompatibility problems when this is done. Can you confirm?*

A. As a rule, you should always partition and format an SCSI drive using the "final" controller. Even though SCSI interfaces are largely identical, the methodology used to format the drives can vary between SCSI adapters (the formatting is not quite as standardized as with EIDE controllers). This means you'll often have to reformat the SCSI drive after replacing the controller with a different model.

Disabling the SCSI BIOS

Q146. *I read somewhere that there are times when I should disable my SCSI BIOS. Is this true? If so, when should an SCSI BIOS be disabled? I don't have an SCSI controller yet, but I've been considering adding SCSI devices to my system.*

A. Generally speaking, an SCSI adapter relies on an SCSI driver, and most SCSI devices also use their own suite of drivers. The main purpose of SCSI BIOS is to support SCSI hard drives, and booting from SCSI hard drives. So if you do not have SCSI hard drives in your PC, you may find it helpful to disable the SCSI BIOS. You may not *have* to do this, but disabling a BIOS may save 16 or 32KB in the UMA for other devices such as video or network adapter BIOS. SCSI BIOS is almost always disabled using a jumper on the SCSI controller, but a few controllers will require a driver to disable the SCSI BIOS.

SCSI Corrective Actions

SCSI Adapters and Lost CMOS Information

Q147. *I recently upgraded a motherboard in a computer with a 540MB*
Maxtor IDE HDD and a Creative Labs SCSI sound card with a
Seagate 1.08GB SCSI hard drive attached. This machine consis-
tently loses CMOS Setup information—especially after having
been moved. This leads me to believe that the battery is faulty,
yet tests show that it's fine. I've heard that Asus motherboards
have a problem with non-Asus SCSI adapters, and I'm beginning
to wonder if this isn't the problem. I have an updated BIOS flash
ready to go, but do you have any information on this SCSI prob-
lem?

A. I've checked with Asus, and I could not find any information to
support problems with non-Asus SCSI adapters. Still, if a BIOS
upgrade is available, it would certainly not hurt to install it.
Before you do flash the BIOS, however, you should rectify the
CMOS problem. According to your description of the problem, it
sounds like the CMOS backup battery on your new motherboard
is not providing power to the system. Since the battery checks
OK, I can only conclude that there is a connection problem. I've
often seen coin cell battery holders where the clip holding the coin
cell in place was not tight enough to establish good contact. In
effect, the battery was disconnected. Remove the battery and *gen-*
tly push the battery clip in to improve tension. Your motherboard
might also have a provision for an external battery pack connected through a small 4-pin header. If so, there is probably a jumper
on the motherboard that allows you to switch between an on-
board battery and battery pack. Make sure that such a jumper is
in the on-board battery position. Finally, check the new motherboard's mounting to be sure that none of the metal standoffs are
shorting out any of the motherboard's printed circuit traces.

DRIVE FORMATS AND SCSI ADAPTERS

Q148. *I need to upgrade my aging SCSI host adapter, but I heard that I would not be able to use my hard drive and that I would need to reformat it. Is this true?*

A.   Yes, it is true. The SCSI interface is very standardized, but the way in which data is translated between an adapter and hard drive is not. Every controller manufacturer uses its own proprietary translation scheme. So a drive prepared on one SCSI adapter may not work at all when used with another SCSI host adapter—even though the SCSI interface is identical. You will probably have to low-level format the SCSI hard drive again once it is connected to the new controller and then restore the drive contents from a backup.

SCSI INSTALLATION PROBLEMS

Q149. *I'm having terrible problems installing my new SCSI hard drive, and I know that part of it is because I've never done this before. Can you tell me how to deal with SCSI problems and make my installation go more smoothly?*

A.   SCSI installations are not terribly difficult, but there are some problems that frequently crop up due to installation oversights. When your installation goes awry, try the following steps:

- Verify that the PC and all peripherals are plugged in and that all power connections secure.

- Verify that the SCSI host bus adapter has been correctly installed—the card should be seated properly. Check for system resources conflicts with the I/O, IRQ, or DMA assignments.

- Ensure the SCSI cables are correctly connected to all devices, and see that the orientation of pin 1 is correct.

- Verify that the SCSI ID jumper setting is correct, and check for ID conflicts.

- Check the termination at the ends of your SCSI chain, and see that the terminator power is adequate.

- Make sure that devices in the middle of the SCSI chain are unterminated.

- Check that the SCSI cable is not too long (typically six meters or less).

- If you receive an error code, check your operating system documentation for an explanation of the error code.

- See that any option jumpers on the SCSI host adapter are installed properly.

- If problems persist, you may have a hardware fault in the SCSI drive or controller board.

SCSI System Not Recognized

Q150. *I just encountered a rather puzzling problem when attempting to install an external 9GB SCSI Seagate hard disk and need your advice. I tried to install that drive on my Compaq Deskpro 90, which has an Adaptec AHA-2940 controller, an internal Toshiba SCSI CD-ROM drive, and an external Iomega Jaz drive. The CD and Jaz drives are terminated. All these devices can be seen by Windows 95, and have been working properly. I installed the Seagate drive before the Jaz drive and rebooted the PC. Windows 95 could see all SCSI devices, except the Seagate. I then removed the Jaz drive, terminated at the Seagate drive, and rebooted. This time, the Adaptec controller only saw the CD drive.*

To be sure that the controller was OK, I installed the Seagate drive on another Compaq (DOS/Win 3.1x), which has an Adaptec AIC-6260. The Seagate was terminated. The same story—the controller could not see the Seagate drive. To be very sure, I added the Jaz drive to the second Compaq, and only the Jaz drive was recognized. I also made sure each SCSI device was assigned a unique SCSI device ID.

A. That's an odd problem—you rarely hear about SCSI hard drives failing to be recognized. I assume that the drive was not identified by the SCSI BIOS display during power up, and you could not run FDISK to partition the drive (Windows 95 won't see anything until the drive is partitioned and formatted). My first thought would be to check the SCSI BIOS to see that it is enabled on the SCSI adapter—you need the SCSI BIOS to run the hard drive. However, since you tried the drive on another system and controller and also could not recognize the drive, I would suggest that the drive itself may be defective or improperly configured. For the sake of your own sanity, take a close look at the documentation for your SCSI controller. Check for any jumpers settings that might interfere with the proper detection of your hard drive. Also check the hard drive for any on-board jumpers that might be preventing proper detection by the controller. If not, try another hard drive.

SCSI BIOS Won't Load on a Non-PnP System

Q151. *I have a PCI-based machine with a non-plug-and-play BIOS (prior to Phoenix 4.05.x), and I'm adding a PCI SCSI adapter. All my SCSI IDs and terminations are correct, but the BIOS on the SCSI adapter always fails to load. What am I missing?*

A. First, check the SCSI adapter itself. Many SCSI adapters provide a jumper which can enable or disable the SCSI BIOS. Make sure the SCSI BIOS is enabled. If the problem persists, you may need to change the PCI slot configuration. Power up the machine and press <F2> to enter the CMOS Setup program. Go to the Advanced Menu and select PCI Devices. Page down until you find the settings for the slot that contains your SCSI adapter. If the IRQ Level is set to None, change it to read 11 (or some other available IRQ). Save the new configuration and reboot.

SCSI Adapter Causes Stack Overflow Problems

Q152. *I recently put an Adaptec 1542C 16-bit ISA SCSI card into a 486SX/25 PC with 8MB of RAM. The PC has DOS 6.22 and Windows for Workgroups 3.11 on it. I now have major problems running DOS applications or accessing the A: drive. To make sure there were no incompatibilities, I removed the Sound Blaster 16 sound card and the 8-bit network card. Still, when I start up, if I type A: to try to access the floppy, I get "Internal Stack Overflow. System Halted." If I try to run DOS applications, they might work for a bit before crashing with the same message. I changed STACKS in CONFIG.SYS, but this seemed to make no difference.*

A. Generally speaking, stack overflows are caused by three things:
(1) bad programming—such as computer viruses, (2) faulty hardware that sends multiple interrupts to the CPU, and (3) misconfig-
ured hardware sending conflicting interrupts or being handled by
the wrong driver. Start your examination by running a current
virus checking utility to rule out the possibility of viruses. If the
system is clear of viruses, suspect a hardware conflict among your
interrupts, DMA channels, or I/O addresses. Compare the hardware settings for your SCSI adapter with the settings of all other
devices in the PC. Any overlap can result in a system crash. In
most cases, this type of problem is due to a hardware conflict. Be
especially suspicious of any other drive controller in the system.
Double-check the SCSI drivers in CONFIG.SYS and see that any
command line switches are set correctly. You may take a moment
to check in with Adaptec technical support (*www.adaptec.com*) to
obtain the latest real-mode drivers for the SCSI adapter. Also
make sure that your STACKS are set to 9256 or better. If the
problem persists, there may be a fault on the SCSI adapter board.

NEW SCSI CONTROLLERS PREVENT DRIVE BOOTING

Q153.   *I have just replaced my motherboard and added a new Adaptec
AHA 2940 PCI SCSI controller card. I have two SCSI drives.
After the upgrade, I cannot boot and get a No Operating System
error message. I can boot from a floppy disk and access files on
the C: and D: drives—I can even run DOS programs. It sounds
like a format is in order, right? I have a backup but would like to
avoid formatting and file restores if possible.*

A. Your problem is one of the most common complaints with SCSI
controller upgrades. New SCSI controllers are often unable to
boot from disks formatted by other SCSI controllers—even
though the SCSI interface itself may operate identically. Since you
have a backup, try running FDISK C: /MBR to rewrite the master
boot record of your C: drive (I doubt that would work because
the partition is readable now, but it's worth a try). If the C: drive
still refuses to boot, use FDISK to repartition the drive, and use
FORMAT C: /S to reformat the drive as a bootable volume. You
can then reinstall your operating system and restore your files.
Since the D: drive is probably not bootable anyway, you may not
need to repeat the process for D:.

INTERMEDIATE

SCSI Drive Not Ready Error

Q154.   *I installed a second SCSI hard drive on my PC. There were no problems with the installation, and the SCSI controller recognizes the second drive, but I get a Drive Not Ready error from that drive. Is the drive defective?*

A.   Possibly, but don't pack up that new drive just yet. Often, an SCSI controller may report a drive error if the drive does not spin up on time. If that new hard drive has a jumper which allows an option such as spin up on power up, select that option so that the drive will be up to speed before the SCSI controller attempts to interrogate it. Also check the SCSI adapter for power-up options that you might enable such as Send Start Unit.

Weird SCSI BIOS Message

Q155.   *When I installed a new SCSI controller board, I got the message "BIOS not intended to run with this card." What does this mean? Do I have a bad card?*

A.   The SCSI controller is probably good. Your error message can sometimes happen when the SCSI BIOS or a real-mode ASPI driver loads (i.e., ASPIxDOS.SYS). This type of error usually means that there is a conflict between your SCSI adapter I/O address and another device in the system. Since you just installed the SCSI controller, change the SCSI controller's I/O address to one not used elsewhere in the system—the error should disappear.

Don't Need the Old Drivers

Q156.   *I just replaced my old SCSI host adapter with a new model, but now I get odd error messages such as "\SB16\DRV\CPS.SYS won't load." Do I need to load the old CTSB16.SYS, CTMM-SYS.SYS, or CSP.SYS drivers?*

A.   No, you don't need to load the drivers for the old host adapter
        since you have removed it. You need to remove the line in CON-
        FIG.SYS that loads \SB16\DRV\CPS.SYS. This device driver looks
        for your old host adapter and can't find it—that's why you're
        getting an error message (most device drivers do not load if they
        cannot find the device they are supposed to control).

SCSI HOST ERRORS AT START-UP

Q157.   When I boot my PC, the SCSI host adapter board displays an
        error message (sometimes it locks up the system). How do I tell
        what's wrong and correct the problem?

A.   Although you don't say exactly what the error message is,
        chances are good that your SCSI adapter is damaged. If your
        SCSI adapter has a diagnostic built into the BIOS (usually acti-
        vated with a jumper on the adapter), run the diagnostic to more
        closely isolate the fault. If the adapter indeed proves to be defec-
        tive, simply replace it outright. If the system hangs up, check
        each SCSI device ID and make sure that there is no conflict
        between device IDs.

"SCSI BIOS NOT INSTALLED" ERROR

Q158.   I just installed a new SCSI adapter to control a page scanner, but
        when the system boots, I get an error message that says "SCSI
        BIOS not installed." What's going on here? Should I take my
        SCSI controller back?

A.   Don't take that SCSI controller back just yet. Normally, SCSI BIOS
        is designed to support SCSI hard drives. If you don't have SCSI
        hard drives in your PC, the SCSI BIOS may not want to load—and
        results in your error message. You may also see other error mes-
        sages like "Drive C: already installed" or "Searching for Target 0."
        These are all related to the fact that there is no SCSI hard drive
        available at ID0. Since your scanner is using SCSI drivers to sup-

ADVANCED

port its operation, you should be able to disable the SCSI BIOS: on
the controller. There are two common means of disabling an SCSI
BIOS: (1) set the appropriate jumper on the SCSI controller or (2)
run a utility at start-up that will disable the SCSI BIOS. Check
with the instructions for your particular SCSI controller.

PHANTOM SCSI HARD DRIVES

Q159.   *Here's an odd one—I'm working on a PC that thinks it has seven
        SCSI drives connected, when in fact, there is only one SCSI drive
        connected.*

A.   Problems like yours can arise when the SCSI protocol is not
        observed. Most conventional SCSI adapters use an ID of 7 (the
        highest SCSI ID) so that the adapter will always win bus arbitra-
        tion—the adapter can always take over the SCSI bus. Every other
        SCSI device in the system uses a unique SCSI ID (0 to 6) which is
        below the SCSI adapter. If a hard drive or other drive is attached
        to the SCSI bus with the same ID as the host adapter, the adapter
        will see phantom devices at IDs where no SCSI device exists. I'd
        bet that your SCSI device is set to the same ID as your SCSI
        adapter. Make sure that the SCSI adapter is set to the highest pri-
        ority ID, and set your SCSI drive to an ID below that. For exam-
        ple, an SCSI boot drive would be ID0.

SCSI NEGOTIATION PROBLEMS

Q160.   *I have a problem with my SCSI system. Why does my SCSI Fast
        and Wide host adapter have problems finding my single-ended
        narrow devices (50-pin connections) when I scan for devices?*

A.   This is a common problem with more recent SCSI adapters
        which ignore the older legacy devices. Chances are that your
        SCSI host adapter has a BIOS utility built into it. Check this utili-
        ty and look for an entry such as Initiate Wide Negotiation. Set this
        entry to No for any SCSI ID that a narrow SCSI device occupies.

DEALING WITH SCSI TERMINATOR ERRORS

Q161. *I have an SCSI host adapter in my system, and I just installed a new SCSI CD-ROM drive. Now when I boot the system, I get an error message that says "More than two terminators," and sometimes the message says "Less than two terminators." I've checked the terminators—there are only two. What's the problem?*

A. For some reason, your SCSI adapter has detected a terminator problem. This is a very serious issue which you must resolve before using any of your SCSI devices. First, see that your terminators are installed only at the *ends* of the SCSI chain (usually the SCSI adapter and the device farthest down the chain). If other devices on the chain have built-in termination, make sure that the termination is disabled. The terminators must be installed completely, and they typically must be receiving adequate power. Your existing terminators may also be damaged, so you might also try installing new terminators. If the problem persists, try moving the SCSI device to another point in the chain (perhaps shuffle around other devices) and reterminate properly.

SYSTEM HANGS UP AFTER SCSI ADAPTER INSTALLATION

Q162. *I just installed a new SCSI controller, but now my system hangs up each time I try to boot it. I removed the SCSI controller and the system boots normally, so I know the problem is with the SCSI controller itself. But can you tell me where I should look for the problem?*

A. Chances are very good that you have a hardware conflict between the SCSI controller and one or more other devices in the system. With the SCSI controller removed, record the IRQ, DMA, I/O, and BIOS address settings. Start the system and run a DOS diagnostic such as MSD, and then compare the IRQ, DMA, I/O, and BIOS information pages to the data you recorded from your SCSI controller. If any of the SCSI controller's settings overlap any of the resources currently in use on your system, *that* is where your conflict is occurring. Reconfigure the SCSI controller to utilize unused resources. Finally, make sure that your scanner ID number is not the same as your controller ID number.

ADVANCED

SYNCHRONOUS NEGOTIATION PROBLEMS

Q163.   *I'm having a problem with my SCSI CD-ROM. The CD-ROM drive is supposed to support synchronous negotiation, but once I enable the synchronous negotiation feature on my Adaptec SCSI host adapter, the CD-ROM refuses to work. Can you tell me why?*

A.   You must disable the synchronous negotiation function on your Adaptec board (typically through a jumper). Disabling the feature does not *prevent* synchronous communication; it only determines what *starts* the synchronous communication.

Video Questions

Video has become a vital element of today's multimedia-driven PC. As resolutions and color depths increase, the video subsystem is being called upon to provide ever-better performance for applications such as MPEG-2 playback, computer-aided design and rendering, and even 3-D games. This chapter examines three important facets of video systems: video board issues, video capture (PC-TV) boards, and monitors.

BEGINNER

Video Boards

UNDERSTANDING VIDEO MEMORY

Q164. *On a video card, what's the difference between DRAM, VRAM, and WRAM, and what are the advantages of each?*

A.   DRAM is Dynamic RAM, which is the most common type of RAM used in SIMMs for your system. DRAM is also used extensively in video boards and sound boards (such as the Creative Labs AWE32). More recently, video boards have moved to use EDO RAM, which is a performance-enhanced version of DRAM. VRAM and WRAM are both types of RAM which have been specialized for your display adapter. VRAM is Video RAM, which typically boasts dual data busses—the VRAM can literally be written and read at the same time. This is a more expensive form of memory and is most effective only at high resolutions. WRAM is Windows RAM, which was developed by Samsung as a means of speeding up video performance under the resolutions and color depths typically used by Windows and Windows 95.

ODD COLORS MAY INDICATE A PALETTE PROBLEM

Q165. *I have a system with 16MB of RAM, 1MB of video RAM, a 540MB hard drive, two hard cards, a scanner, a CD-ROM, a Sound Blaster sound card, and a 14-in VGA monitor. When I run Windows, the VGA display occasionally corrupts and displays some very strange color combinations. This usually happens after loading memory-intensive programs or working with graphics. Sometimes the display corrects itself. I have tried a number of drivers but did not eliminate the problem. What can I do?*

A.   My first impulse would have been to suggest new drivers, but since you've already tried new drivers, I can only imagine you've got a palette glitch. All the colors in your display are recorded in a palette—a table that assigns colors. For a 256-color screen mode, you have a palette of 256 current colors. When some applications load, they take over parts of (or all of) your color palette and can change some of the color assignments. For example, instead of having color 1 assigned to blue, the new program may assign it to a fine shade of pink. When this happens, any area of your display currently showing color 1 will instantly change to the new color. If many colors are reassigned, it can dramatically change the color scheme in your display before the new program is fully initialized. This happens on my systems when I load color-rich programs such as Ventura 7 and AOL 3.1 for Windows 95.

Unfortunately, there's no easy solution to such palette problems, and often rerunning basic Windows applications will reload the original Windows palette (which is why the problem seems to clear itself). The best way to combat palette shifting is to use a higher color depth like 32K, 64K, or 16M colors. However, you *will* need new drivers for higher color depths, and the added data demands of more colors will probably slow down your video performance.

ODD COLORS MAY SUGGEST VIDEO FAILURE

Q166. *I have a situation that I can only attribute to my video card. This is the first problem I have had with my computer since I bought it. On occasion when I am in DOS 6.2 and go to MSD or ScanDisk, they come up in gray tones (normally blue) with some of the text missing. This seems to happen most frequently near the end of a day after I have used the computer for a while. I also can get odd color schemes and graphic "garbage" when working under Windows 95.*

A. Based on your description of the problem, it definitely sounds like a video card issue. Before you go too far though, check the video card itself. Make sure that the card in inserted securely into its bus slot. Also check that the monitor cable is connected properly to the video port. Examine the video cable for any bent or damaged pins. If everything checks out up to this point, I'd say that your video card (probably the video memory) is faulty. Replace your video board.

Drivers or Video BIOS Needed for VESA Support

Q167.   *I'm trying to run a new game on my PC, but I keep getting an error message that says "VESA 2.0 support needed." What does this mean, and what can I do about it?*

A.   Your game is trying to work in an SVGA video mode using 640x480x256 resolution or higher. VESA 2.0 is a standard which defines the programming needed to operate the video board, but the video board doesn't recognize the VESA programming. Today, most video boards incorporate VESA 2.0 programming directly into the video BIOS. Otherwise, you'll need a VESA 2.0 driver (not really a video driver) so that the game software can operate the video hardware. Check the drivers that accompanied your video board—one of those driver programs is likely to be a VESA driver. If you don't have a VESA driver on hand, you can check the video board maker's Web site to obtain the latest VESA driver for your particular video board. You might also check with the game manufacturer's Web site—they might have a generic VESA driver available for download.

Keep in mind that VESA drivers are only needed for DOS applications, and you usually would not add the VESA driver to your start-up files. Instead, you should only load the VESA driver before you start your game. After you have finished playing, you should unload the VESA driver (if there's a command line switch to remove it from memory) or reboot the PC to clear it from memory.

Windows 95 Restarts Needed After Video Changes

Q168.   *Lately, I've been trying to optimize my video under Windows 95, and I've been tweaking video resolution, color palettes, and font sizes. I've noticed that sometimes Windows 95 will need to restart the system, and other times it will not need a restart. Why is that?*

A.   Basically, Windows 95 does not need to restart if you only change the screen resolution. If you change font sizes or color depths, you'll need to restart Windows 95 for those changes to take effect. This is not a problem with Windows 95—but it can be a nuisance if you have to make multiple changes to fonts and colors.

VESA GRAPHICS ERRORS IN DOS WINDOW

Q169. *When I try to run my DOS game in a Windows 95 window, I get an error saying that the program does not detect VESA graphics. But I **know** the board has a VESA BIOS, so what's the deal?*

A.   I'll bet that your game runs perfectly in DOS. Many DOS programs perform a VESA service call to query the video capabilities. Unfortunately, these queries will not be answered from a "windowed" DOS session, so VESA capability is not detected. In order to satisfy the request, the DOS session must take place in full-screen mode so that the BIOS can inspect the video hardware and obtain the correct information. To resolve the problem, configure the DOS program to run in a full-screen DOS session.

JUDGING VIDEO RAM

Q170. *I'm picking out a new video board, and I want to run Windows 95 in 1024x768x256 mode. The problem is that I cannot figure out whether to go with a 2 or 4MB video board. I don't want to spend the money for the extra memory if I don't need it. Can you help?*

A.   That's a great question. There is a quick formula used to calculate video memory requirements:

```
Horizontal resolution x vertical resolution
x bytes per pixel = amount of RAM required
(in bytes)
```

Table 2.1 lists the major figures for bytes per pixel. For your requirements, 1024x768x1 = 787KB (<1MB). So you could actually get away with a 1MB video board. On the other hand, suppose you wanted to view an image in true color (16.7 million colors). The result would then be 1024x768x3 = 2.4MB. So a 2MB video board would not be enough—you'd need a 4MB board. As you can see, color depth plays an important role in video memory requirements. Given the low prices of today's video boards, you should seriously consider a 2MB board as a minimum. If you can justify the 4MB board, it will give you some room for future (more demanding) software.

TABLE 2.1 A COMPARISON OF BYTES PER PIXEL

Colors	Bytes per Pixel
16	0.5
256	1
65K	2
16.7M	3

DISABLING ON-BOARD VIDEO

Q171.   *I'm using the motherboard video system right now, but I want to add a PCI video adapter to my motherboard. How should I disable the on-board video system?*

A.   In many cases, you should be able to install the new video board, and your BIOS will automatically detect the new board and disable the on-board video. However, this is not always the case. You may need to enter the CMOS Setup before adding the new video card, locate the settings for your on-board video system, and then disable the video. Save your changes, and then turn the system off to install the new video board. You will also need to coordinate your changes with Windows 95:

1.   In the Windows 95 Device Manager, disable the on-board video adapter.

2.   Exit Windows 95.

3.   Install the add-in video card.

4.   Run Windows 95. The add-in video card will be automatically detected.

Note   *Some older motherboards do not disable their on-board video system properly, and this causes conflicts with the new video board. If you cannot disable the motherboard video, you may need a BIOS upgrade to correct the problem. Otherwise, you may need to replace the motherboard.*

INTERMEDIATE

3D Video and IRQs

Q172. *I was installing a new 3-D video board when I realized that it needed an interrupt—I didn't think video boards needed an interrupt. What happens if I don't have an interrupt available?*

A. You're right—traditional video boards don't use an interrupt (they just use address space). However, the newest generations of 3-D video boards *do* use an interrupt to support the critical timing needed to handle advanced 3-D features as well as other functions (like MPEG playback). If you do not have an interrupt available, your 3-D video board should still work, but its performance will be severely limited.

Adding a New Video Adapter

Q173. *I've got my eye on a new Diamond video board, and I think it's time to I ditch my old generic SVGA board. The problem is, I've never done a video board installation before. Any advice for a newbie?*

A. Thankfully, it's a lot easier to install video boards today under Windows 95 than it has been in years past. Be sure to turn off and unplug the PC before proceeding, and use an antistatic wrist strap. Disconnect your monitor cable. Remove the old video board, and then insert the new video board. They are really pretty plug and play, and there are almost never any jumpers to set on video hardware. When you restart the PC, Windows 95 should detect the new hardware and install drivers for it—although you should probably use the drivers on the disk enclosed with the new video board. Always make sure to use the very latest video drivers. If your original video hardware is integrated into the motherboard, you will have to disable the motherboard video system (usually with a jumper on the motherboard) before installing the new video card. Keep in mind that some motherboards will not allow you to disable the on-board video system properly without a BIOS or motherboard upgrade.

INTERMEDI

GARBLED ASCII DROPPING FROM WINDOWS 95 TO DOS

Q174. *I typically run a number of DOS programs through Windows 95,
but I get a weird problem when dropping from Windows 95 to
DOS—strange garbled screens with ASCII characters appear. I've
never seen this on other systems. Is my video board bad, or is
this a driver issue?*

A.   This type of problem is more of an inconvenience than a real
fault, and either the video board *or* an older driver may be the
culprit. Always check to see that you have the latest protected-
mode driver installed for your video board. If you do, try modifying your DOSSTART.BAT file with the following line at the top
of the file:

```
MODE CO80
```

This simple command resets the DOS screen automatically. If you
would rather not use the MODE command, you should try a different video board.

You will need to have the MODE utility available on your system.

Note

DIRECTDRAW AND DIRECT3D RENDERING PROBLEMS

Q175. *I'm using programs that operate via DirectDraw and Direct3D,
but the images produced by those applications don't look very
good. Is there a reason for this or a way around it?*

A.   Older versions of the DirectDraw and Direct3D API did not provide the same level of visual quality afforded in current versions.
Make sure to use an up-to-date version of your application
which uses the latest DirectX APIs. The actual parts of your
DirectX system are usually installed when you install your video
board drivers, so your drivers may be current, but the applica-
tion(s) may not be. You might also consider increasing the display refresh rate to 75 Hz or higher (if your video board and
monitor have that capability).

TROUBLE LOADING VIDEO DRIVERS UNDER WINDOWS

Q176. *I just installed a new video board, but I'm having real problems installing the new video drivers under Windows. Do you have any suggestions?*

A.   Since you don't say whether your troubles are under Windows 3.1x or Windows 95, I'll give you some tips for both. Under Windows 3.1x, try booting to DOS and then set Display to VGA in the Windows Setup program. Go into Windows and delete any previous copies of drivers and video utilities for other video adapters and then install the new drivers and video utilities from disk. Make sure to have your monitor information handy. Under Windows 95, you should start in the Safe Mode and then find and remove your old display adapter entry listed in the Device Manager. Next, run the Add New Hardware wizard to identify the new video board and install its drivers. Note that if your new video board is a PnP board, Windows 95 should automatically identify the board and install the proper drivers, so you may simply need to restart Windows 95 normally after removing the old drivers.

DIRECTX REPLACES PCI VIDEO DRIVERS

Q177. *How's this for a problem? I have a Creative Labs video PCI board in my system, and I finally installed my first Windows 95 DirectX game today. The problem is that when I installed the DirectX portion of the game, it replaced my video drivers. Do I need to reinstall the video board drivers?*

A.   This is a fairly rare problem, but it does happen. Fortunately, the original drivers are still there—they've just been disabled. Go to your Control Panel, open the Display icon, select the Settings tab, and click on Change Display Type. Under Adapter Type, click on Change, and select the entry for your Creative Labs video board. Remember to click on OK to save your changes.

Bundled Games Won't Run

Q178. *Now this really makes me mad—I put in a new PCI video board, and it does seem to run. But when I try to use the games bundled with the package, the games won't work (more specifically, the screen goes blank, or the system hangs up). Is this just a bad bundle, or is the video card defective?*

A.   Let's not jump to conclusions just yet. In most cases, the applications that are bundled with new video boards are quite good and have been tested thoroughly with the board. If the games won't work, there's usually a problem with the installation. I think you'll find that the video board (or its PCI slot) is configured poorly or there is not enough conventional memory available for the games. First, check your video board and see if an IRQ is required. Also find out which IRQ is selected by default. Next, see if there are any other devices in the system which are using the IRQ. If so, you'll need to reconfigure the video board to use a different IRQ. If you cannot configure the video board directly (i.e., a PnP video board), you can usually specify an available IRQ for the PCI slot in your CMOS Setup.

MPEG Playback Image Is Dithered

Q179. *I'm trying to play an MPEG movie, but the image quality appears washed out or dithered. Is there any way to improve this?*

A.   MPEG image quality depends largely on your video board and drivers. Most dithering effects are caused by small palettes (i.e., 16 colors). Check your video system and make sure that you're using a 256 color palette as a minimum (you might also try a higher color palette such as 65K color—also known as High Color). If the MPEG player itself offers any picture controls, set up the player's video configuration to achieve the best picture quality.

VIDEO SYSTEM NOT DETECTING MONITOR CORRECTLY

Q180. *I've got a problem with my monitor. Sometimes when I boot my system, my VGA monitor displays everything in black and white. This makes it difficult to use some DOS diagnostics. However, Windows graphics work correctly. My diagnostics tell me that I have a VGA adapter with a monochrome display, but the display is actually VGA. Is my monitor damaged?*

A. Don't panic. The monitor is probably working correctly since Windows runs in color as expected. The problem is probably in your VGA card. When the system powers up, the video card tries to detect the monitor type so that the video card can set its default mode. If the video card detects the wrong monitor type, it will set the wrong mode (monochrome in this case). Try turning your monitor on before powering up the PC. A different type of monitor or video board might clear the problem (although neither device is likely to be defective). Replacing your VGA video board with a newer SVGA graphics accelerator will also improve your video performance. Check with your video board manufacturer to see if they have a utility which can be added to CONFIG.SYS or AUTOEXEC.BAT to *force* the video board's DOS mode.

INTERMEDIATE

NEW VIDEO BOARD CAUSES FUZZY DISPLAY

Q181. *I'm having a problem with my VGA monitor. I just installed a new Windows accelerator card to optimize my old 486 system. The physical installation went well, but when Windows 3.1 loaded, the icons appeared fuzzy. The card and monitor should be compatible. What can I do?*

A. Since you don't really say just which video board you installed, I can only give you the generic overview—but your new video card is probably to blame. Start with your video cable. It should be securely attached to the video board and monitor. The video drivers that came with your video board should be installed (you may need to reboot Windows for the new drivers to take effect). You might check to see that none of the pins on your cable are pushed in or bent. Also double-check your monitor's brightness and contrast settings. Some VL video boards have had problems if the VL bus is being operated over 33 MHz (or if more than one VL device is installed), so if you're running a VL video board, make sure the bus speed is correct. If the problem persists, try changing the video resolution or color depth—some video boards simply do not produce solid images at high resolutions. Remember that with Windows 3.1x, you'll need to reboot each time you make a change to your video drivers.

NEW 3-D VIDEO BOARD CAUSES SYSTEM PROBLEMS

Q182. *I hope you might be able to help me with a problem. I put a Creative Labs 3-D Blaster into my system, and it works correctly. The problem is that every so often, the system hangs up. I've also seen other problems such as the display going blank or displaying garbage. I'd need to reboot the PC to clear these problems. This only happened after installing the 3-D Blaster. Are there any solutions?*

A. There have been a large number of problems reported with 3-D-type video accelerators. In some cases, the board's IRQ may be interfering with another device using the same IRQ. Check your system for hardware conflicts first. Another potential source of problems is the 3-D video BIOS itself. Early 3-D BIOS versions may have problems with certain motherboard chipsets or CPU types. For your 3-D Blaster, check for the latest version of the 3-D Blaster PCI BIOS from the Creative Labs Web site (*www.creaf.com*). For other 3-D video boards, check with the Web site of the respective video board manufacturer.

NEW VIDEO DRIVERS CAUSING SYSTEM LOCK-UPS

Q183. *I've installed a Trident 9680 video card, and using the Windows 95 driver, I get either 16 or 256 colors. When I install the drivers that accompanied the card, or the latest drivers from Trident's Web site, I get a mouse click or two and then the system locks up. Any assistance will be greatly appreciated.*

A.   Your description of the problem sounds like a classic conflict problem (probably generated by the new video drivers). Start Windows 95 in the Safe Mode. I have a feeling that your problem will disappear—if so, you definitely have a driver problem. Try to access your Device Manager and check to see if there are any conflicts between the video adapter and any other devices in the system. Confirm that your original video drivers were removed when the new drivers were installed. You might also try restoring the original Windows 95 native video drivers to stabilize your system. Ultimately, you may need to use a different video card.

3-D Video Board Causing Display Errors

Q184.   *My friend just installed a 3-D video board, and now her system's all messed up—her screen often winds up blank or has colors missing. Sometimes there are missing pixels or text. We're pretty sure it's the video board that's the problem, but do you have any suggestions before she takes the board back?*

A.   Well you don't say just which 3-D board you're dealing with, so I can't give you a specific answer, but there is a trend that you can check. When a video board causes missing colors, pixels, or text, the culprit is often your PCI/VGA palette snoop feature in CMOS Setup. Make sure that the palette snoop feature is *disabled*. If the PCI/VGA palette snoop is enabled, any I/O access on the ISA bus to the video card's palette registers will be reflected on the PCI bus. This will allow overlay-capable cards (i.e., a Creative Labs Video Blaster) to adapt to the changing palette colors. This sometimes causes problems, so disabling the palette snoop may help. Remember to save your changes to CMOS before rebooting the system.

Resolving the Vertical Bar Problem with Diamond Boards

Q185.   *I have just installed a Diamond Stealth 3-D board on my PC (a Pentium 120 with HX chipset and 32MB RAM) running under Windows 3.11. The boot-up sequence is okay. If I run programs under DOS, such as Edit or Dosshell, it's okay. But when I run Windows, I can see (other than the usual things) that there are a*

INTERMEDIATE

lot of evenly spaced vertical stripes about 3 mm apart (in 800x600 resolution). I have tried every single resolution available (also color depth), but it is still the same. However, if I use the generic VGA driver (640x480, 16 color), the display appears to be okay. The driver version that I have is v1.00 for the Stealth 3D 2000 series (Windows 3.1). Is there something wrong with the card?

A. From your description of the problem, it sounds like you're experiencing what's referred to as the *V-Bar Syndrome*, which has been identified with several different types of Diamond video cards. Diamond does not document the problem officially, so the technical reasoning behind the problem is not very clear, but it *is* driver related. Try downloading and installing the latest video drivers from Diamond (*www.diamondmm.com*). Most Diamond cards are based on chipsets from s3, and s3 itself (*www.s3.com/support/enduser/swlib.html*) distributes generic drivers for their chipsets which might also be a solution for you. In some cases, a cold boot (power off for 15 to 20 seconds) may also clear the problem.

There have also been similar reports of problems when mixing video RAM (i.e., adding 1MB of DRAM to a 1MB card to make it a 2MB card). In this case the newer DRAM chips were not compatible, and vertical bars resulted in all modes except plain VGA. If your card has two DRAM chips in brown sockets, try removing them and see if the problem clears up.

SYSTEM LOCK-UPS IN HIGH COLOR MODES

Q186. *I have an Orchid Fahrenheit 64 VLB video card with 2MB of RAM, and I'm supposed to be able to get 24-bit color; however, when I try to set it above 256 colors, my computer locks up and I have to actually power down (CTL-ALT-DEL won't work, nor will pushing the Reset button). I'm using an AMD 486DX4/120 processor on an AMI motherboard, and I've tried checking for card conflicts; there don't seem to be any that I can find. Windows 95 is my OS. I don't really know whether the problem is with my video card, the motherboard, the processor, or even with Windows 95.*

A. You're looking at what is almost certain to be a driver problem. Contact the video board maker, get the newest version of their driver, install it, and those lock-ups will most likely disappear. You can check with Orchid at; *www.orchid.com* for the latest drivers.

3-D Video Adapter Causes Adaptec SCSI Problems

Q187. *I just installed a Righteous 3-D video adapter into my system, and now the system locks up each time the video board is initialized. My system also uses a Supermicro motherboard and an Adaptec SCSI controller.*

A. The problem is with your version of the Adaptec EZ-SCSI drivers. When the Righteous 3-D board initializes, there is a conflict with the Adaptec drivers, and the system crashes. Contact Adaptec and obtain version 4.1 (or later) of Adaptec's EZ-SCSI drivers. According to STB, that should clear the problem.

No System Video with Diamond PCI Board

Q188. *I get no video upon boot-up with my NexGen motherboard and my Diamond PCI display adapter, and my computer beeps eight times.*

A. You've got a video problem. With PCI systems, this is sometimes caused because the CMOS RAM for the system BIOS (sometimes referred to as NVRAM) has recorded information about the PCI cards that is not correct. To force the motherboard to rescan the PCI slots for new cards, hold the <Insert> key while booting. It is also possible that the system BIOS may be outdated and may not have the proper detection for the chipset on your Diamond video card.

Poor MPEG A/V Synchronization

Q189. *I'm trying to play an MPEG movie, and it's not working correctly at all—the playback is slow, and the video and sound are not synchronized. Any ideas on how to fix this?*

ADVANCED

A.   MPEG playback performance really depends on several different factors. First, check the MPEG player itself. If it has a synchronized playback feature (such as the Creative Labs SoftMPEG utility), be sure that the feature is *enabled*. Another factor to consider is CPU utilization. A CPU under high utilization (>70 percent) may not be able to keep pace with the processing demands imposed by MPEG, resulting in choppy, poorly synchronized playback. Older PCs are more prone to these "speed hiccups" than newer systems. Try quitting some of the other background applications that may be running. The CD-ROM is another factor. VideoCDs and MPEG movies typically demand a 4X or faster CD-ROM drive. You may consider upgrading an older CD-ROM. If you are using a Quad Speed CD-ROM or higher, check this under your System Properties:

1.   Double-click on My Computer and Control Panel.

2.   Double-click on System.

3.   Click on the Performance tab.

4.   Click on File System.

5.   Click on the CD-ROM tab.

6.   Under the Optimize Access Pattern entry, see that it is set to "Quad Speed or Higher."

7.   Click on OK.

If you are using a prerelease version of Windows 95 (a beta), you should update your installation with a current commercial version.

Note

System Locks Up When Changing Video Modes

Q190. *My system locks up when changing resolutions or color depths while using the MPEG Playback feature on my PC. Sometimes the system locks up while I'm using the Video Capture function. What's the problem?*

A.   This is a pretty common problem. MPEG and video capture soft-
      ware are notoriously intolerant of video changes on the fly. You
      must close all MPEG and capture functions prior to changing
      resolutions or color depths. In fact, you'd be better off closing all
      applications before changing video modes.

TRITON MOTHERBOARDS AND 3D BLASTER CONFLICTS

Q191. *I've been struggling with a problem for days now with a system*
      that had been upgraded with a Creative Labs 3D Blaster. The
      PCI motherboard uses a Triton chipset. When the system boots
      in Safe Mode to install the drivers, it locks up. Since Windows 95
      is in the Safe Mode, I don't think it can be a driver issue. Can the
      3D Blaster be bad?

A.   It took me a while to track this one down. According to Creative
      Labs, some Triton motherboards do have compatibility problems
      with the 3D Blaster. Such problems occur in the 640x480x16
      mode (exactly the same video mode as the Windows 95 Safe
      Mode. Creative Labs recommends that you replace the Windows
      95 VGA.DRV driver in the \Windows\System directory with a
      specially updated version which should be on the 3D Blaster
      installation CD located in the \VGA_FIX directory:

      1.   Restart your system directly to the DOS mode.

      2.   Insert the installation CD into the CD-ROM drive.

      3.   At the DOS prompt, type in the following command line
            and press <Enter>:

            ```
            COPY D:\VGA_FIX\VGA.DRV C:\WINDOWS\SYSTEM
            ```

      4.   Restart Windows 95 normally.

BEEP CODES SUGGEST FAULTY VIDEO MEMORY

Q192.   *When I boot up, my system makes one long beep and three short ones and then just sits there (nothing more happens). What does this mean? I'm using a Tyan Titan III motherboard, Seagate 2.1GB hard drive, STB Powergraph 64 video board, and 32MB of RAM. Hope you can help.*

A.   Since you don't say what BIOS and version you're running on your system, it's almost impossible to say for sure exactly what the beep code is, but according to our documentation, a series of one long beep and three short beeps usually indicates a memory or video board failure. Start by checking your video board and make sure it is installed evenly and securely in its bus slot. If there is extra memory mounted on the video board, see that it is installed properly. You might even try another video card. If the problem persists, you may have a memory failure on the mother-board. Start by systematically replacing your SIMMs in bank 0 and then move to the higher banks. If the SIMMs are OK replace the motherboard.

PC/TV and Video Capture

VIDEO CAUSES PALETTE CORRUPTION

Q193.   *When I play video on my system, the colors of my background desktop and other applications become corrupted. This is more of an annoyance than anything, but is there anything I can do about this?*

A.   This is a common problem which occurs when using 256-color video drivers. For best results, switch to a 65,000-color video driver (or higher). Note that this will require more video memory and may slow system performance to some degree.

Video Signals and TV Boards

Q194. *I was thinking about adding a PC/TV board to my system; can you tell me what type of signals I need?*

A. Of course, your best option is to study the product box or the product descriptions on the manufacturer's Web site. As a rule, video capture or PC/TV boards designed for use in the United States will accept any NTSC-compatible video source. This means you can display video from cable television, camcorders, VCRs, laser disc players, and so on. PC/TV boards designed for use outside of the United States often use PAL-compatible video. So once again, as long as the video source is the correct format, you can take video from just about anywhere. It is *very* unusual for a single video device to support *both* formats.

Reveal TV Cards Blank the Screen

Q195. *My brother put a Reveal TV board in his computer, but now the display is blank. It works on another PC, and I know he has current drivers. Why would the TV board blank his screen?*

A. This is a known problem with the Reveal TV boards which will only work at 640x480 resolution. I'd bet that your brother's screen resolution is set to 800x600 or some higher value, and the PC his board worked on was running at 640x480. Unfortunately, Reveal is out of business, so there are no patches or upgrades forthcoming. If you don't want to use the TV board at 640x480, you'll have to try a different TV card.

Closed Caption Support Doesn't Work

Q196. *When I activate the closed caption feature on my TV board, closed captioning refuses to function. Do you have any idea as to why?*

A.   From what I've been able to gather about stand-alone video boards and TV boards, the problem has to do with your video board. Some video boards use a type of video overlay feature that prevents closed caption signals from being displayed. Check with your video board maker to see if there is a newer driver that will correct the issue. If not, you may have little choice but to replace the video board with one that *will* permit closed caption signals to appear.

Snow in the TV Window

Q197.   *I've installed one of those new PC TV boards in my computer and had no problems with the installation. But when I try to use the TV, all I get is snow in the video window. Can you help?*

A.   If the TV application seems to be working properly (i.e., windows can be scaled, channel selection works, and so on) but you only see snow in the window, check the coaxial cable from your video source, such as your cable box, TV antenna, or VCR. Make sure that the video source is on and that you have a valid video signal (you can try the video source with any TV). If a stand-alone TV shows only snow, your video source isn't working. If the TV shows a picture, make sure your corresponding video source is selected in the Preferences tab under your Settings dialog. If problems persist, make sure you are using the latest DirectX video drivers. Finally, try a new TV board.

TV Window Is Out of Sync

Q198.   *Here's a strange problem—I installed a PC TV board, but the video window is out of sync. I can't seem to fix the problem. Any ideas?*

A.   PCs must meet several minimum requirements in order to display real-time video. When the video window appears out of sync (or is a solid color, such as magenta), chances are that your PC is violating one or more of the following requirements:

- Your display adapter must support video overlay.

- Your video card's display driver must be Microsoft DirectX-compliant. This is a separate driver that is provided by your video card manufacturer.

- Your computer's hardware interrupts must be correctly configured. To function correctly, both the video card and the TV card probably require hardware interrupts. Make sure there are no hardware conflicts between your system's adapters or components.

- Some 256-color display drivers are not fast enough to allow the proper synchronization and display of real-time video. Most TV cards work best when you set your video display to 65,000 or more colors.

- To obtain a more stable TV picture, lower the refresh rate of your display adapter.

Dark, Scrolling Bands During Video Capture

Q199. *When setting up my external video capture unit, I sometimes get synchronization problems or dark, scrolling bands across the preview screen on my monitor. Any idea about what's wrong?*

A. This is a problem that frequently occurs with external video capture units and is almost always due to magnetic interference in the surrounding environment. The same way that unshielded multimedia speakers can cause image distortion if placed too close to a monitor, signal interference can distort a video signal. Try repositioning the computer or video source. If all else fails, move the setup to another location entirely. For example, I know a user who complained she could never get her capture card working properly in a particular room—directly below a machine shop.

Video Capture Image Looks Torn or Bent at the Top

Q200. *I'm using an Intel SVR II to record image clips from my VCR. But as I look at the video preview, I see that the image looks kind of torn or bent along the top. I've tried different tapes, but the problem continues. What's going on?*

A.   You'll find that the torn-looking image is caused by a weak video synchronization signal coming from the VCR. Check the video cable between the VCR and SVR input. Use a short, good-quality cable, and make sure that the connections are tight. Make sure that the VCR box is checked in the video recording application. If the problems persist, try a different VCR. If a new VCR doesn't resolve the problem, try using an s-video input source (which can be a bit more stable under some circumstances). Try placing the SVR card in a bus slot which is as far away as possible from the power supply and video board, or leave an empty slot on either side of the SVR. If there is a daughter card attached to the SVR, see that the card is secure.

VERTICAL COLORED LINES ON THE VIDEO CAPTURE DISPLAY

Q201.   *I just moved my PC to another room. Everything seems to work, but I noticed that now I see colored bars running from the top to bottom of my video capture display. The image looks OK when monitored on a TV.*

A.   In virtually all cases, the daughter card (a capture module) is not firmly seated on the main video capture card. This is one of the most common complaints with the Intel Smart Video Recorder (SVR) cards—occasionally the daughter card loosens during shipping or other physical moves. Remove the capture card and gently reseat the daughter card. Remember to use good static precautions when working with the SVR card.

TV VIDEO WINDOW WON'T SCALE OR RESIZE

Q202.   *I cannot figure this one out. My video card has a built-in TV tuner and everything works correctly. Lately, I've been tinkering with the TV feature, and I've managed to connect cable to my PC. Although the picture looks OK, I can't seem to resize or scale the picture. I can only get full-screen mode in 640x480 or 800x600 resolutions. Any suggestions?*

A.   I think your trouble is in the resolution itself. Broadcast video is designed with an aspect ratio of 4:3 (four horizontal pixels to three vertical pixels), so the display window automatically resized itself to this closest proportion. The resolutions may also be too low for proper scaling. Try increasing the display resolution. In addition, some ET6000-based video cards (such as STB's Lightspeed 128) will display the TV window in only certain pre-defined ratios.

DirectX Problems with New Video Board

Q203.   *I'm installing some drivers for a new TV board in my PC, but at one part of the software installation, I get an error message that says "a DirectX compatible video driver could not be found." The installation then quits, and I can't use the TV board. I know that I have DirectX drivers installed. What can I do?*

A.   The problem is not with your Microsoft DirectX drivers, but with your video driver. Even though you may have DirectX drivers installed under Windows 95, your video driver is not able to utilize the DirectX features. This is a problem for the TV board because it depends on the video drawing speed afforded by DirectX. The solution is that you need to upgrade your video driver to a more recent version that supports DirectX. Contact your video board maker (or explore the tech support part of their Web site) to see if there are new drivers available for DirectX. If not, you will not be able to use your TV board until you upgrade your video board to a more recent model (whose drivers include DirectX support).

INTERMEDIATE

Dropped Frames During Video Capture

Q204.   *When I try a video capture, my system reports a large number of dropped frames. Is there any way to get around this?*

A.   Dropped frames are typically the result of system resources— there just isn't enough computing power available to save all of the captured video frames in real time. There are a number of issues that can help boost your computing power:

- Shut down any background applications under Windows 95— especially those that demand a lot of RAM or virtual memory.

- Refer to your video capture application and try optimizing video compression, frame rates, and audio quality.

- See if there is a more recent and efficient video capture driver and capture software.

- Add RAM to your system.

- Upgrade your hard drive to a faster model, preferably one with a high data transfer rate (PIO modes 3 or 4).

- Upgrade your CPU.

- Upgrade your video capture hardware.

TV Board Drops Frames or Locks Up System

Q205.   *I don't know what's going on with my video board. It's one of those combined video/TV boards, and when I watch TV, the display looks "jerky," as if it is dropping frames. Sometimes, the system will just lock up. Is there a way to fix this?*

A.   From your description of the symptoms, I'd say you've got a hardware conflict. Chances are that you've got another device using the same IRQ or I/O address as your video/TV board. Check the Windows 95 Device Manager for interrupt conflicts between the video/TV card and other cards in your system. Conflicting devices are typically marked with yellow exclamation marks. You may need to reconfigure the video/TV board in order to clear the conflict.

Interrupt Error When Trying to Capture Video

Q206.   *Here's a tough one. I get an error message that says there's a vertical sync interrupt problem when I try to capture video with my Diamond DVT 1100 board.*

A.   You may have an IRQ conflict. Check the IRQ assigned to the
      video card's PCI slot in the Device Manager under System in the
      Control Panel. If this PCI's slot interrupt is being used by another
      device, you will need to reassign the PCI slot to a different IRQ.
      This can be handled through your system's CMOS Setup. Also, if
      no IRQ is being assigned to the PCI slot, that can also be a prob-
      lem.

      There could also be an IRQ conflict with the Diamond capture
      driver. Look in the Control Panel under Multimedia. Click on the
      Advanced tab and then look under Video Capture Drivers (Fig.
      2.1). There you'll see Diamond Multimedia Capture Driver.
      Double-click on it and then click on the Settings option. You can
      then change the IRQ of the capture driver. Try an unused IRQ.

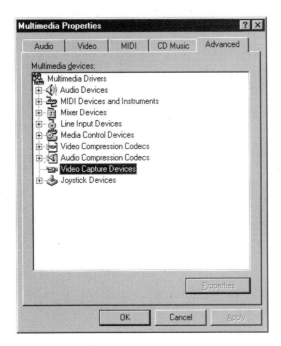

FIGURE 2.1 ADVANCED MULTIMEDIA PROPERTIES DIALOG FOR VIDEO CAPTURE DEVICE

Display Flicker Noticeable During Video Capture

Q207. *My display flickers while I'm using my Diamond DTV 1100 video board, but it doesn't seem to flicker otherwise. Is there any way for me to adjust this?*

A. Not really. This is a limitation of the DTV 1100 itself. The DTV 1100 is designed to run at a 60 Hz refresh rate. Therefore, your graphics card will automatically switch the refresh rate to 60 Hz (no matter what you have currently set under Windows). The refresh rate is switched back to the original setting once the DTV 1100 is no longer in use. Your screen may go blank momentarily while this happens. You'll also probably notice that the flickering will be more noticeable at higher resolutions.

TV Board Not Providing Proper Channels

Q208. *I'm using a Diamond Multimedia DTV 1100 TV/capture card, but I can only get channels 5 and 6 (and they are in black and white). How can I get all the channels.*

A. This is a software problem. Other users report that they can only get channels 14 or 15. You need to contact Diamond Multimedia (*www.diamondmm.com*) and update your DTV 1100 software to version 1.02 or later. With this version, you can change your TV mode under the Tuner Settings. Choose a mode that works correctly with your particular cable provider.

Dealing with "Holiday Lights" in Low Light

Q209. *I'm using a Connectix QuickCam, and I've been very happy with it, but why do I see white dots (they look like Christmas lights) on images in very low-light conditions? How do I adjust my QuickCam for different lighting conditions?*

ADVANCED

A.   The CCD sensor in your QuickCam is suffering from an effect known as *dark current*. Even though no light is falling on the CCD, it picks up minute amounts of random charges. These charges build up and cause some pixels on the CCD to display some color. This shows up as either white specks (on a gray-scale camera) or colored specks (on a color camera) in the image. Specks are an indication that the scene you are trying to capture is too dark. If you were using a 35-mm camera, these are probably the conditions under which you would use a flash. The simplest way to eliminate specks is to increase the light level. Turn on an overhead light or lamp or open a window or door. According to Connectix, the color QuickCam software version 2.02 and later incorporates a low light filter, which should fix this problem.

Monitors

INTERLACED VERSUS NONINTERLACED MONITORS

Q210.   *I have to buy a monitor that will fit within a fixed amount of space, but the only monitor I can find that offers the resolution, color depth, and dimensions I need is an interlaced type. Since I have only bought noninterlaced monitors, I'm really not sure what the difference is. I have heard that there is excessive flicker with an interlaced monitor. What is the effect on a person?*

A.   As you may know, a monitor image is formed by scanning three electron beams (for a color monitor) left to right across the CRT. Each subsequent scan is a bit lower than the previous one. You can visualize scanning the same way in which we read—left to right and top to bottom. A noninterlaced monitor forms a complete image in a single pass. If the screen image is updated 60 times per second, the full image is redrawn (or refreshed) 60 times per second. For an interlaced monitor, images are drawn as two pages—even scan lines on one page, and odd scan lines on the other. It takes two passes of the electron guns to complete an interlaced image. So even though an interlaced monitor may list a scan rate of 84 Hz, each half of the image is only being updated about 40 times per second This is where the flicker comes from.

Now, when sitting and looking at an interlaced and noninter-laced monitor of the same size sitting side by side displaying the same image, you might not see a difference, but if you avert your eyes above or below the monitor (keeping the interlaced monitor in your peripheral vision), the flicker will become clear. Your conscious eye can't really see it, but it's there—and with constant viewing, fatigue and headaches can result. It's no big deal if you just need a data display to review infrequently, but if some poor soul is going to be working with that monitor all day long, hold out for a noninterlaced monitor if possible.

MOVING FROM INTERLACED TO NONINTERLACED MONITORS

Q211. *I have a Packard Bell Legend 2000 that came with an interlaced monitor. Can I upgrade the monitor to a noninterlaced monitor without messing with the video drivers or card?*

A.   That's not always as easy as it sounds. Video display perfor-mance is highly dependent on the combination of your video board *and* monitor. If your video board is generating an inter-laced signal, you can't just plunk a noninterlaced monitor in place. You'd need to update the drivers to provide a noninter-laced signal at the resolution you want to use. If you can't swing a noninterlaced signal at the needed resolution, you *will* need to update both your video board and monitor to more recent mod-els which support the higher bandwidth.

MONITORS AND PHOSPHOR BURN-IN

Q212. *A friend recently told me that today's monitors have very little chance of phosphor damage (phosphor burning) even when images are left on the screen for prolonged periods. Is this true? If so, why are there so many screen savers around?*

A.   Phosphor damage occurs when CRT phosphors are excited with excessive energy (high brightness) for prolonged periods of time. This was prevalent in monochrome monitors used primarily for text displays which showed the same bland screen image day in and day out for years at a time (i.e., a computerized library card file system). With color monitors burn-in became less of an issue since less energy was being used to excite each phosphor, and the use of color allowed programmers to develop more diverse displays, graphic applications, and finally the GUI such as used in Windows. Theoretically, you could still burn in an image, but it would take years of projecting the same image onto the CRT. It just doesn't happen today.

Screen savers are now more of a show rather than a practical tool. They are a way of reflecting your own individual style on your system—sort of like bringing pictures of the spouse and kids to work. Screen savers are harmless and can actually offer a healthy distraction during idle moments. But don't buy a screen saver thinking it will protect your monitor. If you're worried about phosphor damage, turn the brightness down.

CLEANING A MONITOR'S CRT

Q213. *How should I clean the face of my monitor's CRT? Is glass cleaner good enough?*

A. If the CRT is simply smooth, uncoated glass, you should be able to use alcohol or ammonia-based cleaners on a damp, lint-free cloth (do not spray cleaner onto a monitor). It is generally not a good idea to use any detergents or solutions to clean your CRT because you run the risk of damaging the case plastic. However, you should be *extremely* careful with any antiglare coating. Any solution that contains alcohol or ammonia can definitely damage a monitor's antiglare coating. Warm water and a lint-free chamois cloth works the best to polish the monitor CRT in this case. It may take a little longer than using a detergent or spray, but it is the safest way to clean your antiglare display.

UNDERSTANDING MONITOR REFRESH RATES

Q214. *I'm shopping for a new monitor, and I've got my eye on one that seems to fit my needs and budget. Before I buy, I hoped you might be able to tell me what "Vertical Refresh Rate: 50 to 90 Hz automatic" means. I thought monitors used a 60-Hz refresh rate.*

INTERMEDIATE

A.   You're right. Monitors traditionally use a vertical refresh rate of 60 Hz when displaying images. However, more recent monitor designs allow the monitor to operate at higher refresh rates. This minimizes flicker which makes the display easier to look at for prolonged periods, especially when operating at higher resolutions. If you check the documentation that accompanies your video card, you'll see that each video mode uses its own vertical refresh rate. The specification you're referring to indicates that the monitor can shift its vertical refresh rate between 50 and 90 Hz (in several different steps) automatically as needed depending on the video mode being used. In many cases, modern video boards provide a utility for manually boosting vertical refresh rates in order to reduce flicker. If you do enhance the refresh rate, your monitor should adjust itself automatically.

USING VIDEO EXTENSION CABLES

Q215.   *I want to place my monitor on a desk a bit away from the PC, but the video cable won't reach. Can I use a video extension cable?*

A.   In theory, you should certainly be able to use a video extension cable. From a practical standpoint, however, there are some potential problems with poor-quality cables. By their very nature, video signals are high-frequency signals. This means that the physical cabling plays an important role in signal quality. If the video cable (or its extension cable) is damaged or poorly shielded, the video signal quality may degrade and result in ghosting—an echo effect resulting in an outline of images on your screen. When buying a video extension cable, be sure to select a high-quality, shielded, low-impedance one. As a rule, try to keep the overall length of the video cable below 12 feet (under 4 meters)

USING AN SVGA MONITOR ON A 286 SYSTEM

Q216.   *I would like to know if an SVGA monitor will work with an 80286 system. I don't have any brand in mind (any will do for now). I tried this on a Goldstar 230 i286 system and it worked, but I would like to know if it will work for all i286 systems.*

A. You're in luck. An SVGA monitor should work on any i286 system as long as the video adapter is designed to support SVGA video modes (the video card must use the ISA bus because of the 286-vintage motherboard). Of course, the video adapter itself must work properly in the i286 system. In other words, if the computer supports the video adapter, the video adapter will support the monitor.

USING A VGA MONITOR AND SVGA VIDEO BOARD

Q217. *I have a 486DX4/100 system with a Diamond Stealth SVGA video card in it. I need to know it I can use a Packard Bell VGA monitor with it. I am going to use this computer for an organization that I am in to help them save money, so I would be very happy if I didn't have to buy a new monitor.*

A. Yes, you should certainly be able to use a VGA monitor, but you will need to limit the video modes produced by the Stealth board to only those that the monitor can tolerate; otherwise, the resulting overscanning can damage the monitor. For example, you may not be able to drive the monitor above 640x480 at 60 Hz. Fortunately, you should be able to use high color modes with the VGA monitor as long as the resolution and vertical refresh are acceptable.

INTERMEDIATE

UNDERSTANDING MULTISCAN MONITORS

Q218. *I'm shopping for a new monitor and see a lot of units marked "Multiscan." What is this?*

A. Multiscan (often called Multisync) is a technology which enables a monitor to self-adjust to video signal from a variety of graphics boards. This makes it possible to switch between graphic resolutions and color depths without direct user involvement. For example, a multiscan monitor could switch from 640x480x256 to 1024x768x16M as soon as the video signals from the video adapter changed. Most modern computer monitors are capable of some level of multiscan operation.

MULTIFREQUENCY AND AUTOSCANNING

Q219. *I've heard the terms* multifrequency *and* autoscanning *used a lot with monitors. What do they mean?*

A. You're exactly right—these are both monitor-related terms. Multifrequency monitors (often called Multisync, although that's a trademark of NEC) can automatically adjust to the different refresh rates sent from the graphics adapter which indicate different resolutions. As long as those video signals are within the monitor's scanning range, the monitor will automatically adapt. The Term *Autoscanning* is also sometimes used interchangeably with *multisync* or *multifrequency,* but that is not technically correct. Autoscanning is a feature that automatically adjusts the screen at the start of each application to a predefined screen setting determined by the video mode of the application.

THE DIFFERENCE BETWEEN TRINITRONS AND SHADOW MASKS

INTERMEDIATE

Q220. *I'm starting to look at monitor specifications, and most of them make sense. However is there a difference between the terms* Trinitron *and* Shadow Mask? *If so, what is it?*

A. There is a difference between these two technologies, but both relate to the way pixels are isolated on a monitor (Fig. 2.2). A Trinitron CRT uses what's called an *aperture grille*. This grille—designed with long, unbroken slits—allows more energy from the electron beams to reach the phosphors on the screen. In actual practice, this results in purer, brighter, and more colorful images. The Shadow Mask is basically a plate with holes formed in it. This is an older, simpler form of CRT construction which often causes a darker image, with some tendency to color shift (called *doming*).

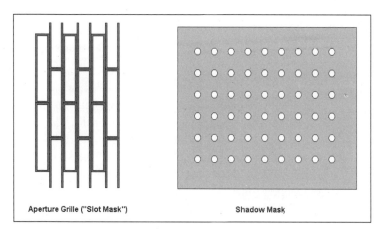

Aperture Grille ("Slot Mask")   Shadow Mask

FIGURE 2.2 APERTURE GRILLES VERSUS SHADOW MASKS

AN INVAR SHADOW MASK

Q221. What is an Invar shadow mask?

A.   Invar is a special heat-resistive alloy. The brighter a CRT picture
        gets, the greater the heat build-up on the shadow mask. If the
        mask gets too hot, it will deform, resulting in a loss of color puri-
        ty. Since Invar resists heat, it does not tend to deform. This
        improves the monitor's quality. Also, the heat-resistive properties
        of Invar allow the monitor to produce brighter images because
        the Invar will not warp from the additional heat.

THE MEANING OF GRAY DISPLAY LINES

*Q222. I have just noticed a thin gray line on the image displayed by my
        Sony computer monitor. It is a horizontal line located about one-
        third of the way up from the bottom of the screen. Is this normal?*

INTERMEDIATE

A.   This is perfectly normal. Sony (and many other manufacturers) use Trinitron picture tubes in their monitors. Trinitron CRTs employ what's called a *horizontal damper wire* to stabilize the aperture grille, which in turn separates the individual pixels. Currently, there are two display technologies designed to isolate individual picture elements (pixels). Together, these pixels form the image displayed on a computer's monitor. Shadow mask technology relies on an opaque sheet with small pinholes to separate pixels both horizontally and vertically. Aperture grille technology employs a series of thin, closely spaced vertical wires to isolate pixels horizontally. The pixels are separated vertically by the nature of the scan lines used to compose the image.

To keep the vertical wires in an aperture grille properly aligned within the picture tube, one or two horizontal damper wires are required. A 14-in or smaller Sony computer monitor employs one such wire. It is located about one-third of the way up from the bottom of the screen. Sony computer monitors larger than 14 in use two horizontal damper wires. These wires are located roughly one-third of the way down from the top and up from the bottom of the screen. Each wire casts a faint shadow that is visible as a light gray horizontal line on the image. This shadow is normally not visible but may become apparent when displaying a lightly colored background.

Video Bandwidth and Scanning Frequencies

Q223.   *I'm curious—can you tell me how video bandwidth, horizontal scanning, and vertical scanning are related?*

A.   A monitor's bandwidth basically specifies the maximum number of pixels that can be displayed on the screen in 1 s. Since pixels are "painted" onto the screen by lines of electrons (horizontal scanning), the bandwidth basically determines how many lines are painted and how quickly. If you can paint a screen full of pixels faster, you can then refresh the entire screen faster (vertical scanning). For example, a monitor with a low bandwidth cannot support high resolutions because it cannot paint the required number of lines in the given time. The higher a resolution you need, the higher your bandwidth should be.

SHADOWS IN THE SCREEN IMAGE

Q224. *The images on my monitor seem to have shadows on them. I'm not sure that shadow is the right word, but that's how it appears. Is there anything that I can do about this?*

A.　Actually, the term *shadow* is very descriptive, and the problem is quite common—especially among larger monitors operating at higher frequencies. There are two typical causes for shadows: the monitor or the video card. For the monitor, a poor-quality video cable, bad cable shielding, or a cheap video extender cable can all cause shadowing. Try removing any extension cable. Also try the monitor on another system or two. If the shadow follows the monitor, you might need to replace the video cable assembly. For the video board, some low-end video boards are not entirely precise with their video signals. There can sometimes be poor signal strength or noise in the video signals. If the monitor works on other systems, you may choose to upgrade the video board itself.

LOCATING MONITOR SCHEMATICS

Q225. *My shop specializes in computer monitors, and we are always looking for new sources of schematics and technical information—specifically, I've had a tough time locating data for KLH MN190 14-in VGA monitor. Any ideas?*

A.　I really had to reach deep into the archives for this one, but it seems that Computer Component Source, Inc., has KLH documentation. Their latest catalog lists a documentation package for the KLH MN190 as part number 86-060 for $35. You can reach CCS at 800-356-1227 or by fax at 800-926-2062. Their mailing address is 135 Eileen Way, Syosset, NY 11791

CARELESS ADJUSTMENTS CAUSE IMAGE DISTORTION

Q226. *I've been using an AST Vision 5L 15-in monitor for nearly 3 years and I'm still quite happy about its performance. One day, I played around with the "easy to use" adjustments. Unfortunately, I cannot revert back to the nearly perfect*

*"square" display (even though I tried to push reset 100 times). I
tried different adjustments with no success. I gave up. Now,
when I focus on the four sides, there are wavy sexy curves—and
they bother me. Is there a way to fix this?*

A.   I'm not clear on what you mean by "wavy sexy" curves, but it
sounds from your description that the edges of the display seem
to pull inward a bit. It doesn't sound like your edges are
"rolling" like waves toward a shore, and it also sounds like your
display is otherwise viewable. If this is a correct evaluation, I suspect you accidentally adjusted the monitor's pincushion setting.
When a flat image is projected against a curved screen, the edges
or the image tend to bow outward. The pincushion adjustment
compensates by pulling those edges in. It you overcompensated
the pincushion, it would pull the edges inward toward the center
of the image (causing an hourglass figure as shown in Fig. 2.3).
Check your monitor's manual for instructions on adjusting the
pincushion setting.

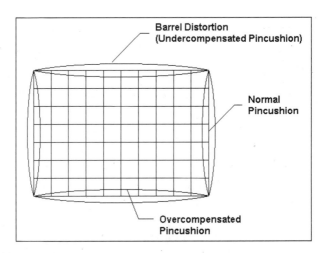

Figure 2.3 An Example of "overcompensated" pincushion

TROUBLESOME MONITOR SCREWS

Q227.   *I cannot unattach the monitor cable from the CPU. One of the
two little screws that holds the monitor cable on the back of the
PC has a stripped head (no groove for the screwdriver). There is
also very little room to work, so little that pliers cannot fit. I*

thought of drilling into the screw, but there isn't enough room for that either. I could take the monitor and PC to a shop where someone with specialized tools can probably take the screw out, but the monitor cable weaves through a slot in a computer desk. The only other suggestion that the staff at our local hardware store could give was to cut the monitor cable and have it replaced. Such a small but vexing problem. Any more elegant solutions?

A.   The little screws for serial cables, monitors, parallel cables, and so on, can certainly cause problems, especially if they are cross-threaded into their hex nut. I believe that you could get the screw out if you had a little more space to work. You can probably take the monitor connector apart by removing the screws that hold the shell together. Once the shell halves are removed, you should have a lot more space to get a "bite" on the troublesome screw and remove it with a screwdriver or needlenose pliers. If you cannot disassemble the monitor connector, you might try a pair of long-nose needlenose pliers, which should fit into even the tightest spaces. You can use the pliers to grab the hex nut into which the screw is inserted and use a fine screwdriver (like a jeweler's screwdriver) to loosen the screw.

HAZY DISPLAY AT START-UP MAY SIGNAL BAD MONITOR

Q228.   *I have a Viewsonic 5e monitor, and just recently it has started getting hazy. The display is cloudy when the monitor is first turned on. I checked all of my connections, and they seem to be all right. After about 30 min or so the display clears up and everything is readable. The monitor is about 4 or 5 years old but does get a lot of use. This may seem weird but the problem also appears to be weather-related—whenever it is very humid or rainy, I have the problem, but when the weather is dry, the problem doesn't occur. Has my monitor just reached its life expectancy?*

A.   It sounds like you've got a problem in the contrast or focus controls of your monitor (I can't really be sure because "hazy" can be interpreted several different ways). It is not unusual for age to affect the reliability of some components—especially resistors and capacitors. As hermetic seals break down, humidity gets into components and changes their characteristics. After the system heats up, humidity is forced from the component, and it returns to its original value.

If you do not choose to work inside of a monitor, you should take the monitor in for service at your earliest convenience. There is no immediate need for service, but it is likely that the problem will just continue to worsen. If you choose to tinker, start by removing the monitor's back cover and check for dust. Vacuum out any dust that may have accumulated on the monitor's main board, and unclog any vents in the case. If you can locate the potentiometer adjustments for focus and contrast, use a good-quality electrical contact cleaner and clean each adjustment thoroughly (be sure to mark the starting point for each adjustment). If the problem persists, you've probably got a capacitor breakdown somewhere on the monitor's main board. Replace the main board, or send the monitor in for service.

Display Snow Not Always Cause for Concern

Q229.   *I just bought a new monitor, and every time my program changes from text to graphics mode, the screen flickers with snow for a moment before settling into its new mode. Is the monitor defective? Should I take it back?*

A.   This is not really a defect, but unfortunately it is a problem that is indigenous to the design of many inexpensive monitors. Each video mode requires different timing signals which are generated by the video adapter. The monitor normally detects these timing signals and changes its operation accordingly. Ideally, the screen should be blanked or faded out until the monitor decides how to interpret new timing signals. However, not all monitors provide such esthetic operations; some just let the snow and retrace lines fly until the new display mode locks in. Chances are that's what your new monitor is doing. If you really cannot live with this behavior, contact the vendor who sold you the monitor. If you elect to return the monitor, many reputable vendors will allow you to return the purchase in 30 to 90 days with no questions asked. Comprehensive product reviews and floor demonstrations will help you choose a better replacement.

Display Shifts to the Right

Q230. *I've got a problem with my computer monitor. It powers up properly but after about 30 minutes, the display will begin shifting to the right. The image continues to shift to the right until it finally cuts out into a jumbled mess. After I turn the monitor off briefly, I can get several more minutes of viewing before the image shifts again (and finally cuts out). Is it time for a new monitor?*

A.   It sounds as if your monitor's horizontal oscillator is suffering from thermal breakdown due to age. A confident fix would be to replace the monitor's raster board—the large main board usually set at the base of the monitor below the CRT. The monitor's horizontal sweep frequency may be off a bit (either from a bad factory setting or due to a component's old age). If you have schematics and a frequency meter, you can measure the horizontal raster frequency and adjust it if necessary. Most component values tend to drift a bit as the monitor warms up—this is normal—and monitors are often adjusted at the factory to compensate for this thermal drift. If the monitor is old, component values may have changed enough to alter the horizontal frequency to a point where it is unstable. As the monitor warms up, the instability becomes severe, gradually worsening until the image just cuts out.

If you're really up for a challenge, try tracking down the defective component with a can of liquid refrigerant (of course, you should have a schematic of the raster circuit in order to locate the horizontal oscillator components). Remove the back of the monitor, power up the system, and wait until the image cuts out. Be *extremely* careful to avoid electrocution since monitors use over 20 kV to drive the CRT. Start with the horizontal oscillator IC (a schematic will tell you which component this is) and squirt a bit of refrigerant on it. Liquid refrigerant cools the part that may have failed due to heating; in many cases, this component can "kick in" again once it's cooled. If the image pops back after a moment or two, you've found your culprit. Replace the defective part. If nothing happens, repeat this procedure with subsequent stages of the horizontal raster circuit until you have isolated the problem part. Of course, if the problem persists, you can still just replace the raster board outright.

MONITOR IMAGE SHIFTS IN CERTAIN VIDEO MODES

Q231. *I'm currently running a P133 with Windows 95. Most of my old DOS programs work OK, but I've got a couple of fairly simple games that when they load, the picture on the monitor moves so far to the right that only half of the screen is visible. I've tried running them in the various DOS modes (including a straight boot to DOS 6.22), all with the same results. I'm assuming that a video driver is involved, but I can't seem to figure it out, especially when booting to DOS 6.22 since I'm not loading any video drivers at all. Any ideas?*

A. Your question is a common one and is related to your video system. The problem is either in your monitor or video board. When a video system changes screen modes (i.e., to play a game), the sync frequencies change. Ideally, the monitor is supposed to lock onto that new sync signal and display the new image accordingly. Sometimes, the video board does not produce the proper sync signals that the monitor needs to make the correct transition. This is not a serious problem but can be annoying. This is probably *not* a driver issue.

First, with your game running, try turning the monitor off for a minute and then turn it on again. If the image comes back properly, the monitor is at fault because it will not resynchronize itself automatically. There is not much you can do about that one except replace the monitor. However, I think that's a drastic measure (and too expensive a solution to play games). If the image remains offset when you turn the monitor back on, the video board may not be producing the correct sync signals to control the monitor. Try the monitor on another PC. If it works properly running the same games (but with a different video board), maybe you should consider a video board upgrade.

ADJUSTING DISPLAY IMAGE SHIFTING

Q232. *The screen shifts about 0.5 in on my XV15 monitor every time that I switch between Windows 95 and DOS. I have to readjust the monitor's dials every time I switch resolutions. Is there a solution to this?*

A.   Your XV15 monitor is what's known as an *analog controlled* monitor. With this type of control, you position a dial at a certain point along a curve. This setting is used across the whole range of resolutions as well as in both the Windows and DOS environments. The problem often associated with this type of control is that the user may make the size and position settings for Windows and then switch to DOS and find that this same dial setting moves the DOS cursor off the screen entirely. This then requires adjustment on the user's part to properly recenter and resize the screen for the DOS environment. In this sort of scenario, the only way you can hope to achieve proper centering and sizing of the image in all environments is by playing around with the frequencies (i.e., refresh rates) for the video card and attempting to match these frequencies as closely as possible to the VESA timing presets for the analog monitor. If the video driver supports setting different refresh rates, you may be able to use a different refresh rate which will minimize this effect. Otherwise, you're stuck adjusting the analog control knob.

DISPLAY IMAGE APPEARS TILTED

Q233.   *My display image appears tilted—one edge of the screen appears lower than the other end. Is there anything I can do before bringing the monitor in for service?*

A.   This is a common complaint, but the cause is easy to understand. The magnetic field from the earth (or anything magnetic near the monitor) may interfere with the magnetic fields generated by the monitor. This can cause the image to become slightly tilted or rotated. Most monitors provide a tilt function control to make the adjustments.

TRACKING DOWN IMAGE JITTER

Q234.   *When I use my monitor at home, the image seems to jump or jitter a bit. But when I try it at my office, the picture is solid as a rock. What's going on here? It isn't the monitor is it?*

ADVANCED

A.   Well it's probably *not* the monitor. Chances are that you're deal-
         ing with an unreliable ac source or some local electromagnetic
         interference. First, check the ac outlet you're using for your mon-
         itor at home. Overloaded power strips can cause problems, so try
         plugging your monitor into a separate wall socket (or other sock-
         et on a different ac circuit in your home). Next, check for elec-
         tromagnetic interference. This is usually caused by things like
         poorly shielded speakers, transformers sitting next to your moni-
         tor, or fluorescent lights hanging close above the unit. Another
         possible (but rarely considered) source is the ac house wiring
         behind the walls near the back of your monitor. As a test, try fac-
         ing your monitor in different directions, or move your monitor to
         a new location. If the problem goes away, you probably have an
         interference problem.

INTERFERENCE PRODUCES THIN SCROLLING LINES ON DISPLAY

Q235.   *What should I do when I see thin lines scrolling down the
         screen? This causes flickering images or wavy displays.*

A.   Interference from appliances or magnetic sources often causes
         irregular images on your monitor. The amount of interference,
         noise, or distortion depends on your monitor's proximity to
         sources such as TV sets, other monitors, refrigerators, large
         stereo speakers, or motor-driven appliances. Faulty fluorescent
         light assemblies can also cause distorted images. Place your sys-
         tem as far as possible from these sources. You might also try the
         monitor in another ac circuit.

JUDGING MONITOR FLICKER

Q236.   *I notice a slight flicker in my peripheral vision when looking
         away from the monitor. I am alarmed by this. Should I ask the
         manufacturer for a replacement?*

A.   First, don't be panicked by flicker, it is a natural side effect of the way in which monitors draw their images and does not necessarily indicate a defect or quality problems with your monitor. Since you found only a trace of flicker in your peripheral vision this suggests that the image probably looks great when viewed directly. If you are satisfied with the image quality, keep your monitor. If the monitor and video board support higher refresh rates, you might consider trying them also.

DEALING WITH SCREEN FLICKER

Q237. *I've got a problem with my monitor. The monitor is supposed to support high refresh rates, but I still see the display flickering. Is there anything I can do about this?*

A.   Just because the monitor supports higher refresh rates doesn't mean that it is actually operating at those refresh rates. The monitor is driven by (or synched to) your video board, which in turn is operated by your video drivers under Windows 95. Select the Display icon from your Control Panel and choose the Adjustment button. If your video system is capable of driving your monitor at a higher refresh rate, you should be able to increase it there. Otherwise, you may need to upgrade your video board (and/or drivers) to match the capabilities of your monitor.

Still, there are other issues that can cause flicker. Try removing or shutting off any nearby electrical devices that could cause flickering (i.e., fluorescent lights or fans). Also make sure you are not using an extension to increase the length of your monitor's video cable. If you are, remove the extender and connect the monitor cable directly to the video port. While you're at it, verify that the video cable is connected properly. Finally, try the monitor's ac power cord in a power outlet that is *not* part of a surge protector power strip.

ADVANCED

SCREEN FLICKER AT HIGH RESOLUTIONS

Q238.   *My display image flickers at higher resolutions under Windows 95. What can I do?*

A.   You will need to change the video refresh rate to reduce your flicker. Check the Display properties under your Control Panel. If your video drivers support such refresh rate changes, you can adjust the refresh accordingly. If not, you will need to download the latest drivers from the video card maker. Keep in mind that not all video boards (or monitors) will support refresh rate adjustment.

HORIZONTAL SYNC PROBLEM CROPS UP IN OLDER VIDEO BOARD

Q239.   *I have just built my first computer and I only have one problem. I am using my old Magnavox VGA monitor (640x480 resolution and 0.42-mm dot pitch) with a Reveal Basic Super VGA card (800x600 16 colors and 640x480 16 colors). The problem is that my monitor has a slight "shimmering" from side to side. The problem persists when I tried a second monitor. Any ideas?*

A.   It sounds like you've got a horizontal sync problem with your video board (perhaps even a dirty video connector). Check the video connector first and see that there are no bent or broken pins. Straighten or clean the pins if necessary. Otherwise, try replacing the video board. A new SVGA video board should provide a superior image and also provide you with a suite of advanced video modes.

SCROLLING, WAVING, OR SHIMMERING ON THE DISPLAY

Q240.   *I don't like my monitor's display. There are "lines" in the image—sort of a wavy shimmer in the image—it's hard to explain. Is this a problem with the monitor?*

ADVANCED

A. I doubt it. In many cases, the mild distortion you're seeing is caused by interference with the display signals. First, try removing or turning off any nearby electrical devices that could be causing the interference. Motors and fluorescent lighting are notorious for this, but other monitors, nearby televisions, and large stereo speakers can also cause such interference. If your monitor is in a "clean" environment, check to see that the monitor cable does not have a cable extension attached to it, and verify that the cable is secure at the video card. Finally, try the monitor's ac power cord in a power outlet that is not part of a surge protector power strip.

CRT DISCOLORATION

Q241. *I've noticed that some areas of my monitor display are showing weird colors. This is most noticeable under Windows 95 with the light grays and white background, but I've also seen discoloration when other colors are displayed. My friend says the CRT is shot. What do you think?*

A. The discoloration symptoms you describe suggest a color purity problem. This is very common and is not necessarily a defect. The problem is that some areas of the CRT's shadow mask can become magnetized. This causes the electron beams to distort and illuminate unwanted color phosphors—that's what's causing your discoloration. The solution is to demagnetize the shadow mask. All color monitors are built with a degaussing coil which serves to briefly demagnetize the shadow mask each time the monitor is turned on. If your monitor has a manual degauss button, just trigger it manually a few times (don't worry when you see the display distort—it should only last a few moments). Note that you should wait about 30 min before pressing the degauss button. If your monitor does not have a manual degauss feature, just turn the monitor off, wait 30 min and then turn it back on.

If degaussing does not help, you may have a failure in the degaussing coil, or there may be some electromagnetic equipment near the monitor (such as unshielded speakers). Try moving any such equipment away, or move the monitor to another location and repeat the degaussing procedure. As a last-ditch effort, you might also try a hand-held degaussing coil. Simply place the coil near the CRT face, switch the coil on and then slowly move the coil away to an arm's-length distance before switching the coil off.

COLORED PATCHES MAY DEMAND DEGAUSSING

Q242.   *I have color spots or "splotches" at the edges of my screen. This can't be normal, can it?*

A.   No, you should have good color continuity across the entire screen area. The color spots (such as those in Fig. 2.4) are almost always caused by magnetic interference—often the CRT's shadow mask is slightly magnetized. The first thing to try is degaussing your monitor. All color monitors automatically degauss them-selves when first turned on. If your monitor has a manual degaussing feature, simply activate it. If your unit does not have a manual degauss feature, simply turn the monitor off for 30 min. and then power it back up again. If degaussing does not help (or if the spots come back after a little while), try rearrang-ing the equipment near your monitor. Devices with magnetic properties (i.e, speakers and transformers) can affect the purity of your monitor.

For best results, you must wait at least 30 min. before degauss-ing manually.

Note

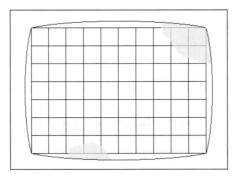

Figure 2.4 An example of color purity problems

CASE OF THE PINK MONITOR

Q243. *There's something wrong with my monitor—the image has developed a pinkish hue. It's still usable, but the color scheme looks terrible (and I'm set to the Standard color scheme). Is the monitor defective, or is there a simple fix that I'm missing?*

A. Assuming that there are no other problems such as low brightness or image distortion, color problems may be caused by connection problems and local magnetization. Check the monitor's connection at the video board and try reinstalling the video connector several times. If the problem persists, make sure that there are no strong magnetic fields near the monitor. Even relatively mild magnetic fields such as those generated by multimedia speakers can eventually cause color problems. Once you're sure the monitor is clear of local magnetic fields, try using a degaussing coil to demagnetize the monitor. If your monitor is still pink, the video drive circuits may need calibration (you may need to take the monitor to a shop for that).

MONITOR SHOWS LIGHT BLUE TINT

Q244. *I have a friend who is using a new Compaq computer with a Compaq SVGA monitor. Everything has been working properly for some months now, but recently, the monitor is showing everything with a light blue tint. What's the problem?*

A. There are a couple of distinct possibilities here. First, check the monitor cable between the monitor and video adapter. Wiggle the monitor cable to see if the blue tint goes away. If that happens, there is probably an intermittent connection in the cable. See that none of the cable pins are bent or broken (thus not making contact with the adapter connector). If you find a broken or intermittent cable, you may have to replace the monitor cable.

If the cable and connector appears intact, try the monitor on another PC. If the blue tint follows the monitor, the monitor is probably defective. If the blue tint goes away when the monitor is used on a different machine, the video adapter on your original PC is probably defective. You can verify this by trying a known-good monitor in place of your suspect one. If the known-good monitor displays with a blue tint on your PC, try replacing the video adapter.

ADVANCED

If you have narrowed the problem to the monitor itself, the trouble is probably in the blue video driver circuit attached to the CRT neck. Excess blue generally means that the blue drive output is shorted or fixed at some level. Ultimately, your best bet is to replace the video drive board (the small printed circuit board which plugs into the CRT neck).

DEALING WITH A DARKENING MONITOR

Q245. *Do you have any suggestions for a monitor that seems to be getting darker?*

A. Display brightness is generally a combination of four factors: high-voltage, screen voltage, CRT quality, and brightness adjustment. I assume you've already tried increasing the brightness control. When a darkening image appears to be "collapsing" around all four edges, the high-voltage level is probably failing, and the monitor will require service. If your image is still strong (though dim), I'd suspect that your high voltage is adequate. Next, there is a master screen voltage adjustment somewhere in the monitor—probably near the flyback transformer. If you can find the screen voltage adjustment, try increasing it in small increments until reasonable brightness is restored. If you continue to have image problems, the CRT may be failing. Of course, if you're uncomfortable at all with the thought of working inside your monitor, I suggest that you simply take the monitor into a shop for service.

Note

Monitors use extremely high voltages in their operation. When working inside a monitor, be very careful to avoid the high-voltage anode at the CRT.

DISPLAY FAR TOO DARK

Q246. *My monitor at home is **not** working properly. It's a Dell 15-in Ultrascan monitor with a built-in antiglare coating The problem is that the screen is way too dark. Even with the brightness dial set at the brightest possible, everything from DOS (white writing is a medium gray) to Windows 3.11 (can't read the current win-*

dow names sometimes, especially if color is set to teal and writing is set to black) to my games (MechWarrior 2 is almost impossible to play). What's the problem? Is there anything I can do to fix it? One other note: The display has gotten progressively darker over the last few months.

A. If one screen mode looked good, but another looked dark, I might have suggested that your video board was using an incorrect refresh rate and urged you to check your drivers or replace the video board. However, if the display is dark in every screen mode (and brightness is at its maximum), that probably means you've got a high-voltage problem with the monitor. If you're not handy with monitor circuitry, you should simply take the monitor in for service. But if you like to tinker, there are a few things to check. Be careful though—the high voltages inside a monitor can be dangerous.

Use a high-voltage probe and measure the anode voltage. It should approximately equal the voltage level marked on the CRT or labeled elsewhere in the PC. If the anode voltage is low, you will need to adjust the high-voltage level (usually through an adjustment on the flyback transformer). Once you know that the anode voltage is correct, look for an adjustment for screen voltage—this is generally the master brightness control. Mark the original position of the adjustment and try boosting the screen voltage. Ideally, brightness should come up. If the adjustments have no effect or you cannot find the adjustments or the thought of playing with 30,000 V scares you, take the monitor in for service.

AMBER DISPLAY LIGHT REMAINS

Q247. *Normally, when I turn on my monitor, the power light appears amber and when I power up the PC, that amber light turns green, and an image appears. When I start my system now, there is no display, and the light remains amber. Do you know what the problem is?*

A. This is actually a very handy troubleshooting tool. The amber light means that there is no video signal (or the signal is not synchronized with the monitor). The green light means that video synchronization is correct. If your light is remaining amber, the video signal from the video card is not reaching the monitor. Make sure that the video cable is secure between the video card and monitor. Also check that the refresh rates being produced by the video card are correct for your monitor (usually between 60 to 76 Hz depending on the video card's resolution and your particular monitor).

Monitor's Crackling Noises Suggest High-Voltage Problems

Q248.   *I have an ADI SM-5514 3e+ monitor. The power LED lights up, and when the unit is powered down, I can hear static electricity crackling as the HV collapses. However, there is no image or raster until the monitor has been powered up for about 1 to 4 h. When the image does show up, it becomes visible slowly (as is typical of a normal monitor power up). Sometimes the image disappears again after 6 to 8 h of operation. The rest of the monitor functions seem to work (i.e, brightness, color balance, and so on).*

A.   For the symptoms you describe, I suggest that your monitor's flyback transformer has failed—the crackling sound you describe is typical of high-voltage electricity arching across the breached insulation of the flyback transformer's windings. The transformer is probably intermittent, which would account for the image snapping in and out over time.

Wrong Refresh Rates Cause Image Problems

Q249.   *I have just finished setting up my new video board, but when I run Windows 95, my display rolls and seems to turn into unreadable static. Multiple screen image ghosts appear. It's hard to really describe it. Do you have any ideas?*

A.   I think you've told me enough. It sounds like the refresh rate being generated by your video board is *not* compatible with your particular monitor. Perhaps you set a resolution which is too high for the monitor. Restart Windows 95 in the Safe Mode (this should use a 640x480 standard VGA display). You should be able to see the display clearly. Open your Control Panel and then use the Display icon to adjust your display settings to a lower resolution which uses a lower refresh rate (check your monitor's documentation for its specific range of operation). If your display is still distorted in the Safe Mode, your video board itself may be defective, try a new video board.

Monitor Synchronization Problems

Q250.   *I've tried a new video mode in Windows 95, but the display is all whitish with haze and blurry lines sort of scrolling through it. However, I can see bits and pieces of the image. What can I do to fix the problem?*

A.   You have a classic synchronization problem. The monitor cannot synchronize to the video signals that are being generated by the video card. This often happens when you try to drive the monitor at a resolution (and horizontal refresh frequency) beyond its capabilities. Reset the video mode to a lower resolution. Start Windows 95 in the Safe Mode (press <F8> when you see the message "Starting Windows 95"), and then open the Display icon under your Control Panel and reset the resolution selection (Fig. 2.5). Save your changes and restart Windows 95. If you had not reset the video mode, I might suggest that the monitor or its video cable might have failed.

Note

*Do **not** allow the monitor to run for prolonged periods in this overdriven mode. Otherwise, the high refresh frequency could damage the monitor.*

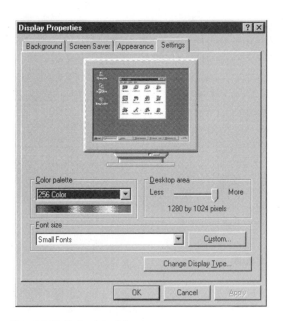

Figure 2.5 Display Properties dialog

IMAGE DISTORTION SUGGESTS SYNCHRONIZATION PROBLEM

Q251. *I'm not getting an image on my monitor, just a scrambled mess. What do I do?*

A.   This is a synchronization problem with the video signal. The first thing to look for is a faulty connection between the computer and monitor. Inspect the video cables to make sure no pins are bent or broken off. If the cable looks OK, contact your video card manufacturer to check the horizontal and vertical scanning frequencies you are running—they may be outside the range of the monitor. Try starting Windows 95 in the Safe Mode, and set the video mode to a different (lower) resolution.

NO MONITOR AUTOSYNC AT 800x600

Q252. *I have a machine that I put together from parts. It's an AMD 5x86 133-MHz system with an OEM STB64 1MB video board. The system is running Windows 95. When I switch to 800x600 with 64 K colors, the video is unreadable (I see only vertical lines). Then I warm boot the system and it's fine. I don't think I'm supposed to have to turn the PC on and reboot it for Windows 95 to work, so I've swapped monitors and video cards, formatted the hard drive, and reinstalled Windows 95. I am puzzled about why it works with a warm boot and not a cold boot. Any ideas?*

A.   I think I may have a solution. Your description of vertical lines sounds like a monitor synchronization problem. If it's an older monitor, it may not have an autosync feature that will configure the monitor for 800x600 operation (but during a reboot, the monitor can resynchronize itself). I suggest that you reconfigure the video board to run at 640x480, or even 1024x768. I have a feeling you'll find that the monitor works properly at a different resolution.

DISPLAY LOSING ITS WIDTH

Q253.   *I have a 14-in monitor which is a few years old now. The left and right sides of the display have a distinctive black area that I cannot adjust out. It has gotten bigger with age. I can push my monitor to 600x800 resolution and make a few adjustments that help, but my system prefers 640x480 resolution. Is it time for a new monitor?*

A.   It sounds like you're losing your high voltage or that your horizontal-size circuits need adjusting. Either way, you're looking at making some adjustments inside the monitor itself. If you're proficient with monitor troubleshooting, you can adjust the high voltage as appropriate. You could then locate the Horizontal Size Hsize adjustment on the monitor's main board and adjust that accordingly to resize the image. Otherwise, take the monitor in for service or replace it outright.

MONITOR IMAGE SHRINKING WITH AGE

Q254.   *I have a 14-in monitor. It is a few years old. The left and right side of the image have a distinctive black area that I cannot adjust out. It has gotten bigger with age. I can push my monitor to 600x800 and make a few adjustments to help, but my system prefers 640x480. Is it time for a new monitor?*

A.   It sounds like you're losing your high-voltage, or your horizontal size circuits need adjusting. Either way, you're looking at making some adjustments inside the monitor itself. If you're proficient with monitor troubleshooting, you can check and adjust the high voltage as appropriate. Then locate the Horizontal Size (or "Hsize") adjustment on the monitor's main board and adjust that accordingly. Otherwise, you may take the monitor in for service, or replace it outright.

FAILED MONITOR PRODUCES A BUZZING SOUND

Q255.   *I am having a problem with a monitor and would like your opin-ion a lot to what I should do. I have a 14-in SVGA Supertron monitor that is about 5 years old. My wife has noticed lately that letters in words flicker when she is using Word for Windows 6.0. Yesterday the monitor went black, the front power light does not light, and the monitor emits a faint buzzing sound from the back of the unit when it is turned on. In fact the buzzing sound is the only way to know that the unit is on at this point since the power indicator light does not light up. The monitor and com-puter had been on for several hours prior to this happening. In other words, the monitor died while it was being used.*

A.   While it's difficult to give a precise answer, I think your symp-toms are clear enough to suspect a power supply problem. The fact that you hear a buzz and the power light stays off is enough to suggest that the power supply has failed (the buzz is probably a 60-Hz hum from your power supply transformer). If your mon-itor has a separate power supply module, you can probably repair the monitor simply by replacing the power supply module. If the supply circuitry is integrated into the main (raster) board, you will have to troubleshoot the circuit, or you can replace the main board—that should do it. Do not be concerned with the high-voltage circuit. It's not working now, but it will come back when the power supply is restored.

HANDLING A DEAD MONITOR

Q256. *I have a Compudyne monitor which has given me years of excellent performance—until today. When I switched it on, there was no power LED, no high-voltage buzz, no picture, nothing. I checked the ac cord and also found that the PC is working (I tried a friend's monitor on the system). What's the deal with my monitor?*

A.   There are a couple of real possibilities. First, suspect the ac fuse in your monitor. The absence of any power LED suggests that power may not be reaching the power supply. If the ac cord is intact, the main fuse may have failed (it can happen spontaneously after long years of use). Make sure the monitor is unplugged and check the back of the monitor for a fuse holder. If there is no externally mounted fuse holder, you will need to remove the rear cover from the monitor and locate the main fuse in the ac filter leading to (or in) the power supply circuit. Observe the fuse carefully; if the fine strand is burned out, replace the fuse. If the fuse is intact (or it burns out again immediately), you may have a short or other failure in the power supply, so try replacing the power supply (or main monitor board).

3

Drive Questions

We depend on permanent storage to hold our operating systems, programs, data files, images, text, and even our virtual memory. Over the last 10 years, drives have increased in size and diversified to fill important storage niches in our PCs. This chapter looks at the terminology, concepts, and corrective actions for the four major drive families: floppy, hard, CD-ROM, and tape drives. You'll also find questions on removable-media drives at the end of this chapter.

Floppy Drive Terminology and General Topics

SUPPORTING FOUR FLOPPY DRIVES

Q257.   *Can my system support four floppy drives?*

A.   Motherboard BIOS almost never supports four floppy devices. In
        most cases, the BIOS supports only two floppy drives (A: and B:).
        However, you can purchase an add-on controller card that will
        give you additional support. For such a card to work, though, it
        must provide its own supplement to the motherboard's BIOS.

SWITCHING FLOPPY DRIVE LETTERS

Q258.   *I have a 386DX/25 Blue Dolphin clone PC with both a 5.25-in
        A: drive and a 3.5-in B:. The A: drive failed, and I would like to
        switch the 3.5-in drive to be the A: drive. Is it just a matter of
        switching data cables and power cables and then reconfiguring
        the CMOS settings, or am I off target?*

A.   You've got the right idea. Exchanging floppy drives basically
        involves two steps. First, you need to exchange the drive posi-
        tions on your floppy cable. The end-most floppy connection is
        the A: floppy, and the middle floppy connection is the B: floppy.
        You'll need to place the end-most floppy cable connection on the
        3.5-in drive. If you plan to replace the failed 5.25-in drive, you
        could make that the B: drive. There's no need to exchange power
        cables. Second, restart the PC and start your CMOS Setup rou-
        tine, then edit the A: drive entry for your 3.5-in drive, and edit
        the entry for the B: drive (if you do not install a new B: drive, set
        the entry as none or not installed). Remember to save your
        changes and reboot the PC. That should be all there is to it.

USING CABLES AND JUMPERS TO REASSIGN FLOPPY DRIVES

Q259. *I need to be able to change my boot disk floppy from the 5.25-in drive (A:), to the 3.5-in (B:) drive. I believe that this would be controlled by a jumper setting on each of the floppy drive's printed circuit boards. Can you reveal the secret of the jumpers?*

A. Swapping floppies should be a relatively simple matter, and you may not need to change the actual drive jumpers to do it. If you have the standard IBM flat cable going to your floppies, you will see that the cable has a "twist" between the two connectors. As shown in Fig. 3.1, the connector before the twist is the B: drive, and the drive after the twist (the end-most connector) is the A: drive. So if all is standard, you must swap the connectors and also swap the CMOS settings. This will effectively reverse your floppy drives without having to adjust anything on the drives themselves.

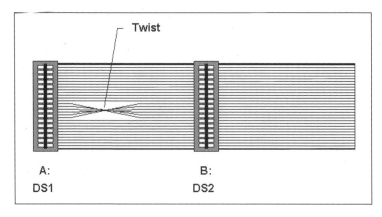

Figure 3.1 Typical floppy drive cable assembly

If you don't have the standard twisted cable, you are correct that the drives should have a set of Drive Select jumpers: DS0, DS1, etc. On a standard (twisted) cable, these jumpers are set to DS1 (on both drives). On a non-IBM (straight) cable, one drive should be set to DS0 and the other to DS1; you would swap the jumper assignments and swap the CMOS settings. This is *not* likely to be the setup on most PCs.

SETTING A FLOPPY ID USING DRIVE JUMPERS

Q260.   *I have an Epson floppy drive (Model SMD-300). It is set to serve
as drive B: What are the jumper settings to set it as drive A:?*

A.   I can't tell you the exact jumper locations for your particular
drive, but look for markings such as DS0 and DS1. DS1 refers to
B: and is the traditional setting for all floppies (the cable twist
turns the end-most drive back to A:). Try changing the jumper
setting from DS1 (B:) to DS0 (A:). You should really only change
drive jumpers if you're using a floppy drive cable *without* a twist.

UNDERSTANDING THE DMF FLOPPY

Q261.   *I want to make a backup copy of the original distribution disks
included with my new Microsoft product; however, the disks are
in that strange DMF (1.7MB) format. I've seen new products out
there that claim to format such disks, but is there a way of estab-
lishing the proper format under current DOS utilities without
having to invest in new utilities?*

A.   Software piracy is a major concern to Microsoft and all software
manufacturers. The ability to copy disks easily has cost the software industry dearly in the last decade. By making disks difficult
to copy, Microsoft hopes to reduce piracy. However, this also
hurts the honest end users who want to create a single (and perfectly legal) backup copy for archive purposes.

Microsoft has not only changed the number of sectors per track
to 21 (from the classic 18), but they have reduced the number of
root directory entries to 16 (instead of 224) and increased the
number of sectors per cluster to 4 (up from 1). This provides
exactly 838 clusters of 2048 bytes per cluster (plus 4096 bytes of
overhead for the boot sector, FAT, and root directory) for a total
of 1,720,320 bytes (or 1.7MB). Unfortunately, DOS will not yet
handle DMF disks, so you *will* need third-party utilities to make
archival copies of the software.

FINDING A REPLACEMENT PS/2 FLOPPY DRIVE

Q262. *We have a PC at work—an IBM PS/2 Model 55. Its disk drive has been ailing for some time, but unfortunately PS/2s have a slightly special disk drive. Purchasing a new one from IBM requires quite a cash advance, so I was wondering if this machine could be fit with a PC-compatible disk drive, which is much cheaper.*

A. You can purchase rebuilt PS/2 drives from a company called PC Service Source. You also have to send in the defective drives after the good drives are received. The price is about $50 each, and their phone number is 800-727-2787.

REVERSING A FLOPPY DRIVE CABLE

Q263. *I have heard that reversing one end of the floppy drive cable can damage the drive. Any comments?*

A. As a rule, you should be very careful about the proper orientation of *all* drive cables. I have *never* seen damage from reversed floppy cables, but I have heard reports of both drive and adapter damage. So the potential for damage is certainly there—it's really a question of drive and controller quality. Higher-quality parts will survive a cable reversal where low-end components may not. Always double-check your cabling before powering up after a repair or upgrade, and if you reconnect a floppy drive and notice that the drive light always remains on, shut down the PC as soon as possible and correct the signal cable.

USING THIRD-PARTY UTILITIES TO SET BOOT ORDER

Q264. *I have a utility called BOOTSET, which basically lets you set A: as bootable or not. If I set A: as a nonbootable drive, my computer will always boot from C:. Now, in your opinion, what is the worst that can happen? Suppose, I have a HDD failure? Will I still be able to boot the system?*

ADVANCED

A.   I'm really not convinced that you need a third-party utility to select your boot order because CMOS should define that for you. If you start the CMOS Setup, you should find an entry such as Boot Order which can be set A:/C:, C:/A:, B:/C:, and so on. If you want the system to boot from a hard drive without bothering with the A: drive, just set the boot order to C:/A:. If the C: drive (hard drive) fails, the system will automatically try booting from the A: drive next. If you can set the boot order, you can omit the use of utilities like BOOTSET.

Floppy Drive Corrective Actions

RECOVERING A WET FLOPPY DISK

Q265.   *I have a 3.5-in DOS disk that has some unknown waterlike fluid in it. Do you have any suggestions about how to make it work long enough to salvage the unbacked up data?*

A.   If the magnetic media itself is damaged, your data may be unre-coverable. Otherwise, remove the wet media from the jacket (you will have to separate both halves of the 3.5-in shell). Rinse the wet media with demineralized water and then set it aside to dry in a dust- and lint-free area. Do *not* use tap water; the minerals and chemicals in tap water will dry into deposits. Also do not wipe the media—any scratches will ruin it—but stubborn accu-mulations of foreign matter can be gently addressed by dabbing with a soft, lint-free swab. While the media is drying, carefully dry the disk shell. You may remove and discard the metal shroud. Once everything is completely dry, you can gently reassemble the disk (minus the metal shroud). Since this is only temporary, feel free to tape the halves of the disk together. Insert the disk and then copy as much data as possible to your hard drive or another disk.

Floppy Operation Is Unreliable

Q266. *I have a 486DX2/50 system with a 503MB HDD (C: drive), a CD-ROM (D: drive), a 5.25-in B: drive, and a 3.5-in A: drive. I am also operating a sound card, a 1MB VL bus video card, a scanner card, a 28.8KB modem, and an Ethernet card that was installed to operate a cable modem supplied by the local cable company as a test. The problem I have been experiencing has been intermittent for some time—even before the Ethernet card was added—and was not apparent immediately after I installed anything. The problem usually occurs when I attempt to reformat a 1.44MB floppy. What happens is that bad sectors start to develop, eventually leaving only about 1.1MB that is usable on the disk. Reuse of these disks has been unreliable; some of the files become unreadable. Sometimes the disk itself becomes unreadable and cannot even be reformatted. I replaced the floppy drive itself, the cable from the controller card, and the ISA controller card itself, but the problem remains.*

A. Try some good-quality disks. It's been my experience that "cheap" disks can present some real problems when it comes to formatting. If good disks don't fix the problem, try simplifying your system by removing the Ethernet card and other devices until your floppy drive operation returns to normal. Once you find the culprit, you can correct the hardware conflict.

Floppy Drive Refuses to Work

Q267. *My floppy drive won't work. The controller is new, and I am positive the 3.5-in 1.44 floppy is good. I checked all the usual things over and over, such as pin 1 on controller to pin 1 on floppy. I also know that the power supply is good. My boot disk works in another system, but not this one. I tried switching a few jumpers (I did not get any documentation with the controller). The controller has two 40-pin connectors marked Primary and Secondary and one 34-pin connector for floppy drives. Right now I don't have a hard drive to connect.*

A.   There are two things that you may not have checked. Start your
      CMOS Setup and check the BIOS settings for your floppy drive.
      If the A: drive is set as none or not installed, the drive will not be
      recognized no matter what you do. Also check the cable position—
      the end-most connector (after the cable twist) is for the A: drive,
      and the middle connector (before the cable twist) is for the B:
      drive. So make sure that the drive set in CMOS is attached to the
      right point on the floppy drive cable. If you are using a memory
      manager (such as QEMM), you may have to exclude some mem-
      ory addresses or just disable all memory management programs,
      since they can conflict with the floppy controller. Finally, try a
      different floppy drive controller.

CORRECTING FREQUENT FLOPPY DISK PROBLEMS

Q268. *I seem to have more than normal problems with floppy
        drives/disks. I usually throw out one out of every six or so flop-
        pies because I either can't format it (invalid track zero) or format
        with enough errors to not be worth it. This happens on many
        machines that I deal with. What is the most common reason for
        this? Is age of the disks a big issue? Is drive speed the most com-
        mon cause? If so, can it be adjusted? What adjustments can be
        made on a floppy drive if any?*

A.   There are a number of factors that can cause such problems.
        Consider your disks first. Some "bargain" disks are really low-
        quality products that provide chronic reliability problems. Try
        some better-quality disks. You should also make it a point to per-
        form a thorough cleaning of the drive's read/write heads. If the
        problem continues, chances are that you've got trouble with the
        drive hardware. Check the floppy drive cable for damage or
        loose connections (try a new floppy drive cable). Your final
        option is to replace the floppy drive outright.

A FLOPPY PHANTOM DIRECTORY

Q269. *When I change the floppy disk, the system still thinks that the
        old disk is inserted, whether I am using DOS 6.22 or WIN-
        DOWS 3.11. When installing software from a floppy, the instal-*

lation program will ask for disk 2, and even though I insert disk 2, the installation program keeps asking for it.

A.   You are dealing with a phantom directory problem. Ordinarily, the FAT is read into cache each time a disk is inserted. When the disk is removed, the disk change line is supposed to clear the cache. A problem with the disk change line will prevent the cache from clearing. Replace the floppy drive cable first. If the problem continues, replace the floppy drive. If you still have trouble, try replacing the floppy drive controller (this is rare).

RECOGNIZING THE FLOPPY PHANTOM DIRECTORY

Q270.   *A customer just brought in a Pentium 100 with an SCSI HDD and Colorado tape backup. Their 3.5-in floppy drive doesn't update the directory when floppy disks are swapped. The only way to read the new directory is to reboot the PC. The whole assembly is in a full tower case, and the floppy cable is stretched to the limit. Any ideas?*

A.   It sounds like you've been hit by the dreaded phantom directory problem. When a floppy disk is ejected, the drive sends a disk change signal back to the drive controller. The next time the drive is read, the disk directory is loaded into a small area of RAM. If the disk change signal is interrupted, the system will not recognize the change—even though the disk is different, the new directory will not be placed into RAM. As a result, the system still "thinks" the old disk is inserted. The most devastating consequence is that writing to an improperly recognized disk can result in unrecoverable corruption of files on the disk.

Since you noticed the strain on the floppy drive cable, that is certainly the most logical place to start. Try moving the floppy drive controller board to an expansion slot closer to the drive. If that is not possible (or the controller is integrated onto the motherboard), try a slightly longer cable. It should have a few inches of slack, but try to keep it reasonably short. If the problem persists, try a new floppy drive cable. If all else fails, replace the floppy drive outright.

INTERMEDIATE

PS/2 Drive Error Message

Q271. *We have an IBM PS/2 Model 90 486 system that will not start up. We get an eight-digit number on the screen (00001700). No other information is given. The machine was being used at home—one day it worked, the next it didn't. What are the possible problems?*

A.   According to my information, that error code relates to a drive system fault (probably a drive controller failure). Try replacing your drive controller. If the problem persists, the drive itself may be defective.

Floppy Problems on Patchwork System

Q272. *I'm trying to get a 486/33 running with parts scavenged from other computers. I've got it working but for one problem—I get error messages such as "packed file corrupt" or "data error reading drive B:" when trying to actuate certain programs on floppy disks. I can take the same disk and it'll work in another computer. I've tried three different 5.25-in drives, two 3.5-in drives, and two controller cards. I also swapped the 3.5- and 5.25-in drives as A: and B:. Both drives are set as DS1 (twisted cable on A:). I also tried different cables, all with the same results.*

A.   It seems pretty clear that your hardware and media should be in good order. Start by checking CMOS Setup. Make sure that your drives are identified correctly. While you're in CMOS, take a look at your cache settings. I've heard reports that changing a cache setting from write-back to write-through (or vice versa) can cause odd floppy problems. If you lose CMOS configuration settings when the power is turned off, consider a new CMOS back-up battery. Check your system configuration next and see if you have any DMA conflicts that might be interfering with the floppy drive (DMA 2). If all else fails, you will have little choice but to replace the motherboard.

System Can't Read from Floppy Drive

Q273. *Lately, I've been having trouble with my floppy drive. It is a 3.5-in drive, and when I try to read a disk, I get a message telling me that it can't read from the drive. I must eject and reinsert the disk several times before I can get it to work. Now, I've tried cleaning the drive, but that has not seemed to help. Do I need a new drive?*

A. Ordinarily, I would recommend cleaning the drive heads thoroughly. But since you've already done that, I suggest that you try reading from a number of different floppy disks. It could be that the particular disk you are trying to read is faulty. If other disks seem to work, chances are that your trouble is on the floppy disk itself. If the problem continues across a variety of different floppy disks, however, you've probably got a failing floppy drive. Before junking the drive, make sure that the floppy cable is installed correctly. Try replacing the cable. If a new cable has no effect, consider a new drive. This is the most economical approach when you have only a single system to worry about. If you work with a variety of floppy problems, you might consider attempting to realign the drive.

INTERMEDIATE

Floppy Drive Won't Detect Disk

Q274. *My system is a Pentium 90-MHz system. The floppy drive doesn't read the disk. When the PC powers up, the LED on the floppy drive lights up. But when I try to put a disk in and read it by typing "dir," the LED doesn't light up at all, and DOS reports: "General error reading drive A:." I have changed to a new floppy drive, and the same thing happens. Another thing I notice is that if I put in a nonsystem disk, when the PC powers up, it doesn't read the disk and goes directly to the C: drive to boot up. Shouldn't DOS report a Non-System Disk error. Another thing I did was run Norton Diagnostic. There is no error message when I run a system board test. When I diagnose drive A:, the program prompts me to insert a disk in drive A:. When I do that, the program can't detect a disk present.*

A. It sounds like several things may be wrong. First, go to your CMOS Setup and check the entry for your floppy drive. It should say 3/5-in 1.44MB (or whatever the case may be). Remember to save any changes before exiting the CMOS Setup. Next, check the installation of your floppy drive cable; one end of the cable may be installed backward. Finally, replace the floppy drive cable outright. Once you get the floppy drive running, you can boot from it by changing the Boot Order entry in CMOS Setup. Swap the Boot Order to A:/C:.

CAN'T BOOT FROM THE FLOPPY DRIVE

Q275. *Here's one I've never seen before: I can't boot from my floppy drive. I know that the boot disk is good. Any ideas?*

A. There are several possible reasons that you may not be able to boot from a floppy disk. First, check your Boot Order in the CMOS Setup. The order should be set to something like A:, C: (where A: is the floppy drive and C: is the bootable hard drive). If the Boot Order is set C:, A:, the system will ignore the A: drive if it finds the boot code on the C: drive. Also check the CMOS Setup and verify that the proper floppy drive type has been entered for A:. If the CMOS Setup is correct, you've got problems with the floppy drive hardware (you don't say whether the drive works after the system boots). Make sure that the 34-pin floppy signal cable is attached securely at both ends. Otherwise, you should try replacing the floppy drive.

SYSTEM WON'T BOOT FROM FLOPPY DRIVE

Q276. *My computer won't boot from the floppy. It can boot from the hard drive, but nothing else. I tried several boot disks, which all work on a different computer (at school). I tried replacing floppy drives, cables, even motherboards. I don't know what else to do. Can you help me?*

INTERMEDIATE

A.   Always start by checking your computer's CMOS Setup (Fig. 3.2). Your floppy drive should have an entry in the Setup screen. Make sure an entry is listed for the floppy drive and that the entry correctly identifies the drive. Next, check for the Boot Order entry. Normally, the Boot Order is A:, C, meaning the A: drive is checked for bootable media first, and if found, the system will boot from A:, otherwise, the C: drive is checked. If the Boot Order is C:, A:; the C: drive will be checked first, and if bootable, the system will boot from it regardless of whether there's a bootable disk in A:. Finally, I can only suggest that you try a new floppy drive controller.

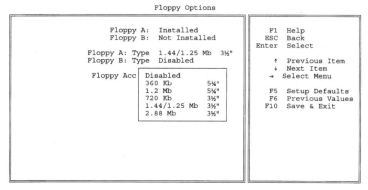

Floppy Options

```
Floppy A:    Installed              F1   Help
Floppy B:    Not Installed         ESC   Back
                                 Enter   Select
Floppy A: Type  1.44/1.25 Mb  3½"
Floppy B: Type  Disabled           ↑   Previous Item
                                   ↓   Next Item
Floppy Acc  Disabled               →   Select Menu
            360 Kb        5¼"
            1.2 Mb        5¼"       F5  Setup Defaults
            720 Kb        3½"       F6  Previous Values
            1.44/1.25 Mb  3½"      F10  Save & Exit
            2.88 Mb       3½"
```

Figure 3.2 Configuring floppy drives in the CMOS Setup

Floppy Error (40)

Q277.   *I have run into a problem getting my new 3.5-in floppy drive to run. I enabled the A: drive as a 3.5-in 1.44MB floppy in CMOS on my system. The floppy does have power (the activity LED lights up), but I get this message at POST: "Floppy disk(s) fail (40)." I suspected the cable so I bought a new one but no luck there. The CMOS Setup entries should be right. Can you tell me what error (40) means?*

A.   While we can't tell the precise meaning of error (40) on your particular system, chances are *very* good that your floppy controller port is faulty. However, before swapping out the controller, take

ADVANCED

a moment to check the floppy drive jumpers. If your drive cable has a twist, make sure the drive is jumpered as DS1 and that it is plugged into the end-most connector (after the twist). You might also check the drive itself by trying it on another PC. If the drive works on another PC, replace the floppy controller. If the drive fails on another PC, the drive's interface electronics may be bad (replace the floppy drive).

601 ERROR INDICATES FLOPPY PROBLEMS

Q278. *I am working on an "antique" Compaq Portable system that has a built-in monochrome monitor. It is an XT compatible. On boot up, it will not access the floppy drives, and it generates a 601 error. This system is not equipped with a hard drive. I don't have any documentation with the system, so can you give me a hint on where to start?*

A.   Table 3.1 lists all the diagnostic codes for the PC. The 6xx series errors usually indicate a fault with the floppy drive or controller (as you probably suspected already). Check the signal cables and power first, try an alternate drive, and then use a new floppy controller card if necessary. I doubt you'll be able to find any "true" replacement parts for a unit as old as yours.

TABLE 3.1 IBM STANDARD DIAGNOSTIC CODES

SYSTEM BOARD (01xx)	
101	Interrupt failure (unexpected interrupt)
102	BIOS ROM checksum error (PC, XT); timer error (AT, MCA)
103	BASIC ROM checksum error (PC, XT); timer interrupt error (AT, MCA)
104	Interrupt controller error (PC, XT); protected mode error (AT, MCA)
105	Timer failure (PC, XT); keyboard controller failure (MCA)

TABLE 3.1 IBM STANDARD DIAGNOSTIC CODES (CONTINUED)

SYSTEM BOARD (01xx)

106	System board converting logic test failure
107	System board adapter card or math coprocessor fault; Hot NMI test failed (MCA)
108	System board timer bus failure
109	DMA test memory select failure
110	PS/2 system board memory problem (ISA); system board parity check error (MCA)
111	PS/2 adapter memory problem (ISA); memory adapter parity check error (MCA)
112	PS/2 watchdog time-out error
113	PS/2 DMA arbitration time-out error
114	PS/2 external ROM checksum error
115	Cache parity error, BIOS ROM checksum error, or DMA error.
116	System board port R/W error
118	System board L2 cache error
119	2.88MB floppy drive installed but not supported by floppy disk controller.
120	CPU self-test error
121	Unexpected hardware interrupt occurred
131	Cassette wrap test (PC)
132	DMA extended registers error
133	DMA verify logic error
134	DMA arbitration logic error
151	Battery, real-time clock, or CMOS RAM failure
152	Real-time clock or CMOS RAM failure
160	PS/2 system board ID not recognized
161	CMOS chip lost power—battery dead
162	CMOS checksum or CRC error

TABLE 3.1 IBM STANDARD DIAGNOSTIC CODES (CONTINUED)

SYSTEM BOARD (01xx)

163	CMOS error—time and date not set (the clock not updating)
164	Memory size error—CMOS data does not match system memory found
165	PS/2 adapter ID mismatch
166	PS/2 adapter time-out—card busy
167	PS/2 system clock not updating
168	Math coprocessor error in the CMOS configuration
169	System board and processor card configuration mismatch
170	ASCII setup conflict error
171	Rolling bit test failure on CMOS shutdown byte
172	Rolling bit test failure on NVRAM diagnostic byte
173	Bad CMOS/NVRAM checksum
174	Bad system configuration
175	Bad EEPROM CRC
177	Bad password CRC
178	Bad EEPROM
179	NVRAM error log full
180x	Subaddress data error in slot x
181	Unsupported configuration
182	Password switch not in the writing position
183	System halted—password required
184	Bad power-on password
185	Bad start-up sequence
186	Password protection hardware error
187	Serial number error
188	Bad EEPROM checksum
189	Too many incorrect password attempts

TABLE 3.1 IBM STANDARD DIAGNOSTIC CODES (CONTINUED)

SYSTEM BOARD (01xx) (continued)

191	Cache controller test failure (82385)
194	System board memory error
199	User-indicated device list not correct

SYSTEM MEMORY (02xx)

201	Memory error (physical location will probably be displayed)
202	Memory address line 0–15 error
203	Memory address line 16–23 error; line 16–31 error (MCA)
204	Memory remapped to compensate for error (PS/2)
205	Error in first 128K (PS/2 ISA) of RAM
207	BIOS ROM failure
210	System board memory parity error
211	Error in first 64K of RAM (MCA)
212	Watchdog timer error
213	DMA bus arbitration time-out
215	Memory address error; 64K on daughter/SIP 2 failed (70)
216	Memory address error; 64K on daughter/SIP 1 failed (70)
221	ROM to RAM copy (shadowing) failed (MCA)
225	Wrong speed memory on system board (MCA)
230	Memory on motherboard and adapter board overlaps
231	Noncontiguous adapter memory installed
235	Stuck data line on memory module
241	Memory module 2 failed
251	Memory module 3 failed

ADVANCED

TABLE 3.1 IBM STANDARD DIAGNOSTIC CODES (CONTINUED)

KEYBOARD (03xx)

301	Keyboard did not respond correctly (stuck key detected)
302	Keyboard locked (AT, models 25 and 30)
303	Keyboard/system board interface error—keyboard controller fault
304	Keyboard or system unit error (keyboard clock stuck high)
305	Keyboard fuse failed on system board (PS/2 50, 60, 80) or +5 V error (PS/2 70)
306	Unsupported keyboard attached
341	Keyboard error
342	Keyboard cable error
343	Enhancement card or cable error
365	Keyboard failure
366	Interface cable failure
367	Enhancement card or cable failure

MONOCHROME DISPLAY ADAPTER (04xx)

401	Memory, horizontal sync frequency, or vertical sync test failure
408	User-indicated display attribute failure
416	User-indicated character set failure
424	User-indicated 80x25 mode failure
432	MDA card parallel port test failure

COLOR GRAPHICS ADAPTER (05xx)

501	Memory, horizontal sync frequency, or vertical sync test failure

TABLE 3.1 IBM STANDARD DIAGNOSTIC CODES (CONTINUED)

COLOR GRAPHICS ADAPTER (05xx) (continued)

503	CGA adapter controller failure
508	User-indicated display attribute failure
516	User-indicated character set failure
524	User-indicated 80x25 mode failure
532	User-indicated 40x25 mode failure
540	User-indicated 320x200 graphics mode failure
548	User-indicated 640x200 graphics mode failure
556	Light pen test failed
564	User-indicated screen paging test failed

FLOPPY DRIVES AND ADAPTERS (06xx)

601	General disk or adapter test failure
602	Disk boot sector not valid
603	Disk size error
604	Media sense error
605	Disk drive locked
606	Disk verify test failure
607	Write protect error
608	Drive command error
610	Disk initialization failure
611	Drive time-out error
612	NEC drive controller IC error
613	Floppy system DMA error
614	Floppy system DMA boundary overrun error
615	Drive index timing error
616	Drive speed error
621	Drive seek error
622	Drive CRC error

ADVANCED

TABLE 3.1 IBM STANDARD DIAGNOSTIC CODES (CONTINUED)

FLOPPY DRIVES AND ADAPTERS (06xx) (continued)

623	Sector not found error
624	Disk address mark error
625	NEC drive controller IC seek error
626	Disk data compare error
627	Disk change line error
628	Disk removed from drive
630	Drive A: index stuck high
631	Drive A: index stuck low
632	Drive A: track 0 stuck off
633	Drive A: track 0 stuck on
640	Drive B: index stuck high
641	Drive B: index stuck low
642	Drive B: track 0 stuck off
643	Drive B: track 0 stuck on
645	No index pulse
646	Drive track 00 detection failed
647	No transitions on Read Data line
648	Format test failed
649	Incorrect media type in drive
650	Drive speed incorrect
651	Format failure
652	Verify failure
653	Read failure
654	Write failure
655	Drive controller error
656	Drive mechanism failure
657	Write protect stuck in protected state
658	Change line stuck in changed state
659	Write protect stuck in unprotected state
660	Change line stuck in unchanged state

Table 3.1 IBM STANDARD DIAGNOSTIC CODES (CONTINUED)

MATH COPROCESSOR (07xx)

701	MCP presence or initialization error
702	Exception errors test failure
703	Rounding test failure
704	Arithmetic test 1 failure
705	Arithmetic test 2 failure
706	Arithmetic test 3 (80387 only)
707	Combination test failure
708	Integer load/store test failure
709	Equivalent expressions errors
710	Exception (interrupt) errors
711	Save state errors
712	Protected mode test failure
713	Voltage/temperature sensitivity test failure

PARALLEL PRINTER ADAPTER (09xx)

901	Data register latch error
902	Control register latch error
903	Register address decode error
904	Address decode error
910	Status line wrap connector error
911	Status line bit 8 wrap error
912	Status line bit 7 wrap error
913	Status line bit 6 wrap error
914	Status line bit 5 wrap error
915	Status line bit 4 wrap error
916	Printer adapter interrupt wrap error
917	Unexpected printer adapter interrupt
92x	Feature register error

ADVANCED

TABLE 3.1 IBM STANDARD DIAGNOSTIC CODES (CONTINUED)

ALTERNATE PRINTER ADAPTER (10xx)

1001	Data register latch error
1002	Control register latch error
1003	Register address decode error
1004	Address decode error
1010	Status line wrap connector error
1011	Status line bit 8 wrap error
1012	Status line bit 7 wrap error
1013	Status line bit 6 wrap error
1014	Status line bit 5 wrap error
1015	Status line bit 4 wrap error
1016	Printer adapter interrupt wrap error
1017	Unexpected printer adapter interrupt
102x	Feature register error

COMMUNICATION DEVICES (11xx)

1101	16450/16550 UART error
1102	Card-selected feedback error
1103	Port 102h register test failure
1106	Serial option cannot be shut down
1107	Communications cable or system board error
1108	IRQ 3 error
1109	IRQ 4 error
1110	16450/16550 chip register failure
1111	UART control line internal wrap test failure
1112	UART control line external wrap test failure
1113	UART transmit error
1114	UART receive error
1115	UART transmit and receive data unequal—receive error

ADVANCED

TABLE 3.1 IBM STANDARD DIAGNOSTIC CODES (CONTINUED)

COMMUNICATION DEVICES (11xx) (continued)	
1116	UART interrupt function error
1117	UART baud rate test failure
1118	UART interrupt-driven receive external data wrap test error
1119	UART FIFO buffer failure
1120	UART interrupt enable register failure; all bits cannot be set
1121	UART interrupt enable register failure; all bits cannot be reset
1122	Interrupt pending—stuck on
1123	Interrupt ID register stuck on
1124	Modem control register failure; all bits cannot be set
1125	Modem control register failure; all bits cannot be reset
1126	Modem status register failure; all bits cannot be set
1127	Modem status register failure; all bits cannot be reset
1128	Interrupt ID error
1129	Cannot force overrun error
1130	No modem status interrupt
1131	Invalid interrupt pending
1132	No data ready
1133	No data available at interrupt
1134	No transmit holding at interrupt
1135	No interrupts
1136	No received line status interrupt
1137	No receive data available
1138	Transmit holding register not empty
1139	No modem status interrupt
1140	Transmit holding register not empty

TABLE 3.1 IBM STANDARD DIAGNOSTIC CODES (CONTINUED)

COMMUNICATION DEVICES (11xx) (continued)

1141	No interrupts
1142	No IRQ4 interrupt
1143	No IRQ3 interrupt
1144	No data transferred
1145	Maximum baud rate error
1146	Minimum baud rate error
1148	Time-out error
1149	Invalid data returned
1150	Modem status register error
1151	No DSR and delta DSR
1152	No DSR
1153	No delta DSR
1154	Modem status register not clear
1155	No CTS and delta CTS
1156	No CTS
1157	No delta CTS

ALTERNATE COMMUNICATIONS DEVICES (12xx)

1201	16450/16550 UART error
1202	Card-selected feedback error
1203	Port 102h register test failure
1206	Serial option cannot be shut down
1207	Communications cable or system board error
1208	IRQ 3 error
1209	IRQ 4 error
1210	16450/16550 chip register failure
1211	UART control line internal wrap test failure
1212	UART control line external wrap test failure

TABLE 3.1 IBM STANDARD DIAGNOSTIC CODES (CONTINUED)

ALTERNATE COMMUNICATIONS DEVICES (12xx) (continued)

1213	UART transmit error
1214	UART receive error
1215	UART transmit and receive data unequal—receive error
1216	UART interrupt function error
1217	UART baud rate test failure
1218	UART interrupt-driven receive external data wrap test error
1219	UART FIFO buffer failure
1220	UART interrupt enable register failure; all bits cannot be set
1221	UART interrupt enable register failure; all bits cannot be reset
1222	Interrupt pending—stuck on
1223	Interrupt ID register stuck on
1224	Modem control register failure; all bits cannot be set
1225	Modem control register failure; all bits cannot be reset
1226	Modem status register failure; all bits cannot be set
1227	Modem status register failure; all bits cannot be reset
1228	Interrupt ID error
1229	Cannot force overrun error
1230	No modem status interrupt
1231	Invalid interrupt pending
1232	No data ready
1233	No data available at interrupt
1234	No transmit holding at interrupt
1235	No interrupts
1236	No received line status interrupt
1237	No receive data available

ADVANCED

TABLE 3.1 IBM STANDARD DIAGNOSTIC CODES (CONTINUED)

ALTERNATE COMMUNICATIONS DEVICES (12xx) (continued)

1238	Transmit holding register not empty
1239	No modem status interrupt
1240	Transmit holding register not empty
1241	No interrupts
1242	No IRQ4 interrupt
1243	No IRQ3 interrupt
1244	No data transferred
1245	Maximum baud rate error
1246	Minimum baud rate error
1248	Time-out error
1249	Invalid data returned
1250	Modem status register error
1251	No DSR and delta DSR
1252	No DSR
1253	No delta DSR
1254	Modem status register not clear
1255	No CTS and delta CTS
1256	No CTS
1257	No delta CTS

GAME PORT ADAPTERS (13xx)

1301	Game port adapter test failure
1302	Joystick test failure

MATRIX PRINTERS (14xx)

1401	Printer test failure
1402	Printer not ready, not on-line, or out of paper
1403	Printer No Paper error
1404	Matrix printer test failure; system board time-out

ADVANCED

TABLE 3.1 IBM STANDARD DIAGNOSTIC CODES (CONTINUED)

MATRIX PRINTERS (14xx) (continued)

1405	Parallel adapter failure
1406	Printer presence test failed

SDLC COMMUNICATIONS ADAPTER (15xx)

1501	SDLC adapter test failure
1510	8255 port B failure
1511	8255 port A failure
1512	8255 port C failure
1513	8253 timer 1 did not reach terminal count
1514	8253 timer 1 output stuck on
1515	8253 timer 0 did not reach terminal count
1516	8253 timer 0 output stuck on
1517	8253 timer 2 did not reach terminal count
1518	8253 timer 2 output stuck on
1519	8273 port B error
1520	8273 port A error
1521	8273 command/read time-out error
1522	Interrupt level 4 error
1523	Ring indicator stuck on
1524	Receive clock stuck on
1525	Transmit clock stuck on
1526	Test Indicate stuck on
1527	Ring Indicate not on
1528	Receive clock not on
1529	Transmit clock not on
1530	Test Indicate not on
1531	Data Set Ready not on
1532	Carrier Detect not on
1533	Clear-To-Send not on
1534	Data Set Ready stuck on

ADVANCED

TABLE 3.1 IBM STANDARD DIAGNOSTIC CODES (CONTINUED)

SDLC COMMUNICATIONS ADAPTER (15xx) (continued)

1535	Carrier Detect stuck on
1536	Clear-To-Send stuck on
1537	Interrupt level 3 failure
1538	Receive interrupt results error
1539	Wrap data compare error
1540	DMA channel 1 transmit error
1541	DMA channel 1 receive error
1542	8273 error-checking or status-reporting error
1547	Stray interrupt level 4 error
1548	Stray interrupt level 3 error
1549	Interrupt presentation sequence time-out

DSEA UNITS (16xx)

1604	DSEA or Twinaxial network adapter
1608	DSEA or Twinaxial network adapter
1624 – 1658	DSEA system error
1662	DSEA interrupt level error
1664	DSEA system error
1668	DSEA interrupt level error
1669	DSEA diagnostics error
1674	DSEA diagnostics error
1684	DSEA device address error
1688	DSEA device address error

HARD DRIVES AND ADAPTERS (17xx)

1701	Fixed disk or adapter general error
1702	Drive and controller time-out error
1703	Drive seek error

ADVANCED

TABLE 3.1 IBM STANDARD DIAGNOSTIC CODES (CONTINUNED)

HARD DRIVES AND ADAPTERS (17xx) (continued)

1704	Drive controller failed
1705	Drive sector not found error
1706	Write fault error
1707	Drive track 00 error
1708	Head select error
1709	Bad ECC returned
1710	Sector buffer overrun
1711	Bad address mark
1712	Internal controller diagnostics failure
1713	Data compare error
1714	Drive not ready
1715	Track 00 indicator failure
1716	Diagnostics cylinder errors
1717	Surface read errors
1718	Hard drive type error
1720	Bad diagnostics cylinder
1726	Data compare error
1730	Drive controller error
1731	Drive controller error
1732	Drive controller error
1733	BIOS undefined error return
1735	Bad command error
1736	Data corrected error
1737	Bad drive track error
1738	Bad sector error
1739	Bad initialization error
1740	Bad sense error
1750	Drive verify error
1751	Drive read error

ADVANCED

TABLE 3.1 IBM STANDARD DIAGNOSTIC CODES (CONTINUED)

HARD DRIVES AND ADAPTERS (17xx) (continued)

1752	Drive write error
1753	Drive random read test failure
1754	Drive seek test failure
1755	Drive controller failure
1756	Controller ECC test failure
1757	Controller head select failure
1780	Drive seek failure (drive 0)
1781	Drive seek failure (drive 1)
1782	Hard disk controller failure
1790	Diagnostic cylinder read error (drive 0)
1791	Diagnostic cylinder read error (drive 1)

I/O EXPANSION UNIT (18xx)

1801	Expansion Unit POST error
1810	Enable/disable failure
1811	Extender card wrap test failure while disabled
1812	High-order address lines failure while disabled
1813	Wait state failure while disabled
1814	Enable/disable could not be set on
1815	Wait state failure while enabled
1816	Extender card wrap test failure while enabled
1817	High-order address lines failure while enabled
1818	Disable not functioning
1819	Wait request switch not set correctly
1820	Receiver card wrap test failed
1821	Receiver high-order address lines failure

TABLE 3.1 IBM STANDARD DIAGNOSTIC CODES (CONTINUED)

BISYNCHRONOUS COMMUNICATIONS ADAPTERS (20xx)

2001	BSC adapter test failure
2010	8255 port A failure
2011	8255 port B failure
2012	8255 port C failure
2013	8253 timer 1 did not reach terminal count
2014	8253 timer 1 output stuck on
2015	8253 timer 2 did not reach terminal count
2016	8253 timer 2 output stuck on
2017	8251 Data-Set-Ready failed to come on
2018	8251 Clear-To-Send not sensed
2019	8251 Data-Set-Ready stuck on
2020	8251 Clear-To-Send stuck on
2021	8251 hardware reset failure
2022	8251 software reset command failure
2023	8251 software error-reset command failure
2024	8251 Transmit-Ready did not come on
2025	8251 Receive-Ready did not come on
2026	8251 could not force overrun error status
2027	Interrupt failure—no timer interrupt
2028	Interrupt failure—replace card or planar board
2029	Interrupt failure—replace card only
2030	Interrupt failure—replace card or planar board
2031	Interrupt failure—replace card only
2033	Ring Indicate signal stuck on
2034	Receive clock stuck on
2035	Transmit clock stuck on
2036	Test Indicate stuck on
2037	Ring Indicate not on

ADVANCED

TABLE 3.1 IBM STANDARD DIAGNOSTIC CODES (CONTINUED)

BI-SYNCHRONOUS COMMUNICATIONS ADAPTERS (20xx) (continued)

2038	Receive clock not on
2039	Transmit clock not on
2040	Test Indicate not on
2041	Data-Set-Ready stuck on
2042	Carrier Detect not on
2043	Clear-To-Send not on
2044	Data-Set-Ready stuck on
2045	Carrier Detect stuck on
2046	Clear-To-Send stuck on
2047	Unexpected transmit interrupt
2048	Unexpected receive interrupt
2049	Transmit data did not equal receive data
2050	8251 detected overrun error
2051	Lost Data-Set-Ready signal during data wrap
2052	Receive time-out during data wrap

ALTERNATE BISYNCHRONOUS COMMUNICATIONS ADAPTERS (21xx)

2101	BSC adapter test failure
2110	8255 port A failure
2111	8255 port B failure
2112	8255 port C failure
2113	8253 timer 1 did not reach terminal count
2114	8253 timer 1 output stuck on
2115	8253 timer 2 did not reach terminal count
2116	8253 timer 2 output stuck on
2117	8251 Data-Set-Ready failed to come on
2118	8251 Clear-To-Send not sensed
2119	8251 Data-Set-Ready stuck on
2120	8251 Clear-To-Send stuck on

TABLE 3.1 IBM STANDARD DIAGNOSTIC CODES (CONTINUED)

ALTERNATE BI-SYNCHRONOUS COMMUNICATIONS ADAPTERS (21xx) (continued)

2121	8251 hardware reset failure
2122	8251 software reset command failure
2123	8251 software error-reset command failure
2124	8251 Transmit-Ready did not come on
2125	8251 Receive-Ready did not come on
2126	8251 could not force overrun error status
2127	Interrupt failure—no timer interrupt
2128	Interrupt failure—replace card or planar board
2129	Interrupt failure—replace card only
2130	Interrupt failure—replace card or planar board
2131	Interrupt failure—replace card only
2133	Ring Indicate signal stuck on
2134	Receive clock stuck on
2135	Transmit clock stuck on
2136	Test Indicate stuck on
2137	Ring Indicate not on
2138	Receive clock not on
2139	Transmit clock not on
2140	Test Indicate not on
2141	Data-Set-Ready stuck on
2142	Carrier Detect not on
2143	Clear-To-Send not on
2144	Data-Set-Ready stuck on
2145	Carrier Detect stuck on
2146	Clear-To-Send stuck on
2147	Unexpected transmit interrupt
2148	Unexpected receive interrupt
2149	Transmit data did not equal receive data

ADVANCED

TABLE 3.1 IBM STANDARD DIAGNOSTIC CODES (CONTINUNED)

ALTERNATE BI-SYNCHRONOUS COMMUNICATIONS ADAPTERS (21xx) (continued)

2150	8251 detected overrun error
2151	Lost Data-Set-Ready signal during data wrap
2152	Receive time-out during data wrap

CLUSTER ADAPTERS (22xx)

22xx	A cluster adapter error has been encountered—replace the cluster adapter

PLASMA MONITOR ADAPTER (23xx)

23xx	A plasma display fault has been detected—replace the plasma monitor assembly

ENHANCED GRAPHICS ADAPTER (24xx)

2401	Video adapter test failure
2402	Video display (monitor) error
2408	User-indicated display attribute test failed
2409	Video display (monitor) error
2410	Video adapter error
2416	User-indicated character set test failed
2424	User-indicated 80x25 mode failure
2432	User-indicated 40x25 mode failure
2440	User-indicated 320x200 graphics mode failure
2448	User-indicated 640x200 graphics mode failure
2456	User-indicated light pen test failure
2464	User-indicated screen paging test failure

TABLE 3.1 IBM STANDARD DIAGNOSTIC CODES (CONTINUED)

ALTERNATE ENHANCED GRAPHICS ADAPTER (24xx)

2501	Video adapter test failure
2502	Video display (monitor) error
2508	User-indicated display attribute test failed
2509	Video display (monitor) error
2510	Video adapter error
2516	User-indicated character set test failed
2524	User-indicated 80x25 mode failure
2532	User-indicated 40x25 mode failure
2540	User-indicated 320x200 graphics mode failure
2548	User-indicated 640x200 graphics mode failure
2556	User-indicated light pen test failure
2564	User-indicated screen paging test failure

PC/370-M ADAPTER (26xx)

2601 – 2672	370-M (memory) adapter error
2673 – 2680	370-P (processor) adapter error
2681	370-M (memory) adapter error
2682 – 2697	370-P (processor) adapter error
2698	XT or AT/370 diagnostic diskette error

PC3277 EMULATION ADAPTER (27xx)

2701	3277-EM adapter error
2702	3277-EM adapter error
2703	3277-EM adapter error

3278/3279 EMULATION ADAPTER (28xx)

28xx	An emulation adapter fault has been detected—replace the adapter

ADVANCED

TABLE 3.1 IBM STANDARD DIAGNOSTIC CODES (CONTINUED)

COLOR/GRAPHICS PRINTERS (29xx)

29xx   A general fault has been detected with the printer or its printer port—replace the printer or adapter port

PRIMARY PC NETWORK ADAPTER (30xx)

3001	Network adapter test failure
3002	ROM checksum test failure
3003	Unit ID PROM test failure
3004	RAM test failure
3005	Host Interface Controller (HIC) test failure
3006	+/-12-Vdc test failure
3007	Digital loop-back test failure
3008	Host-detected HIC failure
3009	Sync signal failure and no-go bit
3010	HIC test OK and no-go bit
3011	Go bit OK but no command 41
3012	Card not present
3013	Digital failure—fall-through
3015	Analog failure
3041	Hot carrier—on other card
3042	Hot carrier—on this card

SECONDARY PC NETWORK ADAPTER (31xx)

3101	Network adapter test failure
3102	ROM checksum test failure
3103	Unit ID PROM test failure
3104	RAM test failure
3105	Host Interface Controller (HIC) test failure
3106	+/-12-Vdc test failure

TABLE 3.1 IBM STANDARD DIAGNOSTIC CODES (CONTINUED)

SECONDARY PC NETWORK ADAPTER (31xx) (continued)

3107	Digital loop-back test failure
3108	Host-detected HIC failure
3109	Sync signal failure and no-go bit
3110	HIC test OK and no-go bit
3111	Go bit OK but no command 41
3112	Card not present
3113	Digital failure—fall-through
3115	Analog failure
3141	Hot carrier—on other card
3142	Hot carrier—on this card

3270 PC/AT DISPLAY (32xx)

32xx	A fault has been detected in the display system—replace the display system

COMPACT PRINTER ERRORS (33xx)

33xx	A fault has been detected in the printer or printer adapter—replace the printer or adapter

ENHANCED DSEA UNITS (35xx)

3504	Adapter connected to twinaxial cable during off-line test
3508	Workstation address error
3509	Diagnostic program failure; retry on new disk
3540	Workstation address invalid
3588	Adapter address switch error
3599	Diagnostic program failure; retry on new disk

ADVANCED

TABLE 3.1 IBM STANDARD DIAGNOSTIC CODES (CONTINUED)

IEEE 488 (GPIB) ADAPTER (36xx)

3601	Adapter test failure
3602	Write error at Serial Poll Mode Register (SPMR)
3603	Adapter addressing problems
3610	Adapter cannot be programmed to listen
3611	Adapter cannot be programmed to talk
3612	Adapter control error
3613	Adapter cannot switch to standby mode
3614	Adapter cannot take control asynchronously
3615	Adapter cannot take control asynchronously
3616	Adapter cannot pass control
3617	Adapter cannot be addressed to listen
3618	Adapter cannot be unaddressed to listen
3619	Adapter cannot be addressed to talk
3620	Adapter cannot be unaddressed to talk
3621	Adapter cannot be addressed to listen with extended addressing
3622	Adapter cannot be unaddressed to listen with extended addressing
3623	Adapter cannot be addressed to talk with extended addressing
3624	Adapter cannot be unaddressed to talk with extended addressing
3625	Adapter cannot write to self
3626	Adapter error—cannot generate handshake signal
3627	Adapter error—cannot detect Device Clear (DCL) message
3628	Adapter error—cannot detect Selected Device Clear (SDC) message
3629	Adapter error—cannot detect end of transfer with EOI signal

TABLE 3.1 IBM STANDARD DIAGNOSTIC CODES (CONTINUED)

IEEE 488 (GPIB) ADAPTER (36xx) (continued)	
3630	Adapter error—cannot detect end of transmission with EOI signal
3631	Adapter cannot detect END with 0-bit EOS
3632	Adapter cannot detect END with 7-bit EOS
3633	Adapter cannot detect Group Execute Trigger (GET)
3634	Mode 3 addressing not functioning
3635	Adapter cannot recognize undefined command
3636	Adapter error—cannot detect REM, REMC, LOK, or LOKC signals
3637	Adapter error—cannot clear REM or LOK signals
3638	Adapter cannot detect Service Request (SRQ)
3639	Adapter cannot conduct serial poll
3640	Adapter cannot conduct parallel poll
3650	Adapter error—cannot DMA to 7210
3651	Data error on DMA to 7210
3652	Adapter error—cannot DMA from 7210
3653	Data error on DMA from 7210
3658	Uninvoked interrupt received
3659	Adapter cannot interrupt on ADSC signal
3660	Adapter cannot interrupt on ADSC signal
3661	Adapter cannot interrupt on CO
3662	Adapter cannot interrupt on DO
3663	Adapter cannot interrupt on DI
3664	Adapter cannot interrupt on ERR
3665	Adapter cannot interrupt on DEC
3666	Adapter cannot interrupt on END
3667	Adapter cannot interrupt on DET
3668	Adapter cannot interrupt on APT

ADVANCED

TABLE 3.1 IBM STANDARD DIAGNOSTIC CODES (CONTINUED)

IEEE 488 (GPIB) ADAPTER (36xx) (continued)

3669   Adapter cannot interrupt on CPT

3670   Adapter cannot interrupt on REMC

3671   Adapter cannot interrupt on LOKC

3672   Adapter cannot interrupt on SRQI

3673   Adapter cannot interrupt on terminal count on DMA to 7210

3674   Adapter cannot interrupt on terminal count on DMA from 7210

3675   Spurious DMA terminal count interrupt

3697   Illegal DMA configuration setting detected

3698   Illegal interrupt level configuration setting detected

SYSTEM BOARD SCSI CONTROLLER (37xx)

37xx   The system board SCSI controller has failed— replace the motherboard

DATA ACQUISITION ADAPTER (38xx)

3801   Adapter test failure

3810   Timer read test failure

3811   Timer interrupt test failure

3812   Binary input 13 test failure

3813   Binary input 13 test failure

3814   Binary output 14—interrupt request test failure

3815   Binary output 0, count-in test failure

3816   Binary input strobe (STB), count-out test failure

3817   Binary output 0, Clear-To-Send (CTS) test failure

3818   Binary output 1, binary input 0 test failure

3819   Binary output 2, binary input 1 test failure

TABLE 3.1 IBM STANDARD DIAGNOSTIC CODES (CONTINUNED)

DATA ACQUISITION ADAPTER (38xx) (continued)

3820	Binary output 3, binary input 2 test failure
3821	Binary output 4, binary input 3 test failure
3822	Binary output 5, binary input 4 test failure
3823	Binary output 6, binary input 5 test failure
3824	Binary output 7, binary input 6 test failure
3825	Binary output 8, binary input 7 test failure
3826	Binary output 9, binary input 8 test failure
3827	Binary output 10, binary input 9 test failure
3828	Binary output 11, binary input 10 test failure
3829	Binary output 12, binary input 11 test failure
3830	Binary output 13, binary input 12 test failure
3831	Binary output 15, analog input CE test failure
3832	Binary output Strobe (STB), binary output GATE test failure
3833	Binary input Clear-To-Send (CTS), binary input HOLD test failure
3834	Analog input Command Output (CO), binary input 15 test failure
3835	Counter interrupt test failure
3836	Counter read test failure
3837	Analog output 0 ranges test failure
3838	Analog output 1 ranges test failure
3839	Analog input 0 values test failure
3840	Analog input 1 values test failure
3841	Analog input 2 values test failure
3842	Analog input 3 values test failure
3843	Analog input interrupt test failure
3844	Analog input 23 address or value test failure

TABLE 3.1 IBM STANDARD DIAGNOSTIC CODES (CONTINUED)

PROFESSIONAL GRAPHICS ADAPTER (PGA) (39xx)

3901	PGA test failure
3902	ROM1 self-test failure
3903	ROM2 self-test failure
3904	RAM self-test failure
3905	Cold start cycle power error
3906	Data error in communications RAM
3907	Address error in communications RAM
3908	Bad data detected while reading/writing to 6845 register
3909	Bad data detected in lower E0h bytes while reading/writing to 6845 registers
3910	Display bank output latch error
3911	Basic clock error
3912	Command control error
3913	Vertical sync scanner error
3914	Horizontal sync scanner error
3915	Intech error
3916	Lookup Table (LUT) address error
3917	LUT "red" RAM chip error
3918	LUT "green" RAM chip error
3919	LUT "blue" RAM chip error
3920	LUT data latch error
3921	Horizontal display error
3922	Vertical display error
3923	Light pen error
3924	Unexpected error
3925	Emulator addressing error
3926	Emulator data latch error

TABLE 3.1 IBM STANDARD DIAGNOSTIC CODES (CONTINUED)

PROFESSIONAL GRAPHICS ADAPTER (PGA) (39xx) (continued)

3927 – 3930   Emulator RAM error

3931   Emulator Horizontal/Vertical display problem

3932   Emulator cursor position error

3933   Emulator attribute display problem

3934   Emulator cursor display error

3935   Fundamental emulation RAM problem

3936   Emulation character set problem

3937   Emulation graphics display error

3938   Emulation character display problem

3939   Emulation bank select error

3940   Display RAM U2 error

3941   Display RAM U4 error

3942   Display RAM U6 error

3943   Display RAM U8 error

3944   Display RAM U10 error

3945   Display RAM U1 error

3946   Display RAM U3 error

3947   Display RAM U5 error

3948   Display RAM U7 error

3949   Display RAM U9 error

3950   Display RAM U12 error

3951   Display RAM U14 error

3952   Display RAM U16 error

3953   Display RAM U18 error

3954   Display RAM U20 error

3955   Display RAM U11 error

3956   Display RAM U13 error

3957   Display RAM U15 error

ADVANCED

TABLE 3.1 IBM STANDARD DIAGNOSTIC CODES (CONTINUED)

PROFESSIONAL GRAPHICS ADAPTER (PGA) (39xx) (continued)	
3958	Display RAM U17 error
3959	Display RAM U19 error
3960	Display RAM U22 error
3961	Display RAM U24 error
3962	Display RAM U26 error
3963	Display RAM U28 error
3964	Display RAM U30 error
3965	Display RAM U21 error
3966	Display RAM U23 error
3967	Display RAM U25 error
3968	Display RAM U27 error
3969	Display RAM U29 error
3970	Display RAM U32 error
3971	Display RAM U34 error
3972	Display RAM U36 error
3973	Display RAM U38 error
3974	Display RAM U40 error
3975	Display RAM U31 error
3976	Display RAM U33 error
3977	Display RAM U35 error
3978	Display RAM U37 error
3979	Display RAM U39 error
3980	Graphics controller RAM timing error
3981	Graphics controller read/write latch error
3982	Shift register bus output latch error
3983	Addressing error (vertical column of memory; U2 at top)
3984	Addressing error (vertical column of memory; U4 at top)

TABLE 3.1 IBM STANDARD DIAGNOSTIC CODES (CONTINUED)

PROFESSIONAL GRAPHICS ADAPTER (PGA) (39xx) (continued)

3985   Addressing error (vertical column of memory; U6 at top)

3986   Addressing error (vertical column of memory; U8 at top)

3987   Addressing error (vertical column of memory; U10 at top)

3988 – 3991   Horizontal bank latch errors

3992   RAG/CAG graphics controller error

3993   Multiple write modes, nibble mask errors

3994   Row nibble (display RAM) error

3995   Graphics controller addressing error

5278 Display Attachment Unit and 5279 Display (44xx)

44xx   A fault has been detected with the display system— replace the display system

IEEE 488 (GPIB) Interface Adapter (45xx)

45xx   A fault has been detected with the GPIB—replace the adapter

ARTIC Multiport/2 Interface Adapter (46xx)

4611   ARTIC adapter error

4612 or 4613   Memory module error

4630   ARTIC adapter error

4640 or 4641   Memory module error

4650   ARTIC interface cable error

Internal Modem (48xx)

48xx   The internal modem has failed—replace the internal modem

ADVANCED

TABLE 3.1 IBM STANDARD DIAGNOSTIC CODES (CONTINUED)

Alternate Internal Modem (49xx)

49xx   The alternate internal modem has failed—replace the alternate internal modem

PC CONVERTIBLE LCD (50xx)

5001	LCD buffer failure
5002	LCD font buffer failure
5003	LCD controller failure
5004	User-indicated PEL/drive test failed
5008	User-indicated display attribute test failed
5016	User-indicated character set test failed
5020	User-indicated alternate character set test failure
5024	User-indicated 80x25 mode test failure
5032	User-indicated 40x25 mode test failure
5040	User-indicated 320x200 graphics test failure
5048	User-indicated 640x200 graphics test failure
5064	User-indicated paging test failure

PC CONVERTIBLE PORTABLE PRINTER (51xx)

5101	Portable printer interface failure
5102	Portable printer busy error
5103	Portable printer paper or ribbon error
5104	Portable printer time-out
5105	User-indicated print pattern test error

FINANCIAL COMMUNICATION SYSTEM (56xx)

56xx   A fault has been detected in the financial communication system—replace the financial communication system

ADVANCED

TABLE 3.1 IBM STANDARD DIAGNOSTIC CODES (CONTINUED)

PHOENIX BIOS/CHIPSET SPECIFIC ERROR CODES (70xx)

7000	Chipset CMOS failure
7001	Shadow RAM failure (ROM not shadowed to RAM)
7002	Chipset CMOS configuration data error

VOICE COMMUNICATIONS ADAPTER (VCA) (71xx)

7101	Adapter test failure
7102	Instruction or external data memory error
7103	PC to VCA interrupt error
7104	Internal data memory error
7105	DMA error
7106	Internal registers error
7107	Interactive shared memory error
7108	VCA to PC interrupt error
7109	DC wrap error
7111	External analog wrap & tone output error
7114	Telephone attachment test failure

3.5 INCH FLOPPY DISK DRIVE (73xx)

7301	Disk drive/adapter test failure
7306	Disk change line error
7307	Write-protected disk
7308	Drive command error
7310	Disk initialization failure—track 00 error
7311	Drive time-out error
7312	NEC drive controller IC error
7313	DMA error
7314	DMA boundary overrun error

ADVANCED

TABLE 3.1 IBM STANDARD DIAGNOSTIC CODES (CONTINUED)

3.5 INCH FLOPPY DISK DRIVE (73xx) (continued)

7315	Drive index timing error
7316	Drive speed error
7321	Drive seek error
7322	Drive CRC check error
7323	Sector not found error
7324	Address mark error
7325	NEC controller IC seek error

8514/A DISPLAY ADAPTER (74xx)

7426	8514 display error
7440 – 7475	8514/A memory module error

4216 PAGE PRINTER ADAPTER (76xx)

7601	Adapter test failure
7602	Adapter card error
7603	Printer error
7604	Printer cable error

PS/2 SPEECH ADAPTER (84xx)

84xx	A fault has been detected in the speech adapter—replace the speech adapter

2MB XMA MEMORY ADAPTER (85xx)

85xx	A fault has been detected in the memory adapter—replace the memory adapter

TABLE 3.1 IBM STANDARD DIAGNOSTIC CODES (CONTINUED)

PS/2 POINTING DEVICE (86xx)

8601	Pointing device; mouse time-out error
8602	Pointing device; mouse interface error
8603	System board; mouse interrupt failure
8604	Pointing device or system board error
8611	System bus error
8612	TrackPoint II error
8613	System bus or TrackPoint II error

MIDI INTERFACE (89xx)

89xx	A fault has been detected in the MIDI adapter— replace the MIDI adapter

3363 WORM OPTICAL DRIVE/ADAPTERS (91xx)

91xx	A fault has been detected in the drive or adapter— replace the adapter and the drive

SCSI ADAPTER (W/32-BIT CACHE) (96xx)

96xx	A fault has been detected in the SCSI adapter— replace the adapter board

MULTIPROTOCOL ADAPTERS (100xx)

10001	Presence test failure
10002	Card selected feedback error
10003	Port 102h register test failure
10004	Port 103h register test failure
10006	Serial option can not be disabled
10007	Cable error

ADVANCED

TABLE 3.1 IBM STANDARD DIAGNOSTIC CODES (CONTINUED)

MULTIPROTOCOL ADAPTERS (100xx) (continued)

10008	IRQ3 error
10009	IRQ4 error
10010	UART register failure
10011	Internal wrap test of UART control line failed
10012	External wrap test of UART control line failed
10013	UART transmit error
10014	UART receive error
10015	UART receive error—data not equal to transmit data
10016	UART interrupt error
10017	UART baud rate test failure
10018	UART receive external wrap test failure
10019	UART FIFO buffer failure
10026	8255 Port A error
10027	8255 Port B error
10028	8255 Port C error
10029	8254 timer 0 error
10030	8254 timer 1 error
10031	8254 timer 2 error
10032	Bisync Data Set Ready (DSR) response error
10033	Bisync Clear-To-Send (CTS) error
10034	8251 hardware reset test failed
10035	8251 function generator
10036	8251 status error
10037	Bisync timer interrupt error
10038	Bisync transmit interrupt error
10039	Bisync receive interrupt error
10040	Stray IRQ3 error
10041	Stray IRQ4 error

TABLE 3.1 IBM STANDARD DIAGNOSTIC CODES (CONTINUED)

MULTIPROTOCOL ADAPTERS (100xx) (continued)

10042	Bisync external wrap error
10044	Bisync data wrap error
10045	Bisync line status error
10046	Bisync time-out error during wrap test
10050	8273 command acceptance or time-out error
10051	8273 Port A error
10052	8273 Port B error
10053	SDLC modem status logic error
10054	SDLC timer IRQ4 error
10055	SDLC IRQ4 error
10056	SDLC external wrap error
10057	SDLC interrupt results error
10058	SDLC data wrap error
10059	SDLC transmit interrupt error
10060	SDLC receive interrupt error
10061	DMA channel 1 transmit error
10062	DMA channel 1 receive error
10063	8273 status detect failure
10064	8273 error detect failure

INTERNAL 300/1200BPS MODEM (101xx)

10101	Presence test failure
10102	Card-selected feedback error
10103	Port 102h register test error
10106	Serial option cannot be disabled
10108	IRQ3 error
10109	IRQ4 error
10110	UART chip register failure

ADVANCED

TABLE 3.1 IBM STANDARD DIAGNOSTIC CODES (CONTINUED)

INTERNAL 300/1200BPS MODEM (101xx) (continued)

10111	UART control line internal wrap test failure
10113	UART transmit error
10114	UART receive error
10115	UART error—transmit and receive data not equal
10116	UART interrupt function error
10117	UART baud rate test failure
10118	UART interrupt driven receive external data wrap test failure
10125	Modem reset result code error
10126	Modem general result code error
10127	Modem S registers write/read error
10128	Modem echo on/off error
10129	Modem enable/disable result codes error
10130	Modem enable number/word result codes error
10133	Connect results for 300 baud not received
10134	Connect results for 1200 baud not received
10135	Modem fails local analog loop-back 300 baud test
10136	Modem fails local analog loop-back 1200 baud test
10137	Modem does not respond to escape/reset sequence
10138	S register 13 shows incorrect parity or number of data bits
10139	S register 15 shows incorrect bit rate

ESDI or MCA IDE DRIVE/ADAPTERS (104xx)

10450	Write/read test failed
10451	Read verify test failed
10452	Seek test failed
10453	Wrong drive type indicated
10454	Controller failed sector buffer test

TABLE 3.1 IBM STANDARD DIAGNOSTIC CODES (CONTINUED)

ESDI or MCA IDE DRIVE/ADAPTERS (104xx) (continued)

10455 Controller failed—invalid

10456 Controller diagnostic command failure

10461 Drive format error

10462 Controller head select error

10463 Drive write/read sector error

10464 Drive primary defect map unreadable

10465 Controller ECC 8-bit error

10466 Controller ECC 9-bit error

10467 Drive soft seek error

10468 Drive hard seek error

10469 Drive soft seek error count exceeded

10470 Controller attachment diagnostic error

10471 Controller wrap mode interface error

10472 Controller wrap mode drive select error

10473 Error during ESDI read verify test

10480 Seek failure on drive 0

10481 Seek failure on drive 1

10482 Controller transfer acknowledge error

10483 Controller reset error

10484 Controller head select 3 selected bad

10485 Controller head select 2 selected bad

10486 Controller head select 1 selected bad

10487 Controller head select 0 selected bad

10488 Read gate command error

10489 Read gate command error

10490 Diagnostic read error on drive 0

10491 Diagnostic read error on drive 1

10492 Drive 1 controller error

10493 Drive 1 reset error

10499 Controller failure

ADVANCED

TABLE 3.1 IBM STANDARD DIAGNOSTIC CODES (CONTINUED)

5.2 INCH EXTERNAL DISK DRIVE/ADAPTER (107xx)

107xx   A fault has been detected in the drive or adapter—
replace the adapter and drive

SCSI ADAPTER (16-BIT W/O CACHE) (112xx)

112xx   A fault has been detected in the SCSI adapter—
replace the SCSI adapter

SYSTEM BOARD SCSI ADAPTER (113xx)

113xx   A fault has been detected in the SCSI adapter—
replace the motherboard

CPU BOARD (129xx)

12901   Processor test failed

12902   CPU board cache test failed

12904   Second level (L2) cache failure

12905   Cache enable/disable errors

12907   Cache fatal error

12908   Cache POST program error

12912   Hardware failure

12913   MCA bus time-out

12914   Software failure

12915   CPU board error

12916   CPU board error

12917   CPU board error

12918   CPU board error

12919   CPU board error

12940   CPU board error

12950   CPU board error

12990   CPU serial number mismatch

TABLE 3.1 IBM STANDARD DIAGNOSTIC CODES (CONTINUED)

P70/P75 PLASMA DISPLAY/ADAPTER (149xx)

14901   Plasma display adapter failure

14902   Plasma display adapter failure

14922   Plasma display failure

14932   External display device failure

XGA DISPLAY ADAPTER (152xx)

152xx   A fault has been detected in the XGA adapter—replace the adapter

120MB INTERNAL TAPE DRIVE (164xx)

164xx   A fault has been detected in the tape drive—replace the tape drive

6157 STREAMING TAPE DRIVE (165xx)

16520   Streaming tape drive failure

16540   Tape attachment adapter failure

PRIMARY TOKEN RING NETWORK ADAPTERS (166xx)

166xx   A fault has been detected with the network adapter—replace the network adapter

SECONDARY TOKEN RING NETWORK ADAPTERS (167xx)

167xx   A fault has been detected with the network adapter—replace the network adapter

PS/2 WIZARD ADAPTER (180xx)

18001   Interrupt controller failure

18002   Incorrect timer count

TABLE 3.1 IBM STANDARD DIAGNOSTIC CODES (CONTINUED)

PS/2 WIZARD ADAPTER (180xx) (continued)

18003 Timer interrupt failure
18004 Sync check interrupt failure
18005 Parity check interrupt failure
18006 Access error interrupt failure
18012 Bad checksum
18013 MCA bus interface error
18021 Wizard memory compare or parity error
18022 Wizard memory address line error
18023 Dynamic RAM controller failure
18029 Wizard memory byte enable error
18031 Wizard memory expansion module compare or parity error
18032 Wizard memory expansion module address line error
18039 Wizard memory expansion module byte enable error

DBCS JAPANESE DISPLAY ADAPTER (185xx)

185xx A fault has been detected in the display adapter—replace the adapter

80286 MEMORY EXPANSION OPTION MODULE (194xx)

194xx A fault has been detected in the memory module—replace the memory module

IMAGE ADAPTER (200xx)

200xx A fault has been detected in the image adapter—replace the image adapter

TABLE 3.1 IBM STANDARD DIAGNOSTIC CODES (CONTINUED)

UNKNOWN SCSI DEVICES (208xx)

208xx   A fault has been detected in an unknown SCSI device—systematically isolate and replace the defective SCSI device

SCSI REMOVABLE DISK (209xx)

209xx   A fault has been detected in the SCSI removable disk—replace the removable disk

SCSI FIXED DISK (210xx)

210xx   A fault has been detected in the SCSI fixed disk—replace the fixed disk

---

NEW SCSI CONTROLLER CAUSES FLOPPY PROBLEMS

Q279.   *I installed a new SCSI host controller, but now my floppy drive doesn't work, and I see an FDD Controller Failure message. When I remove the SCSI adapter, the floppy drive does work. What's going on here?*

A.   I think you've got a floppy controller port incorporated onto your SCSI host adapter. When you install the adapter, the new floppy port is conflicting with your original floppy controller elsewhere in your system. If you are not using the floppy controller on your SCSI adapter, be sure to disable it (usually through a jumper on the SCSI adapter). If you do choose to run your floppy drive(s) from the new SCSI adapter, be sure to disable your original floppy controller.

Parity Errors Booting from Floppy

Q280.   *I've got an odd problem resurrecting my old 386SX/16. I just
installed four 1MB 30-pin SIMMs which seemed to be working
properly until today. I tried to boot from my trusty "bare-bones"
boot floppy to free up some conventional memory for a program
I just downloaded. When trying to boot from this disk, I receive
a PARITY ERROR—SYSTEM HALTED message in huge letters.
This message came after all the POST stuff (all 4MB checked
OK) and appeared right where it should have said "Starting MS-
DOS." The system continues to boot from the C: drive, so only
the A: drive bootup causes this. I tried reseating the SIMMs in
their sockets. Any ideas what's up?*

A.   First, check your trusty bare-bones boot floppy for viruses or at
least try another bootable floppy disk. If another floppy disk
works, you've probably got a problem with the original boot
disk. Check your CMOS Setup next and make sure that your
floppy drive is properly identified. If problems persist, your trouble is likely to be in the floppy drive system itself. Try another
floppy cable and then try another floppy drive (in that order).

Replace Your Dead Floppy Drive

Q281.   *The 5.25-in floppy drive on my 486DX2/66 suddenly quit. It
now gives me the error message "General Failure reading drive
B:." I checked the CMOS setup, ribbon connection, and power
cable connection, and they all seemed to be okay. MSD also
seems to detect the 5.25-in drive correctly. Are there any other
checks I can do before I completely trash this drive?*

A.   For old drives with lots of running time on them, failure in the
spindle motor or read/write heads is not uncommon. If you've
already made sure the cables are snug and tried other disks, you
should take a few minutes to clean the drive's read/write heads. A
simple head cleaning disk will do. Try the drive again. If your
problems persist, your best course is probably to just replace the
drive outright. The 5.25-in drives are *very* inexpensive now, so
price should not be an issue.

COMPUTER REFUSES TO BOOT FROM FLOPPY

Q282. *I wonder if you could help me with a problem that I have. My computer won't boot from floppy. It can boot from the hard drive, but nothing else. I tried several boot disks which all work on a different computer (at school). I tried replacing floppy drives, cables, even motherboards. I don't know what else to do. Can you help me?*

A.   Always start by checking your computer's CMOS Setup. Your floppy drive should have an entry in the Setup screen. Make sure a valid entry is listed for the floppy drive, and that the entry correctly identifies the drive. Next, check for the entry that says "Boot Order." Normally, the Boot Order is "A:, C:" meaning the A: drive is checked for bootable media first, and if found, the system will boot from A:—otherwise, the C: drive is checked. If the Boot Order is "C:, A:," the C: drive will be checked first, and if bootable, the system will boot from it regardless of whether there's a bootable disk in A:. Finally, I can only suggest that you try a new floppy drive controller (or a whole new drive controller board).

CAN'T BOOT FROM THE B: DRIVE

Q283. *I have both A: and B: floppy drives in my old i486DX/33 system. I want to boot from my B: drive, but when I put a bootable floppy in B: and reboot the system, the A: drive light flashes and then the system boots from the hard drive (C:). Is there any way I can set up the system to boot from B:?*

A.   Chances are that your system is new enough that you can select a boot order in CMOS. Your system is probably set to search A: then C:, since bootable media is found in C:, the system boots, and B: is ignored. Start your CMOS Setup and find your CMOS Advanced Settings. One of those entries will probably control the boot order. Once you find the proper entry, you can often change it to B: then C:, A: then B: then C:, B then A: then C:, or something similar. Of course, the selection may simply offer you a choice of which drive to check from first, so you should enter B: in your case. Be sure to save your CMOS settings before exiting and rebooting the computer. If you cannot adjust the boot order, you'll need to reverse your floppy drives (and CMOS entries).

Hard Drive Terminology and General Topics

A QUICK WAY TO DETERMINE DRIVE TYPES

Q284.   *I know there are a lot of different drive types out there, and
sometimes it can get really confusing. How can I tell what type
of hard drive I have?*

A.   When you can't find a description of a drive printed on the drive
itself, the drive signal cable is your best indication of the drive
type. An EIDE or IDE hard drive uses a 40-pin IDC (ribbon)
cable. By comparison, an SCSI drive uses a 50- or 68-pin IDC
cable. A floppy drive uses a 34-pin IDC cable. If you have a *really* old drive such as an RLL, MFM, or ESDI drive, you'll find
two cables, a 34-pin card edge cable (a ribbon cable with a card
edge connector at the end) and a 20-pin card edge cable.

MAXTOR DRIVES AND BUFFER SIZES

Q285.   *I've looked at two Maxtor 2GB drives—one is marked
MXT-72004A, and the other is marked MXT-72004AP. The A
model box is marked 2000MB, while the AP model box is
marked 2GB. I can't tell the difference between these two drives
and the sales person was no help.*

A.   There are two models of those Maxtor drives, one with a 64K
buffer and the other with 128K. The 64K model is the 72004A
and the 128K is the 72004AP. On the shelf of most computer
stores, if you buy the drive in a box, you will see one box that
says "2000MB" and another box that says "2GB." The box that
says "2000MB" is the 64K buffer model. The box that says
"2GB" is the 128K buffer model.

CONFLICTING DRIVE SPACE MEASUREMENTS

Q286.   *CMOS, FDISK, and File Manager in Windows all report less
than the full capacity of my new hard drive, but CHKDSK
reports the right capacity. Which is correct?*

A. This is a common problem which has to do with the way megabytes are calculated. Technically, 1 megabyte (1MB) is 1,048,256 bytes (sometimes called a binary meg), but hard drive makers and CHKDSK use 1,000,000 bytes as 1MB. The result is that the number on your hard drive box (and the number shown by CHKDSK) seem a bit higher than the numbers reported by CMOS, FDISK, or other drive utilities. Table 3.2 illustrates this relationship.

TABLE 3.2 TYPICAL REPORTED DRIVE CAPACITIES

Model	Capacity (MB)	CMOS (MB)	CHKDSK (MB)
AC2850	853.6	814.1	853.6
AC21200	1281.9	1222.3	1281.9
AC32100	2111.8	2035.6	2111.8

MOUNTING LIMITATIONS FOR HARD DRIVES

Q287. *Can I mount my hard drive sideways and upside down?*

A. As a rule, you should be able to mount a hard drive in almost any orientation. The one issue to keep in mind is that you should partition and format the drive *after* it has warmed up in whatever orientation you select. You should *always* make it a point to mount a drive securely to eliminate premature failures due to vibration. Of course, you should also check the drive's documentation for any specific mounting restrictions or precautions.

EXCESSIVE DRIVE WHINE IS CAUSE FOR CONCERN

Q288. *I have a Maxtor hard drive that makes a bizarre sound—like the feedback from an audio speaker. Is this noise normal? What should I do about it?*

A. Hard drives normally make some amount of noise during normal operation—typically a very faint motor noise which is similar to fan noise. You might also detect a bit of "clicking" from the drive heads as the drive reads and writes to its platters. If the drive is whining or squealing noticeably, the spindle motor may be wearing out. This is potentially disastrous because once the spindle fails, your drive will become inaccessible. From your description, I would highly recommend that you back up your hard drive and replace it as soon as possible.

GETTING HARD DRIVE SPECIFICATIONS

Q289. *I need to get my hands on some specifications for the Seagate ST3491A HDD (including such things as its jumper settings and data transfer rate). Can you tell me where I might be able to get this kind of data?*

A. These types of questions come up a lot, especially since drive data can be difficult to sift out of the drive's documentation. Rather then just provide the contact information for Seagate, Table 3.3 lists the Internet contacts for the largest hard drive makers.

TABLE 3.3 INTERNET CONTACTS FOR MAJOR HARD DRIVE MANUFACTURERS

Company	Web Site
Seagate	www.seagate.com
Western Digital	www.wdc.com
Quantum	www.quantum.com
Maxtor	www.maxtor.com

THERMAL RECALIBRATION AND HARD DRIVES

Q290. *What is thermal recalibration of hard drives?*

A. When the temperature of the hard drive changes, the media expands slightly. In modern drives, the data is so densely packed that this expansion can actually become significant—and if it is not taken into account, data written when the drive is cold may not be able to be read when the drive is warm. To compensate for this, many drives now perform thermal recalibration every degree centigrade (or so) as the drive warms up and then some longer periodic interval once the drive has reached normal operating temperature. When thermal recalibration takes place, the heads are moved and the drive may sound like you are accessing it. This is perfectly normal. If you're attempting to access the drive when thermal recalibration occurs, you may experience a slight delay. The only time this becomes important is when you're doing real-time operations such as recording or playing multimedia files.

THE NEED FOR PARTITIONING

Q291. *I bought a 2.0GB hard drive, and I've been told that I should partition it. What is the advantage or reasoning for partitioning? I have a 486 120-MHz system with 16MB RAM running Windows 95.*

A. Yes, you *must* partition any new hard drive. Partitioning is used to divide the physical space of the hard drive into logical drives (or volumes) used by the operating system such as DOS or Windows. You can usually create up to four partitions on a phys-ical drive, and each partition is given its own drive letter by DOS when the system boots up. The actual process of EIDE/IDE drive preparation consists of four steps: Install the physical hard drive in the PC, enter the drive geometry in your CMOS Setup, parti-tion the drive with FDISK, and then format each partition with FORMAT. The drive will then be ready for use.

REMEMBER TO JUMPER

Q292. *I want to add a second hard drive to my system. Do I have to put a jumper on my original drive when adding a new drive to my system?*

A. Most likely, yes. One hard drive—usually the newer larger drive—must be designated as the primary (master) drive and the other as the secondary (slave) drive. You will need to refer to the documentation for your drives in order to determine the proper jumper settings.

Drive RPM Not Best Indicator of Data Throughput

Q293. *I'm planning to build a Pentium soon to make sure I get the best possible performance for my money. As I understand it, hard drives with faster revolutions per minute (RPM) provide faster data throughput; is that right? Is a 7200-RPM drive truly almost 50 percent faster than a 5400-RPM drive, or are there other factors?*

A.   RPM is definitely *not* a good indicator of drive performance. Drive RPM will have a distinct impact on data seek times and the overall speed at which data can be read from or written to the drive platters, so more RPM is generally a good thing. However, drive RPM really doesn't directly affect the speed of the drive *interface*—how fast the drive can send or receive data across its SCSI or EIDE data cable. It is the interface speed which you are *most* concerned with because your system will be held up waiting for the drive to complete its reads and writes. When selecting a new hard drive, look for the specifications that outline its interface.

Connecting EDIE/IDE Devices

Q294. *Does it matter where I connect an EIDE device on the ribbon cable?*

A.   Not really. If you have only one drive on the cable, it is best to put it at the very end (especially when you're using any of the faster PIO modes). For two EIDE devices, it doesn't really matter where you put the drives because an EIDE/IDE cable only supports two drives anyway. Just take care that you plug the drives in the right way: The red (or blue) wire is always pin 1.

Knowing EIDE Drive Jumpers

Q295. *I've heard that I need to change jumpers on the hard drive if I want to add another one to my system. What are these jumpers, and what do I need to set them for?*

A.   An EIDE hard drive port can support two hard drives. One hard drive must be designated as the primary (or master) drive, while the second hard drive must be designated as the secondary (or slave) hard drive. These designations are made with jumpers on the drives themselves. Your original hard drive is probably already jumpered as the primary drive. If you choose to add a second hard drive, the new drive should be jumpered as the secondary drive. You should also check the jumpers on your original drive to see if there is a distinction made between the primary drive in a single-drive system, and the primary drive in a dual-drive system. If so, adjust the original drive's jumper accordingly. More recently, hard drives are providing a Cable Select (CSEL) option. As a rule, you should avoid this selection if possible. You will need to check the documentation for your particular drives to determine the exact location and purpose of each jumper position.

CPU VINTAGE NOT RELATED TO DRIVE PARTITION SIZES

Q296.   *I'm reviving an old 386 PC and dusting off some DOS games for my grandson to play with, but I'd forgotten how large the drive partition should be. What is the maximum size of partition recognized by a 386 PC?*

A.   Partition size is a factor of your operating system, not the CPU. In fact, you can create a partition as large as the OS will allow regardless of the PC's age. For example, early versions of DOS supported only 32MB partitions, DOS 4.0 supported 512MB partitions, and DOS 5.0 and later supports partitions up to 2GB. However, if your hard drive is larger then 528MB, you will need an EIDE drive controller, a new BIOS, or Drive Manager software to make use of the large drives.

TEMPERAMENTAL DRIVE POSITION

Q297.   *My hard drive will work as a secondary (slave) drive but not as a primary (master) drive. Why?*

A.   In almost all cases, you need to update the drive jumpers. The drive will not work as a primary drive if it is jumpered as a secondary drive (or vice versa). If the drive is jumpered as CSEL, make sure to jumper the drive as either a primary or secondary drive as appropriate. Also, the speed and timing of some drives differ drastically during the initial spin-up sequence. This might confuse the system, and one of the drives may not be recognized. The best solution for this situation is to try different combinations of primary/secondary drives until there is a combination the system will accept. In the event that no combination is acceptable, you may need to upgrade the older of the two drives.

COMING TO TERMS WITH BAD SECTORS

Q298.   *I have a homemade Pentium system that has two used Maxtor hard drives. One drive is a 546MB hard drive (D:) and the other is an 840MB drive (C:). I ran Norton Utilities (for Windows 95) and it discovered bad sectors on both drives. I instructed the program to move data out of the bad sectors. What actions damage hard drives to the point that data shouldn't be stored on any part of the hard disk? Does the problem signal a less than perfect hard drive (i.e., low- or poor-quality drive), or is this a pretty normal problem that occurs after normal usage over an extended period of time?*

A.   Since magnetic media begins to slowly degrade the moment it is first written, it is perfectly normal for hard drives to develop bad sectors over the course of time (these are usually referred to as *grown defects*). There are several reasons for grown defects, but all are related to issues such as manufacturing defects, drive age, and wear. In fact, most hard drives reserve several tracks so that defective sectors can be "mapped out" and replaced with working sectors. If you've encountered a few bad sectors after several years of regular use, I'd say you're OK. But if megabytes of bad sectors are cropping up frequently across your drive, that probably signals a serious drive fault, and you should consider replacing the suspect drive as soon as possible. As always, you should back up your hard drive regularly to guard against data loss.

Using EIDE/IDE Drives in Pairs

Q299.   *I've given some serious thought to adding a second IDE drive to my daughter's system, but I've been hesitant because it seems that IDE drives don't work well in pairs. Is this wrong, or should I be worried?*

A.   Don't worry at all. Older IDE drives suffered from incompatibilities such as electrical noise and timing problems. While the drive would work fine by itself, such difficulties often manifested themselves when the drive was combined with a second IDE drive. Perhaps most notorious for dual-drive problems are the older Conner IDE drives (100 to 200MB). However, the drive industry has worked long and hard on refining IDE operation and standards, so unless you plan to use IDE drives made before 1992, you should have no real problems in configuring two current IDE drives. When installing the second drive, be extremely careful to select primary (master) and secondary (slave) jumpers on each drive. Fortunately, there are no terminating resistors or cable twists to deal with, so installation is simplified a bit.

One other issue to consider is hard drive size. Today, hard drives use the EIDE standard, and you'd be very hard pressed to find a drive smaller than 500MB. This means you'll probably be installing a 1.6- to 3.2GB hard drive. You should consider upgrading the drive controller to an EIDE drive controller with on-board BIOS in order to support larger hard drives. If you cannot upgrade the drive controller hardware, you should use the drive overlay software (such as Disk Manager) that probably accompanies the drive. Make the new (large) drive your primary drive, and jumper the original drive as your secondary drive. You'll also need to partition the new drive with an active bootable partition and to format the drive as bootable. Finally, remember to update all the settings in your CMOS Setup to reflect the drive arrangements.

INTERMEDIATE

Mixing EIDE and IDE Hard Drives

Q300.   *My current Pentium system has two Maxtor IDE hard drives
that I salvaged from another system. The drives are performing
with no problems, but I have been told that I will get better performance with an EIDE hard drive. What happens if you mix an
EIDE and an IDE hard drive on the same channel? Can this be
done without sacrificing performance of the EIDE hard drive?*

A.   As a rule, you can certainly mix IDE and EIDE drives on the
same drive channel, but you will not get any increased performance from your EIDE drive. In actual practice, you may not
notice any difference in drive performance, but it may not be
possible to access the enhanced PIO mode 4 data transfers
(16.6MB/s) that make EIDE drives so appealing. If you do
choose to use EIDE and IDE drives in the same system, you
should place the EIDE drive(s) on the primary EIDE drive controller channel and place the IDE drive (and ATAPI devices such
as CD-ROM drives) on the secondary IDE drive controller channel. This tactic allows the EIDE drives to operate at their top
speed and prevents slower devices from interfering.

Identifying an ESDI Drive

Q301.   *I was given an old 760MB hard drive. I thought it was an IDE,
but the connector on the back of the drive is an old card edge-
type connector. It is divided into two sections—the longer one
has 17 contacts, and the second connector has 10 contacts. I was
told by a technician that it's an old SCSI drive, but I don't think
so. Could it be an ESDI drive?*

A.   It's definitely not an SCSI drive—older SCSI drives use a single
50-pin insulation displacement connector (IDC) header for the
signal cable. The connectors you described indicate either an
MFM or ESDI drive. But since MFM drives didn't really get bigger than 80MB, and your drive is a 760MB drive, I'd say the
chances are pretty good that you've got an ESDI drive. This can
pose a problem because you'll be hard pressed to find a controller to support the drive. Even then, the drive's performance
will not be comparable with current EIDE drives.

IDE HDDs Don't Always Work Together

Q302. *I've been piecing together a used system out of spare (a.k.a. old) parts, and I'm having trouble with my IDE drives (both drives are smaller than 520MB). When I install the primary and secondary drives together, the system won't boot, but both drives work alone. I know the jumpering is correct because I've got the documentation, but I don't understand what's wrong.*

A. Chances are that you're using hard drives made by two different manufacturers. Older IDE hard drives often implemented IDE bus timing in slightly different ways. When taken separately, the drives worked, but when used together, those slight timing differences caused the drive system to fail. Since your drives obviously work alone, try reversing their primary/secondary relationship. That should clear the timing issue. Otherwise, you'll need to find another drive that *will* work together with another drive.

Leave Drive Interleave Alone

Q303. *I have heard claims that big improvements in hard disk performance can be achieved by adjusting the interleave. But I also got the feeling that it might be a risky business. I have a Quantum Fireball AT 1.2GB drive that I bought within the last year. Maybe it has no need for any such adjustment. However, if in fact there is something to be gained, how could I go about doing the optimization? Thanks for any help you can give.*

A. Be careful. Older drives (typically MFM or RLL drives) couldn't keep up with systems of the day, so the sectors were alternated (interleaved) around the respective track. This forced the platter to rotate several times before each track could be read completely. When drives used interleaving, performance could be improved by reducing the interleave factor to a minimum (optimum) of 1:1—in other words, no interleaving (all the sectors would be in order). For your 1GB+ drive, the interleave is *certainly* 1:1, and you *won't* get any better than that. Messing with the interleave now would cause more harm than good. Leave the drive's interleave alone.

UNDERSTANDING EIDE

Q304.   *I have heard the terms IDE and EIDE used interchangeably, but I
know they are not the same thing. What is EIDE, and what are
its features? Also, how does EIDE differ from Fast-ATA?*

A.   IDE is the traditional 40-pin hard drive interface used on low-
end PCs since about 1988. In 1993, drive makers introduced a
proposal for a new (but backward-compatible) extension to the
IDE standard. Because this extension was an enhancement of the
existing IDE standard and fully backward compatible, it was
called Enhanced IDE (EIDE). The new standard includes an
expanded suite of drive commands and a new register set. The
new commands and register set ensure that the older systems
(without EIDE) will work with the new EIDE drives. When systems are upgraded with only a new hard disk drive, they must
contend with the limitations of the standard IDE connection.
These limitations can be overcome by upgrading other system
components such as the IDE drive controller and system BIOS.

EIDE offers some valuable features for PC users such as 8.4GB
per device, BIOS translation, logical block addressing (LBA), up
to four devices per system (CD-ROM and tape drives are now
supported), modes 3 and 4 PIO data transfers, and autodetection
of hard drives. Today, EIDE systems have completely replaced
IDE systems.

Fast-ATA is really a subset of IDE; it indicates the ability to run
at higher data transfer rates. As a standard, Fast-ATA does not
include all of the features that EIDE does and primarily focuses
just on faster data transfers.

PREPARING FOR EIDE

Q305.   *I'm helping a friend upgrade an old 420MB HDD. I'd like to
install a cheap 1.6GB hard drive, but I have heard that special
preparations are needed. Otherwise, you won't get more than
528MB from the drive. What do I need in order to prepare for
this large hard drive?*

A.   Hard drives over 528MB are typically referred to as Enhanced IDE (EIDE) drives. In order to take full capacity of the drive, you need to improve your BIOS support. This can be accomplished in one of three ways: upgrade the motherboard BIOS outright, upgrade the drive controller with its own on-board BIOS for EIDE drives, or use a software solution such as Disk Manager or EZ-Drive. If you choose to upgrade the BIOS, be sure to enable LBA mode when configuring the drive in CMOS. It is also important to note that even though EIDE technology should support hard drives up to 8GB, some EIDE BIOS versions will not support drives over 2GB, and some will not support drives over 4GB. Once again, if drive size support is limited, check for a motherboard/controller BIOS upgrade.

CONFIGURING A THIRD IDE PORT

Q306.   *If you already have the primary and secondary EIDE/IDE channels filled up, can you configure your sound card's IDE controller as a tertiary channel and add two more devices (provided you have a spare IRQ)?*

A.   Possibly. It is certainly possible in theory, but there are some limitations that you should keep in mind. First, you *should* be able to configure the sound board's IDE port to serve as a third port, but this requires you to select an IRQ and I/O range that is not being used by any other device in the system. On crowded PCs, this can be a real problem. Second, most CMOS versions that I've ever seen only provide entries for four physical hard drives. If you add a fifth and sixth hard drive, you may not be able to use the drives because you're unable to identify them in CMOS. Instead, you should only place hard drives on the primary and secondary ports and reserve your tertiary port for an ATAPI IDE CD-ROM or tape drive (devices that do not use a CMOS entry). Finally, there's no guarantee that you can use a third port with *every* combination of motherboard and drive controllers—it just may not work in some cases.

INTERMEDIATE

Pinning Down an EIDE Upgrade

Q307. *If I get a new hard drive (larger then the one I have), I heard that I may need a new drive controller to accommodate EIDE. How do I know if I need to get a new drive controller? How do I check? Do I keep my old drive also, or would this just make things more complicated? My finances are tight, and I'd hate to spend the extra money if I don't have to.*

A.   Start your CMOS Setup and check your drive configuration area for entries such as LBA or auto-configure. If you find such entries, chances are that your BIOS will already support EIDE drives. If you cannot find such entries, you generally have three options for supporting EIDE on an older PC: (1) upgrade the motherboard BIOS, (2) add a stand-alone EIDE controller with its own BIOS, or (3) use EIDE partitioning software such as Ontrack's Disk Manager or EZ-Drive. Of the three choices, a new EIDE controller would be the preferred option because you don't have to hunt for a new motherboard BIOS, and the new controller hardware will typically provide the best data transfer performance. You can find good-quality EIDE drive controllers for about $50, so the cost is really not that great. If you really can't spare the extra cash, go ahead and use the Disk Manager or EZ-Drive software that probably accompanied your drive. It will install itself on your large hard drive and overcome the drive size limitations of your older drive controller. As for your original hard drive, you can certainly keep the drive in place and install the large drive as a secondary drive. You could also install the new drive as your primary drive and reconfigure the original drive as a secondary drive (just make sure to set both the drive's jumpers correctly).

Emergency Clearing a Partition

Q308. *I hear that there's a DEBUG script that we can use to clear the partition sector of a hard drive in the event of a virus or other emergency. Can you tell me what that DEBUG routine is?*

A.   Even if you have repartitioned the hard drive, FDISK does not update the entire partition sector after the first time. The following DEBUG script will clear the partition sector (cylinder 0, head 0, sector 1) of the *first* hard drive. This will force FDISK to completely start over. This is sometimes useful for removing Disk Manager or EZ Drive and should also remove any boot sector viruses, providing that the virus is not active in memory (which should be the case if you have booted from a clean, write-protected floppy disk). Although this script clears only the first physical drive, we recommend unplugging other drives to prevent accidental data loss. The Xs in the script should be ignored.

```
C:\>DEBUG

- f 200 L200 0

- a 100

xxxx:xxxx mov ax,301          (ignore segment:offset values at left)

xxxx:xxxx mov bx,200

xxxx:xxxx mov cx,1

xxxx:xxxx mov dx,0080

xxxx:xxxx int 13

xxxx:xxxx int 3

xxxx:xxxx                     (press ENTER an extra time here)

- g=100

                              (ignore register display)

- q                           (quits back to DOS)
```

FDISK should now show "No partitions defined."

Note

This DEBUG script will render all the data on your drive inaccessible. Be sure to perform a complete system backup before attempting any partition work.

BEST PATH TO A NEW HARD DRIVE

Q309. *What is the fastest and easiest way to set up my new EIDE hard drive?*

A.   I'm sure we've touched on this issue elsewhere in the book, but here is the quick and dirty list;

    1.   Copy FDISK, FORMAT, and SYS to a bootable floppy disk.

    2.   Start CMOS Setup. Set the Hard Disk Type to Auto Configure and set the Translation Mode to Auto Detect.

    3.   Boot from the floppy and run FDISK to create at least one active partition.

    4.   Run FORMAT to prepare each of the partitions you created with FDISK.

    5.   Run SYS C: to copy the system files to your C: partition.

    6.   Remove the floppy disk and reboot the system from your C: drive.

EIDE AND CD-ROM TOGETHER

Q310. *Can a hard drive and a CD-ROM drive be installed on the same EIDE data cable? If so, will this arrangement degrade the performance of the hard drive in any way?*

A.   An EIDE hard drive and an ATAPI IDE CD-ROM can be connected on the same cable. The hard drive should be jumpered as the primary (master) drive, and the CD-ROM drive should be jumpered as a secondary (slave) drive. Unfortunately, installing a CD-ROM on the same drive controller port as the hard drive can also cause a reduction of performance in the hard drive. This is because the drive controller port may limit data transfer rates to those of the slowest drive (the CD-ROM) or at least prohibit the highest data transfer modes. Before actually installing a hard drive and CD-ROM together, you may want to contact the drive controller manufacturer and see if there are any reported performance problems. If top performance is an important concern, it may be better to place the hard drive on its own EIDE controller port and place the CD-ROM alone on a secondary drive controller port.

Adding SCSI Support to an IDE System

Q311. *I have a PC with an IDE HDD and CD-ROM drive. I wonder if I can now add an SCSI controller and SCSI hard disk? If this is possible, can I make the SCSI disk bootable?*

A. There is no problem with adding an SCSI adapter and hard drive to your system. SCSI controllers use their own BIOS; so as long as the SCSI controller's IRQ, I/O address range—and so on—do not conflict with other hardware in your system, it should work. Keep in mind that you will *not* add the SCSI drive's geometry to the CMOS Setup. Also remember that you may need to add at least one SCSI driver for the controller (although the use of on-board SCSI BIOS may make this unnecessary), so keep an eye on your conventional memory. Traditionally, you could not boot from an SCSI drive if there are EIDE/IDE drives in the system, but newer SCSI BIOS does allow this option (check your SCSI controller to see if its BIOS will allow booting "over" IDE devices). Finally, remember that adding a drive will change your CD-ROM drive letter. This may require you to update your CD-ROM drivers and reinstall some CD-based applications.

Low-Level Formatting IDE and SCSI Drives

Q312. *I'm confused about low-level (LL) formatting. I've been told that LL formats are not needed for SCSI drives and IDE drives, yet I've seen software that claims to perform LL formats of IDE or SCSI drives. To confuse things even further, I've been told that such LL formatting tools are not always reliable on every drive. What's going on?*

A. That's a great question—and a very important one. The rule of thumb is that you should *not* attempt to low-level format any SCSI or EIDE/IDE hard drive because of the complex way that data is laid out on a modern hard drive. Sophisticated error correction techniques such as sector sparring allow reserved sectors to be mapped in to take the place of defective sectors. Zoned recording improves the use of disk space by allowing outer tracks to hold more sectors and inner tracks to hold less. The trick is that to accomplish these feats, the drive must be prepared at the

ADVANCED

factory. Those old-fashioned BIOS formats using a DEBUG script simply won't work. At best, the drive will just ignore the DEBUG format routine. At worst, the low-level format can damage the drive's layout, causing lost capacity and performance. Once the damage is done, you can't undo it.

Some utilities *claim* to be able to low-level format certain drives, but unless the utility is written specifically for your particular drive, I would strongly recommend that you avoid it. Even different-sized drives made by the same manufacturer can require their own unique low-level formatting. If your drive comes with a preparation utility on disk, that would be the closest tool available for low-level work. Still, you should only use such tools as the very last resort— and *only* after backing up as much of the drive as possible.

CLUSTER SIZE VERSUS PARTITION SIZE

Q313. *I've heard a lot about partitions and cluster sizes. How can I tell what size my clusters are?*

A.   Generally speaking, you can set your partitions for any size supported by BIOS and your operating system. Your choice of partition size will have a direct impact on cluster size. Table 3.4 illustrates the relationship between partition size and cluster size.

TABLE 3.4 CLUSTER SIZE VERSUS PARTITION SIZE

Cluster size (K)	Partition size	FAT type	Notes
4K	16 MB	FAT12	
2K	32 MB	FAT16	DOS versions < 4.0
2K	128 MB	FAT16	DOS versions >= 4.0
4K	256 MB	FAT16	
8K	512 MB	FAT16	
16K	1 GB	FAT16	
32K	2 GB	FAT16	
64K	4 GB	FAT16	

EIDE Hard Drive Partition Not Supported Properly

Q314.   *I have an 850MB hard drive. When I enter my hard drive parameters into Setup and then try to partition the drive, it comes back as 500MB. Am I going nuts?*

A.   I doubt you're going nuts, but you will need to make some changes to your CMOS Setup. If your machine is capable of automatically sensing hard drives, set the drive type to either Auto Sense, Auto Detect, or Type 1. If the machine also has a set-ting for HD Translation Mode or LBA Mode, make sure it is *enabled.* If you can't enable EIDE drive support on your system, you'll need to upgrade your motherboard BIOS or install a new drive controller with its own on-board BIOS extension. Once you are able to configure the EIDE drive in CMOS, be sure to repar-tition and reformat the drive.

Partition Size Limits

Q315.   *I'm trying to partition my new 3.2GB Maxtor drive. The problem is that I can't get partitions larger than 2GB. I know the system supports LBA because the 2.1GB partition works. But if I try anything larger, I get errors and system crashes. Can you help?*

A.   The size of a hard drive's partition is limited by three factors: the size of the hard drive itself, the BIOS, and the operating system. LBA is a BIOS feature that allows drives to be supported over 528MB. In theory, EIDE drives should be supported up to 8GB or so. Even though a BIOS supports LBA, we've been finding that a lot of BIOS versions are artificially limited to around 2 or 3GB. This is a BIOS issue, not an LBA issue. Operating systems are another problem. FAT16 file systems (such as DOS and Windows 95) also limit partitions to 2.1GB (even if the BIOS can support larger partitions). The bottom line here is that you need to have *both* a BIOS and an operating system that support parti-tions larger than 2.1GB. For now, you can simply partition the large drive into two smaller logical drives (both under 2GB).

ADVANCED

Modifying Drive Partitions on the Fly

Q316.   *I am running Windows 95 and I would like to multiboot my sys-*
tem with Windows 95, Windows NT, Linux, and so on. This
means I have to back up everything and then repartition my disk
accordingly (i.e., C: for DOS, D: for Windows 95, E: for
Windows NT, F: for Linux, and so on) and then reinstall
Windows 95 and install the other operating systems. Is there a
utility (not FDISK) which will repartition my disk while
Windows 95 is still running?

A.   You're in luck. Take a look at Partition Magic from Power
Quest. With Partition Magic, you can modify and manipulate
your partitions without damaging existing partitions on the
drive. You can learn more about Partition Magic by visiting the
Power Quest Web site at; *www.powerquest.com,* or you can
place an order at 801-226-8977. However, regardless of what
tool you use to manage your partitions, you should *always* make
it a point to perform a complete backup of your physical hard
drive before attempting to work with any partitions.

Poor Drive Preparation May Cause Controller Errors

Q317.   *I just installed my new Western Digital Caviar drive and entered*
the drive parameters in the CMOS, but the drive will not boot. It
displays the message; "HDD controller failure." Why is that?

A.   You have not prepared the new hard drive correctly. Proper
CMOS settings are just the first step. You will need to boot the
system from a floppy disk and run FDISK to partition the drive
(remember to make your main partition bootable and active).
Next, use FORMAT to prepare the partition for DOS. Finally,
run the SYS utility from your floppy disk (such as: SYS C:) to
place the required boot files on the drive. Your hard drive should
now be bootable.

Lost Drive Space

Q318.   *How come I'm getting an Out of Disk Space message after load-*
ing only 800MB of data onto my 1.0GB hard drive?

A. You are probably seeing the effects of large cluster sizes. In DOS, every file that is stored gets at least one allocation unit (called a *cluster*) no matter what the size of the file is. The size of the cluster grows incrementally with the size of the partition. For a 1.0GB partition, the cluster size will be 32KB. This means that even a 62-byte batch file is going to consume 32KB of storage space (the difference between the 32KB of the cluster and the space that the file really needs is called *slack space*). The only feasible way to reduce the cluster size is to reduce the partition size. For now, you'll simply have to hold off adding new files to your hard drive.

RUN-TIME PROBLEMS WITH FDISK

Q319. *I'm having all kinds of trouble with FDISK. Every time I try to partition my drive, the system hangs up, or I see a message like "Run-time error." What does that mean?*

A. FDISK requires access to the drive's boot sector and master boot record at track 00. FDISK errors almost always indicate corruption or damage to track 00, which can render the entire drive unusable. If your drive has come with a low-level format utility or specific track 00 diagnostic (typically placed on the disk which accompanied your drive), try that utility and see if it clears the problem. If not, the drive may be defective and should be replaced.

UNDERSTANDING PARTITION LETTER ASSIGNMENTS

Q320. *I have a question about the setup of multiple hard drives. My PC system supports two physical hard drives, and when I escape during boot-up to go into Setup, I identify the C: drive (master drive) and the D: drive (slave drive) and their logistics. If I then partition the C: drive (the first physical drive) into say drives C:, D:, and E: drives, what drive numbers do I use for the second physical drive? I cannot use D: drive again, so does it become F:? Are these drive designations separate from the drive numbers used during setup?*

A.   Hard drives have two "realms": physical and logical. The physical realm is handled by your CMOS, which is concerned only about your primary and secondary drives regardless of how many partitions you have on them. On the other hand, DOS (and Windows) are concerned with the logical realm and works with all the logical drives (partitions) that it finds on your physical drives. When you're in CMOS, don't think of the drive in terms of letters—think of them as a primary and secondary drive. The letters are really a convention of the operating system. So the answer to your question is that the drive designations used by CMOS and the operating system *are* separate.

Here's another trick—don't place a primary partition on your secondary drive. Since DOS assigns drive letters to the primary partitions first (and logical partitions second), it will call the primary partition of your first drive C:, the primary partition of your second drive D:, then go back to your first drive to assign other drive letters, and then go to your second drive to assign the rest. If you place *only* extended partitions on the secondary drive, your letters should make more sense.

CHANGING PARTITION LETTERS

Q321. *I want to add a hard drive to my new system, which includes a 2.5GB hard drive partitioned as C: and D:. After installing the new hard drive in my system, the drive letters are changed around. The D: partition on the old drive became E:. Can I change drive letters, or can I install without this problem?*

A.   EIDE hard drives are all BIOS-supported, and all DOS-based operating systems (including Windows) assign drive letters to the Primary DOS partitions *first* and then the extended partitions are assigned drive letters. DOS will not allow you to change drive letters. The only way to get the drive letters to read in order is to create *only* extended partitions on the new drive. This is not a difficult thing to do, and it will not compromise your system's performance. However, there is a drawback to creating only extended partitions on the secondary drive—should you ever decide to make the secondary drive a primary or only drive in the system, you will *not* be able to boot to the drive. Since DOS-based operating systems can only boot to a primary DOS partition, you would have to repartition that new drive.

ASSIGNING DRIVE PARTITION LETTERS

Q322. *Last month I added a 3.1GB hard drive to my P5-133 system. I had to make the new drive C: because I couldn't assign the letter D:. I also had to make a second partition on the drive, but it became E:. How is this possible, and is there any way to fix it?*

A.   The typical computer system BIOS assigns drive letters to all primary (bootable) partitions it finds before assigning drive letters to the extended (logical) partitions. Since both your original drive and new drive have primary partitions, C: is assigned to the primary partition of your master drive (which is now your large 3.1GB drive), D: is assigned to the primary partition of your slave drive, and E: is assigned to the next logical partition of your large master drive. If your new drive was formatted with logical partitions only, it would have been added as the slave drive, and it would have received letters D: and E: in that order. This isn't really a problem, but you can fix it by restoring your original drive as C:, then repartitioning your 3.1GB drive with two logical partitions instead of one primary and one logical partition.

DOUBLESPACE NOT DOUBLING SPACE

Q323. *I recently used DoubleSpace on an old hard disk, and it turned a 120MB HDD into a 240MB HDD. I then copied 100MB worth of files and checked the remaining space. CHKDSK said that the drive only had 80MB left. Why don't I have 140MB left?*

A.   DoubleSpace is probably working correctly here. Keep in mind that the amount of compression that DoubleSpace can provide depends on the *file itself*. Some files by their nature compress better than others. Text files often compress at ratios approaching 5:1, while files that have already been compressed (such as .ZIP files) may not compress at all. The free space on a DoubleSpace disk is determined by the actual occupied space plus the estimated free space. Thus, as files are added to the disk, the total disk space may seem to change out of proportion to the actual file size. If the files placed on disk were already compressed (or compress poorly), the actual occupied space will roughly equal the file space, and the free space will change to reflect a much lower value.

DECOMPRESSING DRIVESPACE 3

Q324. *I am installing a second hard drive in my system, and I want to decompress my existing hard drive. The problem is that I cannot get DriveSpace 3 to decompress. What should I do?*

A. You need to update an .INI file. There is one small (but important) .INI file which needs to be corrected to reflect the new configuration—it is a hidden, read-only file called DBLSPACE.INI and is located in the root directory of the host drive. Chances are that DBLSPACE.INI is still referring to the host drive as H: (or some other label which is no longer valid since a new drive has been added to the system). As a result, DriveSpace 3 looks for a host drive that is no longer there. Simply change the read-only and hidden attributes on DBLSPACE.INI, replace any reference to the old host drive with the new drive letter designation, save the file, restore the R and H attributes, and restart DriveSpace 3.

Drive Enhancement Software

THE ROLE OF OVERLAYS

Q325. *I've heard that I can update my hard drive by downloading and installing an overlay. What is an overlay?*

A. An overlay is a small program that installs into the boot sector of your hard drive (or is loaded by CONFIG.SYS) and can be used to modify the firmware located in the drive's own electronics. The advantage of an overlay is that you can quickly modify the operation of your hard drive without having to physically replace it. However, if you repartition the hard drive (or your start-up files are lost), you will have to reinstall the overlay. Losing the overlay after the drive has been running with it may cause data corruption.

DISK MANAGER VERSIONS

Q326. *I've been using Disk Manager for some time now, and I finally want to upgrade to Windows 95. Will this effect my Disk Manager installation? Should I upgrade Disk Manager?*

A. Disk Manager versions 6.03d or higher should function properly with Windows 95. If you have an older version of Disk Manager, you should upgrade it before installing Windows 95. Check the Ontrack Software Web site (*www.ontrack.com*). If you have version 6.03 through 6.03c, you can get the DMPATCH.EXE upgrade to update the Dynamic Drive Overlay to 6.03d.

OBTAINING OVERLAY SOFTWARE FOR EIDE DRIVES

Q327. *I am upgrading my system, and I am trying to install my Seagate ST5850A 850MB hard drive into an old 386 system. Of course, I now require the software to allow the 386 to access the full 850MB. Can you tell me where I can obtain these drivers?*

A. You are looking for Disk Manager software made by Ontrack. If you did not get a disk containing Disk Manager with your hard drive, you should be able to obtain it from either the Seagate site at *http://www.seagate.com*, or the Ontrack site at *http://www.ontrack.com*.

DISK MANAGER AND DOS UTILITIES

Q328. *I've been told that if I install Disk Manager, I'll no longer be able to use the versions of ScanDisk and DEFRAG that ship with Windows 95. Is this true? Is there any way around it?*

A. No, it is not true. Disk Manager will not interfere with any of the Windows 95 disk utilities. But if the drive came prepackaged with its own suite of OEM disk utilities, you might get better results from them than from the standard Windows 95 disk tools.

WINDOWS 95 AND DISK MANAGER

Q329. *I'm adding a new EIDE drive to my Windows 95 PC, and I want to use Disk Manager so that I won't need to upgrade any other hardware. But a friend told me that Disk Manager won't work with Windows 95. Is that true?*

A. Windows 95 *is* compatible with Disk Manager 6.03 and later. For best results, however, use version 6.03d, which allows Windows 95 to use its protected-mode driver.

SOFTWARE OVERLAYS AND LARGE HARD DRIVES

Q330. *I'm trying to update my 486DX2/66 with AMI BIOS dated 1993. I'm using Windows 95, and I'd like to put in a 2.0GB HDD. I know that the BIOS may be a problem, but I went to a local computer store to ask about sticking a bigger HDD in the system. They suggested going with a 1.3GB and that by using a software overlay the system would work without problems. However, they mentioned that the software overlay wouldn't work with a 2.1GB HDD. What is this software overlay? How does it work, and is it the way to go? Or should I avoid this software overlay and go with a BIOS upgrade? I also phoned another computer store, and they said a BIOS upgrade is not recommended since there may be some problems. What kind of problems can you see?*

A. This has been a very popular question as older PCs are upgraded with current EIDE hard drives. A software overlay is specialized drive software such as Disk Manager or EZ-Drive (both by Ontrack) that will prepare a large hard drive to work in an IDE system that won't support large HDDs through hardware. The advantage of such software is that it almost always comes *free* with the HDD, and doesn't require any additional hardware upgrade. The disadvantage is that you suffer a small performance penalty, and if the overlay is ever corrupted, you'll lose access to your drive.

If you have the choice between using overlay-type software or installing a BIOS upgrade, I usually recommend either a motherboard BIOS upgrade or installing a stand-alone drive controller with an EIDE BIOS on board (which is usually easier). As for potential problems with a BIOS upgrade, the most important problem is handling the physical IC replacement. In order to upgrade an older motherboard BIOS such as yours, you'll probably need to replace the BIOS IC—that can be tricky if you're not used to working with DIP ICs (that's why I say a stand-alone controller with its own supplemental BIOS is easier).

THE NEED FOR EZ-DRIVE WITH WINDOWS 95 AND LINUX

Q331. *I've recently installed a Seagate 32140 HDD as a second drive on my system. I will be changing it to the primary drive shortly. It came with EZ-Drive software to support 32-bit disk access for Windows and to enable recognition of more than 528MB. My BIOS (Phoenix 4.04) recognizes EIDE drives, and Windows 95 doesn't seem to have a problem with 32-bit disk access. Is there any reason to install EZ-Drive? Besides Windows 95, I'm planning on putting in a partition for Linux.*

A. No, as long as you are using Windows 95 and your BIOS provides for logical block addressing (LBA), you do *not* need to use EZ-Drive, and you'll probably get better drive performance without it. Newer versions of EZ-Drive should work with Windows 95, but chances are that it would be incompatible with Linux. On the other hand, Linux will support your hard drive as long as the BIOS does. If Linux gives you an error message about being in an area above 1024 cylinders, ignore it (that's a throwback from previous versions and not applicable to today's Linux versions).

REMOVING DISK MANAGER

Q332.   *I'll be upgrading my PC shortly with a new drive controller that supports LBA, but my drive has Disk Manager installed. How do I remove Disk Manager?*

A.   To remove Disk Manager from your drive, boot from a clean floppy disk (with no CONFIG.SYS or AUTOEXEC.BAT files). Run FDISK from the floppy disk, delete the non-DOS partition, and then run the DOS FORMAT command from the floppy disk. The DDO will be completely removed. Remember that this procedure is destructive to your data, so be sure to perform a complete system backup before proceeding.

GETTING RID OF EZ-DRIVE

Q333.   *Should EZ-Drive be deleted from the hard drive before upgrading to a motherboard with a BIOS that supports large drives, or will the BIOS override it?*

A.   Good question—if you do upgrade your system hardware to support EIDE, you no longer need to use overlay software like EZ-Drive. As I understand it, you *could* leave EZ-Drive in place on the drive without harm. If you choose to remove EZ-Drive, you'll need to backup, repartition, and reformat the drive.

REMOVING EZ-DRIVE 2.03S

Q334.   *I hope you can help with a minor difficulty. I have a Seagate 1GB disk on which I installed EZ-Drive Version 2.03S. This configuration works. I have, however, moved the drive onto a new system that has an advanced BIOS which can handle LBA—so I don't need EZ-Drive. How do I get rid of it?*

A.   According to Seagate, you should be able to remove EZ-Drive using the following procedure. Remember to always perform a complete system backup before attempting any hard drive procedures.

1. Use FDISK /MBR to wipe the master boot record.

2. Change your CMOS drive type to 2 (20MB) and boot from a floppy disk.

3. You should now see a 1MB partition as drive C: that contains several files—look for the SEAMOVE.EXE file.

4. Run SEAMOVE.EXE. This will copy the EZ-Drive installation to floppy and remove the partition.

Unfortunately, it seems that removing the partition means you will have to repartition and reformat. Since you want to use LBA (we assume you also want to use any other advanced BIOS features), you'll really have to repartition the drive anyway. But since you have done a complete backup first, it should be a simple matter to restore the drive contents.

LARGE DRIVE BECOMES SMALL

Q335.   *I've been using my 1.6GB hard drive with Disk Manager, and everything was working until I tried reinstalling DOS 6.22. After DOS installed, the drive was only 504MB. What happened? I can't find a solution to this anywhere.*

A.   The problem is that you booted from disk 1 of DOS 6.22 instead of booting from the hard drive. Once you install Disk Manager, you must always load the dynamic drive overlay (DDO) into memory *before* booting from a floppy. When you boot from the DOS installation disk, the DDO does not have a chance to load, and when DOS writes its boot information, the DDO is lost. Boot from the hard drive initially. When you see the message "press spacebar to boot from disk," press the <Space> key, insert your DOS disk, and then press any key to continue the boot process. This ensures that the DDO loads *first* before the DOS installation starts.

DEALING WITH DDO ERRORS

Q336.   What is a DDO Integrity Error and is there any way to correct it?

A.   This is a failure under Disk Manager where the dynamic drive
          overlay (DDO) fails for one reason or another. Before proceeding,
          always use a current antivirus program to check for boot sector
          viruses. To recover your drive, you'll have to restore the DDO.
          There are several means of accomplishing this. First, run DMC-
          FIG /y, and then follow the prompts to reconstruct the DDO. If
          this is unsuccessful, boot from a bootable DOS floppy disk, and
          then insert the Disk Manager disk in A:. Type DM /m to start
          Disk Manager in the manual mode. When you see the Disk
          Manager status screen, press <Alt>+<C>. At the Main Menu,
          choose hard disk installation, and then select disk 1. Choose parti-
          tion setup and configuration. On line 1, underneath TYPE, con-
          firm that it says *DOS (the * is important). With the highlighted
          bar on line 1 (the line showing *DOS), press the <W> key. The
          <W> rewrites the boot information. The highlight bar should now
          be on the line that says "Save Partition Table and Continue."
          Press <Enter> and then choose <Y> to save. Press <Esc> until you
          get back to the Main Menu, then hit <Esc> again, and exit Disk
          Manager. Remove the floppy and reboot the system. The DDO
          should come up and the system will boot to C:.

DISK MANAGER AND CACHING DRIVE CONTROLLERS

*Q337.   I've been having no end of trouble after installing Disk Manager.
          I read somewhere that a caching drive controller can cause prob-
          lems with Disk Manager. Could that be my problem? If so, will I
          have to replace my drive controller?*

A.   It is true that some caching controllers can interfere with Disk
          Manager, but the issue is rarely serious. Typically, the trouble
          comes with autoidentifying the drive, but there is a list of drives
          that you can choose from. Simply select the appropriate drive
          from the list, and operation should proceed normally. If this pre-
          sents a real problem, you can replace the drive controller (in
          which case you can remove Disk Manager since the new con-
          troller will probably support large hard drives) or disable the
          controller's cache (usually through a jumper on the controller).

Hard Drive Corrective Actions

DRIVE WON'T START UP RELIABLY

Q338. ·My *current C: drive is becoming unstable during the power-up cycle. The hard drive sometimes cannot be read. My current remedy is to bang on the side of the computer—that starts up the C: drive. I'm looking to replace my C: drive with another hard disk, but I don't want to reinstall the software all over again. What is the best way to replace the existing C: drive with a new hard disk? Is it possible for me to do it with just one computer?*

A.   Take a close look at your drive power and signal cables. I'd say you've got a bad connection. You might try disconnecting the cables and reattaching them securely. If you *must* replace the drive, you should back up the drive completely to tape using a tape drive and Windows 95 Backup. Install and prepare the new drive, install Windows 95 (and Backup), and *then* install all the files from your tape (minus the Windows 95 files already on the disk). That's the classical methodology.

NEW HARD DRIVE CAUSING DRIVE LETTER CONFLICTS

Q339. *I installed a 2.5GB hard drive in my PC. The drive is divided into two partitions because it is so large. The problem is that now I get an error message, "Cannot read from drive D:." I also see error messages like "Cannot open file," and "Cannot find file necessary for this application." I get these errors when I try to access the CD. Any ideas?*

A.   You've got a conflict problem with your drives. Your CD-ROM had been configured as D:, but now that you have two partitions on the hard drive (C: and D:), the D: partition is conflicting with the CD-ROM drive. You will need to reassign the CD-ROM drive to another drive letter. You can correct the problem by modifying the Windows 95 Registry:

1.   Choose Start, Run, and type in REGEDIT.

2.   Choose Edit, Find, and type in D:\. Then click on Find Next.

3. When an entry is found, highlight the appropriate key and choose Modify.

4. From the Modify screen, change the D:\ to E:\. Leave the rest of the entry the same so that the paths are not modified. Choose OK to save the changes.

5. Hit function key <F3> to find the next instance, and repeat steps 3 and 4.

6. Continue these steps until the message "Finished searching registry" appears.

7. Exit REGEDIT and restart the system to make sure the changes take effect.

BAD SECTORS SPREADING ON SEAGATE HDD

Q340. *My friend has a Packard Bell Pentium, with a 1.2GB Seagate HDD. The problem is that bad sectors are spreading like wildfire. I booted with a clean, write-protected floppy and scanned with the latest version McAfee antivirus software and it was clean. So what can be causing the bad sectors (1.6MB) in about a week's time? I suspect the HDD is right in the middle of a "heart attack" and that it's physically damaged. Does this seem correct?*

A. Absolutely. My first suggestion would have been to check for viruses (like the Monkey B virus), but since you've already ruled that out, it seems like you're down to the hard drive itself. I've seen this kind of behavior with hard drives before (namely a few Western Digital drives), and in all cases, the drives were failing. Your best bet is to simply back up as much of the drive as you can, and then replace the hard drive outright.

FORMATTING ERRORS WITH MAXTOR DRIVES

Q.341 *I have been given a Maxtor 7850AU, 850MB HDD. I hooked it up as a secondary drive on my backup PC and performed a FORMAT D: /S. The problem is that it will do about 15 percent of the format, and then I get the following message: "Trying to recover allocation unit 9465." This continues for over 2 hours while I hear the HDD chunking away and finally gets up to about 12000 before it ends saying 90 percent completed. Any ideas? Is the hard drive bad?*

A.   Possibly, but there are a couple of things to consider. First, take note of your BIOS version, and then call Maxtor technical support. You may need a firmware upgrade for the drive in order to correct the problem. Otherwise, you may need a motherboard BIOS upgrade. You can also double-check this by trying to repartition and reformat the drive on another PC. If you cannot resolve the problem with a firmware or BIOS upgrade, the drive may indeed be defective.

Overheated Hard Drives and System Lock-ups

Q342. *I heard a rumor recently that HDDs that get overheated will freeze a system. Is that fact or fiction? My father has a 486 system with 20MB of RAM and a brand new Maxtor 1.6GB HDD running Windows 95. The system has started freezing up after about an hour of operation, independent of the application being used. How does one resolve this situation if in fact it is true? Cooling fans? I have heard system cooling fans create more problems than they solve by increasing the heat inside the case.*

A.   Heat is a funny thing, and it can have some odd effects on your system. Let's start with your hard drive. I have heard of some older hard drives (such as Fujitsu and HP drives) becoming so hot that you couldn't write to them. Improving air flow and ventilation spacing helped to correct the problem. Today, drives are generally much more efficient with power and tend to run much cooler. As a result, your first step should be to check the hard drive and see how hot it's *really* getting. If the drive is very hot, you should remount the drive in the most isolated drive bay you can find—perhaps by itself in an internal drive bay. This alone may help the drive case to dissipate excess heat. If problems persist, you might try a fan card to blow air onto the hard drive. Another consideration is your CPU. Overheated CPUs can crash the PC. If you notice that the CPU is getting extremely hot, install a heat sink/fan to help manage the heat. You should consider the possibility of a power problem (a slightly overloaded power supply can cause the system to crash periodically). One more thing—check for dust. Dust is a great thermal insulator, and large accumulations of dust can act like a blanket over components and obstruct air flow and vents.

Overcoming the Problem of "Sticktion"

Q343.   *I have two Quantum Empire ProDrive 1GB hard drives and both have the same problem—they can't get going by themselves. When the PC is started, you can hear and feel the drives trying to start. But what you have to do to get them going is hold them in your hand and give them a quick twist. After a few tries, I can consistently get them to start spinning. At this point, they run until you shut them down, and you need to do the twist thing to get them running again.*

A.   There are two possible problems with your drives: failing spindle motors or a phenomenon known as *sticktion*. If the drives stick immediately after you reboot the system from a cold start, your problem is probably a failed spindle motor. If the drives only stick after they've been sitting for a day or two, the read/write heads are probably sticking to the platter. Sticktion was common on older hard drives with oxide-based media but is not so common today because of the improved media and the way it is applied to the platters. In either case, there is really nothing you can do to fix the drives. You should back up as much data as possible from each drive, and then replace them outright. If the drives are still under warranty (they are probably several years old now), you may be able to get Quantum to replace the drives without charge.

HDD Controller Failure with SCSI Drive

Q344.   *I finished removing my older IDE drives and replacing them with an SCSI adapter and large hard drive. But now when I boot up, I see a message that says "HDD Controller Failure." Does this mean that the SCSI controller is bad?*

A.   Probably not. The HDD Controller Error message is typically an
         IDE/EIDE error that is generated by the motherboard BIOS. This
         often occurs because there are still drive geometry settings in CMOS
         which cause BIOS to look for a drive controller. When BIOS
         decides that no drive controller is responding, it generates the error.
         Check your CMOS Setup. Set any hard drive entries to none or not
         installed. Save your changes to CMOS and reboot the system.

INACCESSIBLE HARD DRIVE IS PROBABLY DEFECTIVE

Q345.   *I am having trouble with a Western Digital WD93044-A IDE
        drive. In the original system it wouldn't boot but would allow a
        floppy boot (I get an Invalid Drive Specification error when
        attempting to access the HDD from a floppy boot). I have
        "SYSed" the drive several times with no effect. The primary par-
        tition is active. I have tried it in three machines with the same
        result. I have tried making it a slave to a working drive, and it
        prevents the master from booting. I can't get to any of the data
        on the drive. What could it be? Am I missing something basic?*

A.   If your CMOS entries and drive jumper settings are correct, I
        doubt that you're missing anything. If you can't access the drive
        from a floppy boot, and it prevents another hard drive from
        booting, I could only conclude that the drive electronics have
        failed, and the drive should be replaced. Unfortunately, there's lit-
        tle that you can do to recover the data at this point.

FAT PROBLEMS MAY SUGGEST FAULTY HARD DRIVE

Q346.   *I'm working with an AST motherboard, AWARD BIOS, EIDE
        I/O card, and an 850MB Western Digital hard drive. The prob-
        lem that I'm having is read/write errors to drive C:. When format-
        ting C:, the system will complete the format and say "Formatting
        complete. Error writing FAT track. Format terminated."*

A.   From your description of the problem and the error message, I'd
        suspect that your hard drive is probably defective. I'd bet that
        even if you tried booting from a floppy disk, the hard drive
        would still be inaccessible. Try booting from another hard

drive—I think the problem will disappear. I certainly doubt that the drive is under warranty from Western Digital at this point, but you should be able to replace the drive with a 1.6 to 2.1GB drive for a very reasonable price.

Large Hard Drive Won't Partition to Proper Size

Q347.   *I don't know what the deal is with my new hard drive. I just installed a 2.5GB Western Digital HDD. The install was success-ful and CMOS shows the correct hard drive size with auto-detect selected, but the drive only shows 504MB after running FDISK. This is driving me crazy—any suggestions?*

A.   This is invariably a problem with your system's BIOS. For exam-ple, Intel Aladdin and Zappa motherboards won't support 2.5GB hard drives while using BIOS older than 1.00.10BROT or 1.00.11BSOT. Upgrade your BIOS. You probably have flash BIOS, so upgrading should be a relatively simple matter once you download a flash file.

Hard Drive Acting Erratically and Refusing to Boot

Q348.   *I got a call because a woman's hard drive was acting up, so I brought the PC down to the lab and tried to boot it from the HDD. No luck—it just locked up without an error message or anything. The HDD was spinning, so I tried to boot from a flop-py. It started to boot and said "Starting MS-DOS..." like it should, but then it just stopped. I tried this again several times, changing BIOS settings (everything that I could think of). I tried booting from the hard drive again, but now it won't even spin. It's completely dead. I am going to give her a new HDD with Windows 95 on it, but I'm still curious about what could cause this. Maybe I can salvage her stuff.*

A.   It sounds like one of two things has happened: either the drive or the drive controller has failed. If the drive was spinning, but now it's not, check the drive's power cables. Try starting the CMOS Setup routine to see that the boot order is set to A:/C:, and try booting from the floppy drive again. If you can boot to floppy and access the C: drive, you've got a chance to back up files and data before replacing the drive. If problems continue, you'll have little choice but to replace the hard drive outright. Try the drive on another PC. If the drive fails on another PC, the drive is probably defective. If the drive works on another PC, you've probably got a faulty drive controller (try a new drive controller board).

PROBLEMS WITH HARD DRIVES OVER 4GB

Q349. *I've had some real problems using hard drives over 4GB. They seem to work well in some systems but not in others. I think it's a BIOS issue, but can you shed any light on the problem? Is there a workaround?*

A. The first EIDE drives larger than 4GB appeared on the market in early 1997. These drives seem to work in some systems and not in others. This problem is not due to a bug in the BIOS but is actually an operating system issue—pertaining to all versions of MS-DOS through 6.22. Windows 95 seems to have the same problem. The problem is that DOS cannot handle a translated drive geometry with 256 heads. You may find that these huge hard drives seem to auto-type correctly in BIOS, and the problem crops up when trying to partition the drive. The partition may seem to be created properly through FDISK, but the system hangs up when rebooting. Although this is an operating system limitation, it appears that the appropriate way to deal with this problem is to account for it in the system BIOS. Fortunately, there is a temporary workaround to the problem (until you get the BIOS upgraded).

 You should first verify that you have a new enough revision to handle drives over 2GB correctly.

Note

To set up a drive over 4GB (under an older BIOS):

1. Autodetect the drive in CMOS Setup.

2. Manually adjust the number of heads from 16 to 15.

3. Multiply the number of cylinders by 16/15 which is 1.06667, and then round down to a whole number.

4.   Adjust the number of cylinders to this larger amount.

5.   Write down these adjusted values for cylinders, heads, and sectors.

6.   Save changes to CMOS and partition and format the drive.

As an example, Table 3.5 illustrates some workaround parameters that can be used with popular models of hard drives over 4GB. While this can be considered a *temporary* workaround, there should be no problem with continuing to use a hard drive set up this way. If an updated BIOS version is used at a later date, it should not be necessary to repartition and reformat the drive.

TABLE 3.5 POSSIBLE WORKAROUNDS FOR HUGE HARD DRIVES

Model	Factory CHS Values	Workaround CHS Values
Maxtor 85120A	9924x16x63	10585x15x63
Micropolis 4550A	9692x16x63	10338x15x63

Note

The important thing to keep in mind in using the above workaround is that you must keep a record of the translation values used so that they can be reentered if the contents of CMOS RAM are lost or if the drive is moved to another system. Write the values on masking tape, and stick the tape on the drive itself.

SYSTEM WON'T BOOT WITH EIDE HDD

Q350.   *I have a PC with a Western Digital 1.6GB HDD, but the system won't boot. I can see that BIOS recognizes the hard drive, and I know the BIOS supports EIDE hard drives.*

A.   I think you may have a problem with your power-on delay. Some hard drives need a longer time to initialize before the operating system starts to load. If the drive is not "ready," it can cause start-up errors. To address this type of problem, you should start your CMOS Setup routine, go to the BIOS Advanced Setup, and adjust the Power-on Delay time to a longer value. This will cause your PC to take more time at start-up allowing enough time for the hard drive to start up.

New Hard Drive Needs a Power-On Delay

Q351. *My brother's got a problem on his P75 system. He put in a second HDD (a 1GB Seagate), and now when he cold boots, the second drive is not recognized until the machine warms up and he boots again. He has a 230 W power supply in the system, and he does not let his printer boot at the same time on his Curtis commander. Any ideas for the missing drive letter?*

A. It sounds like you have a classic power-on delay problem. Many of today's large hard drives need several seconds to initialize after power-up. If the BIOS interrogates the drive before it has a chance to initialize, the drive may "appear" missing. By the time the system boots, the drive has had a chance to initialize, so when a warm boot occurs, the new drive is ready. BIOS versions have also evolved to offer variable power-on delay settings which can hold the boot process for a bit until the drive has time to initialize. Check your CMOS Setup (see Fig. 3.3) and look for an entry such as Drive D: Timeout or D: Power-on Delay. It may be set to disabled. Try entering a number like 5 seconds or 10 seconds, save your changes, and then cold boot the system again. I'd bet the problem goes away.

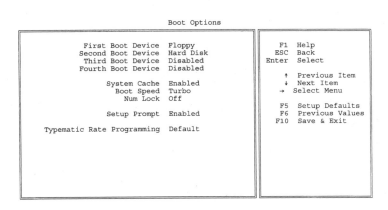

FIGURE 3.3 CONFIGURING BOOT DELAYS IN THE CMOS SETUP

HDD Gives No ROM BASIC System Error

Q352. *I recently obtained a Seagate 1162A IDE HDD. However, when I try to boot my system from the drive, I get the following message: "No ROM BASIC...System Halted." The PC boots from the A: drive, and when I install another IDE drive, the PC boots with no problems, so I know the problem is with the Seagate. Any suggestions?*

A. Well, your isolation of the Seagate HDD certainly makes things a lot easier. For some reason, your PC cannot recognize the logical hard drive. So if there is no other drive (or bootable floppy) available, the system makes a last ditch effort to load BASIC (assuming it is available on your particular BIOS). When even that is not available, the system will simply freeze since it can't do anything else.

Since you're focusing on the drive itself, start with the drive basics. Check the drive jumpers to make sure that the drive is set as the primary (or master), assuming it is the only IDE drive. Also check the drive geometry entered into the CMOS Setup. If the geometry is incorrect, the drive may not be recognized; you may also lose data. Also check the power and data cables attached to the drive and drive adapter. I know this may sound silly, but these simple checks take only a few minutes and can save you hours of troubleshooting.

If everything is right up to now and the Seagate drive still refuses to boot, there is probably a problem with the drive's partition(s)—either there are no valid partitions or the partitions available are not active. Try booting the system from a floppy disk containing FDISK, FORMAT, and SYS and then use FDISK to check the drive's partitions. See that you have at least a primary DOS partition, and that the partition is set to *active*. Once this is done, run FORMAT from the floppy disk to perform a high-level DOS format and then run SYS to transfer the system files to the HDD. You should now be able to boot from the hard drive. Unfortunately, any data that was previously on the drive is now inaccessible.

New Drive Causes Boot Failure

Q353. *I was installing a Western Digital 1.6GB EIDE hard drive and after setting up all the CMOS parameters and using FDISK, I got this error message in big bold letters (and it will not boot up with floppy or hard drive), NO ROM BASIC SYSTEM HALTED. The system refused to boot up no matter how hard I tried. What in the world is that? I consider myself fairly experienced in installing and configuring hard drives, and I had done it quite a few times in the past, but I have never gotten this type of error message. My computer is 5x86 133 MHz with 24MB of RAM. I reinstalled my old hard drive, and it worked perfectly. Can you tell me what's going on?*

A. This is an interesting problem because you have no boot device at all (not even the floppy drive is working). If that's the case, I suggest that you first check your drive controller and all the drive signal cables. Make sure that the drive controller board is installed correctly in its bus slot, and see that all the drive cables are attached properly. The next problem is possibly your drive boot order. Check your CMOS Setup and make sure the boot order is A:/C: so that the system will look for a bootable floppy *first*. If that's the problem, run FDISK again and make sure your partition is active, and then run FORMAT C: /S to make the hard drive partition bootable. That should get you going.

Keep in mind that you are working on a somewhat older system—a 486 motherboard with an AMD 5x86 CPU installed. Your motherboard's BIOS may not be able to support a 1.6GB HDD. You may need to upgrade your BIOS or install an EIDE controller with its own on-board BIOS.

Dealing with a Missing Operating System Error

Q354. *My friend's PC was not booting up; it was continually getting a Missing Operating System error. What can we do about this? Should we reformat the drive?*

A. Before you go through the trouble of reformatting the drive, make it a point to check the drive geometry in the CMOS Setup. Make sure that you have not accidentally lost the CMOS drive settings. If so, restore the settings (or select auto-detect if possible), save the CMOS setup, and restart the system (it is always a good idea to record your CMOS settings on paper before problems arise). If the trouble continues, you should try booting from a floppy disk and then make a complete system backup of the hard drive to tape. You can then rewrite the operating system files by typing SYS C: or reformatting the drive with FORMAT C: /S. Once you can boot from the hard drive again, reload your drive from the tape backup.

FINDING A MISSING OPERATING SYSTEM ON A NEW DRIVE

Q355. *I just finished putting my new system together, and I'm experiencing some problems already. I'm trying to install Windows 95, so I made a DOS partition, formatted my new Seagate hard drive, and installed MS-DOS. But after MS-DOS is done installing and the system restarts, an error message says "Missing operating system." What's the deal with that?*

A. The Missing Operating System error doesn't mean that DOS is not installed. It means that the drive cannot find the three files needed to boot the drive (IO.SYS, MSDOS.SYS, and COMMAND.COM). This happens a lot, and there are several common oversights that can affect you. The first typical mistake is made during partitioning. You must make your first partition active and bootable (it must be a primary DOS partition). If you create any other kind of DOS partition, it will be accessible but not bootable. The second typical mistake is to format without transferring system files. You should use FORMAT C: /S, or use the FORMAT command and then use SYS C: to transfer system files to the drive.

DEALING WITH AN INVALID MEDIA TYPE ERROR

Q356. *What does the Invalid Media Type error message mean? How many possible reasons are there? I'm starting to see this message more and more on my system.*

A. Part of the boot information contained on every disk (hard drive or floppy) includes a media descriptor byte, which identifies the type of media being used. If this descriptor byte is not recognized, the system generates an Invalid Media Type error. This is a very serious error (especially for hard drives) and can easily prevent the disk from booting. Given the intermittent nature of the error, I'd say your drive is having problems reading the disk. For floppy disks, you may simply need to clean the drive's read/write heads. If floppy problems persist, you should replace the floppy drive outright. For hard drives, you should back up the drive, repartition and reformat the disk and then restore the back up. If problems continue with a hard drive, you should replace the drive.

SCSI Controller Causes Second IDE Drive Fault

Q357. *When I put my SCSI controller into the system, my second IDE hard drive fails. What's causing this?*

A. In almost all cases, the problem is related to your SCSI BIOS. If your system is booting from your IDE drive(s), try disabling the SCSI BIOS (usually through a jumper on the SCSI controller). The SCSI BIOS is only needed when booting from an SCSI drive, so disabling the SCSI BIOS should clear the problem and free up space in the UMA.

Hidden Hard Drive

Q358. *I have two hard drives in my computer. When I turn on the computer, only the first hard drive shows up. If I soft boot the system with <Ctrl>+<Alt>+<Del>, both drives show up. What is wrong? How do I get both drives to show up the first time?*

A. If the hard drive starts on a warm boot, but not on a cold boot this can imply a BIOS timing problem. The BIOS may be attempting to access the hard drive before the drive itself has initialized. Check the CMOS Setup screen for any of the following options and set them accordingly:

ADVANCED

Quick Power on Self-Test	Disable
Fast Boot Option	Disable
Hard Disk Initialization time-out	Set to 30 seconds
Above 1MB or any RAM count option;	Enable

SCSI HDD Won't Boot

Q359.   *I've got an HP Pavilion 7020 system using a Morrison mother-board. I want the system to boot from my Quantum 3.2GB Fireball SCSI drive set as ID0. My NCR/Symbios Logic PCI-SC200 Fast SCSI adapter is installed and connected properly (terminations are OK also). One wrinkle—I have an ATAPI CD-ROM drive in the system, but there are no EIDE/IDE hard drives. Why won't the Fireball boot? Is the system trying to boot from the CD-ROM?*

A.   No, the system is not attempting to boot from the CD-ROM, but it cannot boot from the SCSI drive because the NCR SCSI adapter does not have an SCSI BIOS needed by the Fireball in order to boot. Replace your NCR adapter with an Adaptec (or similar) SCSI controller with a built-in SCSI BIOS, and that should enable you to boot the system. Also, AMI BIOS generally does not function well with NCR 810 SCSI chipsets.

Fixing Bad Sectors

Q360.   *I've been having some drive problems, and ScanDisk reports a few bad sectors. How do I go about fixing the problem?*

A.   Bad sectors are caused by such issues as drive age, defective media, or head crashes. The loss of just a few sectors are rarely a problem (although any files recorded there are now damaged), and you will need to run a utility which can perform a surface analysis of the drive and mark out any bad sectors. Today, most drives keep several tracks in reserve and can substitute defective sectors with good sectors from those spare tracks. Most drives provide a specialized utility which can mark out and remap sectors. Such a utility is typically provided on the disk that accompanied the drive or can be obtained from the drive maker's Web site. For example, WDATIDE.EXE is the defect management utility for Western

Digital drives. You may also be able to use the surface analysis feature of ScanDisk to mark out defective sectors, but it may be unable to use spare sectors. Keep in mind that any drive defect management can be destructive to your data, so be sure to perform a complete system backup before using defect management software.

SCSI Drive Size Limits

Q361. *What's wrong with my hard drive? I just added a 2.1GB SCSI drive to my system, and no matter what I do, I just can't seem to use the full drive size. Do you know what's going on?*

A.   Possibly. This is a complaint commonly associated with older SCSI controllers. DOS 4.x and above has a limitation of 1024 cylinders per physical drive. Since older SCSI host adapters utilize a standard of 1MB per cylinder, a limit of 1GB is imposed for every physical drive. You should be able to get around this limit by using a more recent SCSI host adapter (such as an Adaptec AHA-1542B). Keep in mind that if you replace your current SCSI host adapter, you'll probably need to repartition and reformat your SCSI hard drives and install new drivers for other SCSI devices.

Installing Huge Hard Drive Hangs Up System

Q362. *I've got an HDD installation question. I put in a 5.1GB Maxtor as the primary drive, completely removing my current HDD. I made the boot disk, went into CMOS and entered the proper values for the HDD (9924,16,63), saved it, and booted to the floppy. Everything was OK up to there. I then ran FDISK. When it asked if I wanted to make the partition the largest available (at least I **think** that's what it said), I said Yes. It did its thing and now I can't get back to the system. When it boots, it checks A:, reads it for a little bit, and then the whole system hangs up at the blue screen that tells the basic CMOS settings. It won't continue booting from A:. Did I err in asking for the largest partition instead of specifying 2.1GB? How can I get back to the FDISK utility? I just can't get it to boot all the way to A:. I even went back and remastered the boot disk. I tried booting from the original DOS 6.22 disk but still no luck.*

A.   I think your problem has to do with your CMOS Setup entries for the new hard drive. Go back to CMOS when the system first starts and change the drive entry to auto-detect. This causes BIOS to query the drive for its geometry each time the system starts. If you cannot use an auto-detect entry, recheck the drive geometry to see if there might be another translation you can use. While you're in CMOS, check for the boot order entry and make sure it's set to A:/C: so that the system will boot from the A: drive if there is bootable media available. At that point, you should be able to boot to A: and restart FDISK. Erase any existing partitions and (as you suggested) keep your partition sizes to 2.1GB or less—you'd probably make two 2GB partitions, and one 1GB partition.

PROBLEMS GETTING TWO SCSI DRIVES RECOGNIZED

Q363.   *I'm trying to get my Adaptec AHA1542CF to find two SCSI hard drives. One is an IBM DFHS, and the other is an old IMPRIMIS from a Vax. When I hook them up individually and have the AHA BIOS set to scan for SCSI devices, it finds the drive. I can format and use the drive properly. But when I hook both up, I only get the lowest SCSI ID drive assigned to a drive letter. Any ideas here?*

A.   I have personally never configured old Vax hardware for the PC, so I am uncertain as to whether the age of the hardware may cause some incompatibilities when mixed with other SCSI devices, but that is a possibility you should consider. When configuring modern SCSI equipment, there are two major issues that can cause identification problems: the SCSI bus is terminated improperly or both SCSI devices are using the same ID. When two SCSI drives are connected, only the SCSI adapter and end-most SCSI device should be terminated. Check your termination. Also make sure that the two drives are set to ID0 and ID1 (the classic IDs for SCSI hard drives).

Unrelated Boot Failures May Share a Similar Cause

Q364. *Recently, the same chronic behavior has been exhibited by two dissimilar drives in two unrelated systems. On system power-up, the drive is inaccessible (although the drive is spinning and its power supply levels are correct). I found an incorrect entry in the CMOS system setup. When the correct entry was entered and saved, the system was rebooted. However, the drive failed again—even though the correct settings were **still** in CMOS Setup. After several reboots, the system finally uses the hard drive, which works until the next reboot. Any ideas?*

A. Since this problem seems to have started on several systems at the same time, I urge you to run a current virus checking utility on your affected systems—as well as on other systems that you may have recently exchanged floppy disks with. If your systems pass virus checking, you can focus on the hardware attributes of the systems. Start with your drives themselves and see that their signal cables are securely attached at both the drive and controller ends. Make sure that the drive controller boards are inserted into their bus slots completely. You also might try moving the drive controllers to another slot away from other boards and route the drive signal cables away from other devices in the system such as the power supply, cooling fans, and the video adapter. A shorter drive signal cable may also help. If problems persist, try repartitioning and reformatting the drives (make sure to back up the drives completely first). If all else fails, replace the hard drives entirely (although I doubt that you would have to replace two hard drives).

SCSI Hard Drive Suddenly Lost

Q365. *I hope you can help me. I've had an SCSI hard drive working for months now. But yesterday, the PC refused to even recognize the SCSI drive. I need the data on this drive, so I hope you might be able to point me in the right direction.*

A.   That's not a good sign. Sudden failures can be caused by three things: the addition of new hardware or software, the introduction of a computer virus, or a hardware fault in the drive or controller. Boot from a write-protected floppy disk first and run a current virus checker. If your problem cropped up after adding new hardware or software, try removing the offending item—you may have a hardware or software conflict. If the failure was just spontaneous, check the SCSI cable and termination units. Try another SCSI cable if possible. If the SCSI host adapter has a built-in diagnostic, run that diagnostic and see if any faults are detected. A fault would suggest a problem with the host adapter, so replace the SCSI adapter. Otherwise, the drive may have failed. Try a new hard drive in the system to see if the SCSI adapter will recognize it. Without a backup, you may be out of luck with the data.

INVALID DRIVE ERRORS WITH DRIVESPACE 3

Q366.   *I have a hard drive which is compressed with DriveSpace 3. While installed as my secondary (or slave) drive, it worked properly. But when I reconfigured the drive as the primary (master) drive, I get an Invalid Drive error message. I know that I jumpered the drive correctly, so what's the problem?*

A.   You were right to change your jumpers, but it takes more than jumpers to configure your hard drives. Check your CMOS Setup and see that the corresponding drive entry is set with the correct geometry (or set to auto-detect). Also, your secondary drive may not have system files on it. You may need to use the SYS command from a bootable floppy disk in order to transfer the system files to the host drive (the noncompressed portion of your drive). Remember, any time you make changes to the setup of your hard drive, you risk data loss or corruption. You may want to perform a complete backup of your hard drive before proceeding.

"WRITE PROTECTED DISK" ERROR ON COMPRESSED DRIVE

Q367.   *My neighbors asked me to take a look at their computer. They have a Laser 386, and the C: drive has Stacker compression software on it. Boot-up goes directly to DOS rather than Windows.*

*Upon typing WIN, an error message comes up saying that a sys-tem error has occurred: "Write protected disk is in drive C:."
This error message occurs every time I try to access any program
and does not seem to want to go away even after multiple mouse
clicks on the OK button. I ran some of the basis diagnostic pro-grams found in the AMI BIOS, and the hard drive appears to be
OK. Can you offer any suggestions about where I should begin?*

A. Always check for computer viruses first, and eliminate any virus-es that you detect. From your description of the problem, it
sounds like the compressed volume has been damaged. If Stacker
boots up with errors, it will still attempt to boot but will refuse
write permission until any errors have been corrected. This fea-ture helps to keep collateral damage to the STACVOL.DSK file at
a minimum. Once in DOS, find the Stacker directory and run
CHECK /F to check and fix the drive. After CHECK /F runs to
repair your errors, the error message should disappear, and you
should regain write permission.

OLD HDD IN A NEW MOTHERBOARD

Q368. *I have a fairly new PC (one that supports large, or EIDE drives).
However, rather than buy a new drive just yet, I decided to drop
in an older IDE hard drive that I had laying around from an
older PC. The problem is that the system refuses to recognize the
IDE drive. I'm pretty good at drive upgrades and such, so I
know the drive is jumpered right, and it's set to auto-detect in
CMOS Setup. Any other ideas before I dump the drive?*

A. Assuming the drive is jumpered and cabled correctly, I think you
may have a problem with your translation mode in the CMOS
Setup. Many older PC BIOS versions supported *only* the CHS
(Cylinder/Head/Sector) addressing mode for IDE disk drives—even if
the IDE drive itself was capable of supporting a more advanced
translation mode. And when this IDE drive is connected to another
motherboard in auto-detect mode, the drive will tell your system
which translation modes it is capable of supporting. The problem is
that the drive cannot tell the system which mode was being used
when the drive was formatted. This is where I think your problem is:
The BIOS is not identifying the drive with the same parameters used
in your original system, so the drive cannot be read.

There are generally two ways around the problem. First, you can force the new system to use CHS translation mode. To do this, go to your CMOS Setup, set the hard drive type to auto-detect, and set the IDE Translation Mode to CHS (instead of another mode such as LBA). Second, you could simply reformat the drive to use a different translation mode. This is destructive, and any data on the hard drive will be lost:

1.   In the CMOS Setup, the hard drive type should be set for auto-detect, and IDE Translation Mode should be set for CHS.

2.   From a DOS-bootable floppy, use the DOS FDISK utility to delete any existing partitions on the hard drive.

3.   Reset the system and enter the CMOS Setup. Change the entry for the hard drive type to auto-configured, and IDE Translation Mode to auto-detected.

4.   Use the DOS FDISK utility to create at least one new partition.

Hard Drive Stalls Starting MS-DOS

Q369.   *A couple of days ago, I tried to boot up my system. But when I should have seen "Starting MS-DOS," the system just stopped (I am able to boot from floppy). I went as far as reformatting the drive and reloading the OS, but that still didn't help. I also tried another HDD which was known to be working, and the system did the same thing. The odd thing is that I don't get a "Missing operating system" message or anything else to that effect. Does this sound like it could be my IDE controller?*

A.   Whenever you encounter boot problems with a hard drive, it is always wise to check for viruses first. In this case, you did test against another known-good hard drive, so chances are that a virus or drive failure is not the problem, but it would still be prudent to boot from a floppy disk and run a current anti-virus program. Also take a look at your system's CMOS settings and make sure that your setup is correct. Once the system checks clean of viruses and you have verified the CMOS Setup, you can focus on the drive controller. I suspect that the reason you may not have seen an error message is because you did not wait long enough. POST will often take 1 or 2 minutes of checking before registering an error. Try a new drive controller. If your current controller is on the motherboard, you will need to disable the motherboard drive ports before installing the new controller card.

FILES CORRUPTED AS DISK FILLS UP

Q370. *I have an AT&T Pentium 60 system (OPTi motherboard and Award BIOS that supports LBA). Setting it up with DOS, everything seemed OK until I tried to test it by completely filling up the drive. Whenever the drive approached total use, the files would get corrupted. Three different types of drive from two different manufacturers did the same thing. Any ideas?*

A. There's a lot that you haven't told me, but I can give you some pointers. First, check your CMOS Setup and verify that your LBA support is actually enabled. You might also try setting the drive type to auto-detect in order to let BIOS identify the drive. If your CMOS Setup is configured properly, check your DOS version. I seem to recall that an older version of DOS (I believe it was 6.0) had a bug which allowed file corruption when addressing clusters between 65,280 and 65,535. Since your AT&T system probably uses an OEM DOS version, you may need to contact AT&T for a DOS patch.

CD-ROM Terminology and General Topics

THE CD LIGHT

Q371. *I don't understand my CD light. When my PC starts, the green CD light comes on and stays on, but the drive seems to work all right. Is the light supposed to do that, or is the CD broken?*

A.   That's a good question. When a drive light stays on, it often indicates that one end of the signal cable has been inserted backward. But since you mention that the drive works properly, I
believe that the behavior you're seeing is normal for your drive. I
suspect that when you're actually reading the disc, the drive light
flickers. If you take the disc out of the drive and close the door,
I'll bet the light goes out.

CD-ROM LED Stays Lit

Q372.   *My new CD-ROM's drive light stays lit—even when the system
boots. What could possibly cause this?*

A.   You almost certainly have the data ribbon cable reversed. The
red (or blue) strip of the data cable must go to pin 1. Pin 1 is
usually closest to the power connector.

High Sierra versus ISO-9660

Q373.   *I've been looking at documentation for older CD-ROM drives,
and I noticed the term* High Sierra. *I thought ISO-9660 was the
CD-ROM standard. What's the difference between High Sierra
and ISO-9660?*

A.   From a practical standpoint, there's very little difference between the
two standards. High Sierra is the older U.S. standard for CD-ROMs.
Once the standard was submitted to the International Standards
Association, it was accepted (with a few changes) as ISO-9660. An
old CD recorded in High Sierra format should work in any current
CD-ROM drive, but current CDs may not work in CD-ROM drives
manufactured before ISO-9660. Today, virtually all CDs made for
the PC are compatible with ISO-9660 and High Sierra.

The CD-ROM Books

Q374.   *What do all those "colored books" mean for CD-ROMs?*

A.   CD-ROM drives are defined by a series of standards. Each standard is bound in a jacket of a unique color, and the color is often used to designate the standard. You should probably recognize the following standards. Keep in mind that these standards do not apply to DVD discs, which have their own set of standards.

- Red Book is the common name of the Compact Disc Digital Audio Standard. When a disc conforms to the red book standard, it will usually have "Digital Audio" printed below the Disc logo. Most music CDs conform to this standard.

- Yellow Book is the classic standard for program CDs like games and other software discs. When a disc conforms to the yellow book, it will usually say "Data Storage" beneath the Disc logo.

- Green Book is the CD-i (compact disc interactive) standard.

- Orange Book is the standard for write-once compact discs (CD recorders).

- Blue Book is the standard for LaserDiscs (laser video discs, not DVD).

HANDLING THE CD

Q375.   *How should I handle a typical compact disc?*

A.   Compact discs are generally regarded as robust and reliable media, but there are some important precautions that can help to protect your CD investment.

- Keep your CD-ROM discs clean. Use a soft, clean cloth dampened with demineralized water or a commercial disc cleaning solution. Do not use cleaners or detergents.

- Wipe the discs radially from the center straight out to the edge—*never* in a circular motion. A scratch in the shape of an arc could make your disc unreadable. Dry the disc thoroughly before inserting it in the drive.

- Avoid touching the disc surface. Handle discs by their edges.

- Never write on a disc with a ball-point pen or pencil—a scratch on the label side of a disc can damage the data layer.

- Avoid exposing discs to direct sunlight, and avoid storing them in areas subject to high temperature or high humidity.

- Store discs in "jewel" cases to avoid dust, dirt, scratches, and bending. Never bend a disc.

DIRT AND CD-ROM DRIVES

Q376. *Can a dirty CD or dirty lens damage my player?*

A. Not a chance While computer retailers would like you to believe that (and sell you cleaning kits), there's no way that dirt on the CD or optical tracking mechanism can damage the CD-ROM drive. The worse that could happen is that you get Drive Not Ready errors or similar messages. Cleaning the disc or blowing down the optical mechanism with compressed air will help avoid errors.

SETTING THE CD-ROM IN CMOS

Q377. *Even though I have an ATAPI CD-ROM, it wasn't set in the CMOS. I'm wondering if it really matters, since I haven't seen any difference. It works the way it is, and if I do set it in the CMOS, there is no difference.*

A. I'm not surprised. In almost all cases, the CD-ROM is not given *any* assignment in CMOS. Its drive entry is simply left as none or not installed. Instead of BIOS, the CD-ROM is handled by its low-level driver software. This trend is changing with the introduction of "bootable" CD-ROM drives, but my guess is that you do not have the drive or BIOS version necessary to support that feature yet.

IDE CD-ROM JUMPER SETTINGS

Q378. *I just received my 12X IDE CD-ROM drive (a generic model named Maverick 8622K) and have a pretty basic question. I got no documentation with the drive, but it has three jumper positions on it: CS, SL, and MA. If MA is master and SL is slave, what is the CS position? Which should I use for installing the drive as the only device on my secondary IDE channel?*

A.   The CS position means "cable select," which allows the cable (and BIOS) to determine the drive assignment. Considering that EIDE interfaces only support two devices on any one channel, I don't know of any circumstance where choosing cable select would be superior to choosing a master or slave assignment. For your CD-ROM, set it as the master drive on your secondary IDE channel.

CD-ROM Drive Doesn't Depend on LBA

Q379.   *A friend of mine has been told that if she buys an IDE CD-ROM, she will only be able to access the first 528MB of data unless she has a BIOS that supports LBA or unless she uses a disk manager. I think her source is confused. Can you confirm that all of the data is accessible on an IDE interface CD-ROM even if LBA is not supported?*

A.   The drive-size limitation is just for hard drives controlled by the motherboard BIOS. The CD-ROM is not related to the BIOS, and its drivers (and MSCDEX) are not restricted. Still, I would recommend that your friend update her drive controller to a dual-channel EIDE model with its own on-board BIOS. The IDE CD-ROM should be installed as the master drive on the secondary drive channel. This configuration will make it much easier to upgrade the hard drives later on.

Making the Most of an Aztech CD-ROM

Q380.   *I have an old 2x CD-ROM drive (Model CDA 268-01A) manufactured by Aztech Systems. It uses a 40-pin interface, but I'm not sure if it's IDE or not. Can you tell me what type of interface this drive uses, and what kind of controller card it will work with?*

A.   According to our information, the 268-01A is an IDE CD-ROM drive, but its hardware support is limited. The only controller cards that these IDE drives are known to support are Aztech controllers. As a result, you may not be able to use the drive on standard IDE ports. You can find some limited driver support at *ftp.aztech.com.sg*.

Disabling Autoinsert Notification

Q381. *I need more performance out of my system. When the CD-ROM drive is running, it flashes regularly even though there's no CD in it. What's going on here, and is there any way to stop it?*

A.   What you're seeing is known as Autoinsert Notification (AIN). This is a feature of Windows 95 that allows the system to detect new CDs that are inserted into the drive, and to execute Auto Run routines. This is intended to provide a convenience by eliminating the need to manually start installation procedures or launch CD applications. Unfortunately, the system must regularly interrogate the CD-ROM drive in order to determine whether the CD has changed. The resulting overhead slows system performance. For systems that were a bit slow to begin with, the burden of Auto Insert Notification can be frustrating. Use the following steps to disable the AIN:

1.   Double-click the My Computer icon on your Windows 95 desktop.

2.   Right-click the icon representing your CD-ROM drive. A menu appears.

3.   Select Autoplay on the menu.

4.   Follow instructions that appear.

Identifying CD-ROM Ports on a Sound Blaster

Q382. *I've recently come across a Sound Blaster 16 MultiCD sound card that is equipped with three switchable CD-ROM interfaces: Panasonic/MKE, Sony, and Mitsumi. Can you tell me if these are SCSI or IDE interfaces—or something different? I'll be using it with a newer 8X Teac IDE drive connected to the secondary on-board IDE interface but may someday want to connect to the sound card instead.*

A.   All three interfaces on that sound board are *proprietary*—not ATAPI IDE. Creative Labs also makes a card with a true IDE interface or an Adaptec AHA-1510 SCSI host adapter on the card. Be careful; some proprietary interfaces use 40 pins, so it can be easy to confuse them with IDE interfaces. If your CD-ROM came prepackaged with the sound board, you should be able to use the appropriate proprietary interface directly. With IDE drives, you can choose whether to use an IDE interface on the sound card (if it is so equipped) or the IDE interface on your drive controller.

CLEANING A CD-ROM DRIVE

Q383.   *I have an NEC 4X SCSI CD-ROM. Sometimes the CD-ROM cannot read the CD, but sometimes it can with no problem. I use the CD-ROM for Windows 95. I have been checking the Device Manager, but it doesn't show anything wrong. Do you have any ideas?*

A.   I've experienced a similar problem with a Sony 4X CD-ROM in a Compaq system. For 2 weeks it had been sporadically displaying a blue screen saying I need to reinsert the CD or that the CD needs cleaning. So I semi-dismantled the CD-ROM, cleaned the lens with isopropyl alcohol and cotton swabs, then dried the lens with fresh swabs, and put the drive back together. So far it's been working fine. If you don't like the idea of actually getting into a CD-ROM drive, you can try blowing out any dust or debris with a can of photography-grade compressed air. As a side note, always make sure that the CD itself is clean and free of nicks or scratches.

INTERMEDIATE

BOOTING FROM A CD-ROM

Q384.   *I am putting together a new computer based on the Asus T55P2P4 motherboard. In the CMOS Setup where you normally have boot from A then C or C then A, it also lists "CD-ROM" as a third choice (as well as in various combinations). How can I use this feature with an 8x Creative Labs CD-ROM? Does the CD-ROM have to be on the main drive controller channels instead of the Sound Blaster 32 card (although it's an IDE interface)? Can it be used at all with ordinary CD-ROM drives, or must the drive itself support this feature?*

A.   The new generation of BIOS that is appearing today is now supporting bootable CD-ROM. It takes three things to handle bootable CD-ROM: (1) the right BIOS, (2) a bootable CD-ROM drive, and (3) a bootable CD. You already seem to have the right BIOS, but you need a drive and boot CD to complete the picture. Your Creative Labs CD-ROM drive won't work because it still needs a driver loaded in order for the system to talk to the CD-ROM hardware. This means the PC must have already booted. Although you would have a tough time *making* a bootable CD yourself, many of the latest systems are shipping with a boot CD which can be used in emergencies.

CD-ROM Needs an Audio Cable

Q385.   *I connected my NEC CD-ROM, but it won't play music CDs through the speakers. I have everything working except this part. The sound card is by Acer Open. I can play .AVI, .WAV, and MIDI files, but no CD Audio. Since it is playing .AVI files with sound, I believe this is using the audio cable. I also tried headphones for the CD-ROM and it worked playing an audio CD. Am I missing a driver?*

A.   You're real close on this one. Data files like .AVI, .WAV, and MIDI files are *not* CD audio files—they are data which is passed along the CD-ROM's signal cable. Only CD audio uses that narrow, four-wire audio cable (Fig. 3.4) to connect the CD-ROM and sound card. Make sure the CD audio cable is actually attached between the CD-ROM and sound board. You should also make sure that the sound cable is wired properly for the sound board (some OEM sound boards swap the wires for CD audio). Next, check the sound board's mixer applet and see that the CD Audio level is set to an acceptable level.

Figure 3.4 Typical CD audio cable assembly

CD-ROM Changer Cannot Play CD Audio

Q386. *I just purchased an NEC MultiSpin 4x4 CD-ROM changer. It has PIO mode 3 support, and the interface is EIDE. I have it installed with an ISA drive controller board. I connected it as a slave to my IDE hard drive, and it recognizes all four of my drives. I have no manual with the CD-ROM, but the drivers came with it. I will upgrade the motherboard to a Pentium when I can afford it. In the meantime, it will not read CD audio. Can the changer be used on an IDE controller in an ISA slot? I do have a sound card with an IDE controller which I haven't tried yet. Will I have to wait for a motherboard upgrade?*

A. CD audio is handled by a direct cable connection between your CD-ROM changer and your sound board. If that slender, four-wire audio cable is not attached, you won't get CD audio no matter what you do. Some CD audio cables are also incompatible between CD-ROM drives and sound boards (they flip a wire or two that can interfere with sound). You might consider trying a different CD audio cable. Once you have the CD audio cable attached properly, open the sound board's mixer applet and make sure that the CD Audio volume is turned up appropriately.

While I recommend PCI drive controller boards, you should be able to run your hard drive and CD-ROM from an ISA drive controller with no problem. Ordinarily, I would suggest placing the CD-ROM drive as a master device on its own IDE channel, but since the CD-ROM changer is designed specifically to support relatively fast PIO mode 3 data transfers (11.1MB/s), it should coexist with your hard drive on the same channel.

Odd Cable Indicates a Proprietary CD-ROM

Q387. *I inherited a used 2X CD-ROM which I'd like to use on my system for loading software. The drive has a 34-pin interface cable, so obviously it's not a 40-pin IDE drive. I was told that this is an SCSI cable, and the CD-ROM needs its own controller card or the sound card that came with it in order to run. It's a Sony model CDU 33A-01. Is this true? If so, where can I find a controller for it?*

A.   Sony's CDU 33A (and the single-speed CDU 31A) both use Sony
      proprietary interfaces—not SCSI, which would be a 50-pin con-
      nector. The single-speed card is an OPA-344-01, the 2X card had
      a similar number. The problem is that it's virtually impossible to
      find a sound card with an authentic Sony 34-pin interface any-
      more. You can check with the Creative Labs Web site
      (*www.creaf.com*). There may still be a sound card offering sever-
      al proprietary CD-ROM interfaces (i.e., Sony, Panasonic, and
      Mitsumi) which you can find in stores or available through liqui-
      dation sales. Personally, I think that would be a lot of work for
      an old CD-ROM. You could get an 8X IDE CD-ROM drive
      today for a *very* reasonable price.

Moving from Proprietary to IDE CD-ROMs

Q388. *I have a 2X Panasonic CD-ROM drive installed on a Gravis
       Ultrasound Max. A friend is giving me his old 4X Mitsumi since
       he is upgrading. I don't think the Ultrasound will support it, and
       anyway he had it installed on his IDE slaved with the hard drive.
       I currently am running a Tekram EIDE caching controller with
       4MB installed. I have two drives on channel 0 (a master and
       slave drive). If the Gravis doesn't support the CD-ROM, will I
       have any problems running it on the controller channel 1? How
       is it addressed, and what drivers do I need?*

A.   If your hand-me-down CD-ROM drive is indeed IDE, the Gravis
      board will probably not support it, so you should be sure to dis-
      able the Gravis CD interface (if possible) before installing the
      new CD-ROM. Since two hard drives are already installed on
      your primary EIDE/IDE channel, you should jumper the new
      Mitsumi drive as a master drive, and place it on the secondary
      IDE channel. As for drivers, you will need a DOS driver for DOS
      and Windows 3.1x operation and a protected-mode driver for
      Windows 95 (although the Windows 95 installation CD will
      probably have a suitable driver already).

TROUBLE RECONFIGURING A CD-ROM FOR IDE SUPPORT

Q389. *I have an old sound card that apparently will not support my 6X
CD-ROM drive, so I wanted to connect the CD-ROM into the
IDE interface on the motherboard. It didn't work (I got a
buzzing sound at boot, and the system refused to start). Do I
need to change the hard drive to a master drive? I am running
Windows 95. The sound card is an Aztech, and the CD-ROM is
a Turtle Beach. There is only one hard drive in the system, and it
is an 850MB Connor. I am using a BIOS hardware upgrade (an
ISA card) that supports LBA. Any ideas why it doesn't work?*

A. That's a tough one, and I am very concerned with that buzzing
sound you reported. First, you must be sure that the CD-ROM
drive is indeed an IDE drive. Some proprietary interfaces use a
40-pin interface which can resemble an IDE port. If the interface
is proprietary, it will certainly not work without a matching
interface. The fact that your sound card is old suggests that it has
a proprietary interface.

If the CD-ROM is IDE, you should make the hard drive your
master device on the primary drive controller port. If you have a
secondary IDE port in the system, I would highly recommend that
you make the CD-ROM a master device on the secondary IDE
port. If you don't have a secondary IDE port, you might consider
adding a new sound board with a true IDE interface on board. If
the problem persists, you can try making the CD-ROM your slave
device along side of the hard drive, but there are some circumstances where the hard drive and CD-ROM won't work together.

If you still cannot get the CD-ROM to work, try a known-good
IDE CD-ROM drive. When a known-good drive works as
expected, your CD-ROM drive may simply be defective (or not
IDE after all). If the known-good CD-ROM drive also cannot
run, you should consider the possibility of an interface problem
or a power supply overload.

INSTALLING A SECOND CD-ROM DRIVE

Q390. *How would you install two CD-ROM drives on a motherboard with an on-board IDE controller where the existing primary channel runs the hard drive, and the secondary channel runs a CD-ROM? To add another one, would you run it off the secondary channel like a slave drive, or would it be better to run it off the sound card? Could you just "Y" the audio cable to the sound card?*

A.   There are a few things to consider when planning a second CD-ROM drive. First, you *can* connect it as a slave drive on the secondary IDE channel. That makes the cabling pretty straightforward. However, you will need to add a second low-level driver for the new CD-ROM and to update MSCDEX in AUTOEXEC.BAT with a second /D: designation for the new drive's letter. Like IDE drives, not all makes and models of CD-ROM drives are interchangeable. If you have problems getting two CD-ROMs to work together, try reversing their master/slave relationships. Finally, you should not "Y" the audio cable—simply leave one CD with the audio cable connected and leave the other drive disconnected (data cable only). That should take care of things.

CD-ROMs NOT ACCESSIBLE AFTER ADDING SECOND CD-ROM

Q391. *I had a CD-ROM in my system that was working well, but I've installed a second CD-ROM, and now I can't access either drive. What could have happened?*

A.   Check the MSCDEX line in your AUTOEXEC.BAT file. If there was a CD-ROM drive previously installed, there will probably now be *two* lines that load MSCDEX. The problem is that MSCDEX is a terminate and stay resident (TSR) program that can be loaded only *once*; the device names of all CD-ROM drives must be included on the same line after MSCDEX. For example, if the two lines in your AUTOEXEC.BAT file are:

```
C:\DOS\MSCDEX.EXE /D:MTMIDE01

C:\DOS\MSCDEX.EXE /D:MSCD001
```

They should be combined on one line to read:

```
C:\DOS\MSCDEX.EXE /D:MTMIDE01 /D:MSCD001
```

The order in which device names appear is the order in which drive letters will be assigned to them.

Note

RUNNING SCSI AND IDE CD-ROM DRIVES TOGETHER

Q392. *I have a Media Vision Fusion Double CD 16 kit that I installed a couple years ago on my old 486. It's a fairly decent 16 bit sound card (Pro Audio Studio 16) that came with a 2X SCSI CD-ROM drive. The drive is currently plugged into the sound card. Do you know if I could use a 6X or 8X ATAPI drive in addition to this current CD and sound card? Of course, I would have to connect the drive to the secondary channel in this new Tyan Tomcat motherboard. I was just wondering if there's any conflict between sound card and IDE drive. I guess I could always get a new SCSI CD-ROM instead, but the IDE drives are much cheaper.*

A. The answer to your overall question is Yes. You can leave your current sound board and SCSI CD-ROM drive in place and install a new IDE CD-ROM drive on your secondary IDE channel off the motherboard. As long as there is no hardware conflict between the SCSI adapter and secondary IDE port resources, and you install the ATAPI drivers properly, you should be OK. The only real consideration is your audio cable. Since there can only be one audio cable running to the sound card, you must decide whether to continue running audio from the slower 2X SCSI CD-ROM drive or to run from the newer ATAPI CD-ROM drive. If you plan to use games and other multimedia-intensive applications, I suggest that you run your audio from the new CD-ROM.

REPLACING SCSI CD-ROM DRIVES WITH IDE VERSIONS

Q393. *I am trying to solve a problem with my friend's system (Pentium 133, 1.08GB hard drive, 24MB RAM, and Windows 95). She has a Fujitsu SCSI hard drive as her boot drive and was using a*

Mediavison Multimedia kit which included a Mediavision 3D Pro sound card and SCSI CD-ROM attached to the sound card. The SCSI CD-ROM just recently passed away and she would like to replace it. The sound card is working fine, so there is no need to replace this portion of the multimedia kit. Since the motherboard does have primary and secondary IDE adapters present (but they are currently disabled in the BIOS to allow the system to boot from the SCSI hard drive), if I enable one or both of the IDE adapters to connect an IDE CD-ROM, will the system attempt to boot from the enabled primary IDE device, or will it continue to boot off the SCSI hard drive?

A.   You can certainly install an IDE CD-ROM on one of your motherboard's IDE ports. The SCSI drive will remain bootable because there will be no entries in the BIOS for your IDE CD-ROM—you leave the BIOS set as none or not installed. This should be no problem. Just remember to remove the SCSI CD-ROM drivers from DOS (CONFIG.SYS) and Windows 95 before installing the new ATAPI IDE CD-ROM driver. The ATAPI and SCSI drivers should not conflict, but the old SCSI drivers will cause errors when searching for the CD-ROM hardware that no longer exists.

CDRs and Recordable Media

Q394.   *I have heard that generic recordable media is no good for a CDR. Is this true? What type of recordable media should I be using?*

A.   The established standards for recordable media are quite rigid. While no CDR disc can damage the CDR drive, poor-quality CDR discs may result in frequent recording errors and wasted discs. As a rule, stay with name brand media such as Fuji or Maxell. If you do choose to use generic media, be sensitive to recording errors and failures that may suggest a bad disc rather than a bad recorder.

CD Skips When Played in a CD-ROM Drive

Q395.   *I like to play audio CDs while working on my PC, but it seems that my CD-ROM is a lot more sensitive to scratches or dust than my CD player. There's one CD in particular that sounds great on my stereo but skips in the CD-ROM. I do see a scratch on the CD, but I thought that CD mechanisms were supposed to ignore scratches. Is there a problem with the drive?*

A. Probably not. CD-ROM drives *are* much more precise than ordinary audio CD players; they have to be in order to read data without errors. While a CD-ROM drive is supposed to "look past" surface defects, a significant scratch cannot be ignored. For audio players, the scratch may not cause a noticeable difference in the music. When played in a CD-ROM drive though, the same scratch may affect tracking and force the drive to retrack or "hiccup." Ultimately, the CD itself is probably at fault and should be replaced.

CDR Can't Read CDs

Q396. *I installed a Philips CD recorder recently, and I've got a problem that I just can't figure out. It won't work as an ordinary CD-ROM drive. It burns the CDs, and I can see the SCSI adapter and the CDR drive in my Device Manager, but when I try to read an old CD in the drive, it won't work. Any ideas?*

A. I think there's a simple solution—you're missing software. Some CDRs use a particular driver utility which allow them to serve as CD-ROM drives in order to read CDs. I believe that the Philips CDRs use a utility called "CD Creator" that is enclosed on a disk that accompanies the CDR. Install that software under Windows 95, and you should be in business. If there is no such software with your CDR, check the Philips Web site for that software at *http://www.philips.com*

Windows 95 Cannot Utilize CD-I Discs

Q397. *I want to play a VideoCD in my CD-ROM drive, but Windows 95 won't run the movie. In fact, Windows 95 won't even acknowledge the CD-I/VideoCD disc. What can I do?*

A. There are two issues regarding CD-I/VideoCD support: the CD-ROM drive and the CD-ROM driver. *Both* must be capable of CD-I support. Make sure that both the drive and its driver will support CD-I and VideoCD. Otherwise, the player applet will not

ADVANCED

detect the CD-I or VideoCD discs. Also make sure that the drivers are protected-mode versions for Windows 95. Real-mode drivers can definitely affect the drive's performance.

DUAL LANGUAGES HEARD FROM VIDEOCD

Q398.   *I've set up my PC to play VideoCDs. There is one problem though: When playing a dual-language disc, I hear languages from my sound system. This is really annoying. Is there anything I can do?*

A.   In many cases, such dual-language VideoCDs are recorded with the left channel in one language and the right channel in the other (almost never stereo, although this will change with DVD discs). In order to play back a VideoCD and listen to the appropriate language, you'll need to start the sound board's mixer applet and pan the balance of the speakers to either the extreme left or right, depending on the language preferred.

CD-ROM Corrective Actions

CD WON'T EJECT THE DISC

Q399.   *My CD-ROM tray won't eject, what can I do?*

A.   There are several possible issues that can prevent a disc from ejecting, but unless the drive has failed completely, the solutions are usually quite simple:

- Make sure you have power to the CD-ROM.

- Try different power cables.

- Loosen the CD-ROM mounting screws a bit (the case could be warped if the screws are too tight).

- Try the manual CD eject switch (the small hole usually just under the disc tray).

- If the CD-ROM still won't eject, the CD-ROM is probably defective.

CD-ROM Eject Button Problems

Q400. *Here's one that I just can't figure out. There are times when I'll push the eject button on my CD-ROM and the tray will open and immediately close again. Any ideas?*

A. In come cases, you may have simply pressed the eject button twice—this causes the tray to open and close again in rapid succession. Once you press the eject button, it can take a few minutes for the drive to spin down and open, so don't get excited and push the button again. If this is not the problem, your drive may be installed with one or more of the mounting screws overtightened, and this is causing the drive frame to skew. Relieve tension on all the mounting screws, position the drive as level as possible, and then snug the mounting screws down (but do not overtighten them). You might also try to reposition the drive in a roomier drive bay.

Repairing a Scratched CD

Q401. *I've got an important CD that I can't afford to lose, but the CD is scratched—my drive reports Read Errors when I try to read the disc. Is there any way to recover the disc and save my data?*

A. There are some tricks that I've used (and seen used) through the years, but you should understand that *any* attempt to recover a scratched disc should be undertaken *only* as an *absolute last resort*. If you can return the disc for exchange or replacement, you should do so, because after attempting to recover the disc, you will probably no longer be able to return it.

- Try buffing out minor scratches with mild abrasives (i.e., plastic or furniture polish, Brasso metal polish, or even toothpaste). These will totally remove minor scratches if they are *minor* enough. This is probably more effective when the surface has been scuffed or abraded rather than deeply scratched.

- Try applying fillers for deeper scratches (i.e, Turtle wax, car wax, furniture wax). Apply over the whole disc, and buff out with a clean lint-free cloth. Filling larger scratches should be fairly effective, but the disc will be more prone to damage in the future due to the soft wax.

When applying or rubbing any of these materials (as with cleaning a CD), wipe from the center to the outside edge. A CD player can generally track across scratches that are perpendicular to its path reasonably well, but not those that run parallel to the tracks.

Discs Not Read Properly by CD-ROM Drive

Q402. *I have a 486DX4/100 system. Recently it has been having trouble reading the CD-ROM drive. The system itself recognizes the presence of the CD-ROM, and I have two discs that I can put in the drive and they work properly. But if I try using any other disc, the system will not recognize that a disc is in the drive. Is my CD-ROM unit going bad?*

A. Yes, I would definitely suspect your CD-ROM drive. Try cleaning the optical tracking mechanism. If the problem persists, replace the CD-ROM drive—your problem should disappear.

Handling Garbled Speech from CD-ROM

Q403. *When I play digitized files (.WAV files), I get accelerated, or garbled speech. What can be causing this?*

A. Some CD-ROM installations use unusual DMA assignments in conjunction with the sound board. This problem is typically corrected by enabling Single Mode DMA for your PnP sound device. Follow the procedure below:

1. Go to Control Panel, Multimedia, and Advanced.

2. Click + next to the Audio Devices and then highlight the sound driver (Fig. 3.5)

3. Click Properties and Settings

4. Check Use Singe Mode DMA.

5. Click OK.

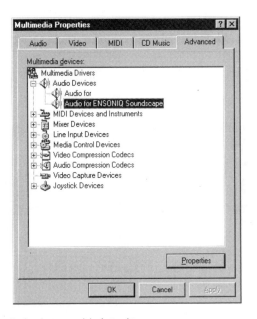

Figure 3.5 Advanced Multimedia Properties dialog for Sound Device

NEW CD-ROM DEVELOPS DATA TROUBLE

Q404. I've installed a Wearnes 8X CD-ROM drive according to the procedure in the instructions. Initially it worked, but after a few CDs, it starts having a problem detecting data CDs. Windows 95 displays an error message stating that D: is not accessible. This problem is intermittent. Red book audio CDs do work.

A.   From your description of the symptoms, I'd say that you're either using dusty or dirty CDs, some dust or dirt has settled on the optical mechanism, or the CD-ROM is failing. Check your CDs first, and make sure they are clean and dust-free. Try some different CDs to make sure. Take a close look at your data cable and confirm that it is connected securely between the drive and controller. Red book audio uses the slim four-pin audio cable between the CD-ROM drive and sound board rather than the data cable. You might also try some photography-grade compressed air to blow out the optical tracking mechanism. If you still cannot get the drive to run data CDs, replace the CD-ROM drive.

Changing the CD-ROM's Drive Letter

Q405. *How do I change the DOS drive letter assigned to my CD-ROM drive?*

A. Add the /L:? switch to the MSCDEX.EXE line in the AUTOEX-EC.BAT (where ? is the drive letter you wish to assign). Remember to adjust your LASTDRIVE= statement if necessary. Here is a sample line, in this case, the CD-ROM is being assigned to drive X:

```
D:\CDR\MSCDEX.EXE /D:DMSCD01 /M:12 /L:X
```

Mitsumi CD-ROM Drive Not Ready

Q406. *I have a Mitsumi FX600S CD-ROM drive, and I am using Windows 95 as an operating system. Lately, I began receiving Drive Not Ready messages when there is a CD in the drive. Sometimes it works, but most of the time it does not. In DOS mode, if I type D: and <Enter>, the prompt will change to D:> and the "Drive Not Ready" message will pop up. The drive is connected on the motherboard's secondary IDE interface. There are no apparent conflicts, and the connections are OK. Where should I look next?*

A. I think you'll find that there are three potential problems here: bad disc, dirty drive tracking, or bad drive. First, try a different CD in the drive—something you know will work in other CD-ROM drives. If known-good CDs work, it could simply be a questionable CD. If known-good CDs still cause problems, you might take a can of photography-grade compressed air and blow down the drive's optical tracking (as well as blow any dust or debris out of the drive). If the problem persists, you may have a drive failure such as the spindle failing to turn at the proper speed. If you really want to tinker, you could try cleaning the rubber spindle clamping mechanism with isopropyl alcohol and a cotton swab. Otherwise, you may simply replace the drive outright.

CD-ROM Generating Drive Not Ready Errors

Q407. *I hope that you can help me with this. I see an error message that says "CDR 101 – Not Ready Drive (X)." I know this is referring to my CD-ROM, but what can I do to fix this? If I try accessing the drive several times, it will finally work.*

A. This is often a drive timing problem. If you have just inserted a disc in the drive, wait a few seconds for the disc to spin up, and try accessing the disc again. Check the disc for scratches, dirt, and fingerprints. Clean the disc if necessary. Make sure the label side of the disc is up. Check to see if the disc is a CD-ROM program disc, not an audio disc (the CD-ROM drive will play CD audio discs, but audio discs are not accessible with DOS commands).

Portable SCSI CD-ROM Reads Erratically

Q408. *I have an older Toshiba XM-3301TA CD-ROM packaged as a CD Technology Porta Drive which is giving me endless difficulty. The drive is connected through an 8-bit SCSI adapter to a 486/33 VESA system. Software interfaces include the Trantor ASPI Manager 1.09 and CD-ROM driver 3.07A. The drive fires up properly but does not read the disc directory or files properly with any consistency, sometimes it works, sometimes it doesn't. Any ideas?*

A. Let's start with the basics. Check the drive to be sure it is clean. Dust or debris on the optical pickup can cause all kinds of random problems. Use a can of photography-grade compressed air to gently blow out any dust that may have accumulated in the unit. The disc itself should be clean, scratch-free, and dust-free. If the problems seem to occur on a certain CD, try another CD. Also, since the drive is on an SCSI interface, check that the cable is connected properly and that any terminating resistor network is installed properly. Try a new SCSI cable between the drive and adapter. Make sure that you are using the latest available drivers for the CD-ROM and SCSI system.

INTERMEDIATE

If problems persist, isolate the problem to your CD-ROM or host computer? Install the CD-ROM setup on another computer and SCSI adapter and see if the problem persists. If so, the drive is probably at fault. If the problem disappears, the problem is probably an incompatibility between the CD-ROM drive and SCSI interface. Try setting up a new SCSI interface with a different SCSI adapter.

DRIVE NOT READY ERROR WITH CD-ROM

Q409. *I have a Mitsumi FX600S CD-ROM, and I am using Windows 95 as an operating system. Lately I began receiving Drive Not Ready messages when there is a CD in the drive. Sometimes the drive works, but most of the time it does not. If I type D: and <Enter> under DOS, the prompt will change to D: and the "Drive not ready" message will pop up. The drive is connected on the secondary IDE interface on my motherboard. There are no apparent conflicts and the connections seem okay. Where should I look next?*

A. I think you'll find that there are three potential problems here; bad disc, dirty drive tracking, or a bad drive. First, try a different CD in the drive—something you know will work in other CD-ROM drives. If known-good CDs work fine, it could simply be a questionable CD. If known-good CDs still cause problems, you might take a can of photography-grade compressed air and blow down the drive's optical tracking (as well as blow any dust or debris out of the drive). If the problem persists, you may have a drive failure such as the spindle failing to turn at the proper speed. If you really want to tinker, you could try cleaning the rubber spindle clamping mechanism with isopropyl alcohol and a cotton swab. Otherwise, you may simply replace the drive outright.

CD-ROM WON'T WORK UNDER DOS

Q410. *I'm trying to get a new 6X CD-ROM running under DOS on a new Intel Gigabyte 100-MHz Pentium motherboard. The CD-ROM works under Windows 95, but won't work under DOS. The sound card is working under both windows and DOS. The machine has two hard disks, 32MB of RAM, PCI video, an exter-*

nal modem, a scanner card, mouse, and so on. All potentially offending devices were removed to test for possible conflicts, but to no avail. The CD-ROM was hooked up to the sound card and also to the secondary on-board IDE controller, but again, no luck. The CD-ROM is from Creative Labs, but the supplied drivers do not appear to work. The CMOS has been changed dramatically to see if this fixed the problem, but it appears it is not a CMOS thing. I must assume that the hardware is functioning correctly because it works under Windows 95. What am I missing?

A.   It sounds like the hardware is installed properly, but you've neglected to install the DOS device drivers for the CD-ROM. The installation disk you received with the drive package should have DOS and Windows 95 drivers. You will need to add the DOS low-level driver to CONFIG.SYS, and add MSCDEX to AUTOEXEC.BAT.

CD-ROM Won't Work After DOS Drivers Removed

Q411. *I installed Windows 95 from a CD-ROM disc using DOS drivers (i.e., MSCDEX). When I removed the real-mode CD-ROM drivers from CONFIG.SYS, the CD-ROM no longer works. How do I get the protected-mode drivers to work?*

A.   Assuming the correct protected-mode drivers are available, the problem is most likely a timing issue concerning just when the real-mode drivers were removed. The basic steps are as follows: Restore the real-mode drivers, and then boot Windows 95 using the real-mode drivers for your CD-ROM and its interface. Using the Add/New Hardware applet in the Control Panel, do a manual hardware addition (do *not* let Windows 95 try to auto-detect the hardware) and install the drivers for the associated CD-ROM interface. Make note of the resources that Windows 95 is assigning to the interface. When the installation is completed, Windows 95 will tell you that it must reboot before the hardware will be available. Do *not* reboot at this time. Instead, drop to the DOS mode and edit out the real-mode CD-ROM drivers in CONFIG.SYS and AUTOEXEC.BAT. Then you can reboot Windows 95.

INTERMEDIATE

New CD-ROM Drive Configuration Problems

Q412.   *I just installed a new Philips CD-ROM, but when I try to access it, I get an error that says "not High Sierra Format." Now I've tried several different CDs (all of which work on other systems), so I know that their format is correct. Is this a defective drive?*

A.   Format errors such as the kind you describe (especially during new installations) indicate a hardware conflict—usually with the DMA setting. Make sure that the hardware settings on the CD-ROM controller match the switches used in your CD-ROM driver command line. For example, if the DMA jumper is set to DMA 5, and the driver is configured to DMA 7, you're going to have an error. You can either change the hardware setting to match the command line switch or change the command line switch to match the hardware setting.

Can't Detect Diamond CD-ROM

Q413.   *I just bought a new CD-ROM, but I can't get it to work with my system. I bought a Diamond 8X Multimedia Kit 8000. I have a 486DX4/100-MHz system with an 850MB IDE hard drive and 28.8KB modem. The sound card seems to be working, but the PC didn't detect the CD-ROM under either DOS or Windows. Could it be a bad CD-ROM? I installed the setup disks without any problem, but I haven't tried to change anything in AUTOEXEC.BAT or CONFIG.SYS.*

A.   Start by checking the CD-ROM jumpers—an IDE drive must be jumpered properly as the primary or secondary drive—and see that the drive is cabled properly. Make sure that the power connector is attached securely. Although you say the software installed properly, do you know if the low-level driver actually installed in CONFIG.SYS or if the MSCDEX driver installed in AUTOEXEC.BAT? Are there any specific error messages produced by the drivers when your system starts? Check to see if there is a hardware conflict between the sound card and the secondary IDE controller channel. If problems continue, try replacing the CD-ROM drive.

IDE CD-ROM Not Always Recognized

Q414. *This 486DX2/50 computer that I'm working on uses an OPTI sound card with an IDE interface. A Mitsumi 4X IDE CD-ROM is attached to the sound card. The system is running MS-DOS and Windows 3.11. The problem is that sometimes the CD-ROM driver loads and sometimes it doesn't—saying it cannot find the CD-ROM. A warm boot will usually find the CD-ROM.*

A. There are a whole series of issues here that can be affecting your system. First, start your CMOS Setup and see if there is any entry labeled Power-On Delay or something similar. If so, extend the power-on delay by several seconds (perhaps by as much as 10 or 15 seconds). Save your changes to the CMOS before exiting and rebooting. The additional time afforded during start-up may be enough for the hardware to initialize properly. If there is no change, set the power-on delay back to its original value.

Since the CD-ROM drive is all by itself on the IDE channel, make sure that the drive is jumpered as the primary (or master) drive. Also see that the IDE signal cable between the CD-ROM drive and sound board is connected securely. Verify the power cable too. If the CMOS Setup and cabling are all intact, you should check for any updated drivers for your CD-ROM drive—perhaps the driver itself is a bit unstable at detecting the drive with an OPTi sound board. A new driver can usually provide faster, more reliable operation. Finally, I'd suspect the OPTi sound board itself. OPTi chipsets do not always provide optimum performance. Try replacing the sound board with a Sound Blaster or other non-Opti board providing an IDE interface.

INTERMEDIATE

System Can't Find IDE CD-ROM

Q415. *I am trying to connect an IDE CD-ROM to an older 486 motherboard. This motherboard has only one IDE port; therefore I want the CD to be the slave device. The CD jumper is set to slave, power is attached, and I have no trouble booting from the C: drive. However, the CD's ATAPI driver reports that it cannot locate the CD. Is there a hardware conflict here?*

A.   Your complaint is a common one. In many cases, older IDE interfaces (and even newer ones) have trouble supporting fast and
slow devices on the same port. In other words, it is not uncommon for hard drives and CD-ROM drives to have trouble working together. Double-check that the CD-ROM drive is attached
correctly, and see that any necessary command-line switches are
set correctly for the ATAPI driver. If problems persist, you should
move the CD-ROM drive to its own drive controller channel.
Since your system only has one IDE port now, your best course is
probably to upgrade your drive controller to a dual-channel
model with on-board EIDE BIOS support. Place the hard drive
on the primary channel. Make the CD-ROM drive a master
device on the secondary channel (you may need to update the
ATAPI driver command line).

IDE CD-ROM Drive Won't Work

Q416. *I just installed an ATAPI IDE CD-ROM drive, but it refuses to
work. Still, I was able to use the drive successfully on another
PC. Any ideas?*

A.   CD-ROM and secondary hard drive problems are quite common,
and since you proved out the CD-ROM on another system, your
problem probably lies in your configuration of the device itself. If
there is already a hard drive on the port, make sure the CD-
ROM drive is jumpered as the secondary (or slave) drive. If the
CD-ROM will be the only device on the IDE port, see that it is
jumpered as the primary (or master) drive. If you are trying to
install the CD-ROM on a fast EIDE port, the performance mismatch between the hard drive and CD-ROM may be preventing
the CD-ROM from being recognized. Try placing the CD-ROM
drive by itself on a secondary IDE channel. Also double-check
your CD-ROM drivers. Finally, there are some instances where
the motherboard BIOS may interfere with some ATAPI IDE CD-
ROM drives. Check with your motherboard or system manufacturer for the latest BIOS upgrade.

There are two known issues involving CD-ROM or secondary hard drives: First, the retail version of Microsoft Windows 95 may not recognize the Intel 82371SB PIIX3 IDE controller used on Intel motherboards. This causes the BIOS to disable the secondary IDE channel. This can result in IDE devices (such as CD-ROM drives) not being detected or disappearing after the system is rebooted. A utility is available from Microsoft to update the MSHDC.INF file and resolve the issue. Second, Windows 95 may also fail to recognize a CD-ROM drive that does not comply *exactly* with the ATAPI specification.

CD-ROM NOT FOUND ON A COLD BOOT

Q417. *I have a 486DX/80 PC with lots of added extras—including a 6X NSA CD-ROM drive. Every time I cold boot my computer, I get a message telling me that it didn't find a CD-ROM drive, and the drivers won't load. If I do a warm reboot (I have QEMM 8), the system finds the CD correctly, then loads the drivers, and everything seems to work perfectly. This is a problem that occurs every single time I do a cold boot. What's the problem here?*

A. One piece of information that's missing is the CD-ROM interface. If your drive uses an IDE-type interface, the BIOS may be trying (and be unable to) identify the drive at POST. Check your CMOS Setup and verify that there are no entries for the CD-ROM drive. If there is an entry for Power-On Delay, try adding a few seconds to the delay. While this feature was intended for the hard drives, it may also give the CD-ROM some additional time to initialize. If the CD-ROM is on the same IDE channel as your hard drive, try moving the CD-ROM to its own controller channel. Check the documentation for your low-level CD-ROM driver in CONFIG.SYS and see if there are any switches you can use to adjust the driver's hardware detection time. If you still cannot resolve the issue, try a different model CD-ROM. Finally, you mentioned that the system was extensively upgraded. It may be that your power supply isn't providing enough current to the system during a coldboot. Try upgrading the power supply to a larger model.

ADVANCED

IDE CD-ROM Won't Run on Sound Board

Q418.   *I just installed a BTC 8X CD-ROM drive along with a Creative Labs 16-bit sound card. When attached to the sound card, the CD-ROM drive is not recognized at boot-up. When attached as a slave device to the HDD controller (IDE), everything works. I'd prefer to have the drive attached to the sound card.*

A.   First, make sure that the drive controller on your sound card is in fact an IDE interface. There are many Creative Labs sound cards with proprietary 40-pin interfaces that could easily be mistaken for IDE. If the interface is a true IDE, you probably need to disable the secondary IDE port on your drive controller board because the sound board's controller is also trying to use the resources assigned to the secondary IDE port. Reattach the CD-ROM as the master device on your sound card, and the problem should be resolved. If you want to keep the drive controller fully operational (i.e., you may be running a hard drive on the secondary IDE channel), you may need to reconfigure the sound card's interface as a tertiary channel rather than a secondary channel, which is typically configured as the default.

IDE CD-ROM Won't Run with Phone Blaster

Q419.   *I want to run my CD-ROM drive from the Phone Blaster board, but I can't get the CD-ROM to work. It's an IDE drive, and I know the Phone Blaster supports an IDE interface, but I just can't get the Phone Blaster to recognize the drive. What's going on?*

A.   The problem is not with your Phone Blaster but rather with your IDE driver. The SBIDE.SYS 1.08 driver supports only a few IDE drives: Creative CD220E, Goldstar R540B, Mitsumi FX400, NEC CDR271 and CDR272, Panasonic CR574B and CR581, and the Toshiba XM5302. Other IDE drive models (especially those produced by other manufacturers) may not work with the SBIDE driver. Check with the Creative Labs Web site (*www.creaf.com*) to see if there are any updated IDE drivers for the Phone Blaster. If not, you can always use an IDE CD-ROM through your regular IDE drive controller. Otherwise, you may need to limit yourself to one of the supported drives.

COMPUTER CRASH DISABLES THE CD-ROM DRIVE

Q420.   *My computer crashed, and now it won't acknowledge that I have an E: drive (which is my CD-ROM). What should I do?*

A.   If a CD-ROM cannot be recognized, it usually means that either or both the low-level CD-ROM driver (in CONFIG.SYS) and the CD-ROM DOS extension MSCDEX (in AUTOEXEC.BAT) are not loading. The question now is *why* they aren't loading. Since you didn't tell me what you mean by "crashed," I have to assume your hard drive failed, and it is no longer working (or has been replaced). If that is the case, you need to replace the AUTOEXEC and CONFIG files on your new hard drive. At the very least, you'll need to reinstall the CD-ROM software from the disk that accompanied the drive. If the C: and D: drives are working, you may have a corrupted driver or MSCDEX file—try reinstalling them. If you can't get *any* of your drives to work, you may need to replace a defective drive controller board.

CD-ROM CAUSES EIDE DRIVE TO FAIL

Q421.   *I've finally replaced my proprietary CD-ROM drive with an ATAPI IDE drive, but when I install the CD-ROM drive, the 2.3GB EIDE hard drive refuses to boot. At this point, I haven't gotten the CD-ROM drivers installed because I haven't been able to get the system to boot. Is the CD-ROM defective?*

A.   Probably not. If I understand your problem, you have connected the IDE CD-ROM and EIDE hard drive to the same drive controller channel—this can be a problem. IDE CD-ROM drives have much slower data transfer rates than EIDE drives, and in many cases, the slower CD-ROM causes the EIDE drive to fail when it tries to communicate with the controller. Remove the CD-ROM drive from your EIDE channel—your system should now boot normally. Rather than making the CD-ROM drive a secondary (or slave) device on the primary drive controller channel, make the CD-ROM your primary (or master) device on the secondary IDE channel of your drive controller. That way the EIDE drive has its own controller channel (you can always add another EIDE drive later), and the CD-ROM has its own controller channel. The system should boot this way, and you can proceed to install your ATAPI drivers.

ADVANCED

Can't Find a SCSI CD-ROM

Q422.   *When I start up my PC, I can't find my new SCSI CD-ROM. I'm
pretty sure that it's installed correctly, but I can't seem to get the
system to recognize it. What's wrong?*

A.   There are several possible reasons why your SCSI device is not
being detected. Always check your power first. If the device is
internal, make sure that a power cable is attached. If the device is
external, see that its power supply is attached, and turn the power
switch on. Next, check for your SCSI IDs and verify that there are
no duplicate IDs. Termination can play havoc with SCSI devices,
so check that each end of your SCSI chain is terminated properly.
While you're at it, check the SCSI cable. Try a new SCSI cable if it
appears frayed or damaged at any point. Finally, make sure that
you've installed the necessary device driver(s) for your particular
SCSI device. You might try reinstalling the driver(s).

System Won't Boot After Adding External CD-ROM

Q423.   *This one blows my mind. I added an external SCSI CD-ROM
drive to my server, and **now** the server won't boot from the SCSI
hard drive. What's the deal?*

A.   This is a common problem when external SCSI devices are added
to previously internal SCSI systems. You probably forgot to
remove the termination from the SCSI host adapter. All SCSI systems must be terminated at the *ends* of the SCSI chain. In most
SCSI systems, the devices are all internal, so the ends of the SCSI
chain are at the host adapter and the last device on the ribbon
cable. When you add an external SCSI device, however, the ends
of the SCSI chain are now different. The internal ribbon cable
end remains the same, but the other end moves off the SCSI host
adapter to the last *external* device in the external portion of the
chain. Remove the termination from the host adapter, and terminate the external CD-ROM properly.

ADVANCED

CD-ROM DRIVE NOT READING

Q424. *I'm trying to figure out what could be wrong with my 2X CD-ROM. It's in a Compaq Presario 833 CDS running Windows 95 with 16MB of RAM. The CD-ROM drive steadfastly refuses to read anything (data or audio) even though the activity LED indicates life when a disc is inserted or ejected and when Windows starts up. The Device Manager indicates that there are no problems with the drive. I have cleaned the lens and checked all cables and connectors. The problem started several months back with intermittent failures to read CDs and now nothing is read at all. Is there some simple fix I have overlooked, or is it just time to chuck the old one and install a new one?*

A.   I had the same problem with several CD-ROM drives throughout the years, and the problem turned out to be that the CD was not spinning in the drive. A simple way to check this is to put the CD in the drive with the lettering on the disc straight up (as you would read it). Close the tray, let the drive try to access the disc, and then eject it. If the disk is in the same straight up position, it isn't spinning (try it two or three times to be certain). To temporarily fix the problem, I removed the cover of the CD drive, inserted a CD, closed the tray, and gave the disc a clockwise spin with my finger. Once the disc started spinning, the drive took over and worked. This would work for varying lengths of time (sometimes weeks) before the problem would reappear. Ultimately, I replaced such afflicted drives, and your most economical solution is certainly to replace the drive outright.

However, if you're in the mood to tinker, you can dismantle the drive enough to get to the rubber disk which sandwiches the CD against a nylon bushing. This rubber disk can become dirty and "smoothed" from friction when the drive spins, and the CD won't spin normally. Use isopropyl alcohol and cotton swabs to clean both the rubber disk and nylon bushing. If there is a belt between the drive motor and spindle, try to remove the belt from the drive motor and clean it with alcohol as well. This may restore some operation to the drive—at least temporarily.

SCSI CD-ROM NEEDS DRIVERS

Q425. *I've been trying to install a new SCSI CD-ROM drive for days now. I know that the cabling is right, the power is good, and the termination is set properly, but the PC simply won't recognize the CD-ROM drive. However, my SCSI hard drive works (so I also know that the SCSI adapter is good). I'm at my wit's end here.*

A. It sounds like you forgot a key part of the installation—the ASPI *drivers* for your CD-ROM. Most SCSI devices require drivers in order for the SCSI adapter to recognize them. The SCSI adapter will recognize SCSI hard drives because the SCSI BIOS provides the necessary firmware, but everything else (i.e., CD-ROM drives, tape drives, and so on) demands a driver. Check the installation disk that probably accompanied your SCSI CD-ROM and try installing that software. You may also need that installation disk to provide the protected-mode drivers for installation under Windows 95. Finally, if the SCSI CD-ROM still refuses to work, try a different SCSI CD-ROM.

SCSI CD-ROM DRIVERS HANG THE SYSTEM

Q426. *I've been running an SCSI system (adapter and SCSI hard drive) for months now, but I just installed a driver for a new SCSI CD-ROM, and now the system hangs up. Any ideas?*

A. This sounds like a classic driver conflict. The new SCSI driver is probably conflicting with another driver in your system. First, check your CONFIG.SYS file and see that the driver is only being loaded once. Also make sure that any command line switches needed for the driver's command line are set correctly. Try systematically disabling other drivers in CONFIG.SYS to see if you can isolate the conflict. Finally, check to see that you are using the latest driver version.

SCSI CD-ROM WON'T RUN UNDER DOS

Q427. *I have a Western Digital WD7197 SCSI host adapter and an NEC MultiSpin 6Xi CD-ROM drive. I cannot get the CD-ROM to run under DOS. It runs under Windows 95, so I do know that the hardware is working. Is this a driver problem?*

A. I think you've certainly got a DOS driver problem, but the SCSI host adapter adds another real-mode wrinkle. The real-mode driver for the host adapter must be loaded *before* the CD-ROM's real-mode driver. Otherwise, the host adapter may recognize the drive, but the drive won't run. Check your CONFIG.SYS file and see if you have a configuration such as:

```
device=c:\wdscsi\wd296.exe

device=c:\coreldrv\cuni_asp.sys
```

The WD296.EXE file is an ASPI manager. You may be using a different ASPI manager, but the point is that the ASPI manager must load *first*. The CUNI_ASP.SYS file is the CD-ROM low-level device driver. The CD-ROM driver must load *after* the ASPI manager. You might also check to see that the LASTDRIVE statement has a free drive letter for the CD-ROM. In AUTOEXEC.BAT, make sure that you are loading MSCDEX.EXE such as:

```
c:\dos\mscdex /D:MSCD001
```

If you are using the CorelSCSI package, that line might appear like:

```
c:\coreldrv\corelcdx
```

CDRs AND BUFFER MISCOMPARE ERRORS

Q428. *I have a CDR which sometimes produces a Buffer Miscompare error message when I make a CD or try to run the CDR diagnostic utility. Otherwise, the CDR seems to be working. What does this error mean, and how can I correct it?*

ADVANCED

A.   CD recorders often use SCSI adapters and DMA channels to transfer data. In many cases, the data buffer suffers an error when the DMA channel transfer speed is too high or if there is a DMA channel conflict with another device in the system. First, check for DMA conflicts—you might try selecting a different DMA channel for your SCSI adapter. Next, lower the DMA transfer speed to 3.3MB/s or so. Finally, your SCSI adapter is probably a PCI bus master. Make sure that the adapter is plugged into a bus master slot and see that the slot is configured properly.

Tape Drive Issues

TAPE DRIVE WILL NOT ACCEPT A CARTRIDGE

Q429.   *My tape drive will simply not accept any of my tape cartridges. What can I do?*

A.   It's probably safe to say that you're using a helical scan drive such as an 8-mm DAT. First, check your power and make sure that the drive is powering up normally. Assuming that there is not a tape already in the drive, part of the tape-handling mechanism may be jammed or broken. You are probably best advised to return the drive for service.

TAPE BACKUP FLEXIBILITY

Q430.   *I am thinking about getting a tape drive for my system and I have a question for you. Can you back up and retrieve files one at a time or do you have to back up an entire drive at one time? I am looking for a way to put all the miscellaneous files I have on 1.44MB floppies in one place.*

A.   Just about every tape drive on the market today comes with software that allows you to back up and restore files one at a time— even to different directories. If you use Windows 95, make sure that the software is designed expressly for Windows 95 so that it preserves the long file-name structure.

ADDING A FLOPPY-BASED TAPE DRIVE

Q431. *I have two floppy drives in my PC, but I'd like to add a floppy-based tape drive. Do I have to remove one of my floppy drives to support a floppy-based tape drive.*

A. That really depends on the type of hard drive that you choose. Since tape drives don't need any CMOS support, most current tape drives using a floppy interface can exist as a floppy cable extension in *addition* to your two floppy drives. Older floppy-based tape drives may not be able to coexist with two floppy drives quite so nicely. The bottom line is that you need to study the documentation that accompanies your tape drive. If the tape drive won't run with your floppy drives, you can always install a four-channel floppy controller or a dedicated tape controller board.

TAPE DRIVE SPEEDS WITH FLOPPY INTERFACES

Q432. *I've been thinking about adding a tape drive with a floppy drive interface to my system, but it seems that they are pretty slow devices. How fast is a tape drive? Will a dedicated controller improve this?*

A. Floppy interfaces provide several classes of speed to a tape drive. Classic floppy interfaces (supporting up to 1.44MB drives) can transfer 500KB/s. Later floppy interfaces (up to 2.88MB drives) will usually support 1MB/s. If you need even more performance, you can use a dedicated floppy accelerator board which can handle data transfer rates up to 2MB/s.

DETERMINING TAPE LENGTH

Q433. *I've seen lots of different tapes and tape drives, but how does the drive or backup software know how long the tape is?*

A. Tape length is not really detected—that is, there are no codes or data that tell a tape drive how long a tape will be. In practice, the *ends* of a tape are detected by an infrared sensor. Holes at each end of the tape will allow the infrared signal through, and this signals an end-of-tape (EOT) condition. In fact, if the infrared sensor is damaged or fouled with dust, the tape drive may not detect the tape end, and this can cause the tape to "reel off" the cartridge spool.

TAPE DRIVE READ/WRITE ERRORS

Q434.   *I've been using my Travan tape drive for some months now, but lately I've noticed that I seem to be getting Read/Write errors when accessing the tape. The problem has been getting more frequent recently. I tried different tapes, but the problem is still occurring. What do you think?*

A.   From the symptoms that you describe, I'm almost certain that your trouble is with dirty R/W heads in the tape drive. Oxides from the media eventually wear off onto the heads and cause read/write problems. Try cleaning the read/write heads thoroughly, and then try your tapes again. I bet you'll find that the problem has gone away. You should incorporate routine tape drive cleaning into your weekly or monthly system maintenance ritual (the instructions with your particular tape drive will provide specific cleaning directions and schedule recommendations).

USING A TAPE CLEANING CARTRIDGE

Q435.   *Here's a quick question: How many times can I use the cleaning cartridge for my tape drive.*

A.   Generally speaking, an average-quality tape cleaning cartridge should not be used more than 30 times. Afterward, it should be discarded. Lower-quality cartridges should often be discarded after as many as 10 uses.

TAPE CAPACITY AND DATA COMPRESSION

Q436.   *I have a 2GB tape drive, but when I try to make a complete backup of my 2.1GB hard drive to tape, I run out of space on the tape just before I reach the 1.6GB mark. Why can't I fit my entire 2GB worth of files onto the tape?*

A.   This is a common complaint about tape drives. The problem is that your 2GB tape capacity is *compressed* capacity—the tape cartridge itself is probably a 1GB tape. The result is that the tape drive tries to fit 2GB of data onto a 1GB tape using data compression. That's fine as long as the drive can compress data at a 2:1 ratio. But not all data can be compressed that well and may use lower ratios like 1.6:1 or 1.3:1. Some files (such as .ZIP files which are already compressed) cannot be compressed at all. Since your tape could not halve your file sizes, it could not fit all the data onto the same tape. Select fewer files for backup, or plan on using several tapes to back up your system.

HANDLING LOW TAPE TENSION ERRORS

Q437.   *This one's got me stumped: I'm using a tape backup with a 1.3GB 3M tape, but each time I try to back up, I get a Low Tape Tension error. I retensioned the tape using the backup software, but the problem remains. Before I run out and drop another $20 on a new tape, do you have any ideas of what I might check?*

A.   You're right—that's a good one. Believe it or not, I think the tip-off is your mention of the 3M tape. According to my information, 3M had problems with some tapes dated November and December 1995. You can find the dates stamped on the metallic casing of the tape. If you *do* have a tape dated late 1995, contact 3M at 800-328-9438 for a replacement tape. Otherwise, you should start by cleaning the drive's capstan and read/write heads. Accumulations of oxides and debris can affect tape tension in extreme circumstances. If cleaning doesn't help, you should try another tape with a very recent manufacturing date. Format and retention the new tape as you would normally, and then try your backup. If a new tape fails to solve the problem, there is probably a mechanical fault in the tape drive. Replace the tape drive.

TAPE BACKUP ERRORS AND POWER CONSERVATION

Q438.   *My sister got a CMS Jumbo 1400 tape backup unit to save her Pentium system, but she regularly gets Error 92 failures about 15 or 20 minutes into her tape formatting. The bottom line is that*

*she just can't complete a format (or a backup). She's tried differ-
ent tapes and even tested the drive on her spare 486 system—
which worked perfectly. Is this a system problem or what?*

A.   There is a known problem with the CMS Jumbo 1400 tape drive
and Aladdin or Zappa motherboards. The problem occurs when
Advanced Power Management is *enabled*. As power management
starts to kick in, the tape drive generates an error. Your sister's
best solution is to disable the advanced power management with
the following steps:

1.   Turn on the system, and press <F1> to enter CMOS Setup.

2.   Select the Advanced option in CMOS.

3.   Select the Power Management Configuration option.

4.   Hit <Enter> and change the setting from Enabled to
Disabled.

5.   Save the changes, and allow the system to reboot.

6.   Format the tape, and perform the tape backup.

7.   Reboot the system and follow steps 1 through 4 to reenable
power management later.

DIVIDE ERRORS AND TAPE BACKUP PROBLEMS

Q439.   *An IBM 100-MHz Pentium computer with 16MB of RAM was
recently transferred to our office. The operating systems on the
machine are OS/2 and PC-DOS 6.3. Since I am not familiar with
OS/2, I run Windows 3.11 for Workgroups over the PC-DOS 6.3.
I had an external tape backup system installed along with a sound
card and speakers since it had a 4X CD-ROM drive already
installed. My tape backup system appears to be running normally.
However, when I try to run PC-Backup from Windows, I get an
Integer Divide by 0 message and the program freezes up. The
DOS version of the backup software also doesn't work.*

A.   There's lots that you haven't said about this system, so I'll try
and cover several different issues. Start with the basics—make
sure the external drive is powered up, connected to the system,
and has a tape cartridge inserted properly. If the tape drive is

external, it's probably a parallel port drive. If you have a parallel port drive, make sure that your new sound board isn't using the same IRQ used by the parallel port. LPT1 uses IRQ7, and LPT2 would use IRQ5 (most frequently used by a sound board). This kind of conflict isn't always easy to spot and can prevent the backup software from finding your drive (thus generating an error). Next, make sure that the PC-Backup utility you're using is *compatible* with the tape drive, and has the proper drive type selected. Tape drives rarely use drivers, relying instead on software specifically written for particular drives. You might want to try a different backup utility which is known to be compatible with your drive.

No Tape Drive Power LED

Q440.   *My internal tape drive uses a power LED that always comes on when the PC starts. The other day I noticed that the LED did not come on, and the drive has stopped working. I opened the system and I checked the drive's power cable—it seems nice and tight. Can you point me in the right direction to this problem?*

A.   In virtually all cases, the loss of your power LED indicates a power failure in the drive. Either the power cable has come loose, the power supply is failing, or the drive's internal circuitry has failed. Since the power connector is attached properly, and other drives are running correctly, I suspect you have an issue with the drive itself. The drive's internal fuse has probably blown—that can happen if there are surges or spikes in the power or if the power supply is on the verge of failing. Return the drive for service, and take a close look at your power supply voltages.

Flashing Tape Drive LEDs

Q441.   *I have a Sony SDT-5200 tape drive, and when I power the system up, the drive refuses to work, and I see that LEDs are flashing. Do you know what these flashing patterns mean? Is the tape drive defective?*

A.   Well I don't know the precise meaning of each flashing LED off-hand, but I can tell you that there's a problem. Before you panic, check the tape drive power cable, signal cable (try a new signal cable), jumpers and settings, and the proper insertion of your tape cartridge. If the tape drive still refuses to function, you can get an index of LED patterns by calling the Sony Fax Retrieval System at 800-883-7668 (document 5871). For other tape drives, contact your manufacturer or their technical support Web site for specific LED codes.

Other Drives and Drive Issues

PARALLEL PORT ZIP DRIVE CONVENIENCE

Q442. *Can you use a Zip drive to copy files back and forth between computers? If I only have one Zip drive and need to transfer files between two PCs, do I have to install a lot of software to the other computer?*

A.   The parallel port version of Iomega's Zip drive is largely regarded as one of the best portable drives available, and it allows you to copy 100MB to a single Zip disk. In actual practice, the Zip can be connected to a PC, and the *guest* software can be loaded in a matter of minutes.

MOVING TO RAID

Q443. *I've heard about something called RAID. What is it and will my Pentium 166 MHz, 32MB of RAM, 3.2GB SCSI system support it?*

A.   In the PC industry, RAID stands for redundant array of independent disks. This is a backup method which mirrors the contents of one hard drive to another in real time—providing a level of redundancy to your system's data. If one disk fails, one of the redundant disks can be accessed for backup data without having to make or restore tape backups. The use of redundant hard drives is a serious expense; they consume serious power, and they use up lots of drive bays. As a result, RAID is typically used only on minitower and tower server-type systems.

As to whether or not your system will handle RAID, it is a question of space, power, controllers, and software. Assuming you have the drive space and power available, you'll need to check with your SCSI controller maker to see if it supports RAID. If not, you'll need to upgrade your SCSI controller to a version that will support RAID. If it does support RAID, you will need some third-party RAID software. Typically, SCSI controllers will support RAID levels 0, 1, and 5.

POWERING UP A ZIP DRIVE

Q444. *Zip drive instructions state that you should always plug in a Zip drive's power just after powering up the computer to which it is attached. What problems are caused by leaving the Zip drive plugged into power constantly and starting the system as needed with the drive already plugged in? Does it damage the drive or the system to leave the drive plugged in or to boot with the drive already connected to power? Does it cause the system to hang up if power is applied to the Zip drive before starting the system?*

A. I've talked to several owners of Zip drives, and most tend to keep their Zip drives plugged in at all times (regardless of whether the PC is on or not) with no ill-effects. According to my information, it shouldn't cause any problems to leave the Zip drive on constantly, but it wastes electricity, and can shorten the life of the Zip drive's electronics. Since there's really no point in keeping the drive on constantly, I suggest that you simply place the Zip drive on the same power strip as your PC—that way you'll control power to both the PC and Zip drive together.

SCSI Zip Drive Recognition

Q445. *I just installed an external Iomega SCSI Zip drive, but my SCSI adapter refuses to recognize it. I'm using a WD7193 SCSI adapter. Do you know what the problem is?*

A. I've got a pretty good idea what the problem is. Try setting your Wide Negotiation for ID6 (usually the Zip drive) to None. Also see that the Zip drive is not selected as the boot drive. Device 0x80h is the boot drive, and it should be the SCSI or EIDE hard drive. Since the Zip drive is external, you should also check that your termination is correct.

4

Communication Questions

With the emergence of on-line resources like America Online (AOL) and the Internet, PC communications has taken on a whole new importance. The ability to communicate with other PCs and networks around the world allows everyday users to exchange e-mail, download files and patches, gather information, and even play games against other human players. With this new importance comes a host of questions and problems, so this chapter deals with on-line questions and then moves on to PC-specific modem hardware. The chapter concludes by examining serial ports and UARTs.

On-line Issues

Can't Connect to BBS

Q446.   *I'm having difficulty using a BBS. I tried Hyper-Terminal under Windows 95, got connected, and received about a half screen of garbled text and then the connection got hung up. I tried Dial-up Networking and got disconnected before the connection was complete. I'm using a 14.4KB modem. Any help you can give will be appreciated.*

A.   Trouble with BBS connections can be due to many different reasons. First, try at several different times of the day—perhaps there is interference somewhere along the telephone system. Make sure that your communication software is configured for hardware flow control and ANSI BBS terminal emulation, that the data rate is correct, and that you are using an 8/N/1 data frame. Check the modem's initialization string to see that it is using data compression and error correction as required for 14.4KB+ connections. If all else fails, you might also try connecting at a slower speed.

Choose Terminal Emulation Carefully for BBS Work

Q447.   *I see ASCII garbage on the screen when I attempt to sign onto local bulletin boards. I am able to connect without a problem but cannot read the instructions or menus in order to register or access files. I assume that if I am making the connection, the problem is not related to software or configuration. I am using an inexpensive Askey external 14.4KB modem which I just purchased from a mail order catalog. The phone cables are new—the phone company has checked our lines and indicated the lines are clear. At their suggestion, I switched from a portable phone to a regular one, but the problem still exists. The phone is one of three connected to the same line. Could this be the reason?*

A.   Since you clearly seem able to dial and establish connections at the expected speeds, I seriously doubt that the modem or phone line is defective. I think the answer to your problem is very simple: You've selected the wrong terminal emulation in your communication software. All the other attributes of your serial connection are probably correct (i.e., baud rate, stop bits, parity, and so on). Otherwise, you simply wouldn't be able to establish a connection. But BBS communication software has several different ways of interpreting those extended ASCII characters which are so often used to create menus and other pseudo-graphics effects. When connecting to a BBS, try using ANSI BBS terminal emulation.

INTERNET CONNECTIONS AND FILE TRANSFER SPEEDS

Q448.   *My question concerns Internet connection speeds. I presently connect to the Internet through IBM Global Network services using a 28.8KB modem. I've just got a new computer (100-MHz Pentium) and it seems to me (it may be my imagination) that my connection is slower than what it was with my old computer. The IBM dialer indicates that I'm connected at 28.8, but I'm not sure. I've done several file downloads—usually late at night—and the download reports speeds of approximately 1.6Kbps. Before, I was getting 2.5 to 3.0Kbps.To test further, I downloaded a program called Anyspeed which "pings" selected URLs and reports back speeds. I was averaging 1.5 to 1.8Kbps and peaking around 2.1Kbps. Am I really connected at 28.8?*

A.   Your question comes up a lot, and the answer to your question is almost always Yes. Your modem reports its true connection speed when the modem-to-modem negotiation is established, so when you see a message like "Connected 28800," you can be pretty confident that the speed is accurate. However, the actual transfer of data from place to place is dependent on a number of factors such as server traffic load, phone line quality, and the overall quality of your modem. The Pentium system itself should have *very little* to do with your overall connection speed since modems are vastly slower than Pentium PCs. I suggest that you try your testing repeatedly over the course of several days (perhaps at different times of the day)—you will probably find that some days are faster then others.

ERRORS AND DISCONNECTIONS DURING LONG-DISTANCE FILE TRANSFERS

*Q449. When doing Z-modem file transfers with this particular comput-
er, the transfer is always rough, and I get a lot of CRC errors—so
many that I'm finally disconnected by remote host. This happens
with long distance calls (local calls don't seem to have this problem). Could it be the phone line or the other modem or computer? Both modems are 14.4KB.*

A.   There are a whole variety of factors that contribute to communication problems, but since you seem to be able to communicate
with local BBS and other on-line facilities, I would say that your
PC and modem are working fine. The only variable then becomes
your long distance telephone connection and the modem at the
other end of your connection. Try connecting to other long distance resources and see if the problem continues. If so, you probably have poor phone line service, and it may be necessary to
force your communications at slower speeds (i.e., 9600 baud). If
you *can* connect to other long distance resources properly, I'd
suspect a problem with the remote PC or modem. You might try
contacting the system sysop for that system and asking for a
check of the system. It may also be that your modem and their
modem simply don't interact well (this is fairly rare, but does
seem to happen from time to time).

FULL-DUPLEX SOUND BOARD AND INTERNET PHONE

*Q450. I plan to install a new 33.6KB full-duplex voice/fax/data modem
(replacing the old 14.4KB modem). I also have a new full-duplex
sound card on the way. If you have a full-duplex modem, do you
have to have the full-duplex sound card as well to talk on the
Internet? What does full-duplex mean anyway?*

A.   That's a very popular question—and one that will become even
more important as modem speeds increase to support more data
across the Internet. Basically, the term *full-duplex* means simultaneous send and receive (much like your ability to talk and listen
at the same time using your telephone handset). Since Internet

talk takes voice in and sends voice out through the sound board, you *will* need a full-duplex sound board (and full-duplex drivers) to take advantage of your full-duplex modem and to talk over the Internet.

INTERNET VIDEO PHONE QUALITY VARIES

Q451. *The audio and video quality of my Intel Video Phone is usually terrible, but it seemed OK while I was on-line yesterday. What happened?*

A. You've almost certainly got a bandwidth problem with your Internet connection. The quality of a phone call across the Internet can vary from moment to moment. For the best possible quality, the Internet must transmit all the audio and video data without losing any portion of that data. The problem is that your bandwidth on the Internet is *dynamic,* and is affected by factors such as the amount of traffic on the Web at that particular moment. As more people connect to the Internet to access a growing range of services, you might have problems getting information through the congested services. For phone calls over the Internet, this can result in long delays or poor audio quality.

When audio and video quality degrade, you can maximize the available bandwidth for audio by stopping the video (ask your calling partner to do the same). This stops the video in both directions. You will most certainly experience improved audio sound. You can restart the video from time to time to test the video quality.

WEB BROWSERS AND DRIVE SPACE

Q452. *I am using Netscape Navigator and Windows to access the Internet. When I disconnect from the Internet, I notice my HDD has fewer bytes free even though nothing has been downloaded. Is there an answer for this?*

A.   I don't know what version of Netscape or Windows you're using, but it sounds like you're dealing with a caching issue. While you may not have downloaded any particular files, you have downloaded images and text—Netscape reuses those "pieces" as you revisit those sites to speed access times. Eventually, those temporary pieces will be deleted, but if you do a lot of surfing, the cache can become rather large. You can set the size of the cache or flush it at will—in Netscape, this is under the Network Preferences option. Note that making a very small cache (or reducing it to 0) can significantly slow your browsing because every graphic will have to be reloaded each time you visit a page. Ultimately, you should not be terribly concerned with this issue unless you desperately need the space immediately.

BROWSER TROUBLE WITH ANIMATED GIFs

Q453.   *My elderly 486DX2/66 Gateway with 6MB of RAM and still oodles of room on the hard drive can't handle Netscape 2.0. It seems to get confused with the new "moving" types of ads and any other type of message on the site that moves. The hard drive makes noises, and the red stop light on the top of the screen goes on and off, and it seems to be reloading the little files that move over and over again. If I try to change sites while these things are moving, the message "General Protection Fault" will show up. What is happening? Is my computer missing something? Why can't it handle the little moving ads on the Internet?*

A.   The problem is with your version of Netscape—it cannot handle animated GIFs. You should download version 3.0 or later. Go to the Netscape site (*www.netscape.com*) and download the latest version or Netscape. Move your BOOKMARK.HTM file to a temporary location and then uninstall your current version of Netscape completely. Use ScanDisk to correct any defective hard drive sectors and then defragment the hard drive. Finally, reinstall Netscape from your download. This should correct the problem. If trouble continues, you should use a comprehensive diagnostic to check the hard drive. If it is bad, it should be replaced.

NETSCAPE 3.0 AND WINSOCK ERRORS

Q454. *I'm running Netscape Navigator 3.0 on Windows 3.1. During the last few days, every time I start Netscape it crashes after a short while, and the only thing I can do is terminate it using <Ctrl>+<Alt>+<Del>. The error message I get in Winsock (2.0) is "Task Netscape(1E47) did not call WSACleanup." There are also other numbers like (1DFF), (1FA7), and (1FDF). How can I find out which program is causing the problem, and what can I do to fix it?*

A. First, did you load any new applications that could have a conflicting winsock? If so, check the date of the winsock against the one in your Netscape directory or dialer/connection directory. Moving the client application's winsock to its native directory (out of the Windows directory can help). Also search for all your winsocks—this may shed some light on a potential conflict or memory error (remember that you only want to have *one* winsock loaded at a time). There may also be a drive problem. Run ScanDisk and Defrag to check and organize your hard disk. Clear your disk cache in Netscape. Finally, you may want to add more RAM to your system if there is less than 16MB.

NETSCAPE 3.0 AND FILE ATTACHMENT PROBLEMS

Q455. *I can send e-mail with attached files but cannot receive them. If I send an attached file to myself, it is OK, but when others send attached files, they are received as garbage. Any help would be appreciated.*

A. Try changing to a MIME-compliant setting. Select Options, Mail and News, choose the Composition tab, then choose the MIME Compliant setting. If you had Allow 8-bit selected, this would explain why mail sent to yourself is OK, but when others send to you, you see the file coding instead of a picture or a viable file attachment. Supposedly, the MIME-compliant setting will process UUENCODE attachments. If you select View in the Mail window and Attachments as Links, you can load the file to your hard drive and be prompted to Save As automatically.

USING PHONE BLASTER WITH THE INTERNET

Q456. *I want to use my old 14.4KB Phone Blaster modem to access the Internet—I only need it for e-mail. The problem is that I can't figure out how to configure the Phone Blaster in Trumpet Winsock. Any suggestions?*

A.   Yes, you will need to edit the LOGIN.CMD file in the Trumpet directory. Near the beginning of the LOGIN.CMD file, you'll find a modem string of ATZ. You will need to replace it with the following string:

```
AT S37=11 S46=138 S48=7 W1 L3 N0 &R1^M
```

Remember to save your changes. This string should configure the Phone Blaster for 14.4KB operation.

REMOTE STATIC HEARD WITH WEBPHONE

Q457. *I'm working over the Internet using WebPhone with my PhoneBlaster 28.8 board. Everything works, but I'm getting reports that static is being heard on the other end. I don't think it's my microphone since I record WAV files with it that sound clean. I also don't think it's the phone connection because this seems to happen all the time. Any way to stop this?*

A.   I've seen this kind of problem with other types of sound boards, and it is almost always due to noise on the LINE-IN input. The noise is mixing with your voice and is being transmitted to the remote end. Start the mixer applet for your sound board, then MUTE the LINE-IN input. If you don't have a specific MUTE control, bring the LINE-IN volume down to zero. This should cut off the LINE-IN and prevent any unnecessary signals from mixing with your voice at the MIC-IN input.

Sound Volume Too Low Under RealAudio

Q458. I've been unable to adjust the volume control on my sound board to a high enough volume. I have a 16-bit Ensoniq Vivo 90 Wave 32 sound card and had no problems until I downloaded RealAudio in order to follow Danish news on the Danish Radio channel. Everything worked for several weeks, but over the last week, the sound setting is barely audible (even at the highest setting). Can you help?

A.   Here's a list for checking sound volume:

- Check the master volume control on your sound board—make sure it is turned up properly.

- Most sound boards have a "mixer" application that is initialized when the PC starts. Find that mixer application and see that the digital audio volume is set normally (Fig. 4.1).

- Check the cables that connect your speakers to the sound board—you may have a broken or loosened speaker cable.

- Make sure the speakers are powered properly.

- Finally, you may just have a failure in the sound board. The way to find out is to try another sound board.

- One last note: If your trouble's only under RealAudio, make sure the RealAudio volume control is turned up.

Figure 4.1 Typical mixer "applet" in operation

INTERMEDIATE

IMPROVING THE PERFORMANCE OF INTERNET EXPLORER

Q459. *I use Internet Explorer to surf the Web, but it seems so slow—even at 33.6KB. Is there any way to improve the performance of IE besides getting an even faster connection?*

A.   The most common cause of poor performance in Internet Explorer 3.0 is the many large pictures, sounds, videos, or other multimedia files that appear when you access a Web page. To improve browsing performance under IE 3.0, you can prevent pictures and multimedia files from being played when you access Web pages. Try the following procedure:

1.   On the View menu in Internet Explorer, click Options.

2.   On the General tab, click one or more of the following check boxes in the Multimedia area to clear them: Show Pictures, Play Sounds, and Play Videos.

3.   Click the Security tab and then click one or more of the following check boxes in the Active Content area to clear them: Allow Downloading of Active Content, Enable ActiveX Controls and Plug-ins, Run ActiveX Scripts, and Enable Java Programs

4.   Click OK.

CANNOT USE INTERNET EXPLORER THROUGH AOL

Q460. *I cannot use Internet Explorer through AOL; I get a message that says "Internet Explorer cannot open the Internet site."*

A.   You're running AOL version 3.0 for Windows instead of AOL 3.0 for Windows 95, so Internet Explorer 3.0 (for Windows 95) won't run. AOL for Windows uses a 16-bit version of WINSOCK.DLL. The 32-bit version of Internet Explorer does not run with this WINSOCK.DLL file. AOL 3.0 for Windows 95 also uses a 16-bit version of Winsock but installs an AOL adapter in Network properties that allows 32-bit browsers to work. If you upgrade your version to AOL for Windows 95, your Internet Explorer should work properly.

INVALID PAGE FAULT ERROR IN INTERNET EXPLORER

Q461. *I downloaded and installed Internet Explorer, but now when I start Windows 95, I get an Invalid Page Fault message.*

A.   In every case like this that I've ever heard of, the history folder or the cache folders used by Internet Explorer are damaged, or the index files used to track the contents of the history folders are damaged. To work around this problem, follow these steps:

1.   Empty the history and cache folders. Click Options on the View menu in Internet Explorer. Click the Navigation tab, and then click Clear History in the History area. Answer Yes in the dialog box that appears. Click the Advanced tab, click Settings in the Temporary Internet Files area, click Empty Folder, and then click Yes.

If the problem persists:

2.   In Control Panel, double-click Add/Remove Programs.

3.   Click Internet Explorer 3.0 in the list of installed programs and then click Add/Remove.

4.   After Internet Explorer has been removed, restart the computer. When you see the Starting Windows 95 message, press the <F8> key, and then choose Command Prompt Only from the start-up menu.

5.   Type the following commands, pressing <Enter> after each command;

Note

When you press <Enter>, you should be prompted to confirm that you want to delete the folder.

```
cd \windows

smartdrv

deltree tempor~1

deltree history
```

ADVANCED

```
cd system

ren mshtml.dll mshtml.old

ren shdocvw.dll shdocvw.old

ren inetcfg.dll inetcfg.old

ren actxprxy.dll actxprxy.old

ren wininet.dll wininet.old

ren cachevu.dll cachevu.old

ren inetcpl.cpl inetcpl.old

ren shlwapi.dll shlwapi.old

ren url.dll url.old

ren urlmon.dll urlmon.old

ren wsock32n.dll wsock32n.old
```

6. Press <Ctrl>+<Alt>+<Del> to restart your computer and then start Windows 95 normally.

7. Reinstall Internet Explorer.

Modem Terminology and General Topics

UNDERSTANDING ESSENTIAL MODEM TERMS

Q462. *I am confused by the terms* bps, baud, *and* cps. *Would you please explain the difference (if any) once and for all?*

A. The term bps means bits per second. This represents the actual number of digital 1s and 0s that a modem transmits each second. The term *baud* refers to the number of signal changes per second. It is vital to understand that the number of signal changes does not necessarily (almost never today) equal the number of bits per second since it is possible to carry 2, 4, 6, or more bits on any one signal transition using various frequency, phase, and amplitude modulation techniques (as well as data compression). As a result, one baud may carry several bits per second. For example, a 2400-baud modem may be able to carry 4800 or 9600 bps. While bps and baud are used to measure the speed of a modem, *cps* (characters per second) indicates the speed of the actual file transfer using protocols such as X-modem or Z-modem. For example, you will usually see the transfer speed in characters per second when downloading a file from a BBS or on-line information service.

INTERNAL VERSUS EXTERNAL MODEMS

Q463.   *I've been contemplating a new modem so that I can finally go on-line, but I'm confused about internal versus external modems. Some of my friends swear by internals and others by externals. Can you explain the difference and tell me what type of modem is best?*

A.   Let's start by saying that internal and external modems serve exactly the same purpose—they allow your PC to communicate over telephone lines. Internal and external modems will work exactly the same way so long as their performance specifications (i.e., data rate, error correction standards, and V. compatibility) are all equal. So neither type is really better, but there *are* times when an internal or external modem is better-suited to your particular PC's configuration. First, a modem needs two parts—a serial or COM port to transfer data to and from the PC and a modulator/demodulator to translate the data to and from audible signals that actually travel over the telephone lines. While most PCs today can support four serial ports (COM1 to COM4), a PC—practically speaking—can only use two serial ports at any one time because only two IRQ lines (IRQ3 and IRQ4) are available.

Here's the trick: If your PC has only one serial port (say the mouse is using COM1), you can use an internal modem, which provides both a modulator/demodulator and serial port on one plug-in board. You can then set the modem board to use another available COM address port (say COM2), and the modem should work properly. Internal modems are less expensive and take up no extra room outside of the PC.

Now things get a bit more complex. Most of today's PCs are equipped with two COM ports (say COM1 and COM2). That means the COM ports are using both available IRQ lines. Sure, you could add an internal modem as COM3 or COM4, but you would have to use one of the IRQ lines in use already, giving you the groundwork for a classic hardware conflict. In this scenario, you can use an external modem which would simply plug into the second serial port. Since the external modem is just the modulator/demodulator part, it does not care about COM ports and IRQ lines. External modems are a bit more expensive and take up extra room outside of the PC. They also need an extra ac outlet for a power adapter. On the plus side, external modems provide an array of status LEDs which allow you to track the progress of a call.

OK, say that there are two serial ports in the PC, but all you've got is an internal modem. If you disable the second serial port (usually through a jumper on the motherboard), you can then configure the internal modem as that same serial port—effectively, the internal modem would assume the identity of the port you just disabled. This tactic lets you avoid hardware conflicts. The time things get really bad is when there are two serial ports in the system, but both of them are in use. Sure, there are still two unused COM port addresses, but you're out of IRQ lines. If you can free one of the serial ports (i.e., change the serial mouse for a bus mouse), you can then use an external modem in the open port.

UNDERSTANDING MODEM FIRMWARE UPGRADES

Q464. *I have seen some modems advertised as being upgradable using some Flash ROM BIOS (or something like that). Do you know how these would be upgraded in the future—I mean, what would I have to do to upgrade a modem? Are these upgraded modems as dependable as nonupgradable ones? Would I be better off getting one without the upgrade feature?*

A.   Modems are largely governed by their firmware—the software permanently recorded in the modem's Read Only Memory (ROM). By altering the firmware, a modem can often be upgraded to handle additional commands, fix any bugs in the original code, or add new functions (such as operating at higher speeds). Firmware upgrades are typically handled in one of several ways: The modem may be sent back to the manufacturer for upgrade, the manufacturer will mail you a new firmware IC with instructions on how to physically replace it, or you can download and run a Flash file which will rewrite the firmware without having to ever touch the IC. According to our experience, flashed or otherwise upgraded modems are every bit as dependable as other modems, so there is no real reason to avoid choosing an upgradable modem.

FASTER MODEMS DON'T ALWAYS YIELD FASTER CONNECTIONS

Q465.   *I have a Logicode 2814HV modem that has been upgraded to 33.6KB with a new EPROM. The problem is that I can only connect with my ISP at 24.0KB. I know that our town has great phone service, so I can't think of a reason why the connection would be so slow.*

A.   There's more to Internet connections than the quality of your local telephone line. In most cases, your call to an ISP must pass through several telephone company switching offices. Older switching equipment and wiring problems may limit the bandwidth of your telephone line just enough to prevent the fastest modem connections. Choosing a different (perhaps more local) ISP might relieve some of those problems. Another important issue about modems that is often overlooked is that a connection can only be as fast as the *slowest* modem. If you're dialing into a 28.8KB modem at the remote end, there's no way you can take advantage of your faster modem. Maybe your ISP needs to upgrade their facilities, or there might be a different telephone number to call for 33.6KB access—check with your ISP to be sure.

INTERMEDIATE

MODEM WON'T WORK UNDER DOS

Q466.   I'm pretty good with computer problems, but I'm still baffled about this one. I have Windows 95 and my modem works correctly, but I need to use my modem for a DOS program. Why wouldn't it work? It has the standard settings for COM1. The echo command doesn't work.

A.   It sounds like you're using a Winmodem—which relies on Windows 95 resources for proper operation; it will not work under DOS. If the modem is a conventional modem, be sure that your COM software settings match the modem settings and then see that the modem initialization strings are configured properly.

TELEPHONE WIRING AND MODEM PROBLEMS

Q467.   *I replaced a working 14.4KB modem with a new 28.8KB modem (an internal model) which worked 10 percent of the time and only initialized the modem but did not dial properly most of the time. After frustrating hours of checking, rechecking, and replacing drivers all over the place, I returned the modem for another of the same model and have the same problem.*

A.   This is actually a fairly common complaint. Some modems are very sensitive to telephone line polarities. Try the modem on another telephone line. If it works, try reversing the line polarity (by reversing the tip and ring—red and green—wires). If a new telephone line doesn't do the trick, check the modem driver(s) and initialization strings. You may find that when you installed the new modem, the software was not updated properly or that the modem initialization string is not correct.

SELECTING THE RIGHT COM PORT

Q468.   *I'm installing a Zoom V34.I and am encountering obstacles with my COM port choices. Is there any sure-fire way to know which port to use? I have a mouse, printer, and sound card—and that's it. How exactly do I choose the port to use?*

A.   Be careful when installing a new internal modem—you will need to set the modem's jumpers to select a particular COM port, but you will also have to disable any corresponding COM ports in the system. This is one of the major disadvantages with internal modems. If you set the modem to use COM2, you will need to disable any other serial port set as COM2 in your system. Otherwise, the two COM ports will probably conflict, and the new modem will refuse to work. The printer is on a parallel port, and the sound card does not use resources typically used by COM ports, so your only real concern is the mouse. If the mouse is installed on COM1, you should set the modem as COM2. Conversely, if the mouse is installed on COM2, set the modem as COM1.

Running Two Fax/Modems

Q469.   *I would like to do some broadcast faxing. Is it possible to simultaneously run two fax/modems on my Gateway 2000 P75 computer?*

A.   The answer to that question is not so simple because of the myriad of hardware and software combinations that are available. Technically, the answer is Yes. You should be able to install two modems and run two instances of communication software to operate them. From a practical standpoint though, modems need a lot of configuring. And in many cases, two identical COM packages looking for two identical modems are likely to become confused and generate errors. Your best chance of success is to use two *different* modems and two *different* pieces of communication software (each configured for a specific modem). By using dissimilar products, you should be able to prevent hardware confusion. You also need to run a multitasking operating system like Windows 95, Windows NT, or OS/2.

Phone Blaster, Not Plug-and-Play

Q470.   *I just installed one of those Phone Blaster boards from Creative Labs, but Windows 95 refused to recognize the hardware. How do I get Windows 95 to recognize the Phone Blaster?*

A.   According to Creative Labs, the Phone Blaster is not a PnP device. This means you will have to configure it manually under Windows 95. You would accomplish this by opening your Control Panel and running the Add New Hardware wizard. This will identify your Phone Blaster to Windows 95 and allow you to load the drivers that accompanied your board.

When running the Add New Hardware wizard, do *not* let the wizard try to auto-identify the Phone Blaster.

Note

ADVANCED

MODEM-TO-MODEM TRANSFERS WITHOUT PHONE LINES

Q471.   *Can you just plug a phone line directly from modem to modem to transfer a file, or do you need to use two phone lines. If you can make a direct connection, how do you make it? This is not an attempt to replace a network; it is just a one-time thing.*

A.   In order to handle modem-to-modem communication without the support of the telephone company's phone lines, your modems will both need to handle leased line operation. It is very easy and can even be done from DOS. Assuming you have two PCs each with a modem and you join them directly with a simple telephone cable, use the following procedure:

- Connect the phone line cable between the two modems.

- Run your modem communication software on both PCs.

- Go into terminal or manual mode.

- You may reset modems to factory default first by sending AT&F to both modems.

- Send ATA on one modem and ATD on the other modem.

- The modems will start handshaking and establish connection.

- Start file uploading on one side and file downloading on other side.

Modem Corrective Actions

RESTORING A MODEM'S FACTORY DEFAULTS

Q472.   *Recently, I used some communications software that edited my modem's NVRAM (it's a US Robotics Sportster 14.4KB external unit). Now when I use Telix to call local bulletin boards, I get a screen full of garble that looks like an ASCII mess (instead of the usual ANSI graphics). I tried AT&F and then AT&W0 (I heard that this would reset to factory default, but it obviously didn't). Any help would be greatly appreciated.*

A.   I think you're using the wrong commands. Instead of &F or &W0, try &F0 and &F1 (referred to as extended AT commands) in your initialization line to load the modem's defaults back to NVRAM. For example, use AT&F0 or AT&F1.

Unable to Utilize Modem in MS-DOS Based Application or Game

Q473. *I've got a 33.6KB modem that I've been using for several months under Windows 95. The modem's been working flawlessly, but I can't get it to work under DOS. Someone told me that I've got a Winmodem, which will only work under Windows. Is this true? Will I have to replace the modem to work under DOS?*

A.   From your description, it does sound like you've got a Windows-only modem that depends heavily on Windows resources for proper operation (the modem driver is provided as a .VXD file). If you need to use a modem under DOS, you will have to replace the modem outright.

Lightning Still Damaged Modem

Q474. *I live in an area that gets a lot of lightning storms. Ever since I got my new Pentium PC, I have always unplugged it from the wall outlet when I'm not using it. The problem is that we got a storm the other day, and now my modem's not working. I replaced the modem (so I know the modem was bad), but I don't understand why the modem failed if the PC was unplugged.*

A.   I think the answer to your question is very simple—you unplugged your ac power line but forgot to unplug the modem from its telephone line. Remember that power surges and spikes can easily travel along telephone lines just as well as they can move down power cables. You almost certainly took a power surge from your telephone line. In the future, you should use a high-quality surge protector that provides ac and telephone line protection. If you would rather not trust a surge protector, you should continue to unplug both your ac power and your modem telephone cable.

No Sound from Scavenged Modem

Q475.   *I have a modem which I liberated from an NEC Ready 9522. It is
now installed in my Tyan Tomcat I system. The modem is working except I am not getting any audio from it. It would be nice to
hear the negotiation of each connection (I don't know if the
speaker ever worked). Any advice?*

A.   I'm assuming that you know what kind of modem you're using
and that you've installed the proper drivers for it. Modem sound
is generally controlled by two AT commands, as shown in Table
4.1: M*n* and L*n*. The M command defines when the speaker is
on, and the L command sets the speaker volume. These commands can be included in the modem's initialization string. By
default, most modems use M1 and L2, so you generally should
hear the connection and negotiation. The only reason a speaker
would be quiet is if the initialization string contains an M0 or if
the speaker is damaged. Check the modem's initialization string
in your communication software and make sure the commands
M1 and L2 or L3 are included. You might also enter the terminal
mode for your communication software and type the command
AT&F to load the factory configuration for the modem (which
will probably include M1 and L2 modes).

Table 4.1 Typical AT speaker commands

Command	Definition
M0	Speaker always off
M1	Speaker on until carrier detected
M2	Speaker always on
M3	Speaker on during answering
L0	Low volume
L1	Low volume (same as L0)
L2	Medium volume
L3	High volume

MODEM HANGS UP WITH MS PHONE

Q476. *I'm having trouble using MS Phone on my modem—the modem has a tendency to hang up. The modem works with other communication programs. How can I fix this?*

A. This is actually a common complaint about MS Phone, and it is because the line detection sensitivity is set too high. This makes the modem think that the caller has hung up, and the modem subsequently disconnects the phone line. You will need to download and install the latest patch for MS Phone.

TWO MODEMS APPEAR IN WINDOWS 95 CONTROL PANEL

Q477. *I don't understand what's going on here. I've been having trouble getting my new modem to work, and I noticed two entries for my modem under the Device Manager. The Diagnostics tab shows both modem entries set for COM2. Could this be what my problem is? How do I get rid of the extra modem entry?*

A. Yes, the extra entry can be causing your problem, so you'll need to remove the second entry under your Device Manager. Open your Control Panel, select System, select Device Manager and then double-click on Modem. You will want to highlight and Remove the second modem entry (or the modem entry that does not pertain to your system). If you are not sure which modem listing is correct, remove both modem entries and then allow Windows 95 to identify and reinstall the correct modem.

MODEM CAUSES MOUSE MALFUNCTION

Q478. *I installed a new internal modem into my PC, but now the mouse refuses to work. Is this a hardware conflict?*

A. This is perhaps one of the most common problems with internal modem installations. When a new modem is installed, it must be configured to use a COM port. There are typically two COM ports ready to go in a PC (although most PCs will support at least four COM ports). In many cases, the modem is accidentally configured to use the same COM port resources used by the COM port controlling your mouse. This causes a hardware conflict that can prevent the mouse, the modem, or both from working. Check to see which COM port the mouse is using (probably COM1) and then set the modem to an unused COM port (usually COM2). If your motherboard already has a connector for COM2, you may have to disable that COM port so that *it* does not conflict with the modem when you reconfigure it. You may have to disable a conflicting motherboard COM port through CMOS Setup or through jumpers on the motherboard itself.

WEIRD MODEM TONES SUGGEST BAD POWER DISTRIBUTION

Q479.   *I've replaced my internal 14.4KB modem with a new 28.8KB model using a Rockwell chipset. The new modem refuses to dial, and the dial tone is very low and highly distorted through the speaker. However, the 28.8KB modem seems to work on other PCs. Similarly, other modems (like a USR modem I've had laying around) work in my system. So I can't tell whether the modem or the motherboard are at fault. This is very confusing. Any ideas?*

A.   Yes. I've seen this kind of problem before, and it has to do with the voltages being provided by your power supply. Normally, a PC power supply produces +5-, −5-, +12-, and −12-V levels. In today's motherboards, however, the −5-V power supply is virtually unused except for the analog amplifier circuitry of some modems. If the −5-V power supply is low or absent, it can greatly disturb the operation of any modem that tries to use it (not all modem designs rely on the −5-V power supply). That would also explain why the modem would work in other systems, and other modems (which probably don't use the −5-V power supply) will also work in your system. Check the −5-V output from your power supply which is connected to the motherboard. If the output is low or absent, you should replace the defective power supply. If the −5-V level is present from the power supply, check the −5-V pin at your ISA ports (pin B5). You may have a faulty ISA port or a signal break elsewhere on the motherboard.

CHOPPY SOUND WHEN USING MODEM AS SPEAKERPHONE

Q480. *I have a modem which doubles as a speakerphone. In the data mode, the modem works perfectly. But in the voice mode, the sound is choppy (or there is no sound). I've checked the modem drivers and hardware installation—everything seems all right. Is the speakerphone defective?*

A. Your modem probably uses a technique called *dynamic echo cancellation* to avoid feedback from the microphone when operating in the speakerphone mode. However, if the volume on the speakers, the microphone's gain, or the ambient noise level is too high, the microphone picks up a high level of local feedback from the speakers. To counter this, echo cancellation automatically lowers the speaker volume (also lowering the volume of sound coming from the other end of the telephone line as well). When the modem realizes this, it raises the volume again. This up and down fluctuation in volume is what you hear as choppy sound. Adjust your microphone gain and speaker volume based on your particular environment in order to smooth out the choppy sound.

TRACKING DOWN SPEAKERPHONE PROBLEMS

Q481. *When I use the speakerphone feature in my modem, I can hear the person calling in, but that person cannot hear me. What's the problem?*

A. The most common cause of this problem is a wiring error. Double-check the following items:

■ The phone line from the wall should plug into the Line slot on the back of the modem.

■ The microphone should plug into the Mic-in port on the back of the modem.

■ The cable that connects the modem to the sound card should be secure.

■ Make sure to answer the phone with the speakerphone software before other answering applications pick up the line.

■ Additionally, once you turn on the speakerphone, be sure to check the volume settings in your mixer applet.

INTERMEDIATE

No Dial-tone Error When Dialing Out

Q482. *I can't dial out with my modem. When dialing starts, I cannot hear the dial tone. The dialing tones start and then I see a No Dial-tone error message. Why can't I get a dial tone?*

A.   First, check other phones that may be using the same phone line and see if any of those phones can draw a dial tone. If so, your problem is probably in the modem. If not, you've got a bad connection somewhere within your house wiring, or another phone (or other device) is off hook and interfering with your phone system. If only the modem can't draw a dial tone, check the modem's telephone cord (try replacing it with one from a working telephone). Also make sure that the modem's initialization string is correct and optimized for your particular modem (i.e., avoid using generic or Hayes-Compatible initialization strings). The modem may be "frozen"—try a cold reboot of the PC. Finally, the modem itself may be defective, so try replacing the modem outright.

USR Internal Modem Needs Re-seating

Q483. *I've got a USR Sportster modem and every now and then it quits—just "disappearing" from the system. Finally, I have to shut down and reseat the modem before it "comes back." Can you tell me why this is, and is there anything I can do about it?*

A.   Take a close look at your modem. Often, expansion cards may not fit perfectly into a card slot or seem to stop when only partially inserted. This makes it easy for system vibrations to "shake" the card loose. Make sure that the modem is seated *completely* in its slot, and its bracket is secured properly with a screw (if the bracket doesn't fit properly against the chassis, that's a good sign that the card is not installed completely). If you must remove the modem, check its gold-plated contact "fingers." You might try cleaning the contacts with a good-quality electronics contact cleaner and a cotton swab. Finally, try the card in a different slot—you may find that the slot is defective. If all else fails, try a new modem.

INTERNAL MODEM NOT WORKING AFTER A MOVE

Q484. *We just moved the motherboard, drives, and modem to a new case. When we power up the computer, it does not recognize the internal modem or its COM port assignment. We didn't change any of the jumpers or any other settings that were originally set.*

A. Hardware moves are a frequent source of problems such as yours. Start at the beginning and examine the modem. It should be seated evenly and completely in its bus slot. Some motherboards use oversized ISA bus connectors which allow a board to be inserted crooked or incompletely. Try reinserting the board from scratch. Also see that the modem's bracket is secured with a screw. Are you using a new video board with 8514 emulation? This causes a known conflict with COM4. If the modem is configured as COM4, it might be worth reconfiguring the modem to use a different COM port.

You might also try moving the modem to another ISA bus slot. If problems persist, try the modem in another PC. If it works in another system, you still have an installation problem. If the modem refuses to work in another system, you may have accidentally damaged the modem with electrostatic discharge during the move.

MODEM NO LONGER CONNECTING RELIABLY

Q485. *I have been using a NewCom 28.8KB fax/modem since late 1995 and consistently connected at 28.8KB. However, lately for no apparent reason, this modem just quit connecting reliably at any speed. After several tries, it will connect at no higher than 16.8KB—and often at 12.0KB. I checked and rechecked all the modem and Windows settings, and they are the same as before I had the problem. Also, the modem will not make any connection to BBS facilities at all. It will dial and attempt to make the connection and then will give me the No Carrier message. Is there a Web address for NewCom?*

A.   The first issue to consider is software or hardware conflicts—if
you installed any software or hardware recently that might have
coincided with the onset of your modem problems, you should
remove the hardware or software and see if the problem disappears. If the problem continues, I suspect that the modem itself
has failed. When modem connection speeds suddenly become
erratic, the modem hardware itself is usually at fault. Try a different (name brand) modem and see if the situation improves.
You can reach the NewCom Web site at *www.newcominc.com*.

CREATIVE LABS MODEM HANGS UP AFTER RECEIVING DATA

Q486.   *Here's one that's been bothering me a lot—when I receive a lot of
data, my Modem Blaster hangs up. I don't understand what's
going on here.*

A.   This is a simple problem that plagues both the Modem Blaster and
the Phone Blaster from Creative Labs. In most cases, the flow control setting for the product is set improperly. Make sure that your
communication software is configured to use RTS/CTS (hardware
flow control) and *not* DSR/DTR flow control. When the communication buffer is full, your computer will drop DTR to signal the
modem to stop sending data. Unfortunately, the modem interprets
this as an order to hang up the line. Under Windows 95, you may
also change the flow control setting in the Properties dialog of your
modem under the Connection, Advance setting.

MODEM CANNOT TALK TO OLDER FAX MACHINES

Q487.   *I recently built a system for a client using a Digicom Scout 33.6
modem, and now I have a strange problem—the modem does
not work properly with older fax machines. It will connect and
appears to be transmitting, but after it reaches 100 percent complete, it will give an error. I've tried a number of programs, but
all have the same problem. It has no problem connecting to other
fax/modems. I've tried changing the initialization string, but I
can't think of any setting that would cause this problem.*

A.   I'm not sure if you're using Windows 95, but if you are, you
     must alter the flow control method in the Registry for the
     Digicom Scout to work with Windows 95. To make this change,
     you must use REGEDIT and change the Setup Command key to
     ATS7=255&D3*F2 under the following entry:

```
KEY_LOCALMACHINE\SOFTWARE\Microsoft\AtWork Fax\
Local Modems\TAPIxxxxx
```

After making the changes, you must restart Windows. If the entry
is already set properly, or if this change fails to correct the problem, your modem is probably defective and should be replaced. If
you are using Windows 3.1x, you should simply enter the modem
initialization string above into the communication software.

Modem Works but Fax Doesn't

Q488.   *I purchased a Compaq Presario 7170 a couple weeks ago. I
        upgraded it to Windows 95 with the CD that came with it. Now
        the modem works, but the fax feature does not—it returns a
        Modem in Use message when I try to send a fax. Any help will
        be appreciated.*

A.   If the modem is a plug-and-play unit, remove the after-market
     fax software that it came with (if any), and use Microsoft Fax
     (part of Windows 95). Open Control Panel, System, and Device
     Manager, and double-click on the modem until you get to the
     Properties screen (Fig. 4.2). You'll want to manually select a con-
     figuration (you'll see a number of them listed). Select the one that
     corresponds to the traditional settings for the desired COM
     port/IRQ (i.e., COM2/IRQ3, COM1/IRQ4). We've found that
     that fixes the problem that you're having about 90 percent of the
     time. The other 10 percent of the time, you will need to revise
     the modem's initialization string, or you have a defective modem.

INTERMEDIATE

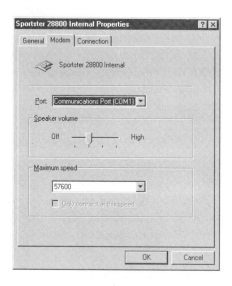

Figure 4.2 Modem Properties dialog for modem configurations

TRACKING DOWN MODEM ERRORS

Q489. *I recently inherited a used i486DX2/66. The system contains a standard IDE drive and adapter board, 8MB of RAM, and a VL video board with 1MB of video RAM. My modem is a 14.4KB unit. Unfortunately, I've discovered that my hand-me-down system is suffering from communication overrun and data framing errors. I have been able to calm these problems somewhat by lowering the data transfer rate from 57600 to 38400, but since the modem supports V.42bis and MNP compression, I did not think that would be necessary. Any ideas?*

A.   Well, it takes two computers to communicate. Framing errors are often caused when the frame bits (start, stop, and parity bits) are not set the same way at both ends of the communication link. Double-check the frame settings of your modem against the frame settings of the remote end, and make sure they match. Take a look at your flow control method—modems should use hardware flow control rather than software (XON/XOF) flow control. Another common problem is a speed mismatch between your PC and your modem. If the host PC passes data to the modem too quickly, the modem can easily overrun and misinterpret the data frame. As you noticed, slowing the data transfer rate relieved some of your problem—I would not be surprised to see you drop that value of 38400 down another notch to 19200. That will still be fast enough to support a 14.4KB transfer rate between computers. You're right that the latest communication standards support very fast data transfer, but that does not mean the transfer *must* be that fast. Try dropping the data transfer rate another notch, and I think you'll see the problem disappear.

CLEARING A "FROZEN" MODEM

Q490. *From time to time, my modem "freezes" and locks up the telephone line. What should I do if the modem locks up the phone line?*

A. Occasionally, you will notice that a modem might not disconnect properly. As a result, you continue to hear the modem squealing when you pick up the telephone receiver. The easiest way to resolve this problem is to use a modem command to disconnect the modem manually. Follow this procedure to resolve this problem:

1. Click on Start button, and then choose Programs from the menu.

2. Choose Accessories and then HyperTerminal.

3. Double-click on the HyperTerminal icon.

4. Enter a name in the Name field, and then click on the OK button.

5. Enter a phone number, and then click on the OK button.

6. Click on the OK button on the Connect screen.

7. Enter the following command: ATH.

8. Wait for the OK response.

9. Wait a moment, pick up the receiver, and check the phone line. The line should be clear.

ADVANCED

MODEM NEGOTIATES BUT WON'T CONNECT

Q491. *Maybe you can help me with my modem problem. I've got a 28.8KB USR modem. It dials, and I can hear the two modems negotiating, but they just keep negotiating—a connection is never established. What can I do?*

A. There are generally three problems that prevent modems from connecting: (1) your modem is configured (initialized) improperly, (2) the line conditions are terrible, or (3) the modems may simply be incompatible with one another. Check your modem's setup (especially the initialization string). You might want to check with USR and obtain the preferred initialization string for your particular modem. If the modem is set up correctly, try calling a different modem in another location. If you can connect to other modems, you may have serious line problems between your modem and the remote modem. You might want to try that modem again at another date. Finally, try calling the remote modem from a different local modem. If you can connect with a different local modem, it may be that your original modem and the remote modem are simply incompatible—it's rare, but it does happen.

REDETECTING SERIAL EQUIPMENT CAN CLEAR MODEM PROBLEMS

Q492. *According to the literature, a US Robotics Winmodem 28.8 is supposed to be plug-and-play. I tried installing it on a Gateway 2000 P-60 today, and it just wouldn't take. I tried manual installation, changed COM ports, and so on, but still no luck. I tried installing it on a different Windows 95 machine—pulled the old modem out and installed the Winmodem. Windows 95 recognized the modem at boot up and asked for the install disk. I'm confused.*

A. While this might sound like a complex problem of hardware conflicts, the answer is pretty direct—plug-and-play just failed to detect your Winmodem. This can happen on some PnP BIOS versions and motherboard designs. Start your CMOS Setup and make sure that all of your available serial ports are enabled under BIOS. Go to your Device Manager and *remove* the COM ports (highlight the devices and select Remove) along with any instance of the modem (look under Modem & Other Devices).

Now reboot Windows 95 and allow it to redetect the ports and modem—you will probably find that Windows 95 will sort everything out and successfully detect the Winmodem.

PnP Modem Disabling Hard Drive

Q493. *I recently purchased a plug-and-play modem and am having trouble installing it. I have purchased an ASPEN 28.8KB PnP modem. When I plugged it in a slot in my motherboard, my Seagate IDE hard drive failed. When I pulled the modem out, the hard drive worked properly. I have tried to plug the modem into different slots, but the modem still knocks out the hard drive. I have a GXA486SG motherboard with an AMD 486DX4/100 MHz CPU and AWARD BIOS v.4.50G.*

A.   First, make sure that your BIOS is compatible with PnP devices. If not, you should upgrade the BIOS before using your PnP modem. You may also need PnP drivers for the modem. When using a PnP device under DOS (or Windows 3.1x), you need low-level PnP drivers to assign resources to the PnP device. For example, my CONFIG.SYS file uses the following command line to enable my Ensoniq PnP sound card:

```
DEVICEHIGH=C:\PLUGPLAY\DRIVERS\DOS\DWCFGMG.SYS
```

My guess is that you failed to install the DOS PnP drivers for your modem in CONFIG.SYS. The DOS PnP drivers assign interrupts and I/O addresses during system start-up. Otherwise, the modem may be "guessing" at the settings and using resources that conflict with your hard drive controller. If problems persist, try a non-PnP modem instead.

Some Winmodems Require a Firmware Upgrade

Q494. *I have the Zoom 14.4 PC fax/modem and have had problems with AOL. After a "lively" conversation with the technical support people at AOL, they sent me some information on RPI modems in general, and it also included some helpful suggestions for the Zoom 14.4 PC. They basically said that you need to download the Windows RPI driver to replace the Windows*

*COMM.DRV driver. The snag I ran into is that the Windows
RPI driver won't work with firmware version 1.403 (of course,
that's the one I have). What should I do now?*

A.   If it's not one thing, it's another. Now that you know what driver
you need to use, you'll need to contact Zoom technical support
and order a firmware upgrade for your modem. In actual practice, the upgrade isn't that hard. You just need to replace an IC
(much like replacing a BIOS IC in a PC). The whole process
shouldn't take more than a few minutes.

ZOOM ROCKWELL MODEL GIVING CONNECTION PROBLEMS

Q495. *I have a Zoom 14.4KB PC fax/modem that gives me a lot of
connection problems. I'm not sure if it is my service or the
modem, but I've heard that Zoom modems with the Rockwell
RPI software-controlled data correction are very picky. If this is
true, what should I look for in a new modem, or is there anything I can check to determine where the connection problem is?*

A.   The Rockwell Protocol Interface (RPI) basically moves data compression and correction from the hardware layer into the software
layer. This allows a modem to be implemented as a single-chip
solution, but it makes greater processing demands in the Windows
95 environment. According to technicians that I have talked to, the
RPI-type modems work quite well when configured properly in a
system with adequate resources but can prove difficult to manage
otherwise. Before you take action with your modem, check the
phone connection by trying different locations. If you can get into
other on-line resources properly, it may be a problem with just that
BBS or service. If you have troubles with other on-line resources,
have your telephone company check the phone lines.

You might also try some different communication software which
might provide better support for the modem. For example, I've
seen RPI-type modems have trouble with AOL's front-end software, but after upgrading the RPI drivers downloaded from
AOL, the modem's performance improved dramatically. If all else
fails, you might consider a new 33.6KB modem with all the classical functions implemented in the modem's hardware.

ADVANCED

Serial Ports/UARTS

IDENTIFYING OLDER UARTs

Q496. I looked through some modem cards the other day, and I noticed that some of the cards had a device labeled as a 16C450. Now, I know that modems today use a 16550A UART, so what is the 16450? Is it an older UART?

A. Yes, it seems that you have come across an older modem board. The 16450 is indeed a Universal Asynchronous Receiver/Transmitter (UART). It was used primarily in AT (i286) modems as the successor to the 8250B UART which was so popular in XT modems. The C in the number simply designates that the IC is fabricated with low-power CMOS (no relation to CMOS Setup) technology. If you have a 16450-based modem, it is probably quite old by today's standards (probably under 9600 bps), and should only be applied in low-end applications.

CONNECTING SERIAL PORT CABLES

Q497. My new Tyan Tomcat's manual makes no reference to hooking up serial port cables. I am assuming they should plug into the motherboard's COM1 and COM2 connections since this is the logical location and is the only thing the cables fit on. Is this the correct place to plug in the cables?

A. If the motherboard has 9-pin (or 25-pin) subminiature D-type connectors, you should certainly be able to connect the serial cables directly to your motherboard—it's a pretty foolproof setup. However, if your motherboard only offers serial "headers" for a ribbon cable, you'll need to pick up a serial connector adapter at your local computer superstore. A serial connector adapter is basically a serial connector mounted in a bracket that fits into an expansion board opening on your chassis. A thin ribbon cable attaches the D-type serial connector to the serial header on your motherboard.

UPDATING A UART

Q498. *I remember that some UARTS have trouble at high speed, but I don't remember what the limitations of the chips are. I seem to be having a problem with a 28.8KB modem attached to a serial port with a 16450 UART. I've seen other serial ports with 16550s, so I know a 16450 isn't the latest and greatest. The port is on a Toshiba laptop. If I need to replace it, how much of a problem is that?*

A.　You're right on target with your UART issue. You'll need a late-model 16550A to handle communication with a 28.8KB modem. The bad news is that your laptop probably solders the UART right to the main board (if it's not integrated into another high-density IC). Either way, I think you're stuck back at 9600 or 14.4KB until you invest in a new laptop. Your only *possible* way around it is to install an internal 28.8KB modem in the laptop—disabling the corresponding COM port and using its own high-speed UART.

UPGRADING AN OLD UART

Q499. *I am presently using COM ports based on a 8250 UART chip. Is it possible for me to buy a high-speed serial port and fully take advantage of a 28.8KB external modem? My machine is a 486/33.*

A.　You can easily accomplish a UART upgrade by installing an internal modem. This will require you to disable the corresponding COM port in the system. If you are using an external modem, you will need another I/O card. Fortunately, multi-I/O cards are readily available and inexpensive. Since a multi-I/O card typically offers several options such as two serial ports, a parallel port, a joystick port (and more), you will need to see that *all* the unused ports are *disabled* before installing the card (otherwise you'll wind up with hardware conflicts). You will also need to disable the corresponding COM port on your motherboard. For example, if you install a multi-I/O board to serve as COM1, you'll need to shut down everything on the multi-I/O board except for a serial port, configure the serial port as COM1, and then disable COM1 already in your system.

Refitting Old COM Ports

Q500. *I just rebuilt an old Zenith Data Systems 286, and I was thinking about using it for a simple BBS system. I want to use an external 28.8KB modem I have laying around. My problem is that both COM ports use the 8250 UART, which I know won't support high-speed modems. Can I replace the UARTs with 16550s?*

A. Check to see if the 8250 UARTs are in sockets. If so, you should be able to replace them directly with 16550 UART ICs. If not, you will need to replace your existing COM ports by using an I/O board that has 16550 UARTs. Many older PCs provided COM ports using an I/O board. If this is the case, you can just remove the old I/O board and install the new one. When the 8250 UARTs are installed on the motherboard, you will have to disable the motherboard's COM ports before installing the high-speed I/O card. If a new I/O board has other ports on it as well (such as drive controllers and parallel ports), be sure to disable them before installing the I/O card.

Keeping COM Ports from Interfering

Q501. *Will a mouse on COM1 (IRQ4) interfere with a modem on COM3 with the same IRQ? When will it not interfere? If I'm not using the mouse, will it still interfere? Will the modem interfere with the mouse when not being used?*

A. Modems and mice each demand exclusive use of their respective COM port. If you had the modem on COM1 and the mouse on COM2 (or vice versa), there would be no problem since each device would use its own IRQ. When you attempt to use both devices with the same IRQ, however, a hardware conflict will invariably result. Even when only one of the devices is being used, the presence of the idle device can (and usually will) cause conflict problems. Your best course is to rearrange the mouse and modem so that one device is running from COM1 (IRQ4), and the other device is running from COM2 (IRQ3).

ADVANCED

Increasing the Available COM Ports

Q502. *I've got a question about my motherboard. It has two serial port connectors installed right on the motherboard (COM1 and COM2). Can I add more COM ports to the system, or am I stuck with the two ports I have already?*

A.   The technical answer to your question is Yes, you can certainly add a multi-I/O board with one or two additional COM ports which you could assign as COM3 and COM4. This would give you a total of four COM ports. The problem is that COM ports share IRQs—COM1 and COM3 use IRQ4, and COM2 and COM4 share IRQ3. What this means is although you can have four COM ports, you can only *use* two COM ports at any given time. Real technophiles will argue that you *can* use all four COM ports (just as long as you don't use the devices on COM1/COM3 or COM2/COM4 simultaneously). I always believed that was an invitation for trouble, so if you can live with the two COM ports already on your motherboard, I would advise you *not* to add the extra COM ports.

5

Motherboard Questions

Each new generation of PC demands ever-more complex motherboards to support more powerful CPUs and chipsets, more memory, faster busses, and other performance-oriented features. Keeping track of the changing specifications and components can be a full-time job, so there is never a shortage of motherboard-related questions. This chapter answers BIOS and chipset issues, examines motherboard planning and operations, and then takes an extensive look at system memory and cache.

BIOS and Chips

UNDERSTANDING A ZIF SOCKET

Q503. *I've been looking into a CPU upgrade, and I've seen a lot about ZIF sockets. This may sound like a silly question, but what is a ZIF socket?*

A.   ZIF stands for zero insertion force and ZIF sockets are used to simplify removal and replacement. Lifting a lever on the socket relieves tension on the IC so that it can be removed. When the new IC is installed, you return the level to its locked position to secure the IC. Most current motherboards incorporate a ZIF socket for the CPU. In cases where a CPU is hard-soldered to the motherboard a ZIF socket is frequently provided for an OverDrive processor.

TX vs. HX CHIPSETS

Q504. *I know that this can be a complicated question, but can you tell me the basic difference between a TX and HX chipset? Do you need a TX chipset to make use of MMX CPUs?*

A.   The Intel 82430HX chipset is a bit older and is usually considered to be the best Pentium classic chipset (dubbed Triton2). It is renowned for providing great performance for Pentium motherboards with up to 512MB of RAM. The 82430TX is a similar chipset, but it is designed to support true MMX processors and SDRAM. A TX chipset also integrates a whole series of intelligent system features such as System Bus Management (SMBus), Dynamic Power Management Architecture (DPMA), and Advanced Configuration and Power Interface (ACPI). You can get MMX compatibility by using a Pentium MMX OverDrive CPU on your ordinary Pentium motherboard. But if you want the *best* MMX performance, you'll need a true MMX processor with the TX (or similar) chipset.

GETTING POSITIVE ID ON A CPU

Q505. *My Tyan Tomcat motherboard came with the Pentium 133 CPU already installed and the heat sink/fan on top. I don't suspect that anything is wrong, but how can I tell if the CPU is indeed a 133-MHz Pentium?*

A. There are a few options for you. First, check your BIOS display in the moments following your system start-up. Often, modern BIOS versions will display information like the CPU type and speed, memory configuration, BIOS version, and so on. Check there for your CPU ID. If that fails, you can use a current diagnostic utility to query the CPU ID and report the results. A current version of Norton Utilities, WinProbe, TuffTest, or any number of up-to-date shareware diagnostics can provide detailed CPU information. If all else fails and you need a handle on your CPU immediately, you can always just remove the heat sink/fan and read the part number directly (then replace the heat sink/fan assembly).

UNDERSTANDING THE CPU SOCKETS

Q506. *I've been working with PCs for a few years now, and I see a lot about Socket 7. What is Socket 7 and are there other sockets that I should know about?*

A. That's a great question. Socket designations have been used by Intel for some years since the introduction of their 486 CPU. Figure 5.1 illustrates the eight major socket types, and Table 5.1 explains how each socket is used. Today, Socket 7 is a popular Pentium socket which accommodates low voltage CPUs up to 100 MHz and OverDrive CPUs to 166 MHz. One new socket which is not listed here is Slot 1—a new 242-pin edge connector type of CPU socket used for the Pentium II.

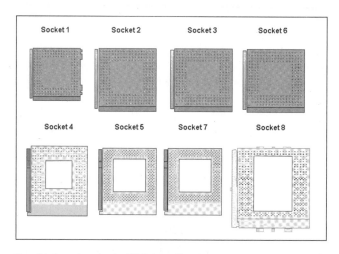

Figure 5.1 Comparison of major CPU Socket configurations

TABLE 5.1 COMPATIBILITY DETAILS FOR MAJOR SOCKETS

Socket	Pins	Volts	CPU	Compatible OverDrive Processor(s)
1	169	5	486 SX	BOXDX4ODP75, BOXDX4ODP100
			486 DX	BOXDX4ODPR75, BOXDX4ODPR100
2	238	5	486 SX	BOXDX4ODP75, BOXDX4ODP100
			486 DX	BOXDX4ODPR75, BOXDX4ODPR100
			486 DX2	BOXPODP5V63, BOXPODP5V83
3	237	3/5	486 SX	BOXDX4ODP75, BOXDX4ODPR75
			486 DX	BOXDX4ODP100, BOXDX4ODPR100
			486 DX2	BOXPODP5V63, BOXPODP5V83
			486 DX4	n/a

TABLE 5.1 COMPATIBILITY DETAILS FOR MAJOR SOCKETS (CONTINUED)

Socket	Pins	Volts	CPU	Compatible OverDrive Processor(s)
4	273	5	60 /66 MHz Pentium	BOXPODP5V133
5	320	3	75 /90 /100 MHz Pentium	BOXPODP3V125 BOXPODP3V150 BOXPODP3V166
6	235	3	486 DX4	n/a
7	321	2.5/ 3.3	75 /90 /100 MHz Pentium	BOXPODP3V125 BOXPODP3V150 BOXPODP3V166
8	387	2.5	Pentium Pro	n/a
Slot 1	242	n/a	Pentium II	n/a

CYRIX CPU MISIDENTIFIED UNDER WINDOWS 95

Q507. *Why is my IBM P100 CPU reported as a 486 CPU in Windows 95?*

A. This is a common problem and is typically caused by the age of Windows 95. The entire line of Cyrix/IBM 6x86 CPUs will be reported as 486s under Windows 95. Reboot your system and look for the CPU to be identified in the BIOS setup screen. If BIOS identifies the CPU as a 6x86/100 MHz device, the BIOS should support your CPU properly and performance should not be adversely affected under Windows 95. If BIOS doesn't recognize the 6x86 CPU correctly, you should consider upgrading your BIOS. Future versions of Windows should identify the Cyrix CPUs correctly.

SECURING A DISLODGED HEAT SINK/FAN

Q508. *My heat sink/fan fell off my CPU while in transit the other day. The heat sink was originally glued on. I have a 486DX2/80 AMD CPU. Do I really need a heat sink/fan for this CPU? If so, are there new heat sink/fans with clips rather than glue to hold the assembly to the CPU?*

A.   I doubt that your heat sink/fan was just glued in place. I'd bet that glue was thick white paste—it probably has a little bit of an acrid smell. If so, that's thermal grease which is used to improve the heat transfer between the CPU and heat sink/fan assembly. Leave the thermal paste in place when you replace the heat sink/fan. The actual heat sink/fan should clip onto the CPU or latch to the CPU socket once the CPU is set into place. If you have no means of securing the heat sink/fan to the CPU, you should replace the assembly with one that has working clips.

EXCHANGING FANS BETWEEN CPUs

Q509.   *Would you tell me if the fan on a P75 CPU will fit on a P133 CPU? I know they have the same pin layout and fit in identical sockets, but as I understand, the P75 IC case dimensions are different.*

A.   Physically, the heat sink/fan assembly should attach to a P133 just as well as a P75. The only problem is that of heat dissipation. You should be sure that the P75 heat sink is large enough (with enough surface area) to dissipate the additional heat created by a P133. Otherwise, you may need a larger heat sink or more robust fan to handle the additional heat. Also remember to attach the heat sink/fan using a thin layer of thermal grease between the CPU and heat sink.

CPU COOLERS SHOULD NOT HAVE GAPS

Q510.   *I'm putting together a P166 system. The CPU fan that was supplied slides onto the CPU before it is installed, but it is very loose on the CPU. I put some silicone heat sink compound between the CPU and heat sink and had to push against the edge of the CPU when I pushed the socket lever down so that the heat sink/fan would not move around. There is still a small gap between the heat sink and CPU. Is this normal? Isn't the heat sink supposed to butt right up against the CPU?*

A.   This is a very common (and unnecessary problem) with today's heat sink/fans. Cheap heat sink/fans have fixed-height clips, but any variation in the CPU's case thickness basically leaves the heat sink/fan useless. Thermal grease is only effective when there is a tight seal between the heat sink and CPU to begin with. I suggest that you replace the heat sink/fan assembly with one using spring-loaded clips—this allows the heat sink to adapt to minute variations in the CPU height. Since you just bought the CPU and cooling unit, you should be able to send it back for a suitable replacement.

Replacing a Broken Heat Sink/Fan

Q511. *The CPU fan attached to the heat sink on my 100-MHz Pentium (not overclocked) is broken and has been temporarily removed. This is in an Enlight midtower case. There is a secondary fan in the front of the case which is a few inches from where the CPU is. It seems to be blowing more air into the case than out. Should I worry about not having a CPU fan when there is a heat sink attached to this type of processor and given the secondary fan?*

A. The general rule of thumb is that any 486DX4 CPU or later should have a heat sink/fan. I will grant you that the remaining heat sink and external fan will help, but you need to take a close look at the heat sink itself. If the heat sink is hot, you should certainly get a new heat sink/fan assembly. If the heat sink is really only warm, it's more of a judgment call. Still, $10 to $15 for a new heat sink fan is cheap insurance against random system lock ups and crashes caused by CPU overheating.

Understanding Flash BIOS

Q512. *I'm considering a motherboard upgrade for my older i486 system, and all the Pentium motherboards I see sport something called Flash BIOS. I know what BIOS is, but what is flash BIOS? Is it faster than ordinary BIOS?*

A. Traditionally, BIOS was fixed in a ROM IC which was inserted into the motherboard. In order to upgrade the BIOS, you would have to purchase new BIOS ROM ICs and then insert them into the motherboard yourself. Flash BIOS is reprogrammable memory which can be reprogrammed by the computer user while the flash BIOS IC is still in the motherboard. This technology allows you to actually upgrade your BIOS in a matter of minutes without ever opening the computer. In order to update a flash BIOS, you simply need to download the updated BIOS file from the system maker, decompress the update file, and then run the update file. Keep in mind that if you are given the opportunity to make a backup copy of your existing BIOS before flashing it, you *should* do so.

PENTIUM PRO INTERNAL CACHE

Q513.   *I've heard a lot about the Pentium Pro and the "power" of its internal L2 cache. Now I always thought that L2 meant "outside the CPU." Is the cache really inside? If so, how does that improve the Pentium Pro's performance?*

A.   Traditionally, L1 cache is internal cache which is located in the CPU die, and L2 cache is external somewhere on the mother-board. The Pentium Pro changes the rules a bit by placing 256KB of cache inside the Pentium Pro assembly. However, since the cache is located on a die, which is *not* the same die as the Pentium Pro, it is considered to be L2 cache (even though it is packed in the same IC). This close proximity to the actual CPU allows the Pentium Pro to communicate with the L2 cache at top speed for best performance.

PLACING AN MMX CPU IN A PENTIUM MOTHERBOARD

Q514.   *Can a Pentium motherboard accept a Pentium-MMX chip?*

A.   That can be a confusing issue. A true MMX CPU requires dual voltages and a chipset capable of supporting the enhanced MMX features. As a result, you cannot use a true MMX in a regular Pentium motherboard. However, you *can* install a Pentium MMX OverDrive CPU on an ordinary Pentium motherboard. The OverDrive module handles the voltage conversion and does not use all of the enhancements found in a true MMX.

CHECKING FOR FLASH BIOS

Q515. *I'd like to upgrade my motherboard's BIOS, but I don't know if I have flash BIOS or not. How can I tell what kind of BIOS I have?*

A.   There are several ways to tell. First, check the documentation that came with your motherboard or system—the list of features will probably identify a flash BIOS. If the documentation also lists a jumper such as a flash jumper, BIOS programming jumper, or something similar, you have a flash BIOS. If that fails, you can probably tell by looking at the BIOS IC itself. Find the BIOS IC on your motherboard. It will usually be a 28- or 32-pin DIP IC in a socket and will probably have a sticker on it from a BIOS manufacturer (i.e., Phoenix or AMI). Compare the IC's part number prefix with those in Table 5.2.

TABLE 5.2 TYPICAL BIOS IC TYPES BY PART NUMBER

Part Number	Description*
28Fxxx	12 V flash
29Cxxx	5 V flash
29LVxxx	3 V flash (these are rare)
28Cxxx	EEPROM (similar to flash)
27Cxxx	EPROM (you'll see a quartz window)
	* Anything without a quartz window that doesn't have a 28 or 29 as the prefix number is most likely a standard ROM.

INTERMEDIATE

SHARING A BIOS BETWEEN MOTHERBOARDS

Q516. *I'd like to try my current BIOS on another motherboard. The ICs look to be the same size. Can I move a BIOS from one computer to another?*

A.   A BIOS is very closely tied to the particular motherboard hardware, especially the chipset. As a result, it is virtually impossible to transfer a BIOS between dissimilar motherboards. While the actual BIOS IC may fit in, the actual BIOS code will probably not even boot an alien motherboard. You would be better off to obtain a generic third-party BIOS (such as one from Mr. BIOS, *www.mrbios.com*) for your other motherboard.

BIOS Is Not Portable

Q517.   *I want to upgrade my BIOS, but I can't find a suitable replacement for my system. Can I use a BIOS from another more recent PC?*

A.   Not a chance. The BIOS is very closely tied to the hardware, especially the chipset installed on your motherboard. A current BIOS will almost certainly prevent an older motherboard from booting. In fact, even exchanging BIOS ICs between different motherboard models of the same current product line will almost always prevent those systems from starting. If there is no update for your existing BIOS, your best course if to leave the system alone or replace the motherboard outright.

Precautions When Installing an Old Motherboard

Q518.   *I inherited an older motherboard from a friend at work. The motherboard has all the documentation. I haven't really thought of a place to use it yet, but given that the motherboard has been around for a while, are there any special considerations to keep in mind when setting it up?*

A.   Yes, there are several issues to keep in mind if you do choose to resurrect any older motherboard:

■   You'll almost certainly need a new CMOS backup battery. Don't buy or install one until you're ready to install the motherboard.

■   Carefully reseat *any* DIP-type ICs on the on the motherboard, including BIOS, keyboard controller, and so on. This prevents corrosion between the sockets and IC pins which might cause bad connections.

- Reseat all cable connections such as the power supply, floppy drive, hard drive, and so on. This also helps prevent contact corrosion from causing bad connections.

- Before installing new expansion boards, use some good-quality electronics contact cleaner in the bus slots to help clear away any corrosion.

- When you finally do use this motherboard, power it up first with only a bare minimum of equipment needed to boot a PC (i.e., video board and floppy drive). Allow the motherboard to burn in for a few days before completing the assembly.

TROUBLE WITH THE FLASH UPGRADE

Q519. *I want to upgrade my BIOS, so I downloaded and ran the flash program, but my system hangs up every time I try to run the flash program. What do I do now? Is my BIOS damaged?*

A. If the BIOS upgrade program refuses to execute (and your PC continues to boot normally), chances are that your BIOS is OK. In many cases, flash BIOS utilities *must* be executed without any memory managers (i.e., HIMEM, QEMM, or EMM386), drivers, or TSRs in memory. Try booting the system from a bootable diskette that doesn't have any CONFIG.SYS or AUTOEXEC.BAT files and *then* try running the flash utility. Remember, if the utility gives you an opportunity to make a backup of your current BIOS, do so before flashing the new BIOS. That way, if there are any unforeseen problems with the new BIOS, you can always restore the original BIOS.

FLASHING THE BIOS ON AN ACER 970

Q520. *I want to flash the BIOS to upgrade my Acer 970. The problem is that the AFLASH utility doesn't want to work. How can I upgrade my BIOS?*

A. I really had to dig for this one. Although the AFLASH utility for an AcerNote 970 is built into the BIOS, you cannot use the AFLASH program on a model 970. Instead, use the following procedure:

ADVANCED

1. Power up the 970 and then press <Fn>+<F2> to enter CMOS Setup.

2. Select the System Security option, and change the Flash New BIOS entry from disabled to enabled.

3. Save the CMOS setup during exit.

4. Power down the 970 by closing the display lid.

5. Prepare a formatted disk (*not* a bootable disk) with the new desired BIOS binary file *.BIN on it.

6. Power up the 970 again (with the data disk in drive A:) by opening the display lid.

7. The 970 will flash the new BIOS. You'll hear four beeps if the new BIOS has flashed successfully.

8. After flashing, the 970 should automatically shut down. If not, reset the system.

9. Remove the data disk and restart the 970.

10. Make sure to change the Flash New BIOS entry back to disabled.

FLASH BIOS DISASTER

Q521. *I'm in trouble. I started a flash utility to upgrade my BIOS, but in the middle of the process, the system crashed and rebooted. Now my PC won't boot at all. What can I do?*

A.   Well you're right, you *are* in trouble. One of the cardinal rules when flashing a BIOS is to *never* reboot or power down the system. The BIOS must be *completely* rewritten before rebooting. When you rebooted in the middle of your flash process, you left the BIOS only partially rewritten. As a result, the BIOS is corrupt, and your PC won't boot because there's effectively no BIOS. You will need to replace the BIOS IC on your motherboard. Even if you get the same version you had, you can always reflash that once the system is booting again.

New BIOS Causes Rustling Sound

Q522. *My system has an Intel Advanced/EV motherboard, and a good-quality sound card. Originally, I had a problem installing Windows 95. However, I noticed that the BIOS was older, and after I upgraded the BIOS to 1.00.06.CB0, Windows 95 installed correctly. But now I have another problem. I get a rustling sound from my speakers every time I move the mouse or press keyboard keys. This never happened with the old BIOS. Any suggestions?*

A. First, I assume that you did not make any hardware changes to the system before installing Windows 95, so chances are that the problem is software-related. If this problem occurs under DOS and Windows 95, I'd suspect your BIOS upgrade. Check for an even later BIOS upgrade from Intel. If the problem occurs only under Windows 95, check the Device Manager for hardware conflicts between the system timers and sound board. You might also try removing the sound board (and its drivers), and then reinstalling your sound system from scratch using the latest Windows 95 drivers for your sound board. Intel recommends that you perform an NVRAM Clear, which will load the defaults for your CMOS Setup. You can find the procedure in Q108. Remember that clearing the CMOS in this fashion will also clear a CMOS area used by PnP and may require you to reinstall Windows 95.

Busses and Bus Mastering

Why So Many Slots

Q523. *Why do almost all motherboards support three or four PCI slots? I haven't been in the PC business that long, but every motherboard I have seen has the HDD, FDD, and usually even video connectors on the motherboard already. Maybe you need one PCI slot for a video board and perhaps one for a SCSI adapter. Are there any more devices that use PCI? I sure haven't found any; it seems to me that they just waste space that could be used for ISA or more SIMM slots.*

A.   I totally disagree. One of the reasons that PCs became so popular was due to their expandability—the potential to add and upgrade new devices in a system without having to start from scratch. That fact alone demands that there be at least a few extra slots available. You're correct that many motherboards now integrate many controllers right out of the box, but that doesn't negate the need to upgrade a system later on with newer and more powerful video and drive adapters (or replace a controller that may have failed on the motherboard). But if you consider that a video board, SCSI adapter, and drive controller would take up three slots, that only leaves a forth slot unclaimed, which is typically used by a network board. Ultimately, there's very little wasted space on today's motherboards.

MAKING USE OF EISA SLOTS

Q524.   *A friend of mine just got an old Acer 1200 handed down to her. A cursory inspection reveals only EISA slots. Are sound cards and internal modems available for this type system?*

A.   As a general rule, ISA boards should work in EISA slots (that was supposed to be EISA's advantage over MicroChannel slots). So regular ISA sound boards and modems will probably install properly. The problem is that EISA slots need to be specifically configured. The system should have an EISA configuration utility program that will allow you to properly configure each slot. Whenever you add or remove a card from a slot, you need to run the utility again to properly configure the slot. If you don't have the utility, you're going to have a tough time setting up the system.

USING ISA BOARDS WITH VL OR EISA MOTHERBOARDS

Q525.   *I'm always piecing together PCs out of used parts and subassemblies. The problem is that it's tough to find EISA and VL boards to replace old or failed parts. Some friends say I can use ISA boards in EISA or VL slots, but I've never heard of this. What's the deal?*

A.   Yes, you *can* put ISA cards in both EISA slots and VL bus slots, since both buses were specifically designed to be 100 percent backward-compatible with ISA. However, you should understand that ISA devices are low-bandwidth devices, so you will not get nearly as much performance from an ISA board in an EISA or VL bus slot as you would from an EISA or VL board. Also remember that when using EISA systems, you'll need to run an EISA configuration utility after making any changes to the system's configuration.

Handling an EISA Configuration Error

Q526.   *I'm using an EISA system, and I've made some changes to it. Now my machine gives a Configuration Error for Slot 16. I know the PC doesn't have anywhere near 16 slots. What's the problem?*

A.   This is a minor quirk of many EISA-based machines. While a BIOS upgrade should correct the problem, it isn't serious, and there's nothing wrong with your hardware. You only need to run your EISA Configuration utility once to get rid of the message.

Using ISA Boards with MCA Motherboards

Q527.   *I'm working on a MicroChannel PC that looks like it needs a new video board, but all I've got are some old ISA video boards. Finding new MCA video boards has proven to be almost impossible. Before I replace this antique motherboard, can I use an ISA video board instead?*

A.   No. ISA and MCA bus architectures are totally different. It looks like you'll be replacing that motherboard after all.

Three Bus Types on the Same Motherboard

Q528.   *I've purchased a motherboard that has a VESA Local Bus, three ISA bus slots, and three PCI bus slots—all powered by an AMD 5x86 CPU. The system is up and running with an AMI BIOS. Although I'm not experiencing any problems with the system, I'm just wondering if there's a catch somewhere.*

INTERMEDIATE

A.   The answer to your question is Yes. Since there must often be a
       "bridge" between the PCI and VL bus systems, PCI performance
       tends to suffer. I don't have hard numbers handy to explain the
       differences, but the difference is noticeable. Chances are good
       that your motherboard will continue to work adequately, but I
       would recommend avoiding those kind of "trio" motherboards
       in the future.

Understanding the USB

Q529.   *I've been looking at new motherboards recently, and one feature
        I see a lot is a USB port. What is a USB port, and how do I use it?*

A.   The universal serial bus (USB) is a relatively new bus architecture
        developed by Compaq, DEC, IBM, Intel, Microsoft, NEC, and
        Northern Telecom. The idea behind USB is that you can simply
        plug in a peripheral to a bus *outside* the PC and then the PC will
        automatically recognize and configure the USB device. USB is
        also designed for "hot" insertion and removal, so you wouldn't
        even have to power down or reboot the system after inserting or
        removing a USB device. According to the specifications, a USB
        port allows up to 127 devices to be connected simultaneously.

        In theory, just about any peripheral device could be designed to
        accommodate the USB. Telephones, modems, keyboards, mice,
        CD-ROM drives, joysticks, tape and floppy drives, scanners, and
        printers are just a few such devices. USB offers a 12-Mbit/s data
        rate, and this allows a whole new generation of peripherals
        including MPEG-2 video-based products, data gloves, and digitiz-
        ers. Also, since computer-telephone integration is expected to be
        a big growth area for PCs, the USB is expected to provide an
        interface for integrated services digital networks (ISDNs) and dig-
        ital PBXs.

        Unfortunately, the move to USB has been painfully slow. Even
        though a growing number of motherboards and BIOS versions
        are supporting USB, early releases of Windows 95 do not, and
        very few important USB devices are available. That situation will
        probably change through 1997 into 1998.

CONTROLLING YOUR BUS MASTER

Q530. *What is bus mastering and how does that relate to PCI devices?*

A.   Simply stated, bus mastering is taking control of the bus operations. Most older PC busses were dependent upon the CPU for
constant direction and control; bus devices (such as video
adapters) were unable to take control of the bus. The
MicroChannel (MCA) bus was the first PC bus architecture (used
with PS/2 systems) that allowed bus mastering. Unfortunately, the
MCA bus never caught on. The high-performance PCI bus used
with late model i486 systems and virtually all Pentium systems
also allows bus mastering. A PCI bus master device can take control of the PCI bus and execute data transfers independently of
the CPU. This not only boosts performance by allowing higher
data rates during long transfers, but it also frees up the CPU to
handle other tasks in the meantime. You can usually enable or
disable PCI bus mastering through the CMOS Setup.

PCI HANG-UPS

Q531. *I've got a problem with my new PCI drive adapter: It won't
work when I plug it into the system. It will work on another system, so I know that the hardware and drivers are good, but I
can't imagine what might be wrong on my system.*

A.   It may very well be that your PCI slot is not configured properly.
Most PCI systems automatically configure cards plugged into a
PCI slot, but some systems require you to go in to the CMOS
Setup menu and manually configure each PCI slot. Generally, you
must have the drive adapter in a bus mastering PCI slot. The slot
must be assigned a unique IRQ—often 9,10 (0Ah), or 11 (0Bh),
and an I/O address. If you are running Windows 95, settings in
the Resources tab in System Properties must match the settings in
the CMOS Setup menu as far as IRQs and I/O addresses.

CHOOSING THE RIGHT PCI SLOT FOR VIDEO

Q532. *I've installed a new video board in a PCI slot, but video is still being produced by the motherboard. Why is this, and what can I do about it?*

A.   First, you may need to disable the motherboard video via a jumper on the motherboard or by shutting down the video system in your CMOS Setup. If the problem persists, try installing your video board in PCI slot 1. PCI slots are typically prioritized, and slot 1 gets the highest priority. In some motherboard designs, the add-on video system must be added to slot 1 and will automatically disable the motherboard video system.

PCI SCSI DEMANDS BUS MASTERING

Q533. *I just installed a Western Digital WD7197 PCI SCSI controller in my system, but now when I boot the PC, I see the following message right after my hard drives are shown: "Auto-Configuration Error 03:03 Bus#:00 Device#:06 Function#:00." What is this error, and how can I fix it?*

A.   One of the problems with PCI is that some controllers require bus mastering in order to work. Your error suggests that the PCI adapter is not in a bus mastering slot. Try placing the controller in a PCI slot that has been configured for bus mastering, or reconfigure the current slot for bus mastering through your CMOS Setup.

Implementation Issues

FINDING YOUR BIOS VERSION

Q534. *I'm thinking about upgrading my flash BIOS, but before I download a new BIOS file, I need to know the current BIOS version. How do I determine the current BIOS version?*

A.   The current BIOS manufacturer name and version are one of the first pieces of information to be displayed during initialization. The display may only last for a few moments, but there should be enough time for you to record the version number.

Math Coprocessors and System Performance

Q535.   *Would a math coprocessor speed up my machine?*

A.   Math coprocessors (called MCPs or NPUs) are probably one of the most misunderstood parts of the PC. An MCP will greatly improve the performance of mathematic operations *if* the particular *application* is specifically written to use it. So just running out and adding an MCP won't necessarily improve anything. 486DX and all Pentium CPUs incorporate an MCP already, so you don't need to add an MCP separately.

Planning for 2000

Q536.   *I've been hearing a lot about the problems posed by the year 2000 rollover. How do I know if my system can support the next century or not?*

A.   There are three elements to the year 2000 problem: your real-time clock (RTC), your BIOS, and your operating system/applications. You can test your hardware using the following procedure:

1.   Set your date to December 31, 1999, and set the time to 11:59 p.m.

2.   Wait a minute or two and then check the date. If the date says January 1, 2000, you can go on to the next step. If the date says 1880 or 1980 or some other bizarre date, you will probably need a motherboard upgrade to provide you with a new RTC.

3.   Once you know that the date rolls over correctly, try rebooting the PC cold and check the date again. If the date holds, chances are that your BIOS is adequate. If the reboot causes a weird date, you may need a new BIOS. Check with the motherboard or system manufacturer for a BIOS update.

4.   Even after your hardware is proven out, your operating system and applications will have to be reviewed on a case-by-case basis. Older applications will need to be upgraded as required.

Award BIOS and the Year 2000

Q537.   *I've got a new Award BIOS in my system. Can you tell me if there is anything special I need to do to accommodate the year 2000?*

A.   Since you haven't told me the specific version number or date of your BIOS, I'll give you the general breakdown depending on the release date of your BIOS:

- If your BIOS was released *before* April 26, 1994, you only need to reset your system clock once. Turn the system off before midnight on 31 December 1999. Turn it back on some time after midnight on January 1, 2000. Then reset the system date in CMOS Setup.

- If your BIOS was released *between* April 26, 1994 and May 31, 1995, you need to obtain a BIOS update (or reset your system clock every day after the year 2000).

- If your BIOS was released *after* May 31, 1995, its calendar automatically rolls from 1999 to 2000 at midnight on December 31—the version is year 2000-compliant, and you don't need to do anything.

Phoenix BIOS and the Year 2000

Q538.   *How can I find out if my computer supports the year 2000? The system is using a Phoenix BIOS.*

A.   If your owner's manual doesn't mention this issue, and you can't call the computer manufacturer for some reason, take these steps:

- Set the time on your computer to 3 minutes before midnight (23:57:00), and the date to December 31, 1999.

- Turn your computer off and wait for 5 minutes.

- Turn your computer on, booting from a clean floppy disk (DOS only with no CONFIG.SYS or AUTOEXEC.BAT files).

If the date prompt displays 2000 as the year, you have nothing to worry about. If it displays any other year, you have to upgrade your BIOS. Phoenix (and most other BIOS makers) fixed this problem in February of 1995, but some OEM customers may be using source code purchased before February 1995. Keep in mind that there is no BIOS version number that guarantees your system will report the proper date in the year 2000.

The Relationship Between Chipsets and CPUs

Q539. *Could you tell me the difference between a chipset and a CPU? I've heard the terms used often enough, but I'm just not clear on the difference.*

A.   I can understand why you'd be confused—the CPU and chipset are *very* closely related. The CPU is the central processing unit, which is a single, large (and very complex) IC. As a program is executed, the CPU handles all of the logical and mathematical processes that go on in your computer. But a CPU needs lots of support in order to interact with memory, cache, and all of the various ports and functions of a motherboard. The chipset is tailor-made to support the CPU by handling all of the critical operations that occur outside of the CPU. For example, a chipset can be made to run EDO RAM or provide interfaces for EIDE and floppy drives. The actual list of functions provided by current chipsets is far too long to mention here. A chipset is typically composed of three or four large ICs (in addition to the CPU) which replace over 150 discrete ICs needed on older motherboards. Fewer ICs make motherboards much cheaper to manufacturer and dissipate less power. Today, motherboards are often classified by their CPU and chipset (i.e., Pentium Triton II motherboard).

INTERMEDIATE

Disabling a BIOS Start-up Logo

Q540. *I'm working on an Acer system with Windows 95, and I'm completely perplexed by the Acer start-up logo. The logo appears as soon as the system starts and continues through until Windows 95 starts. The problem is that I can't see any BIOS ID or power-up information about the system. Is there any way to stop this silly logo?*

A.   Some OEM BIOS versions such as the kind used by Acer provide
      a customized start-up screen which generally serves two purpos-
      es. First, it's a nice little advertisement. Second, it prevents the
      normal boot-up messages which might cause curious do-it-your-
      selfers to tinker with the system. Fortunately, you can usually dis-
      able the start-up logo through CMOS Setup. For the Acer, use
      <Ctrl>+<Alt>+<Esc> to enter the CMOS Setup routine.
      Somewhere in the Basic System Configuration section, you'll see
      an entry such as Quiet Boot, and another like Configuration
      Table. Set the Quiet Boot to Disable, and set the Configuration
      Table to Enabled. Save your changes and reboot. This should
      show the normal BIOS boot information. Keep in mind that
      some systems may be labeled differently or only use one entry to
      enable or disable the logo.

BIOS AND OEM MOTHERBOARDS

Q541. *I've got an Intel OEM motherboard that's a few years old now,
       and the OEM has since gone out of business. I want to upgrade
       my BIOS; can I use a standard Intel BIOS?*

A.   That's a tough question because there's no way to tell what the dif-
       ferences are between the OEM and "stock" versions of the moth-
       erboard, but chances are that the answer is No. Unfortunately, if
       the OEM has gone out of business and disappeared without a
       trace, you have no support. The most trouble-free means of
       upgrading your system now would be to upgrade the motherboard
       with a later stock model.

IRQs AND YOUR PARALLEL PORTS

Q542. *I just installed a second printer port in my computer, but Windows
       95 shows that it's not assigned an IRQ. What does an IRQ do for
       a parallel port, anyway? Is it used for regular inkjet printing?*

A.   As a rule, printer ports (a.k.a. LPT ports) do utilize hardware
       IRQs. LPT1 uses IRQ7, and LPT2 uses IRQ5. However,
       Windows 95 doesn't need an IRQ for printing. Instead, it polls

the LPT ports with software. But even though Windows 95 does-n't use IRQs for printing, the IRQs are *still* assigned to the hard-ware, so you can cause odd hardware conflicts if you allow other devices to use the same IRQs as your printer ports.

INSTALLING A NEW CPU

Q543. *I have the possibility of buying the motherboard and the CPU* separately. *How do I install the CPU? Do I only snap it on the* *motherboard?*

A.   There are several issues to consider when installing a CPU. First, since you're buying the CPU and motherboard separately, you should make sure that your CPU will operate properly in the motherboard (check the motherboard documents and see how to configure it for the CPU). Next, CPUs rarely snap into place or plug into sockets. Today, virtually all CPUs are mounted in zero insertion force (ZIF) sockets. By lifting a lever on the socket, a CPU can easily be removed and replaced, and then the tension lever can be locked down to hold the new CPU in place. The most important part of installing a new CPU is to align it proper-ly. Typically, the CPU and socket will be slightly notched (or keyed) to indicate the alignment. There may also be extra pins on the CPU and socket that will prevent installation in other than the proper orientation, but once again, you should be sure that the motherboard documentation outlines the proper installation of a new CPU.

INTERMEDIATE

MOTHERBOARDS AND SDRAM

Q544. *I'm looking for a new motherboard that supports state-of-the-art* *SDRAM. What motherboards can use SDRAM?*

A.   Most motherboards based on Intel's 430VX (Triton VX) chipset and the VIA Apollo chipset are configured to use SDRAM DIMMs. These chipsets are designed to work with synchronous DRAM, EDO DRAM, and standard DRAM. The motherboard must have at least one 168-pin DIMM socket to accept the

SDRAM module. The new Intel Triton TX chipset and the Intel Natoma LX will also support synchronous DRAM. SDRAM is expected to become the mainstream memory architecture of the next few years.

SELECTING THE BEST CHIPSET

Q545. *Which chipset is better for me, FX, HX, or VX?*

A.   That's a tough question because it really depends on your specific needs. Generally, the chipsets are ranked in the following order:

- **VX.** An inexpensive chipset targeted toward home or entertainment use. It is designed for a low-cost computer with limited high-end features and expandability and is a great computer for end users like college students who don't need all the power of the FX or the expandability of the HX.

- **FX.** A more powerful and versatile chipset targeted toward the midrange system user who uses the computer primarily for games and home office use. This is a midrange computer with the power and expandability options (mainly RAM and cache) that satisfies your growing needs when they arise.

- **HX.** A slightly older but perhaps the most versatile chipset targeted toward the professional or power user who needs the highest performance and expandability at an affordable price. The HX is best suited for CAD/Graphics and engineering uses because of the large amount of supported RAM.

HAL ERRORS WITH MULTIPROCESSING MOTHERBOARDS

Q546. *I just installed an AMI multiprocessing motherboard, and I'm installing NT 4.0. Why does Windows NT give me an incorrect HAL error during installation?*

A.   In almost all cases, HAL errors are the result of configuration problems when installing NT. If you're installing one CPU only, use a Custom Installation, and specify Standard PC instead of

MPS1.1 compliance. Also make sure to disable the APIC feature (usually with a jumper on the motherboard). If you're installing *two* CPUs, check the System Configuration window under NT for two CPUs. Enable the APIC feature (check the motherboard jumpers), and try an Express installation. If problems continue with a dual CPU installation, try using two matched CPUs that are recommended by the motherboard manufacturer.

DIAGNOSING A DEFECTIVE MOTHERBOARD

Q547. *I have an old 386SX motherboard that's not working at all. Is it possible to run a diagnostic test on that board and find the problems?*

A. Always be sure to check the basic things like your power supply and power connections to the motherboard. Also see that the CPU, cache, and memory are installed properly. Remove any extra expansion boards from the motherboard aside from a video board and drive controller (and make sure the monitor is attached). If the system is powering up but still refusing to boot, your only real course is to install a POST board and then try to boot the system. Check the code that appears on the POST board—the last code to be displayed is the point at which the system failed. You can then check the code against the codes for your BIOS, which should explain the failure. If you still have problems (or don't have access to a POST reader board), replace the motherboard.

INTERMEDIATE

DEALING WITH INTERNAL STACK OVERFLOW ERRORS

Q548. *When I boot up my system, the boot process gets part way through and then freezes. If you hit <Left Shift> during a boot, it says "Internal Stack Overflow. System Halted." I have tried rebooting several times, I have tried changing the AUTOEXEC.BAT and CONFIG.SYS files, and I have tried booting from a known-good boot disk—all with no success. By the way, this occurred after hooking up an Iomega Zip drive using the GUEST program. I am running in DOS 6.2 and Windows 3.1 with a Phoenix BIOS.*

A.   In a PC, the stack relates to interrupts. When an interrupt is called (by hardware or software), the CPU has to suddenly drop what it's doing and attend to the matter which called the interrupt. The current state of the CPU is saved in the stack which is a small area of memory set aside for that purpose. However, it is possible to have multiple interrupts occur before the current interrupt is handled—in which case the CPU just keeps pushing more and more conditions onto the stack in order to deal with higher-priority interrupts. Eventually, stack space can run out, and you see the result. I believe that your installation of the GUEST software for your Iomega Zip drive has caused the problem, so you should check your start-up files (AUTOEXEC.BAT and CONFIG.SYS). Make sure that you have added any necessary command line switches as required or simply remark-out any references to the GUEST program using the REM command. You might also try disconnecting the Zip drive.

OverDrive CPU Causing Parity Errors at Start-up

INTERMEDIATE

Q549.   *A friend of mine has a 486DX4 system which was upgraded from a DX2 some time ago. When he runs this machine at its highest speed, he often receives memory parity errors at start-up. He's checked to see that the SIMMs are seated well, so that's not the problem. Could his computer require faster SIMMs than what he currently has installed, or is this a hardware failure problem?*

A.   Before you start tearing down hardware looking for bugs, start by running a current virus checking program to look for viruses on disk as well as in memory (loaded into memory when the PC starts). If the system is clean, you can search for a hardware solution. I suggest that you start your CMOS Setup routine and add a wait state to your memory configuration. Save the changes and reboot. If the parity errors go away, your SIMMs may indeed be too slow for the demands of the processor. At that point, you can leave the new CMOS settings and keep your RAM or install faster RAM and return to a smaller number of wait states. This will optimize your system's performance. If the parity errors persist even with a larger number of wait states, I would suspect a fault on one of your SIMMs, so try some new RAM.

HUGE HARD DRIVES AND INTEL MOTHERBOARDS

Q550. *I've got an Intel motherboard which is a few years old now, and I want to upgrade my 1.6GB HDD to one of those new 3.2GB drives because the price is terrific. The thing is, I remember seeing a notice or warning that I couldn't use drives over 2GB, but I can't find it anywhere now. Is there any truth here, or am I wrong?*

A. Well you're not wrong. Intel motherboards issued prior to their current Advanced products will not support EIDE drives over 2GB. This is due to limitations in the motherboard BIOS, but there are no BIOS upgrades planned to correct the issue. Several symptoms have been noted when larger drives are installed:

- In a system where only a single IDE drive is being used, or where the drive is configured as a slave in a master/slave pair, the hard drive will not be recognized by the BIOS or by your operating system's partitioning utility.

- If the hard drive is a master in a master/slave configuration, the system may freeze during boot.

Note

You may be able to get around this problem by using the disk management software (i.e., EZ-Drive or Disk Manager) which usually accompanies large drives today.

MMX ON PENTIUM PRO MOTHERBOARDS

Q551. *Will the Tyan Titan Pro motherboard support the MMX chip?*

A. Absolutely not. The Titan Pro is a Pentium Pro-based motherboard, which is not compatible with the Pentium classic line of processors. A MMX Pentium Pro is scheduled to be released, but compatibility with the Pentium Pro MMX CPU and the Titan Pro line of motherboards has not yet been determined. Check in with the Tyan Web site periodically (*www.tyan.com*) for the very latest developments.

Problems Installing Windows 95 on a New Motherboard

Q552. *I've just replaced my motherboard with a Tyan Titan TX moth-erboard, but I can't seem to get Windows 95 running. Why does Windows 95 have problems operating or installing on this motherboard?*

A.   Windows 95 relies heavily on drivers to operate normally. With the addition of a new Intel chipset (the TX), Windows 95 is unable to recognize it as any currently "known" hardware device. Because it does not know what chipset is being used, Windows 95 replaces these requirements with generic drivers, which may cause system sta-bility and installation problems. To correct this problem Tyan has prepared drivers as a workaround. The new TYAN TIDE bus mas-ter drivers take care of this problem, as does the new TX fix which was just recently made available on the Web at *www.tyan.com*.

Memory Issues

Parity Versus Nonparity RAM

Q553. *What is parity RAM and why would I want it? All the new machines seem to come with nonparity RAM. If one were to look for the "best" motherboard, would it use parity RAM?*

A.   Without going into a long technical explanation, parity is a form of memory error checking that adds an extra bit to every byte of memory. You've probably seen this marked as 2Mx9—there are 8 data bits *plus* 1 parity bit for every address. A device like 4Mx36 uses 32 data bits (4 bytes) with one extra bit for each of the four bytes (32 + 4 = 36). Parity works by calculating a parity bit for each byte on the fly and then comparing that with the parity bit stored in memory. If the two match, the data is assumed to be good. Otherwise, a memory error is generated.

Parity is a somewhat old technique and is criticized as unneces-sary because memory errors are so rare. Still, I would rather have error checking in place to catch a rare error and halt my system

than allow memory errors to go unchecked (which would ultimately crash the system anyway). If you have the choice, I would
recommend using parity memory. However, parity checking is an
all or nothing proposition. If you have parity memory in your
system and choose to add nonparity memory, you will have to
disable *all* parity checking in the system.

MIXING PARITY AND NONPARITY SIMMS

Q554. *I have parity RAM in my system, and I'd like to add some hand-
me-down SIMMs from a friend's system. The problem is that her
RAM is nonparity. Can I use nonparity and parity SIMMs in my
system at the same time?*

A.   If the memory type and speed are compatible with your system,
you should be able to use parity and nonparity RAM together in
the same system, but you will have to disable *all* of the parity
checking—so memory errors will no longer be detected and
reported. You can disable parity checking through your CMOS
Setup routine (probably under the Advanced Chipset menu).

IDENTIFYING PARITY VERSUS NONPARITY SIMMS

Q555. *I have been given four 30-pin 1MB SIMMs that I will use in a
system I'm resurrecting for a friend. The markings indicate that
they are 70-ns RAM, but I have no idea if they are parity or
nonparity SIMMs. I know the difference between the two types,
but is there any way to tell just by looking at the SIMMs?*

A.   The rule of thumb for 30-pin SIMMs is this: Eight identical ICs
on the SIMM means nonparity, and nine identical ICs on the
SIMM means parity. Of course, to be absolutely certain, you
should cross-reference the SIMM part number with the manufacturer or local computer store. They should be able to give you a
description of the part based on its number. If the description
carries a 9 (like 1Mx9), the SIMM offers parity. If the description
carries an 8 (like 1Mx8), the SIMM does not offer parity.

DETERMINING PARITY VERSUS NONPARITY MEMORY

Q556. *A friend of mine is having memory problems with her 486 120-MHz system. She has 16MB, but it appears that 8MB might be parity. I know parity and nonparity memory do not mix, so is there any coding on the memory chip to let me know which is which?*

A.   First, parity and nonparity memory *will* work together in the same system (as long as other factors such as memory type and speed are compatible), but if there is *any* nonparity RAM in the system, *all* memory parity checking must be disabled through a motherboard jumper or CMOS Setup. You can determine parity based on the SIMM layout. Any layout ending with a 32 (i.e., 4Mx32) is a nonparity SIMM. Any layout ending with a 36 (i.e., 4Mx36) is a parity SIMM (the extra 4 bits are for parity).

ECC VERSUS PARITY

Q557. *What is ECC, and how does it compare to parity? Can I use my parity SIMMs in an ECC system?*

A.   Simply put, ECC stands for error correction code. It refers to an advanced technique used to find and correct single-bit memory errors and to even detect multibit errors. By comparison, parity just allows for single-bit error checking and does not support any error correction at all. To use ECC, your motherboard and SIMMs must be capable of supporting ECC. An ECC motherboard will almost certainly support parity SIMMs, but you cannot invoke ECC using parity SIMMs.

UNDERSTANDING THE AREAS OF MEMORY

Q558. *I'm just starting to learn about computers, and I'm totally baffled by the memory terms. Can you tell me the difference between conventional, upper, high, extended, and expanded memory?*

A.   PC memory can be a real source of confusion. In general, PC memory is divided into two zones: the first 1MB and everything else. The first 640KB within that initial 1MB is referred to as conventional memory (also called DOS memory). MS-DOS and all DOS applications need to use this 640KB space. The remaining portion of that first 1MB (that 384KB above the 640KB mark) is called upper memory. This space is used by the various BIOS ICs in your system (motherboard BIOS, video BIOS, SCSI BIOS, and so on). Of course, there's no guarantee that *all* of the upper memory area will be used, so by installing memory managers in conventional memory (i.e., HIMEM and EMM386), unused portions of the upper memory area can be recovered and used for DOS drivers and TSRs. This frees up more conventional memory for use by DOS applications.

High memory is really an anomaly, an accident that developed because of the way older CPUs addressed memory. A CPU can address one 64KB segment *above* the 1MB mark. This high memory is typically made accessible with memory managers and is used to relocate part of DOS. By relocating DOS, even more conventional memory space is freed up for use by applications.

Both extended and expanded memory represent the remaining memory space above the 1MB mark. The difference is in the way that memory is used. Extended memory (XMS) is typically considered as Windows memory because Windows uses that space to load and run applications directly (something DOS cannot do). Windows 3.1x requires memory managers to use XMS, but Windows 95 does not. By comparison, expanded memory (EMS) is treated as DOS memory because DOS can load data and programs into EMS. However, DOS cannot execute programs in EMS; the programs must be transferred into conventional memory (one 64KB page at a time), executed there, and then returned to EMS and replaced with the next EMS page. EMS is the only means DOS has of using the memory above 1MB.

INTERMEDIATE

THE ROLE OF UPPER MEMORY

Q559. *I'm learning about computers, and there's a lot of talk about the first 1MB or RAM, and the first 640KB. So what happens to the 380KB left over?*

A. That 384KB between 640KB and 1024KB is called the upper memory area (UMA). In actual practice, the UMA is taken up by the different BIOS that resides in a typical PC (motherboard BIOS, video BIOS, SCSI BIOS, network BIOS, and so on). The space left over can be used by DOS, drivers, and TSRs (though you need a memory manager like HIMEM.SYS to take advantage of the UMA).

Upper Memory on a 286 System

Q560. *A friend of mine has an Epson Equity 286 system. At start-up, the computer displays a 1024KB memory check, but I haven't been able to use more than 640KB from DOS. The documentation says it has 1MB of RAM. Do you know if I have to use a special driver to access this extra memory?*

A. The space of memory between 640KB and 1024KB (or 1MB) is known as the upper memory area (UMA). This space is reserved for such things as video BIOS, controller BIOS, motherboard BIOS, and all the other odds and ends that the PC needs. Normally, that 384KB UMA is not filled entirely, and memory managers like HIMEM.SYS and EMM386.EXE allow drivers or TSRs that would ordinarily reside within the 640KB conventional memory space to be loaded "high" to occupy unused space in the UMA. You need DOS 5.0 and a 386 or later PC to take advantage of that memory management. For a 286 system, you may need to use an older memory manager such as QRAM, or system-specific memory managers like EMM286.EXE and STARTEMM.EXE, which may buy you an extra 50KB or so, but in general, your 286 is pretty much stuck with its 640KB limit.

Advantages of EDO RAM

Q561. *I'm thinking about getting some EDO memory to upgrade my system because everyone seems to think it's superior. But can you tell me why EDO RAM is better than ordinary DRAM?*

A.   Extended data output (EDO) RAM is designed to prolong the time
      which data is available from RAM. This eliminates some of the
      delays that were required in the memory controller IC on your
      motherboard, and allows a net improvement in system performance
      of as much as 10 to 15 percent. In actual practice, the improvement
      is more like 5 to 10 percent. In order to use EDO RAM, you need a
      motherboard with a chipset designed to handle EDO. Today, virtu-
      ally all motherboard chipsets are EDO-compatible.

THREE-CHIP VERSUS NINE-CHIP SIMMs

Q562.   *I've been trying to buy more memory for my PC, but one salesperson
        asked me whether I wanted two- or three-chip or eight- or nine-chip
        SIMMs. That's one I've never heard before. Is there a difference?*

A.   The difference is in the density of the individual memory ICs on
      the SIMM. SIMMs with two or three chips on them are using
      denser memory components but are usually limited to 4MB or so.
      The eight- or nine- chip SIMMs generally offer just as much stor-
      age (or more), but each IC on the SIMM is typically smaller. In
      theory, there should be no difference between these SIMM types.
      After all, 4Mx9 SIMMs all provide 4MB of memory regardless of
      how many chips are used. In actual practice, however, the SIMMs
      with smaller chip counts can present problems to some mother-
      board designs (especially when mixed with larger chip count
      SIMMs). As a rule, get SIMMs with chip counts that are similar
      to those already in your PC, or go with the larger chip count
      devices.

USING NINE- AND THREE-CHIP SIMMs TOGETHER

Q563.   *I've heard the at nine-chip and three-chip SIMMs won't work
        together. I have never tried it, but is this true?*

A.   In theory, there should be no difference between nine- and three-
      chip SIMMs, but not all motherboards support both types equal-
      ly. From a technical standpoint, there are two reasons why this

INTERMEDIATE

incompatibility can occur. First, some motherboards do not supply enough refresh address bits for a 4Mx1or a 1Mx4 DRAM. These are generally older motherboards that will not work with 4MB nine-chip SIMMs or 1MB three-chip SIMMS. Second, some inexpensive motherboards do not have proper terminations on the lines which drive the DRAM array. These boards often have only marginal compatibility with various SIMMs (not working with all perfectly good SIMMs you try). What this means in actual practice is that you shouldn't be surprised if three-chip SIMMs cause memory problems when used in your system. You might find that a solution is to use SIMMs one speed level faster than the manual calls for. This should help compensate if the motherboard cuts things too close.

THE DIFFERENCE BETWEEN SINGLE-AND DOUBLE-SIDED SIMMS

Q564. *I've heard of single- and double-sided SIMMs. What's the difference? Is one type better than another?*

A.   That's a great question because most motherboards are using 72-pin SIMMs. All 72-pin SIMMs are 32-bits wide (36 bits with parity), but double-sided SIMMs have four row address strobe (RAS) lines instead of two. This can often be thought of as two single-sided SIMMs wired in parallel. But since there is only one set of data lines, you can only access one "side" at a time. Usually 1, 4, and 16MB 72-pin SIMMs are single-sided, and 2, 8, and 32MB SIMMs are double-sided. Note that this only refers to how the chips are wired. SIMMs that are electrically single-sided may still have chips on both sides of the board.

Most 486 motherboards use memory in banks of 32 bits (plus parity), and may treat a double-sided SIMM as two banks (see your motherboard's manual for details). Some motherboards can take four SIMMs if they're single-sided but only two if they're double-sided. This can really be a problem because double-sided SIMMs can limit the amount of RAM that can be added. Pentium motherboards are a bit more forgiving because SIMMs must be used in pairs anyway. Neither type of SIMM is really better than another, but double-sided SIMMs may cause memory errors on some motherboards.

MIXING SINGLE-AND DOUBLE-SIDED SIMMs

Q565. *I have a UM4981 motherboard using an AMD 486DX2 80-MHz processor and an 8MB double-sided SIMM. The SIMM is mounted in one of the slots (bank 3). Can I mount a ordinary 16MB SIMM in some of the other banks?*

A. Possibly. Mixing double- and single-sided SIMMs can sometimes be a tricky proposition. It really depends on the particular motherboard. Double-sided SIMMs can sometimes be treated as two banks in a 486 system. This may prevent you from adding another SIMM in the next subsequent SIMM slot but may not prevent you from adding a single-sided SIMM in another bank. The rule is that you should check your motherboard documentation for specific limitations or cautions when using double-sided memory. If you can't mix single- and double-sided SIMMs, your best bet is to install all single-sided memory.

SELLING OFF USED MEMORY

Q566. *I have accumulated a number of SIMMs from years of upgrades, and frankly I haven't got a clue what to do with them. A friend suggested that I can sell off the memory. Is that true? Is there a place to sell memory?*

A. If you search through mainstream computer catalogs (like Computer Shopper), you will find a number of organizations that trade-in or buy-back RAM. One such company is The Memory Broker (*www.compbroker.com*). This is most popular with companies that repackage the older RAM onto newer SIMM boards. However, memory costs have dropped significantly in the last few years, and you will probably only receive a small fraction of what you originally paid for the memory.

IDENTIFYING MEMORY TYPES

Q567. *I've learned that all the RAM in my PC should ideally be the same type (i.e., standard DRAM, EDO, or FPM). Is there an easy way to identify which kind of RAM is already installed when you are upgrading memory?*

INTERMEDIATE

A.   Unfortunately not. Memory types are not intuitively obvious and cannot be determined by visual inspection. The way to tell is to cross-reference the SIMM part number with a database like the kind you'd find with Kingston (*www.kingston.com*) or PNY (*www.pny.com*) or take the part number to computer store like CompUSA or ComputerCity that sells memory. Once you can cross-reference the part number, the corresponding description will usually identify the memory type (DRAM, EDO, FPM, and so on).

DRAM VERSUS VRAM

Q568.   *I've been hearing a lot in the PC media about DRAM and VRAM. What are they? Are they the same thing?*

A.   They're close, but not the same. *Dynamic RAM* (DRAM) is used as main system memory (on motherboards, video boards, and SIMMs). *Video RAM* (VRAM) is used in high-end video boards. Both forms of memory are almost identical, but there is an important difference in the data bus. DRAM uses a single data bus—there is only one set of data lines. As a result, the DRAM is either reading or writing at any given point in time. On the other hand, VRAM uses two duplicate data busses. This means that data can be read from the IC while data is being written to it simultaneously. This makes VRAM very fast (and very expensive). You may also hear the term *static RAM* (SRAM). SRAM is much faster then DRAM or VRAM and is often used as L2 (or external) cache.

PREPARING FOR SDRAM

Q569.   *Just when I was realizing that extended data output (EDO) RAM was the way to go for high performance systems, Dell has changed the rules? What is synchronous dynamic RAM (SDRAM)? Are the Pentiums I've built with EDO (Intel boards) going to be able to handle SDRAM? Assuming the SDRAM comes in 72-pin SIMMs, will the upgradeable BIOS support it?*

A.   SDRAM is a fast-memory technology that promises to offer higher system performance than EDO RAM by providing valid outputs at any portion of the clock cycle and through a "pipeline burst" mode which can greatly accelerate memory transfers. Unfortunately, SDRAM is only supported by specific chipsets (like the 430VX or TX). So older chipsets like the 430HX will *not* support SDRAM. However, the 430TX will handle a mix of EDO and SDRAM. As a consequence, your older Pentium motherboards will probably *not* support SDRAM, and a BIOS upgrade will not be enough to provide support.

DISSIMILAR SIMM METALS

Q570.   *I went shopping for new SIMMs the other day, and the sales person asked if I needed tin or gold SIMMs. What's the difference, and which should I get?*

A.   That's not an odd question, but unfortunately it's often treated as an afterthought. When you "mix" metals (i.e., tin SIMM contacts with motherboard gold contacts or vice versa), oxidization can occur, resulting in signal problems and system crashes. If the contacts on your motherboard SIMM sockets are tin, you should install SIMMs with tin contacts. If the contacts on your motherboard SIMM sockets are gold, you should install SIMMs with gold contacts. Today, cost-conscious manufacturers are doing everything they can to reduce costs, so tin connections are by far the most common. So if you don't know what SIMM contacts to get, choose tin.

INTERMEDIATE

MIXING MEMORY CONNECTOR METALS

Q571.   *I posted to a PC forum regarding the tin/lead compatibility question in order to get some extra feedback, and I got several responses which said that mixing tin sockets with gold RAM connectors had not affected their computers. One person said he had been using such a setup for 2 years, another for 3. A couple of people said that the tin/gold connector problem was more of a problem on Intel motherboards than on other boards. So I am here asking you for any further feedback or advice which you might care to pass along. Based on the responses I have received so far, it doesn't seem like this metal compatibility is an extremely serious problem.*

A.   Well I'm not a metallurgist, so I can't explain the science behind this effect, but according to my understanding, you should attempt to match *all* connector metals wherever and whenever you can (including things like expansion boards and jumpers). If you mix contact metals, one of the metals (probably the tin) will begin to oxidize and can gradually raise the contact resistance until signal errors begin to occur. In actual practice, the quality of the opposing metals can play a huge role in this effect. Some cheap tin sockets might only work for a few months when gold SIMMs are installed, while other sockets which might use a tin alloy or other variant that reacts much better and can run for years without trouble. Intel technical support specifically warns against mixing contact metals in their motherboard SIMM slots.

INSTALLING SIMMS BACKWARD

Q572.   *I've been thinking about upgrading the memory in my PC. I can do this by adding some SIMMs, but how do you know if the SIMMs are installed properly? Can you install a SIMM backward?*

A.   No, all SIMMs are notched on one side. You'll also notice that SIMM holders are similarly notched. This prevents you from installing SIMMs backward. However, be sure to have your PC turned off and unplugged before installing new SIMMs, use an antistatic wrist strap whenever handling SIMMs, and be sure to seat the SIMMs completely into their socket before *gently* easing them back into place. Both sides of the SIMM should clip into the SIMM holder.

MAKING THE MOST OF SIMM ADAPTERS

Q573. *I'm on a very limited budget and after buying some new equipment for my PC, I don't have enough for more memory. I do have four 4MBx9 30-pin 60-ns SIMMs, and I'm looking at using an adapter (or stacker) for those SIMMs (30-pin to 72-pin). I know this isn't best, and I also know that this will most likely slow my system down, but is this a feasible way to go?*

A. SIMM adapters are generally a well-accepted technology, but you should select an adapter with on-board buffering logic. This is a bit more expensive, but it will limit the timing penalty imposed by the adapter. If you get a simple pass-through SIMM adapter, it will be less expensive, but you can expect a timing penalty of about 10 ns (so your 60-ns SIMMs would act like 70-ns devices on the adapter). A timing penalty may require you to add a wait state to your memory configuration in CMOS Setup. Also remember that SIMM adapters require a large amount of space, so you'll need to select an adapter with size and orientation characteristics that best fit the available space on your particular motherboard.

UNDERSTANDING DIMMs

Q574. *Can you tell me what a DIMM memory unit is? Dual in-line memory module? What is it used for? I have seen several motherboard ads describing these as available on-board.*

A. You're right. DIMM stands for Dual in-line memory module. While 30-pin SIMMs are 8-bit memory devices and 72-pin SIMMs are 32-bit memory devices, DIMMs are 64-bit memory devices. For a Pentium CPU (or other 64-bit CPUs), a single DIMM covers the entire data bus, so one DIMM can fill a bank. Multiple DIMM sockets represent multiple banks. DIMMs can use all of the advanced memory types we know today (i.e., EDO, FPM, SDRAM). One of the advantages of DIMMs is that they can hold a tremendous amount of memory (32MB, 64MB, and more), so one DIMM can supply you with the equivalent of several SIMMs.

INTERMEDIATE

Mastering DIMM Keying

Q575. *I'm looking over some new Pentium Pro motherboards for my server, and many of them use DIMMs instead of SIMMs for adding memory. The problem is that there seem to be several different types of DIMMs. I've seen references to 5-V DIMMs, 3.3-V DIMMs, and buffered and unbuffered DIMMs. How many types are there, and how do I tell the difference between them?*

A. I've done some checking, and there are generally three types of DIMMs: buffered 5 V, buffered 3.3 V, and unbuffered 3.3 V. The DIMMs are differentiated by key notches placed in different locations along the connectors (seen looking at the front or component-side of the DIMM). Buffered 5-V DIMMs use a centered notch to indicate that the DIMM is buffered and left-offset notch to indicate 5-V operation. Buffered 3.3-V DIMMs use a centered notch to indicate that the DIMM is buffered, and a centered notch to indicate 3.3-V operation. Unbuffered 3.3-V DIMMs use a right-offset notch to indicate that the DIMM is unbuffered and a centered notch to indicate 3.3-V operation. The use of these key notches means that you cannot install the wrong DIMM type on your motherboard.

Getting a Grip on Memory Issues

Q576. *I just want to make sure I have this straight: EDO SIMMs give an average of 3 percent performance increase and can only be used with Intel's Pentium processors. Parity SIMMs don't give a performance boost but do provide parity checking, which will uncover a memory fault almost as soon as it happens and they can also be used in any 72-pin SIMM slot around. As a result, parity SIMMs are the better, more versatile investment, even if they do cost somewhat more. Did I get it right?*

A. You're very close, but there are a few little points to correct. First, EDO RAM is not limited to Pentium processors—instead, they are limited by the motherboard's chipset. If the chipset can detect and use the EDO RAM (and the BIOS supports it), you'll see a slight system performance improvement. You should be able to use EDO RAM in many non-EDO motherboards, but there will be no performance improvement. Parity checking will reliably uncover single-bit memory errors *as soon as* they occur (not almost as soon). Parity SIMMs can fit into any 72-pin SIMM slot, but for parity to be of any use, the motherboard must be configured to check for parity. If parity is shut off on the motherboard, your memory will not be checked for parity. If you use *any* nonparity memory on your motherboard, *all* parity checking must be disabled. Finally, I would agree with your statement that parity SIMMs are the superior investment for memory. Although memory faults are somewhat rare, detecting the fault can seriously reduce the chances of data corruption.

MIXING AND MATCHING EDO RAM

Q577. *I frequently find myself upgrading PCs with components I mix and match from other systems. Can I use regular DRAM in an EDO motherboard? Could I also use EDO RAM on a non-EDO motherboard?*

A. Generally speaking, you can use regular DRAM in a motherboard which is compatible with EDO RAM. You simply will not receive any performance advantages. Similarly, you should be able to use EDO RAM on a non-EDO motherboard. Again, you won't receive any of the performance advantages that EDO RAM can offer. However, I would strongly advise against mixing memory types in the same bank or even in the same system. For example, if you need two SIMMs to fill a bank, you could probably use two EDO SIMMs or two DRAM SIMMs, but using one EDO SIMM and one DRAM SIMM could cause problems.

MIXING RAM TYPES

Q578. *I'd like to know if you have installed EDO RAM in 486 boards or know of any incompatibility when doing so. It seems to me that with the minor memory cycle modification that EDO memory implies (with respect to FPM), it should also work in motherboards which don't benefit from EDO. In addition, EDO and FPM memory can't be easily distinguished, so would they work together on the motherboard?*

A.   You're really asking several questions here. First, you want to know if EDO RAM can be used in non-EDO motherboards. The answer to that is generally yes. EDO RAM should work in most motherboards—the operative word being *most*. While the EDO RAM will probably work, you won't receive any performance benefit from it. Non-EDO motherboards that are custom-manufactured for specific PC manufacturers (i.e., Compaq, Dell, Packard Bell) stand a higher chance of rejecting EDO RAM.

As for mixing EDO and FPM RAM, the answer is very much the same. In most cases, you must place similar RAM types in the same bank but can use different types in different banks. In other words, you probably could not mix EDO and FPM RAM in bank 0, but it is likely that you could fill bank 0 with EDO RAM and fill bank 1 with FPM RAM. Still, there are some motherboard designs (especially older motherboards) which can be extremely sensitive to any memory mixing. The bottom line is that you simply have to *try*. If the configuration doesn't work, try using only a single memory type.

EDO MEMORY AND NON-EDO MOTHERBOARDS

Q579.   *Is it possible to use EDO RAM in a conventional motherboard? I have a 486 PCI board that accepts parity or nonparity RAM, but I'd like to know if EDO will work. I realize I wouldn't get the performance out of it that a Triton board would.*

A.   According to all of the documentation that I have seen and technicians I have talked to, EDO RAM should work properly on a non-EDO motherboard. You simply do not get the performance advantage that EDO offers. Of course, the SIMM itself must be the correct size, and provide the right speed. Make sure you use enough EDO RAM to fill a complete bank.

USING EDO RAM ON A NON-EDO MOTHERBOARD

Q580.   *I have a Soyo 486 DX4 motherboard with non-EDO SIMMs. The chipset is made by SiS, and it was not intended to support EDO RAM. I can buy new 16MB EDO SIMMs for a very reasonable price. Do you think that those SIMMs will work without compatibility problems?*

A. According to all the information I've seen, you should be able to use EDO RAM in almost any non-EDO motherboard without problems; however, you will not be able to take advantage of the performance benefits offered by EDO RAM. The one nice thing about using EDO RAM now is that you can always transfer the RAM to a new motherboard later on which *does* support EDO.

MIXING EDO AND FPM MEMORY

Q581. *After reading all the discussions about Fast Page Mode and EDO memory, I have a question about mixing them together. If I put a pair of 70-ns Fast Page Mode SIMMs in one bank and a pair of 60-ns EDO SIMMs in another, what would the accessing speed be?*

A. Mixing memory types and speeds can always be tricky. If you must mix speeds, place the slower RAM in bank 0, and then place the faster RAM in subsequent banks. You may also need to add wait states in your CMOS Setup to accommodate the slower memory. In theory, that should work. When you bring various memory types into the discussion, there is no universal rule that will give you an answer. The two memory types *should* coexist properly if your motherboard chipset will support both types, but in actual practice, their compatibility will be affected by the chipset, motherboard timing, size of the SIMMs—a myriad of factors that you have no way to predict. You may be able to mix very successfully on some motherboards but not at all on others. You're just going to have to test that for yourself.

CHOOSING TO USE CACHE MEMORY

Q582. *I have a Pentium 100-MHz system with an Intel motherboard, 24MB of EDO RAM, and no cache memory. When I purchased the computer in December of 1995, I was told that the pipeline burst cache on their 120-MHz systems would only give me a 3 percent performance increase and wasn't an option on their 100-MHz systems. Since that time, I have read that I might actually expect to get about 30 percent better performance if my system contained 256KB of cache memory. Is this possible? What is your opinion?*

A.   I am very surprised that your system doesn't have cache. Cache has been a vital performance enhancement on virtually every PC since the early 486s—even the Pentium you're using has a small amount of internal (or L1) cache. As for a 30 percent performance increase, I'm not entirely certain that's true, but adding 256 to 512KB of cache to your system should yield a major improvement. First, run a benchmark program and establish a baseline for your system's performance. Start the CMOS Setup for your system and see if there are options to enable or disable L1 cache (the CPU cache). If it is disabled, try enabling it and run your benchmark again—you should notice some small improvement (I say small because the CPU's internal cache is only 8KB). Next, go back to your CMOS Setup and check for an option to enable or disable L2 cache (the external cache on the motherboard). If there is no such entry, there may well be no provision to add L2 cache (although that would be a surprise). If there is an L2 entry, check your documentation that came with the system to see if there really is a provision for adding L2 cache; it wouldn't be the first time PC users have gotten bad information from their place of purchase. You may even be able to purchase the components from any local computer store. Once the cache is installed, you can enable the L2 cache and run your benchmark a third time. This will give you a final before and after picture of how cache affects your system.

UNDERSTANDING CACHE MARKINGS

Q583.   *I've been trying to decipher the markings on my motherboard cache ICs, and I wonder if you can help. The markings on my cache RAM are as follows: UM61512AK-15, 9603L, and MBS05.*

A.   That's a 512KB 15-ns static RAM chip made by UMC (you probably have 512KB of cache on your motherboard). There are faster devices out there, but it's a good, basic, middle-of-the-road SRAM chip for a cache. We've seen similar cache in nonsynchronized burst motherboards with very good results.

UNDERSTANDING A COAST MODULE

Q584. What is a COAST module?

A.   COAST stands for cache on a stick. It was a design originated by Intel to standardize the modularized L2 (external) cache provided in Pentium-based computers. Physically, a true COAST module should be about 4.35 inch wide, and 1.14 inch long. At first glance, a COAST resembles a SIMM, and it fits into a COAST slot on the motherboard.

THE DIFFERENCE BETWEEN CELP AND DIMM

Q585. What does CELP and DIMM mean?

A.   The two terms are totally unrelated. CELP stands for card edge low profile. It is the physical socket specified by the COAST standard, so if you upgrade to a motherboard with a CELP socket, the motherboard accepts L2 cache in the form of COAST modules. DIMM stands for dual in-line memory module. This is a memory device which is physically larger than SIMM, and can pack large amounts of memory on-board. A DIMM also provides many more signals than a SIMM because the contacts on each side of the DIMM are electrically independent (unlike SIMMs where contacts on both sides of the SIMM are tied together).

SYNCHRONOUS VERSUS ASYNCHRONOUS CACHE

Q586. What are the differences between synchronous and asynchronous cache modules?

A.   Synchronous cache modules base their operation on signals derived directly from the Pentium's clock and can generate burst addresses internally. This makes synchronous cache very fast; it is able to exchange large amounts of data with the CPU with fewer clock signals. Asynchronous cache must wait for burst addresses

ADVANCED

from the motherboard's chipset, and while they're as good at holding data as synchronous cache, the asynchronous cache can be much slower when it comes to transferring large amounts of data.

ESTIMATING CACHE SPEED REQUIREMENTS

Q587. *I'm going to be adding cache to my motherboard shortly. Now I can order the parts from my PC maker, but I'm wondering if you can tell me how fast the cache should be for my Pentium motherboard.*

A.   There is no single formula that defines the absolute cache speed under every condition, but there are some guidelines that might help you. A 33-MHz motherboard will work with 25-ns data cache and 20-ns tag cache. A 40- or 50-MHz motherboard typically uses 20-ns data cache, and 12- to 15-ns tag cache. If you're not sure, it doesn't hurt to use faster cache than your manual calls for. If your manual says 20-ns and you only happen to have 15-ns parts, it's OK to mix the speeds, but keep in mind that faster parts will not yield higher performance.

WRITE-THROUGH CACHING VERSUS WRITE-BACK CACHING

Q588. *I've been hearing a lot about EIDE and write-back cache. Is write-back caching worthwhile? How does it compare to write-through caching?*

A.   Yes, write-back caching is a valuable drive performance enhancement, and most EIDE and SCSI drives have a multisegmented write-back cache right on board the drive electronics. Write-back caching is a way to speed-up drive access by holding onto data in RAM until the system has an idle moment to write it to the drive. In other words, the system hands off data to the disk drive, which receives this data in RAM memory and immediately informs the system that the data was written. Then, at a later time (when the system is idle), the drive writes the cached data to the platters. The important thing to remember is that RAM is *much* faster than the actual drive media itself. The result is a dramatic improvement in apparent system performance.

You should understand how write-back caching compares to write-through caching. The write-through cache is not really a cache at all. The data is written through to the platters with no caching whatsoever. Write-through caching is desirable for mission-critical applications where the write-back caching would pose a potential danger of data loss if the power were lost while data that hadn't had a chance to make it to the platters was still in the cache.

CHECKING OUT YOUR SYSTEM CACHE

Q589. *I am concerned about whether or not I actually have an L2 cache in my system. I have an i430VX motherboard and an Award 4.51PG BIOS. Power-on text indicates the presence of L2 cache, but there are no numbers to confirm the exact amount. Is there any diagnostic to check this?*

A. Most full-featured commercial diagnostics like TuffTest (*www.tufftest.com*) will report the amount and speed of cache in your system, but there are some shareware alternatives. You can get the CTCM utility from Tom's Hardware Performance Pages (*www.sysdoc.pair.com*). As I recall, CTCM will not work with IBM/Cyrix CPUs (although an update may be available by now). You can also obtain NUCACHE.EXE from the PC Build Web site (*http://nospin.com/pcbuild.html*).

FITTING SIMMs TO A MOTHERBOARD

Q590. *I've really just started tinkering with PCs, and I have a question about memory. Am I correct in thinking that a 486 motherboard can take SIMMs one at a time because of their 32-bit bus, but a Pentium motherboard must have SIMMs installed in pairs because of a 64-bit bus? If so, can I install one 4MB SIMM and one 8MB SIMM on a Pentium board, or do they have to be the same size?*

A. The rule is that there must be enough memory data bits to accommodate the data width of the CPU. For example, an i486 is a 32-bit CPU, so a single 72-pin SIMM is "wide" enough to service the CPU. If you have a 486 motherboard that uses 72-pin

SIMMs, you can add them one at a time. If your 486 motherboard uses 30-pin SIMMs, you'll need to add 30-pin SIMMs in sets of four. On the other hand, a Pentium is a 64-bit CPU, so it takes two 72-pin SIMMs to service the CPU (i.e., to form a bank). When installing multiple SIMMs within a bank, the SIMMs must be of the same size and speed. As a result, you should *not* mix 4 and 8MB SIMMs.

MAKING USE OF OVERSIZED SIMMS

Q591.   *I have been offered the use of some SIMMs for my home computer. According to the motherboard manual, mine can take two 16MB 72-pin SIMMs at the maximum. I have been offered two 32MB 72-pin SIMMs. I have been told by another source (and have once seen it work) that the motherboard would just utilize both 32MB SIMMs as 16MB SIMMs. Is this true? If so, would it cause any harm to the system or RAM?*

A.   You don't say how old your motherboard is, but if it is only capable of handling a maximum of 32MB (two 16MB SIMMs), I'd say the motherboard is more than a few years old. Unfortunately, there is no certain answer to your question except to say that it *should* work. Even though the motherboard can only address 16MB SIMMs, the SIMM pin layout should be identical between the 16- and 32MB SIMMs, so the extra 16MB per SIMM will probably be ignored. Ordinarily, I would say that's a terrible waste of RAM, but if you're only borrowing the SIMMs, and they're free to use, it's not really a bad deal.

MEMORY AND PRESENCE DETECT SIGNALS

Q592.   *I'm looking into a memory upgrade for my Compaq PC, and I'm seeing references to presence detect. What is it and how does it relate to the speed of my new memory?*

A.   There are two factors that affect the speed of memory. One is the actual speed of the chips, and the other is called *presence detect*. Most SIMMs are now using 60-ns chips. A 60-ns chip is designed to run at 60 ns, but through a set of presence detect signals, we can reconfigure the SIMM. Presence detect defines the size of the SIMM (i.e., 4, 8, or 16MB), as well as the speed at which the computer will access the memory (i.e., 60, 70, or 80 ns). Even though the chips may be rated at 60 ns, presence detect lines can control how the computer sees and uses the memory. With some systems such as Compaq and IBM, it is imperative that you have the presence detect set up correctly; otherwise, the system will not function properly or perhaps will fail to recognize the memory at all.

Knowing What the Numbers Mean

Q593. *What do the numbers of the RAM chip mean? For example, do 2x32 or 2x36, and so on, refer to speed?*

A.   That's an important question when planning to upgrade your memory. PC memory is designated as depth x width, so a 2M x 32 SIMM means that there are two million memory addresses which are each 32 bits wide. Since 8 bits are a byte, a 32-bit device offers 4 bytes. As a result, that memory device would be a (2M x 4 byte) 8MB SIMM. Computers frequently use parity checking as a means of testing memory integrity, so for each byte, an extra bit is added for parity. For example, a 2M x 36 SIMM offers the same 32 bits of memory, plus an additional 4 bits for parity, but the parity bits are ignored in the overall calculation of RAM size, so the device would still be considered an 8MB SIMM. You can say that any device labeled x32 is nonparity, while any device labeled x36 is parity.

It's a similar situation for smaller 30-pin SIMMs. A 1M x 8 SIMM offers 1 million memory addresses which are each 8 bits wide. Since 8 bits are a byte, an 8-bit device offers 1 byte. That memory device would be a (1M x 1 byte) 1MB SIMM. If the device is designated with 9 bits (i.e., 1M x 9), it offers the same 8 bits for data and an extra bit for parity. You can say that any device labeled x8 is nonparity, while any device labeled x9 is parity. The bottom line here is that these numerical designations specify the device's size only—they have nothing to do with speed. Speed is usually designated as a two-digit code following the part number. For example, xxx 60 is a good indication of 60 ns. Table 5.3 illustrates some popular SIMM sizes.

ADVANCED

TABLE 5.3 POPULAR SIMM SIZES

Designation	Size (MB)	Note
1x8	1	Nonparity
1x9	1	Parity
2x8	2	Nonparity
2x9	2	Parity
4x8	4	Nonparity
4x9	4	Parity
1x32	4	Nonparity
1x36	4	Parity
2x32	8	Nonparity
2x36	8	Parity
4x32	16	Nonparity
4x36	16	Parity
8x32	32	Nonparity
8x36	32	Parity
16x32	64	Nonparity
16x36	64	Parity

ESTIMATING MEMORY SPEED REQUIREMENTS

Q594. *I'd like to add memory to my system, but I'm not sure just what speed memory I need. Any ideas?*

A.   While there are no hard and fast rules for selecting memory speeds, there are some guidelines to keep in mind: 25-MHz motherboards will use 80-ns RAM, 33-MHz and some 40-MHz motherboards use 70-ns RAM, and many 40-MHz and faster motherboards use 60-ns RAM. Today, you can count on a Pentium system to use 60-ns EDO or FPM SIMMs. The very latest motherboard will use SDRAM.

CHECKING RAM SPEED

Q595.   *Is there a way to check the speed of my RAM? I think the two*
         8MB SIMMS I have now are 70-ns. I asked the salesperson what
         speed the new SIMMS were, and was told they were 60 or 70 ns.
         They are PNY SIMMs. I went to the PNY Web site and found
         out how to decode the part numbers but could not deduce the
         speed. That salesperson also told me if the 8MB SIMMS already
         installed were 70 ns, the motherboard would recognize all the
         RAM as 70 ns. Is that correct?

A.   You can check RAM speed, but it requires a rather sophisticated
         piece of diagnostic equipment that costs about $2000. PNY
         (*www.pny.com*) should be able to take their part number and tell
         you everything (including the speed). But if you have to guess
         yourself, check the SIMM's part number. If it ends with a 60 or
         06, it's probably a 60-ns device. If it ends with a 70 or 07, it's
         probably a 70-ns device. Your salesperson was basically correct
         about memory speeds. When you mix memory speeds, the rule is
         to install your slowest memory in bank 0, and the system will use
         that as a reference for all other banks. However, you should also
         remember that some of the more advanced motherboards avail-
         able today can operate at "split" speeds (i.e., run faster for the
         faster RAM and run slower for the slower RAM).

MIXING RAM SPEEDS

Q596.   *I have an old 486/33-MHz system and have been seeing lock-ups*
         and parity errors. I took about an hour today and swapped out
         the 8MB of memory to see if I could get rid of the problem. I
         found that I had 4MB of 80-ns RAM and 4MB of 70-ns RAM. I
         thought that it was maybe a paging problem, but I could not get
         rid of the parity errors. Then I checked some of the BIOS set-
         tings, disabled the above 1MB memory test, and the problem
         went away. I can't figure it out.

ADVANCED

A.   RAM can be very finicky when you start mixing speeds. If your 80- and 70-ns RAM are mixed within the same bank, you need to fill a bank with memory that is all the *same* speed. If you do have a bank filled with the same speed already, the slower memory should be in bank 0. Once the memory is organized properly, try adding a wait state in your CMOS Setup. This slows the system to accommodate the slower RAM (which also reduces system performance). If you need top performance from your system, replace the slower RAM with 80-ns devices, and your parity problems should disappear.

THE GOOD AND BAD OF FAKE PARITY

Q597.   *OK, here's a new one. I was calling around to price some memory, and a salesperson cautioned me to avoid SIMMs with emulated parity. I was told to only buy SIMMs with true parity. What is emulated parity, how do I tell the difference on a SIMM, and should I be worried?*

A.   Parity is a rather primitive means to check the integrity of a data byte. Computer designers originally embraced parity because it was relatively simple and did not demand significant processing overhead. However, parity is only effective at finding single-bit errors, so it is not 100 percent reliable. That is the reason designers went to CRC as the error-checking technique of choice. That is also the reason why some current systems abandon the use of parity. Traditionally, for every 8 data bits, there is a parity bit. Thus, if you have a 1MB SIMM, and each DRAM IC is 1MBx1 bit, there will be eight ICs on the SIMM, plus a ninth IC for parity (referred to as a 1MBx9 SIMM). In a 16-bit system, adding 1MB of RAM involves installing two of those 1MBx9 SIMMs. Your own RAM configuration is probably different, but you get the idea. This is what your salesperson referred to as true parity. If you find a SIMM with nine identical DRAM ICs, chances are pretty good that it is a true parity SIMM. If the ninth IC is not the same as the other eight, or there are only eight ICs, you may have an emulated parity (or fake parity) SIMM.

Fake parity is a relatively new cost-cutting technique which abandons the RAM used for parity in favor of a parity generator IC (a much simpler and less expensive device). When SIMM data is read, the parity generator looks at data on the fly and produces a parity bit based on the data. While this results in cheaper SIMMs, the problem here is that the SIMM's parity bit will always match the parity bit generated by parity checking circuitry on the motherboard. There will *never* be a memory error, even if the data in RAM is wrong.

In actual practice, RAM is tested with the POST during system initialization (and after initialization with commercial diagnostics) by writing data and reading it back. If read data matches written data, the RAM is good. So parity is purely a secondary line of defense against memory failures. If a parity error arises during normal operation, the system halts, so whatever you were working on is lost anyway. However, I would rather see the system halted and run the risk of losing a file or two than allow faulty instructions or data to corrupt the entire system. With this in mind, I would recommend against the use of fake parity. True parity, in spite of its limitations, is better than none at all.

USING SLOWER RAM IN A NEW SYSTEM

Q598. *I suspect that my 16MB of 70-ns RAM SIMMs won't be fast enough in moving from a 486 to 586 system. Can I use the slower RAM, or should I look at trading up to faster memory?*

A. As a rule, 70-ns RAM from a 486 PC is probably not *ideal* for Pentium systems (which usually prefer 60-ns RAM). But if you're in a pinch, it *will* work as long as the slower RAM is placed in bank 0. The most important thing you may need to do is add a wait state in your CMOS Setup. This slows the PC down a bit, so it's not the best for performance, but it will get you going until you can line up faster RAM.

ADVANCED

Parity Errors and RAM Speed

Q599.   *I just tried to add four 4MB SIMMs to a board that originally had eight 1MB SIMMs. I was hoping to leave four of the 1MB SIMMs to end up with a total of 20MB. At first, I got a System Halted—Parity Error message right after the POST. I disabled parity checking in the CMOS settings and the system booted, but Windows 3.1 gave me its parity error message and the system froze. I reset the parity check in CMOS, and then the system refused to even recognize the new SIMMs. I tried them alone and got no POST errors (but three short beeps). Finally, I adjusted the wait states in CMOS and the new SIMMs will work on their own, but I cannot get them to work with the old 1MB SIMMs. The vendor assures me they are true parity SIMMs. One thing I noticed is that two of the chips on each SIMM have the number 70 while the third has 60. Is that a reference to the speed or something else? And if it's the speed, why aren't they consistent?*

A.   There are several issues here. First, make sure that all of your SIMMs use the same type of memory (such as EDO or FPM). Mixing memory types can cause problems. If your older SIMMs are slower than your newer SIMMs, you should place the older SIMMs in bank 0, and then place the newer SIMMs in subsequent banks. All of your memory must be either parity or nonparity. If any memory is nonparity, you must disable all parity checking. Finally, some motherboards are *very* restrictive about the combinations of RAM that they will accept. In theory, your idea should work, but in practice, your motherboard may simply be unable to accommodate 4- and 1MB SIMMs together. Check the memory upgrade table that probably accompanies your system. It is unlikely that your new SIMMs are defective since you indicate that they will work properly on their own.

Employing RAM Expansion Boards

Q600.   *I'm working on an HP 286 for a friend, and it has all of the RAM memory (30-pin SIMMs) on an expansion card. This seemed a little unusual to me. Could this type of card and memory be used on another 286 or other computers also? It certainly seems to help make this fancy little 286 with VGA video, a SCSI adapter, a Sound Blaster, and Windows 3.1 work quite well.*

A.   Generally speaking, these were 16-bit memory expansion boards for 286 systems with only 1MB of RAM on the motherboard. When more memory was needed, PC companies often employed a variety of proprietary and ISA bus solutions. Many companies used highly proprietary memory expansions, so if your memory board is plugged into a non-ISA slot, chances are that you cannot use the board in other systems. If the memory expansion board is plugged into a standard ISA slot (such as an AST RAMpage board), you may be able to use the board in other systems.

However, there are some serious problems with this recycling. First, those RAM expansion boards (at their best) offered only a few megabytes of additional RAM—less than the equivalent of a single SIMM today. Second, the memory was slow (usually 100 ns or slower), so you would actually need to slow down later PCs by adding wait states—a *lot* of wait states. This combines with signal delays added by the use of the ISA bus slot itself, and you may need one or more real-mode drivers to access the board. PC performance would be dramatically reduced. In short, there is no economy in compromising the performance of your system to gain only a few megabytes, so I would suggest reserving the board for other 286-class PCs.

UNDERSTANDING BAD CACHE ERRORS

Q601.   *I have an AMI series 727 Atlas PCI II motherboard. When the system starts, I am getting a Bad Cache, Do Not Enable Cache error at POST. What's the problem?*

A.   If you've added cache or altered your cache configuration, you'll probably need to adjust the cache setting jumpers on your motherboard. Your specific setting will probably depend on the cache module type (i.e., asynchronous or pipelined). You can tell the cache type based on the module's appearance: 256K asynchronous cache modules often have seven chips on one side and four on the other, 256K pipelined burst cache will typically have three chips on one side only, and 512K pipelined burst cache modules often have two chips on one side and three chips on the other. If the problem persists, you've probably got a faulty cache module. Try replacing your cache.

SYSTEM HANGS UP WITH 256KB L2 CACHE MEMORY

Q602.   *I just upgraded my motherboard from 128 to 256KB of cache RAM, but now the system hangs up during initialization.*

A.   There are two common problems when upgrading cache: The new cache is too slow (i.e., 20 ns when 15 ns is needed), or the new cache is faulty. As a temporary measure, you can remove or disable the additional cache, but you will need to replace the cache with approved components before you can take advantage of the full cache amount.

SYSTEM ONLY RECOGNIZES 128 OF 132MB OF MEMORY

Q603.   *I'm doing an upgrade on a PC that I use for high-end graphic design work. I've put in 136MB of RAM, but I can't get the PC to identify more than 128MB. There's no answers anywhere— can you help?*

A.   There's only one issue that comes to mind. Your system is probably not capable of supporting more than 128MB of RAM (the extra RAM will be ignored); 128MB is a lot of RAM, so a motherboard that's a few years old may just not support the extra memory. Check with your PC manufacturer and determine the maximum amount of RAM your system can handle.

VALUE POINT MEMORY PROBLEMS ARE NOT ALWAYS BAD MEMORY

Q604.   *My IBM PS/Value Point systems has been suffering from frequent lock-ups, along with a message such as "Memory Parity Error, System Halted." When these faults occur, I am forced to turn the PC off and perform a cold start, losing everything I've been working on up to that point. I know that the SIMMs are the correct speed for my system, and I have had them tested (they are OK). The lock-ups occur most often under Windows using large applications. Before I take the system to the shop, do you have any suggestions?*

A.   The easiest place to start is with CMOS Setup. Go to the Advanced Setup or Advanced Chipset areas of your setup and check the settings for your Wait States. Most contemporary systems work well with one wait state (sometimes two). If you have zero wait states, the RAM will probably not be fast enough to keep pace. Try adding wait states one at a time, save the CMOS, and reboot the system each time. See if that takes care of the parity problems. If you do not have a CMOS entry for wait states, they are probably set by one or more jumpers on your motherboard.

Even though you had your RAM tested, you did not say how they were tested. Unless you used a first-rate SIMM checker such as SIMCHECK from Innoventions, you may have been wasting your time. Just dropping the SIMMs into a different PC and powering it up is not an adequate test. Try pulling out the SIMMs in pairs (or individually depending on your system), and test the PC. You may find that one or two SIMMs are actually bad. Once this process of elimination reveals a faulty SIMM, you can replace it. Windows is a much more demanding platform for memory than DOS, which is why so many memory problems are reported under Windows.

There is another issue that relates specifically to Value Point systems. IBM manufactured some early Value Point units with faulty external cache. The IBM Help Center BBS (919-517-0001) has a program called PARITYFX.EXE (run in AUTOEXEC.BAT) that seems to correct the questionable cache problem.

2MB OF RAM DISAPPEARS

Q605.   *I noticed that my home-made PC is short about 2MB of DRAM. This Acer motherboard "ate" 2MB somewhere. Please help me to locate it. I dual boot to NT4.0/Win95 and when I upgraded to 128MB of RAM, I only saw 126MB. When booting, BIOS shows 129024 instead of 131072. I use the same SIMMs in all four slots.*

ADVANCED

A.   I don't think you're 2MB short. Instead, I think your system is using the 2MB as a memory hole for ISA boards or for memory shadowing. Check your CMOS Setup and try disabling some of the more advanced memory features such as ISA Memory Hole, Video Shadowing, or BIOS Shadowing (at least temporarily). I think you'll get your 2MB back, although there may be a performance decrease. You can always reenable those features later once you've demonstrated to yourself that your 2MB is not missing after all.

6

Sound Questions

The PC has always been a natural platform for entertainment, and a big part of entertainment is sound. Music, voice, and sound effects have become major elements of all multimedia software and will become even more important as the new generation of DVD drives takes its place on the PC. Sound boards have been around for many years now, but sound boards often incorporate several different functions (i.e., sound, joystick port, and CD-ROM interface), each demanding resources and drivers. This places sound boards at the focus of many hardware conflicts and upgrade problems, so sound-related questions are always plentiful. This chapter breaks down the various sound board questions into software and hardware issues.

Software and Driver Issues

ADDONICS WEB SITE INFORMATION

Q606. *I am trying to install an Addonics Sound Vision 500 card. It did not come with any DOS drivers for this card. Can you tell me if they have a location to download a DOS driver for this card?*

A.   I did some searching, and I was able to find a download site for Addonics drivers. Check out their Web site at: *http://www.wco.com/ ~atc/tech2.html.*

FINDING DRIVERS FOR OLD SOUND BLASTERS

Q607. *I've inherited a Sound Blaster 16 (#CT1740). However, as is the case with most hand me downs, there is no literature, instruction booklet, or drivers. Can you point me in the right direction?*

A.   You should be able to find drivers and information for most of the Creative Labs product line by visiting the extensive Creative Labs Web site at *www.creaf.com.* If you want to try by telephone, you can contact technical support at 405-742-6622.

CAN'T LOAD THE SOUND MIXER

Q608. *I'm befuddled by this one. I wanted to adjust the various levels of different inputs to my sound board, but I can't seem to get the Windows 95 mixer applet to start. I've used it before (long ago), but it just won't run now. Any ideas?*

A.   If you cannot find the mixer applet in your Start menu, you'll need to install it. This may mean reinstalling the software that accompanied your sound board. If you see the mixer applet in your Start menu (perhaps under the sound board's entry) and it just refuses to launch, chances are that you've accidentally deleted a file needed by the applet. Try running ScanDisk and see if any file associated with your mixer may have been cross-linked (and therefore corrupted) by another file. If so, delete the mixer applet, defragment the disk, and then install the mixer applet again. If not, simply reinstall the mixer applet.

TROUBLE INSTALLING NEW CREATIVE LABS DRIVERS

Q609. *I downloaded SB16UP.EXE, which had the full-duplex drivers with it, and CTCMBBS.EXE; both have Creative Lab's version of plug-and-play control software. When trying to install both packages, the INSTALL.EXE program comes back with "Critical DOS error occurred. Press <ESC> to quit." I have used the software and hardware on another system, so I am confident that they do work, but do you have any other ideas?*

A. That's a tricky one, and the answer probably lies with your install program. Some install programs will crash if you have virus protection utilities running in memory (MBR virus protection in CMOS is usually OK). If you're loading any sort of antivirus software (such as f-prot 2.22), try disabling it temporarily and then try installing your software. I think you'll see your problem disappear. Remember to reenable your antivirus software after the installation is complete.

GETTING SOUND DRIVERS FOR INTERNET PHONE

Q610. *I finally decided to get Internet Phone and try it out. It doesn't mention anything about this on the outside of the box, but inside it says for full-duplex operation (both people talking at once like on a real phone), your sound card needs to be able to handle full-duplex voice. It didn't even say in the directions which cards did—I have a Creative Labs AWE32. Do I need to use a second sound card or replace my existing sound card?*

A. As it turns out, the AWE32 is capable of full-duplex voice operation. You simply need the proper drivers. Check out the Creative Labs site at *www.creaf.com* or check the Creative Labs FTP site at *ftp.creaf.com*. Get the AWEUP.EXE file for your AWE32 under DOS or Windows 3.1x, or get SBW95UP.EXE for the SB16 or AWE32 under Windows 95.

FINDING NT DRIVERS FOR OPTi SOUND CARD

Q611. *I have a plug-and-play OPTi sound card that is recognized during hardware initialization, but Windows NT has no drivers for it. To put it simply, there is no sound. Do you have any suggestions (other than sound card replacement)? I could not find anything meaningful at the OPTi site. The card has no obvious model number, but it is accepted as an OPTi with 16 bits. Note that I have NT set up using NTFS, and DOS is not present.*

A. This is a common complaint with NT. It simply wasn't designed as a multimedia operating system. As a result, you often have to hunt for NT video and audio drivers. Identify the card model by its chip or chipset number (i.e., 925 or 931) and then look at the OPTi FTP site at *ftp://ftp.opti.com/pub/multimed* for the proper (or closest) NT driver. If you cannot find working NT drivers, you will need to replace the sound card with one that *does* have NT drivers.

CAN'T PLAY .WAV FILES ANYMORE

Q612. *I'm running Windows 3.1, and I have recently installed an AudioWave sound card. Theoretically, it installed properly and I could listen to a few sound files I had for a few days. Then I got the following message:"No wave device that can play files in the current format is installed. Use the Drivers option to install the wave device." I have no idea what I might have done wrong. I've looked at AUTOEXEC.BAT and CONFIG.SYS, and they seem to be set up as suggested.*

A. Since you apparently had the sound board working, it seems like you may have accidentally disabled or erased the driver. If you installed any other software which may be interfering with your sound board, try disabling or removing that software. The driver file may also have accidentally been cross-linked to other files and may now be corrupt. Try removing the driver outright through your Windows Control Panel, and then use ScanDisk to check the disk for problems. Correct any disk problems, defragment the drive, and try reinstalling the driver.

NEW SOUND BOARD WON'T STREAM FROM THE INTERNET

Q613.   *I finished building my 5x86-133 system with 32MB of RAM, a
        4MB video card and the new Ensoniq PCI sound card. The sound
        card works in Windows and with games, but when I go on the
        Internet and try to use QuickTime on the CNN site, the page just
        freezes up and won't load. Vivo Player streams the images, but I
        get no sound (RealAudio says that I'm out of memory). What am I
        doing wrong, or does that PCI card really need more memory?*

A.   Sound cards can be finicky devices under Windows, especially
        when being used for Web-based applications. Since this is an
        issue with the Internet, I first wonder whether the clip you're
        playing actually has sound. I suspect it does, but it's worth a san-
        ity check. Next, see if you're running any other unnecessary
        applications while trying to run the clip. You *may* be short on
        RAM if there's a lot running in the background. Also see if you
        can configure the Vivo Player to use reduced bandwidth (this will
        speed things up and reduce memory demands). Finally, make sure
        you've got the latest version of the Vivo Player.

Hardware Terminology and General Topics

LOOKING FOR CRYSTAL AUDIO WAVE TABLE CARDS

Q614.   *Does any manufacturer make wave table cards that will augment
        the Crystal Audio chipset on an Advanced/AS motherboard?
        Apparently, Crystal Audio no longer does.*

A.   The 4CDs company offers a Crystalake wave table card
        (*www.4cds.com*). Star Multimedia Corporation also has a selec-
        tion of wave table cards (408-946-8288). Both products should
        be compatible with Crystal Audio, but be sure to check very
        carefully before ordering. Also make sure that your vendor has a
        liberal return policy if the product fails to work.

INTERMEDIATE

WAVEBLASTERS AND THE AWE32

Q615. *I heard that I can extend the capabilities of my AWE32 by adding a WaveBlaster. What is a WaveBlaster, and what can it really do for my sound?*

A. Simply stated, a WaveBlaster is a module that plugs into the AWE32. The additional circuitry increases the AWE32 to a 32 channel sound board and gives you access to a second set of sampled sounds. The net result is that you can add a lot more "instruments" to your "orchestra," and the resulting sound and music can seem much fuller. Note that the Value Edition of the AWE32 does not have a WaveBlaster connector on it.

PREPARING FOR AN AWE 64

Q616. *I want an AWE 64 PnP sound card from Creative Labs; however, I understand that it will only run correctly on a computer equipped with a genuine Intel Pentium 90 or faster chip. Here is my problem: I currently have an Acer Acros Pentium 75 with 24MB of RAM, an 850MB hard drive, and I'm running Windows 95 as my OS. In order to have the AWE 64 sound card run correctly, I figure I have three options: get an OverDrive chip, buy a new CPU and motherboard, or overclock the existing CPU.*

A. You left out a forth option: get a lower-end sound board. Even an AWE 32 is a fine alternative. If you feel that you really *have* to have the AWE 64, check the documentation for your system and see if the motherboard will accommodate a Pentium 90. If so, your cheapest "out" is probably to buy the new CPU. If not, you'll need a motherboard that will accommodate a faster CPU.

You should avoid overclocking a CPU if at all possible. While many users have overclocked their CPUs successfully, I strongly discourage it because it tends to drive the CPU beyond its rated parameters, and this can cause unpredictable operation.

DETECTING BLOWN SPEAKERS

Q617. *Why would the Device Manager list under Windows 95 say that everything is working properly if the speakers were blown? Would there be a diagnostic anywhere?*

A. Speakers are strictly output devices, and there are no signals provided back to the sound board to indicate whether the speakers are working or not. As a result, there are no speaker diagnostics, because there is really nothing to check. If your sound board is installed properly, your drivers are configured correctly, the speakers are powered normally, and the volume is set right, you should hear sound. Otherwise, you'll need to check those four factors to track down the problem.

UPGRADING MEMORY ON AN AWE32

Q618. *I've got a Creative Labs AWE32 sound board, and I'd like to upgrade its memory. How much memory can I add, and what type of memory should I use?*

A. The AWE32 has two standard SIMM slots which allow you to add up to 28MB more DRAM (note that the AWE32 Value Edition does not allow you to expand memory at all). The SIMM demands are a bit less stringent than main system RAM. You can use ordinary 30-pin 80-ns (or faster) DRAM SIMMs. You may use two 1MB SIMMs, two 4MB SIMMs, or two 16MB SIMMs. One issue to remember is that you cannot mix SIMM sizes. After you add the SIMMs, you'll need to adjust a memory selector jumper on the sound board.

INTERMEDIATE

AWE32 AND CD-ROM SUPPORT

Q619. *I want to upgrade my PC with a new CD-ROM drive and AWE32, but my current Sound Blaster is supporting my CD-ROM, and I want the upgrade to be configured the same way. Can you tell me what CD-ROMs are supported by the AWE32 or recommend which one I should get?*

A.   In general, Creative Labs has gone through several evolutions of CD-ROM drive support with *all* their sound boards, including the AWE32. The first AWE32 models supported only proprietary CD-ROM drives: Creative Labs brand, Sony, and Mitsumi. Each drive had to be connected to its respective interface on the sound board. The next generation of AWE32 (the CT3900 model) supported IDE and Creative Labs brand CD-ROM drives. Today, AWE32 boards support only IDE CD-ROM drives. As I understand from Creative Labs, there are no plans to support SCSI CD-ROM drives. If you have the choice, you should support IDE CD-ROMs. This allows you to mix and match any IDE CD-ROM drive with your sound board, and it also gives you the ability to interface the CD-ROM to your IDE drive controller instead.

MEMORY AND WAV FILE PERFORMANCE

Q620.   *I've got an AWE32 sound board from Creative Labs, and I've been thinking about upgrading its memory. I'm always looking for more performance from my system; will adding memory improve .WAV file editing or manipulation?*

A.   That really depends on what you consider to be "performance." More DRAM in the AWE32 will allow you to hold more SoundFont data and larger samples. However, this will have no effect on the speed of those samples or your ability to manipulate them. That's still based on your overall PC's performance.

MIDI SEQUENCERS WITH THE AWE32

Q621.   *I want to use a DOS MIDI sequencer with my AWE32 board. I've got a sequencer that works in Windows 95, but I need to use a DOS sequencer for the work I'm doing now. The AWE32 won't respond to the DOS sequencer. Am I missing a driver or something?*

A.   Theoretically, Yes, but there are no DOS MIDI drivers to buffer your sequencer program (at least none that I know of). As a result, your sequencer needs to have *direct* support for the

AWE32 board already built into the software. You may need to find a more compatible MIDI sequencer or check in with the sequencer maker and see if there are any patches or upgrades to support the AWE32.

AN SB16 INSTALLATION WITHOUT LITERATURE

Q622. *I've inherited a Sound Blaster 16. However, as with most hand-me-downs, there is no literature, instruction booklet, or drivers. Can you help with an installation?*

A. Generally speaking, all that is required to install a SB16 sound card is that you open your system and configure the card to use the proper resources. In most cases, an IRQ of 5, a DMA channel of 1, and an address setting of 220h should be appropriate. You'll need to find those jumpers on the board itself. If the board has a built-in joystick port, you'll probably want to keep that disabled, especially if you already have a game port working in your system. Install the card in your PC and then turn the power back on. If you have an audio cable from your CD-ROM, be sure to connect it to the sound board as well before continuing. If you're running Windows 95, you can use the Add New Hardware wizard in your Control Panel to install the Windows 95 default drivers for Windows operation. If you need the latest drivers, you can download them from *www.creaf.com* (look for the Creative Labs TechLab page).

SWITCHING TO A STAND-ALONE SOUND CARD

Q623. *My motherboard uses an on-board sound system, but it's a bit older now, and I'd like to upgrade to one of the new Sound Blaster boards such as the AWE32. Is there anything I need to watch out for when installing the new sound card?*

A. You bet. If you were replacing an existing sound card, you'd simply remove the old card (remove the old drivers if necessary) and then install the new sound card and sound software. When the sound system is integrated into the motherboard, you need to ensure that the motherboard sound is *completely* disabled before installing the new sound card; otherwise, you'll have a serious hardware conflict problem. Disabling the motherboard sound can usually be accomplished by changing one or more jumpers on the motherboard or disabling the motherboard sound in your CMOS Setup (or a combination of the two). If you cannot disable the motherboard sound system properly through CMOS Setup, you may need a BIOS upgrade before continuing.

LPT2 AND SOUND CARDS

Q624. *I'm trying to install Reveal's SC400 (rev3) sound card into my Intel Premiere/PCI II motherboard. I can't seem to get the sound card or the Sony CD that is hooked to the sound card to work. The motherboard seems to be using IRQ5 for the second printer port (LPT2). I don't know how to disable it in the BIOS (AMI dated 1992) so that IRQ5 would be available. Any ideas?*

A. Disabling a parallel port is usually very simple, but it comes down to a question of how LPT2 is implemented in your computer. If LPT2 is actually a port on your motherboard (I've never seen a motherboard with *two* LPT ports), you should be able to disable LPT2 through a jumper on the motherboard. Your motherboard manual should have all of the jumpers listed. If LPT2 is on a stand-alone multi-I/O board, you should have no problem disabling the port with a jumper on the I/O board.

AWE32 UNDOCUMENTED JUMPERS

Q625. *I have an AWE32 sound board, and I have found three jumpers on the board that I cannot identify in the documentation: JP6, JP8, and JP9. I'm wondering if you can tell me what these undocumented jumpers do?*

A. According to the information I've been able to dig out from Creative Labs, JP8 is a digital output from the EMU8000 chip (SPDIF). It is not a jumper, but rather an actual signal source which I believe is used for diagnostic purposes. Pin 0 is the signal line, and pin 1 is the signal ground. JP9 is a jumper, and it controls the mixer volume on the AWE32. When pins 1 and 2 are jumpered, the mixer volume is increased. When pins 2 and 3 are jumpered, the mixer volume is decreased. Finally, JP6 is an audio feature connector. Like JP8, the JP6 is a port rather than a jumper. The pinout is listed in Table 6.1.

TABLE 6.1 AUDIO FEATURE CONNECTOR PINOUT

Pin	Purpose
1	AG (analog ground)
2	Line out (right)
3	AG (analog ground)
4	AG (analog ground)
5	Line out (left)
6	AG (analog ground)
7	-12 V
8	Reserved
9	Mic In
10	+12 V
11	AG (analog ground)
12	AG (analog ground)
13	AG (analog ground)
14	AG (analog ground)
15	PC Speaker In
16	Mono Speaker Out

INTERMEDIATE

Hardware Corrective Actions

SOUND COMING FROM ONLY ONE SPEAKER

Q626. *I've set up a new sound board and installed the speakers, but I'm only getting sound out of one of my speakers. Any idea why?*

A.   First, check the mixer applet that was probably installed when you installed the sound drivers. Make sure that the output volume for your left and right channels are both set evenly. Next, test your speakers on an alternate source such as a Walkman or portable stereo. If both the speakers work, the problem may be with your sound card output (try replacing the sound board). Try switching the input cable end for end. If the speakers still don't work, replace the speakers.

Speakers Work but Volume Control Doesn't

Q627.   *I just installed some new speakers on my system, but the volume controls don't work. I've never had volume controls to contend with before, so I don't understand what could be wrong.*

A.   I'll bet that you forgot to install batteries or provide power to the speakers. Speakers with volume control require a source or power to run the volume control. Also make sure that the speaker power is turned *on.* If you still can't control speaker volume, you may have a fault in the speakers themselves.

Loose Volume Adjustment May Mean Faulty Speakers

Q628.   *I've got a problem with my audio speakers. The volume control is terribly noisy, and I can't adjust the volume properly without wiggling the control. The speakers aren't that old, and I'd hate to have to replace them if I can help it.*

A.   Unfortunately, that sounds like exactly what you need to do. The type of symptom you're describing sounds like a faulty volume control, and these problems will only get worse with time. Your best bet is to just replace the speakers. If the speakers are under warranty, have the manufacturer replace them.

DEALING WITH AN UNCOOPERATIVE MICROPHONE

Q629. *I've got a microphone connected to my Sound Blaster sound board. I know the microphone is connected to the right input jack, but I can't seem to record anything. How can I get my microphone working?*

A. The easiest way to test a microphone is with the Sound Recorder (Fig. 6.1) accessory in Windows 95 (Start, Programs, Accessories, Multimedia) or any sound recording applet accompanying your particular sound board. Press the right-most button to start recording, speak into the microphone, and watch the green line on the screen. If the line doesn't move, the computer isn't "hearing" anything at the sound board. Make sure the microphone is plugged into the MIC jack on your sound card (I know you checked, but check again). Also check the sound mixer program applet included with your sound board to make sure that the microphone input level is turned up and the recording source is set to the microphone.

Figure 6.1 The Sound Recorder applet in operation

If this is a new microphone that you're trying out for the first time, also make sure you have the correct type of microphone. Most microphones are the condenser type, but there are also carbon microphones, and your sound card may have a preference or setting that determines which one to use. Also check the microphone's specifications against the sound card's requirements. The specification that trips most people up is the impedance rating, for example, a 2-KΩ microphone in a sound card rated at 600 Ω simply will not work.

Selecting a Sound Board DMA Setting

Q630.   Is it better to set the DMA channel of a sound card to 0 or 1?

A.   Traditionally, DMA0 is assigned to memory refresh operations. While this is no longer as important a factor as it used to be, it would still be helpful (especially when working with older motherboards) to keep DMA0 free and use DMA1 instead.

Sound Card and SCSI Adapter Conflicts

Q631.   I've noticed that my sound is conflicting with my Adaptec SCSI controller at 300 to 330h. What should I do to clear this conflict?

A.   You probably discovered the conflict in your Windows 95 Device Manager. Sound cards rely on those address ranges to provide MIDI (MPU401) compatibility. As a result, you are usually better off to reconfigure the SCSI adapter to clear the conflict. Set the I/O range for your SCSI adapter to a different (unused) range, and update its configuration in Windows 95. You may need to reboot the system. After you reconfigure the SCSI adapter, the conflict should disappear.

Disabling an Integrated Motherboard Sound System

Q632.   I have an Intel Advanced/AS motherboard fitted with a Pentium 133 MHz CPU and an on-board sound system by Crystal Subsystem. I have just added a Sound Blaster 32 PnP card to the system and need to disable the motherboard sound. Unfortunately, the manual that came with the PC contains no details about the jumpers needed to disable the Crystal chips. I have tried using Device Manager under Windows 95 to remove the Crystal device. This is fine until I reboot; Windows 95 detects it as new hardware and reinstalls it. Can you help?

A.   Well, first let's point you in the direction of the Intel Web site. You can get detailed information on the Advanced/AS motherboard at *http://www.intel.com/design/motherbd/as/index.htm.*

Disabling motherboard features is sometimes a BIOS-related problem, so check your BIOS version code when the PC first powers up. According to Intel, BIOS version 1.00.07.CL0 is the latest BIOS version for the Atlantis motherboard, and the flash file can also be found on the Intel site.

To disable the on-board sound using ICU software (this is pre-ferred for MS-DOS and Windows 3.1x systems), you should check your CMOS Setup. The Plug and Play Configuration sub-menu found in the Advanced menu for your CMOS Setup should have Use ICU for Configuration Mode, and Boot With PnP OS should have None selected:

1. Install and run the ICU software. Go to Card Configure.

2. Under Motherboard System Devices, highlight the CS4232 entry, but do not hit <Enter>.

3. Click on Modify.

4. Under card configure are four choices. Click on each choice to disable all four.

5. Save and exit.

To disable the on-board sound using the Windows 95 Device Manager (this is preferred for Windows 95 systems), you should check your CMOS Setup. The Plug and Play Configuration sub-menu found in the Advanced menu for your CMOS Setup should have Use ICU for Configuration Mode, and Boot With PnP OS should have Windows95 selected:

1. Double-click on the System icon in the Control Panel folder.

2. Expand the Sound, Video, and Game Controllers entry by clicking on the + sign.

3. Highlight the Crystal PnP Audio System CODEC entry.

4. Select Properties and uncheck the Original Configuration box.

5. Highlight the Crystal PnP Audio System Control Registers entry.

6. Select Properties and uncheck the Original Configuration box.

7. Highlight the Crystal PnP Audio System Joystick entry.

INTERMEDIATE

8. Select Properties and uncheck the Original Configuration box.

9. Highlight the Crystal PnP Audio System MPU-401 Compatible entry.

10. Select Properties and uncheck the Original Configuration box.

11. Save your changes.

12. Using a text editor, add REM in front of the following CONFIG.SYS entry:

```
C:\win95\cs4232c.exe /w /x
```

MOTHERBOARD DOESN'T "LIKE" SOUND BOARDS

Q633. *I have a PC system with a AMD 5x86 P75 on a 486 PCI bus motherboard that is designed to also handle the AMD 5x86 chip. The system consists of two hard drives, a Logitech serial mouse, a US Robotics 28.8KB modem, a Trident PCI video card, a 12X CD-ROM drive, and a generic sound card. I cannot get Windows or DOS to find the sound board at the suggested I/O address 220h or any other address that the system will allow me to enter. I have replaced the motherboard and also used another sound card. I tested the sound boards in a 486DX4 system, and they worked. I had even disabled the CD-ROM drive. I have swapped out almost everything except for the 5x86 chip. Can you offer any suggestions?*

A. It sounds to me like you have a very unusual hardware conflict. There are rare occasions when a motherboard may simply not like a particular peripheral (often the peripheral's chipset) for one reason or another. Clearly the motherboard works and the sound card works (which means the drivers also work). I suggest moving from a generic sound card to a different brand (perhaps a name brand). I think that would be the best way to resolve the problem.

GAME WON'T RUN WITH MOTHERBOARD SOUND

Q634. *I bought a game for my daughter that doesn't run on my computer. I get a message which says that there is an error in CS32BA11.DRV. The sound requirements for the game are an*

MPC-compatible sound card, but I ran another game by the same company and this game worked with my Intel Atlantis motherboard and its internal sound system. The sound requirements for that game are Sound Blaster/Sound Blaster Pro. Any help would be greatly appreciated.

A.   First, the Crystal Sound system on your motherboard should be fully compatible with Sound Blaster/Sound Blaster Pro architecture. Before you go too far, check your BIOS version when the system powers up. The latest BIOS version is 1.00.07.CL0. If your BIOS is older, it may be worth upgrading the BIOS before proceeding. You can find the flash BIOS upgrade file on the Intel Web site at *http://www.intel.com/design/motherbd/as/as_bios.htm.*

You should also consider the game itself. If you get sound but not with that particular game, chances are that the game is not configured properly. Most games (especially DOS games) require that you set up the game to run your particular sound system. Check your game's configuration or setup menu and make sure that you select the Sound Blaster/Sound Blaster Pro entry. If you get no sound at all (from any application), the motherboard's on-board sound system may not be configured:

- Click the Start button and then move the cursor to Settings.

- Click on Control Panel.

- Double-click on the System icon.

- Click on the Device Manager tab.

- Click on the + sign next to the Sound, video and game controllers entry.

Find the Crystal PnP Audio System CODEC. If this option is not present, you need to reconfigure the Crystal audio hardware with the latest drivers.

High-Pitched Noise from System Speaker

Q635.   *My late-model IBM PC emits an unexpected high-pitched noise from the speaker. I can't find anything about this in my system manual. Do you have any ideas?*

A.   I went digging for this answer, and it seems that this is a known problem with the audio circuit of some motherboards in IBM's 7xx series systems. You should just press the Mute button until you can replace the motherboard with an upgraded version. If you cannot replace the motherboard, you may be able to disable the sound feature and install a sound board.

Sound Blaster Makes Noise After BIOS Upgrade

Q636.   *I've upgraded my motherboard's BIOS, but now the Sound Blaster is making all kinds of noise. I rebooted again, but nothing seems to help. What's going on here?*

A.   This is a problem with some older sound cards. Motherboard peripheral controllers are programmed through ports 26Eh/26Fh or 398h/399h. Different motherboards are wired to use one set of ports or the other. On most sound cards, FM music can be accessed through I/O port address 388h and 389h. This is implemented on Sound Blaster cards for compatibility with Adlib cards and on other cards for compatibility with Sound Blaster cards.

On certain older Sound Blaster and Sound Blaster Pro sound cards, writes to I/O address 398h/399h are incorrectly decoded as writes to I/O address 388h/389h due to a bug in the sound card's address decoding logic. This causes the FM synthesis subsystem of the Sound Blaster card to be accidentally programmed while the BIOS is programming the peripheral controller chip. The BIOS programs this chip during and after the POST test. The new BIOS may write data to this chip in a different order or at a different time than the original BIOS. This can result in a "generator" noise issuing from the sound card—sometimes starting at boot-up, at Windows start-up, or at some other time. Once the noise starts, it stays on until you reboot the system. There is a workaround to the problem. Load (and then immediately unload) the FM driver in AUTOEXEC.BAT by adding these lines:

```
C:\SBPRO\SBFMDRV
C:\SBPRO\SBFMDRV /U
```

Of course, you could also replace the sound board with a newer version.

Sound Blaster Produces Noise After Pentium OverDrive Upgrade

Q637. *My Sound Blaster sound card gives me garbage from the speakers after I installed a new Pentium OverDrive processor. Why is this? What can I do to fix the problem?*

A. The problem is with your Sound Blaster drivers; they are not compatible with the new OverDrive CPU. You'll need to go to Creative Labs Web site at *http://www.nt-ca.creaf.com/wwwnew/tech/ftp/ftp.html* to acquire the latest Sound Blaster drivers for your sound card. Once new drivers are installed, the noise should stop.

No DOS Sound from Mwave Sound Card

Q638. *My Mwave sound card sounds good under Windows 95, but I can't get any sound at all under DOS. Are there any tricks to DOS sound?*

A. Your Mwave card is configured to run in the Windows 95 environment only. The DOS drivers for the sound card are available but are not fully activated. Follow the steps below to enable sounds in MS-DOS mode:

■ Click Start, Settings, and Control Panel and select the System icon.

■ Select the Device Manager tab and check the IBM Mwave Digital Signal Processors section.

■ Note the resources allocated for the IBM Mwave DSP, Audio Control, and DOS Games devices.

■ Make sure the SET BLASTER environment settings in the AUTOEXEC.BAT correspond with these resources.

■ Remove the REM from the CONFIG.SYS line:

```
REM device=c:\mww\manager\dwcfgmg.sys
```

■ Restart the system to Windows 95, and then restart to MS-DOS mode.

■ Type FASTCFG and then press <Enter>. A series of selections will appear.

ADVANCED

- Select Advanced Audio and then click OK.

- Select Yes to the question "Use these settings when rebooting system to MS-DOS mode?"

- Configure the MS-DOS mode program for SB Pro Sound and General Midi Music.

The modem feature of your Mwave card will not be functional under MS-DOS mode when Advanced Audio is selected. For modem applications, select Standard Configuration and configure the MS-DOS mode program for SB Pro Sound and music.

INTERWAVE AUDIO MALFUNCTIONS AFTER RUNNING DOS GAMES

Q639. *I have problems with my sound after playing my DOS games. My system is a Compaq Presario 8700 (with InterWave audio). In some cases, the system locks up after playing games. Any suggestions?*

A. Compaq Presario 8700 PCs with InterWave audio may not function properly after running multiple DOS games under Windows 95 or running a DOS game in DOS mode. The problems include loss of audio and system lock-ups. This is caused by DOS games not properly releasing the InterWave audio resources when the game is shut down. To prevent audio problems with DOS windows under Windows 95, make sure that only *one* DOS window is open at any time. Always close the first DOS window before opening the next one. To stop problems with DOS games, type IWINIT at the DOS prompt after ending a game (and prior to starting a second one). This resets the audio and allows it to be used by other applications.

GRAVIS ULTRASOUND CAUSING A LOUD SQUEAL

Q640. *I just installed a Gravis UltraSound card, but now when I start Windows 95, I hear a sharp, loud-pitched squeal. Why?*

ADVANCED

A.   This is caused because one or more of the Gravis UltraSound PnPs devices are disabled (or in conflict). When the plug-and-play feature is initialized, the Gravis drivers are almost always the culprit. Check in with Gravis for some updated UltraSound drivers. In the meantime, if you are not using the IDE interface on your UltraSound PnP board, open the IW.INI file and make sure the following lines are all set accordingly. This will ensure that the interface circuit is disabled and should prevent the noise problem:

```
CDBase=0

CDIRQ=0

CDDMA=4

ATAPIBase=0
```

If you are using the IDE interface, you'll need to simply turn down the sound volume until you can update your driver.

SOUND BOARD CAUSING SYSTEM LOCKUPS

Q641. *I have a 486 PC which has had a problem with frequent lock-ups. When I remove the sound card, the problem disappears. It is a Sound Blaster 16 (CT2230). Anyone had similar problems? Suggestions for reconfiguring the card?*

A.   System lock-ups are always tough problems because so many things can contribute to the cause. If your system has stabilized after removing the sound board, you've probably found the culprit, but that's only half the problem. You still need to reconfigure the sound card to avoid such conflicts. You will need to check each IRQ, I/O, and DMA assignment on the sound board against the other resources used in your PC. The complicated part about sound boards is that there are resources assigned for sound, MIDI, and a drive interface, any of which can be conflicting. Anything assigned on the sound board that is *also* assigned to other devices in the system will have to be adjusted. You can use the Device Manager in Windows 95 to check the hardware assignments of other devices.

ADVANCED

7

Input Devices

As computers become more sophisticated, so do our means of interacting with them. The ability to get data into a computer and make selections in a quick, easy manner is vital for small-office/home-office (SOHO) businesses and companies of all sizes. This chapter examines the three major types of input devices: keyboards, mice, and joysticks. While the essential operating characteristics of these devices have really changed very little through the years, there are always new issues and questions to address.

Keyboard Issues

KEYBOARD CONFUSION

Q642.   *I bought a new inexpensive keyboard with some Windows 95
        keys for my old PC, and was surprised to discover a 6-pin mini-
        DIN connector. My old PC and my new Tomcat system use a 5-
        pin standard-DIN connector. I assume all I need is an adapter,
        but why does this keyboard have a PS/2 connector in the first
        place? Aren't there any standards for keyboards?*

A.   Yes, there are two general standards for keyboard connectors: 5-pin
        AT-type connectors and 6-pin PS/2 type connectors. I can't answer
        the question of why your new keyboard has a PS/2 connector rather
        than an AT- type connector, but today I would expect PS/2 key-
        board connectors (PS/2 connectors are the most common).
        Fortunately, all you need to do is pick up a simple PS/2-to-AT
        adapter for your keyboard, and you should be in business.

TURNING OFF THE KEY CLICK

Q643.   *A customer sent in a system for an upgrade and asked me to turn
        off an annoying clicking sound each time a keyboard key is
        pressed. Well, the upgrade's done, but I'll be darned if I can fig-
        ure out how to turn off the key click. Any ideas?*

A.   When you say "key click," I presume you mean that the system
        speaker is emitting a short squawk each time a key is pressed.
        This is usually controlled either through the CMOS Setup (in the
        Advanced Configuration area) or is being produced by a short
        TSR being loaded in AUTOEXEC.BAT. Check your CMOS Setup
        first. If you cannot disable the clicks there, start a text editor
        such as DOS EDIT and look for a TSR that you can disable. If
        the actual clicking sounds are coming from the keyboard itself,
        keep in mind that some keyboards are designed specifically to
        make light clicks each time a key is pressed. This is referred to as
        tactile or positive feedback, and you may not be able to stop that
        without replacing the keyboard.

CLEARING REMAPPED KEYS AND MACROS

Q644. *A lot of Gateway 2000 systems come through my shop for upgrades, but they all use those Anykey-type keyboards. How do you clear the macros or remapped keys that are entered into the keyboard?*

A.   These Anykey keyboards are programmable—any of the keys can be reprogrammed as macros, or can be remapped to other keys. Most people do not use these features, but it is *very* common to find that any number of keys have been accidentally remapped. When it comes time to upgrade the system, keyboard tricks can have some unexpected results (for example, if the <F1> key is re-mapped, you may not be able to get into CMOS Setup). So it helps to know how to clear any keyboard programming.

To clear all macros and remapped keys, press <Ctrl>+<Alt>+<Suspend Macro>. The Program light on the key-board will blink for a few seconds, and all macros and remap-pings are then cleared. It sounds simple enough, but if the Program light does not blink, the <Ctrl> or <Alt> keys may be remapped. To reset them:

1.   Press REMAP once.

2.   Press <Ctrl> twice.

3.   Press <Alt> twice.

4.   Press <Remap> once.

5.   *Now* press <Ctrl>+<Alt>+<Suspend Macro> to clear all macros.

BOOTING A PC WITHOUT A KEYBOARD

Q645. *I've got a networked PC that I don't want anyone to physically access. Can I fake a keyboard so my computer will boot without it?*

A.   Sometimes a PC needs to be set up as a turn-key system with no keyboard for security reasons or simply because the application doesn't need a keyboard. This causes a problem when the system is booting—the BIOS will detect that there is no keyboard and display the message "keyboard failure—press <F1> to continue," and the system will halt until you reboot. There is usually an option for disabling the keyboard test located in your CMOS Setup. If your BIOS can't shut down the keyboard, you should update the BIOS with a version that will. As a last-ditch alternative, you could always make use of a keyboard lock (if your PC supports it). You can boot a system with the keyboard enabled and then "lock out" the keyboard with the key switch. There is really no other means of faking a keyboard.

Rascally Rodents and Keyboard Cables

Q646. *My nephew's pet rat chewed through the computer keyboard cable, so I removed the damaged wire sections and resoldered the wires—making sure to match all of the colors. When I tested it on my computer, I could type letters and numbers, but I could not use <Alt>+<Tab> between open programs in Windows. When the repaired keyboard was reinstalled in my nephew's computer, it would not boot, and the system would give a 3, 2, 4 beep at approximately 100-Hz frequency (a low tone, not the usual higher pitched beeps you hear during a normal boot). When the keyboard is removed, the computer boots, but then reports a keyboard error. When a known, good keyboard is installed, the same 3,2,4 beep is reported.*

A.   It sounds like a blown keyboard fuse. There's a small fuse on the motherboard which protects the +5-V power supply from short circuits at the keyboard. If you examine the motherboard in the area of your keyboard connector, you'll probably notice a tiny cylinder (it looks like a little 1/4-W resistor) called a *pico fuse*. When Rat Boy chewed through the keyboard cable, the +5-V line probably shorted to ground and popped the fuse. This also explains why a known, good keyboard doesn't work. If you can identify the pico fuse in your motherboard's documentation, you can pick up a replacement fuse at your local electronics store or order it from the PC manufacturer and then solder it into place yourself. Otherwise, you'll need to replace the motherboard.

DEALING WITH KEYBOARD FAILURES

Q647. *My sister-in-law has a Digital PC with an IBM keyboard. When she boots up, a message saying; "(10) Keyboard Failure" appears. The boot-up process continues without any other problems, but you can't use the mouse or keyboard. Could this be a BIOS problem, a motherboard problem, or another problem?*

A.　You haven't given me a whole lot of information about the system, but the fact that both the keyboard and mouse don't work is really a bad sign. I don't think the keyboard is bad, but you should try a new keyboard just to be sure. If the error message disappears when a new keyboard is used, the keyboard may well have failed, and you just have a coincidental mouse problem. But I suspect you have a system setup problem that's jamming your keyboard and mouse at the same time. Start your CMOS Setup, record the current setup, and then select the Default or Automatic setup options if your CMOS provides it. Save your changes and reboot.

KEYBOARD NOT FOUND ERROR

Q648. *I have a problem. When I boot my 486 machine, it replies "Keyboard not found." The keyboard is plugged in, and I'm afraid the motherboard may have a bad interrupt controller or something. Is there an easy way to fix it, or should I throw the motherboard out and replace it?*

A.　Always check for loose connections at the keyboard controller. Before you toss your motherboard, try the keyboard on another PC. If you can confirm the keyboard is running, the problem is most likely in the keyboard controller. You may be able to get a replacement keyboard controller (since they are usually socketed), but you may also replace the motherboard outright.

INTERMEDIATE

RANDOM CHARACTERS APPEAR WITH WIRELESS KEYBOARD

Q649.   *I've installed a wireless keyboard with my PC, but the keyboard seems to type random, erratic characters on the screen. Is the keyboard defective? Is there anything I can do about this before I replace the original keyboard?*

A.   Wireless equipment suffers from the same noise and radio inter-ference problems as cordless telephones. Cordless equipment usu-ally provides several different channels to choose from. Take a look at the channel settings for the wireless keyboard and receiv-er. First make sure that both are set to the same channel. Next, try different channels until you find a more stable setting. If there is any electrically noisy equipment in the area, try moving it away from the keyboard. If the problem persists, replace the original keyboard.

WIRELESS KEYBOARD BEEPING MAY SIGNAL BAD BATTERY

Q650.   *I've been using a wireless keyboard for some time now without any difficulty, but recently I've noticed that the keyboard has started to beep when I'm typing or using the built-in touch-pad. What does this beeping mean, and is there anything I can do about it?*

A.   My guess is that your beeping means a low battery condition in the keyboard. Since the keyboard is wireless, it must work on batteries. Try replacing the batteries in the keyboard.

PC EXPERIENCES DELAYED KEYBOARD RESPONSE

Q651.   *When I'm typing, my keyboard suddenly stops working properly. It can take 1 or 2 seconds for the letters to appear on the screen. This happens several times a day. I replaced the keyboard, but the problem is still there.*

A. Would you believe that this is often a printing-related problem that creeps in when you're running an Office 95 application under Windows 95. In most cases, you'll find that the system's LPT port is configured for ECP (and a printer is attached and on). As you probably noticed, you can clear the problem by rebooting the PC, but you'll need to replace the printer port driver with an updated version for a more permanent fix. In the meantime, you might try keeping the printer off or changing the LPT mode to bidirectional.

Keyboard Refuses to Work

Q652. *I am having a keyboard problem. I have a Tyan Tomcat motherboard. When I first start my PC, instead of one beep followed by a memory check, I get a continuous beep with a continuous memory check that pauses for a fraction of a second between completed memory counts. If I unplug the keyboard, the memory check runs normally and is followed by a No Keyboard error message. I have tried switching keyboards and keyboard cables, and am even using that keyboard right now on another PC without a problem. I am using a keyboard with a PS/2 plug connected to an extension cable plugged into a adapter and then plugged into the motherboard. It's not unusual for one of these connections to become loose despite my efforts to keep these connections together.*

A. Start by removing your extension cable and connecting the keyboard directly to the adapter. Also check the adapter to see that it is connected securely to the motherboard. It is very possible that the extension cable or adapter has suffered a short which is causing your boot problems. If the trouble continues, you may have a faulty keyboard controller. Try booting the system with a POST reader and see if the POST process stops with a keyboard controller (KBC) test. If the KBC is bad, you might be able to obtain a replacement from the motherboard or system manufacturer (most KBCs are DIP-style ICs that can be replaced easily). Otherwise, you may simply have to replace the motherboard.

NATURAL KEYBOARD CAN'T USE WINDOWS KEY ON TOSHIBA 8500

Q653.   *I'm using a Microsoft Natural Keyboard, but the Windows keys do not function on my Toshiba 8500 Desktop.*

A.   Some function keys and Windows keys on the Microsoft Natural Keyboard do not work properly on Toshiba 8500 desktop machines. This is a problem with the Toshiba keyboard BIOS. The Toshiba 8500 recognizes the keyboard during the power-on self-test (POST); however, it does not recognize some of the keys, including certain function keys and Windows keys. The solution is to replace the Toshiba's keyboard BIOS with a later version.

CAN'T SWAP TASKS WITH THE NATURAL KEYBOARD

Q654.   *The Windows keys on my Microsoft Natural Keyboard will not start the alternate task swapping feature.*

A.   This was a tough one, but I managed to track down an answer. When you are using the Natural Keyboard, you cannot use the Windows key to start task-switching software other than TASKSW16.EXE. Only using <Ctrl>+<Esc> or double-clicking the desktop may start the task-switching program you want. The Windows key on a Natural Keyboard will not start another task-switching program if TASKSW16.EXE can be found on the path. To start a different task-switching program:

■   Open the SYSTEM.INI file in any text editor (such as Notepad) and modify the line that reads

```
TASKMAN=TASKSW16.EXE
```

to read

```
TASKMAN=<task manager>
```

where <task manager> is the name of the executable file you want to start when you press the Windows key.

■   Rename the TASKSW16.EXE file, or move it to a directory that is not in the path.

■   Save and then close the SYSTEM.INI file and then restart your computer.

Mouse Issues

DEALING WITH MOUSE STALLS

Q655. *The mouse cursor doesn't move properly when I move my mouse. It seems to "stick" or "stall." I checked the cable and it's installed tightly, and I know the mouse driver is loading because the cursor appears. Is there anything I can do before replacing the mouse?*

A.   Your mouse is dirty. This is a common problem which plagues all mice and trackballs eventually. Fortunately, you can clean the mouse easily. You need to clean the mouse ball, the X- and Y-axis rollers that press against the mouse ball, and the little pressure roller that presses against the mouse ball and blow out any dust within the mouse housing.

Turn the computer off.

1.   Remove the O ring that locks into place on top of the mouse ball itself.

2.   Remove the mouse ball from the socket and try blowing some compressed air into the mouse to remove dust particles, pet hair, and other debris that may have settled into the unit.

3.   Clean the mouse ball with a light ammonia-based glass cleaner, and dry it thoroughly with a lint-free cloth.

4.   Clean all three rollers inside the mouse with isopropyl alcohol on a clean cotton swab.

5.   Replace the cleaned mouse ball and secure it with the plastic O ring.

Turn the computer on.

HESITANT MOUSE NEEDS BETTER CLEANING

Q656. *I've got a mouse problem that just won't go away. No matter how many times I clean my mouse ball, the cursor still seems to jump around the screen. What else can I do to clean my mouse properly?*

A.   Before you get out the cleaning fluid again, take a look at the
        mouse software. An old mouse driver may not be compatible
        with new software that is available. Check with the mouse manu-
        facturer and make sure you have the latest version of the driver—
        you can probably download it from their own BBS or Internet web
        site. When you install the new driver, make sure that any configu-
        ration questions or command line switches are set properly.

        If the driver software is not at fault, the mouse may need a more
        comprehensive cleaning. Remove the mouse ball again and take a
        look inside the mouse enclosure. The mouse ball is probably rest-
        ing against three rollers or wheels (an X roller, a Y roller, and a
        pressure roller). Debris easily accumulates on the rollers, result-
        ing in choppy or erratic movement. Clean all three rollers care-
        fully, and see that none of the debris falls into the mouse hous-
        ing. Finally, take a can of photography-grade compressed air and
        blow out any dust or debris that may still be interfering with the
        mouse's optical sensors.

SERIAL VS. PS/2 MOUSE

Q657.   *I'm shopping for a new mouse. I've been using an older serial
        mouse with great success, but I see lots of PS/2 mice around.
        What's the difference between serial and PS/2 mice, and which
        one would you recommend? By the way, my system will support
        a PS/2 mouse.*

A.   Technically, there's no real difference between a serial mouse and
        a PS/2 mouse. Both are serial devices, but the actual port used for
        communication is a bit different. A serial mouse use a 9-pin sub-
        miniature D-type connector and the classic COM1 or COM2
        resources, while the PS/2 mouse uses a 6-pin barrel-type connec-
        tor with IRQ12 or some other non-COM port resources. But
        regardless of the interface type, both mice only use the same
        three or four wires, and I've seen serial mice adapted to PS/2
        ports without any problem at all. If you need to free up a COM
        port (and your PC has a PS/2 mouse port), use a PS/2 mouse. If
        you don't have a PS/2 port, or you can spare the serial port, go
        ahead and use a serial mouse.

ENABLING A PS/2 MOUSE CONNECTOR

Q658. *I recently put together a new PC using a Biostar MB-8500TVX motherboard and a Cyrix P150 CPU. The system is running Windows 95 with the Plus Pack. The problem is that this motherboard does not see my PS/2 mouse. The only reference to a PS/2 mouse in the manual is a pinout of J5—a 5-pin straight connector near the motherboard's serial port connectors. What can I do about this?*

A. This happens a lot on low-end motherboards. In most cases, you have to enable the PS/2 connector through your CMOS Setup (usually in the Advanced Chipset Features or some similar area). Keep in mind that enabling the PS/2 port will free a COM port, but the PS/2 port will demand another IRQ (often IRQ12). You will also need to adjust your mouse driver to accommodate the PS/2 mouse.

PS/2 PORTS AND IRQs

Q659. *I have a Tomcat 1 motherboard and have a question about PS/2 ports. Do they require an IRQ to operate? I'm running out of IRQs, and I am just not ready to go SCSI with the machine I have now.*

A. Yes, PS/2 ports *do* require an interrupt and traditionally use IRQ 12, although many motherboards will allow you to select from several possible IRQs.

PS/2 MOUSE LOCKS UP

Q660. *I've been having periodic lock-up problems with my Microsoft PS/2 mouse (version 2.1A). When I boot the system, the mouse works, but after no more than 30 minutes, it freezes. After a soft reboot, the mouse works again. The motherboard is an Asus P/I-P55TP4XE with the PS/2 port.*

A. It is very possible that you have a defective mouse. I suggest perhaps borrowing a PS/2 mouse from a friend and see if the problem persists. If a new mouse clears the problem, you can discard the original mouse. If the problem persists (even with another mouse), make sure the latest mouse driver is loaded. If the problem continues even with the latest driver, you may have trouble with the PS/2 port. In that case, try replacing the PS/2 mouse with a serial mouse, otherwise you'd have to replace the motherboard.

DOS Mouse Driver Won't See Mouse

Q661. *I have an Intel Advanced/EV motherboard with a 133-MHz processor, and I am trying to install the game Privateer II. It requires a DOS mouse driver, but I can't seem to get the driver to see the mouse. I've tried it with and without the ICU, manual/auto configuration, and so on. The mouse works in Windows 95. I've tried just about everything I can think of. Do you have any suggestions?*

A. Since the mouse works under Windows 95, it's safe to say that the hardware is fine. Make sure that your DOS mouse driver is the correct driver for your particular mouse, and try to use the latest driver version. Also try booting directly to DOS by pressing the <F8> key when you see the "Starting Windows 95" message—and then selecting Command Prompt to start DOS. If this works, you may need to put your mouse driver in the DOSSTART.BAT file so the driver will run once Windows 95 shuts down to DOS.

If all else fails, you may want to try an NVRAM Clear procedure for the Advanced/EV motherboard. According to Intel, jumper 4 on your motherboard is the Clear CMOS jumper. This jumper allows CMOS settings to be reset to default values. In the *off* position, the current CMOS settings are maintained. In the *on* position, CMOS is reset to default values. Normally, the jumper is in the *off* position.

1. Note your current CMOS settings.

2. Turn power off.

3. Set jumper 4 to *on.*

4. Turn power on.

5. After the system boots (you will see an error), turn power off.

6. Set jumper 4 to *off*.

7. Turn system on and enter the CMOS Setup to change any of the default settings as required (i.e., hard drive parameters).

If you are running Windows 95 and you perform an NVRAM Clear, you may have to reinstall Windows 95 because Windows 95 stores system configuration data in the plug-and-play configuration area that will also be cleared.

Mouse Buttons Won't Work

Q662. *I'm having trouble with my mouse. Sometimes when I boot up, the left mouse button will not work. I can click on things with my right button to open menus. At boot up, my system detects the mouse. I have a refurbished Packard Bell with a P/S-style mouse. Could it be a port conflict? When this happens, I can reboot (it might take a few times) and the mouse will work.*

A. I seriously doubt that you've got a port or driver issue. I think it's your mouse. If the mouse works OK except for the left button, I would guess that the micro switch or whatever activates the left button is faulty. I threw away a mouse about 6 months ago that exhibited the same symptoms. Try a different mouse, and I believe you'll find that you'll get normal operation back.

Mouse Not Initializing

Q663. *I have a 486DX2/66 with a generic motherboard. I use a Logitech two-button mouse. When the machine is cold-booted, the mouse will not initialize 50 percent of the time. The DOS driver loads but doesn't see the mouse connection. The problem cannot be solved with a reset. Only another cold-reboot solves the problem (again only 50 percent of the time). This has also happened on a previous motherboard while using the same mouse.*

A.   Normally, the mouse driver doesn't load if it can't detect the mouse hardware. When a driver loads but does not detect the mouse, there is almost invariably a connection problem—either the mouse contains a faulty connection or the PC's mouse port has a faulty connection. Since this problem occurred with the same mouse on another motherboard, my money is on the mouse. You could check the mouse for wiring problems, but it is faster and cheaper to just use a different mouse (and mouse driver). That should take care of the problem.

MOUSE FAILS AFTER RETURNING FROM SUSPEND MODE

Q664. *I'm using a serial mouse with my laptop PC. The mouse works, but it stops after my laptop comes back from the suspend mode under Windows 95. I'd really rather not mess with my system setup if I don't have to, but is there anything I can do?*

A.   This is usually due to an issue with your mouse driver. The driver shuts down when your PC enters its suspend mode and does not reestablish communication when your PC exits the suspend mode. Remove whatever mouse driver you're using now and use the standard serial mouse driver that ships with Windows 95. If your particular mouse has an updated driver from the manufacturer, you can try that instead.

INTELLIMOUSE WHEEL DOES NOT WORK AFTER INSTALLING F-PROT

Q665. *I just installed F-Prot on my system, but now my IntelliMouse wheel refuses to work. What's going on here?*

A.   To work around this problem, you need to restart MSWHEEL.EXE:

1.   Press <Ctrl>+<Alt>+<Del> to open the Close Program dialog box.

2.   Click MSWHEEL, and then click End Task.

3.   Click the Start button, and then click Run.

4.   In the Open box, type in mswheel.exe and then click OK.

New Pointing Device Causes Erratic Pointing Behavior

Q666. *I just got a new Toshiba Pentium laptop that uses Windows 95. The built-in pointing device (called an Accupoint) is so difficult to control that I added a Microsoft serial mouse to the system. Now I notice that occasionally the mouse pointer suddenly migrates to the top or left side of the screen for no reason at all. Is there a purpose I am not aware of for this behavior? Is there a way to make adjustments in Windows 95 that would stop this annoyance?*

A. I've seen this type of behavior, and it's virtually always due to a conflict between your pointing device drivers. Go to your Device Manager and verify that there is only *one* pointing device. If you have an entry for both a serial mouse and the Accupoint, you're going to see odd pointing behavior as the devices fight each other for control of the pointer. Remove the Accupoint device from your device list, and I think you'll find that the serial mouse works perfectly.

GlidePoint Driver Causes GPF

Q667. *I get General Protection Fault messages after loading my Alps GlidePoint driver.*

A. The problem is that your driver is conflicting with other pointing drivers. Go into your SYSTEM.INI file. Under the [386Enh] section, there is a statement that reads:

```
mouse=scvmd.386
```

Change that to:

```
mouse=vmd.386
```

That should fix the problem.

Older GlidePoint Driver Worked Better Than Newer One

Q668. *I've been using a GlidePoint driver for a while now, and it's been fine, but I just recently upgraded the driver, and now I have problems with the GlidePoint. What's the problem?*

A.   I'd bet that the new driver is installed on top of the old driver, and it has caused a conflict. Always deinstall any existing driver first and *then* install the later driver. To accomplish a deinstall, go into your Control Panel and then open the Mouse Properties box. Under the General page, select Change. Select a Microsoft Mouse. This will rewrite your files and put your system back to an original configuration. Once that's done, reinstall the new GlidePoint driver.

INTEL MOTHERBOARD WON'T FIND IRQ12

Q669.   *The documentation for the "stripped" version of an Intel Advanced/EV motherboard says that if no PS/2 mouse is used, IRQ12 will be available. Still, no matter how much I try, I cannot get Windows 95 to acknowledge IRQ12.*

A.   You probably need to order Windows 95 to explicitly release the port addresses and interrupt that would have been used by a PS/2 mouse:

1.   Click on the Start button.

2.   Move the cursor to Settings.

3.   Click on Control Panel.

4.   Double-click the System icon.

5.   Click on the Device Manager tab.

6.   Highlight the PS/2 Compatible Mouse Port entry under Mouse in the device tree (if PS/2 Compatible Mouse Port is not seen, expand the tree by clicking on the + sign or by double-clicking on Mouse).

7.   Click on the Properties button (Fig. 7.1 appears).

8.   Uncheck the Original Configuration (Current) box.

9.   Click OK.

10.   Shut down and reboot the system.

11.   The PS/2 Compatible Mouse Port entry will now have a red X through it, which means the device is not being used.

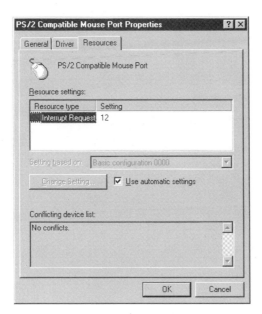

Figure 7.1 PS/2 Compatible Mouse Port Properties dialog

If you use the Remove option in Device Manager, the PS/2 controller will again be autodetected and installed on the next reboot.

Note

WINDOWS 95 INSTALLATION CAUSES TRACKBALL PROBLEM

Q670. *I just installed Windows 95 on my Aero and the trackball no longer works properly.*

A.   The Contura Aero uses an integrated trackball. If the integrated trackball on your Aero computer is no longer responding correctly after installing Windows 95, try using the other trackball button. When Windows 95 is installed, it swaps your mouse buttons so that the rear one is now set as the primary mouse button. To swap the buttons back to the way they were, go to Control Panel, double-click on the Mouse icon, and then choose Left Handed under Button Configuration.

ADVANCED

Joystick Issues

BEGINNER

Looking for a Joystick Pinout

Q671. *I've been looking everywhere for a joystick pinout. Do you have one handy?*

A.   Sure do. Table 7.1 shows the pinout for a typical PC joystick that would be used with an ordinary 15-pin gameport. Have fun.

Table 7.1 A typical joystick pinout

Pin	Function
1	+5 Vdc
2	Joystick A, button 1
3	Joystick A, X axis
4	Gnd
5	Gnd
6	Joystick A, Y axis
7	Joystick A, button 2
8	+5 Vdc
9	+5 Vdc
10	Joystick B, button 1
11	Joystick B, X axis
12	Gnd
13	Joystick B, Y axis
14	Joystick B, button 2
15	+5 Vdc

Disabling a Jumperless Joystick Port

Q672. *I'm using an Ensoniq VIVO sound board. The sound board works, but it also has a joystick port. I've already got another joystick port in the system, and I'd like to disable the VIVO's joystick port, but there's no jumper for that on the VIVO. How do I disable the joystick port without a jumper?*

A. There are a few jumperless boards that are controlled exclusively through drivers. The VIVO also uses drivers to disable certain functions such as the joystick port. Use the following steps to disable the VIVO's joystick port:

1. Leave Windows 95 and enter the MS-DOS mode.

2. Edit the SNDSCAPE.INI file in the \Windows directory. Change the line JSEnable=true to JSEnable=false.

3. Save the file and reboot the system. The joystick will be disabled.

Setting Up a Joystick in Windows 95

Q673. *I want to use a joystick with Microsoft Flight Simulator for Windows 95. How do I set up my joystick in Windows 95?*

A. If a joystick icon appears in your Control Panel, this step is already done, and you can skip to the Game Controller Setup. If you have not yet added your PC game port as New Hardware in the Windows 95 Control Panel, you should do this first:

1. Click the Start button.

2. Select Settings, and then Control Panel.

3. In the Control Panel, look for a Joystick icon. If it's there, skip to the Game Controller Setup. If not, double-click the Add New Hardware icon to start the Add New Hardware wizard.

4.   When prompted to have Windows search for new hardware, select NO. Click Next to continue.

5.   Select Sound, Video and Game Controllers and then click Next.

6.   Select Microsoft as the Manufacturer and Gameport Joystick as the model. This will add the game port as a device. Click Next.

7.   If resource settings are given as 0201-0201, click Next. Windows will look for the required files. If it can't find these files, it will ask you to insert your Windows 95 CD or disk.

8.   When the files have been installed, click Finished.

9.   Shut down your computer and restart Windows 95.

Once your game port driver has been added, a joystick icon appears in your Control Panel. Use this to set up and calibrate your joystick as follows:

1.   Double-click the Joystick icon in the Control Panel.

2.   In the Joystick Configuration section, choose the appropriate joystick type from the list.

3.   After selecting your Joystick configuration, click the Calibration button and carefully follow the on-screen instructions.

No Response from the Joystick

Q674.   *There's no response from my joystick. What should I be checking?*

A.   There are some important points to check when the joystick malfunctions.

   ■   The joystick must be securely connected to port A of your computer's game card.

   ■   Check the joystick with any joystick utility (such as GravUtil from Gravis). If it doesn't work, there is a problem with your joystick or with your game port.

- If the joystick responds normally to a utility or other application, the problem is with your game software setup or calibration.

- If you are running Windows 95, make sure that you have loaded the correct driver in your Control Panel.

- Check that you have selected the correct joystick type (i.e., CH Flightstick Pro) in the Joystick icon under your Control Panel. Run the Windows 95 joystick calibration routine.

- In your game's setup, make sure you have selected joystick as your control device and that you have followed the joystick calibration program in your game. For a game to work properly with a joystick, the joystick must be calibrated correctly.

JOYSTICK NOT CONNECTED ERROR

Q675. *I'm using my joystick under Windows 95, but I'm getting a Joystick Not Connected error with my CH Flightstick Pro. I know that the joystick is definitely connected, so what does that mean?*

A. The Windows 95 driver looks for a three-axis joystick when you tell it that the joystick is a CH Flightstick Pro. Use a diagnostic (like GravUtil from Gravis) to make sure that the X and Y joystick axes (and the throttle Y axis) are active. If the throttle is not active, this is your problem. Try to unplug the joystick, and just push the connector on without securing the screws. On some machines, when the screws are used to tighten the connector, the plug twists and starts to pull away enough to disconnect one of the axis wires. The Y axis on the B (throttle) side is usually first. If just pushing the connector on does not produce a Y axis, the game port may be substandard or faulty, so try a new game port controller.

INTERMEDIATE

8

Installation and Upgrade Questions

If you're like most PC users, sooner or later you'll want (or need) to upgrade your system. This may involve something as straightforward as adding more memory or may be as complex as replacing the entire motherboard. When it comes to installing and upgrading the PC, there are endless questions—and problems. This chapter starts off by reviewing some background information and answering basic questions about upgrading. You'll also find a large number of answers about CPU/motherboard, drive, video, RAM, and modem installations and upgrades.

General Topics

CHOOSING MAIL-ORDER PARTS

Q676.   *I am about to build my own Pentium system and can't decide where to buy the mail-order parts. I have looked through Computer Currents and see that there is a great disparity in the prices of components. For instance, I am thinking of purchasing a Intel Marl ATX motherboard with 120-MHz Pentium CPU and have seen prices range from $305 to $399. Another example is a Matrox Mystique 2MB video card with prices ranging from $130 to $219. Are these cheaper prices legitimate, or is something sneaky going on?*

A.   You are correct that prices vary a lot—and purchasing through mail order can often be a tricky proposition. Price disparity can arise for many reasons, such as special deals, volume discounts, overhead, and so on. The best advice we can give you is this:

■   If you order by mail, choose a source that has been in business a long time (mail order is a magnet for fly-by-night companies).

■   Choose companies with good warranties and liberal return policies so you don't get stuck.

■   Choose companies with ample stock. If a mail order company doesn't seem to have stock available, that's a bad sign.

■   Check out their tech support before making a purchase. If you can't get through or they don't return your call, that's a warning to look elsewhere.

LOOKING FOR THE BEST CASE

Q677.   *I am planning to build a new PC to network with the one I have right now. I want to stick to a desktop case configuration, and I was hoping you could give me some pointers on what to look for.*

A.   While all computer cases perform the same function, they are certainly not all alike. When choosing a case, quality is an important concern. Select a case that uses heavy gauge metal which is welded or bolted together for optimum strength. Saving a few dollars on a super-thin case that's only pop riveted together is hardly ever a deal. Also make sure that your power supply and motherboard will fit in the case's available space, and see that there are enough drive bays for all the drives you plan to add. If you can buy the case and power supply together as a set, that will save you a step by ensuring that the power supply will fit (but does not guarantee that the power supply will be reliable).

GETTING GOOD MIDTOWER CASES

Q678.   *I'm planning on building two Pentium systems this month, and I would like to use midtower cases with good intake filters. Can you point me in a good direction?*

A.   There are several fine case manufacturers that can provide you with good-quality products. Check out the following Web sites: PC Power and Cooling (*www.pcpowercooling.com*), Amtrade Products (*www.amtrade.com*), Fong Kai Industrial (*www.fkusa.com*), and InWin Development (*www.in-win.com*).

CONNECTING THE CASE LED FOR A HARD DRIVE

Q679.   *I recently installed a SuperMicro P5STE motherboard in a midtower Enlight case. My problem is the case's hard drive light connector has only spaces for two pins, but my motherboard has four pins. Is it OK to try to put the connector on pins 1 and 2 and leave the rest free? Will it short out anything?*

A.   If I understand you, the LED drive light on your case has a two-wire cable and connector, but your motherboard has a four-pin header for the drive activity light. You will almost certainly not damage anything if you place the LED across the wrong two pins or get the connector backward, so start across pins 1 and 2 as you suggested. If the LED doesn't light, reverse the connector on pins 1 and 2. If the LED still won't light, repeat the process with pins 3 and 4. Keep in mind that you really don't *have* to connect the drive activity LED—it's more of a cosmetic feature than anything else.

Understanding the Turbo Switch

Q680. *My computer has a turbo switch. With the turbo switch off, my computer runs very slowly. If I have a 486DLC/40 CPU, does turning the turbo switch on mean that it is running above 40 MHz? How is that possible? By the way, does an i486DX4/100 need a heat sink and fan?*

A. With the turbo switch off, your PC will run at a clock rate below the CPU's maximum speed. With turbo on, the CPU runs at its maximum rate. The turbo mode doesn't run a CPU above its maximum clock rate—this is known as overclocking, and I strongly discourage it. Finally, Yes, please do use a heat sink and fan with a 486DX4/100.

Connecting a Turbo Switch to a New Motherboard

Q681. *I recently purchased a Cyrix 6x86 P150+ CPU and a PA-2002 PCI motherboard. While installing them, I could not find a place to hook up my turbo switch from the case. There was a place for the turbo LED but not for the switch. Does this motherboard not have a place for the switch, or am I just overlooking it?*

A. I don't have direct experience with that particular motherboard, but I'm going to go out on limb here and say that if there's an LED, there's probably a switch to go with it. Take another look through the documentation. However, don't be flustered if you can't find it because there *are* systems that forego the switch and LED (like my Gateway 2000 P5/166). I think the whole turbo idea is phasing out of the industry.

CONNECTING A TURBO SWITCH

Q682. *I'm installing a new motherboard into my existing case, and I'm confused about the turbo switch. My motherboard manual shows a two-pin connector for the turbo switch, but the switch on the case has a three-wire connector. How do I know which two of the three leads actually connect to the motherboard or can I even use this turbo switch on my motherboard?*

A. First, don't panic. Your motherboard will probably work even without the turbo switch connected. When a turbo switch is arranged like yours, the center connector is usually neutral, and one side of the connector is normally open (NO), while the other side of the connector is normally closed (NC). Try installing pins 1 and 2 of your switch to the motherboard first. If the turbo mode kicks in with the turbo switch in the off position, you know the switch is backward, so connect pins 2 and 3 to the motherboard's turbo connector instead. You cannot damage anything on the motherboard by trying this.

THE NEED FOR A SECOND COOLING FAN

Q683. *I'm going to be upgrading my PC shortly to add a second hard drive and more memory. I noticed that the PC has space for a second cooling fan. Should I also be adding another fan to the system?*

A. A second fan wouldn't hurt, but it may not be necessary. Let the system run for a while and feel the air exhausting from the current fan. If the air is very warm, go ahead and take the plunge for another fan. My guess is that you won't need it unless your system is already heavily loaded with lots of drives and expansion devices.

THE CASE FOR MORE FANS

Q684. *I'd like to add an extra cooling fan in my newly built PC. It's a Cyrix 6x86 CPU (which I've heard runs a little hot anyway). I've currently got a heat sink/fan that came with the CPU, and the only other fan in this Enlight midtower is the small one in the power supply. The data sheet for the case shows three possible locations for other fans—one 6 cm and two 8 cm (I assume that means the diameter in centimeters). Are these generic cooling fans that can be obtained at a computer parts shop, or do I have to get one specific to this case? Do they just hook up to one of the existing power cords for the drives?*

A.   As a rule, cooling fans are relatively generic devices, and I have bought many replacement fans from computer parts shops and have even stripped fans from obsolete computer cases. Before you buy a fan, *do* make sure that it is a +12-V unit and that it will use a standard four-pin Molex connection rather than a specialized ac cord. Also take care to avoid splitting drive power to operate a fan. Fans generate a lot of electrical noise (and draw a lot of current), so using a Y splitter to run a hard drive and fan can easily result in data corruption and system problems. If you have the power connectors available, I'd suggest that you buy two fans. Position one fan at the bottom of the case blowing in and another fan at the top of the case blowing out. This provides the best ventilation for heated air. If you cannot find the right fans or do not have enough power cables to drive them, you might consider using fan cards. These are simply fans built right onto ISA, VL, or PCI boards that can plug into any available card slot.

New Busses Demand a New Motherboard

Q685.   *I want to upgrade my i486DX PC from an ISA-only system to include a VL or PCI bus for better video performance. What is the best way to do this?*

A.   There is really no way of adding new busses to an ISA-only motherboard. If you want to take advantage of the newer bus architectures available today, you're going to need a new motherboard. Today, you can upgrade to a Pentium motherboard, CPU, and PCI 3D video card for under $500. Not only will you enjoy terrific video improvements, but you'll see dramatic performance improvements across the board, and your system will support large EIDE hard drives if you decide to upgrade later.

CHOOSING A CPU FOR WINDOWS 3.1X NUMBER CRUNCHING

Q686. *I need to build the fastest computer I can because I have a customer who needs a bare bones system for crunching numbers in Excel (under Windows 3.11). The system must also operate on a Novell network. They tried on a Pentium 133, and a typical session took 2 hours. I was planning to build a bare bones Pentium Pro 200 with a VENUS motherboard. Should I do that, or should I get a Pentium Pro 150 or 180? Also, how well will Windows 3.11 run on those chips?*

A. Hold off on that Pentium Pro. If your client insists on running Windows 3.1x instead of a Windows NT Workstation, the way to go is with a Pentium 200 or 233 (or an AMD K5 or Cyrix 6x86 with a similar P rating) using a Marl or later motherboard. I doubt that an MMX processor would offer any real bonus for your type of work. Pentium Pros are seriously optimized for 32-bit performance and can actually suffer diminished performance under older versions of Windows. Also keep in mind that RAM can have a serious impact on processing, so be sure to add lots of RAM (at least 32MB) to your bare bones system.

One other thing, you might get even more performance by optimizing the spreadsheet itself. Things like more efficient algorithms and relaxed convergence criteria can significantly speed processing on *any* system.

MEASURING 486 OVERDRIVE IMPROVEMENT

Q687. *My 486 VLB motherboard has a ZIF CPU socket and AMI BIOS. The motherboard manual says it will support 486DX2, DX, and SX processors at speeds of 25, 33, 40, 50, and 66 MHz through the ZIF CPU socket. If I replace the current 33-MHz processor with a DX2/66-MHz coprocessor, will I see a marked increase in speed? How can I measure the difference? Would it be possible to pop in a DX4/120-MHz processor even though the manual (written back in 1993) doesn't list it?*

A.   Yes, you will see a noticeable improvement in speed, but the overall system improvement will be marginal. Remember that even though the DX2 CPU may be running at twice the motherboard clock speed, the remainder of the system is still running at the original clock speed. You would measure this improvement by running a benchmark (or set of benchmarks) before the upgrade and then running the same set of benchmarks after the upgrade. The difference represents the improvement for your particular system. You will probably notice that CPU-specific benchmarks show the most substantial improvements, while related benchmarks like drive access and video performance will show far less dramatic improvements.

When it comes to running an "unlisted" CPU, that's a bit more problematic. Your motherboard supports the 40-MHz clock that would be needed to run a DX4/120, but you may need to make sure that your CPU socket would provide the right voltage, and you may need a BIOS upgrade to identify the faster OverDrive. Even then, other issues like the motherboard chipset or CPU socket pinout may not be fully compatible. Your best avenue is to contact the motherboard (or system) manufacturer and check in with technical support to see if a DX4/120 has been tested with your system. Given the cost of a CPU—even an older CPU—it's not worth taking the gamble without more detailed information.

486 System Upgrade Suggestions

Q688. *I wonder if you can help me with a system upgrade. I have a 486/66-MHz system with 16MB of RAM and about a 600MB HDD, along with a CD-ROM drive and sound board. I would like to spend under $500, so what can I do to maximize processing speed?*

A.   This is a real blanket question, but I'll give it my best shot. PC performance is generally limited by three factors: the CPU, the motherboard, and the external busses (like the ISA bus). As a starting point, you can upgrade the CPU with a Pentium OverDrive for 486 systems. Keep in mind that your current motherboard will have to support such an upgrade. Another alternative is the AMD 5x86 CPU (though the motherboard *still* has to support the new CPU, and the AMD processor may require a new motherboard BIOS). The problem with CPU-only upgrades is that you're still stuck with older-motherboard clock speeds, chipset, and so on. A more aggressive upgrade would be to replace the motherboard outright with a real Pentium motherboard. You can shop around and get the board, CPU, and cache for about $500. Since the majority of processing elements are located on a motherboard, replacing the motherboard should yield your most dramatic performance increase. The only wrinkle with a Pentium motherboard is that you'll probably need new 72-pin SIMMs instead of the 30-pin SIMMs you're likely using in the 486 system. This will push your budget up a bit, but the improvement will be worth it.

UPGRADING A 486 FOR MULTIMEDIA TITLES

Q689. *I've been trying a CD-ROM multimedia demo on an older 486 PC, but I can barely understand the sound because it constantly cuts in and out. Should I upgrade the CPU, CD-ROM, or video board? The CD-ROM seems to work on my other CD-ROM titles.*

A. We've become so used to fast Pentium systems and 12X to 16X CD-ROM drives that it's easy to forget what a nightmare multimedia can be. Traditionally, the video and audio involved in multimedia are extremely data-intensive, and an ample amount of computing power is required to handle the multimedia properly. If you do choose to upgrade your older 486 PC, there are several avenues that will aid multimedia applications. A faster CPU should be the first order of business. If your motherboard is OverDrive-ready, you can probably install a DX2 or DX4 processor—perhaps even an AMD 5x86. You'll need to check your system documentation for specific CPU compatibility. Of course, you can also choose to upgrade your entire motherboard to an entry-level Pentium.

A faster CD-ROM is also a definite plus. Chances are that you're using a 2X CD-ROM right now. You can find dirt-cheap 4X CD-ROMs and very low-priced 8X CD-ROMs which can significantly boost the data speed available from the CD. If your 486 has a VL bus slot available, you can also improve performance with a VL graphics accelerator (your motherboard is probably too old for the PCI bus). If your motherboard only offers ISA slots, you probably wouldn't see much improvement with a new graphics board (not that you can find ISA video accelerators anymore). You don't say how much RAM is in your system, but ample system RAM under Windows (probably 3.1x in your case) will also help.

486-to-Pentium Upgrade Suggestions

Q690. *Currently I have a 486/33 MHz system with 8MB of RAM, a 1.6GB HDD, a generic video card, a Sound Blaster 16, an old Edison SVGA monitor, and an Internal 14.4KB modem. I'd like to upgrade this to a Pentium class machine (Maybe a 100 or 133 MHz) with 16MB of RAM, a decent video card, and a 33.6KB external modem (I've got the modem and just need to get the serial port). Any suggestions?*

A. Well I don't like making product recommendations, but there are some hints that I'll pass along to you. First, you can almost certainly find a 133- to 166-MHz Pentium motherboard for a very reasonable price. Just make sure that it will fit the space available in your case. If you are able, you should also get a motherboard which can be upgraded with processors with clock speeds up to 200 MHz or so. Don't worry about the serial port for your modem. Your new motherboard will have at least one serial port available on it. If you don't want to spend the money to get a true Pentium MMX motherboard (which I think start at 166 MHz), you should at least plan on getting a Pentium MMX OverDrive processor for your Pentium motherboard. This will at least keep you compatible with MMX software as it becomes available.

486-to-Pentium Motherboard Upgrade Advice

Q691. *I'm planning to upgrade several 486-class PCs with a new Pentium P5-75 motherboard. Could you give me some pointers on what to look out for during such an upgrade?*

A.   Before you go too far, you might consider replacing just the CPUs
       rather than the entire motherboards. You could probably
       upgrade the CPUs with AMD 5x86 133 MHz CPUs, which
       benchmark about at the level of a P75. You can obtain 5x86
       CPUs for well under $100. If you must upgrade your mother-
       boards, there are some more typical issues to keep in mind:

■   *Consider the physical dimensions.* You've probably done
       this already, but it's vital that the new Pentium mother-
       boards fit into the older cases. Not only must they fit in the
       available spaces, but the mounting points must line up, and
       the case openings for serial ports, parallel ports, mouse
       port, and so on, must all align properly.

■   *Consider your video boards.* Chances are you're moving
       from ISA or VL video boards to motherboards with PCI.
       Your ISA video boards would work but performance would
       be poor. If you have older video boards in your 486 sys-
       tems, you'll need to upgrade the video boards to PCI bus
       versions (probably 3-D video boards).

■   *Consider your RAM.* The older 486-class motherboards
       often used 30-pin SIMMs, while late-model 486 and
       Pentium motherboards use 72-pin SIMMs. If you only have
       30-pin SIMMs on the old motherboards, you'll need to pur-
       chase some new 72-pin SIMMs for the Pentium mother-
       boards (or use SIMM adapters to convert the 30-pin
       SIMMs into 72-pin SIMMs).

■   *Consider your controllers.* Chances are that your new
       Pentium motherboards offer on-board floppy and hard
       drive controller ports. If so, you can discard any older
       stand-alone ISA or VL drive controller cards. If the Pentium
       motherboards won't support your drives, you'll need to get
       PCI drive controllers. SCSI is rarely supported on the moth-
       erboard, so you can transfer any ISA SCSI controllers over
       to the new motherboards or buy PCI SCSI controllers for
       top performance.

INTERMEDIATE

HOW MUCH L2 CACHE FOR A PENTIUM MOTHERBOARD

Q692. *I just ordered a new Pentium motherboard and was told by the salesperson that I should only get 256KB of pipeline burst cache instead of the 512KB I was planning on. The reason was that the second 256KB would not be recognized since I only have 16MB of RAM. I would need 32MB before the system would use the second 256KB. Can you verify this? If it is true, could you enlighten me as to why this is the case?*

A. Since you have not said exactly which type of motherboard you have ordered, I cannot be absolutely certain whether this is the case or not. However, I have learned that some low-end motherboards will operate this way. Fortunately, the performance jump from 256 to 512KB of cache is not that great, but if you are looking for the absolute maximum possible performance from your motherboard investment (or feel you may have trouble installing more memory and cache later on), you may decide to select a different motherboard. If you don't need absolute peak performance, the loss of cache will probably not affect you that much.

MOTHERBOARD DEAL MAY DEMAND NEW BIOS

Q693. *A friend of mine is trying to build a computer. He got what he called a "deal" on a 486 motherboard and Cyrix 5x86/100 CPU. The BIOS is AMI (dated 1993). He can't get the computer to do anything. The hard drive powers up, but there is no display or beeps. He says he double-checked all jumpers. I told him a BIOS that old will not support a 5x86 CPU. Will my friend have to send this deal back, or will a BIOS upgrade do the trick?*

A. Cyrix and AMD CPUs often need a BIOS upgrade before they'll operate in older motherboards. According to the information I've got here, your friend will need a BIOS dated June 1995 or so. His current 1993 BIOS is a real red flag. I am also concerned about CPU voltages. A 486 motherboard typically run at 5 V, but the 5x86 takes 3.3 V. Your friend should have set the CPU socket on the motherboard for 3.3 V (if the motherboard supports it) or used a voltage regulator module between the socket and CPU.

Otherwise, the CPU could have already been damaged. He might also want to check those motherboard jumpers again to make sure the clock is set to 25 MHz (for a 5x86/100 CPU).

SYSTEM SOMETIMES FAILS TO BOOT

Q694. *I just assembled a system using a PCI 486 motherboard with 8MB of RAM, a Phoenix NuBIOS, and running an AMD DX4-100 CPU. At times the system fails to boot (i.e., there is just a blank screen and no beeping from the speaker). The system can only boot after a few cycles of switching off and on the power supply. Any hints or pointers?*

A. You've got a whole selection of things to check. First, make sure that your power supply works and that its cables are connected securely to the motherboard. If the power is intermittent, replace the power supply. Check the motherboard next to see that none of the metal standoffs are shorting any printed circuit traces on the motherboard. Check the RAM and CPU to see that they are all installed completely and secured into place. If the problems persist, try a new motherboard.

NEW MOTHERBOARD NIGHTMARE

Q695. *I got a new motherboard, a Pentium K5 P75 upgradeable to 200 MHz with 32MB of RAM, 256KB of cache, an Epoch 4MB video card, a used Sound Blaster and CD-ROM drive. The power supply is new. The system had been running really well until I downloaded a video. Then it went nuts. It locks up. I reboot, and it is missing HIMEM.SYS, so I get my start-up disk and restore HIMEM.SYS, and still it freezes. The A: drive light is on, but there is no response. I shut down and start back up and still no-go. I ran ScanDisk, which found a few bad sectors on the hard drive, so I removed all partitions and reformatted using DOS 6.22. The formatting took a very long time, and the system still freezes up. I even installed an older hard drive, and that still doesn't help. I checked for viruses, and the system is clean. Any suggestions will be helpful at this point.*

A.   As I understand it, you upgraded your motherboard, and now your system is extremely unstable. Since this is the result of a major upgrade, I first suggest that you recheck your installation. Check the motherboard mountings for any shorts, recheck your cable installations, make sure any expansion boards are mounted correctly, and so on. Also check your power supply (you said it's new). Use a multimeter and make sure that every output from the power supply is at the correct level as shown in Table 8.1. If any of the power supply outputs are low or absent, the power supply may be defective. Next, try booting from a floppy. If that works and the system is stable, run a diagnostic like TuffTest (*www.tufftest.com*) to check for faults. If the system checks clean, you might take a long hard look at your hard drive controller and cable to see that the hard drive is installed correctly (intermittent connections or power at the hard drive can cause all sorts of problems). If a motherboard error surfaces (or if problems persist), I would have to suggest that you replace the motherboard. It's new, so you can probably get it replaced.

TABLE 8.1 POWER SUPPLY LEVELS AT THE MOTHERBOARD

Wire Color	Voltage (V)
Black	Ground
Red	+5 V
White	–5 V
Blue	–12 V
Yellow	+12 V

VINTAGE CONVERSION WON'T BOOT

Q696.   *A friend gave me an old XT with an NEC V20 CPU, but with a VGA monitor, etc. I have lots of small parts, boards, and such, so I purchased an old 386 motherboard to make this relic Windows 3.11- and Netscape-capable so my mother can get into e-mail and do some surfing. It gets to where it should boot (graphics adapter is up, memory is checked, etc.), hits each drive once, and stops. It started with ST225 and ST238 drives, but I switched to a Quantum drive and an IDE controller.*

A.   There are a few issues to consider with conversions of this sort. Start by checking your power supply and see that it is in the 200-W+ range. Older XTs often used smaller power supplies, and such underpowered ones can sometimes be overwhelmed by later motherboards and drives. I personally don't think that power is your problem, but you should check the situation before proceeding.

Next, IDE drives must be configured in CMOS, so you must start your CMOS Setup routine (for a 386-vintage motherboard, you may need a setup disk). Make sure that all the drives and memory settings are correct. You'll need to enter detailed geometry figures for your IDE drive. Boot the PC from a bootable disk that contains FDISK and FORMAT. You can then partition the disk with FDISK and format it with your FORMAT utility. Use FORMAT C: /S to make the drive bootable. You should then be able to remove the disk and boot directly from the hard drive. At that point, you can install DOS and Windows 3.1 to the system.

Newly Built PC Is Dead

Q697. *I have started building my first computer, and I am not having any luck. I bought a 486 Deep Green motherboard. The motherboard uses a 486DX2/88 CPU and an AMI BIOS. I installed everything in the case, and hooked up all the wires just as the user's guide indicated. I checked all the jumpers on the motherboard and powered it up. I then got a beep error (1 long and 2 short). I determined that this was a memory failure, so I reinstalled the SIMM and the beeps stopped. Now when I turn on the power, I get nothing—no lights on the front of the case, no beeps, and no video. The power supply works and the CPU cooler works too. What can I do next?*

A.   When there is no response from the system at all, start by checking the power supply connectors at the motherboard. Make sure they are all installed securely. Also check the metal standoffs which mount the motherboard to see if any of the standoffs are shorting the printed traces on your motherboard. You may want to insert thin, nonconductive washers between the metal standoffs and the motherboard. Also check that your video board is inserted correctly into its expansion slot. If problems continue, check the flash ROM voltage selector jumper used to program the flash BIOS. If that jumper is set incorrectly, the system may hang up awaiting the code needed to reprogram the BIOS. Be sure to set such jumpers to their proper positions.

CPU and Motherboard Upgrades

WORKING WITH METAL OR PLASTIC STANDOFFS

Q698.   *I built my first P166 PCI system last week, and it's humming along perfectly the except for a registry error I am working with. My real problem lies with a second case and motherboard I bought from another supplier that looked like a better deal. The first case came with the plastic standoffs I needed, and they screwed into the plate from the cabinet. This new case has slide-in plastic standoffs, and only three of the corners line up. There are also some metal standoffs that line up with taped holes in the case. Should I be using these, or did the supplier stick me with incompatible parts. This also got me questioning the first mother-board I put together. It had similar metal standoffs that were not needed. It started me to wondering if the motherboard should be insulated from the case, or does it need the metal standoff for grounding.*

A.   No, the motherboard does *not* need to be grounded to the PC's metal chassis (you can operate a motherboard quite nicely out-side of a case). In actual practice, the motherboard receives its electrical ground from the power supply connected through the power cables. While the metal chassis should also be grounded, that is typically accomplished for the sake of electrical safety, so it is not sound to "common" the grounds between the case and motherboard. There should be absolutely no difference between using plastic or metal standoffs when mounting the motherboard. The problem comes in when metal standoffs accidentally short circuit printed circuit runs on the motherboard. This can often result in intermittent operation or a "dead" system. Experienced PC builders frequently use plastic washers between metal standoffs and the motherboard anyway. If you have the choice, use plastic standoffs that screw into place for a little more rigidity—slide-in plastic standoffs allow the motherboard to move, and this can stress your plug-in expansion boards. As far as whether the mounting points actually line up, *that* is another matter entirely and suggests that your case may not be designed or machined properly for your particular motherboard.

Isolating the Motherboard and Case

Q699. *I have just successfully installed a Tyan Tomcat motherboard, and as this is my first motherboard installation, I have a question to clarify a few uncertainties. Must the Tyan be isolated from the case chassis, and is this true of most motherboards?*

A. As a rule, a motherboard should not *short circuit* to the case or any of the metal standoffs. In the rush to create new motherboards, designers often run their printed circuit traces a bit too close to the mounting holes. When the board mounts to a metal standoff, the standoff shorts against one or more of these close traces, and the system won't start or acts erratically. To prevent this from happening, I always recommend the use of thin, nonconductive washers between the metal standoffs and the motherboard. If you *really* want to be cautious, you can also place a nonconductive washer between the mounting screw and the motherboard as well.

Upgrading from a 486DX2 CPU

Q700. *I am running a 486DX2/66 VESA local bus system which has 20MB of RAM and 4MB cache on my hard drive controller. I want to upgrade my CPU and am able to go with an Evergreen 586/133. From all I have read, this processor will give me about the same performance as a P75. My other option is to upgrade to an AMD 486/100 or 486/120 Enhanced CPU. Would I notice any appreciable performance difference between the 486/100 Enhanced and the 586/133? The AMD 486/100 chip costs about $30 and the Evergreen 586/133 is about $200.*

A.   There are several important points to keep in mind here. First, the AMD 5x86 133 costs about $45 to $60—the $200 price quoted you is probably with a motherboard. Second, you'll need to watch your CPU voltages. If you're running a DX2/66 motherboard, the CPU socket is almost certainly running at 5 V and the Evergreen/AMD 100/120/133-MHz processors must run at 3.3 V. This voltage difference requires you to get a voltage regulator (or upgrade your motherboard). Since you are able to support a 5x86 133, that would probably be the preferred CPU because of its performance. Finally, you'll need a good-quality heat sink/fan to properly cool your new CPU.

OVERCLOCKING A 486SX2 CPU

Q701.   *I am planning to do a major system upgrade within a month. But in the meantime, is it possible to overclock a 486SX2/66 to a 486SX2/80? I often hear of overclocked Pentiums and Cyrix chips but never 486s.*

A.   Of course overclocking is *possible,* and it is often desirable, but it is almost never wise. All you'd really need to do is change the clock frequency from 33 to 40 MHz (if your motherboard supports 40 MHz). While many supporters claim success with overclocking, it is an inherently unreliable technique. Overclocking places additional stress on the CPU and causes added heat dissipation. Some CPUs can tolerate overclocking, some will work unreliably (causing data corruption and system lock-ups), and others will just not start at all. I personally do *not* advocate CPU overclocking, but if you insist that you *must* try it, I urge you to use a heat sink with your 486SX2 CPU.

DON'T IGNORE HEATING WITH OLDER PENTIUMS

Q702.   *I'm planning to upgrade an older PC to a basic Pentium 120-MHz motherboard. I know that the newest Pentium CPUs need a heat sink/fan to keep them cool, but do I still need a heat sink/fan for the P120?*

A.   Yes, even the established Pentium CPUs like the 100- and 120-MHz models can still run extremely hot. Since a good-quality heat sink/fan runs about $15 to $25, it is well worth the investment to use one with any Pentium CPU. Be sure to include a thin layer of thermal grease between the CPU and heat sink to aid heat transfer.

AMD K5 vs. 5x86

Q703.   *I've been seeing a lot about the AMD K5 and the AMD 5x86. Are these the same CPU? If not, what are their differences?*

A.   Both are similar processors, but there are some important differences. The AMD 5x86 is basically a 586 Lite, which is a 32-bit CPU built around an enhanced 486 design. It delivers much better performance than a 486 but not as good as a true 64-bit CPU. By comparison, the AMD K6 is a true 64-bit CPU designed to be at least equivalent to the Pentium. As a rule, 486 motherboards will usually benefit from the AMD 5x86, while Pentium motherboards can employ the AMD K5.

Considering a 5x86 Upgrade

Q704.   *Do you have any experience with the Evergreen 5x86/133, which is supposed to upgrade a 486 to 586 levels of performance? Clock speed is increased to 133 MHz in the new chip. They supply the CPU, a voltage regulator, and a fan/heat sink combo. Evergreen's part number is 248. I want to use this to upgrade my old 486DX/33 with its generic motherboard, AMI BIOS, and 16MB of 30-pin RAM.*

A.   Generally speaking, the 5x86 class of upgrade processors yields an impressive improvement on most motherboards—often providing performance around the level of a 75-MHz Pentium. The CPUs are considered to be reliable and effective devices. However, keep in mind that not all systems will accept the 5x86 flawlessly. Some CPU upgrades need a BIOS upgrade as well to better support the 5x86, and a few users report periodical Windows kernel faults after performing an upgrade.

Understanding the K5

Q705.   *I've got an older Pentium system (a P5/66), and I want to upgrade the CPU. A friend recommended an AMD K5, but can you tell me if that is a good choice?*

A.   The AMD K5 line of CPUs is designed to compete with Intel's Pentium line of CPUs. Over the years, AMD has established a place for themselves with the K5, which has proven to be fully compatible with DOS and Windows as well as with many BIOS and chipset versions developed for Pentium-class motherboards. At this point, it is reasonable to say that the K5 is a sound alternative to the Pentium. Before changing over from an Intel CPU to an AMD CPU, make sure that the CPU voltage is appropriate for the K5 (you may need a voltage regulator module between the socket and K5). You should also make sure that the BIOS is fully compatible with the K5. Check with your original motherboard or system manufacturer to see if there are any cautions or special instructions for K5 upgrades. Finally, you may need to make changes to your motherboard clock speed or CPU Type setting to accommodate the K5.

AMD K5 Voltages

Q706.   *I'm replacing my Pentium CPU with an AMD K5/133-MHz model, but I'm unclear about the voltages. The Pentium uses 5 V, but I think the K5 uses less. Is this true? If so, how do I reduce the voltage requirements? Finally, if the working voltage is lower, will I still need to use a heat sink or fan with it?*

A.   The K5 line of CPUs work within a narrow range between 3.52 and 3.6 V. If the voltage falls too low, the CPU (and your entire system) may not work reliably. If the voltage rises too high, the CPU may be permanently damaged. As a rule, there are two methods of controlling CPU voltage. First, there may be a CPU voltage regulator built into the motherboard. If so, there is probably a jumper that will allow you to switch between 5 and 3.5/3.6 V. If there is no on-board voltage regulation, you will need to add a voltage regulator module—packaged to resemble a socket that fits between the motherboard's CPU socket and the CPU itself. You should still employ a good-quality heat sink/fan with the K5 and use a thin layer of thermal grease between the CPU and heat sink to achieve best heat transfer.

Understanding the K6

Q707. *I've just heard about the K6 CPU from AMD. What is it, and how does it compare to Intel's CPUs?*

A. The K6 processor from AMD (*www.amd.com*) is designed to deliver performance that is competitive with Intel's Pentium Pro CPU under Windows 95. In addition, the K6 processor contains an industry-standard high-performance implementation of the new multimedia extensions (MMX) instruction set, which enables a new level of multimedia performance. AMD designed the K6 processor to fit the low-cost, high-volume Socket 7-type motherboards. This enabled PC manufacturers and resellers to use the K6 quickly. The initial K6 CPU family includes the K6 166-, K6 200-, and K6 233-MHz versions, with higher speeds coming soon.

MMX Possibilities

Q708. *I've been hearing MMX mentioned a lot lately in the popular media. I know all about the 57 new instructions it offers and its on-chip enhancements. But I want to know what the practical applications of the MMX are.*

A. MMX will be a tremendous boost to data-intensive applications like games. Imagine playing your favorite 3-D walk-through game at high resolution in 24-bit TrueColor mode. MMX also improves simultaneous activities, so imagine multiple channels of audio, high-quality video or animation, and Internet communication, all running in the same application. As a rule, some of the applications that benefit most from MMX technology are 2- and 3-D graphics, audio, speech recognition, video codecs, and data compression. Of course, it may take some time before the potential for MMX is fully realized in the actual software.

MMX Software on Older CPUs

Q709. *I just ran across my first MMX game program in the store yesterday. It looks really good. The thing is, I've got a Pentium 120
system, and I haven't upgraded to a Pentium MMX OverDrive
yet. Can I run the game on the Pentium 120 (at low performance) until I have a chance to upgrade the CPU?*

A. Unfortunately not. MMX software uses the instructions which
are specific to MMX processors, so there is no backward compatibility between MMX software and older CPUs. The MMX
software won't even run. You will need to upgrade your CPU
before you even consider installing that new software.

CPU Voltage and Cooling

Q710. *I'm building my first PC, and it will be a 486DX4/100. I have the
CPU chip, but an article I read said that I need to get a voltage
adapter board and a heat sink/fan for the CPU because of the voltage. Why, when I can set the CPU voltage on the motherboard?*

A. If your motherboard already supports 3.3 V CPUs, there should-
n't be voltage problems. But, you SHOULD use a heat sink/fan
anyway because the DX4 CPU will still run very hot. You should
also put a thin layer of thermal grease between the CPU and heat
sink/fan to aid in heat transfer.

Choosing Intel, AMD, or Cyrix CPU Upgrades

Q711. *I have a Gateway 2000 system with an Intel 486SX/33 CPU.
Should I stick with Intel and upgrade to the Pentium OverDrive
83-MHz CPU? Are Cyrix or AMD chips worth looking at?*

A. The rule of thumb that I have always used is that for top-of-the-
line speed and performance, go with Intel. For general-purpose
upgrades of existing CPUs, AMD is usually the way to go. Cyrix
has some real issues with heat and math coprocessor performance, but their newer M2 CPU promises to be more competi-

tive. The real question is just *which* CPUs your motherboard will actually support. Check the documentation that accompanied your system and look for a list of suitable upgrade CPUs. If the AMD 5x86 is listed, that's often an excellent solution. You may also wish to check with Gateway technical support to find if there are any newer CPUs (that had been released after your system was built that will work). You may also need a BIOS upgrade to support CPUs like the AMD 5x86. Keep in mind that you can also upgrade to an entry-level Pentium motherboard and CPU for a very reasonable price.

UPGRADING TO PENTIUM PRO

Q712. *I've got a Pentium system, but I run Windows NT. I hear that the PentiumPro performs better with NT. Can I upgrade my Pentium to a Pentium Pro? Is there even such an animal out there?*

A. Although Intel is renowned for their OverDrive line of CPUs, there is no Pentium Pro OverDrive available. According to Intel, no such OverDrive is even planned. If you really want to use a Pentium Pro system, you'll need to upgrade both your motherboard and CPU.

PENTIUM AND PENTIUM PRO SOCKETS

Q713. *I've been looking everywhere for a motherboard that will accept either a Pentium or a Pentium Pro, but I haven't been able to find one. Will the Pentium Pro fit in a Pentium socket (or vice versa)?*

A. Not a chance. The Pentium Pro is a much larger device than the Pentium classic, and the two are not even close to being pin-compatible. As a result, there are no motherboards that will support either a Pentium or Pentium Pro; it must be one or the other. This will demand two completely different motherboards with specialized sockets and chipsets. By contrast, you will find Pentium MMX OverDrive CPUs which will replace existing Pentium classic CPUs without any changes to an existing Pentium motherboard at all.

Setting the Clock Multiplier on a New Pentium System

Q714.   *I'm installing an Intel Pentium 75-MHz CPU on a motherboard with an Intel Triton chipset. On the CPU speed selection jumpers, I have a choice of 66, 60, or 50 MHz. On the Internal Clock Speed selection jumpers, my choice is 2.0X, 1.5X, 2.5X, or 3.0X external clock speed. What's a safe bet for my 75-MHz CPU?*

A.   That's a great question with so many users upgrading their CPUs. Setting up a Pentium CPU requires the proper setting of both the clock speed and multiplier. For a P75, you should set a clock speed of 50 MHz and a multiplier of 1.5X (50 x 1.5 = 75). If you install a 100-MHz CPU, leave the clock speed set to 50 MHz and just change the multiplier to 2.0X (50 x 2.0 = 100), and so on.

Adapting AMD CPUs to an Intel System

Q715.   *I have an Intel 486DX2/66 processor which I would like to upgrade to a 486DX4/100. Intel stopped producing this chip this year. AMD has a chip that is priced very competitively, but it is a 3.3-V CPU as opposed to my present 5.0-V chip. I'm told that I may be able to use a voltage regulator, but I wanted to check first.*

A.   First, you will need to ensure that the CPU you plan to buy is pin-compatible with the Intel DX2 you're removing. You should not have to adjust the motherboard clock [which should already be set to 33 MHz for the 66-MHz clock doubler, or 99- (~100) MHz clock tripler]. However, if the new CPU is not precisely pin-compatible, you may need to set a jumper on your motherboard to select the CPU Type (see your PC manual for the exact jumper and its recommended position). Next, if the CPU is a 3.3-V model, you *will* need a voltage regulator. Fortunately this often fits as an interim plug between the new CPU and its original socket, and you can buy it along with the new CPU. Finally, you will need a heat sink/fan that is attached to the top of the new CPU. Don't skimp on a heat sink/fan spend a couple of extra dollars and get a ball-bearing fan. By the way, you may be able to find some real close-out bargains on Intel 486DX4/100 CPUs in magazines like *Computer Shopper*.

K6 Software Compatibility

Q716. *I see that AMD has released its K6 MMX CPU. I'm considering an upgrade when my budget allows, but can you tell me if the K6 will run all of my existing software—especially since the K6 is an MMX CPU?*

A. AMD has taken great pains to ensure that their K6 MMX CPU will be backward-compatible with all major operating systems such as MS-DOS, Windows 3.1x, Windows 95, and Windows NT, as well as their respective applications. The MMX extensions simply provide the added versatility to improve the performance of multimedia applications. While AMD has earned a lot of respect in the PC industry with their K5 line of CPUs, it is always prudent to wait a bit until major motherboard manufacturers have had an opportunity to develop a new generation of motherboards and identify any possible BIOS, CPU, or chipset issues.

Upgrading K5 to K6

Q717. *I have a motherboard with an AMD K5 CPU. Now that AMD has released its K6, I would like to upgrade. Can I use the K6 with my existing motherboard?*

A. That's a very difficult question to answer decisively because the K6 is so very new. Both the K5 and K6 CPUs are made for Socket 7-type motherboards, so the K6 should fit your existing K5 motherboard. The problem is that it takes more than CPU sockets to determine CPU upgradeability. Other motherboard factors such as BIOS versions, CPU voltage settings, and chipsets must also be considered. So it is entirely possible that even though the K6 may physically fit your motherboard, you may encounter any of three problems: (1) the K6 would be damaged by incorrect voltage levels at the CPU socket, (2) poor chipset compatibility may cause poor system performance or crashes with the K6, or (3) the BIOS or chipset (or both) refuses to run with the K6 at all, and your system won't even start. Your best option is to check with your original motherboard manufacturer to see if they have tested the K6 on your motherboard model. A new voltage regulator module and/or BIOS upgrade may be needed, or you may need a new motherboard entirely.

INTERMEDIATE

Considering a Pentium OverDrive Upgrade

Q718. *I'm thinking of upgrading my 486 with a Pentium OverDrive CPU. The problem is that I don't have any documentation for my system, and the manufacturer went out of business some time ago. Is there any way to tell if the motherboard will support a Pentium OverDrive?*

A.   That's a particularly tricky question, and you're really going to have to dig for an answer. Take a look at the 486 socket. If the socket is noticeably bigger than the 486, the socket will probably accommodate a Pentium OverDrive. If the 486 socket is just the right size for your existing 486, it will probably not accommodate a Pentium OverDrive. The problem is that even if the socket *will* support a larger CPU, there's no clear way to configure the motherboard clock and CPU Type jumpers properly. You should check out the Intel Web site (*www.intel.com*) and search for the System Upgrade List. If you can find your system model listed, any compatible CPU upgrades will also be listed. You may also be able to determine any particular jumper changes.

INTERMEDIATE

P5/120 Crashes—Fact or Fiction

Q719. *I'm in the process of upgrading all the major components of my 486 machine. I have purchased a Pentium motherboard (Tyan Triton III) and I am considering an Intel P5/120 CPU. A service representative at a local computer store told me that they stopped installing the Intel P5/120 chip because customers were experiencing system crashes which were attributed to that particular CPU. Currently, the store sells and installs all other Intel P5 chips. Can you confirm or deny this issue? I was also told that the chip was designed primarily for laptop machines.*

A.   I have used the P5/120 CPU, and seen it working in other systems. There have been no problems. I suspect that your salesperson is either misinformed or that they are using questionable motherboards that have problems with the 60-MHz clock needed to operate the CPUs. I personally would opt for the P5/133 because it is a faster CPU and uses a 66-MHz clock (and runs the PCI bus at 33 MHz instead of 30 MHz as the 60-MHz clock does). As a result, the jump from 120 to 133 MHz shows a noticeable increase in overall performance, but the P5/120 should work more than adequately. I can also tell you that the P5/120s were *not* designed for laptop use because of the heat they generate.

Choosing a Motherboard for MMX

Q720. *I want to upgrade my motherboard to support a Pentium MMX CPU. What features do I need to look for?*

A. Pentium MMX-compatible motherboards generally use an Intel 430VX chipset (or similar) and provide two voltages to the CPU (2.8 and 3.3 V). Recent Pentium motherboards which are not *directly* compatible with true Pentium MMX processors will still benefit from a line of Pentium MMX OverDrive CPUs which are now available.

MMX and Advanced/EV Motherboards

Q721. *I have an Intel Advanced/EV motherboard, and I want to upgrade to MMX. Will the Advanced/EV motherboard accept an MMX chip? I have looked all over the Intel Web site and could not find the answer.*

A. According to Intel, the Advanced/EV motherboard will *not* accept a true Pentium MMX microprocessor, but it will accept a Pentium OverDrive with MMX enhancements. If you need a true MMX CPU, you'll need to upgrade your motherboard.

New CPU vs. New Motherboard

Q722. *My son uses his 486DX/33 multimedia VLB system for school work and games. Today he showed me the latest game catalog in which 80 percent of the games require a 66-MHz system as a minimum. I realize that the best solution is to buy him a Pentium system, but I can't afford that now—I am looking for a cheap temporary fix. I figure I can use all of the present components*

INTERMEDIATE

but am not sure of the eight 30-pin 80-ns SIMMs. The two·
choices that I am considering are simply replacing the 486DX/33
CPU with a Cyrix 586/100-MHz CPU for $159 or replacing the
motherboard with an AMD 586/133-MHz motherboard for
about $180. If one of the two choices can still use the eight old
SIMMs, I will go in that direction. What are your thoughts on
this matter?

A.   As a rule, you will receive better performance when upgrading a
CPU and motherboard rather than just upgrading the CPU alone.
With a price difference of only about $20, the new CPU/mother-
board combination seems like a natural choice. But there are two
issues to consider. First, the new motherboard may provide PCI
busses (not VL), so you will need a new video card. Also, the
AMD 586 CPU is a 64-bit CPU, so the new motherboard may
employ 72-pin SIMMs instead of 30-pin SIMMs. The 80-ns
memory may also be too slow for the new CPU (this can be corrected by adding wait states, but performance will suffer). In
either case, a new motherboard is the better choice, but it may
wind up costing you more than you realize. If money is the
absolute bottom line, you should have good luck with the CPU-
only upgrade. Remember that you may also need a voltage regulator adapter between the new 3.3-V CPU and your old 5-V CPU
socket.

BIOS UPGRADE OPTIONS

Q723.   *How can I upgrade the system BIOS? Is it just a matter of*
replacing the old BIOS with the new one? Is there anything I
should watch for?

A.   Typically, updating a BIOS involves a direct replacement of the
motherboard BIOS. There are two popular methods of accom-
plishing this: physical replacement, and flash BIOS. Physical
replacement is just what the name implies. You remove the original BIOS IC(s) and insert a new one (or a set). The cost runs
from $40 to $100 depending on the BIOS manufacturer. This is
relatively simple; you need only be concerned with installing the
new IC(s) properly. Flash BIOS is the preferred technique, using
reprogrammable BIOS ICs (virtually all current motherboards

provide flash BIOS). You can download updated BIOS files from on-line sources and run a programming routine to install the new BIOS files automatically. The advantage of flashing a BIOS is that you never have to open the PC. When obtaining a new BIOS, you need to know the *exact* motherboard receiving the upgrade. Plugging in or flashing the wrong BIOS version can render the system inoperative.

Cyrix CPU Overheating

Q724. *I just got a Cyrix 6x86 P150+ CPU and plugged it into a Triton chipset motherboard. Everything works except that the heat sink on the CPU becomes very hot several minutes after the power is turned on. By comparison, the Pentium 133-MHz CPU on the same motherboard is just a little bit warm after a 1-h run. My concern is that the heat on the Cyrix CPU can cause damage, or does it matter?*

A. Heating is always an important consideration for *every* fast CPU. The Cyrix CPUs tend to run hotter than comparable Intel and AMD CPUs. That's probably why the CPU is getting so hot after such a short time. If the CPU gets too hot, it can cause system crashes and eventually failure. I suggest that you use a heat sink/fan mechanism, which forces air through the heat sink (vastly improving cooling efficiency). Invest in a good-quality ball-bearing heat sink/fan. You should also use a thin layer of thermal grease between the CPU and heat sink/fan to improve heat transfer. One other alternative is to exchange your current 6x86 for a 6x86L, which is an improved low-power version of the CPU.

INTERMEDIATE

OverDrive CPU Demands Low-Voltage Operation

Q725. *I am helping a friend upgrade her HP Vectra VR/2, currently running with a 486SX/33 CPU. The manual indicates that the motherboard will accept an Intel 486DX4/100 CPU. The only CPU matching this description (that is still available through channels that I know) is listed as a 3.3-V chip. I assume that the CPU socket is 5 V. Will one of these CPUs work in the computer?*

A.   The news is mixed. According to the information I've been able to dig out from Intel, the 486SX is a 5-V CPU. In order to accommodate a 486DX4/100 upgrade, the socket would need to be a Socket 1 or Socket 2, both of which are 5-V sockets. This probably means you'll need to find a BOXDX4ODP100 CPU for the upgrade. This will probably have all the internal regulation needed for the OverDrive processor. However, you must still read the documentation accompanying the new CPU for any particular cautions. If you find for some reason that your OverDrive CPU demands a 3.3-V socket, you will need to add a regulator between the socket and the CPU.

FLASHING THE BIOS

Q726.   *I hope you might be able to answer a question about flashing a BIOS upgrade. I have a BCM SQ588 OEM motherboard in my Tagram Thunderbolt PC. I paid a visit to the BCM Web site and downloaded a newer version of my BIOS. How can I find out what the newer BIOS is supposed to "fix" and/or improve, and where can I download a flasher (and how do I use it)? I also want to download the code from the current BIOS just in case I trash it during flashing. Can I do that? Where can I get the utility that will allow me to do it?*

A.   Let's start with your list of fixes. Unfortunately, that kind of information isn't always available. Some technical support pages will offer a list of fixes or an explanation of the problems. In other cases, there is a README file zipped up with the flash file which you downloaded. After you decompress the ZIP file (I assume it was ZIPped), look for a README, which usually lists the fixes and offers a general flash procedure.

As far as the flasher is concerned, that is part of the flash file that you downloaded, and after you decompress the file, you'll probably find a COM or EXE file that will actually do the work, along with a .ROM file which contains the new BIOS code. You should copy all of the unzipped flash files to a floppy disk.

The actual flash process may vary a bit from system to system, but it usually involves setting the program jumper on the motherboard and then booting the PC with the flash file on disk. The flasher will start automatically and begin the upgrade process. *It is very important to not reboot or kill the power while the flash process is proceeding.* Otherwise you'll damage your existing BIOS, and the system won't start—ever (you'll need to replace the physical BIOS). Once the flash is finished, you'll usually hear one or two beeps. Shut the system down, reset the program jumper, and you're done.

Finally, it is *always* a good idea to make a backup of your current BIOS if the flash program will allow it. Remember to backup the BIOS file to a floppy disk. The problem is that a BIOS backup will not get you out of trouble if the new BIOS refuses to work. You need to boot the system successfully before you can run any kind of flash program. The real reason for keeping a BIOS backup is so that if new bugs or incompatibilities are discovered, you can restore the older BIOS if necessary.

A BIOS Upgrade for Tucson Motherboards

Q727. *What are the reasons to upgrade a BIOS, and should I do it? I have an Intel Tucson motherboard and have been having problems. My errors include Windows 95 registry errors and the inability to run MMX software with my P5/166 MMX chip. Can this be BIOS-related? Any good solutions?*

A.   The main reason for upgrading a BIOS is to resolve BIOS bugs or hardware incompatibilities that may lead to system problems. For example, you may need a BIOS upgrade in order to support AMD or Cyrix CPUs on your motherboard. While registry errors can be caused by a number of different factors, an MMX motherboard and MMX CPU that refuses to run MMX software may very well indicate a BIOS upgrade is needed. According to Intel, BIOS version 1.00.06.DH0 is the latest BIOS for the TC430HX (or Tucson) motherboard. You can find detailed information about the motherboard (and the new BIOS file) at *http://www.intel.com/ design/motherbd/tc/index.htm*. Take a look at your current BIOS version numbers when your PC first starts up. You can perform a BIOS upgrade and clear the CMOS with the procedure below. You may also wish to perform the CMOS clear procedure to see if that resolves your issues. Remember that this procedure does not apply to all motherboards.

ADVANCED

1. Locate CMOS Clear jumper on the motherboard. For the Tucson, this is J10C1-A.

2. Move the jumper from pins 4 and 5 to pins 5 and 6, and turn the system on.

3. When the system reports "NVRAM cleared by jumper," turn the system off and return the jumper to pins 4 and 5.

4. Run the system normally.

UPGRADING A COMPAQ MOTHERBOARD

Q728. *I have a Compaq Presario CDS524 which is a 486DX2/66-MHz system. I'd like to upgrade my motherboard with an Intel Pentium 200-MHz model. Can you tell me what I need to know in order to accomplish such an upgrade?*

A.   The most important issue in selecting a new motherboard is to determine the "form factor" of your current motherboard—the documentation that came with your system will probably tell you what kind of motherboard is installed. For example, a Presario-vintage motherboard probably uses a baby-AT or low-profile motherboard. Since the motherboard is matched to the case, choosing the correct motherboard form factor will ensure that the expansion slots, ports, and mounting points will all line up. The other issue is to consider where the CPU is located in relation to your expansion cards. Some motherboards place the CPU such that its heat sink/fan will obstruct full-length expansion cards. If you're interested in Intel motherboards specifically, you might consider the Advanced/EV (the baby-AT Endeavor) or the Advanced/AS (the baby-AT Atlantis).

TROUBLES REMOVING AN OLD CPU

Q729. *I'm trying to replace my CPU, and I have a chip puller that I got in a kit (kind of like tweezers but with a bend at each end). I have tried for about 30 min, applying upward pressure and rock-ing back and forth. I have repositioned the chip puller toward the end and then back in the middle and rotated it 90 degrees, but I haven't budged my chip. I am even deflecting my motherboard, which I know isn't good. I decided I'd better quit for now and ask for comments on how to go about this. I apparently haven't damaged anything yet because I'm using the same computer to send this.*

A.   Stop now and check your socket. Many CPUs are mounted in a zero insertion force (ZIF) socket. Look for anything that even remotely resembles a handle or little lever that you might be able to lift in order to relieve pressure on the IC's pins. After you lift the lever, you can probably lift the CPU right out, drop the new CPU into place, resecure the lever, and away you go. If your motherboard doesn't have a ZIF socket, you're going to have a devil of a time removing the CPU. What you need is a little bit of leverage. Use a wide, flat-blade screwdriver between the CPU and socket, insert the blade just under the CPU and then turn the blade slightly to rock out one side of the CPU just a bit. Then proceed in a clockwise (or counterclockwise) fashion to each side of the CPU, easing out progressively more of the CPU. Eventually, the CPU will pop out (the whole process will likely take 5 to 10 min). Keep in mind that this will probably leave some noticeable marks on the plastic socket. You should be *extremely* careful when installing the new CPU because you'll probably need to ease it into place using the same gradual process.

JUMPERS FOR A PENTIUM OVERDRIVE

Q730.   *I'm planning to install a new Pentium OverDrive CPU in my system. Will I need to make changes to my motherboard jumpers to accommodate the OverDrive? If so, what will I need to change?*

A.   Not too long ago, new CPUs would require you to make changes to the motherboard's clock setting and CPU Type settings, both selected through motherboard jumpers. But today, Pentium OverDrives (and the motherboards they work in) are becoming more versatile. The Pentium OverDrive processors made for current Pentium systems are intended to serve as drop-in replacements. If you select the proper OverDrive for your system, you

ADVANCED

can probably replace the CPUs directly without having to make jumper changes. However, 63- and 83-MHz Pentium OverDrive processors intended to replace the i486 *will* probably require a jumper change. To be absolutely safe, check the manual that came with your motherboard or system to see what jumpers are available for CPU-related changes. You should also check with your vendor to see if there are any particular jumper changes required. Intel provides an index of jumper settings at *http://www.intel.com/overdrive/upgrade/index.htm.*

Recognizing a New AMD 5x86 CPU

Q731. *I have a Deep Green VESA 486 R407E mainboard which works pretty well. I just took the Intel 486DX2/66 chip out and replaced it with an AMD 5x86 133-MHz 3.3-V chip. I don't know how to get the system to recognize the new chip properly. The manual for the board says it's compatible with AMD DX4 chips and shows the jumper settings, but it does not specify the newer 5x86 line. The BIOS (Award modular BIOS v4.50G) reports that the system is running a 486DX2 at 120 MHz. Is the system actually running at 133 MHz but only reporting it wrong, or do I need to change something? What do I need to do?*

A.   First, it sounds like your PC is running—that's always a good sign, and it means you don't have a voltage problem (i.e., plugging a 3.3-V CPU into a 5-V socket). Since your DX2 ran at 66 MHz, the motherboard was set to 33 MHz. Since the 5x86 is a clock quadrupler, your AMD should be running at 33x4, or 132 MHz. This should be exactly right for the 5x86 CPU, so I expect it would be safe to leave the system this way. As for the CPU reporting problem, it is also not uncommon for the BIOS (or any reporting software) to misreport the CPU performance. Since the 5x86 is not listed in the motherboard manual, the BIOS probably isn't recent enough to recognize the CPU. This can probably be corrected with a BIOS upgrade. *Also don't forget to use a good heat sink and cooling fan on the CPU.*

Pentium OverDrive Causes Windows 95 to Fail

Q732. *I just installed a Pentium 83-MHz OverDrive in my 486DX2 computer running Windows 95. The motherboard manual indicates that this chip will work, and I set all the appropriate jumpers. However, it locks up trying to load Windows 95 (with an 0E error). I cannot even get Windows 95 to boot up in Safe Mode, but it will boot to DOS. Is there something I need to adjust in the BIOS after installing this chip?*

A.   Well, it stands to reason that if your PC will boot to one operating system (DOS), it should boot to another operating system (Windows 95). Check the BIOS start-up screen to see if the BIOS identifies the OverDrive CPU correctly. If not, you should investigate a BIOS upgrade for your motherboard. If it does, I suspect that Windows 95 needs to detect the new CPU from an installation standpoint, so I suggest that you reinstall the original CPU and perform a full system backup to tape and then install the new CPU and try reinstalling Windows 95 as an upgrade. Allow Windows 95 to detect the hardware and reinstall it. That may clear the problem.

MMX CPU Upgrade Hangs Windows 95

Q733. *I just upgraded my Micron Pentium 90-MHz PC with a Pentium MMX OverDrive CPU. The problem is that the Micronics M54Si motherboard detects the new CPU at only 80 MHz and hangs up when loading Windows 95. Is there anything I can do about that?*

A.   This problem is caused by the BIOS on your Micronics motherboard. You will need an upgrade in order to detect and use the new MMX CPU properly. Try downloading the 05.ZIP file from the Micronics M54Si PCI BIOS File Update area at *http://www.micronpc.com/support/file_lib/bbs/micm54si.html*. There are two versions available, one of which adds some resources for support of IDE CD-ROM drives.

ADVANCED

PENTIUM MMX OVERDRIVE NOT IDENTIFIED PROPERLY

Q734.   *I've installed a new Pentium MMX OverDrive CPU, but the PC identified it as an Intel 486 CPU. What can I do? Did I do something wrong with the upgrade?*

A.   You probably didn't do anything wrong, but there are some things to check. Check your CMOS Setup and verify that the system configuration (i.e., L1 and L2 cache enabled, and so on) is the same before and after the Pentium MMX OverDrive installation. Also make sure the bus speed and CPU voltage pins haven't been changed. If everything checks properly, you will need a BIOS upgrade. Contact your motherboard or system manufacturer for the new BIOS version.

PENTIUM MMX CPU IDENTIFIED AT THE WRONG SPEED

Q735.   *I installed a Pentium MMX OverDrive, but now the BIOS identifies the processor as running at the wrong speed.*

A.   Some BIOS versions use a look-up table or timing loop to determine the speed of a processor. These may not always provide the correct value (this is known to happen on the ALR Optima, Intel Zappa, Aptiva 2168, and Aptiva 2768). Try running the OverDrive processor diagnostics that accompanied the OverDrive. This should report the CPU speed correctly. The long-term solution for this problem is to upgrade the BIOS. The Aptiva 2168 and 2768 need a BIOS update equal to or greater than BGOUS1H (this is available from IBM at *http://www4.pc.ibm.com/aptips/4b66_5ea.html*).

PROBLEMS WITH A NEW CPU

Q736.   *I want to upgrade my CPU, so I checked the processor on my motherboard and found it was an Intel 486SX/33. Then I contacted both Dell and Intel, and both suggested that I use the PODPV 25-MHz Pentium overdrive. So I bought one and mounted it, but the system doesn't work. Before this, I upgraded the BIOS and then upgraded the hard disk (using EZ-Drive to support large HDDs). Maybe I need to restore the original BIOS?*

A. I seriously doubt that restoring your original BIOS would help your new CPU. There are many reasons why the new CPU might not work. I suggest that you first restore the original CPU. If the original CPU works, you know the new CPU is the problem. When installing a new CPU, you typically need to make CPU Type and clock speed changes on the motherboard and to mount the new CPU correctly. Check your new CPU position and orientation in the socket, and see that you made the proper motherboard jumper changes. If problems persist, the new CPU is probably defective.

NEW CPU FAILURE FREEZES SYSTEM

Q737. *I have two nearly identical 486DX/33 systems (Micronics ISA motherboards). I replaced the CPU on system 1 with a Kingston clock quadrupler 133-MHz upgrade. Operation is flawless, and I'm very pleased with the result. I did the same upgrade on system 2 with the same excellent result. However, after about 2 weeks of 24 hour/day operation, the system hung up in the middle of a process which we run daily to update a database. Attempts to reboot met with partial success on the first two tries, after which the system was totally dead—not even a video logo or BIOS identifier on power-up. Any idea what the problem might be?*

A. I'd be willing to bet that your new CPU failed. Try putting the original CPU back in your system 2. If the system starts up normally, you'll need to exchange that defective 5x86 with Kingston. Sometimes even new CPUs fail spontaneously. Make sure to have a good-quality heat sink/fan on the CPU to keep it from overheating.

NEW CYRIX SYSTEM FREEZING UP

Q738. *My new Cyrix 6x86 166+ is freezing up on me. The CPU is mounted on a SuperMicro P5STE motherboard. It freezes at different times—sometimes during boot-up and other times when the machine has been running a while—so I don't think it's excessive heat. It has a Cyrix fan/heat sink. Doesn't this usually mean it's a hardware problem?*

ADVANCED

A.   Yes, I'd certainly say you've got a hardware problem brewing there, but it's very hard to tell where the problem might be. In this case, you'll need to cover all the angles. Start by checking the installation of your CPU, cache ICs, and SIMMs. Take a look at any expansion boards and verify that they are sitting evenly in their expansion slot(s). Make sure that everything is installed securely. Also check to see if anything is shorting your motherboard (such as your metal standoffs mounting the motherboard to the chassis). Finally, I'd suggest you check your power supply—a low or marginal power supply voltage may easily allow the system to freeze at random points.

New BIOS Won't Run System

Q739.   *A customer flashed his BIOS with a download from a manufacturer's Web site. After the flash, the system didn't POST or do anything. I assumed that the customer had chosen the wrong BIOS for his motherboard and had just totally messed up his system. What might have happened, and is there anything the customer can do to correct the problem?*

A.   This is a *very* sticky problem, and there is little that can be done to fix it. If the wrong BIOS was installed (or the POST process was interrupted), the original BIOS is trashed and the system simply won't boot. In virtually all cases, the BIOS IC on the motherboard must be replaced (the system manufacturer may be able to sell your customer another BIOS IC). Your customer can then try flashing the BIOS again.

New OverDrive Causing Floppy Drive Problems

Q740.   *I just replaced the 486 CPU in my system with an 83-MHz Pentium OverDrive. The system boots and runs, but I noticed that the floppy drive won't work. It works with the original CPU in place. What's going on?*

A. I really had to dig for this one. Some older 486 motherboards use the SIS 85C471 controller IC. Unfortunately, this chip doesn't use the write-back cache correctly, and the most common result is floppy problems when the CPU speed is high enough. Intel reports that the problem can be resolved by installing what they call an Interposer Socket between the motherboard socket and CPU. You can order the Interposer Socket from Intel at 800-321-4044. You can also find more contact information at the Intel Web site at *www.intel.com*.

New OverDrive Causing Windows Video Errors

Q741. *I just put in one of those Pentium OverDrive chips, but now I get video problems in Windows 95. Everything was working properly before. How can I fix these problems?*

A. There are two possible problems that can account for your video issues: Either the video driver is dated, or the video hardware itself cannot accommodate the higher speed afforded by the Pentium OverDrive. Try starting Windows 95 in the Safe Mode (you might also try disabling the L1 internal cache through your CMOS Setup). If the video problem goes away, your video driver is probably dated, so contact your video board maker for an updated video driver for Windows 95. If the video problem remains even in the Safe Mode, chances are that your video adapter cannot operate properly at the higher system speed. Try a different video adapter in the system.

SCSI CD-ROM Fails with the OverDrive

Q742. *I installed a Pentium OverDrive 133-MHz CPU, but now my SCSI CD-ROM drive is refusing to work. I checked all the cabling and power, and everything seems right. Why would this happen?*

ADVANCED

A.   Your problem is not uncommon, but the most frequent cause is often overlooked. Some SCSI adapter drivers (or SCSI BIOS) will not operate properly at the higher CPU speeds. You may need to install a more recent SCSI driver or replace the SCSI BIOS. If the problem remains (or there are no driver/BIOS updates available), you may need to replace the SCSI adapter entirely.

TYAN TOMCAT II+ S1562 AUDIO PROBLEM

Q743.   *Following the installation of my Pentium MMX OverDrive, my system emits feedback when playing sound files from the CD-ROM drive. This is really annoying. The CD-ROM drive is a Panasonic 6X IDE drive plugged into a Tyan Tomcat II. The drive was plugged directly into the motherboard using the primary on-board connector. All hard drives on the system are SCSI rather than IDE, which enabled the CD-ROM drive to access the primary IDE controller by itself. A separate SCSI CD-ROM was installed and ran sound files without any feedback. The latest AWE32 drivers from Creative Labs were installed, but this did not resolve the problem when using the IDE CD-ROM. Also, the latest Adaptec SCSI drivers didn't reduce the distortion. How should I handle this?*

A.   It seems that the bus mastering drivers included with Windows 95 are causing feedback which causes noise on the expansion bus—resulting in bad data, which translates to sound noise. Check in with the Tyan Web site (*www.tyan.com*) to download the latest bus mastering drivers for your motherboard, or remove the drivers to shut down bus mastering (though this may cause some devices in your system to stop working).

SYSTEM STALLS AT POST WITH PENTIUM OVERDRIVE

Q744.   *I've got a problem upgrading my PC. I replaced my older CPU with an 83-MHz Pentium OverDrive, but now the system locks up during POST. I exchanged the OverDrive, but the problem still remains. The original CPU still works, so I know the problem is with the new CPU. What have I missed?*

A.   I'd almost be willing to bet that you've got a BIOS problem. One of the first tasks performed by BIOS during the POST is to identify and test the CPU. Some BIOS versions will not correctly identify the Pentium OverDrive or test the new CPU properly, and this causes a system lock-up. If you were to install a POST reader board and check the last POST code to be executed, you'd probably find that the system halts just before or during the CPU test. In most cases, you can get a BIOS upgrade from the motherboard or system manufacturer, which can solve the problem. Unfortunately, if there is no BIOS revision available, you may not be able to use the OverDrive with your particular system.

SYSTEM WON'T BOOT WITH NEW PENTIUM OVERDRIVE

Q745.   *I really need your help with this one. I just upgraded a friend's Pentium 60-MHz system with a 133-MHz Pentium OverDrive CPU. The problem is that now the system won't boot. When I restore the original 60-MHz CPU, things work, but that new CPU just won't run. Is the CPU bad?*

A.   You've hit on a really rare problem that only seems to crop up when upgrading the first-generation (60- to 66-MHz) Pentium systems. I think you should first see if the CPU is good by trying it on another PC. That will eliminate the possibility that the CPU might be defective or accidentally damaged in handling. If the CPU is OK, your problem is probably with the original Pentium motherboard itself. You may need what Intel calls an Interposer Socket between the CPU and motherboard socket. The Interposer Socket stabilizes and filters some critical signals passing to and from the CPU. Fortunately, the Interposer Socket is easy to install. You can call Intel Technical Support at 800-321-4044 or visit the Intel Web site at *www.intel.com* for international contact information. Keep in mind that Intel will need to know your BIOS revision and the part number (i.e., that AA number) from your motherboard when you place your order.

ADVANCED

New Motherboard Causes Invalid System Disk Error

Q746. *Recently, I switched motherboards, using the same memory, CPU, hard drive, floppy drive, and CD-ROM. The second motherboard constantly gives an Invalid System Disk message. It does not respond to any disk placed in the floppy drive. It also appears that the floppy drive is inoperable. I tried a second working floppy drive and disk, and received a similar message. I went into the BIOS settings several times with no luck or responses. The cable was checked and replaced with another working cable. Any idea what I might be doing wrong?*

A. Whenever you change a motherboard, you *have* to enter the CMOS Setup routine and log all of the drives and other system parameters. While you mention that you did update the CMOS, I'm not sure that you actually saved any of your changes before rebooting the PC. Double-check your entire CMOS Setup configuration, and be sure to save your changes. Aside from a CMOS Setup problem, the only other issue could be your drive controller. You don't mention whether the drive controller is on the motherboard or a stand-alone board. Make sure that there is only *one* set of drive controllers in your system. If you have both motherboard and expansion drive controllers in the system, be sure to disable the motherboard drive controllers.

System Dead After Case and Power Supply Upgrade

Q747. *Several months ago, I purchased a new case and power supply for my PC. I tested the power supply before installing the motherboard, and it worked. Then I switched the motherboard and other components from my old case to the new one, plugged it in, turned it on, and nothing happened. The system acted as if were not getting any power (no fan or anything). I checked all the connections, but nothing was wrong.*

A. Start by checking your ac cord between the wall outlet and power supply. I've seen loose cords cut off electricity to the power supply. If the ac cord is secure and the power switch is on, but your system is still dead, check the motherboard power connections and drive power cables. Also check the installation of all your expansion boards. Discount expansion boards are not always designed with optimum dimensions. This allows the board to be inserted improperly. When an expansion board is inserted incorrectly, pins can short and result in serious power problems. Check that all boards are inserted correctly and completely. If the problem continues, try your original power supply (the new power supply may have failed prematurely).

Extra Drives

Considering a 2.88MB FDD

Q748. *My cousin has been using a 2.88MB floppy drive for months now and has had great success with it. I've been thinking about upgrading to one myself, but I see they're hard to find—especially the 2.88MB disk. Is it a good idea to invest in the 2.88MB floppy drive?*

A. My advice is to save your money. The 2.88MB FDDs were a good idea whose time never really came. The 2.88MB floppy drives were always a bit pricey and often demanded a 2.88MB floppy drive controller. Even though most current floppy ports will support a 2.88MB floppy, the availability of the drives and the media just never made them popular. Now that you can get an Internal Iomega 100MB Zip drive or a 1GB removable media Jaz drive, the extra 1.44MB afforded by a 2.88MB floppy just seems terribly limited. The one advantage that 2.88MB floppy users have is that they are still backward-compatible with older 3.5-in disks.

Choosing a New Hard Drive

Q749. *I currently have a Conner 1.2GB EIDE hard drive. I was considering purchasing a 4GB EIDE hard drive. Which manufacturer and model would you recommend? I have downloaded information on the Quantum Fireball and the Seagate ST34250.*

A.   Generally speaking, all the major drive makers such as Maxtor, Seagate, Quantum, and Western Digital produce hard drives of roughly equal size and quality. I suggest that you compare the quality of their technical support and length of their warranties before making a final choice. Also keep in mind that you will need to partition your 4GB physical drive into at least two 2GB logical drives.

IDE Drive Cable Not Long Enough

Q750.   *I want to hook up my second hard drive to the primary channel, but the IDE cable drive connectors aren't far enough apart on the ribbon cable to reach between the two drives. I need about another 1 in. Is it possible to move the slave drive's connector a little further down on the cable to reach? If not, is there such thing as a pass-through connector that would allow the use of two single cables on one channel? I'd rather not relocate the hard drives if possible.*

A.   This happens a lot, especially in larger minitower and full-tower PCs where there are many drive bays, and the distance between drives and controllers can be quite significant. If you had an insulation displacement connector (IDC) crimping tool, you could install another female connector further down the cable to suit your needs. However, there are no pass-through or other cable modifications available. I suggest that you simply purchase a longer drive cable or contact a full-service PC shop that could make one for you. This will cause the least fuss and get you running reliably.

Faster CD-ROM Drives Don't Always Mean Faster Searches

Q751.   *I am thinking of upgrading to one of the new 16x CD-ROM drives, but I wonder how much a faster drive would help with my CD database searches. Will it do a boolean search faster?*

A.   Hold on before opening your checkbook. CD-ROM drives are rated by their data transfer speed and seek time. Faster CD-ROMs will yield faster data transfers and shorter seek times. But this does not necessarily translate to faster logical searches. A search depends on the search algorithms used in the search software and the number of criteria involved in the search.

CHOOSING A CD-ROM FOR LOADING SOFTWARE

Q752. *I'm going to buy two CD-ROM internal units for our depart-
ment here, and their primary use will be for loading software
rather than for entertainment. Do I really need one of the latest
and greatest 12X or 16X CD-ROM drives, or can I get away
with an older technology?*

A. If you're only going to be loading software, virtually *any* CD-
ROM will do, but in order to make sure you have the current
drivers and operating system support, I'd suggest that you buy at
least a 4X drive. You can probably find a name brand 8X drive
for well under $100. If you swap CDs frequently, I might also
suggest a 4X CD-ROM changer, which can support four CDs
and is available from companies like NEC for under $100.

CHOOSING A REPLACEMENT CD-ROM AND INTERFACE

Q753. *I have a CR-563-B 2X CD-ROM drive that failed some time
ago, and it is time for a upgrade. The problem is that my computer is a few years old and doesn't support the current
Enhanced IDE interface. I would like to use the Panasonic,
Mitsumi, or Sony interfaces available on my Sound Blaster 16
card. I'm not an expert, but it seems that you can't find these
kinds of CD-ROM drives out there anymore. Is it worth hunting
for one of these drives?*

A. You may be able to find proprietary interface CD-ROM drives at
close-out sales or in warehouse liquidations, but you're unlikely to
find them on the shelf in today's computer stores. Proprietary CD-
ROM drives have largely been abandoned in favor of the more standard IDE interface. This presents you with a bit of a dilemma. Your
best solution is to buy a new EIDE controller board (one with the
EIDE BIOS supplement on board) and a new ATAPI IDE CD-ROM
drive. You can find drives in the 8X to 12X range at very reasonable
prices. You should disable the CD-ROM adapter function on your
sound board, install the new drive controller, switch your hard drive
over to the primary channel, and then connect the CD-ROM drive
as the master device on the controller's secondary channel. After you
install the ATAPI drivers (and protected-mode Windows 95 drivers),
your new CD-ROM should work without problems.

PARALLEL OR SCSI ZIP DRIVE

Q754. I am thinking of buying an external Zip drive for my PC. Which one do you suggest—the SCSI or the parallel port version? Speed is not important, but I do want to access it fairly quickly. Currently, I don't have a SCSI card on my PC. My main purpose for the Zip drive is to use it as a backup storage medium. What do you suggest?

A.   If you want an external drive (perhaps something that can be transferred between PCs) and don't have SCSI capability, you're going to need a parallel port Zip drive. Data transfer is slower, but the parallel port approach is more versatile. If you really want top data transfer speed and are willing to invest in a SCSI adapter, a SCSI Zip drive will serve you well. By the way, you really don't want to be running applications from the Zip drive, although you can access it for data files as needed.

TAPE DRIVE SOFTWARE AND FLOPPY DRIVE INSTALLATION

Q755. I have just recently purchased a tape drive, but this is my first time installing one. Does it require any type of software driver, and if so, where can I find one? I also bought a Panasonic 3.5-in 1.44MB floppy disk drive but can't configure it to run as the B: drive on my 486DX2/50.

A.   For the tape drive, there is rarely a driver for the drive itself (usually it is installed as an external device on the parallel port or an internal device connected to your floppy system). If the drive is a high-end device (with an interface such as SCSI), you *may* need a driver. Check the disks that accompany the drive. More likely, you simply need to install a backup application (such as Backup under Windows 95) that will recognize the drive mechanism. You should also have a backup utility on the disk(s) that came with the drive. Once installed, pop a tape in the drive and test the software. If the drive responds and can record and verify a file, you're home.

As for your floppy drive, you must connect the data cable to the middle connector, attach a power cable, and enter the drive as B: in your CMOS Setup. You must specify the type and size of drive correctly (i.e., 3.5-in 1.44MB) and then reboot the PC for the changes to take effect. If you've already done this and the drive still won't work, try a different drive (it may be bad). If you are using a 2.88MB floppy, you will need a new floppy controller to support it.

UPGRADING AN I/O BOARD

Q756. *I am hoping that you can help me with some questions I have. My machine is an old 486SX/25 (with DX2/50 OverDrive CPU) and a built-in IDE controller on the motherboard. I recently upgraded my modem to an external 28.8KB model, and to ensure quality connections, I installed a high-speed I/O controller (SIIG) to make use of the 16550 UART chip. This controller also has a IDE interface (zero wait state 50 MHz, ANSI ATA 3.1, pipeline read ahead and posted write). Would I be gaining performance by using the IDE interface on the I/O controller instead of the one built in? If so, should I disable the built-in IDE controller?*

A. Performance is always a tricky issue. Generally speaking, a VL or PCI controller with on-board EIDE BIOS will yield measurably better performance then a basic IDE-type interface. For a 486SX motherboard, I doubt you have PCI bus capability. If your I/O controller is VL, you'll probably note a significant speed improvement. If it's an ISA bus board, your improvement may be only marginal (if you notice it at all). However, it wouldn't hurt to try it. To use the add-on drive controller, you *will* need to disable the motherboard's IDE controller. This is almost always accomplished with a jumper on the motherboard (but check your CMOS Setup for other on-board controller entries). If your hard drive is under 528MB, you should not have to change any of your drive parameters in CMOS.

IDE VERSUS SCSI CD-ROMS

Q757. *Any thoughts on IDE versus SCSI CD-ROMs? I'm planning to upgrade over the next few weeks, and I can go either way since I have a SCSI board in my PC. The price difference seems to be quite high, and I'm trying to decide if the SCSI performance would make the extra cost worthwhile.*

A. Both the SCSI and IDE interfaces are capable of transferring data *much* faster than a CD-ROM. For example, a 2X CD-ROM transfers data at 300KB/s, while a 12X CD-ROM transfers data at 1.8MB/s. By comparison, SCSI and EIDE interfaces can handle data at 10MB/s or higher. So from a performance point of view, one interface offers no real advantages over another. The issue is really convenience. IDE drives are quick and simple to install, but you can only fit two devices on the same channel. SCSI is a versatile bus that can handle a variety of devices and can provide superior support in multitasking environments. If CD-ROM performance is vital, save some money and go with an IDE model.

HDD UPGRADE SUGGESTIONS

Q758. *I have a 486SX system that was custom-built a few years ago by someone else. I have upgraded from 8- to 16MB of RAM without any real knowledge of what I was doing, but now I would also like to add another (second) hard drive. It appears as simple as mounting it, connecting it to the ribbon cable, and formatting it to be the E: drive. Could it really be that simple?*

A. Well, Yes and No. Given the vintage of your system, I assume you have an IDE drive system in place. Since virtually all hard drives available today are Enhanced IDE (EIDE) drives, you should consider upgrading your PC to support EIDE. This typically involves a motherboard BIOS upgrade or the addition of a new drive controller board with its own EIDE BIOS. After upgrading your drive controller system, you would *then* be ready to add another drive. From a physical standpoint, adding a second hard drive is very straightforward. The new drive must be jumpered as the secondary (or slave) drive, mounted in an available drive bay, connected to power, and connected to a signal cable. Once the physical installation is complete, the drive must be entered into your CMOS Setup and then partitioned and formatted with software. Finally, your new hard drive will probably be drive D: rather than drive E:. This will displace your CD-ROM drive's letter. You will need to update the CD-ROM's driver to make it the E: drive. This change may also require you to reinstall some CD-ROM-based applications.

HARD DRIVE UPGRADE QUESTIONS

Q759.   *I've just ordered a Seagate Medalist Pro 2520, an ATA-2 2.5GB drive that I researched carefully for quality before spending my money. It should arrive today. From what I gather, Seagate's software makes it pretty easy to get up and running, but I have three questions. First, should I make the new drive my master or slave, since I plan on keeping my Western Digital 1.6GB drive? Second, I have heard a lot of good things about Partition It 3.0. But can I partition my drive in a more economical way since it is running Windows 95 with FAT16 support only? Finally, I am taking for granted that my EIDE controller for the old drive will also handle the new drive as either a slave or the new master. ATA-2 is a type of EIDE, right? I'm also presuming that WD and Seagate are compatible. All the help I could get here would be appreciated.*

A.   Since your new Seagate drive is likely to be faster than the Western Digital drive, it would probably be most effective as the new primary (or master) drive with your current WD the secondary (or slave) drive. This would require a complete backup and then a repartition and reformat of your drives, a reinstallation of Windows 95 and your backup software, and finally restoring your system to the new drive. This can be done, but it demands a considerable amount of work. The quickest and easiest upgrade would be to keep your WD drive as the primary drive and install the Seagate as the secondary drive (be sure to check your drive jumpers). In either case, the new hard drive will add at least two drive letters to the system, so you may also need to update your CD-ROM drive installation and software applications. When the new drive is installed, start up to DOS using a boot disk and use the DOS FDISK on the floppy disk to partition your new drive into two drives. It's a quick, clean, and easy process.

Your drives should work together with no problems. ATA-2 is actually a subset of EIDE, so your Seagate should be supported by the existing EIDE controller. Now that EIDE timing is much more defined than it was in the early days of IDE, you should have no compatibility problems running the WD and Seagate drives on the same EIDE channel.

CONNECTING A SECOND HARD DRIVE

Q760. *I'm trying to add a second hard disk to my computer so that I will have a master/slave setup. I do not have any manuals for my computer because it was assembled by a friend 2 years ago. My BIOS supports hard disks up to 2GB. Currently, I have an IDE Western Digital 420MB hard disk. How do I add another 1.6GB hard disk to my current system? I know I will have to change the CMOS and set a few jumpers on the hard disks, but do I connect the second hard disk to the controller card, or do I connect it to the IDE WD 420MB hard disk? On my controller card, there doesn't seem to be any more connectors for a second hard disk. Do I need a new controller card? If I can connect my new hard disk to my existing hard disk, can I add an EIDE drive to an existing IDE drive?*

A.   Here's the basic procedure. Turn off and unplug the PC. Jumper your existing drive as the primary (master) drive in a two-drive system. Jumper the new hard drive as the secondary (slave) drive. Mount the new hard drive. Find the empty 40-pin connector on your hard drive cable and connect that to the new hard drive (be sure to align pin 1 in the proper orientation). Connect a power cable to the new drive. Power up the system, start the CMOS Setup, and set the drive entry to autodetect. Reboot the system and use FDISK to partition the new drive (careful to partition your *new* drive, not your existing drive). Use FORMAT to format the drive for DOS. The new drive should now be accessible, and you're done.

Now, the slower IDE drive does not have the same data transfer speed as the newer drive, so the overall performance of the new drive may be limited by the maximum data rate of the old drive—that may or may not be a problem for you. If you need peak performance from the drive, you can update the drive controller with one offering a primary (EIDE) port and a secondary (IDE) port. You can then put the EIDE drive on the primary port (you'll need to partition and SYS the drive to make it bootable) and put the IDE drive on the secondary port. You will also need to install the operating system on your EIDE drive if you choose to pursue this alternate arrangement.

Watch out for this one. Check to see if you have a special device driver for your IDE drive controller loaded in the CONFIG.SYS file. The new drive may not be compatible with it, and you can get strange error messages in Windows. When using Windows 95, you can safely disable this driver and use the default Windows 95 IDE drivers.

INSTALLING A SCSI HARD DRIVE

Q761. *How do I install my Fujitsu SCSI hard drive on my PC?*

A.   Well, you asked for it. Installing a SCSI drive can usually be broken down into seven distinct steps:

■   *Set the SCSI ID.* If your drive is to be the boot device, set the SCSI ID to ID0. If not, set the drive to ID1 (although any unused number from 0 to 6 can be used). The SCSI interface is normally ID7 and should not be changed. The factory default for Fujitsu drives is zero, but always check the jumper or switch settings before installation. If you have more than one device on the SCSI bus, verify that no other device has the same ID number.

■ *Configure the drive termination.* If your new hard drive will be the only device on the SCSI bus, it must be terminated. The factory default for Fujitsu drives is to have the termination enabled, but if you have more than one device on the SCSI bus, only the devices on *each* end of the bus are terminated. Devices not on the ends of the bus *must* have termination removed or disabled. Note that the SCSI interface card is also considered to be a SCSI device. Select your Termination Power—often abbreviated as TRMPWR. This can be set three ways: supplied from the interface card only, supplied from the drive only, or supplied by both. Most SCSI drives come with termination power enabled by default. If you use an Adaptec SCSI interface, disable termination power from the drive using the proper jumper.

■ *Check the SCSI parity.* Parity checking is used to verify the accuracy of data transfers on the SCSI bus. Disable parity checking if *any* device on the SCSI bus does not support it.

■ *Set the SCSI BIOS.* If this will be the boot device, make sure the SCSI BIOS and SCSI Boot option on your SCSI interface are enabled.

■ *Configure your IDE devices (if any).* If you have no IDE drives, the CMOS should be set to None or Not Installed for C and D. If you have one IDE drive, the CMOS setting for drive D should be None or Not Installed. If you have two IDE drives, make no changes to the CMOS.

■ *Configure the SCSI hardware.* If you are running DOS or Windows 3.1, run the setup software that came with your SCSI interface to add the needed ASPI drivers. If you are running Windows 95, go to Control Panel and double-click on Install New Hardware. The dialog box will offer to have Windows scan your system and automatically install the correct protected-mode drivers. This is recommended, but have your Windows 95 installation floppies or CD-ROM handy. At this point, install any software that came with your SCSI interface card.

■   _Prepare the drive._ If your SCSI drive is the boot device (and/or the drive ID is 0 or 1 and the SCSI BIOS is enabled), run the DOS FDISK command to partition the drive. If you create more than one partition, be sure the first one is assigned as the active (bootable) partition. Finally, format the drive using the DOS FORMAT command. If this will be the boot device for DOS 6.xx, you can begin installing DOS at this point, and it will format the drive for you. Otherwise, start up the CD-ROM from a bootable floppy disk and start the Windows 95 CD-ROM installation.

TRANSFERRED FILES TAKE UP MORE DRIVE SPACE

Q762.   _I transferred the files from my old 200MB hard drive to my new 1.06GB hard drive, and they took up much more space on the new drive. Why is that?_

A.   Chances are that you've lost the extra space in larger clusters (known as slack space). The larger the size of a partition created using FDISK, the larger the cluster size created by the FORMAT command. All files stored on a drive occupy a minimum of one cluster. Even if the file size is smaller than the cluster size it is assigned, the entire space in the cluster is committed, and no other file can use the unused space. If you store many small files, it is a good idea to create at least one small partition (200 MB or less) to store them on in order to minimize slack space.

INTERMEDIATE

EIDE CONTROLLER WON'T SUPPORT THIRD DRIVE

Q763.   _I am having trouble setting up a third hard drive on my EIDE controller. I can't get the system to recognize the drive on the second channel even though the drive is cabled, powered, and jumpered as the master drive. The system is a 486DX4/100 with two drives already in it. I could really use the space since I only have a 340MB and a 250MB drive available, so any help would be greatly appreciated._

A.   I have been through some of this when adding a CD-ROM to a
       supposed EIDE card. I learned that an EIDE controller doesn't
       necessarily give you a second channel for drives 3 and 4. Check
       your card to make sure it really supports four drives *simultane-
       ously.* I bought (and later returned) two EIDE boards which
       claimed to support four drives on the package, but when you
       read the documentation, you found that only two drives are sup-
       ported at a time—you had to set a jumper to select which set of
       two drives you want to activate. You probably have an older
       EIDE controller in your system. Today there are many full-fea-
       tured EIDE controllers to choose from which provide ample sup-
       port for two drive channels.

Installing an IDE CD-ROM Drive

Q764.   *Could you please explain how to connect the CD-ROM drive to
        the secondary IDE port rather than the sound card? Does the
        hard drive remain the master drive? Does the CD drive get set
        for master, slave, or Csel? Is there anything I need to change in
        the CMOS settings?*

A.   When installing an IDE CD-ROM drive, you really need to do
        nothing to the existing hard drive. Set the CD-ROM drive as the
        primary (or master) drive and then cable it to the secondary IDE
        port on your hard drive controller using a standard 40-pin IDE
        cable (remember to align pin 1 properly at both ends). If there is
        already a hard drive on the secondary IDE port, you should set
        the hard drive to the primary (master) drive in a two-drive sys-
        tem and then jumper the CD-ROM as the secondary (slave)
        drive. If you have a sound card installed with a built-in IDE
        interface, be sure to disable that interface so that it does not con-
        flict with the secondary IDE port on your hard drive controller.
        For CMOS settings, leave the drive entry set to None or Not
        Installed. You'll be installing drivers to handle your CD-ROM.
        The only exception is when you are using bootable CD-ROM
        drives, but you need the suitable CD-ROM, a BIOS that supports
        CD-ROM booting, and a CD with boot code and an operating
        system on it.

INTERMEDIATE

CD-ROM Installation Causes Out of Environment Error

Q765. *I get an Out of Environment message when I hook up my Mitsumi IDE CD-ROM drive as a slave device and enter the driver's command line in the CONFIG.SYS file. After booting, my 486DX4/100 runs Windows 95 at a snail's pace.*

A.   Environment errors such as yours are generally due to an excessive number of CD-ROM buffers being loaded at start time. Try editing your CONFIG.SYS file and adding the following lines:

```
BUFFERS=22,0

shell=c:\command.com /P /e:256
```

The BUFFERS change should allow for only a minimum number of buffers, while the /e switch in the shell statement should increase the available environment space.

Installing a New HDD with Windows 95

Q766. *I'm planning to tackle a second hard drive installation on my Windows 95 PC, but I've heard that Windows 95 can be a real problem. Before I get into trouble, can you give me a rundown on installing a new second drive in a Windows 95 system?*

A.   Since you're only adding a second hard drive, the process is considerably easier then replacing the only hard drive outright. First, jumper the second drive as the secondary (or slave) drive, and see that the original drive is jumpered as the primary (or master) drive for use in a dual-drive system (some hard drives make this distinction). Mount and power the new hard drive and then attach the signal cable. You can power up the system and add the drive entry to CMOS Setup. In many cases, simply indicating autodetect will be sufficient. When the system reboots, use a DOS version of FDISK to partition the new drive. Reboot the system and use FORMAT to prepare each of the partitions you created. You may also choose to format through Windows 95. At this point, each of the new drive's partitions should be available with its own drive letter. The only thing you need to watch out for is that you'll need to change your CD-ROM drive letter and probably reinstall any of your CD-ROM applications to reflect the new CD-ROM letter.

COMPLEMENTING A SCSI DRIVE WITH EIDE

Q767.   *I need advice about how to add an EIDE drive to a system that already contains a SCSI drive. The SCSI drive is a stacked 212MB drive with C: (compressed) and G: (host). I'd like to keep the SCSI drive and use the EIDE drive for storage, keeping the big programs on it. Is this possible? If so, what must I consider?*

A.   First, it is certainly possible to add an EIDE drive to your system so long as you have an EIDE controller port (possibly on your motherboard), but there are some wrinkles to think about. First, an EIDE device will want to be the boot device (the motherboard BIOS will normally give precedence to EIDE drives over SCSI drives). However, the newest SCSI adapters *do* offer a BIOS override which can keep the SCSI drive bootable. You may need to update your SCSI controller to keep your SCSI drive bootable, or you may choose to forego the SCSI drive entirely in favor of the huge EIDE drives that are now available. If you really *want* to keep your SCSI drive bootable and don't want to fuss with EIDE or new SCSI controllers, spend a few extra dollars for a huge SCSI hard drive (3GB+). You can easily install the drive as a secondary SCSI drive (ID1) and keep all of your existing SCSI files in place on the original drive.

DRIVE OVERLAY SOFTWARE AND WINDOWS 95

Q768.   *I want to put an EIDE hard drive into my mother's i486 system so that she can get a few more years out of it. But will that system support an EIDE drive? Do I need to use software like Disk Manager or EZ-Drive to support an EIDE hard drive?*

A.   In actual practice, i486 systems are a tough call for EIDE support—some support EIDE drives and some do not. Start the CMOS Setup for your mother's system and look at your hard drive area for references such as LBA or EIDE. If those capabilities are detailed in the CMOS, the system probably supports large hard drives already. Otherwise, you'll need to add support for the EIDE. There are three ways to upgrade a PC for EIDE support: upgrade the motherboard BIOS (especially if you're using a drive controller on the motherboard), upgrade the drive controller board with its own EIDE BIOS, or add software such as Disk Manager. The cheapest solution is to use software support since most hard drives come with a version of Disk Manager or EZ-Drive right in the box. The problem is that you don't get top performance from a software solution. If you do opt for software support, make sure that you are using the very latest version of the software so it will support Windows 95 properly should you choose to upgrade.

SYSTEM WON'T RECOGNIZE A CDR

Q769. *I have installed a SCSI CD recorder in my system. While the installation seemed to go correctly, and everything else in the system seems to be working correctly, the system refuses to recognize the CDR. Any ideas?*

A. You probably have overlooked something in your SCSI configuration. First, if the SCSI adapter is being used exclusively for the CDR, check the SCSI driver at system start-up to see that the driver is loading. You may also want to check the SCSI adapter in your Device Manager. If there is a yellow exclamation mark or red X on the SCSI adapter entry, the SCSI adapter driver is not loading. Check that the driver's command line switches match the SCSI adapter settings. Next, check the SCSI IDs and make sure that no two SCSI devices are using the same SCSI ID.

Set up a recording session and choose to simulate recording rather than actually creating the CD. If the simulation is successful, but there are still errors while recording, lower the maximum transfer rate of the SCSI controller to 5.0 or 3.3MB/s. This is done through the setup for the controller card itself. Check to make sure cable is short (1 m or less) and good quality. Replace the cable if it appears worn or damaged. Check for proper termination at the ends of the SCSI chain. Finally, turn off the synchronous negotiation feature on the host adapter card.

ADVANCED

MIXING HARD DRIVES AND CD-ROM DRIVES

Q770.	*I recently bought a 1.6GB HDD for use as a master drive and use a 540MB drive as a slave drive. Since I didn't have any connectors available on the data cable for two drives and one CD-ROM, I put the 540MB drive by itself with one controller, and the CD-ROM and 1.6GB drive together. When I boot cold in the morning, I get an HDD failure. I can't seem to clear the problem. Any suggestions?*

A.	You won't find an IDE cable with connectors for three drives because each IDE channel can only handle two drives. However, I've always asserted that it was a good idea to put EIDE/ATAPI CD-ROM drives on a separate channel from hard drives. Due to the timing differences between hard drives and CD-ROM drives, mixing the two on a fast EIDE channel may cause one or both drives to not be recognized. Try putting your 1.6GB and 540MB drives on your primary EIDE channel. Leave the 1.6GB as the master drive, and set the 540MB drive as the slave drive. Then place your CD-ROM drive on the secondary IDE channel jumpered as the master drive. In your CMOS Setup, make sure that the drive entry corresponding to your CD-ROM is marked None or Not Installed.

PROBLEMS WITH A NEW FLOPPY DRIVE INSTALLATION

Q771.	*I'm having a problem with a floppy drive I just installed. It's new, and I have it on a new controller card. When I start the system, it gives the message "Floppy disk(s) fail (40)." I have changed the card, and I have set the drive up as A: and B: with no luck. The controller card sees my hard drive and COM ports with no problems, so I'm at a total loss.*

A.	My first piece of advice would be to make sure that the floppy disk controller portion of your new controller card is enabled. You may have forgotten to disable any other floppy controller in the system (or on the motherboard). If your new controller is the only floppy port in the system, check the CMOS Setup and make sure that you have the proper entry for the new drive. For example, if the floppy were cabled as A:, there should be a corresponding entry for A: in the CMOS. If the proper entry is in place, you should check the power cable at the floppy and try a new floppy drive signal cable next (and ensure that both ends of the drive cable are inserted with pin 1 in the proper orientation). If problems persist, the new floppy drive may be bad. Try the floppy drive on another system. If the floppy drive checks on another system, try another drive controller.

SYSTEM WON'T RECOGNIZE NEW HARD DRIVE

Q772. *I'm trying to install a Western Digital Caviar 21200 (1281MB) hard disk on a Gateway 486DX/33 using a Phoenix BIOS version 0.10 G21-2. But every time I want to save the new setup and reboot, the computer won't recognize the hard drive and gives me the following error message: "No boot sector on Hard drive, press <F1> to reboot or <F2> to enter setup utilities." Can you help me?*

A.   If I understand your symptoms properly, you installed the drive and entered its parameters in CMOS, but the system won't boot. Make sure you've entered the right drive parameters. Try booting from a floppy disk containing FDISK and FORMAT. Prepare the drive by partitioning it with FDISK and then format the drive using FORMAT C: /S. This should prepare the drive and make it bootable to DOS. Many do-it-yourselfers forget that they need to prepare the new hard drive before it can be accessed. Now here's the wrinkle. If you can't boot the system at all (or the system still refuses to recognize the drive), you probably need a BIOS upgrade for your Gateway's motherboard or an EIDE drive adapter with its own on-board EIDE BIOS.

HOME-BREW SYSTEM CORRUPTING HARD DRIVE FILES ON START-UP

Q773. *I discovered that I had enough spare parts around to build an extra system. It is a 386DX/40 Micronics motherboard (ISA only). I have a simple 512KB Cirrus Logic video card, a Teac floppy drive, a Maxtor 120MB HDD, and a Winbond ISA drive controller card. Every time it reboots, it corrupts the system files—it deletes the first line of the CONFIG.SYS and AUTOEX-EC.BAT, replacing it with odd ANSI characters. I reloaded DOS, ran ScanDisk, ran a virus program, and double-checked all my hardware connections and CMOS settings. But it still corrupts the system files.*

A.   I've seen this type of problem before, but it can be caused by several possible sources. First, check the drive cable between the hard drive and controller—try a new cable if possible. Second, check those CMOS settings for the drive geometry one more time and make sure the geometry is set *precisely* for the exact drive you're using (rather than just close). Third, try a different drive controller (some controllers have been known to have chipset problems with certain hard drives). Fortunately, drive controllers are dirt cheap. If the problem still persists, replace the hard drive itself (it is defective, i.e., not communicating properly with the controller).

Can't Make the Hard Drive Bootable

Q774.   *I got a used 520MB Quantum hard drive and installed it in the system I just built. The drive was already formatted because I could access C: and read a directory. I ran FDISK and then formatted the drive with the FORMAT C: /S command. The drive finished formatting and the system files were transferred. However, when trying to boot without the boot disk, I got the message "Missing operating system." I reformatted with the DOS 6.0 setup disk using the FORMAT C: /S command. The system files were transferred again, but when trying to boot from C:, I got the message "Drive Not Ready." What do I need to do?*

A.   There are three issues when preparing a drive for a system. First, make sure that the drive geometry entered into CMOS is correct for your particular drive. This is probably already correct since you were able to read from the drive. Second, when using FDISK, make sure that the primary DOS partition is active and bootable. You may want to erase your current partitions and repartition the drive again. Third, I have heard of situations where the FOR-MAT C: /S command does not work. Try the FORMAT command alone and then run SYS C: to transfer your system files. That should get the drive going.

Unusually Long Pause When Loading CD-ROM Driver

Q775.   *I just finished building a Pentium 100-MHz system with an ASUS motherboard, and my troubles began after installation of a 6X Aztech CD-ROM drive which I placed as the slave device with the hard drive. However, the CONFIG.SYS file stalls for 25 seconds when it loads the driver for the CD-ROM, and then eventually the CD is recognized. Any ideas?*

A.   Several things come to mind. First, it sounds like you've placed your CD-ROM on the primary drive controller channel. This may be a problem because slow devices like a CD can sometimes interfere with the data transfer rates of fast devices like hard drives (this might also interfere with device detection). I suggest that you make your CD-ROM drive a master device on the secondary drive channel and leave the hard drive as the master by itself on the primary drive channel. Test the system start-up again. You may find that separating the two drives speeds things up. If problems persist, check your CD-ROM driver for any command line switches that might be causing the unusual delay. If not, the driver itself may be the problem. Check with the Aztech Web site for any updated CD-ROM drivers.

Old Partitions Not Recognized by New System

Q776.   *I just finished putting together a new Pentium 133-MHz system to replace my old 486, which I have handed down to one of my daughters. Everything on the P5 is new with the exception of a 1.3GB HDD which I pirated from the original computer. I figured that she will not need as much storage for her schoolwork, so I left her with the 540MB slave drive instead. I had originally partitioned the 1.3GB drive into three logical drives, so I expected to see C:, D:, and E: drives when I first powered up the new system. However, all I saw was the C: drive. Is there any way I can get the other drives back without starting from the bottom again?*

A.   My only suggestion is to check the drive entry in your CMOS Setup. Your 1.3GB drive is an EIDE unit, so you should be using LBA access in CMOS, and the drive should ideally be autodetected. If the CMOS is set for ordinary IDE addressing, it won't recog-

nize more than 528MB of drive space (which I'd bet is pretty close
to what your original C: partition was). Remember to save any
changes before exiting CMOS and rebooting the system. If BIOS
recognizes the full size of your drive, but partitions D: and E: are
still unavailable, try repartitioning and reformatting the drive.

SWAPPING HARD DRIVES REQUIRES A CMOS UPDATE

Q777. *I have a client's 486DX4/100 machine which had a 340MB master drive and a 540MB slave drive. I have removed the 340MB
drive, made the 540MB drive the master, and set the drive
jumpers accordingly. Then I ran FDISK and formatted the drive
using the /s parameter to make it bootable. Now I try to boot the
PC with this drive, it runs through the POST, and then the system just hangs up—no Starting MS-DOS message, just a blank
screen. The system boots from a floppy; I just cannot seem to get
it to boot from the HDD. The drive is a Conner CFS540A and
the PC is an IBM 350. Any suggestions ?*

A. My first suggestion is that you check your CMOS Setup. It
sounds like you forgot to update the CMOS when you swapped
your drives around. Enter the drive geometry for your 540MB
drive as the first drive and then be sure to set the second drive as
None or Not Installed. You may need to repartition and reformat
the drive after the settings are corrected. Also double-check the
drive jumper. If you can choose between a master in a dual-drive
system and single master, select single master. Note that not all
drives make that kind of distinction, but it's one thing you should
check for. Next, you should take one more look at the power and
signal cables, to see that they are installed properly. Finally, I
question your partitioning technique. Run FDISK again and confirm that your primary DOS partition is active. Afterward, you
may need to SYS the drive again or run FORMAT C: /S to make
the drive bootable.

CD-ROM INSTALLATION FREEZES SYSTEM STARTUP

Q778. *I installed an EIDE BIOS card, and now I'm trying to install a CD-ROM as a slave drive to my HDD using the same cable for HDD and CD-ROM. I have been told to install a sound card and then to put a CD-ROM on it, but is there any other way to do this (I don't need sound on this machine anyway)? I changed the settings of BIOS—I set the second HDD as Auto. Subsequently, my system stops after the memory count. All I see is a cursor blinking. Is there any way to restore my BIOS setup?*

A. I think the problem is your CD-ROM and hard drive coexisting on the same channel. Also, the CD-ROM entry in CMOS Setup should be None or Not Installed for the CD-ROM. When you set it to Auto, it expects to find a hard drive. I suggest that you rearrange the hardware to place your CD-ROM as the primary (or master) drive on your secondary drive controller channel all by itself and leave the hard drive by itself as the master drive on the primary channel. Once you rearrange the hardware, you should be able to enter your CMOS Setup in the moments after your system boots. If you cannot, the BIOS is probably searching for a secondary hard drive and should produce an error message after a minute or two. Clear that Auto entry for the CD-ROM, and select None or Not Installed. Once the system boots, you can install your ATAPI CD-ROM drivers.

HARD DRIVE UPGRADE NIGHTMARE

Q779. *I purchased a second HDD for my system about 2 weeks ago, a 3.2GB IBM drive. I already had three IDE devices on the motherboard controllers—a 2.1GB HDD, a SyQuest internal 135MB EZ-Drive, and a CD-ROM. I also have a floppy drive and tape drive in the system. Ever since installing the new IBM drive, I have had terrible problems with my system being unstable. I ended up placing the 2.1GB drive as the master on the primary controller, the 3.2GB drive as the master on the secondary con-*

troller, the EZ-Drive as the slave drive on the primary controller, and the CD-ROM on the IDE controller of my Sound Blaster 16 card. This was the only way the machine would recognize all four devices. Some combinations resulted in the drives only being visible in Windows, but not in DOS (which I still don't understand). After adding the new drive, I had problems with lockups, GPFs, internal errors, and every other error message you can imagine. I ended up reformatting both the 2.1GB and 3.2GB drives and reinstalling Windows 95. Even after reformatting, I get lots of lock-ups and internal error messages. It almost seemed like a virus to me, but I checked my system with three different virus scan programs—it seems to be clean. Do these symptoms sound like some type of impending hardware failure or what?

A.   Let's start with what we know. The system was working before the new drive was installed, and it's not working after it was. That being the case, I can offer the following comments. First, I would be very suspicious of your drive controllers. You've got three different controllers running at the same time. It can be done, but the resources become a problem since you need unique IRQs and I/O addresses for each controller. If you have two controllers using the same IRQ or I/O space, or another device in the system is using those same resources, you'll get a hardware conflict that causes intermittent operation or lock-ups. Take a close look at the way your PC is configured.

Second, I'd be very suspicious of the power supply. You've got a number of drives there, and drives take power. If your power supply is overloaded (or is failing), that can also cause intermittent system operation. Try disconnecting the power to your less-used drives like your floppy and tape drive. You might even try disconnecting power from the SyQuest drive. If the system stabilizes, you might consider upgrading to a larger power supply.

Finally, you might try rearranging your drives. Put the two hard drives on your Primary EIDE controller. Put the SyQuest drive on your secondary IDE controller. Leave the CD where it is.

System Trouble with a Second HDD

Q780. *My new motherboard is giving me fits. I installed a Tyan Tomcat I (a Triton II chipset) with a P166, 512KB pipeline cache, Matrox Millennium (4MB WRAM), 32MB EDO RAM, Sound Blaster PnP with 8X CD-ROM, and a 2.1GB Seagate HDD. After some basic glitches, the system is up and running, but I cannot add a second hard drive, and after removing the second drive, the system now won't work. I think it's the power supply.*

A. You added a second drive, the system refused to boot, and now the system won't boot even though the drive is removed. You've got several things to check. First, check the CMOS Setup and delete any extra drive references (make sure that only your current drives are listed). If that's not the problem, you'll need to do things the hard way. Check the power supply outputs, and confirm that the power supply is connected to the motherboard and your other drives. If any of the power supply outputs are low or absent, replace the power supply. Check all of your expansion boards and cables (especially your drive controller and cables). Reseat any board or cable that appears to be loose or incompletely inserted. I've seen mentions of some motherboards that won't boot if the drive cable is reversed or installed improperly. Also check the motherboard to see if any printed traces are shorting against the case or any metal standoffs. Try booting the PC from a floppy disk. If the system boots, you may have a fault in the boot drive or cable. If the system still won't boot, your new motherboard may be defective (but one hopes still under warranty).

Once you do get the system to boot, you should try reinstalling the second hard drive to eliminate any chance that you may have installed it wrong in the first place. If the system refuses to boot even though the second hard drive is installed correctly, you may *still* need to upgrade your power supply to accommodate two hard drives.

New Video Systems

HEADING OFF NEW VIDEO PROBLEMS

Q781.   *I'm planning to upgrade my video board soon to one of those new 3-D video accelerator cards, but I'm understandably nervous since this will be my first upgrade. Some friends have told me that new video cards can cause display problems, weird fonts, and system lock-ups. Can you provide some pointers for a newbie?*

A.   In the majority of cases, video upgrades are very quick and smooth, but I can give you a rundown of the most frequent troubles. There are three areas related to video (and video problems): hardware, firmware, and software. For hardware, you will probably need to exclude a memory range in the upper memory area (usually A000h through C7FFh). You can accomplish this exclusion by adding the exclude switch to your EMM386 command line in CONFIG.SYS. Also make sure that no other devices (such as SCSI BIOS) are utilizing that excluded memory range.

Your PC firmware (BIOS) can also be a source of problems. If your video installation meets with trouble, go to your CMOS Setup and disable features like video cache, video shadow, byte-merge, palette snoop, and hidden refresh. If PCI bus-bursting is assigned to the video bus, you should disable this as well. If an IRQ is being assigned to the PCI video bus in CMOS Setup, make sure the assigned IRQ is not in use by some other device.

For software, make sure that your video drivers are correctly installed, and you may also need to add the line: EMMExclude=A000-C7FF to the [386enh] section of SYSTEM.INI. If you are using QEMM as your memory manager, be sure to turn the Stealth mode off.

DISABLING PACKARD BELL VIDEO

Q782.   *I have a Packard Bell Pentium computer which has video on the mainboard. That was fine for a while, until I decided to upgrade to a Diamond Stealth 3D video card. I read the manual and probed inside the computer itself in order to find the jumpers to disable the old on-board video, but I couldn't find any. Then I disabled the on-board video in the Control Panel of Windows 95. That did the trick until I turn on the computer again. Plug-and-Play "finds" the old video and reinstalls it. Is there any way of disabling Packard Bell's on-board video?*

A.   You've got a real problem on your hands. While Packard Bell makes a fine entry-level PC, their systems are not known for versatility. Upgrades such as yours are sometimes problematic. There are three methods of disabling on-board video systems: motherboard jumpers, CMOS settings, and autodetection. You've already ruled out motherboard jumpers. Start your CMOS Setup and check for any options that may allow you to disable the video (poor BIOS design in some systems may still prevent this from working). Finally, newer motherboards will look for "add-on" video cards and disable the on-board video automatically. Apparently, this is not the case either. If you cannot disable the video through CMOS, you've got little option but to live with the existing on-board video or replace the motherboard outright.

Video Board Upgrade Causes Boot Problems

Q783.   *I've been upgrading my nephew's PC. It's a 386DX/33 system with an AMD CPU, AMI BIOS (5/5/91), and 4MB RAM. I recently installed a leftover Hercules Dynamite Pro 2MB video board with its own BIOS (10/29/93). After installing the board, the system sometimes fails to initialize correctly. For example, the system may beep up to six times and fail to boot until the reset button is pressed. Any ideas?*

A.   Check the installation of your video board one more time. Make sure that the board is inserted into its slot properly and completely. Also check to be sure that no part of the board is touching any other adjacent board. Try the board in a different slot. If the board's physical installation is correct, there may be a fault in the board itself. Test the board on another similar system. If the board works on another system, there may be an incompatibility between your motherboard and video board. Contact AMI to see if there are any reported problems or a BIOS upgrade you can use. If the board also fails on another system, the fault is on the board. Try another video board.

Video Lost After Installing New Video Board

Q784.   *I just installed a new video board (one of those Creative Labs 3D Blasters). The problem is that after I installed the board, I don't get any video (even under DOS). I'd hate to have to take the PC into a shop, so is there anything you can advise?*

A.   Not to worry. Problems with video upgrades are really very common, and I think your problem is very simple. First, you should have removed the old video board from the system and set it aside. If you forgot to remove the old video board, turn the system off (and unplug it) and remove the old video board. If your motherboard had provided your video, you must disable the motherboard video system (usually through a jumper on the motherboard itself). Refer to the manual for your system to find exactly how to disable the motherboard's video. Check the new video board to see that it is properly and completely inserted into its new PCI slot. Sometimes a board can look deceptive. If that metal bracket at one end of the video board does not sit flush against the chassis, that's a good sign your video board isn't inserted properly. Be sure to bolt down that metal bracket. Finally, you should double-check that the monitor's video cable is securely attached to the new video board's video port. Once you have made these checks, you should at least get DOS video when powering the system up.

New Video Board Restarted in 16-Color Mode

Q785.   *I installed a new video board along with its drivers, but when Windows 95 restarted, it started in the 16-color mode instead of the 256-color mode. What's going on here?*

A.   In virtually all cases, you've got multiple video board entries logged in your Device Manager, and this is confusing Windows 95. To clear the problem, you'll need to clean up your Registry by eliminating repeat entries in your Device Manager:

1.   Start Windows 95 in the Safe Mode.

2.   Open your Control Panel, and select the System icon.

3.   Select the Device Manager page, and double-click the Display Adapters entry (Fig. 8.1).

4. When you see the entries under Display Adapters, remove any other entries listed *except* for your *current* video board.

5. Save your changes and restart Windows 95 normally.

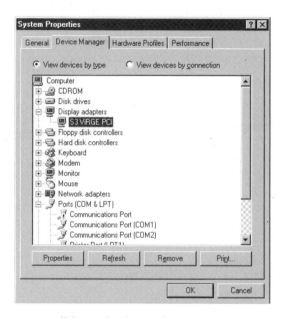

Figure 8.1 Highlighting Display Adapters in the Device Manager

VIDEO BLASTER AND SOUND BLASTER WON'T WORK TOGETHER

Q786. *I just installed a Creative Labs Video Blaster RT300 in my Pentium 120-MHz PC. Not only does the Video Blaster refuse to capture video, but the system performance is sluggish, and I'm not getting any sound from my Sound Blaster 32 board. Any idea what might be wrong?*

A. You almost certainly have a hardware conflict. The Sound Blaster 32 is configured by default to use IRQ 10 for the IDE interface. The Video Blaster also defaults to using IRQ 10. The result is that you have two devices probably trying to use the same interrupt, and the system is performing poorly (I'm surprised that it hasn't crashed). In order to resolve this problem, verify the settings used by your Sound Blaster and Video Blaster. If you indeed find that the Video Blaster is using the same IRQ as the Sound Blaster's drive controller, reconfigure the Video Blaster to use a different IRQ.

New Video Upgrade Possibly Incomplete

Q787. *I have a friend who recently upgraded a video card from mono-chrome to VGA with a different monitor. When he boots up the computer, everything seems to work. In DOS mode, the text is shown in the proper colors. Here is the problem: When he tries to start Windows, the monitor only displays garbage. What can he do to correct the problem?*

A. It sounds to me like your friend installed the new video card proper-ly but forgot to update the video driver in Windows (I assume your friend is using Windows 3.1x). Try running the Windows Setup utili-ty from DOS, and set up the Windows video driver for the new video board. The board probably came with a disk containing Windows drivers. Otherwise, just select a generic 640x480x16 dri-ver. That should get Windows started without the garbage.

More Memory (RAM)

More Memory for an AT&T System

Q788. *I'm going to a computer show next week and a woman I work with wants me to pick up some memory for her, but she's not sure what she needs. She has an AT&T Pentium that's about a year old with 8MB of memory. Does AT&T typically uses stan-dard SIMMs in their computers? I assume they do, but when it comes to computers there are always exceptions.*

A. I suspect that you'll have trouble. One of the problems with AT&T computers has been that they were *very* proprietary. That was one of the reasons AT&T eventually failed in the PC market-place. I urge you to refer to the upgrade section of your friend's user manual and determine *exactly* what kind of memory devices are required. It would also be helpful to take an actual SIMM (or picture of a SIMM) with you to identify an exact match. Since some highly proprietary motherboards can only support a limited number of SIMM geometries, you should check for particular SIMM sizes (i.e., 4Mx9) that the user manual confirms will be able to work with the memory devices currently installed.

UPGRADING MEMORY IN A COMPAQ PRESARIO

Q789. *Can you please tell me if the Compaq Presario uses a type of SIMM that is different from the conventional 72-pin SIMMs? A friend of mine tried to upgrade her PC from 8 to 16MB. The local Compaq office told her that 8MB of Compaq RAM costs $800— way out of the current market value for standard 8MB RAM.*

A. According to my information, Compaq Presarios use convention-al 72-pin 60-ns DRAM. As a result, you should be able to use any standard DRAM SIMM for your upgrade. These days, you should be able to get 8MB of DRAM for around $140. If you're looking to do some specific shopping, you should visit the PNY site (*www.pny.com*) and use their Memory Configurator to deter-mine the exact parts you need.

REGULAR SIMMS IN A PAGE-MODE SYSTEM

Q790. *I recently bought two 8MB SIMMs for my computer. I pretty much depended on the salesperson for help, but I later realized that my motherboard supported fast-page mode RAM. What will happen if I bought regular SIMMs, or is there a difference? I'm just worried that I got the wrong ones. The computer seems to say "OK" when it makes a memory test.*

A. Page-mode RAM is basically turbo-charged DRAM. If the moth-erboard is designed to accommodate page-mode operation (and the CMOS Setup is configured accordingly), you may see a per-formance improvement with page-mode RAM—sometimes a good improvement. However, if you simply buy ordinary DRAM instead, the system should almost universally accept it. You just won't see any real performance increase.

HANDLING A BROKEN SIMM SOCKET

Q791. *I have a computer with four SIMM sockets. The computer was purchased with 8MB of RAM in two of the sockets (4MB each). I purchased two more 4MB SIMMs which I tried to put into the remaining sockets. During the attempted installation, I snapped off a latch pin on one of the sockets, rendering it unusable. Since*

I must install memory in pairs, I am now dead-ended. I know I can purchase two 8MB SIMMs and replace the original pair of 4MB SIMMs, but is there any way around this problem other than buying a new motherboard?

A.   As long as you have not damaged any of the electrical contacts or printed wiring on the motherboard, you can use virtually any means to hold the SIMM in place. I advise against using any form of tape, since tape eventually becomes gummy and loses its adhesive power (the SIMM will just slip out). Rather, I like to suggest using an elastic band to keep the SIMM in place. Elastic has good holding strength, is nonconductive, and will not get gummy over time.

REUSING RAM IN A NEW CONSTRUCTION

Q792. *I'm just about to start building my first Pentium using some components from my 486, and I have a question about RAM use on a Tyan Titan III motherboard. I have four 1Mx36 70-ns pari-ty SIMMs that I'd like to reuse in four of the six available SIMM slots. This should fill two banks and save a bit of money on memory, but with RAM prices being low now, I'm considering buying two more 8MB SIMMs for the other two slots. Should I get 60- or 70-ns EDO RAM (the current SIMMs are 70-ns)? Should I get parity or nonparity RAM?*

A.   The general rule with memory is that your system will only run as fast as your slowest memory, so if you've already got 70-ns RAM, buying more 60-ns RAM won't hurt, but you'll get no added benefit in your system. The biggest advantage behind buy-ing faster RAM now is that you can always reuse the faster RAM in future systems. Since you're already using parity RAM, I'd suggest that you buy more parity RAM as opposed to non-parity RAM. You should be able to use parity and nonparity RAM in the same system if necessary, but you'll need to disable all parity checking.

UPGRADING MEMORY IN A 486 SYSTEM

Q793. *I have a 486DX PC with eight 30-pin SIMM slots. The system has eight 1MB SIMMs in it now filling up all eight slots. Each 70-ns SIMM has three memory chips on it. Is there any way I can upgrade this machine to 16MB of memory and still use some or all the SIMMs it has now.*

A. As I understand it, you have 8MB in the PC now and no available SIMM slots left. You can't get more memory with the SIMMs you have now, but you could probably buy four 30-pin 4MB 70-ns SIMMs and replace four of the 1MB SIMMs. This would give you four 1MB SIMMs in bank 0 and four 4MB SIMMs in bank 1, giving you a total of 20MB (4MB + 16MB). This is a bit more than you needed, but it should work out. If you need exactly 16MB, you'd need to replace all eight SIMMs with 2MB 30-pin SIMMs. No matter what SIMMs you buy, you should be sure to match the parity. For example, if your original SIMMs are nonparity, get new nonparity SIMMs. If the original SIMMs are parity (which I suspect they are), get parity SIMMs.

REARRANGING MEMORY IN A 486

Q794. *I have an old generic 486DX2/60 motherboard that I just installed in a 386 computer case. Four 4MB 30-pin SIMMs came with the motherboard, but I elected to put my eight 1MB 30-pin SIMMs in the slots. Can I put the four 4MB SIMMs back in the first four slots and leave four 1MB SIMMs in the remaining four slots? I was always told that you cannot mix the SIMMs.*

A. The answer to your question is almost certainly Yes. A 486 is a 32 bit CPU, which means you need four 30-pin SIMMs to fill a bank. So you must match four SIMMs at a time in size and speed. As long as you follow that rule (and the motherboard can support the total amount of RAM you add), you should be fine. If your motherboard cannot detect the extra RAM automatically, you'll need to update your CMOS settings. The time you get into trouble mixing memory is when you add RAM that is too slow, mix memory types within the same bank (i.e., EDO and FPM), or mix parity and nonparity devices without disabling the motherboard's parity checking.

POSITIONING A PACKARD BELL RAM UPGRADE

Q795. *I want to upgrade the RAM for my Packard Bell Legend 68CD (Pentium 60). It came with 8MB of RAM. I want to upgrade to 16MB. However, when I opened the case, I saw four empty 72-pins slots. The markings on the motherboard read "2 bank A and 2 bank B." Where is the preinstalled 8MB of RAM? Can I upgrade by installing one 8MB 72-pin SIMM, or do I need two 4MB 72-pins SIMMs? Since I have no idea what the original 8MB of RAM is, what type of memory should I buy (i.e., parity, nonparity, or EDO)?*

A. Packard Bell traditionally incorporates the base RAM for their systems right on the motherboard (as opposed to generic motherboards that often use SIMMs exclusively. For your Packard Bell system, all the memory *over* the base RAM is installed as SIMMs. For a Pentium PC, you'll need to install RAM as a set of two SIMMs—single SIMMs will not work—so if you want to add only another 8MB to the system, you would add two 4MB SIMMs. If you can afford two 8MB SIMMs, you can bring the total amount of RAM in your system to 24MB. This would be a great plus for Windows 95. As far as the specifications for new memory, you really *should* refer to the system documentation to be sure, but you'd probably be pretty close with 60-ns FPM nonparity memory.

WHERE TO INSTALL MEMORY FIRST

Q796. *I'm using a Pentium 133-MHz system, and I want to install another set of 8MB 72-pin SIMMs to give me an additional 16MB of RAM. The problem is that my manual doesn't show me where to place the new SIMMs. There are already two 16MB 72-pin SIMMs on the motherboard for a total of 32MB. Should I just place the new SIMMs next to the existing ones?*

A.   That's not a bad bet, but you should do some investigating first. Memory banks are not always organized in numerical order. Your current two SIMMs are almost certainly installed in bank 0, so you're looking at placing your new SIMMs in bank 1. Check your manual again for a diagram of the motherboard, and see if you can find bank 1 called out anywhere. You should also check the silk-screening on the motherboard itself for written markings near the SIMM slots. If you absolutely cannot find markings to guide you, try installing the SIMMs next to the existing SIMMs.

MEMORY UPGRADES SOMETIMES DEMAND IDENTICAL DEVICES

Q797.   *I've put more memory into my Gateway Solo PC, but now I get some memory failure error. It can't be the memory because I've used exactly the same size memory modules as it says in the manual—the system just won't recognize them. What can I do?*

A.   Although memory is supposed to be universal, there can be subtle differences between memory made by various manufacturers—even when the memory modules are exactly the same size as the existing memory. This is especially common on systems that use proprietary motherboards like the older Gateway 2000 systems. Assuming that the system has been configured properly, you should attempt to use memory that is made by the same vendor as the existing memory.

INTERMEDIATE

NEW SIMM CAUSES MEMORY MISMATCH

Q798.   *I just installed an 8MB 2Mx32 70-ns 72-pin SIMM in my 486DX4/100 for a total of 16MB. On boot-up, I get the message "CMOS memory size mismatch—Run Setup utility." I can enter the setup utility, exit without making any changes, and proceed with the boot sequence normally. The SIMM is of the type specified in the motherboard manual for installation. The system recognizes the memory (the memory check at boot-up verifies the total of 16MB before displaying the CMOS memory size mismatch statement). Windows 95 also recognizes the additional memory.*

A.   Believe it or not, that's a very common problem with newer BIOS versions. Traditional BIOS required users to enter the exact amount of RAM, but that was largely abandoned in 486 and later systems because it was easy enough to autodetect available memory. The problem is that you still need to let your CMOS adjust to the new memory size by *saving* your CMOS contents before exiting the setup routine. Even though you aren't making any specific changes yourself, the CMOS needs to save the new amount of RAM that has been detected. Once you save and exit, your error message should disappear.

FASTER MEMORY CAUSING PROBLEMS

Q799.   *I just replaced several 100-ns SIMMs with their 70-ns equivalents, but now I get a memory error message when the system tests memory during initialization. I thought that faster memory should not be a problem—what do you think?*

A.   You said that you replaced several SIMMs. You must replace *all* the SIMMs. If you leave older SIMMs in the system and reduce wait states to accommodate the newer RAM, the system will operate too quickly for the older RAM, and that will generate all manner of data errors. In fact, the system may even refuse to boot.

If you *did* replace all the SIMMs, I would suspect a fault with at least one of the SIMMs that you just installed. If you did not discharge yourself to a grounded metal chassis or use an antistatic wrist strap, it is very possible that one or more SIMMs have been damaged by electrostatic discharge (ESD). Take a new 70-ns SIMM and rotate it through each SIMM location until the error disappears. The 70-ns SIMM that you removed when the error disappeared is the faulty module. You can then buy another SIMM (or exchange the faulty one). Be careful when exchanging SIMMs. Make use of an antistatic wrist strap, and make sure not to damage the SIMM socket(s).

NEW MEMORY NOT RECOGNIZED

Q800. *I just added another 8MB to my system, but it does not recognize the additional memory. What am I doing wrong?*

A. There are a number of important issues to consider whenever adding memory to your PC. You must add enough SIMMs to fill an entire bank, the RAM speed (in nanoseconds) must be as fast as or faster than your existing memory, and the memory type (i.e., EDO or FPM) must match the other RAM in the system. As if that weren't enough, you must match the lead material on the SIMMs with the leads in the SIMM sockets (typically, tin or gold)—mismatching the SIMM and socket materials can result in oxidization and SIMM problems. Finally, few motherboards recognize all possible SIMM combinations. Check the documentation for your system to see which size and configuration of SIMMs are allowed in each bank.

NEW RAM NOT RECOGNIZED IN BANK 1

Q801. *I have a DTK PM35S motherboard—a 100-MHz Pentium. I just installed another 16MB (two 8MB SIMMs) in bank 1 to complement the 16MB (two 8MB SIMMs) already in bank 0. The motherboard won't recognize bank 1. I've checked and rechecked the motherboard jumpers and BIOS setup, I've swapped the memory chips in every conceivable fashion, and checked the SIMM sockets for damaged pins and cleanliness. Is there anything that I've missed?*

A. There are several common reasons why new memory isn't recognized. Examine your new SIMMs, and make sure that they're actually in bank 1—some motherboards allow you to configure different jumper orders. Perhaps you've accidentally installed the SIMMs in bank 2 or bank 3. Check your memory types next. I've seen situations where EDO and FPM memory won't mix in the same system—even though they're in different banks. Another trick is to check your CMOS Setup and turn the BIOS and video shadowing features off. This may slow the system a little bit but may allow the system to recognize over 16MB. Finally, contact DTK and check the specifications of your motherboard. It may not be able to handle 8MB SIMMs in bank 1. You may need to replace them with 4 or 16MB SIMMs.

SINGLE SIMMs MAY NOT BE RECOGNIZED

Q802.   *I bought a SIMM for my Pentium PC and installed it last night.
But no matter what I do, the memory is not recognized. What
am I doing wrong?*

A.   You said SIMM—not SIMMs. Pentiums are 64-bit CPUs, so
you'll need two 72-pin SIMMs (each of which are 32 bits wide)
to accommodate the Pentium memory bank. If you just installed
one 72-pin SIMM, it shouldn't damage anything, but the memory
would not be recognized. Check the layout of your memory
banks in your motherboard manual and then install a second
SIMM. You may also have to change the amount of installed
RAM in your CMOS Setup (although many current BIOS versions will find RAM automatically).

*Some of the most recent BIOS versions and motherboard
designs are able to utilize half of a memory bank.*

Note

NEW 30-PIN SIMMs ARE NOT RECOGNIZED

Q803.   *When installing 30-pin memory in the second four slots of an
Acer 486DX/33 system with AMI BIOS dated 11/20/92, I cannot get the system to recognize the extra memory. There were
four 1MB SIMMs in the first four slots and they are working
properly. I switched chips and the first four slots continue to
work, but I still can't get the second bank recognized.*

A.   There are several issues to consider when adding memory to any
computer. First, the memory type and speed should be the same
as the existing RAM. Since you swapped the new SIMMs in
place of the original SIMMs, and the new SIMMs worked, I'd
say that's not your problem. The trouble is in getting the system
to recognize the second bank. First, make sure that you are actually installing the SIMMs in the *next* contiguous bank. I've seen
motherboards that use odd bank orders (i.e., bank 0, bank 2,
bank 1, and bank 3) or allow bank orders to be reassigned using
motherboard jumpers. Even though the next physical bank may
seem like bank 1, you may accidentally be placing the new
SIMMs into a higher bank without realizing it. Next, check your

CMOS Setup routine and look for any entries that define the amount of RAM installed, or check for motherboard jumpers that might enable or disable the next bank. Finally, make sure that you can actually *use* your new SIMMs in the next bank. Often, PC memory banks can only use a limited variety of SIMM configurations (such as 2 or 8MB but not 4MB). The manual that accompanied your PC probably has a table that lists the acceptable SIMM combinations needed to achieve different total amounts of RAM in the system.

INSTALLING RAM IN A PENTIUM SYSTEM

Q804. *I have a Pentium that has two 4MB 72-pin 70-ns SIMMs already installed. They have chips on only one side. I recently got an 8MB 72-pin 70-ns SIMM, but it has chips on both sides. I installed it, but the computer doesn't see it. Is this a compatibility problem?*

A. I doubt that. The first issue you need to address is the fact that 72-pin SIMMs must be installed in pairs on a Pentium motherboard. Since you only installed one SIMM, the bank is incomplete, and the BIOS probably ignored it. Try adding a second SIMM. Next, I suspect that when you mention compatibility problems, you are suggesting that the new SIMM is double-sided. That is a bit of a misconception because double- and single-sided SIMMs are a function of the overall size—not whether there are RAM ICs on one side or two; 1, 4, and 16MB SIMMs are generally single-sided, and 2MB, 8MB, and 32MB SIMMs are double-sided. Since you're adding 8MB SIMMs, there *may* be an incompatibility, but check the documentation that accompanies your motherboard for memory expansion information. If you can't add double-sided SIMMs, you might elect to invest in 16MB SIMMs instead.

GETTING A MEMORY UPGRADE TO WORK

Q805. *I removed four of the existing 1MB SIMMs (60 ns) from bank 1 and installed four 4MB SIMMs to that bank (intending to raise the total RAM to 20MB). The motherboard manual said that four 1MB SIMMs had to be in bank 0 and four 4MB SIMMs in bank 1 in order for this configuration to work. The system immediately*

*stalled at boot-up with a: "System Halted, Parity Error" message.
I switched the 4MB SIMMs to bank 0 and tried to boot the system with just 16MB RAM, but I got no video and a repetitive series of three short beeps. I disabled the parity in the CMOS settings and the memory worked. I returned to my vendor, who suggested trading four of the original 1MB (60 ns) SIMMs for four 1MB (70 ns) SIMMs and seeing if these would work with the 4MB SIMMs. They didn't at first but did when I raised the number of Wait States in CMOS Setup. So I have 20MB of parity RAM now, but more wait states. Yesterday the "System Halted, Parity Error" reappeared. I tested the RAM using AMIDiag, and it reported a parity error at a certain address (I got the same result several times). I am returning the 4MB SIMMs and asking that they be exchanged. Should I get faster memory?*

A.   As you noticed, motherboards can be very demanding when deciding which SIMM sizes will operate in which banks. That's why you had a beep problem when installing the 4MB SIMMs in bank 0. Your first problem seems to be that the memory is too slow. You're using 70-ns RAM, and since you needed to add wait states, you could probably use 60-ns RAM, and remove the extra wait state. This will also improve your overall system performance. Based on your description of symptoms, it does seem like at least one of your 4MB SIMMs has failed. Take this opportunity to return all of your SIMMs for exchange and get faster memory.

Blindly Adding SIMMs Is a Shot in the Dark

Q806.   *I want to know if I can add two 8MB SIMMs (72-pin) to my two 4MB SIMMs on my PCI motherboard. I have misplaced my motherboard handbook, and I not sure if I can do this. I have found someone who will supply me with 8MB SIMMs, and I am keen on having 24MB of RAM on my PC, but I'd like your comments before proceeding.*

A.   That's a tough call without a motherboard manual. In theory, you should make out OK, but motherboards can be extremely particular about the size of SIMM that can be accommodated in each bank. For example, it's not uncommon for older motherboards to support 2- and 4MB SIMMs in one bank, and only 4MB SIMMs in another. That's what makes the motherboard documentation so vital. If you decide to try the 8MB SIMMs, be sure that you can get a return authorization (and your money back) if the new SIMMs don't work out.

USING PARTIAL MEMORY BANKS

Q807. *I have a question about memory. I'd like to install a new 72-pin 16MB SIMM in my system for more memory. But a friend told me I need to install two 72-pin SIMMs in a Pentium motherboard. Is this true? There are only four SIMM slots on the motherboard (two slots are filled).*

A. Yes, your friend is correct. Pentium CPUs are 64-bit devices, so two 72-pin (32-bit) SIMMs are needed to fill a bank. Inexpensive motherboards often limit the number of SIMM slots available to save on cost, and since 72-pin SIMMs are easily 16 to 32MB today, it is still possible to install a substantial amount of memory with few SIMMs. I have heard of some motherboards being designed to support partial banks, and using one SIMM. This feature is handy if a SIMM should fail, but performance would be seriously reduced. Try adding the one SIMM. This won't damage anything, and chances are you'll get a parity error or some other type of memory error. The error should disappear when a matching SIMM is added. If the system *does* boot up and use a partial bank, you should notice reduced performance when the memory in that bank is accessed (so you'll still need to add the second SIMM for best performance).

NEW SIMMS REFUSE TO WORK, BUT OLD SIMMS DO WORK

Q808. *After replacing the two original 8MB SIMMs on a SQ599 motherboard with two new 16MB EDO 60-ns SIMMs, the system won't start. I don't get anything at all on the monitor, not even the BIOS information. If I go back to the two original 8MB SIMMs, the system does work. The 16MB SIMMs do work in another PC.*

A.   If your new 16MB SIMMs check out on another PC, you've pretty much confirmed that the new memory works, which means there's a reason why the SIMMs won't work on *your* motherboard. My first guess is that the motherboard won't support 16MB SIMMs in the bank you've chosen. Check the documentation that accompanied your motherboard and look for a memory table which outlines the acceptable combinations of SIMM sizes. I'd bet that 16MB SIMMs just aren't supported (or are supported in a different bank). If you do find this to be the case, you can probably use the 8MB SIMMs in conjunction with the new 16MB SIMMs or return the 16MB SIMMs for another size. It may also be possible that the motherboard doesn't support EDO SIMMs. In most cases, you should be able to use EDO SIMMs (even on non-EDO motherboards), but your motherboard may be an exception to that rule. The solution here is also to try different RAM sizes.

PENTIUM MOTHERBOARD WON'T RECOGNIZE OVER 16MB

Q809.   *I have a PCI54PL Pentium 100-MHz motherboard using an AMI BIOS. I have installed a total of 48MB of RAM (all known-good SIMMs). The POST counts all 48MB, but the boot screen only shows 15MB. DOS, Windows 95, and BIOS probes like Snooper also see only 15MB. Snooper fails to correct the CMOS memory size, and all combinations of caching have been tried. Any ideas?*

A.   Since POST recognizes all 48MB, you may have a setup problem. It sounds like you're on the right track with your CMOS Setup. Look for any CMOS entries related to memory holes and enable them. Otherwise, turn off all video and BIOS caching (such as video shadow or BIOS shadow memory). If you are simply out of options in your current CMOS, check with the motherboard maker to see if there is a BIOS update available that might correct the problem. The answer is somewhere in your BIOS.

RAM UPGRADE PROBLEMS

Q810.   *I've bought RAM to upgrade my PC from 8 to 16MB. After upgrading, I encountered errors running some applications under Windows 3.11, and sometimes the system hangs up. I exchanged one of the SIMMs, and the problems under Windows 3.11 disap-*

peared, but then occurred in DOS applications instead. I replaced the SIMM again, and now all applications are running correctly. Any idea what the problem might have been?

A. I have to believe that you encountered two faulty SIMMs during your memory upgrade. The first SIMM probably had a fault in an area used by Windows, while the second one probably failed in an area used by DOS. It is really unusual to encounter two faulty SIMMs in a row. Whenever you are working with memory, be sure to use antistatic precautions (such as antistatic wrist straps and antistatic bags) to protect the memory. You should also remember to purchase memory (and all PC products) from reputable vendors with liberal return policies. Just to be safe, I'd also suggest that you use a good-quality PC diagnostic and run an extensive memory test to weed out any intermittent or marginal memory while the SIMMs are still under warranty.

New Memory Causes System Crashes

Q811. *I just finished adding some new RAM to my PC, but now the system crashes periodically with those awful blue screen errors in Windows 95. Do you have any suggestions before I return these SIMMs and get my money back?*

A. Don't pack up those new SIMMs just yet. Check the new SIMM type (i.e., EDO, FPM, or SDRAM) and compare it against the memory type already in the system. Mixing memory types can cause intermittent problems on some systems. Also check the new SIMM speeds. For Pentium systems, you should be using a 60-ns memory or faster. Memory speed that is borderline might cause intermittent crashes. You can try adding a memory wait state in your CMOS Setup. If the problem goes away, you have a speed problem (get faster memory). If not, try memory from a different manufacturer. Quality *does* vary between manufacturers.

Compaq System Locks Up After Upgrading Memory

ADVANCED

Q812. *My system is a Compaq Deskpro XL unit. After upgrading memory from the original 16MB to 40MB, the machine locks up after starting to load Windows 95. Any ideas?*

A.   This is a problem with Compaq systems when a Matrox Millennium video board is installed. The Compaq doesn't configure the video board with the Matrox drivers installed, so you'll need to disable the Matrox drivers before upgrading your memory:

1.   Before installing the additional memory, remove the Millennium video driver from the Device Manager.

2.   Shut down the computer.

3.   Install the additional memory.

4.   Start the computer and run its EISA Configuration Utility to configure the additional memory.

5.   Save the changes and restart the system.

6.   Windows 95 will be initialized in VGA mode and will autodetect the Millennium card.

7.   Follow the instructions and reinstall the Millennium video driver.

8.   Save the changes in Windows 95 and restart the computer.

There's another alternative:

1.   When installing the additional memory in the computer, move the Millennium video card into another PCI slot first.

2.   Start the computer and run its EISA Configuration Utility to configure the additional memory and reconfigure the Millennium video card.

3.   Save the changes and restart the computer.

4.   The computer will now initialize Windows 95.

UPGRADING MEMORY IN A GATEWAY COLORBOOK

Q813.   *I've got a Gateway 2000 Colorbook laptop with 8MB of RAM. I bought a 16MB RAM module to upgrade the system to 24MB. But after I install the 16MB RAM module, the system refuses to boot. Any ideas about what might be wrong?*

A.   Unfortunately, you'll need to remove your existing memory module before installing the 16MB module. Your Gateway

Colorbook is probably using two 4MB piggy back modules which allow additional modules to be stacked together. The problem is that stacking a 16MB module on top of a 4MB module just doesn't work. Try installing the 16MB module alone and then try stacking the 4MB module(s) on top of that. At the very worse, you'll be able to use the 16MB RAM module by itself.

MEMORY CARDS AND IBM THINKPADS

Q814. *I finally got around to upgrading the memory in my IBM ThinkPad. The memory card was a snap to install—nothing to it really—but now I get a 201 error. What's a 201 error?*

A. Based upon IBM's traditional diagnostic codes, a 201 error indicates a memory error, but given the ThinkPad's design, I suspect that you just haven't configured the memory properly. During power-up, hold down the <F1> button until you hear a beep and then release button and enter the easy setup. Select Configuration, Select Memory, and Disable Parity. Exit and save your changes, and then reboot the ThinkPad. Many of the ThinkPad series computers can use either parity or nonparity memory cards. You probably installed a nonparity card in a system preconfigured with parity checking enabled. If the problem persists, the memory card may be defective.

Modems

NO ROOM FOR A MODEM

Q815. *I want to install an internal modem on my PC, but I already have two COM ports on the motherboard, and both are being used. How can I install the new modem without causing a hardware conflict?*

A. That's not so easy. If COM1 and COM2 are on the motherboard, you could set the modem to use COM3 or COM4. Unfortunately, COM1 and COM3 share an IRQ, and COM2 and COM4 share an IRQ. So even if you set a different COM port, you'll still have an

ADVANCED

IRQ conflict if COM1 and COM2 are both in use. There are really only two ways out at this point. First, you could remove one of the serial devices and assign the COM port to your modem. For example, if you're using a mouse on COM1, you might install a bus mouse instead and place an external modem on COM1. As an alternative, you might use a modem which can be configured with IRQs *other than* the traditional IRQ4 or IRQ3. So you can set the COM3 I/O address but use an entirely different IRQ. That would overcome the hardware conflict, but Windows 95 and your communication software may have a great deal of difficulty in utilizing the unusual IRQ. Ultimately, I think you'll find yourself rearranging your serial devices.

OUTFITTING A 286 FOR ON-LINE WORK

Q816.   *My dad has an old 286 machine that I want to put my used 14.4KB modem into, but I've been told that his 286 PC won't work with "fast" 14.4KB modems. Does my dad need to buy a new PC just to go on-line with AOL at a reasonable speed?*

A.   Not necessarily. The problem is with your modem's universal asynchronous receiver/transmitter (UART). The UART is responsible for channeling all the data between your modem and system busses, so you need a fast UART such as a 16550A in order to achieve the data rates needed by 14.4KB modems and higher. If you choose to use an external modem, you will probably need to disable your system's original COM ports and update the COM ports with a high-speed I/O card. You can find inexpensive I/O cards with 16550A UARTS that will plug into an ISA port. If you have an internal modem, the UART is integrated onto the modem itself, so you need only disable the corresponding COM port in the system. For example, if you install an internal modem as COM1, you need to disable any other COM1 in the PC.

PHONE BLASTERS AND SOUND BLASTERS TOGETHER

Q817.   *I've got a Phone Blaster in my PC, which I use mainly for its modem. The sound is OK, but I'd like to upgrade to an AWE32 or Ensoniq Soundscape or to some other sound board. The problem is that I can't find a documented way to disable the sound portion of my Phone Blaster board. Any ideas?*

A.   This is going to be a problem for you. According to my information, there is no way to turn the Phone Blaster's sound portion off—largely since sound is a key part of the board's function. As a consequence, you're going to have a difficult time installing another sound board. However, since the Phone Blaster has a relatively old modem speed, you may find it more cost-effective to simply remove the Phone Blaster entirely and install a separate 33.6KB or faster modem, as well as a separate sound board.

MODEM INSTALLATION POINTERS

Q818.   *I recently received an internal modem, and I'd like to put it in my system. I already have a good idea how to handle the physical installation, but how do I configure the modem to a COM port and IRQ address?*

A.   The COM port and IRQ settings will probably have to be done manually. If the card has no jumpers or DIP switches, it is a full PnP card and should be handled by your Windows 95 operating system. Otherwise, the jumpers or DIP switches have to be set to the desired configuration. When configuring the modem, remember to avoid using COM ports or IRQs that are used by other devices in the system. You will also need to disable the corresponding COM port already in your PC to avoid a hardware conflict. Table 8.2 illustrates the relationship between COM ports and IRQs. The most important point to take from the table is that while there are four recognized COM ports, only two COM ports can be used in the system at any one time because COM ports share IRQs.

INTERMEDIATE

TABLE 8.2 COM PORTS VS. IRQ ASSIGNMENTS

Port	Standard IRQ
COM1	IRQ4
COM2	IRQ3
COM3	IRQ4
COM4	IRQ3

New Modem Isn't Recognized

Q819.   *A friend has a 486 running Windows 95. The system has two physical COM ports with a mouse on COM2. She has an internal 14.4KB Hayes Accura modem in a slot, configured (at least to Windows' taste) as COM4. It works like a charm. I come over with a nice, newer 28.8KB internal modem (a Logicode). We remove the old modem and put in the new modem (configured as COM4). We do the hardware wizard thing and violá—it won't work. I reconfigure the modem and everything else as COM3. The modem now works, but the mouse dies whenever the modem is up and running. I assume the modem and mouse are demanding the same IRQ.*

A.   Right. You said the PC has two physical COM ports. When you installed the new modem, I'll bet you didn't disable the corresponding physical COM port. With COM1 and COM2 on the motherboard, you could install a modem as COM4 without a conflict *if nothing is using COM2*. My bet is that the mouse is actually on COM1, and COM3 shares an interrupt with COM1, so the modem has a big hardware conflict. Remember, COM1 and COM3 share an IRQ, and COM2 and COM4 share an IRQ.

First, find out exactly what COM port the mouse is on and then configure the modem for a complementary COM port. For example, if the mouse is on COM1, set the modem for COM4. If the mouse is on COM2, set the modem for COM3. Of course, you can make sure to stick the mouse on COM1, disable COM2 on the motherboard, and configure the modem as COM2. That should clear things up.

9

Configuration and CMOS Questions

The proliferation of equipment available for the PC today is truly astounding. In order to start and run correctly, the PC must be "told" exactly how it is configured and to retain those configuration settings at all times (even when system power is off). The CMOS RAM in a PC is responsible for retaining the system's configuration data with the help of a small backup battery. This chapter examines PC time-keeping and provides answers for a wide array of CMOS RAM issues.

Keeping Time

Clock Stops When Power Is Off

Q820.   *The real-time clock on my Intel Advanced/EV P100 motherboard*
stops whenever the power is shut off, and I have to reset the
clock each time I turn on the PC. I have changed the battery, but
the problem persists.

A.   Apparently, your CMOS Setup is maintaining your system configuration when power is shut off, so that pretty much confirms
that the battery is good. If the time runs correctly when the PC is
on, but stops when the PC is off, chances are that the RTC itself
may be defective (you may need to replace the motherboard). If
the time runs erratically (or stops) when the PC is on, check for
viruses, and boot the system "clean" to see if any drivers or TSRs
may be interrupting IRQ0 (the 54.926-ms clock that updates
time) or the memory area where time is stored.

Date and Time Won't Update When Power Is Off

Q821.   *I was given a 486DX2/66 motherboard. It originally had prob-*
lems retaining the CMOS settings, but I fixed that by connecting
an external 6-V lithium battery. Now I find that the system date
and time are "stuck" when the machine is turned off. The CMOS
still retains its contents, and time-keeping works when the
machine is on. Is the battery-operated system clock on the BIOS
chip, and will replacing the AMI BIOS chip solve the problem? If
not, can the battery clock chip be replaced?

A.   Your system date and time are kept by a real-time clock (RTC)
chip which is powered by the CMOS backup battery. It is *not* a
part of your BIOS, so replacing the BIOS will have no effect.
However, when the RTC fails to keep time, it's a pretty good
indication that the CMOS battery is failing. Often a marginal
battery will maintain the CMOS settings but not provide enough
energy for the RTC. I would advise you to back up your CMOS
settings and then replace the CMOS battery. Also make sure that
the battery is connected securely.

PC Clocks Are Rarely Accurate

Q822. *Why is it that my computer clock loses time every day? I synchronized the computer clock to 12:00 p.m. yesterday, and today it lost 20 s. And it doesn't lose 20 s a day but 20 s on day 1, 23 s on day 2, 28 s on day 3, and so on. I just put in a new motherboard battery because the old one died (the motherboard is 4 yr old). Also, the CMOS time and DOS time are not synchronized and become unsynchronized after a day if I synchronize them. Could you tell me why?*

A.   The time on your PC is maintained by a chip called the real-time clock (RTC). The RTC is updated every 50 ms or so, but the timing that updates your RTC is hardly precise. It can vary by a few milliseconds here or a few milliseconds there. At the end of a day or a week, you really notice the difference. In other words, PC clocks are just not known for their accuracy. The fault is not really with the RTC itself but rather with the mechanism (an interrupt from your motherboard) which updates the RTC. The battery was a good guess, but I think you'll need to replace your motherboard if you want more accurate time keeping, but even then, there's no guarantee of accuracy.

Poor PC Time-keeping

Q823. *Why does my computer clock lose time every day? I synchronize the computer clock to 12:00 pm yesterday, and today it lost 20 s. And it doesn't just lose 20 s per day, but 20 s on day 1, 23 s on day 2, 28 s on day 3, and so on. I just put in a new motherboard battery because the old one died (the motherboard is 4 yr old). I hoped the new battery would fix things. Can you help?*

A.   The time on your PC is maintained by a chip called the real-time clock (or RTC). The RTC is updated every 50 ms or so, but the timing that updates your RTC is hardly precise. It can vary by a few milliseconds here or a few milliseconds there. At the end of a day or a week, you really notice the difference. In other words, PC clocks are just not known for their accuracy. The fault is not really with the RTC itself but rather with the mechanism (an interrupt from your motherboard) which updates the RTC. Replacing the battery was a good guess, but I think you'll need to replace your motherboard if you want more accurate time keeping, but even then, there's no guarantee of accuracy.

CLOCK LOSES TIME UNDER WINDOWS 95

Q824. *I'm working on a Windows 95 system that just won't keep the right time while the PC is running. It seems to keep the right time while power is off, so I figure the CMOS backup battery is good, but I just can't figure out why I lose time when the system runs.*

A. That's an unusual problem, but it should be fairly simple to track down. The first issue to check for is DOS programs. If you're running DOS programs in a window under Windows 95, the DOS program can sometimes cause Windows 95 to lose time. Stop using DOS programs in a window, and see if the time-keeping improves. Not all DOS programs will do this, and there may be a patch or upgrade available for the DOS program that will stop the problem. Otherwise, you should make it a point to run the program only from the DOS mode rather than through a window. Also check for DOS TSRs or other real-mode programs loaded by CONFIG.SYS or AUTOEXEC.BAT which might be interfering with the time under Windows 95. You may need to disable any such DOS utilities. Next, check the power saving configuration settings under your CMOS Setup. If you have an entry for System Suspend Timer, be sure it is set to *off*. If the suspend feature is left on, the PC's clock will halt whenever the system enters its suspend mode. The clock will resume when you exit the suspend mode, but the clock will not correct itself.

HANG-UPS TRASH DATE AND TIME

Q825. *I am running a Supermicro P55T2S motherboard with S6Y08T BIOS. Whenever I reboot after a hang-up or crash, the time and date settings have been altered and need to be reset—everything else is OK. Can you suggest cause?*

A.   There are two attributes of your PC that are supported by a back-up battery: the CMOS RAM, which holds information such as hard drive parameters, and the real-time clock (RTC). If reboots and crashes are effecting the RTC only, I suspect you have a defective RTC. Just to be on the safe side, contact your PC maker and see if there have been any problems reported with your BIOS. This is an unlikely symptom, but BIOS calls can set date and time, and a BIOS bug *might* be responsible. Once you clear the BIOS as a suspect, you may need to replace the RTC chip on your mother-board. If you don't know how to do that, you may have to take the PC to a shop or replace the motherboard outright.

CMOS RAM Issues

Understanding CMOS RAM

Q826. *What is CMOS?*

A.   CMOS stand for complementary metal oxide semiconductor. CMOS RAM is a special kind of low-power memory maintained by a battery after you turn the computer off. The BIOS uses CMOS RAM to store the settings you define in the Setup routine. The next time you turn on your computer, the BIOS looks in CMOS RAM for the settings you selected and configures your computer accordingly. If the battery charge runs too low, the CMOS contents will be lost, and POST will issue a CMOS Invalid or CMOS Checksum Invalid message. If this happens, you may have to replace the battery and restore the CMOS settings from scratch.

Understanding the CMOS Setup

Q827. *What is CMOS Setup?*

A.   CMOS Setup is an interactive BIOS program which allows you to configure (and optimize) your particular computer. The CMOS Setup supports three major functions: changing the hardware on your system (i.e., installing a new disk drive), changing the behavior of your computer (i.e., changing the date or time or turning special features on or off), or enhancing your computer's behavior (i.e., speeding up performance by turning on shadowing or caching). The actual Setup program varies considerably from computer to computer, depending on which company writes the BIOS. Be sure to run CMOS Setup before you make any changes to your system hardware or if you see an error displayed during POST.

CMOS Survival Tactics

Q828.   *I've been working with PCs since 1988, but to this day I don't know where to turn to optimize those cryptic BIOS settings. Is there an on-line FAQ or any other resource that puts these settings into simple terms?*

A.   I've got the perfect solution for you. Check out *The BIOS Survival Guide* at *http://www.lemig.umontreal.ca/bios/ bios_sg.htm.* This site provides some great detailed information on even the most current BIOS settings.

NVRAM Versus CMOS RAM

Q829.   *Can you describe the difference between NVRAM and CMOS RAM?*

A.   NVRAM is nonvolatile RAM. It is an electrically erasable form of memory (similar to an EEPROM) typically used in modems for holding the modem's configuration settings such as S-register values. There is usually enough NVRAM provided in a modem to hold several different configurations. By comparison, CMOS RAM is true RAM which is used on the motherboard to hold a PC's setup variables (like drive parameters). CMOS RAM is called true RAM because it will lose its contents when power is removed. In actual practice, CMOS RAM contents are maintained with a small battery.

Understanding ESCD

Q830. *When my computer boots up, before it displays the Staring MS-DOS message, it displays "Updating ESCD." What does ESCD stand for, and what does this message mean?*

A. ESCD stands for extended system configuration data, and it refers to a portion of CMOS used by plug-and-play operating systems and devices. PnP BIOS versions support an ESCD. For all practical purposes, you should not be concerned with this message, it simply means that the PnP configuration is updating.

Handling Invalid System Configuration Data Errors

Q831. *What does this message mean: Invalid System Configuration Data?*

A. Your extended system configuration data (ESCD) is a storage space for the configuration data in a plug-and-play system. Once you have configured your system properly, the plug-and-play BIOS uses your ESCD to load the same configuration from one boot to the next. If this error message is displayed, take these steps:

1. Go into Setup and find a field labeled "Reset configuration data."

2. Set this field to Yes.

3. Save and exit the CMOS Setup program. The system restarts and clears the ESCD during POST.

4. Run whatever PnP configuration tool is appropriate for your system:

    - If you have Windows 95 (a plug-and-play operating system), just restart your computer; Windows 95 will automatically configure your system and load the ESCD with the new data.

    - If you don't have Windows 95, run the DOS ISA Configuration Utility (ICU) to reset the ESCD.

TRICKS TO ENTER CMOS SETUPS

Q832.   *I work on a lot of different PCs, and I often have to enter CMOS configurations while updating or replacing parts. The problem is that with so many different BIOS versions, it's hard to keep track of all the key combinations available. Any guidelines for us bench technicians?*

A.   I've compiled a list of CMOS setup codes for the most popular BIOS types in the table. When you're stuck and cannot enter CMOS with any of the key combinations in Table 9.1, you might be able to "force" the CMOS Setup routine by causing a configuration change (such as removing a SIMM or two). This sometimes causes a CMOS error and allows you to proceed to the setup routine. If you have an older 386 or 286 system, you'll need to use a setup disk to access the system CMOS configuration. You can obtain freeware setup utilities at *oak.oakland.edu:/SimTel/msdos/at* or *ftp.uu.net:/systems/msdos/simtel/at.*

TABLE 9.1 TYPICAL CMOS SETUP KEY SEQUENCES

BIOS	Key Sequence
AMI BIOS	\<Del\> key during the POST
Award BIOS	\<Ctrl\>+\<Alt\>+\<Esc\>
DTK BIOS	\<Esc\> key during the POST
IBM PS/2 BIOS	\<Ctrl\>+\<Alt\>+\<Ins\> after \<Ctrl\>+\<Alt\>+\<Del\>
Phoenix BIOS	\<Ctrl\>+\<Alt\>+\<Esc\> or \<Ctrl\>+\<Alt\>+\<S\>

ACCESSING THE CMOS SETUP FOR A SONY PC

Q833.   *I'm working on a Sony PC, and I need to access the CMOS Setup to make some hard drive updates. The problem is that I can't access CMOS with any of the traditional keystrokes (i.e., \<Del\> or \<F1\>). Do you have an answer?*

A.   According to Sony, you should hit the <F3> key while the PC is
       first starting (when you see the Sony logo) and then press the
       <F1> key.

ACCESSING THE CMOS SETUP FOR A 286 PC

Q834.   *I've been tinkering with an old 286 for my young nephew, and I*
        dropped in an EGA card for simple color graphics. The problem
        is that I can't get into Setup in order to update the CMOS set-
        tings. How do you get into Setup on an IBM AT?

A.   You're going back a way on this one. As I recall, all 286 and
        most early-model 386 systems required a setup disk in order to
        change CMOS settings. You would boot the PC from its setup
        disk in order to launch the CMOS Setup routine. I've done some
        searching at the IBM Web site, and it seems you can download
        the setup file SETUPNU.COM from the IBM FTP site at
        ftp://ftp.pc.ibm.com/pub/pccbbs/dos_util/

ACCESSING THE CMOS SETUP FOR A LEADING EDGE 286 SYSTEM

Q835.   *I have a Leading Edge 286 system that I'm trying to add a 3.5-in*
        floppy drive to, but I can't figure out how to reach the CMOS to
        tell it that it's there. Can you help me? I've tried all of the hot
        key procedures I know.

A.   This question comes up a lot with folks trying to breathe new life
        into their old PCs. The problem is that 286-class PCs required a
        Setup disk. Setup routines were not integrated into motherboard
        BIOS until after the 386-type PCs were released. What this means
        is that you can press key combinations all day, and you won't be
        able to access the CMOS Setup without booting a setup routine
        from disk. If you do not have the original disks for the PC and
        cannot get a CMOS Setup utility from Leading Edge support
        (since Leading Edge is out of business), you may be able to use
        the classic IBM AT setup utility SETUPNU.COM from the IBM
        FTP site at *ftp://ftp.pc.ibm.com/pub/pccbbs/dos_util/*. A number of
        commercial and shareware diagnostics also incorporate a utility
        which can be used to adjust at least the basic CMOS settings.

INTERMEDIATE

One other problem—286 system BIOS cannot support 3.5-in high-density (1.44MB) floppy drives. If you're installing such a drive, you won't find it listed as one of the available drives. To get around this, you can use the DOS DRIVPARM utility to identify the drive as a 1.44MB unit after the PC boots. Keep in mind that you cannot use 1.44MB boot disks.

Accessing CMOS Setup for a GRiD Laptop

Q836.   *Can you tell me how to enter the CMOS Setup routine for a GRiD 386 laptop? It has a Phoenix BIOS LAP386SL V1.01 dated 06/24/93, and I don't have any other documentation.*

A.   As a rule, you should look at the display during the first few moments after start-up. The CMOS key sequence will usually be displayed (i.e., "Press <Del> for CMOS Setup"). The Phoenix CMOS Setup usually is called by pressing <Ctrl>+<Alt>+<s> in the few moments after system start-up. Act fast; the window of opportunity for starting CMOS Setup is typically only a few seconds. If you cannot access CMOS with a series of keystrokes, you may need to boot the laptop with a start-up disk.

Accessing CMOS Setup for a Sony PC

Q837.   *I'm working on a Sony PC, and I need to get into the CMOS Setup. Any guidance?*

A.   The CMOS utility screen can be accessed while the computer is powering up and before Windows 95 starts. Power up the PC (or restart it). While the computer is starting, the Sony logo appears with instructions to hit <F3> to access the CMOS. Do so, and the CMOS Setup routine should open in a few moments.

Note

If you have a floppy disk in the A: drive, remove it before restarting the computer.

Accessing CMOS Setup for an ALR Computer

Q838. *How do you access the CMOS Setup program on an ALR computer?*

A. I had to really do some digging at ALR, but I think I have an answer for you. On a PCI-based machine, you will be prompted to hit the <F2> key while the machine is booting up. If you do not hit the key in time, you will have to reboot the machine to access the Setup. On a machine that does not have a PCI bus, press the <Ctrl>+<Alt>+<Esc> keys simultaneously. If that fails to launch the Setup program, try rebooting without loading your AUTOEX-EC.BAT or CONFIG.SYS. There are two ways to do this:

■ If you are running DOS 6.0 or higher, when the machine gives you the Starting MS-DOS message, hit the <F5> key.

■ If you are running DOS 5.0 or earlier, format a floppy with the command FORMAT A: /S and boot from that "clean" disk.

Accessing CMOS Setup for a Presario

Q839. *I'm working to upgrade a Compaq Presario, and I need to access the CMOS Setup. How do I get into CMOS?*

A. For newer Compaq products like the ProLinea, Deskpro, Deskpro XL, Deskpro XE, or Presario, you need to press the <F10> key in the moments while the cursor is in the upper right hand corner of the screen. This happens just after the initial two beeps when booting.

Setup Utility for GRiD Computer Systems

Q840. *I'm stuck working on an old GRiD computer, but I don't have the utility to access the CMOS Setup. Any pointers?*

A. Most GRiD systems require an external program to access CMOS setup—it is not built into the BIOS as on most systems. Setup programs for GRiD computers are available on the Web at *http://support.tandy.com/grid.html,* and also at *http://www.ast.com/americas/files.htm.*

*Some of the files at the those sites are in the form of .COM files,
so it may be necessary to use a special technique to download
them. If using Netscape, <Shift>+Left Click (hold down the
SHIFT key while clicking the left mouse button) on the file to
download it. If you just click on it, you will be viewing the file.*

SETUP UTILITY FOR IBM PS/2 COMPUTER SYSTEMS

Q841.   *I have an IBM PS/2 system, but I cannot get it running because it
does not have the CMOS Setup utility handy. Where can I find
the CMOS Setup files?*

A.   You can download a copy of the PS/2 Setup utility from the IBM
site at *http://www.pc.ibm.com/files.html.* This is an extensive site,
and you should be able to find a selection of diagnostic and troubleshooting information as well.

SETUP UTILITY FOR PANASONIC COMPUTER SYSTEMS

Q842.   *I've got an old Panasonic system to work on, but I don't have
the utility to access the CMOS Setup. Where can I find a
Panasonic Setup utility?*

A.   A lot of older 286 and 386 computers require an external program to access CMOS Setup (on newer systems, Setup is built
into the BIOS). You may be able to find a generic setup utility at
most BIOS manufacturer's Web sites, but those are not compatible with all systems—especially the more proprietary ones. Setup
programs for Panasonic computers are available on the Web at
http://www.panasonic.com/host/support/.

DEFEATING AN AMI BIOS PASSWORD

Q843.   *My client has a new AMI BIOS (A37D 18:00:00 04/29/96). She
changed the password, and now we can't get into the system. I
thought AMI was a default password, but that didn't work
either. Any suggestions?*

INTERMEDIATE

A.   If the password option had simply been enabled, but the actual password had not been changed, AMI should have been the default. You can also try the "CMOS Clear" method of overcoming a BIOS password by removing the CMOS battery and allowing the CMOS contents to clear. Unless there is a jumper to force a short, you will have to wait anywhere from 15 min to several hours for the CMOS to fully discharge (I've seen some CMOS RAM retain its contents on a latent charge for days). After ample time for the CMOS to clear, reinstall the battery and power up the system. You'll need to reenter your CMOS settings, but the password should be gone. If you still have trouble, you may be able to find a password cracking routine for AMI BIOS at *http://nospin.com/pcbuild.html.*

CLEARING THE PASSWORD ON AN ACER 970

Q844. *I've got an AcerNote 970 notebook PC which I inherited from a colleague who left the company. Unfortunately, he used a password which he "forgot" to share before leaving. How do I clear the password and start from scratch?*

A.   The procedure to clear an Acer 970 password is a bit involved because there is no DIP switch to enable or disable passwords. Remove the bottom housing of the Acer 970 by unscrewing seven screws. You'll see two DIMM slots—there is a PAD21 marking printed between the two DIMM slots. All you need to do is to short the PAD21 contacts and then power up the 970 to clear the password. Make sure you remove the PAD21 short to reenable password setting.

CLEARING THE PASSWORD ON AN ACER 950

Q845. *I've tried clearing the password on my AcerNote 950, but it won't clear—even when DIP switch SW1 is set to disable the password. Is there any way around this?*

A.   The procedure for clearing a 950's password is a bit convoluted. Read the procedure carefully and make sure you understand everything before proceeding.

1. Reset the SW1 DIP switch so that pin 1 at the bottom is set
    off and pin 2 at the top is set on (by default, both pin 1 and
    2 are set off).

2. Start the 950. When you see the Starting Windows 95 mes-
    sage, press <F8> and select Command Prompt Only.

3. Once in DOS mode, type the following DEBUG script:

    ```
    C:\>debug
    -o 70 22
    -o 71 45
    -o 70 12
    -o 71 21
    -q
    ```

4. Now you can enter CMOS Setup using the <F2> key
    (although it shows "Checksum error and default values
    loaded" when you start system).

5. Clear all passwords and disable Password on Boot.

6. Save the CMOS changes, and restart the system to verify.

7. Change DIP switch SW1 back to its default settings.

SPEEDING THE CMOS DISCHARGE

Q846. *I've lost my password, and I've removed the battery to discharge
the CMOS RAM in order to clear it. But each time I turn the PC
on (without the battery), the CMOS RAM is still intact. It's been
24 h—what to I need to do?*

A. This is not unusual. I've seen some CMOS RAM hold onto a
    latent charge for days. You can typically speed the discharge of
    your CMOS RAM by removing the battery and *then* jumpering
    across the + and – battery contacts with a 10-kΩ resistor. Leave
    the resistor attached for an hour or so and then try the PC again.
    Remember, don't replace the battery until the CMOS contents
    have been cleared.

CONFIGURATION ERRORS AFTER REMOVING FLOPPY DRIVE

Q847. *I recently removed a 5.25-in floppy drive from my cousin's 386 system (a 3.5-in drive remains). I entered Setup and adjusted the configuration to eliminate the 5.25-in drive (set to none). Now when I boot the system, I get an error message telling me that the system configuration is no longer correct and that I should be running Setup. Did I mess up the configuration?*

A.   First, enter your CMOS Setup routine again and check your floppy drive entries. You may have forgotten to save your changes before exiting and rebooting the system, so the 5.25-in floppy drive may still be entered (don't worry, this is a common mistake). Make sure that the 5.25-in drive entry is eliminated. Also check to see that you didn't accidentally change any other settings while in CMOS. If problems persist, try placing the remaining floppy drive at the end of the drive cable (making it A:), and be sure to update the CMOS Setup accordingly.

LOOKING FOR THE CMOS BATTERY

Q848. *I know that motherboards need battery power to back up the CMOS settings, but I have an old 486 VL bus motherboard that doesn't have a battery on board—yet it retains the CMOS information. Where would the battery be? If there's no battery to remove, how would I clear the CMOS?*

A.   I'm not sure that's exactly right—all motherboards *do* need a battery source to maintain the CMOS settings while system power is off, so the battery has to be somewhere. If you don't see a battery on the motherboard, and you're not using an external power pack, chances are that you're motherboard has a Dallas Semiconductor CMOS/RTC module. Dallas is renowned for integrating the battery with the CMOS on the same device. If you study the motherboard carefully, look for a particularly thick, narrow IC (probably mounted on a DIP socket) marked "Dallas" along with the part number. If you find such a device, the battery is inside the IC. Since you cannot remove the battery to clear CMOS, Dallas-type modules often have a jumper on the motherboard which can be shorted to clear the CMOS.

CMOS Battery Replacement Pointers

Q849.   *Can you give me some information on how to change the CMOS battery. A message comes up on the computer that the CMOS battery is low, and I know that it needs to be changed. How am I to change it without losing all the hardware data when I remove the old battery?*

A.   Ultimately, there is really no way to prevent the loss of data when replacing a CMOS battery—although not all motherboard designs will lose CMOS contents in the few minutes it takes to actually exchange the battery. Your best course when replacing the battery is to first back up the CMOS contents. You can simply go through each page of the CMOS Setup and take a <PrintScreen> to compile a hard copy of the contents.

Next, open the PC and locate the battery. It may be a coin cell, or a cylindrical battery soldered to the motherboard. If the battery is a coin cell, simply slide the old coin cell out, and slip a new one into place (be sure to note the proper polarity of the old coin cell). Do *not* lift or bend the metal arm holding the coin cell in place. This can cause a bad connection with the new battery, and your CMOS may not hold its contents. If the battery is hard-soldered to the motherboard, you should install an external battery pack, which typically connects to a four-pin header plug located near the original battery. You will also need to move a motherboard jumper to enable the external battery. Always remember to turn off and unplug the PC before attempting to replace the battery. Also be sure to use a well-grounded, good-quality antistatic wriststrap to prevent accidental static discharge from damaging the motherboard.

Once the new battery is in place and secure, power up the PC. Go into the CMOS Setup and check its contents against your hard copy and then correct any discrepant information. If you have backed up CMOS contents to a floppy disk, you need only boot from the floppy and run the CMOS backup utility to restore the CMOS data. Be sure to replace the cover and any hardware before returning the system to service.

CMOS BATTERIES AND ADDING MORE RAM

Q850. *When I change the CMOS battery, are there any files that will be lost, or are you allowed enough time to replace the battery? Several years ago I had to change the CMOS battery and had a headache getting the system back up and running. I would also like to add more RAM (SIMMs) to my system, but I'm not sure how much to add. My system is a 486 Packard Bell Legend 23CD with 8MB RAM. It looks like I only have one more slot for SIMMs. Could I replace my original ones with say a 16MB SIMM and add another 16MB SIMM in the other slot? I never seem to get the same answer twice whenever I inquire about this.*

A.   Before replacing the CMOS backup battery, you should enter the CMOS Setup routine and take <PrintScreen> shots of every page of your setup—that way you have all of the original settings documented. After you replace the battery, you can go back into CMOS Setup and restore everything in a matter of minutes. Some CMOS devices are very good at holding latent charges and won't loose their contents if the battery is removed for a few minutes, but other CMOS RAM may not be so forgiving. *Never* assume that your CMOS RAM will hold its contents once a battery is removed.

As for memory, you probably don't need more than 16MB total with your Packard Bell 486 system, so try adding an 8MB SIMM to your open slot. Of course, check with the Packard Bell manual first to see if that slot will support an 8MB SIMM. I would be very concerned with adding 16MB SIMMs to a Packard Bell system unless the manual explicitly calls out that arrangement.

CAN'T ORIENT A BATTERY PACK CONNECTOR

Q851. *When I disconnected my external battery from an older 486 motherboard, I didn't label the wires, thinking I would never use it again. Now I want to set it up as a second machine, and I forgot which way the battery pack connects. The motherboard has a four-pin male connector labeled pins 1 to 4, and the battery pack is a 4.5-V alkaline from Rayovac using a four-pin female socket (a red wire at one end and a black wire at the other end; the middle two holes are empty). So, is it red or black to pin1?*

A. First, I suspect that all four pins are available on the mother-board's four-pin header, and there is no "key" on the battery pack connector. Generally speaking, pin 1 is the positive connection, so the red wire would go there. If your CMOS RAM will not hold its contents when PC power is turned off, you should try reversing the battery connector.

CMOS Won't Stay Set After BIOS Flash

Q852. *I have an ABIT SM5A motherboard with 16MB of RAM, a Sanyo CD-ROM drive, a Western Digital 3.1GB hard drive, a Cirrus PCI 5440 video card, and a 3.5-in floppy drive. The problem is that when I start up the unit, it gives an error: "CMOS Checksum Errors. Default setup loaded." The strange thing is that if you reboot it after you have let it run for a minute or two, it doesn't repeat the error. In fact it could be off for an hour or so, but more than that and the error returns. My first guess was the battery (which I have replaced). The contacts look clean since it is a new motherboard. But I noticed this problem started when I installed a new BIOS file. This unit has the Award flash BIOS. I obtained the latest BIOS file from ABIT and installed it as instructed. It appeared to flash correctly, but it seems to lose contents after being off for a while.*

A. A CMOS checksum error is a natural result of updating a BIOS. If I understand your question properly, you simply allow the CMOS to load the defaults, but you are not actually starting your CMOS Setup routine to check and tweak your entries. First, I suggest that you review your new battery installation carefully. If it is installed backward or not connected securely, the battery will not maintain CMOS contents (even the default contents) after power is removed. Since CMOS is a low-power form or memory, it will sometimes retain its contents using only the latent charge from the system. The effect can last several hours, and I've seen it last several days. Once you have the battery installed in the proper orientation, go into your CMOS Setup, make any changes you need to, then *save* your setup and exit to reboot the system. If the problem persists, you may need to perform a *complete* CMOS clear (sometimes referred to as an "NVRAM clear"). Consult your user manual for specific instructions on how to accomplish this for your system.

ADVANCED

CMOS Values Won't Hold in 286 System

Q853.　*Here's a blast from the past. I've got an i286 system using AMI BIOS. I'm trying to get the system running for a ham radio application. The system seems to run properly, but I can't get the CMOS configuration settings to hold when the system is turned off. I can warm-boot the system, but after power is removed, I have to boot from the setup disk and reenter CMOS values before I can use the system. I've measured the battery, and it reads 4.2 Vdc. Any Ideas?*

A.　There are always a few important issues to consider when it comes to CMOS backup batteries. First, the 4.2 V you measured should be close to the rated battery voltage. In other words, if the battery is supposed to be 4.5 V, 4.2 V is probably OK. If the battery is supposed to be 6 V, 4.2 V probably demands a replacement. If you're in doubt, try a new battery anyway. Also make sure that the battery is securely attached to its connector and inserted in the right polarity (a reversed battery can act like it's not even there). Check the motherboard for an "external" battery connector. There's probably a jumper to switch between the motherboard and external battery. It sounds like your battery is on the motherboard, so the jumper should be set to internal (otherwise, set the jumper to external).

Dealing with Autodetected Memory Upgrades

Q854.　*I just added another 4MB of RAM to my wife's Pionex 486SX/25 (OverDrive 50-MHz) system. The original 4MB was in 1MB SIMMs in sockets 1 through 4. I added four 1MB SIMMs in sockets 5 through 8. At boot-up, the added RAM is automatically detected, and POST shows 7808KB followed by the message "CMOS memory size mismatched. Run setup utility. Press <F1> to resume." When I press <F1> and enter Setup, the display shows 7168KB of memory and seems to not allow any changes. After exiting Setup without changes, the system continues to boot normally and appears to operate normally. It won't boot now without going through Setup.*

A. It used to be that whenever you added more memory to a PC, you'd need to enter the new memory total in CMOS Setup. Today, BIOS is perfectly capable of detecting the total amount of installed memory in a PC, but you still need to confirm the new total by entering the CMOS Setup and saving with changes (even though you made no specific changes yourself). Once you save the changes and reboot the computer, your CMOS error message should disappear.

DEALING WITH A CMOS MISMATCH ERROR

Q855. *I'm building a 486DX2/66 from spare parts, and I'm getting an error message. Does a CMOS Memory Mismatch error mean a bad SIMM?*

A. Generally speaking, a CMOS Memory Mismatch error usually means that the PC did not find the hardware it expected to find based on the entries in your CMOS Setup. This can occur for a number of reasons. You might have forgotten to update your CMOS when you finished assembling the system, and the CMOS still expected to find the hardware from its old incarnation. The CMOS battery could have failed, causing the CMOS RAM to lose its contents. You might also have inadvertently changed a CMOS parameter (or set it incorrectly) when updating your CMOS Setup. Finally, you might indeed have a hardware fault (such as a bad SIMM).

Check your CMOS Setup and make sure that if there is an entry for Installed RAM, the correct amount of RAM is entered. Most PCs perform a RAM Count during start-up. If you know how much RAM should be in the system, watch this RAM count and see where it stops. If it counts *less* RAM than you know you have, a bad SIMM may well be your problem.

UNDERSTANDING A CMOS MISMATCH ERROR

Q856. *Does "CMOS memory mismatch" mean a bad SIMM? I'm building a 486DX2 system from spare parts.*

A.   A CMOS memory mismatch usually means that the PC did not find the hardware it expected to find based on the entries in your CMOS setup. This can occur for a number of reasons. The CMOS battery could have failed, causing the CMOS RAM to lose its contents. You might have inadvertently changed a CMOS parameter (or set it incorrectly) when updating your CMOS Setup. You might also have a hardware fault (such as a bad SIMM). Ignore no possibility.

Check your CMOS Setup and make sure that if there is an entry for Installed RAM, that the correct amount is entered. Most PCs perform a RAM Count during startup. If you know how much RAM should be in the system, watch this RAM count and see where it stops. If it counts *less* RAM than you know you have, a bad SIMM may well be your problem.

PRESERVING YOUR CMOS BATTERY

Q857. *I've been told that I should keep my PC on in order to prevent the internal CMOS battery from draining. Is this true, and should I be concerned?*

A.   The battery in your desktop PC is referred to as the RTC/CMOS backup battery. It is typically a small lithium cell (or pack of lithium batteries) which maintain essential elements of your PC's configuration in a small amount of low-power (CMOS) RAM on the motherboard. Most motherboards attempt to preserve battery life by using main power to maintain CMOS contents while the PC is on (and only draining the battery while the PC is off).

However, a battery will still self-discharge even if it is not being drained (although at a much slower rate), so even if you leave the PC on full time, the CMOS battery will still eventually go dead. In the meantime, you are paying far more in energy costs than the cost of any new battery. Under average daily PC use, a CMOS battery should last 3 to 5 yr (sometimes longer). As a result, it does not pay to buy a spare battery and keep it on the shelf. You can buy compatible backup batteries for most systems at almost any computer store.

ADVANCED

Losing a configuration can easily disable your system, but a bit of advance planning can make CMOS battery failure and replacement a painless process. Your best protection against CMOS battery failures is to enter your CMOS Setup mode and take a <PrintScreen> shot of the configuration settings *now,* and then tape the pages to the inside of your enclosure. That way, when the battery does eventually fail, you will have a written record of all settings that you can easily restore once a new battery is installed.

ALTERNATIVE REPLACEMENTS FOR SOLDERED BATTERIES

Q858.   *When the CMOS cannot retain any settings, does it mean I have to replace the CMOS battery? It's the solder-in type. Is there any other alternative, because I am not good at soldering?*

A.   Soldered batteries are probably one of the worst moves the PC industry has ever taken. Fortunately, most motherboards do incorporate a four-pin header connection for an external battery pack. The battery pack may be preassembled with the right voltage for your motherboard (or can be loaded with common AA-type batteries), attached to the PC chassis with a piece of Velcro, and then connected to the external battery connector through a short cable. Keep in mind that many motherboards provide a jumper for switching between external and internal batteries. You can leave the internal battery in place, switch the motherboard jumper to its external position, and then attach the battery pack. You can then reset the CMOS normally.

One caveat: A few motherboards use a rechargeable NiCd battery which is charged while the PC is on. If the PC is left off for several months, the battery may discharge and lose CMOS settings. You then must leave the system on for 24 h or so to recharge the battery before it will hold CMOS settings again.

Using Various Backup Battery Types

Q859. *Our old Zenith 80386/16 has a dead CMOS battery. It's a Tadiran Lithium Inorganic 3.6 V (AA size). Would be okay to use a standard 3.6-V AA to replace it, or do I need a specialty computer battery?*

A.   Generally speaking, the battery configuration should not matter as long as the proper voltage is available to the motherboard. As a result, if you started with a 3.6-V lithium battery, you can install any battery arrangement (via an external battery pack) as long as 3.6 V are available. Also keep in mind that lithium batteries are typically not rechargeable, so avoid using NiCd cells. Of course, to ensure the best fit, you should replace the battery with an exact replacement. I believe that you can order replacement batteries from a local Radio Shack. If not, you can contact Battery Specialties for Tadiran replacement parts at 800-279-2561.

Battery Leakage Problems

Q860. *Is there a wide-spread problem of this battery leaking after a number of years? My mom lost her 386 motherboard because this type of battery started leaking. I've heard this story about a number of other machines too.*

A.   As you discovered, battery leakage is a serious matter, and it happens most frequently with low-quality or overstressed batteries. The chemicals used in batteries (even small batteries) are acidic. If the battery container breaches and allows those chemicals to spill out onto the motherboard, it can easily eat away at the printed wiring and ruin the motherboard. However, I would suspect that this happens most frequently with motherboards that have been sitting unused for some years. By the time a battery container fails, the battery is virtually always dead, so the idea is that you'll lose your CMOS contents and replace the dead battery long before the actual container opens up. I would be very surprised if your mom's CMOS Setup had not been lost regularly for some time.

ADVANCED

There are two rules to help prevent battery damage. First, replace your CMOS backup battery regularly (every 2 or 3 yr). Second, if you must remove and store the motherboard for any length of time, take a <PrintScreen> of all your CMOS Setup pages and then remove motherboard. Remove the battery from the motherboard and place it in a separate container, and then store the motherboard in an antistatic bag along with the printed CMOS Setup pages.

FIXING A BROKEN BATTERY HOLDER

Q861. *I have a customer who felt the need to pull the battery out of his motherboard. This is the round flat type of battery that slides into a compact connector on the motherboard. The customer, however, believed that the positive connector arm was a type of lever and pulled it open to remove the battery. Needless to say, the contact is terrible now, and the BIOS loses its settings on a regular basis (not always). I've tried to bend the contact back without any luck. Any other suggestions?*

A. Chances are that the contact has broken (or the soldering points on the motherboard have been strained. If you really want to tinker, you can try bending that contact back once again and then reheating the battery connections on the motherboard with a soldering iron. If you'd rather stay clear of soldering, I'd suggest that you simply remove the coin cell entirely and use an external battery pack instead. Just remember to set the motherboard to use an external battery pack and secure the pack with a bit of Velcro.

CMOS ACCIDENT LEAVES SYSTEM INACCESSIBLE

Q862. *My home Pentium runs Windows 3.1. It has a Micronics motherboard with the PhoenixBIOS 4.03. I'm on-line, and I realize the time is off an hour. I figure I'll exit out and run Setup to change the clock. I changed the clock in Setup and then apparently hit the wrong key; I don't think I saved the changed values. Instead, I think I either hit some button that restores ancient defaults or just blitzed everything. My system reboots, it finds memory and my various SCSI cards, and then it can't find the operating sys-*

tem (it's dead in the water). I'd made a Norton rescue disk a few months before. I run it, and now I get

```
CMOS checksum bad—run setup.

Error: incompatible BIOS translation detected.
```

What is going on here? How do I get my hard drive back?

A.   Start the system and enter your CMOS Setup. In the drive portion, set the entry for your drive to LBA Mode if it's available and then select autodetect for your translation geometry. This eliminates your having to enter specific geometry figures for the EIDE drive. As long as you haven't tried fiddling with hard drive partitions, the drive should come back and bring your system with it. My guess is that the defaults loaded a drive geometry that wasn't the same as the drive actually in your system. The result is that the system couldn't read the hard drive and boot to your operating system. The next problem is tweaking the rest of your CMOS values, but as long as you keep track of each change you make, you should have no trouble restoring your system. Once things are optimized again, you should take a PrintScreen of each CMOS Setup screen and file those prints with your PC's documentation.

System Loses Some Settings After Playing Game

Q863.   *After I play some of my DOS-based games, my system loses some of the CMOS settings. I've never heard of this before— what could have happened?*

A.   There are several games and other programs on the market that *can* reset at least some CMOS locations. One solution is to contact the program maker and see if there is a patch or fix that will prevent CMOS access. Another solution to this problem is to exclude the C000h to CFFFh range in the EMM386 device line in your CONFIG.SYS file. This prevents programs from accessing the section of memory that the BIOS uses for shadowing. Here is an example:

```
DEVICE=C:\DOS\EMM386.EXE X=C000-CFFF
```

ADVANCED

SETTING THE CACHE READ CYCLE

Q864.   What should I set the cache read cycle to in my CMOS setup?

A.   That depends on your computer. The clock cycle has four inter-
        vals. These intervals are called T1, T2, T3, and T4, and this sets
        the "rhythm" for every operation in the computer. The cache
        read cycle is made up of four numbers displayed like this: *x-x-x-
        x*. Each *x* represents the number of steps required for a specific
        read operation. For example, the first *x* represents how many
        clock steps to delay when looking at the Tag RAM (basically a
        directory listing for the cache memory).

        The other three x's represent the delay in looking at the SRAM cache.
        For faster systems, use a faster setting (such as 2-1-1-1 or 3-1-1-1). If
        you notice the system locking up intermittently, consider a slower set-
        ting (like 2-2-2-2 or 3-2-2-2). Your system will run faster if the cache
        read cycle is set properly. Remember that if cache cycles are set incor-
        rectly, the computer may experience intermittent lock-ups.

CONFIGURING SHADOW RAM

Q865.   How do I configure Shadow RAM in the CMOS Setup?

A.   Shadow RAM is a technique used to improve system performance
        by mapping slower ROM (BIOS) contents into faster RAM. Not
        only the motherboard BIOS, but *all* BIOS (Video BIOS, SCSI
        BIOS, and so on) can be shadowed. Before configuring shadow
        RAM, you should know the locations of the BIOS in your system.
        Often a utility like MicroScope (*www.micro2000.com*) can reveal
        the active ROMs in your system. You may see entries like

```
VGA Adapter          A000-AFFF
Adaptec SCSI BIOS    D000-D7FF
```

        The trick is to enable shadowing *only* for the BIOS devices in
        upper memory. This leaves the rest of the upper memory area
        available for drivers and TSRs. If you configure the address
        ranges of your different BIOS devices so that they are all contigu-
        ous, you can shadow the whole range of BIOS addresses, while
        leaving the *maximum* amount of upper memory area available.

ADVANCED

10

Windows 95 Questions

Today's hardware is highly dependent upon the operating system. Windows 95 has proven to be a very effective and versatile operating system for general-purpose computing, but it also has its share of problems and limitations. This chapter examines Windows 95 concepts and then looks at some answers to driver and applet issues. You will also find answers to a number of important installation issues. The chapter also covers answers to networking, communication, and multimedia questions.

Terminology and General Topics

Identifying Windows 95 Versions

Q866. *I've been seeing odd designations for Windows 95 lately like 95a and 95b. Have I missed something? How many versions of Windows 95 are there?*

A.   Well you're certainly not alone. The multiple labels assigned to Windows 95 are confusing a lot of people. Generally speaking, there are three major designations that you should be familiar with, depending on which Windows 95 add-ons you have installed. There is the main retail version of Windows 95, which is simply 95. If you have installed the Microsoft Plus Service Pack, the installation is 95a. If you have installed OSR2 (or gotten it with a new system), the installation is 95b.

Memory Requirements with Windows 95

Q867. *I've been upgrading older (i486) systems to Windows 95 for a while now. In most cases, I notice that performance is usually a bit slower, but only rarely does Windows 95 really bog down the performance of an older PC. Yet I see claims that Windows 95 needs 32 or 64MB or more to run properly. What's the real story with memory?*

A.   Technically speaking, Windows 95 needs 4MB of RAM to operate, and 8MB are recommended (this is on the Windows 95 product box). However, the general rule for all Windows-based operating systems is that more memory is better. There are several reasons for this. More memory allows multiple applications to be running simultaneously, it supports larger, more complex applications, and reduces the dependence on virtual memory—all of which can only help performance. I'd bet that if you tried opening more than one application or tried to use a data-intensive application on your older 4 to 8MB systems, you'd see very poor performance. In practice, 16MB seems to work quite well;

it's enough to run a diverse selection of applications and handle a few applications simultaneously, yet it does not depend on virtual memory too heavily. If you're using high-end applications or doing design work like CAD or solid modeling, you should seriously consider 32 to 64MB of RAM.

MORE RAM IS BETTER UNDER WINDOWS 95

Q868. *I have 32MB of EDO RAM for my new system and can't wait to assemble it, but I am wondering if I should go to 48MB for my new system. Picking up another 16MB would be cheap right now. If I am running Windows 95, will it use the extra memory effectively? I do work with graphics, which is why I got 32MB with a 4MB Matrox Millennium video board.*

A.   A total of 48MB of RAM will certainly not hurt a Windows 95 platform, but it may not be an urgent addition. If you can afford the extra memory, your graphics applications will benefit, and if you want to diminish your dependence on virtual memory (the permanent swap file on your hard drive), you should go ahead and add the extra 16MB now. Otherwise, 32MB will probably take you a long way, and you can add the extra memory later as your budget allows.

INTERMITTENT LOCK-UPS WHEN OPENING A DOS WINDOW UNDER WINDOWS 95

Q869. *When I try to open a DOS window under Windows 95, the PC locks up. I've got a Compaq Presario 4400 running Windows 95.*

A.   This is a video driver problem with Presario PCs using an IR remote control port and an internal modem. When you select Start, Programs, and the MS-DOS prompt, the system hangs up. In fact, Compaq says that new serial devices (like a mouse) can make the problem even more pronounced. To clear the problem, you need to use <Ctrl>+<Alt>+<Del> twice to reboot the PC. You should resolve the problem by updating your video driver with a patch from Compaq.

INTRODUCING FAT32

Q870. *When will FAT32 debut? I thought I heard it would be released in the OEM version of Windows 95 only. Why would Microsoft do this?*

A.   FAT32 appeared early in 1997 as part of Microsoft's Service Release 2 (also called OSR2). The release is not yet available commercially. Instead, Microsoft is releasing it through PC vendors who can install OSR2 with new systems. Although I cannot speak for Microsoft, I suspect they made the choice to OEM their OSR2 in order to minimize the number of support calls that would otherwise be generated by the installation and use of OSR2. However, FAT32 has had its share of problems, and as of this writing, FAT32 is not yet stable enough to recommend for all systems. Among the serious limitations of FAT32 is the inability of other operating systems (even older Windows 95) to read FAT32 partitions. All drive-related tools and utilities would also have to be updated for FAT32.

WINDOWS 95 WON'T AUTOSTART SOFTWARE

Q871. *I'm installing some new drivers from CD, and the PC is supposed to reboot and launch a setup utility. Well, the drivers install OK and the system reboots, but the setup utility does not launch automatically. How can I launch the setup utility manually?*

A.   This is a common problem that occurs when the CD autoinsert notification feature under Windows 95 is disabled or does not detect the CD when the system reboots. You can launch the setup utility manually by opening the folder for your CD-ROM and then double-clicking on the setup utility icon.

POOR COLOR SCHEME HIDES TEXT UNDER WINDOWS 95

Q872. *I'm typing text under Windows 95, but I can't see the text in the display unless I highlight it. Do you have any idea what's going on? I can see the text cursor moving.*

A. I haven't heard this one in a while. I'd bet this only happens under Windows, and you're using an unusual or custom color scheme in your display. Check the color scheme selected by right-clicking on the desktop. Click on Properties and then the Appearance tab. Set the scheme to Windows Standard, and click on OK to return to the desktop. The text should now appear normally. This fix can be attempted with any application, as long as the symptoms are similar to yours.

MISSING SHORTCUT ERROR

Q873. *I have a Pentium 133-MHz PC with 32MB of RAM, a 1.6GB HDD, and Windows 95. A couple of days ago, I started getting the following error message: "Missing Shortcut: Windows is searching for the file FAGUARD.EXE. To locate the file your-self, click Browse." After a few seconds, the following appears: "Problem With Shortcut: The file or folder FAGUARD.EXE that this shortcut refers to cannot be found." I've used the Find fea-ture and cannot locate any reference to FAGUARD on my hard drive. I even went to my last tape backup (about 2 weeks old) and still couldn't locate any reference to the missing file. All of the programs on the computer run fine and I've not had any problems previously. Any idea as to what the cause of these error messages could be?*

A. It sounds like you have lost part of a shortcut. Each icon on your desktop corresponds to a brief shortcut designation which allows you to launch an application directly from a desktop icon rather than having to walk through your Start menu. The type of error you're seeing suggests that one or more of your shortcuts may have been lost or corrupted. Also, if you recently erased an unused application (but forgot to delete its shortcut), Windows 95 may simply be indicating that it can no longer use that short-cut—and you should send the dead icon and shortcut to the Recycle Bin. You might also run ScanDisk to check for any cross-linked files. You may find that FAGUARD.EXE may have been corrupted by another file. If so, delete the cross-linked file, defragment the disk, and then reinstall the file from a backup.

IDENTIFYING A MISSING SHORTCUT

Q874.   *A couple of days ago I started getting the following error messages after turning on my computer (a Pentium 133-MHz, 32MB RAM, 1.6GB HDD, Windows 95, and so on):*

"Missing Shortcut: Windows is searching for the file FAGUARD.EXE. To locate the file yourself, click Browse".

After a few seconds, the following appears:

"Problem With Shortcut: The file or folder FAGUARD.EXE that this shortcut refers to cannot be found".

I've used the Find feature and cannot locate any reference to "Faguard" on my hard drive. I even went to my last tape backup (about two weeks old) and still couldn't locate any reference to the missing file. Note that all of the programs on the computer run fine and I've not had any problems previously.

A.   It sounds like you have lost part of a "shortcut". Each icon on your desktop corresponds to a brief shortcut designation which allows you to launch an application directly from a desktop icon rather than having to walk through your Start menu. The type of error you're seeing suggests that one or more of your shortcuts may have been lost or corrupted. Also, if you recently erased an unused application (but forgot to delete its shortcut), Windows 95 may simply be indicating that it can no longer use that shortcut—and you should send the dead icon and shortcut to the Recycle Bin. You might also run ScanDisk to check for any cross-linked files—You may find that FAGUARD.EXE may have been corrupted by another file.

FINDING A LOST TASKBAR

Q875.   *I've lost the Taskbar from my desktop. How can I get it back?*

A.   A nice feature of the Windows 95 Taskbar is that you can move it to any of the four sides of the desktop, and you can also resize it by dragging the border anywhere from half the screen to almost nothing. Curiously, when some people resize it to nothing, they panic and think that their Taskbar has gone completely. Not so—the Taskbar's border will always be there. Look carefully at the edges of the desktop (especially on the side where you last saw your Taskbar). There will be a thin gray line (or whatever color the Taskbar happened to be). This is the Taskbar's border. If you point to the border with the mouse, the mouse cursor will change to a double-pointed arrow . You can then hold the mouse button down and drag the border to resize the Taskbar again.

Shutting Down Windows 95 Without a Mouse

Q876. *I work on a lot of PCs—many have mouse problems with the mouse or the COM or PS/2 port. How can I work in Windows 95 when the mouse won't work?*

A. The first thing you need to know is how to open and close programs and how to shut down Windows. The first keystroke you need to learn is <Ctrl>+<Esc>. This will pop up the Start menu. From there, you can type <R> and then type the filename of the program you want to launch, followed by <Enter>. Otherwise, type <P> to open the Programs submenu. In each menu you can either use the up or down arrows to move to the item you want or can type the first letter of the item. To open the next menu level, either press the right arrow or <Enter>. To back up from a menu, press the left arrow. When you finally reach the program you want to open, press <Enter>.

The fastest way to close a program that's active is to press <Alt>+<F4>. Another way of closing a program is with the Close Program window. Press <Ctrl>+<Alt>+<Delete> (only from in Windows 95 and be sure to only press it *once*) to get to Close Program. Then use the arrow keys to highlight the program you want to close, and press <Alt>+<E> to End it. Note: Two programs (Explorer and Systray) should not be closed in this way—they have special functions in Windows 95. Shut down Windows as follows:

- Press <Ctrl>+<Esc> to open the Start menu.

- Type <U> to get to the Shut Down dialog.

- If you want to go into DOS mode, type <M> at this time.

- Type <Y> to confirm.

An alternate way to shut down Windows is:

- Press <Ctrl>+<Alt>+<Delete> to open the Close Program window.

- Press <Alt>+<S> to Shut Down.

If you want to switch from one program to another without closing the current program, hold down <Alt> or <Shift>+<Alt> and then press <Tab> repeatedly. This will display a gray box containing icons for all the programs that are running, and the selected program will have a box around its icon as well as its name displayed in a box below. Once you have selected the program you want to switch to, let go of the <Alt> key. That should keep you going for a while.

CHANGING RESOLUTION AND COLOR DEPTH UNDER WINDOWS 95

Q877. *I'm kind of new with Windows 95, and I just bought a new system with a high-end video adapter in it. Now that I have this terrific video system, I want to tinker with the resolution and color depth for my 17-in monitor. Can you tell me how to alter the resolution and colors?*

A. You can change your Windows 95 display properties through the Display icon in your Control Panel, but you can also use the steps below:

1. Right-click the mouse button anywhere on the desktop (not over an icon).

2. Choose Properties.

3. Click on the Settings tab.

4. Move the scroll buttons in the Display Area until you have selected the correct resolution.

5. Select the desired color depth in the Color Palette area.

6. Click Apply to apply the changes and OK to close the screen (Fig. 10.1). You may need to reboot your system for the changes to take effect.

7. If you do reboot your system and there is a video problem, start Windows 95 in the Safe Mode and reset the resolution and color depth to lower, less-demanding settings.

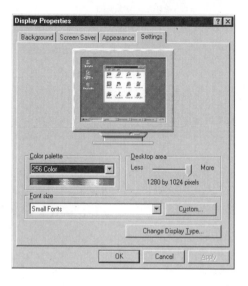

Figure 10.1 Setting the Display Properties

ADDING A SECOND PARALLEL PORT

Q878. *I was told you could add a second parallel port card to a computer running Windows 95, but I was not told how to set it up (configure the second piece of hardware). Any guidance for a novice?*

A. Adding a second LPT port is pretty simple. You'll need an LPT board. If you use a multi-I/O board, you'll need to be sure to disable any of the unused ports on the board (i.e., game port, serial ports, and so on). You can set the parallel port to LPT2 via a jumper on the new board. When Windows 95 starts, it should recognize the new port and adjust its configuration accordingly. If not, you'll need to run the Add New Hardware wizard in your Control Panel.

The only *warning* here is that sound boards use IRQ5—the same IRQ used by LPT2. If you have a sound board in the system, you may need to change the sound board's configuration to an unused IRQ (and update the drivers as well). You may have the most luck removing the sound hardware first and letting Windows 95 recognize that it's gone. Then install your LPT2 and let Windows recognize that. Finally reconfigure and reinstall your sound board, and let Windows 95 recognize that.

Examining Hard Drive Activity

Q879. *My hard drive light goes on and it makes noises when I'm not doing anything. Is this normal? It's a fairly new PC running Windows 95. Sometimes it starts when I'm on-line chatting with someone. Is someone getting into my computer and getting information, or am I just being paranoid? It also happens when I'm in the other room—I'll hear it grinding for no reason.*

A.   That's a great question. Operating systems like Windows 95 rely heavily on the hard drive for virtual memory, which means it will frequently shift programs and data back and forth between the hard drive and system RAM—this is perfectly normal. Windows 95 also uses a *dynamic* swap file for virtual memory, which means that the swap file will grow and shrink as the need for virtual memory changes. This also causes the hard drive to go through spurts of activity—often during idle times. You might notice increased drive activity on-line because your browser tends to cache images and text to the hard drive (this speeds up the apparent operation of the browser). I seriously doubt that anyone is trying to get into your PC.

Perking Up System Performance After a Windows 95 Upgrade

Q880. *I've installed Windows 95 on my brother's PC, and I'm really not too satisfied with the system's performance now. Windows 95 seems to work all right, so I can't pin down any particular symptoms, but are there any ways to perk up the performance?*

A.   There are many issues that effect the performance of Windows 95, and since it is a more demanding operating system, it is natural for some aspects of system operation to appear a bit slower—especially on older 486 systems. Memory is always a big issue for Windows 95. You should really be using 16MB as a minimum, but 32MB of RAM would be a real plus. Additional RAM also reduces dependence on virtual memory (the Windows swap file). Heavy use of virtual memory (with an older, slower hard drive) can seem to slow system performance. You might try disabling virtual memory, running ScanDisk and DEFRAG to check for disk problems, and then restoring virtual memory. There should be at least 50MB of free space on the drive to handle the Windows permanent swap file. Check your cache next. Windows 95 should be using at least 256KB of external (L2) cache. If you have less cache on your motherboard, consider adding more. Finally, video has always been a data bottleneck for Windows and Windows 95. If you're using an ISA video board and your motherboard has advanced busses like VL or PCI, consider adding a VL or PCI graphics accelerator.

BACKING UP WINDOWS 95 REGISTRY FILES

Q881. *I've been told time and again that I should back up my Windows 95 registry files. Is this true? Can you give me a quick and easy procedure for this?*

A. The registry is a vital part of Windows 95, and it may crash or refuse to start entirely if the registry is damaged or corrupted. The registry is *so* important that Windows 95 automatically creates backup registry files each time it starts successfully. However, it is possible that system crashes and glitches may corrupt both the working and automatic backup copies of your registry files. As a result, you should make it a habit to back up your registry files to disk periodically. You can easily back up to disk using the REGEDIT registry editor utility under Windows 95. Click Start and then Run. Type REGEDIT and <Enter>. This will bring you a screen showing My Computer and a number of hot keys. Select My Computer and then Registry. Then select Export Registry File. I always back up to the desktop (by default). The file *must* have a .TXT extension (i.e., REGBAKUP.TXT). This backup will then appear as an icon on the desktop—and perhaps remind you to do it regularly.

ADVANCED

From there, you can easily copy the backup to floppy disk. Keep in mind that your registry is a dynamic file. It changes often and can easily become quite large. If your backup is too large to fit on a single floppy disk, you can compress the file (using PKZIP or WinZIP) and then copy the file to diskette. If disaster strikes, boot into DOS mode (<F8> or emergency boot disk) and type REGED-IT REGBAKUP.TXT. This will restore the registry to the most recent backup state. Keep in mind that you may need to decompress the floppy file back to your hard drive before restoring.

DirectX Applications Causing Performance Problems

Q882.   *Maybe you can help me with this. I have several DirectX applications installed on my Windows 95 system now. When they are run individually, they all work properly. But when I try to run more than one DirectX application at the same time, my system performance seems to slow down noticeably. Can you give me any advice?*

A.   This is generally a problem with Windows 95—the DirectDraw API simply wasn't designed to run more than one DirectX application at a time, and this can cause Windows 95 to behave unpredictably. As a rule, you should only run one DirectX application at any given time.

CD-ROM Drive Refuses to Play Audio Under Windows 95

Q883.   *I just got a good price on an Acer 525E CD-ROM drive, and it installed with trouble on my Windows 95 PC. The problem is that I can't play any CD audio. I know the cables and interface are good because I tried another CD-ROM (a Mitsumi drive), which did work. I can use data disks without any difficulty—it's just a problem with CD audio. Any suggestions?*

A.   The Acer 525E 2X CD-ROM drive is incompatible with Windows 95, and audio from the CD will be muted. Fortunately, this does not affect data CDs, and the problem does not appear under Windows 3.1x. All of the current Acer CD-ROM drives

(743E, 747E, 645A, 655A, and 665A) are tested to work with Windows 95. You can either live with the loss of CD audio or replace the CD-ROM drive with another more recent model.

No Sound in Windows 95

Q884. *This is driving me crazy. I can't hear sound under Windows 95. Can you give me some pointers on what to look for?*

A.   In most cases, sound problems are the result of hardware configuration problems or driver conflicts. You don't say whether your sound card was ever working or if you have just installed it or have installed other hardware or software which may have precipitated the problem. So I'll just cover everything. If the sound card had been working, check the sound board's mixer application under Windows 95 in the Programs menu (virtually all Windows 95 sound boards have them). Make sure that the master volume for your sound card is up at a reasonable level. If you have separate controls for other inputs (i.e., CD audio, mic inputs, and so on), those inputs should also be set adequately. Check the sound board's master volume control on the sound board itself. Also check your speakers. They must be turned on and properly connected to the sound board (you wouldn't be the first person to accidentally yank out a speaker cable kicking your feet behind a desk). Speaker volume must also be set adequately. You might try a set of headphones or alternate speakers just as a test.

Next, the correct drivers for your sound card must also be installed. Open the System icon in your Control Panel. Click on the Device Manger button. Double click on the Sound, Video, and Game Controllers entry. The drivers that are listed should be appropriate for your sound card. Otherwise, you should remove those drivers and install the correct drivers. Always make sure that you are using the latest drivers for your sound board.

Could you have recently installed hardware or software that might be conflicting with the sound setup? If you lost your sound after installing new hardware or software, you might try removing that hardware of software or reconfiguring it so that it will not conflict. If you just installed the sound board, it may be that the sound board is conflicting with other devices in the system. Check and correct the sound board's configuration. Here's another wrinkle if you have a sound system integrated into your motherboard. Check the CMOS Setup and make sure that any references to your sound system are set to Auto or Enabled.

Exception Error Caused by Corrupt Registry

Q885. *I'm getting this "blue screen" error message at various times: "An exception has occurred at 0028:C10602AB in VxD ESDI_506(01)+00000D4F. This was called from 0028:C117CE70 in VxD SCSILP(03)+ 00000678. It may be possible to continue. Press any key to continue." I can't seem to stop this problem from cropping up. Any ideas would be appreciated.*

A. I just saw the same kind of problem on another system. It turned out to be a corrupt registry. You will need to restore the SYS-TEM.DAT and USER.DAT registry files from a backup or Windows start-up disk that was made before the problem started. Before actually attempting the registry restore, you may want to run ScanDisk to check for any disk file damage, and then run DEFRAG to decompress your hard drive. Once the hard drive checks properly, you can proceed with restoring the registry.

Note

Working with the Windows 95 registry always carries some element of risk. Incorrect or obsolete registry files may cause newly installed hardware or software to be ignored or may prevent the Windows 95 platform from booting at all.

Handling a Divide By 0 Error

Q886. *Every time I shut down my computer, I get an error message that says; "Integer Error Divide by 0". Can you tell me what this means?*

A. A divide by 0 error is a software problem. The CPU is trying to execute a mathematical computation that cannot be done, and it hangs up the system. Try starting Windows 95 in the Safe Mode and see if the problem remains. If not, you probably have a corrupt driver somewhere in the system. If you still have a problem, one of your core Windows programs may be defective. If newly installed software started the problem, try disabling or uninstalling the software. Try running CHKDSK to find any cross-linked files. If cross-linked files are part of the Windows system, that's probably your problem. Try erasing the offending files from DOS, defragment the disk, and then reinstall them from the Windows 95 installation CD.

Device Drivers

VIDEO DRIVERS WON'T LOAD WITH WINDOWS 95 OSR2

Q887. *I'm installing one of those STB TV Pro video boards on my system, and I get an error saying the drivers cannot be found. But I've installed this board on another Windows 95 system without problems. The only difference I can think of is that my target system is using the OSR2 version of Windows 95. Could that be the problem?*

A.   Yes, that is very likely to be your problem, but the fix is really quite simple. When the Setup Wizard requests new drivers, the OSR2 version of Windows 95 automatically looks in the directory from which Windows was originally installed. Obviously, the new drivers are not there but rather on a disk or CD accompanying the new product. All you need to do is to change the default driver installation directory to the root directory for the STB TV Pro. For example, make sure the directory is D:\ instead of D:\WIN95\SETUP.

FINDING REVEAL DRIVERS

Q888. *Can you help me with Windows 95 drivers for Reveal SC400 products? They have gone bust, and the only Web site I can find is asking for credit card numbers for supplying drivers.*

A. If I'm not mistaken, the SC400 sound card works using the Aztec Sound Galaxy Nova 16 drivers included with Windows 95 (except for the 4r). If you can't get the drivers from your Windows 95 installation CD, you might try the drivers for the SC400 4G available at the OPTi FTP site (*ftp://ftp.opti.com/pub/multimed/*). The drivers for the OPTi 82C929 are the ones needed. Look for the file 929W95.EXE. You might also try the German site at *http://www.vobis.de/bbs/firmen/reveal.*

Dealing with Obsolete Drivers

Q889. *I've been thinking about upgrading my video board, but I friend of mine who's done it says that you also need to get rid of the old drivers—and that can be a pain. Is this true with Windows 95? How can I get rid of the old drivers?*

A. Old drivers can be a pain, but Windows 95 usually deals with them automatically. When a new PnP video board is installed, Windows 95 will detect it automatically and try to install the appropriate new drivers (disabling and removing the old drivers in the process). In this case, you really don't need to deal with the old drivers. However, if the new video board is *not* PnP (and Windows 95 is unable to detect it), you may have to specifically tell Windows 95 what's going on. With the *original* video board still installed, look for any uninstall utilities for your video board. If you have the original driver disks (or CD), run the installation and select uninstall if you can. After the drivers are gone, you can shut down and replace the video board. If you cannot uninstall the original video drivers automatically, you can highlight the video system under your Device Manager, and click the Remove button.

Protected-Mode ASPI Drivers Won't Load

Q890. *I can get my real-mode ASPI drivers to load, but the protected-mode ASPI drivers will not load at all. What's wrong here?*

A.   Since real-mode drivers are loading properly, we can assume that the SCSI hardware is working correctly. Make sure that the resources for the protected-mode driver under the Device Manager are set exactly the same as the card (you may have to change the driver settings to match the card). Also check the Performance tab under System Properties to see if the system is infected with a virus. Windows 95 will not load any protected-mode drivers if the system is infected. Finally, make sure that the latest version of protected-mode ASPI drivers are being used.

DISABLING PROTECTED-MODE DRIVERS HIDES PARTITIONS

Q891.   *I recently upgraded my hard drive system, and during the upgrade, I disabled my protected-mode disk drivers. The problem is that now when I run FDISK, it hides the partition table. What's going on here? How do I get my partition table back?*

A.   This is almost always a problem with your BIOS version. The best answer is to check with your system manufacturer and see if there is a BIOS upgrade available that would resolve that problem. In the mean time, do *not* use the Disable all 32-bit protected-mode disk drivers option under Windows 95.

DISABLING PROTECTED-MODE DISK DRIVERS HIDES PARTITION TABLE

Q892.   *I ran the FDISK utility through a DOS session under Windows 95, but I don't see the partitions that I created. Any ideas?*

A.   This is a known problem which can occur if your computer has a Phoenix BIOS Plus version 0.10 GLB01, and if you have selected the Disable all 32-bit protected-mode disk drivers option on the Troubleshooting tab in System Properties. You can correct this problem by upgrading the computer's BIOS or leaving the Disable all 32-bit protected-mode disk drivers option unselected.

Checking the SCSI Driver in Windows 95

Q893.   *I can't get my new SCSI hard drive to work under Windows 95.*
When I look at the Device Manager, I see a yellow exclamation
mark over the SCSI adapter entry. What does this mean, and
what can I do about it?

A.   The yellow exclamation mark generally means that there is a
problem in loading the corresponding device driver—often
because of a problem such as a hardware conflict or failure.
Check the SCSI adapter and make sure that there are no hardware
conflicts with other devices in the system. You might want to try
the SCSI adapter at other resource settings. Also check the device
driver references and see if you missed any important command
line switches. Try a new SCSI adapter in the system. If a new
adapter works, the old SCSI adapter is defective. Also check that
you are using the latest version of the SCSI host driver.

Getting Out of Compatibility Mode

Q894.   *When Windows 95 starts, it says that I'm operating in DOS*
compatibility mode. What does this mean, and how do I stop it?

A.   This is not necessarily an error message. The DOS compatibility
mode is invoked by Windows 95 whenever the system loads a
real-mode driver. This would happen quite normally when
Windows 95 does not have an equivalent 32-bit protected-mode
driver to replace the existing real-mode driver. Click on the
Performance tab under the System icon for details about what
devices are affected when there is a real-mode device driver at
work. Highlight the message in the details box and click the
Details button for information on that particular issue.

The way to escape the DOS compatibility mode is to replace all
of the real-mode drivers with protected-mode drivers. The first
places to check for questionable real-mode drivers are your
CONFIG.SYS and AUTOEXEC.BAT files. Once you isolate the
offending driver(s), you can contact the driver maker(s) or visit
their Web sites to obtain the latest protected-mode driver(s).

HARD DRIVES AND COMPATIBILITY MODE

Q895. *I have a generic clone PC, and I noticed that the hard drive is running in compatibility mode under Windows 95. Can you tell me what the problem is and how to fix it?*

A. Windows 95 may use its DOS compatibility mode on large EIDE hard disks (hard disks with more than 1024 cylinders) in some computers. This situation may occur because of invalid drive geometry translation in the system ROM BIOS that prevents the protected-mode IDE device driver from being loaded. In most cases, an updated BIOS will correct the problem. Check with your system manufacturer (or a third-party BIOS maker) for a BIOS update or flash file.

NEW EIDE DRIVE IN COMPATIBILITY MODE

Q896. *Here's a real confusing problem. I've had my Windows 95 system working properly for months now—it had a 1.6GB HDD in it. Recently, I removed the 1.6GB HDD and installed a brand new 3.2GB HDD and EIDE controller. There were no installation problems, but now Windows 95 says that the new EIDE hard drive is running in DOS compatibility mode. Why is this, and how can I fix the problem?*

A. The bottom line here is that Windows 95 does not have a protected-mode driver that is suitable for your new hard drive controller. The IOS.INI file (located in the \Windows directory) contains a list of device drivers that Windows 95 can safely remove from the CONFIG.SYS file and replace with its own protected-mode device driver (usually a .PDR file). If the real-mode device driver name is not present in the IOS.INI file, Windows 95 will continue to use the real-mode device driver in CONFIG.SYS, and the devices attached to the controller will operate in compatibility mode. Unfortunately, if you simply add the name of the real-mode device driver for the EIDE controller to the IOS.INI file, you may risk data loss, data corruption, and performance degradation.

Another issue to consider is that a Windows 95 protected-mode EIDE driver needs to use the Int 13 hardware interface to communicate with the drive controller. If another device driver is intercepting these calls, the Windows 95 protected-mode driver will not be able to communicate directly with the device. As a result, all devices attached to the controller will use the compatibility mode.

It is also possible that a virus may be interfering with protected-mode support. If a virus is present on the system or in its master boot record (MBR), Windows 95 will receive incorrect information about the EIDE controller and the device(s) connected to it and will fail to load the protected-mode device driver. Run a virus detector to clean the system. If your MBR is not infected by any viruses, it is possible that the manufacturer of the EIDE controller has updated drivers for 32-bit disk access.

Finally, your EIDE controller itself may be causing the compatibility issue. If it is possible to select different modes of operation (i.e., normal, fast, turbo, etc.), you may be able to correct the problem by setting the controller to a different mode. If problems continue, you might consider using a different EIDE controller.

CD-ROM Message Indicates Real-Mode Drivers

Q897.   *A message appears when booting Windows 95 stating that my CD-ROM can run but results may not be as expected. What is wrong?*

A.   Nothing is "wrong," although the system is not running in an optimum fashion. This is just a warning message that means that you are using real-mode (DOS) drivers instead of protected-mode (Windows 95) drivers. If protected-mode drivers are available for the CD-ROM's interface, these should be used instead to ensure peak performance from your CD-ROM subsystem.

Windows 95 and 32-bit Disk Access

Q898.   *No matter what I do, I just cannot get 32-bit disk access on my 1.0GB HDD running under Windows 95. What am I missing?*

A.   Chances are that you're using a plug-in drive controller with a
        drive controller disabled on the motherboard as well. Check the
        motherboard drive controller settings in CMOS to see that the
        motherboard is not using LBA settings (also confirm the mother-
        board controller is indeed completely disabled). Check the drive
        controller BIOS setup next and see that LBA is enabled. The bot-
        tom line here is that only *one* drive controller should be set to
        use LBA. Finally, don't forget to check for any obsolete 32-bit
        drivers which may no longer be needed and could be deleted
        from the SYSTEM.INI file.

INSTALLING A JOYSTICK DRIVER IN WINDOWS 95

Q899.   *How do I install my joystick driver in Windows 95?*

A.   Use the following process to install a joystick under Windows 95:

1.   Click Start, Control Panel, and Add New Hardware.

2.   Click Next.

3.   When asked if you want Windows to search for new hard-
        ware, select No. Then click Next.

4.   From the list of hardware, select Sound, Video, and Game
        Controller, and then click Next.

5.   From the list of manufacturers, select the corresponding
        manufacturer.

6.   From the Models list, select Gameport Joystick, and then
        click Next.

7.   Click Next on the Properties screen.

8.   If prompted, provide the path to the Windows 95 CD-
        ROM or floppies.

9.   Click Finish.

10   You may be asked to restart Windows 95 for changes to
        take effect.

Note

Go to Control Panel and then Joystick. You should be able to calibrate the Joystick at this point.

WINDOWS CONTINUES TO DETECT DISABLED HARDWARE

Q900. *I have turned off my integrated PCI Ethernet Adapter in my PC's CMOS Setup utility, but every time I run Windows 95, it turns the adapter back on. What do I do?*

A. You'll need to make some changes to the device configuration under Windows 95. Start your Device Manager, locate the entry for your network card, remove the checkmark on Use Original Configuration, and save your changes. During reboot, enter <F10> to start the CMOS Setup and disable the PCI Ethernet Adapter again. Save your changes and reboot again. The following reboot should bring up Windows 95 without the PCI Ethernet Adapter.

SUDDEN DRIVER CONFLICT DISRUPTING WINDOWS 95

Q901. *A conflict has developed out of nowhere between a Windows 95 file and the sound driver (MVIWAVE.DRV). This causes Windows 95 not to load. When I remove the MVIWAVE.DRV file, Windows 95 works OK, but there is no sound. The specific error is "MGR32.EXE has caused a general protection fault due to conflicts with MVIWAVE.DRV at xxxxxx."*

A. It is very rare that conflicts should crop up between software for no reason. First, restore your MVIWAVE.DRV file and try starting Windows 95 in the Safe Mode. If the problem disappears in the Safe Mode, you have a software issue. Otherwise, you probably have a problem with your sound board. If you determine the problem to be software-related, run ScanDisk to check for any cross-linked files that may have corrupted your .EXE or .DRV files. If you find cross-linking or lost allocation units, go to DOS, delete any indicated files, defragment the disk, and then restore the files you deleted. When you restart Windows 95, the error should be gone. If there are no disk problems, you probably have a corrupted registry. Restore backups of your SYSTEM.DAT and USER.DAT from a recent backup of the Windows start-up disk. If that fails, you will need to reinstall Windows 95 from scratch.

HANDLING SOUND DRIVER CONFLICTS

Q902. *I have a Yellow exclamation mark on my Multimedia Sound driver in the Device Manager. How can I eliminate this ?*

A.   Chances are that you've got a resource conflict with the system sound board. You'll need to check the Device Manager to isolate the problem:

1.   Go to Control Panel, System, and Device Manager.

2.   Highlight the device that has the yellow exclamation mark.

3.   Click on Properties and then Resources.

4.   Uncheck Use automatic settings if it is checked.

5.   Highlight each device IRQ, DMA, I/O address until you find the one that shows a conflict in the conflicting device list.

6.   Double-click the device that has the conflict.

7.   Then adjust the value to a free resource.

8.   Click OK.

9.   Restart the system if necessary.

INTERMEDIATE

Disk Utilities and Applets

THIRD-PARTY TOOLS AND WINDOWS 95

Q903. *I often use system tools like Norton Utilities, but now that I bought a new Windows 95 PC, can I use the same tools under Windows 95?*

A.   Ideally, the answer to your question is Yes. However, you should avoid using the Windows 3.1x versions of those tools because they do not support the added desktop and file features found with Windows 95 (such as long file names). Get the Windows 95 versions of those tools you plan to use. Remember that most software makers offer very reasonable competitive upgrades for their older software packages.

THE BEST SCANNING AND DEFRAGMENTING

Q904.   *What is the best procedure for scanning and defragmenting using Norton Utilities? Should I scan first using the Disk Doctor and then defragment with the Speed Disk, or the other way around? Will this do any harm to my computer?*

A.   Generally speaking, you should check the disk first using ScanDisk, and then defragment. This allows you to recover any lost allocation units and correct any cross-linked files before reorganizing the clusters with DEFRAG. Of course, you could also use third-party tools such as those included with Norton Utilities.

THE SAFETY OF DRIVE DEFRAGMENTING

Q905.   *Is it safe to defragment a hard drive? What is the likelihood of a mishap? I have a 1.2GB hard drive with a little over 200MB free, so there's a lot I just can't afford to lose.*

A.   One of the most important rules of computing is to always *back up* whatever you cannot afford to lose. Don't ever trust in any utility to be flawless, even a utility as tried and true as DEFRAG. The answer to your question is Yes, it is safe to use DEFRAG, but you should use the version of DEFRAG that accompanies your primary operating system. For example, if you run Windows 3.1x, you should use the DOS version of DEFRAG that comes with DOS 6.22. If you run Windows 95, you should use the Windows 95 version of DEFRAG found in your Programs, Accessories, System Tools folder. When you start DEFRAG, it will report the percentage of file fragmentation. Don't bother defragmenting a disk with less than 10 percent fragmentation. From 10 to 20 percent, it's more of a judgment call. Above 20 percent, you'll probably notice a loss of performance due to file fragmentation.

ALLOWABLE FILE FRAGMENTATION

Q906. *Depending on how much free space you have on your hard drive, at what percentage of fragmentation would you see an increase in performance after defragging?*

A.   I have always used a 10 percent rule. If more than 10 percent of the files are fragmented, I'll take a few minutes to defrag. I see very little performance change after defragmenting at this level because I don't let the drive get fragmented enough to really hurt performance in the first place. However, I would not recommend allowing over 20 percent fragmentation.

WHEN TO DEFRAGMENT AND RUNNING .ZIP FILES

Q907. *I find myself defragmenting a lot. I use Windows 95, and it tells me that my hard drive is fragmented between 2 to 5 percent, and that I don't have to defragment yet, but I can if I want. I go ahead and defragment, then 2 days later, I have a 2 to 5 percent fragmented hard drive again. What wrong? I also downloaded a shareware video game from the Internet (it's a .ZIP file). I can't get it to run. Someone told me I have to unzip it. I don't know what to do. Can you help?*

A.   Let's look at both of your questions. First, don't worry about 2 to 5 percent fragmentation. It is a natural (but undesired) side effect of DOS which allows the various clusters containing a file to become scattered around a drive as space is used and freed again. You will start to notice a problem when the drive reaches 20 percent or higher fragmentation. There should be no need to defragment a drive every day unless you are working with some huge files.

INTERMEDIATE

As for your game question, you will need a decompression utility such as PKUNZIP.EXE to unzip the file. You can get a copy of PKUNZIP from many different on-line sources. Create a directory for the game and copy the .ZIP file there. Copy PKUNZIP to that same directory. Run PKUNZIP such as PKUNZIP [filename], where [filename] is the name of your game's .ZIP file. That should decompress the .ZIP file into its constituent files, and you can proceed to install or run the game as appropriate.

Halting a RAM Doubler

Q908. *I'm working on a customer's PC with RAM Doubler on it, and I'd like to disable RAM Doubler to perform some tests. How can I stop RAM Doubler from loading without removing the software (which I'd not be able to reinstall)?*

A.   According to my information, you can simply hold down the <Esc> key as Windows begins to load. Let go of the key when you hear a beep, and you'll see the message "RAM Doubler load canceled by user request." If that process doesn't work for you, check your product documentation for the specific key sequence.

AMIDiag Can't Work with VESA Video

Q909. *My question is about running AMIDiag 5.0 system diagnostics software. I have a Cyrix 5x86 computer system running Windows 95. Every time I try to initialize the AMI software (installed on hard drive from floppy disk, the initialization freezes at the screen "INITILIZING VESA VIDEO." My system has to be rebooted. I tried running the software on another computer, and it loaded without a problem. I called AMI, and they say I have a bad video card or driver. I have had no problem with my video display with any other program, and I have also run AMIDiag 4.0 on this system with no errors.*

A.   It seems that AMIDiag 5.0 is attempting to test your video board for VESA compatibility, and the board is not responding—thus you're getting the system crash. Do you use DOS programs that need a separate VESA driver (like UNIVESA) to be loaded first?

If so, you may need to load that driver before running AMIDiag. If not (i.e., the VESA mode is built into the video card), the card may be using an older implementation of the VESA standard. The reason AMIDiag works under Windows is because Windows uses video and video drivers differently than DOS does. I think AMI is essentially correct. AMIDiag 5 doesn't "like" your video board. The board itself is probably not defective in the classic sense, but AMIDiag is not seeing the response it expects from your video hardware in VESA mode.

Replacing the video board with a newer model would probably clear the problem but may not be necessary if the board is clearly operational. Check your AMIDiag installation for any sort of an INI or configuration file—even command line switches that you can use to force AMIDiag to skip the VESA test. If you find any, the problem will probably go away.

RUNNING ICU UNDER WINDOWS 95

Q910.   *I installed a new PnP board, but part of the installation required me to install what they call an ICU in CONFIG.SYS. But now I'm having trouble with Windows 95 crashing. Can you point me in the right direction?*

A.   As you probably suspect, the ISA Configuration Utility (ICU) is the cause of your problem. An ICU (such as the DWCFGMG.SYS file) is used to provide plug-and-play capability under DOS and Windows 3.1x. It should *not* be used with Windows 95 and will actually conflict with Windows 95's configuration manager. Disable the ICU and let Windows 95 find and allocate resources for your PnP device. If you run under DOS, use a boot disk configured with the ICU, or place the ICU reference in the DOSSTART.BAT file to run it when the PC exits Windows 95 to DOS.

NEW INSTALLATION CAUSES ERROR LOADING FROM FILE MESSAGE

Q911.   *I just installed a new device under Windows 95, but now I get an error message that says "Error Loading From File." What does this mean, and how can I fix it?*

A. Since you don't say just *which* device you installed, I'll have to give you the generic answer. In virtually all cases, the drivers accompanying your new device were installed incorrectly. To fix the problem, right-click on My Computer and select the Device Manager page. Look down the list for your device entry (you may need to expand parts of the device tree to find it). Your new device probably has a yellow question mark in front of it. Select your new device entry and hit the Remove button and then select OK to remove that device. Next, hit the Refresh button, and Windows 95 will bring up the New Hardware Found window. Select the option Driver from disk provided by hardware manufacturer and then enter the drive letter and path to your new drivers. The Selected Device window should then list your new device, and you should click OK. If an Insert Disk window comes up, just click OK and reenter your CD ROM drive letter. Windows 95 will then install the drivers and probably prompt you to reboot your system.

TROUBLE WITH WINDOWS 95 FDISK

Q912. *I have been planning a second hard drive for my Windows 95 system, but I have heard that there have been some problems with the Windows 95 version of FDISK. Is this true? If so, how can I get around it?*

A. You are correct. There have been some problems reported with early versions of Windows 95's FDISK. Specifically, when FDISK creates a second partition, it partially overwrites the first partition. Things are fine until you attempt to do file transfers to the second partition—some data on the first partition gets overwritten, and you end up with corrupted data. Also, there have been instances reported where FDISK creates mirror partitions. These are phantom partitions that reflect exactly what's in the original partition, but they show up as a different drive letter. Use the version of FDISK that ships with DOS 6.2x to partition your hard drives.

FDISK PROBLEMS WITH WINDOWS 95

Q913. *I've just installed a 2.5-in Western Digital AL2540 HDD in a 486. I am running it as a slave on the primary EIDE channel with the original HDD as a boot drive. The secondary IDE controller has a CD-ROM on it. My problem is that Windows 95 is reporting two copies of the new drive. Have you seen this problem? How do I fix it?*

A.   I have seen this problem with the original release of FDISK for Windows 95. If you partitioned the second drive from Windows 95, a fault with FDISK may be responsible. Go into your Control Panel and then select your System icon. Click the Device Manager tab. Under the Disk Drives entry, make sure you only have the two existing drives listed. If there are more listed, highlight and remove them. You should only have your master, slave, and CD-ROM drives listed. As an alternative, you can try running the Windows 95 FDISK with the /X switch, which disables extended FDISK features. You can also delete the new partitions and run DOS 6.22 FDISK from the DOS mode.

According to my information, Microsoft should have fixed the FDISK problem in their OSR2 release of Windows 95.

Note

PLUGGING A MEMORY LEAK

Q914. *I was in Netscape 2.01 using Trumpet Winsock 3.0 to make a PPP connection. Afterward, I exited Netscape and closed down Trumpet Winsock (my modem was disconnected). Later I went into Microsoft Tools and ran the virus checker. When I selected C:\ to scan I had a Not enough memory to scan C:\ error. My system is a 486DX2/50 with 24MB of RAM. How could this problem occur?*

A.   It sounds like you have either of two problems in your system: a memory leak or virus infiltration. Start by checking for viruses using a current antivirus tool on a bootable write-protected floppy disk from DOS. If the system checks clean, you should suspect a memory leak under Windows. A memory leak occurs when a

Windows program is assigned memory when the program is loaded but won't release the memory after the program terminates. This is usually due to a bug in the program. Check for memory leaks by starting Windows and examining your system resources (especially the free memory). Run Netscape and Trumpet Winsock normally and then exit and check your system resources again. Ideally, you should have the same amount of free memory as when you started. If you have measurably less, one of your applications is refusing to release its memory. Try installing updated versions of Netscape and Trumpet Winsock.

Virus Protection

CURING THE LAROUX MACRO VIRUS

Q915.   *Do you know where to get the add-on for combating the Laroux virus for Excel 7 with Windows 95?*

A.   Go to *www.microsoft.com/excel/productinfo/vbavirus/add_in.htm* and you will find the add-on available for download.

ANTIVIRUS SOFTWARE KEEPING FLOPPY DRIVE LIGHT ON

Q916.   *I've got a problem with my floppy drive. I installed VirusScan for Windows 95 from McAfee and Associates, but now the floppy drive light stays on all the time, or until I quit to DOS. I can't seem to find any configuration options to shut the floppy drive off. What's happening, and is there anything I can do about it?*

A.   McAfee's software can be set to continuously check your drives. Unfortunately, this includes the floppy drive as well. You will need to reconfigure VirusScan for Windows 95 using the following steps:

1.   Click on Start and Programs.

2.   Scroll to and highlight the McAfee VirusScan95 group folder.

3.   Click the VShield Configuration Manager program icon.

4. Click the Detection tab.

5. Under the Scan Disks On... section, clear the check boxes on Access & Shutdown.

6. Click on the OK button.

This should stop the continuous checking of your drives (and will probably enhance system performance too).

FILE EXTRACTION PROBLEMS POSSIBLY RELATED TO VIRUS SOFTWARE

Q917. *I have a problem with a new PC build that is probably software related, but I thought I would cover all the bases. When I extract .ZIP files (and particularly self-extracting .EXE files), they become corrupted even though they extract successfully. This is a Windows 95 setup with Norton Anti-Virus, and it is the anti-virus program that I suspect to be responsible. There are no other problems with the PC.*

A. I've never actually experienced this effect myself, but I have heard reports that Windows 95 and anti-virus software can sometimes have some unexpected results. Of course, the way to test the problem is to disable Norton Anti-Virus and see if the problem disappears. If so, you should contact Symantec for an update (*www.symantec.com*).

WINDOWS 95 ERRORS GETTING PROGRESSIVELY WORSE

Q918. *I have had problems lately with a 486DX4/100 running Windows 95, which suggests a possible infection of my system (although McAfee and Norton both say there is no virus present in the system). My last encounter occurred during the last week of October, and 1 month later it is back. Everything was working well, and then slowly over a period of about 2 days the error messages increased until eventually the system would not load without crashing. An attempted reinstall of Windows 95 from the CD caused a system crash about 80 percent of the way through, which resulted in my reformatting the C: drive. After a reinstallation of Windows and other programs, the system worked properly until now. I have begun to get the error messages again at an alarming rate. The only things which I have on the C: drive are programs which are easily recovered. Any files which I would like to keep are on the D: drive, but I fear transferring them to disk if a virus does exist in the computer and infected the boot sector of the disk. Any ideas?*

A.   It seems like only your C: drive has been affected by problems. My first suggestion is to get the very latest virus update for your antivirus utility and try running the utility from a "clean" write-protected bootable disk. Check your C: and D: drives. I have a feeling that both drives will check clean. Instead, I think it's more likely that your C: drive is faulty. The mention that you were not able to reinstall Windows 95 until the disk was reformatted probably means that you've got bad clusters multiplying like rabbits. You can try running ScanDisk (for DOS) first to see just how bad the media is. Try a new C: drive. I'd bet that your problem will go away.

DEALING WITH AN MBR VIRUS

Q919.   *While installing Windows 95 on a machine, I discovered that it had a virus resident in the MBR. Since McAfee Virus Scan couldn't clean the virus, I decided to try removing all partitions and repartitioning the drive in hopes that it would get rid of the virus, but of course, it didn't. Is there any way to clean a virus from the MBR without doing a low-level format or similar?*

A.   There are three rules when dealing with virus eradication: use a virus-free, write-protected floppy disk to boot the system, always use the *latest* version of your antivirus tool, and always make a complete backup of your files before proceeding (even an infected backup is better than none). Boot the system from your clean, write-protected boot disk and run FDISK /MBR. This should rewrite the master boot record in the system and eliminate the virus. This is not a cure-all, and in some cases you're going to find this leaves you with a blank drive (but at least you've got your backup). After the MBR is rewritten, start the CMOS Setup routine and look for a Boot Sector Write Protect feature. If you find such a feature, enable it. If you prefer to avoid using FDISK /MBR, select a virus tool that *will* clean the MBR automatically.

Installation Issues

VxD Error When Installing Windows 95

Q920. *I have an Intel Advanced/MN motherboard with 1.00.01.BT0 BIOS, and it has been working with Windows 3.11. However, when I try to load Windows 95 as the operating system, the PC completes the installation, only to give me a VxD error which always refers to C000. I have tried to reinstall Windows 95 repeatedly, and each time the problem returns. Can you help me?*

A. According to my information, the Intel Morrison motherboard has problems with Windows 95 when older BIOS revisions are used. The current Advanced/MN BIOS is 1.00.09.BT0, so your version may simply be too old to support Windows 95 properly. You can get the flash BIOS file from *ftp://ftp.intel.com/pub/bios*.

BIOS Upgrade Requires BIOS.VXD

Q921. *I've just upgraded my BIOS with a PnP BIOS, but now I'm getting a BIOS.VXD Error message from Windows 95. What can I do about this?*

A. After installing a plug-and-play BIOS upgrade, Windows 95 will need to make some adjustments. It may be necessary to tell Windows 95 to detect new hardware by choosing Control Panel, Add New Hardware. This will cause Windows 95 to become aware of the PnP BIOS, which may cause Windows 95 to demand an additional file, BIOS.VXD. Windows 95 will usually ask for the installation CD-ROM or disk to be inserted so that it can copy this file to the hard drive. Windows 95 is sometimes not able to locate the file. This may be due to a bug in Windows 95, or it may be caused by using a different media or version of Windows 95 than what was used during the original installation.

The BIOS.VXD file is contained within a CAB (cabinet) file on the Windows 95 CD-ROM or disk, but different versions of Windows 95 may place the file in different places. Table 10.1 lists some typical locations of the BIOS.VXD file. Here is the command to extract the file and place it in the proper directory:

```
EXTRACT /L C:\WINDOWS\SYSTEM\VMM32 D:\WIN95\WIN95_09.CAB
BIOS.VXD
```

This command would be adjusted according to the source and destination of this file. The example assumes a CD-ROM drive on D:, the BIOS.VXD file in WIN95_09.CAB, and Windows 95 installed to C:\WINDOWS. On the disk versions of Windows 95, the CAB files are not in subdirectories, so the above example would be adjusted to

```
EXTRACT /L C:\WINDOWS\SYSTEM\VMM32 A:\WIN95_10.CAB
BIOS.VXD
```

TABLE 10.1 TYPICAL LOCATIONS OF BIOS.VXD FILES

Retail upgrade CD-ROM	WIN95_09.CAB
OEM CD-ROM	WIN95_09.CAB
Full version on disk	WIN95_10.CAB (Disk 10)
Retail upgrade from Gateway 2000	WIN95_15.CAB

WINDOWS 95 WON'T INSTALL TO A HARD DRIVE

Q922. *Windows 95 will not install to my SCSI hard drive. I get an error saying Windows 95 Setup cannot find any SCSI devices. How do I get Windows 95 to install?*

A.   I don't think that this is a SCSI issue since the drive apparently works. Check the CMOS Setup and look for the Boot Sector Virus Protection entry. If the boot sector protection is enabled, *disable* this before starting the installation. Also disable any power management features during installation. After successfully installing Windows 95, you may reenable both features.

Installing Windows 95 with Disk Manager

Q923. *While installing Windows 95, Disk Manager was not able to complete the installation of DDO 6.03d. In the manual mode of the older Disk Manager version (DM /m), I discovered the problem was caused when the system file IO.SYS was copied to hard disk. What should I do about this?*

A. The Windows 95 version of IO.SYS is too large for Disk Manager 6.03d to handle, so you will have trouble installing Windows 95. Therefore, use a DOS boot disk when Disk Manager prompts for a systems disk. Then to install Window 95, reboot and let the DDO load, hit the Space bar to halt the boot, insert the Windows 95 disk, and proceed to install the rest of Windows 95.

Copying Your Windows 95 Platform

Q924. *I want to upgrade my existing 850MB HDD by replacing it with a 4.0GB Maxtor drive, and I want the new drive to be the only drive in the system. The problem is that I need to transfer my Windows 95 files over to the new drive. My friends have told me that it's a real pain to transfer an established Windows 95 platform to a new hard drive. How can I do this? There has to be a way.*

A. You're right. There is a way to accomplish a complete Windows 95 transfer. In fact, this is one of the most frequent questions that I ever receive. The procedure below outlines a method for copying files over to a new drive and then making the new drive your primary (master) drive. Keep in mind that this process may not work on all PC platforms, and you should perform a *complete* system backup before proceeding.

- Install your new drive as the secondary drive in your system (remember to jumper the hard drives and set up your CMOS parameters accordingly).

- Use FDISK and FORMAT to prepare the new drive. When partitioning, do not make the primary partition active just yet.

INTERMEDIATE

■ Create a boot disk (a rescue disk) by selecting My Computer, Control Panel, and Add/Remove Programs, then click the Startup Disk tab, select Create Disk, and follow the instructions.

■ Use the SYS command to transfer system files to the new drive. Open a DOS window and type

```
sys d:
```

■ Close the DOS window and double-click on My Computer again.

■ Double-click on Control Panel and then System.

■ Click on the Performance tab and Virtual Memory button and select "Let me specify my own system memory setting" to disable virtual memory.

■ Restart Windows 95, click Start, then select Run, and type

```
xcopy c:\*.* /e /h /k /r /c d:
```

■ Click OK. This command line copies all your files to the new drive. If your original drive is fairly large, this operation could take some time. *Do not power down your system during this operation.*

■ Once this operation has completed, shut down Windows 95, turn off your PC, and change the jumper settings on your drive so that the new drive is the primary (master) drive. If you wish to keep your original drive in the system after all, you can jumper it as the secondary (slave) drive. If you choose not to use the original drive, you should remove it now and return it to its protective packaging.

■ Place your boot disk in the floppy drive and turn on the PC, edit the CMOS settings to reflect the change in master/slave drives and then continue booting with your start-up disk.

■ At the A: prompt, type FDISK and select option 2 to make the primary partition on your new disk drive the active partition, then exit FDISK, and reboot.

- Windows 95 should boot from the new hard disk. It is a good idea to allow Windows 95 to determine your Virtual Memory settings, so double-click on My Computer, Control Panel, and the System icon.

- Click on the Performance tab and Virtual Memory button, and then Click on "Let Windows specify my own system memory setting" (Fig. 10.2).

- You should be in business.

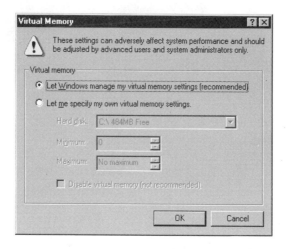

Figure 10-2 Virtual Memory Dialog

REINSTALLING WINDOWS 95 DOESN'T DETECT CD-ROM

Q925. *I installed a retail version of Windows 95 on my system, but now my system will not recognize the CD-ROM drive. What should I do?*

A.   This happens a lot. The retail version of Windows 95 often does not recognize a controller on the motherboard (such as the Intel 82371SB PIIX3 controller). Windows 95 will identify the controller; however, Windows 95 cannot identify the function of the controller. As a result, Windows 95 usually identifies the controller as a legacy (non-plug-and-play) card, and the CD-ROM drive will not function. You can obtain an update for Windows 95 from the following Web site *http://developer.intel.com/design/motherbd/ideinfup.htm.*

MOVING A WINDOWS 95 HARD DRIVE TO A NEW PC

Q926. *Can you tell me if it is possible to take a hard drive already loaded with Windows 95 from a 486DX machine and put it into a Pentium 90 machine? Someone told me that this is not possible because Windows 95 is hardware specific. Would this mean that I would need to reload the operating system on the Pentium?*

A. Moving Windows 95 is always a challenge because Windows 95 does expect to see certain configurations of hardware and drivers. However, there is one tactic that might work out for you. First, perform a complete system backup of the drive (probably to tape). Next, prepare a boot disk that will start the Pentium and add the appropriate CONFIG.SYS and AUTOEXEC.BAT files that will enable the CD-ROM drive. Then "unhide" the registry files using the ATTRIB command such as

```
attrib *.dat -s -h -r
```

and rename your registry files (SYSTEM.DAT and USER.DAT). Do *not* attempt to start Windows 95 again on that drive. Install the drive in your Pentium and then enter your CMOS Setup to change the drive parameters. When you save your CMOS changes and reboot, boot to the floppy disk and run the Windows 95 installation CD as an upgrade. This should allow Windows 95 to redetect existing hardware and modify the drivers for the Pentium's environment but not lose any of your applications or program groups in the process.

INVALID SYSTEM DISK WITH WINDOWS 95

Q927. *I'm installing Windows 95, and during the first boot of Windows 95, I got an Invalid System Disk error message. What does this mean?*

A. If during the first reboot in Windows 95 setup (or when you boot from the start-up disk), you receive the following error message:

```
Invalid system disk
Replace the disk, and then press any key
```

your system may be infected with a boot-sector virus, running virus-protection software, or using hard disk management software (such as Disk Manager, EZ-Drive, or DrivePro) for logical block addressing (LBA) support. These tools provide support for hard disks that have more than 1024 cylinders. To correct a virus infection, use an antivirus program to detect and remove the virus and then reinstall Windows 95 system files. If the system is running virus protection software, boot the system using the start-up disk created during Windows 95 setup and then use the SYS command from the start-up disk to restore the system files to the hard disk.

Windows 95 may not detect disk management software and may overwrite the master boot record (MBR). Refer to the documentation for the disk management software you are using for information about restoring the MBR. To reinstall the Windows 95 system files, follow these steps:

- Boot the system using the Windows 95 Emergency Boot Disk.
- At the MS-DOS command prompt, type the following lines:

```
c:
cd\windows\command
attrib c:\msdos.sys -h -s -r
ren c:\msdos.sys c:\msdos.xxx
a:
sys c:
del c:\msdos.sys
ren c:\msdos.xxx c:\msdos.sys
attrib c:\msdos.sys +r +s +h
```

- Remove the emergency boot disk and reboot the system.

INTERMEDIATE

Monitor Not Listed with Windows 95

Q928.   *I'm installing a new NEC MultiSync monitor, but when I scroll through the list of NEC MultiSync monitors in the Change Display Type dialog, I do not see my model on the list.*

A.   You probably have a MultiSync monitor that was released after the Windows 95 operating system. However, NEC does maintain an up-to-date .INF (information) file which contains the profiles of their latest products. You can download the latest Windows 95 .INF file (called NECMONTR.INF) from the NEC FTP site (*ftp.nectech.com*) or the NEC Web site (*www.nec.com*). Go to NEC Support, then to Drivers and Upgrades, and finally to NEC Graphics Files. Once you have the file, here is what you need to do to install it:

1.   Click the Start button, highlight the Settings option, and then select Control Panel.

2.   Double-click on the Display icon in your Control Panel.

3.   Select the Settings tab in your Display Properties window.

4.   Click on the button labeled Change Display Type.

5.   Now locate the Change button located next to the Monitor Type selection (Fig. 10.3).

6.   Click on the Have Disk button, and browse to the directory containing the new .INF file. Double-click on the file.

7.   Make sure that the Show All Devices radio button is selected.

8.   Scroll through the list of manufacturers until you find NEC Technologies. Select this option.

9.   Listed in the right window are the NEC monitors. Make the appropriate selection.

10. Click on the OK button in the Select Device window. Click on the X in the top right-hand corner of the Select Display Type window. Finally, click on the OK button of your Display Properties window.

11. Restart your computer.

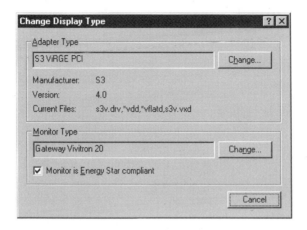

Figure 10.3 Change Display Type dialog

REMOVING WINDOWS 95

Q929. *I've been using Windows 3.1x for years now, but with all the new software geared for Windows 95, I decided to move forward and upgrade to Windows 95. The problem is that I'm really overwhelmed by Windows 95, and I can't seem to be productive in it. Can I remove Windows 95?*

A.   Yes, you can remove Windows 95—if you saved the original system files. During the Windows 95 setup, you are asked whether you want to save your computer's system files. If you choose to save the system files, Setup saves them in a hidden, compressed file on the hard disk. Keep in mind that you will not be asked to save the system files if you are installing Windows 95 into an empty directory, if you are not running MS-DOS version 5.0 or later, or if you are reinstalling Windows 95 over itself. To remove Windows 95, follow these steps:

■   Click the Start button, point to Settings, and then click Control Panel.

■   Double-click the Add/Remove Programs icon.

■   On the Install/Uninstall tab, click Windows 95, and then click Remove.

You can also remove Windows 95 by starting your computer with the Windows 95 Startup Disk and then typing "un-install" at the command prompt.

Can't Upgrade with New CPU

Q930.   *I have a friend who is trying to set up a computer with a Cyrix 6x86/120 CPU and cannot get Windows 95 installed. The computer appears to be set up properly. I even removed all cards except for the video card. I swapped the RAM. Nothing seemed to work. The system appears to install Windows 95, but it generates a GPF in USER.EXE or PROGMAN.EXE during the install. I have had problems like this when there were hardware conflicts before. That's why I took out everything but the video card.*

A.   A Windows 95 installation can fail for a great many reasons. While it is very versatile when it comes to accepting hardware, it will not accept *all* hardware (or all combinations of hardware). There are instances where an old video board can cause the problem. For the sake of argument, try another video board and see if the problem disappears. Windows 95 can also fail when there are faults on the motherboard, in cache, and in other integral components that may not have shown up as bad during the POST. Try a good system diagnostic like TuffTest from Windsor Technologies (*www.tufftest.com*) and see if any faults are revealed. You may also wish to try a different CPU (although the probability of a compatibility problem here is slim). Another concern is the hard drive. If it already contains data, try making a full system backup and then try repartitioning and reformatting the drive.

Networking and Communication

Using More Than One Modem

Q931.   *Is it possible to have more than one modem in a PC? My cousin says no, but I say it can be done.*

A. Technically, the answer is Yes, but you'll have to configure the two modems separately using different COM ports (with unique IRQ and I/O address settings). You'll also need to configure your communication software very carefully. To run both modems, you'll need to load two instances of your communication software (preferably different communication applications)—one configured for each modem.

FIXING A DIAL-UP PASSWORD

Q932. *My dial-up window asks for my password and gives me the option of saving it for later but never remembers it the next time I log on. I've got Windows 95 with Service Pack 1 installed. How can I make my computer remember my log-on password?*

A. I think your problem may actually be with Service Pack 1 itself. SP1 contained several changes to the password encryption used by Windows 95, so it may simply be refusing to acknowledge the older passwords. Try deleting your password files (the *.PWL files in your C:\Windows directory). After you delete those files, run ScanDisk to check the drive and correct any errors. You may also want to defragment the drive. Then restart Windows 95. The restart should force Windows 95 to create new password files. Of course, you'll need to reenter your password from scratch, but it should remember the passwords from now on.

RED X ON COM PORT NOT CAUSE FOR CONCERN

Q933. *I see a red X on COM1 in my Device Manager, but I don't understand why it's there. I disabled COM1 on the motherboard and installed an internal modem as COM1, and the modem works correctly. I'd assume this means that there's no trouble with the COM ports. Should I be worried?*

A. Probably not. That red X is a natural response from your Device Manager. In the CMOS Setup, your COM1 is disabled so that the internal modem can use its settings. In Windows 95, the operating system will look for all COM ports whether they are active or not. It will see your modem (COM1), your COM2, and your nonactive COM1, which it will mark with an X. There's nothing wrong with your system in this case.

Can't Get Direct Connect to Work

Q934.   *My sister is trying to link two Windows 95 machines. We are using a parallel cable and the Direct Cable Connection feature in Windows 95. Everything went smoothly until we get to the connect screen. The computers will not connect. We are both using our LPT1 connection, which we know is a good port on both computers because we can use a printer on it. If you have any advice or know of a better way that would not be too expensive, I would appreciate it.*

A.   Start by checking the parallel port setups in the CMOS Setup of each machine. They should be set for bidirectional operation. Next, check the actual cable being used to connect the two machines and see that the cable is working properly. Finally, there is probably still a configuration problem with your Direct Connect feature. Check your setup again or try an alternate connection software such as Laplink for Windows 95. If you can get alternate software to work, you know the problem is in your Direct Connect setup.

Restoring a Modem from a Windows 95 Crash

Q935.   *One of my main problems right now is that Windows 95 crashed last week, and I had to reload it. I have been unable to get the computer to recognize my Zoom ComStar 28.8 voice/fax/ modem. I've spent 3 entire days downloading upgraded software, changing COM port info, and checking CONFIG.SYS and AUTOEXEC.BAT. I'm just out of ideas.*

A.   I just saw this problem in another system, and the solution depends on whether you have a PnP BIOS. If so, go into the BIOS and reselect the COM ports as Present. Save your changes and reboot. Next, go into Windows 95 and remove the modem drivers through your Device Manager (highlight the device entry for your modem and click the Remove button). Reboot and reinstall the drivers for the modem once the new hardware is detected. If Windows 95 doesn't detect your modem automatically, use the Add New Hardware wizard to identify the modem and install your drivers. On a non-PnP system, just remove the drivers through your Device Manager, reboot, and then reinstall the drivers.

An Insert Your Modem Error with HyperTerminal

Q936. *I have a problem with HyperTerminal. It was working until I reinstalled my fax/modem. Now every time I try to dial using HyperTerminal, I get a message saying "Please insert your modem now. Click Cancel to quit dialing." What did I do wrong?*

A. If you installed the Windows 95 drivers for your fax/modem more than once (perhaps when you reinstalled your modem), HyperTerminal may be looking for the last installation. From HyperTerminal, click on File, Properties, Phone Numbers, and Connect and choose the *highest* number version of the modem (i.e., Fax Modem 2).

Network Server Looses Time

Q937. *Our 3-year-old Novell NetWare 3 server using a 486DX/33 (due for an upgrade) has to have the clock reset each morning since it loses about a half hour per day. Any ideas here?*

A. Ordinarily I'd tell you to try replacing the CMOS backup battery. However, since the server is apparently running full time, the PC would never be turned off, so the system isn't using the CMOS battery in the first place. I did some checking and discovered that this is a known problem with NetWare 3 servers which are heavily utilized (such as an overburdened 486). On a NetWare server, the drive I/O interrupts get priority over all other interrupts. The clock in the server operating system runs late while the RTC stays on time. There is a utility that will bring the two clocks into sync if it is employed. Now, if it is the RTC that loses time, suspect some odd software that may be reprogramming the RTC hardware or timing. Ultimately, I'd say that once you upgrade to a faster server platform, the problem should go away.

INTERMEDIATE

Multimedia

WORKING WITH .PDF FILES

Q938. *I've visited a Web site to download several files about mother-boards. These file have the extension .PDF and I can't print them. What application should I use to print out .PDF files?*

A.   The .PDF file extension is an Adobe Acrobat format which is frequently used for the electronic publishing of documents. Chances are that the site providing those .PDF files also has a link where you can download the Adobe Acrobat viewer (it's free). If not, try *www.adobe.com* or search for them in Yahoo at *www.yahoo.com.*

CONVERTING .AVI FILES TO .MOV

Q939. *How can I convert Video for Windows (.AVI) to QuickTime (MOV)?*

A.   Now that multimedia is in the mainstream, more and more users will want to convert .AVI files (Video for Windows) to .MOV (Mac QuickTime) files. You can get an .AVI to .MOV conversion utility called SmartVid from Intel (at *http://www.intel.com/ pc-supp/multimed/indeo/smartvid.htm*). SmartVid is a codec-independent utility that can be run from the DOS command line. You can get an .AVI-to-QTV (QuickTime for Windows) converter (from *ftp://mirrors.aol.com/pub/info-mac/gst/mov/avi-to-qt-converter.hqx*). Have fun

UNDERSTANDING VIDEO SCAN CONVERTERS

Q940. *I do a lot of computer graphics, and I'd love to record my animations to video tape. I understand that I need a scan converter for this, but can you give me some unbiased details about what a scan converter is?*

A.   A scan converter converts the SVGA output from your video board into a signal format used by a television or VCR (i.e., NTSC or PAL). Using a scan converter, you can display your computer monitor's display simultaneously on a television or record it to video tape. Scan converters are frequently used in education and business presentations since you can hook your PC or laptop to a scan converter unit and display your presentation on a large-screen TV. You'll find that good-quality scan converters are external devices that can easily be transported. In fact, you can probably find scan converters at your nearest computer superstore (like CompUSA or Computer City).

VOICE RECORDING SPACE ON A HARD DRIVE

Q941.   *Can you tell me how much space (in megabytes) 1 h of voice mail storage will take up on my hard drive?*

A.   It's hard to provide a precise figure because it depends on the quality at which the voice is digitized, and if any compression is being used. For straight voice capture at 22 kHz, 60 s require about 2MB, so for 60 min, figure 2MB x 60, or 120MB. Of course, that figure is just a guesstimate. For CD-quality recording at 44 kHz, 60 s demand about 4MB, so 60 min need about 240MB. With today's 2 to 4GB hard drives, you should have plenty of space for recordings.

ESTIMATING DRIVE SPACE REQUIREMENTS FOR IMAGES AND VIDEO

Q942.   *How much hard drive space is required for a still picture? For a 10-s video?*

A.   A precise answer is difficult to give because the actual file size will vary with a number of factors such as the color depth, file format, and image size. For video, other factors include the frame rate, compression type, addition of audio, and CPU speed. Still, I've assembled some general guidelines in Table 10.2.

TABLE 10.2 SOME TYPICAL FILE SIZE ESTIMATES

Image Size (pixels)*	Format	Colors	File Size (kilobytes)
320 x 240	JPEG	Millions	27
320 x 240	BMP	Millions	230
320 x 240	JPEG	Thousands	29
320 x 240	BMP	Thousands	230
640 x 480	JPEG	Thousands	82
640 x 480	BMP	Thousands	900

* Each 10 s of video at 640x480 with audio (compressed) ~ 2 to 3 MB. Each 10 s of video at 640x480 with audio (uncompressed) ~ 10 MB.

A WORD ABOUT PC CONVERGENCE

Q943. *Over the last few years we have seen the PC consume several single purpose machines (like the word processor, the fax machine, and the answering machine) into it's capabilities. Do you feel that this will inevitably happen with the TV, or will the TV digest the PC with products that combine TV and Internet access?*

A.   Your question is about a trend called *convergence,* where different forms of media (i.e., PCs, telephones, TVs, cable, and so on) are all blending into one device. In truth, it is very difficult to tell just *where* convergence is headed because there are so many powerful industry players struggling to control and direct the path toward convergence. My guess (don't hold me to this) is that there will eventually be two schools of devices: PCs with TV, telephone, and other features built in as standard equipment and TVs with computer-like keyboards having limited Internet, e-mail, phone, and applications-processing capability. I don't believe that any *one* type of device will dominate—at least for a while.

CONNECTING AUDIO FROM TWO CD-ROM DRIVES

Q944. *I am going to add a second CD-ROM drive to my current system and I have a question regarding the CD audio. I already have my original CD-ROM patched to the sound card's CD audio input using a long, four-wire audio cable. I don't have a second audio connector on the sound card, but is there any way to get audio from the new CD?*

A. Possibly. You can't splice the existing audio cable, but you probably could run a cable from the amplified headphone jack on the front of your new CD-ROM drive to the Line Input connector on your sound card. You would then need to start the mixer applet that accompanies the sound board and raise the Line Input level for proper volume. I admit this might look a bit awkward, but it should work.

VIDEO BOARD CAUSING LOCK-UP PROBLEMS UNDER WINDOWS 95

Q945. *I'm working with a PC using a new STB video board (don't know which type), but it's causing some random system lock-ups. Any ideas?*

A. If the drivers are all current and installed correctly, try turning down the Windows 95 Hardware Acceleration setting found under Systems Properties, Performance, and Graphics. Certain users with non-Intel processors (i.e., AMD or Cyrix products) may experience compatibility difficulties. Contact your PC maker for specific CPU compatibility issues.

VIDEO MODES LIMITED IN WINDOWS 95

Q946. *My ALR Optima system only lets me use a video resolution of 640x480 at 16 colors in Windows 95, and I can't improve anything through the Display icon. How can I get higher resolutions and color depths? I know the ATI Mach 64 video board is capable of far superior performance.*

INTERMEDIATE

A.   That's a great question. The ATI Mach 64 driver included with
         Windows 95 is *not* compatible with the current version of the
         ATI chipset. You will need the ATI-specific driver included on the
         disks that came with your machine. The drivers are also available
         from ALR and ATI's Web sites. As a rule, you will always get
         better performance from a video board by using the latest drivers
         available directly from the video board maker.

IDE Versus EIDE Performance for Video Applications

Q947.   *If we have to choose between an IDE and an EIDE drive for*
         video applications, (assuming we don't want SCSI), what should
         we choose? Furthermore, is it possible to connect an IDE drive
         on an EIDE controller?

A.   There's no doubt at all the EIDE drives and interfaces will yield
         superior data transfer rates in PIO mode 3 or PIO mode 4.
         Upgrading an existing IDE drive installation to EIDE drives and
         controllers will aid virtually all data-intensive applications, espe-
         cially real-time multimedia such as video. It is possible to connect
         older IDE devices to EIDE interfaces, but you should be aware
         that sharing an interface in this way may cause the older IDE
         device to slow down the top speed of the interface and take away
         performance from the faster EIDE device. If performance is your
         top concern, I suggest that you install an EIDE controller with
         two ports (a primary EIDE port and a secondary IDE port). Place
         your EIDE device(s) on the EIDE port, and place your older IDE
         device(s) on the IDE port.

Halting Feedback from a Multimedia System

Q948.   *I'm getting some horrible feedback from my Acer sound sys-*
         tem—the one where the microphone and speakers are integrated
         into the monitor. What can I do to stop the feedback?

A.   The problem is that your microphone is not being muted in the
         system's playback mixer, so sound from the speakers is being
         picked up by the microphone and fed back through the speakers

again, and you hear the results. Use the following procedure to mute the Acer microphone:

- Double-click on the Speaker icon located next to the clock on the Taskbar (usually in the bottom right corner of the screen).

- Click on Options and then click on Properties.

- See that there is a check in the small box next to Microphone.

- Click OK.

- Now you will see a microphone setting in the Volume Control Panel.

- Place a check in the Mute setting under microphone. If there is already a check next to Mute, uncheck and then recheck it.

- This should clear your feedback problem.

GETTING A SONY CD-ROM TO RUN WITH A SOUND BLASTER UNDER WINDOWS 95

Q949. *Do you have any hints on where to find a Windows 95 driver for a Sony ATAPI IDE CD-ROM that came with my Sound Blaster 16 sound card? I have tried the Creative Labs FTP and Web sites and have even called their technical support (a 30-min waiting time). They say that for some "contractual reasons," they cannot supply this driver. Sony has a similar problem. Since I bought the drive from another company, they won't give me a driver either. My current driver is a 16-bit driver which forces Windows 95 to run in a DOS compatibility mode for the CD-ROM drive. I'd like to get top performance out the drive and would prefer to run with a 32-bit driver.*

A.   I hunted everywhere for a solution. Ultimately, you'll need to set up the Sony CD-ROM drive manually. I believe the following procedure should work:

1. Click the Start button, choose Settings, and then click Control Panel.

2. Double-click the Add New Hardware icon, and then click the Next button.

INTERMEDIATE

3. Click the No option button, and then click Next.

4. Click CD-ROM Controllers, and then click Next.

5. In the Manufacturers box, click Sony. In the Models box, click Sony Proprietary CD-ROM Controller, and then click Next.

6. Click Next, and then click Finish.

7. When you are prompted to restart your computer, click No.

8. Click the Start button, choose Settings, and then click Control Panel.

9. Double-click the System icon.

10. On the Device Manager tab, double-click the CD-ROM Controllers branch, and then double-click Sony Proprietary CD-ROM Controller.

11. Click the Resources tab.

12. In the Settings Based On box, click Basic Configuration 0.

13. Click the Use Automatic Settings check box to clear it.

14. Use the Change Settings button to modify the resources to match the CD-ROM drive's settings.

15. Click OK.

16. When you are prompted to restart your computer, do so.

Sound Problems When Using Xing 2.03

Q950. *When I play a video CD in my system, the sound stops after about 30 min, but the video continues to play. I have to click the sound icon in the Xing 2.03 software and click again to resume the sound. This is more annoying than anything. Any solutions?*

A.   It sounds like you're using an obsolete version of Xing. Download and install the Xing 3.02 (or later) upgrade. You can download the upgrade from the following Web site *http://www.xingtech.com/ technical_support/mpegplayer_download.html*.

File May Be Corrupted Error Playing MPEG

Q951. *I'm using the SoftMPEG utility to try to play MPEG files, but I get an error that says "This file cannot be played on the specified MCI device. The file may be corrupted, or not in the correct path." What can I do about this if the MPEG file is on CD?*

A.   That's a tough one. In most cases, any error message that suggests file corruption is usually correct. The way to tell for sure is to try another CD with an identical MPEG file. If the new CD plays, the original CD is probably defective. If you cannot get another CD, you should override the problem by removing the corrupted MPEG file from your playlist.

Device In Use Error Playing MPEG

Q952. *I started an MPEG player program and tried to run an MPEG file, but I get an error that says "The device needed to play the file is already in use. Wait until it is free, and then try again." Well, how can the MPEG player already be in use if I just started it?*

A.   This type of error occurs when there are multiple MPEG players at work in the system. Only one MPEG player should be running at one time. My guess is that you've already got another application open that is capable of playing MPEG files and the MPEG drivers are in use. When you start another player, the drivers are inaccessible, and that forces the error. Try closing any open applications, and just run one MPEG player.

System Freezes During Xing MPEG Playback

Q953. *I just recently purchased an STB Velocity 64V PCI 2MB VRAM graphics card (the final component of my recent PC building project). It was bundled with Xing MPEG playback software. The system freezes every time I attempt to resize the playback window in any way (including maximizing it). If I disable video acceleration in the playback options, this problem does not exist, but video quality gets bad and "choppy." The board is marketed as being a video acceleration board with full motion MPEG and video playback.*

A.   As I recall, there were some issues with early versions of Xing MPEG software. I suggest that you contact STB or visit their Web site (*www.stb.com*), and you should find an updated version of Xing—as well as other updated drivers for your Velocity board. Once you update your software, the problem should disappear.

Can't Play CD-I Movies Under Windows 95

Q954.   *Why can't I play CD-i movies under Windows 95? I get an error message saying "Format Unrecognized." I've got a pretty new CD-ROM—shouldn't that support CD-i?*

A.   Not necessarily. This is a limitation of the CD-ROM extension built into Windows 95. It won't allow you to play video in a streaming format (such as CD-i or video in a Green Book format). There's really nothing you can do about this. It will, however, allow you to play video in a file format, such as videos labeled "Video CD" or in the White Book format. You can be sure that a CD-ROM with video will work if it's labeled "Video CD."

DOS and Windows Questions

While Windows 95 has emerged as a major force on today's desktops, there are a myriad of older PCs still in service which are unable to run Windows 95, and in some cases, systems are dual-booted to intentionally run older versions of DOS and Windows. This chapter examines a variety of questions about the operations of DOS and Windows and then covers related issues such as communication and multimedia. If you work with older PCs, this chapter may cover questions that you can't find in books anymore.

Terminology and General Topics

CORRECTING MULTIPLE POWER-UP PROMPTS

Q955.   *Maybe you can help me with a prompt problem I've been having.*
        When my PC powers up, I get a set of three prompts such as

        C:\>

        C:\>

        C:\>_

        What is causing this, and how can I fix it?

A.   These multiple prompts are a harmless side effect of multiple car-
        riage returns in your AUTOEXEC.BAT file. Load your
        AUTOEXEC.BAT file into a word processor (such as DOS EDIT
        or Windows Notebook) and remove any extra carriage returns.
        You may see these as extra (blank) lines between AUTOEXEC
        statements. Eliminating these extra lines should make the extra
        prompts disappear. Be sure to resave the AUTOEXEC.BAT file
        before exiting your word processor, and reboot the system to see
        that your fix has worked.

DISPOSING OF THE WINA20.386 FILE

Q956.   *I'm trying to streamline my brother's old PC, and I keep seeing*
        the file WINA20.386 in the root directory of Windows 3.1x, but
        I do not understand what this file is or why it is there. Do we
        need it at all?

A.   It depends. WINA20.386 is a driver needed to run Windows 3.0 in
        the 386 enhanced mode—this is the file's *only* purpose. You do *not*
        need WINA20.386 if you are running any other version of
        Windows, or if you run Windows 3.0 in the standard mode. Today,
        Windows 95 is the dominant operating system, and the number of
        Windows 3.1x installations is dropping as new systems are pur-
        chased and new systems are upgraded. There are almost no installa-
        tions of Windows 3.0 still in service (except perhaps on old 286 sys-
        tems that can't handle the enhanced mode of Windows 3.1).

INSTALLING DOS UPGRADES

Q957. *If all new DOS versions must be installed over an existing version of DOS, how can I install DOS on a second or new hard drive? I have DOS 6.22, which is an upgrade, and I cannot get it installed on a hard drive which I have partitioned and formatted.*

A.   Unfortunately, the upgrade versions of an operating system require a preexisting version of an operating system before the install will proceed. A full-install version should require no preexisting DOS version to be present. I suggest that after properly partitioning and formatting your new hard drive, you try booting from disk 1 of your DOS disk. If it complains that there is no prior version of DOS, you'll need to obtain a full version of DOS, or install an older full version first and then run your upgrade.

NEW SYSTEM FREQUENTLY HANGS UP DURING HIMEM

Q958. *I'm having trouble with a newly built system. It hangs up when HIMEM tests extended memory (it does this about 50 percent of the time); the test never completes and says "done." Could this be a bad SIMM unit? I've checked and reseated all the boards and SIMMs numerous times. It's an Intel P5 75-MHz CPU on a Triton motherboard and uses two 2MX32 70-ns 8MB SIMMs (for a total of 16MB). The RAM is non-EDO. Is this memory OK to use with this motherboard?*

A.   It could be a bad SIMM, but I'd suspect that even when the system does boot normally, it would probably stall or crash later on. As you suspect, it's a good idea to check your SIMMs first, so use an aggressive diagnostic like TuffTest (*www.tufftest.com*) or other good commercial diagnostic to stress test your RAM. If you find a failure and can get the failure to repeat during subsequent tests, replace the defective memory. Your 70-ns RAM should be adequate for the Triton motherboard. Check the HIMEM command line for any unusual switches. If HIMEM is running the HIGHSCAN feature, remove the feature and reboot the system—PCs often have trouble when running HIGHSCAN.

HIMEM Problems Suggest Memory Conflict

Q959. *I cannot run HIMEM.SYS without a /MACHINE:1 switch. When I use the switch, my system tells me that HIMEM is installed and that 64KB are available. However, the DOS MEM function reports that 1MB is available in contiguous extended memory. If I try to use a UMB switch in the DOS= line of CON-FIG.SYS, I am told that HIMEM is not available. I also have problems with EMM386.EXE locking up the entire system. I am using MS-DOS 5.0.*

A.   You have a memory conflict in your system. The clue here is your need to use the /MACHINE:1 switch, but that is the *default* for PC/AT-compatible systems anyway. Start with the basics; check the memory to be sure that it is fast enough for your system (usually 70 ns or less). Next, check that your memory is properly installed in your system and that every possible jumper or DIP switch is set correctly. Check your CMOS memory settings as well. You may need to use a different memory setup. Also check the versions of HIMEM.SYS and EMM386.EXE that you are using. They should be the current version distributed with your operating system (check the file dates against COMMAND.COM). Finally, check your driver order in CONFIG.SYS. The order should be HIMEM, EMM386, and then DOS=. If your problems continue, boot the system with a clean disk and then run an aggressive diagnostic to stress test all of your system memory.

Cannot Access A20 Line Handler Errors

Q960. *I have a 386 machine with 1MB RAM that was brought to me. The system keeps getting Cannot access A20 Line Handler messages and then loads DOS 5.0 low. I have checked CONFIG.SYS, and HIMEM.SYS is there. Any suggestion on how I can get access to high memory?*

A.   If only 1MB is available in the system, HIMEM will only give you access to free space in the upper 360KB (the upper memory area). If HIMEM has only just been added to the system and never worked properly, make sure that HIMEM is the first device driver loaded in CONFIG.SYS. You may need to specify a different A20 handler by using the /MACHINE:x switch. Your DOS 5.0 user manual probably specifies up to 20 different entries for the /MACHINE:x switch. Find the correct entry for your system. If HIMEM has worked in the system before (and only failed recently), there may be a fault in the system's memory or memory control circuitry. Run a diagnostic and check the memory thoroughly. Remember that you'll need over 1MB of RAM in that system before DOS will load high. Until then, use the DOS=UMA command line after HIMEM and EMM386.

HIMEM Problems May Need Gate Handler Switch

Q961. *Recently, my friend bought an IBM Blue Lightening CPU (i486DX2/66) with an SIS motherboard. When she installed IBM DOS 5.0, there were no problems. Then, after upgrading to DOS 6.22, the computer hangs up when HIMEM.SYS is testing the memory. We tried changing CONFIG.SYS to ignore HIMEM.SYS, and the system boots properly. We also tried to install Windows, but the installation failed. Any suggestions?*

A.   HIMEM.SYS problems are often the result of incorrect A20 gate detection or handling. In most cases, HIMEM can detect the A20 gate for just about any kind of system, but there are some systems for which HIMEM must explicitly define the type of machine in use through the /machine:xx switch. Normally, the syntax for HIMEM is

```
device=c:\dos\himem.sys
```

Try adding the /machine:*xx* switch where *xx* is one of the machine numbers in Table 11.1. If your system is like 90 percent of the systems out there, the following would be the proper syntax (assuming the DOS directory is on C:):

```
device=c:\dos\himem.sys /machine:1
```

TABLE 11.1 MACHINE SWITCH SETTINGS FOR TYPICAL PC SYSTEMS

Code	Machine	A20 Handler
at (standard)	1	IBM AT
ps2	2	IBM PS/2
pt cascade	3	Phoenix Cascade BIOS
hpvectra	4	HP Vectra (A and A+)
att6300plus	5	AT&T 6300 Plus
acer1100	6	Acer 1100
thoshiba	7	Toshiba 1600 and 1200XE
wyse	8	Wyse 12.5 MHz 286
tulip	9	Tulip SX
zenith	10	Zenith ZBIOS
at1	11	IBM AT (alternative 1)
at2	12	IBM AT (alternative 2)
css	12	CSS Labs
at3	13	IBM AT (alternative 3)
philips	13	Philips
fasthp	14	HP Vectra

EMM386 ERROR MAY SUGGEST SEVERAL PROBLEMS

Q962.   *I have an Austin 486DX2/50 at work that has been giving me a perplexing error message at boot time when I run EMM386. The message is as follows: "EMM386: Unrecoverable privileged operation error #00—press ENTER to reboot." The system will not warm boot using either the suggested <Enter> key or <CTRL>+<ALT>+<DEL>. I have tried stepping through the CONFIG.SYS and AUTOEXEC.BAT, but that tells me very little. The error message does not appear until AUTOEXEC.BAT tries to boot Microsoft Anti-Virus or other utilities.*

A.   That's a tough one. It sounds like one of your applications (probably one in your AUTOEXEC.BAT file) is having trouble loading into memory. Unfortunately, this is probably due to a fault somewhere in memory. It is not uncommon for the BIOS memory test to miss such a fault, especially if the memory is marginal. Before planning on serious downtime, try booting your system and remarking-out one statement at a time. If the problem is limited to one or two specific utilities, make sure that you have the system resources to run those utilities, and try reloading those utilities. If you cannot narrow the problem that way, get a good PC diagnostic and put your system's memory through a thorough stress test. If a fault is located, replace the faulty SIMM.

If a diagnostic can't find a problem, things get a bit more complicated. Use a write-protected bootable floppy and scan the system for viruses. File corruption caused by virus infiltration can result in bizarre system behavior. If the system passes a virus check, boot the system from a clean bootable floppy disk and run a utility like PC Tools or Norton Utilities to check the disk for bad sectors, cross-linked files, and disk fragmentation. Map out any bad sectors and clear any cross-linked files (files in bad sectors and cross-linked files may be corrupt and have to be reloaded from a protected backup), and then defragment the drive.

EMM386 Errors After Running MEMMAKER

Q963. *After trying to load several games (such as CD-ROM Wolfpack and Seawolf), a message came on each time saying that I was short of memory. I then decided to run Memmaker to see if that would help. When I did that, I got the following message: "EMM386 has detected an Error #12 in an application at memory address 5052:7BC5. To minimize the chance of data loss, EMM386 has halted your computer. For more information, see the README.TXT file." What can I do to correct error #12?*

A. MEMMAKER has caused a problem with your memory configuration, and this in turn is causing a serious issue with EMM386. In order to clear the problem, you will need to undo the changes MEMMAKER has made to CONFIG.SYS (and possibly AUTOEXEC.BAT). If you made backup copies of these files, it should be a simple matter to copy those backups to the current CONFIG.SYS and AUTOEXEC.BAT files. Once you clear the error, you will have to tweak your CONFIG.SYS and AUTOEXEC.BAT files manually to try to free additional conventional memory.

EMM386 Problems with the HIGHSCAN Switch

Q964. I'm using EMM386 with the following command line in CONFIG.SYS:

```
DEVICE=EMM386.EXE RAM HIGHSCAN I=B000:B7FF
```

After booting, Windows will not start, simple DOS commands like EDIT freeze the computer, and the DELETE command produces this message: "EMM386.EXE has detected error #06 in an application at memory address 00B8:802D. To minimize the chance of data loss, EMM386 has halted your computer. Press restart..." The computer works without the HIGHSCAN command. Norton's comprehensive memory check reported no problems with the SIMMs. Any ideas on what this could mean?

A.   As you suspected, the problem is with your HIGHSCAN switch. The HIGHSCAN switch is probably there because you told MEMMAKER to scan the upper memory area aggressively. Unfortunately, HIGHSCAN will often incorrectly identify areas of upper memory that are not actually available. Try removing the HIGHSCAN switch from EMM386. This should stabilize your system and restore Windows.

MSCDEX Causes the System to Hang Up

Q965. I'm having trouble getting a CD-ROM drive to work. When the MSCDEX.EXE file is accessed in AUTOEXEC.BAT, the system hangs up. Could the file be corrupt? Is there a virus that targets MSCDEX? How can I get a new MSCDEX file?

A.   Start by examining the MSCDEX command line in AUTOEXEC.BAT. Make sure the command line arguments match those used with the low-level CD-ROM driver in CONFIG.SYS. If everything matches, try moving the command line to the end of the AUTOEXEC file. Some users have reported problems when using MSCDEX as the first line in AUTOEXEC.BAT.

If problems persist, try running CHKDSK and check for cross-linked files. If MSCDEX is cross-linked with another file, it may indeed be corrupt. You may try reinstalling MSCDEX to correct the file. If you are concerned with the version, try reloading MSCDEX from your MS-DOS 6.22 disks, or use the installation disks that came with your CD-ROM drive (whichever is more recent). As a last resort, you can download MSCDEX from the Microsoft Web site (*www.microsoft.com*).

Excluding DOS Upper Memory

Q966. *I'm having no end of trouble configuring my network card. Someone mentioned to me that I should be excluding an area of memory since the network card is using that particular area. Unfortunately, I have no idea how to do this.*

A. Excluding memory is a rather simple detail that you can handle by setting a command line switch for your EMM386.EXE file called in CONFIG.SYS. By adding the /x switch (followed by the range of memory that needs to be excluded), EMM386 will leave that defined area alone so that other hardware (i.e., video boards, SCSI adapters, and network cards) can use it exclusively. For example, suppose CONFIG.SYS shows the following line:

```
device=c:\dos\emm386.exe
```

You can exclude memory by adding /x=aaaa-bbbb where aaaa is the starting hex address you need to exclude, and bbbb is the ending address that must be excluded. For example,

```
device=c:\dos\emm386.exe /x=d800-dfff
```

The problem now is determining exactly which area of memory to exclude. Although the range D800h to DFFFh is typical for network cards, you should check the manual accompanying your network card for exact settings.

INTERMEDIATE

NEW GAME NEEDS EMM TO RUN

Q967. *I've just installed an IDE CD-ROM in my son's system (a Packard Bell 770 Elite). Like most PB systems, the IDE controller is built into the motherboard, and the controller only supports two hard drives, which it has (234MB as master and 420MB as slave). But the CD-ROM (a Sony CDU-55e) came with a secondary IDE adapter. I installed the adapter and set the drive to be master as the installation guide said to do if the drive was alone on its own card. I then installed the CD drivers and window drivers. Everything was working until my son tried to install a game demo from a demo CD. It wanted a hard drive space to put some files on, so he entered E:, which is a partition on his master HDD. All went well until he tried to play the demo. The game started with some opening video from the CD, but when it went to the hard drive, he got the message "SHARING VIOLATION READING DRIVE E," then he got "ERROR: NO EMM FOR USE". What can I do about this?*

A.   Start by checking your CONFIG.SYS file. It may be that your extended memory manager driver is not installed. The first two lines in your CONFIG.SYS file should look something like this:

```
DEVICE=C:\DOS\HIMEM.SYS
DEVICE=C:\DOS\EMM386.EXE NOEMS
```

The NOEMS switch tells the driver *not* to configure any expanded memory. If your game requires expanded memory, do not include this switch. Also, many games require a certain amount of free conventional memory to run. At the DOS prompt type MEM. Check the line that says Largest Executable Program Size. This tells you how much free conventional memory you have. Check your game's README file for the amount of conventional memory required to run your game and make sure there's enough.

EMS #6 ERROR MESSAGE UNDER WINDOWS 3.1x

Q968. *I get an EMS #6 error code when I'm in the Windows 3.1 Program Manager and I try to access the A: drive. I have put this*

*disk in another laptop and it works correctly. I have also
changed disk drives, and still the same error occurs. What do I
need to do to fix this? I have an NEC V/50 laptop with 16MB of
RAM and an 810MB HDD. This error just started for no reason
that I can see.*

A.   I'm not familiar with the NEC error code specifically, but EMS is
used by DOS applications to allow paging into high memory and
is invariably related to memory management (by comparison,
Windows 3.1 uses XMS). When a memory problem materializes
for no reason, it means one of three things: (1) your memory
manager has become corrupt, (2) you have a fault in memory
above the 1MB mark, or (3) you have introduced a driver or
TSR that might be interfering with EMS. Check your memory
manager if you're using an advanced memory manager like
QEMM, try a more basic manager like EMM386. If the memory
manager is using a feature like Stealth or HIGHSCAN, try disabling those aggressive memory tools. Defective memory can trigger an EMS fault, so try a DOS diagnostic which will thoroughly
test your RAM. If you detect defective RAM, you should replace
it. Finally, try disabling any recent drivers or TSRs that might
have been installed before the error started.

Error Using the LASTDRIVE Statement

Q969.   *I am trying to set up a Novell Network. I have the server loaded
and operating OK, but I am having a problem setting up a workstation in Windows 95. I know that the CONFIG.SYS file must
have the entry LAST DRIVE=Z, but when I put that in, I get an
error message from Windows 95 that I have an error on that
line. I have tried every setting that I can think of in Windows
95's Network settings, but to no avail. Any suggestions?*

A.   Only one. I see from your question that you used the term LAST
DRIVE (with a space between the words *LAST* and *DRIVE*). If
you used the same space in your CONFIG.SYS file, your system
won't recognize the command as *LASTDRIVE=Z*. I strongly suspect that's why you're getting an error. Correct the LASTDRIVE
command line and try again.

Boot Disk Won't Run Start-up Files

Q970.   *I'm having a bizarre problem making a boot disk for my system. I've formatted the floppy disk and copied the start-up files. I also copied the files needed by AUTOEXEC.BAT and CONFIG.SYS, but now that the hard drive has really failed, the floppy boot disk also decided to fail.It produces a bunch of warnings that it can't find files like HIMEM.SYS and EMM386.EXE, but the files are on the disk. What can I do?*

A.   This is a common oversight with start-up files (AUTOEXEC.BAT and CONFIG.SYS). Simply copying the DOS files to a floppy are not enough. You also have to change the directory path for each file. Traditionally, a start-up file reference looks like

```
c:\dos\himem.sys
```

If you copied this reference to the floppy disk, the floppy disk will be looking for the files on the *hard drive* and not the floppy disk. While the hard drive was working, it was totally transparent to you. Now that the hard drive has failed, the oversight has appeared. If you have access to another system, load your floppy disk start-up files into a text editor and check the directory references for each command line. If you see references pointing to the hard drive, change them to reference the floppy drive. For example,

```
a:\himem.sys
```

Resave the start-up files and try your boot disk again.

MSD Won't Check for Pentiums

Q971.   *I usually make use of the Microsoft Diagnostic (MSD) to check my PC's configuration, but after I tried MSD on my new Pentium system, MSD reported a 486DX. I looked inside the PC, but the CPU itself is covered by a large heat sink, so I can't tell if the CPU is right or not. How can I check the CPU?*

A.   Chances are very good that your system is indeed using a Pentium. You're probably just using a slightly older version of MSD (written before the Pentium went into commercial systems). According to Microsoft, MSD version 2.11 should detect a

Pentium properly. Version 2.11 is included with MS-DOS 6.22. If you do not choose to upgrade your DOS version, you can download MSD version 2.11 from CompuServe (GO MICROSOFT) or the Microsoft Web site at *http://www.microsoft.com*

MEMORY AVAILABILITY PROBLEMS WITH MSAV

Q972. *Why do I receive an Insufficient Conventional Memory error message when I try to run Microsoft's Anti-Virus utility in Windows?*

A. I presume that you're running Windows 3.1x. This is a common problem with the Microsoft Anti-Virus application when run through a DOS window. The problem is that after the Windows kernel and supporting software are loaded, there really isn't enough memory left to run MSAV. One tactic that seems to work is to lower your video resolution from 65K colors to 256 or 16 colors. If the problem persists (or you don't want to mess with your video configuration), run MSAV from a DOS prompt.

DEALING WITH ENVIRONMENT SPACE PROBLEMS

Q973. *I can't use the PCSETUP utility of PROCOMM PLUS. I get the following message: "RUN-TIME ERROR R6009—NOT ENOUGH SPACE FOR ENVIRONMENT. EXTERNAL PROGRAM ABORTED. TERMINAL RESET." What or where is the problem?*

A. This error was reported by PROCOMM when it accesses your DOS environment while running PCSETUP. Type SET at the command prompt and you will see your current DOS environment. Something in that list is conflicting with what PROCOMM needs, or the list is so large that it takes up too much room. Try booting your system from a bootable floppy disk without CONFIG.SYS or AUTOEXEC.BAT files to give your system the minimum possible environment space. Change to the PROCOMM directory and try running PCSETUP again. If environment space is a problem, PCSETUP should work properly now. You can also edit the CONFIG.SYS file in the root directory and remark (disable) one line at a time until you find the conflict. Remember that you will have to reboot the computer after each change.

You may also need more memory. Either there is not enough memory in the system or too many things are loaded into conventional memory. Use MEM (for DOS 5.0 or 6.0) or CHKDSK (DOS 3.3 or lower) to see how much memory is available. There may be a bad copy of one or more PROCOMM files. You may wish to try reloading your copy of PROCOMM. Finally, there may be a computer virus at work in your system, especially if the same problems seem to be occurring in other programs. Use antivirus software to check your system.

CD-ROM Caching Problems with SmartDrive

Q974.   *I'm a bit of confused about CD-ROM caching. The other day, I was running a CD-ROM diagnostic which told me that the CD-ROM drive was not cached and that I should take advantage of SmartDrive's CD caching ability, but I thought I was already doing that. When reviewing the SmartDrive entry in AUTOEXEC.BAT, I found the /u switch in the SmartDrive command line. What is this switch for, and how can I get SmartDrive to cache my CD-ROM?*

A.   First, I'm assuming that you're using Windows 3.1x—Windows 95 doesn't use SmartDrive at all. While older versions of SmartDrive were not designed to cache CD-ROM drives, current versions (with DOS 6.2 and later) are perfectly able to cache most CD-ROMs. The /u switch in your SmartDrive command line forces SmartDrive to disable CD-ROM caching. Try removing the /u switch, and make sure that SmartDrive is loaded *after* MSCDEX.EXE, as shown in the following AUTOEXEC fragment:

```
loadhigh C:\SB16\SBCONFIG.EXE /S

loadhigh C:\SB16\DRV\MSCDEX.EXE /D:MSCD001 /V /M:15

PROMPT $P$G

loadhigh C:\DOS\SMARTDRV.EXE

SET MOUSE=C:\MSMOUSE

loadhigh C:\MSMOUSE\MOUSE
```

If you want a complete explanation of SmartDrive and a breakdown of its command line switches, type

```
help smartdriv
```

at the DOS prompt.

Keep in mind that caching generally slows performance of sequential CD-ROM reads but improves overall performance of random reads. Now, many of today's multimedia CD titles rely on large sequential reads for video and audio data, so it may actually turn out that you are better off with CD-ROM drive caching disabled. Also consider that CD-ROM performance is affected by the /m parameter of MSCDEX, which specifies the read-ahead buffer for the CD-ROM. A read-ahead buffer will read more data than is requested on the assumption that the reads are sequential and the next request will already be in memory. For example, if the buffer is 10 sectors, a request to read sector 100 will result in sectors 100 to 109 being read into the buffer. That way, if the next request is for sector 101, followed by 102, and so on, the system saves the time it would have take to physically read the drive again. The trade-off is that increasing the size of the buffer increases the amount of memory that MSCDEX will require. In the AUTOEXEC fragment above, the /m switch is set to 15.

OUT OF MEMORY ERRORS RUNNING DOS APPLICATIONS THROUGH WINDOWS

Q975. *I am having trouble when I try to run my DOS application through Windows. Each time I start the DOS application, I see an Out of Memory error message. I know that there's plenty of RAM in my system. What am I doing wrong?*

A. It sounds like a classic case of NOEMS. DOS applications rely on expanded memory provided through the use of EMM386.EXE, but Windows works directly with extended memory. By using the NOEMS switch with EMM386.EXE in your CONFIG.SYS file, you are preventing DOS from accessing high memory, thus, you have an Out of Memory error. When you try to start a DOS application under these circumstances, the application may simply refuse to load (as you found), the application may load and run but fail when particular functions are used, or it may run some DOS applications but not run others. Try using the RAM switch instead of the NOEMS switch.

ADVANCED

DOS Applications Through Windows Causes Split Screen

Q976. *I am using a DOS program through Windows 3.1, but when I close the DOS application, Windows goes into a split screen (top to bottom) which I cannot clear. I have no choice but to close and restart Windows in order to clear the problem. Any ideas?*

A.   It sounds like you are using an old or corrupted Windows 3.1x video driver. Part of a video driver serves as a "grabber" which stores the Windows video mode before the DOS application starts and restores the Windows graphics mode when the DOS application is finished. If this grabber file is obsolete (i.e., a Windows 3.0 file) or corrupt, you can experience that kind of problem. Contact your video board manufacturer to see if they can provide a new set of video drivers and DOS grabber files. You may be able to download updated files from the manufacturer's BBS, CompuServe forum, or Internet Web site.

Intermittent Drive Problems Loading USER.EXE

Q977. *The error message "Failure to load USER.EXE, you must reinstall Windows" has been popping up—not every time, but several times a day for at least 2 months. After much effort (and hair pulling), replacing the hard drive has cured the problem. Could you please shed some light on what might have been happening?*

A.   I've got a good idea. I suspect that one or more of the sectors containing your USER.EXE file were marginal (that is, they had almost failed). By replacing the drive and reinstalling your software, you eliminated any potential hardware problems with the original drive. You might try popping the old drive back in and running ScanDisk for a low-level media check to see if it can identify bad media and remap the bad sectors to new sectors. If you can successfully map out the bad sectors, you may be able to repartition and reformat the drive and then use it as a handy second hard drive.

PINNING DOWN GPFS

Q978. *Why do I get GPF error messages so erratically? I get them frequently—referencing Netscape much of the time while on the Internet—but they appear while I'm using other software as well. I am using Windows 3.11 with Netscape 2.02 on a 486DX4/100 system with 28MB of RAM.*

A.   The phrase general protection refers to the way in which Windows manages RAM in a PC and how it keeps track of which programs are running in what memory space. General protection errors usually occur for two reasons: (1) one badly coded program is "stepping on" the memory space used by another program, or (2) there is a problem somewhere in your system RAM. Try a DOS diagnostic to test your system RAM (concentrate your testing on all memory over the 1MB mark). Feel free to stress test the RAM. If a fault is revealed, you will need to replace the offending SIMM(s). If memory is good, you will have to focus on pinpointing bad software or bad drivers under Windows. First, make sure that you are running as few applications as possible and see that any unneeded drivers are disabled; then make sure that you are using the latest major Windows drivers (i.e., video drivers). If your problems persist, you may need to reinstall Windows and your applications to relieve the problem.

GPFS WHEN WORKING WITH QUATROPRO

Q979. *I just installed a Desk Jet 682C on Windows 3.11 with QuatroPro for Windows, and I'm getting GPFs (like Exception Trapped, Execution Resumed) and GPFs with the HPFW04.DLL when I try to print or load files. Can you help me?*

A.   If you're only getting errors under QuatroPro, check the configuration of that application. You may even try reinstalling it. If you're getting GPFs printing from any application, your Windows 3.1 platform does not like the printer driver. Open your printer control panel and select a generic printer driver.

ADVANCED

You'll loose some capability, but that'll nail down the problem if those errors go away. At that point, you'll need a new printer driver from Microsoft (*www.microsoft.com*) or direct from Hewlett-Packard (*www.hp.com*).

GPF Shuts Down MS Word Permanently

Q980. *Recently, Word decided to crash while I was typing a term paper. It gave me the message of "General Protection Fault." I have a program called First Aid which (theoretically) catches the crash before it causes damage or lost data, automatically fixes the problem, and allows you to restart where you left off. Well, I was able to shut down Word, but when I tried to restart Word, I received the GPF, and now I can't even open Word. I installed WordPerfect (just to give me a word processing program), but when I tried to open it I still got the same GPF. Please help.*

A.   A general protection fault is *always* related to memory—specifically something in memory has become corrupt or damaged. Although I can't tell you *why* your GPF occurred, it seems that you've got a corrupt driver. My guess would be a bad printer driver. Try removing and reinstalling your printer driver(s), and I think the GPF will clear.

Look Beyond Memory for GPFs and Lock-ups

Q981. *I have a Cougar 486BL motherboard. The documentation that came with it says to use single-density 256Kx36, 1Mx36, or 4Mx36 SIMMs. I currently have two 1Mx32 SIMMs in the PC (those were what I had when I got the motherboard). I am having problems with GPFs and the computer locking up. Can I attribute the problems I am having to the memory? If so, will I be doing any major damage to the SIMMs or the motherboard while I save the money to replace the memory?*

A.   Stop right there. I'm not sure just *why* you've targeted your memory for suspicion, but Windows general protection faults and system lock-ups can be caused by a staggering number of potential hardware and software problems. If your problems started after installing this Cougar motherboard, you might try entering the CMOS Setup and systematically disabling some of the advanced features (like internal cache, external cache, video shadowing, BIOS shadowing, and so on).

As a general rule, if the system locks up while working under DOS, chances are that you've got a hardware problem, so check the entire system for loose boards, SIMMs, and cable connections. If the system works soundly under DOS, your hardware is probably working properly, and there is an issue with Windows drivers, TSRs, or applications that is causing your problems.

Adding RAM Causes System Slowdown

Q982. *I added 8MB to a 8MB machine (bringing the total RAM to 16MB) and the computer actually slowed down. The system uses DOS 6.2x and Windows 3.11. I can't get any help from the manufacturer, so I hope you might have some suggestions.*

A. This is an unusual problem, and I searched all over the place for an answer. I've discovered that some systems with Windows 3.11 swap files can actually slow down when RAM is added. I suggest that you remove the permanent swap file by disabling virtual memory. You will probably notice a speed improvement. At that point, I suggest that you run ScanDisk to check your drive and then use DEFRAG to defragment the disk. Then try recreating the swap file. If speed drops again, you can disable virtual memory again and leave it disabled, or reduce the size of your swap file.

File Management and Virtual Memory

Cleaning Out the Rubbish

Q983. *I am about to totally wipe my hard drive because I feel that there is that much rubbish on it, and it's almost full. I currently use DOS 6.22 and Windows 3.11. I was thinking about trying to partition my drive so that I could have DOS, Windows, and my other main software in one partition and other not-so-important software in the other. Would this cause problems when installing programs in the second partition, would they find the WIN.INI file, and so on?*

A.   That's actually a common housekeeping technique and should present no real problem. However, adding the partition will add a drive letter, so if your PC has a CD-ROM, you'll need to reconfigure the CD-ROM drivers to reflect the new CD-ROM drive letter. For example, a CD-ROM that was D: would become E:. As long as your installation routine knows where to find the Windows directory, software installations should proceed properly. However, keep in mind that the only technical advantage to your plan is smaller clusters because your partitions will be smaller. Still, this will not save you significant slack space unless you deal with a large number of very small files.

Floppy Disks Not the Best Choice for Long-Term Backups

Q984.   *I have been backing up files onto floppy disks for several years now. A friend just told me that floppy disks are only reliable for a few years. Is this true? Should I be backing my files up on tape or some other media?*

A.   Theoretically, a good-quality floppy disk that has been recorded from a clean, properly aligned drive should be readable indefinitely. In actual practice, however, there are a myriad of factors that effect a disk's readability. The disk's quality, drive wear and alignment, and the disk's handling and storage conditions will all effect data retention. Under average conditions and reasonable storage, it's reasonable to expect a 10-yr life span from floppy disks. Under harsh conditions or consistent use, 3 to 5 yr is more realistic. Since tape is also a magnetic media, it suffers from the same limitations as floppy disks. In fact, data integrity on tape tends to be somewhat less than on disk since the data on closely wound tape tends to degrade a bit faster. The advantage to tape is its great capacity, not its life span.

If you want an ideal mix of capacity and life span, consider a recordable CD-ROM. A single disc can hold over 600MB (over 1GB with compression), and the disc material is rated to last over 100 years with proper storage. Later in 1997 or early in 1988, recordable DVD drives (with several GB of recordable capacity) should be available.

TAKING CARE OF THE SWAP FILE

Q985. *I've been cleaning out my hard drive trying to make some more space, and I came across a file called 386SPART.PAR. Any idea what this file is or if I can erase it?*

A.   Don't erase that file. That's your Windows permanent swap file (PSF) which is *absolutely essential* for providing virtual memory in your Windows environment. *Never* erase this file unless you disable virtual memory from within Windows *first*. Once you've disabled virtual memory, you can erase the file, defragment the hard drive (or use ScanDisk to check for disk errors), and then reenable virtual memory to recreate a new PSF from scratch the next time you start Windows.

DEALING WITH CORRUPT SWAP FILES

Q986. *Whenever I boot Windows 3.1, I get the error message "Permanent Swap File is Corrupt." I have tried to deal with the problem by going through the 386 enhanced utility with no results. Even after resetting the swap file by way of 386 enhanced and then circling back and going into the Virtual Settings of 386 enhanced, the message comes back up indicating that the permanent swap file is corrupted. What do you think?*

A.   I'm not sure exactly *what* you did under 386Enh, but you're on the right track. You need to *shut down* the PSF completely. This should effectively erase the PSF. At that point, go to DOS and run ScanDisk to correct any cross-linked files or missing allocation units. Defragment the drive, *then* restart Windows, and restore a new PSF by restarting virtual memory under 386Enh.

Manually Correcting a Corrupt Swap File

Q987.   *Here's an odd problem. I had to restore my Windows 3.1x sys-tem files, and when I did, I found that the permanent swap file was corrupted. I tried to fix the swap file but couldn't. Any sug-gestions?*

A.   You may be able to get around this problem by manually deleting the swap file under DOS and then defragmenting the disk. Once DEFRAG is complete, you can reboot the system and start Windows 3.1x. This will register an error indicating that the swap file is missing and should give you an opportunity to create a new swap file. Reset your swap file, and the problem should disappear.

Compressed Swap File Crashes Windows 3.1x

Q988.   *I finally decided to use DoubleSpace to compress my hard drive. The compression created drive C: (compressed) and drive I: (uncompressed). I then decided to increase the size of my perma-nent swap file, so I selected the 386 Enhanced option from the Control Panel and then went in to change the Virtual Memory size. I filled in the size I wanted* without *changing the drive to I:, so the PSF change went through on drive C:. Now the system boots to DOS, but Windows crashes every time I start it. What can I do to fix this mess?*

A.   That is a very easy mistake to make. Start a DOS text editor and load the SYSTEM.INI file located in the /WINDOWS subdirecto-ry. Search the [386 Enh] section of the file. You will probably find two entries: PermSwapDOSDrive=C and PermSwapSizeK=<whatever you entered for PSF size>. Remove these two lines and enter the line Paging=Off to temporarily dis-able Windows use of the swap file. You will also have to delete the existing permanent swap file 386SPART.PAR before attempt-ing to create a new one. The PSF is a hidden file, so use the /A switch with DIR to locate the hidden file (i.e., DIR 386SPART.PAR /A). Use the DOS DELTREE command with the /Y switch to eliminate the file (i.e., DELTREE /Y 386SPART.PAR). You should now be able to restart Windows and create a new PSF on the uncompressed drive I:.

Also remember that you can only create a PSF that is less than 50 percent of the available uncompressed drive space. If you only have 8MB of uncompressed space free, you will only be able to create a PSF up to 4MB. If you need more uncompressed space to create a larger PSF, use the DoubleSpace control panel to alter the drive compression parameters to free more uncompressed space before creating a PSF.

DEALING WITH A 32-BIT DISK ACCESS ERROR

Q989. *Windows 3.1x gives me an error message about the 32-bit disk access driver whenever it loads. How can I correct this?*

A. The standard Windows 3.x driver for 32-bit disk access was designed to be compatible with an older Western Digital controller standard. EIDE drives (larger than 528MB) are not compatible with this driver. Enabling 32-bit disk access with larger drives requires a driver written by the manufacturer of the drive. Contact your drive manufacturer for 32-bit disk access drivers. You can usually download the 32-bit driver directly from the manufacturer's Web site.

WINDOWS APPLICATION QUITS IMMEDIATELY

Q990. *I spent a little time cleaning out excess files yesterday, but now I can't get one of my Windows 3.1 applications to run. The icon is still there, but when I start the program, it just bombs out immediately—there isn't even an error message. What could I have done?*

A. This happens all too often. Chances are that while cleaning out unneeded files, you accidentally erased one or more .DLL files from the application directory. When the program starts, it uses a .DLL file. If the file is not there, the program usually just quits outright. Fortunately, this is easy to rectify. You can find a copy of the .DLL file (if one exists elsewhere on the drive) and copy it to the application's directory. Otherwise, you can just reinstall the application from scratch. Keep in mind that installing an application over itself can reset preferences and clear data files, so you may want to back up the remainder of the application's directory before reinstalling it.

WINDOWS ERRORS LEAD TO HDD FIRMWARE UPGRADE

Q991.   *Periodically, I receive an error message in Windows stating that some of my program groups are damaged or missing. I don't see anything missing (everything is still there). Is there a problem with Windows or my Quantum 730MB hard drive?*

A.   You've hit upon a little-known problem with some of the early Quantum EIDE drives—specifically, this problem is present in some of the Quantum Lightning 540MB and 730MB hard drives. You can correct this issue once you download, extract, and install the firmware update from Quantum (*www.quantum.com*).

CORELSCSI BACKUP ERRORS

Q992.   *I'm using the CorelSCSI tape backup program on my system, and every time I try to back up, I get a Fatal Error. Do you know what this means or how to fix it?*

A.   In virtually all cases, you've got a problem with one or more SCSI drivers failing to work with CorelSCSI. I have heard that older versions of DOS ASPI managers can cause CorelSCSI to fail. Check the dates on all of your real-mode SCSI drivers, and make sure that you are using the latest versions of each.

DRIVER ERRORS FOUND WHEN SETTING UP WINDOWS 3.1x PSF

Q993.   *Recently, while attempting to set up a Windows permanent swap file (or PSF) on a Gateway 486DX2/66 with 8MB RAM, we received the following message: "07,1-32 bit driver corrupted." This appeared when the permanent (using 32-bit access) virtual memory type was selected. Any idea how to get around this or get the driver reloaded?*

A.   Windows 3.1x incorrectly detects several types of hard drives as being compatible with FastDisk when they really are not. This is why Windows does not automatically enable FastDisk. Whenever you notice hard disk errors or file corruption, disable FastDisk *immediately* and check with Gateway (or the drive/controller manufacturer) to find if the drive system is compatible with FastDisk. Once you disable FastDisk, it may be necessary to delete and recreate the PSF again. If the drive system is compatible with FastDisk, the file WIN386.EXE may actually be corrupted. Reinstall WIN386.EXE manually. If the problem persists, you may need to reinstall Windows 3.1x.

FLOPPY ACCESS PROBLEMS UNDER WINDOWS 3.1

Q994. *A friend of mine has a 486DX266 that has been behaving strangely. It is running Windows 3.1, and often when the A: drive is accessed, it reports that the drive cannot be read. The drive has been replaced, but the problem continues. The system has a sound card, CD-ROM, and an Ethernet card. Any help would be appreciated.*

A. Floppy drive access problems may be the result of a computer virus, so boot from a clean write-protected floppy and run a current antivirus program. If the system is clean, you can check the floppy drive hardware. Make sure that the drive controller is installed properly (a moot point if the floppy controller is already on the motherboard). Also see that the floppy drive cable is in good shape and connected securely at both ends. You've already replaced the physical drive, so you should not have a floppy drive failure. Try accessing the floppy drive under DOS. If the drive works under DOS but not under Windows, you've got a driver or utility problem to deal with. If you cannot access the drive under DOS either, there's definitely a hardware problem with the floppy system.

LINUX PARTITION NOT SEEN BY DOS

Q995. *My system has been using C:, D:, and E: drives. The CD-ROM used E:, and C: and D: were for hard drives. C: is the primary drive with Windows 95, and D: is the secondary drive, which has just been repartitioned for Linux. Yesterday when I booted the system, the secondary drive was not there; C: is still the primary drive, and D: became the CD-ROM. When I went to CMOS, the drive was detected there with all its parameters. I went to File Manager and found that I had only two drives, hard drive C: (primary) and D: for the CD-ROM. Please help.*

A.　As I understand it, you had two hard drives, but "lost" the secondary hard drive after you repartitioned it. If so, I think the answer to your problem is very simple. You didn't format the new partition. For example, if you partition a drive, you still can't access the drive letter until you successfully format the partition. Since you repartitioned the secondary hard drive but did not format the partition, your system has no way of assigning a drive letter. Try it. Partition and format the drive for DOS, and I think you'll see the D: drive return. Now there's another problem. Even when you *do* finally install Linux, I'm not sure that DOS will see the Linux partition and assign a drive letter. But that's an operating system issue you'll need to deal with between Linux and DOS.

Communication Issues

REQUIREMENTS FOR HEAD-TO-HEAD PLAY

Q996.　*I have a DOS game that features "head-to-head" play, and I want to play it with my sister-in-law across town. What do I have to do to play head-to-head with my modem?*

A.　Since you don't say what the game is or who makes it, I can only give you a general overview. You will need to find the game's configuration screen and enter all of the operating details for your modem such as COM port, IRQ, I/O address, connect speed, data frame, player name, and so on. Your sister-in-law will have to do the same thing. Then one of you will probably have to initiate a new game and then have the other "call" and connect to the first modem in order to join the game. This is also the way things go with serial cable connections (you just need a serial cable and null modem instead). If the settings do not match precisely, the computers won't connect. Here's a hint: Start your connections at a slow speed and then reconnect with consecutively faster speeds until you find the fastest connect speed that will work for both of you.

Modem Not Seen in Windows 3.1x

Q997.   *I've configured my modem properly and I know that there are no hardware conflicts, but my Windows 3.1x communication software refuses to identify the modem. This is driving me crazy. Can you help?*

A.   It sounds like your port and hardware settings do not match. Open the Control Panel—it is usually in the Main program group. Double-click on the Ports icon and then click on the picture of the COM port that you actually set the modem to. Change to IRQ and I/O address settings from their default settings to the settings that the modem is actually set to. You may also have to make the same changes in your communication software if necessary. Once that is done, you may have to restart Windows. At that point, you modem should be active.

Network Card Lock-up Problems

Q998.   *I have a 3-yr-old AST Advantage Pro 486DX/33. I am trying to install an Ethernet adapter card and am having conflict problems at every setting that is mutually available to me in DOS and WFWG. My Ethernet card came with DOS software that sets the IRQ and I/O address and checks them to make sure they are conflict-free in DOS. I then go to WFWG network setup and match the settings with every available setting match, I have a conflict which locks up the computer as soon as I load Windows. A cold boot is needed to restart the system. I had no problems installing this card in another machine. Any help is appreciated.*

A.   Generally speaking, when a hardware device works trouble-free under DOS (and in other systems), the device is operating properly. It is usually Windows itself which is at the root of the problem. Specifically, there may be a driver loaded in SYSTEM.INI (or other .INI file) which is causing the conflict that is locking up your system. Chances are that the software used for the network card is also working if you can get the board to run on other systems. Check SYSTEM.INI and other communication-related .INI files for any networking entries that might cause a conflict. You might also contact the network card maker (or visit their Web site) and see if there are any known driver conflicts. That may help speed your search.

Multimedia

SYSTEM LOCK-UPS CAN BE TRACED TO VIDEO SYSTEM

Q999. *I've pieced together a system from spare parts. It's an AMD486DX2/80 system using an SIS 85C471-based VESA VL motherboard and a Trident TGUI9400CXi VESA video card. When running Windows 3.11, the system locks up periodically. Lowering the bus speed to 33 MHz didn't help. But when I put my older Cirrus Logic VGA ISA card in there, everything runs like a charm. Any ideas? What is the tech support number for SIS and/or Trident?*

A.   First, you should always make sure to update the Windows video driver when installing a new video board. A disk of Windows 3.1x video drivers should have accompanied the video board. You can also download the very latest drivers from the manufacturer's BBS or Internet site. If the problem persists, check to see if there are any memory exclusions needed for the video board (entered as EXCLUDE switches in EMM386 command line). Update the EMM386 command line in CONFIG.SYS if necessary. If that does not solve the problem, the video board itself may be defective. Try another video board. If you need help or new drivers from Trident, call their BBS at 415-691-1016. You can download Trident drivers from the Internet at http://www.cs.usask.ca/grads/philip/trident.html.

SCREEN BLANKS WHEN WINDOWS CLOSES

Q1000. *I've got a video problem. Whenever I close Windows (or open a DOS window), the display blanks out. Why is this? How do I fix it?*

A.   From your brief description of the symptoms, it seems that the video system works fine until you shift from Windows mode to DOS mode. In virtually all cases that I have ever heard of, this type of problem is due to a buggy video driver (or other display TSR software). Check the software that is running your display, and upgrade to the very latest version of that software.

Windows 3.1x Program Icons Lost with High Color Depth

Q1001. I'm using Windows 3.1, and I'm having trouble with my
enhanced video drivers. The video works at 256 colors, but when
I try to use a 65K or 16M color mode, I see an error message
that says "Extremely Low on Memory. There is not enough
memory to convert all the program icons. The icons which are
not converted will appear black...." And some icons do appear
black. I know that I have plenty of memory. What's wrong?

A.   The problem is with Windows 3.1x. The Program Manager
reserves only 64KB of memory for each icon group in Windows.
When you use higher color drivers, each icon requires much
more memory than an icon in 256 color mode. So if Program
Manager runs out of memory, it paints some icons black and displays that error message. Unfortunately, choosing File Properties
as the message instructs does not solve the problem. You will
need to revert to a lower color driver, use fewer icons in each
group, or upgrade to Windows 95.

Windows 3.1x Icons Disappear in High Color Palettes

Q1002. I've got a problem with my Windows icons. When I switch to a
32K color driver, some of my icons turn black, and I get a mes-
sage saying that there is not enough memory to display all the
icons properly. The problem is that my video board has 1MB of
RAM, which seems to be OK for 32K colors. Am I doing some-
thing wrong?

A.   Well, yes and no. The problem is not with your video memory
Rather, it lies in the basic design of Windows and your main system RAM. A program group window will only accommodate as
many icons as will fit into a 64KB space (that's system RAM not
video RAM). Since the amount of memory needed for each icon
is dependent on the screen mode (higher modes need more data
to represent each pixel), higher modes can limit the number of
icons in the group. An icon file (.ICO) defines a 32x32 matrix of
pixels. When the icon is copied into a group file, each pixel gets
between 4 and 32 bits—EGA and VGA offer 4 bits per pixel,
SVGA 256 colors use 8 bits per pixel, and so on. This means an

icon can demand from 512 to 4096 bytes, depending on the color depth being used. Table 11.2 illustrates this relationship. If your program group has more icons than can be represented in a 64KB space, the remaining icons will appear black. Your only course then is to reduce your color palette or move some of the "extra" icons to a separate program group. This will vary a bit in actual practice due to variations between video adapters, but you get the idea. Note that Windows 95 eliminates this issue.

TABLE 11.2 COLOR DEPTH VERSUS ICON MEMORY REQUIREMENTS

Colors	Bytes/pixel	Bytes/Icon	Icons/Group
16	.5	512	128
256	1	1024	64
32.8K	2	2048	32
16.7M	3	3072	21
16.7M	4*	4096	16

* Note that some 24-bit (3-byte) color systems actually store each pixel in 4 bytes, with the fourth byte reserved. Therefore, the icon limit is a bit less than expected when some 24-byte color cards are installed.

VIDEO BOARD ICON WON'T APPEAR IN WINDOWS 3.1X

Q1003. *Maybe you can help me figure out the problem with my video board. I just put a Kelvin Video64 board in my PC and installed the drivers under Windows 3.1, but I can't get the Kelvin installation icon to appear. Do you have any ideas?*

A. While I don't have a specific solution for your Kelvin Video64 problem, I have seen this sort of problem crop up before—almost always because of memory manager problems. When you use EMM386 or QEMM, you need to exclude the video adapter's memory range. This is typically accomplished through the memory manager's command line in CONFIG.SYS. Try excluding the address range from A000h to C7FFh and adding the exclude switch (i.e., x=a000-c7ff) to your EMM386 or QEMM command line. Another problem with memory managers is their special features. With QEMM, the Stealth feature (ST:M or ST:F) can cause problems. You may need to add the XST=C000 switch to your command line. With EMM386, the HIGHSCAN option may also be an issue. If you are using the HIGHSCAN switch under EMM386, try removing it.

NO SOUND VOLUME WITH DOS GAME

Q1004. *Maybe you can help me with a sound problem. My Ensoniq sound board has been working for months now (ever since I first got my system). It works under Windows 95 perfectly and under DOS 7.0 when I run DOS games. The problem is that I just installed a new DOS game which demands a Sound Blaster 100 percent compatible system. I thought the Ensoniq was compatible with Sound Blasters—I've run other games that way. Can you shed any light on this?*

A.   I've seen this one crop up more than once, and it is almost always a fault of the application. In this case, your game is using a sound library that requires a true Sound Blaster. The Sound Blaster clones simply won't work. My advice to you is just to return the game and get a refund. It's not worth replacing your Ensoniq board.

PLAYING CD AUDIO SLOWS WINDOWS

Q1005. *A couple of friends have commented to me that when playing a music CD on their systems, Windows slows down considerably. I've never noticed this when I play audio CDs, but is this true?*

A.   I don't hear this kind of complaint often, probably because so many users have plenty of processing power today for CDs and multimedia in general. Since you don't say anything about the age of your friends' computers or what version of Windows they're running, I have to assume these are older systems with Windows 3.1x.

First, audio CDs are typically played through an applet (a simple application). In some cases, these applets are not written very well and can tie up an unusual amount of resources, especially if the applet is left open on the desktop (or Program Manager for Windows 3.1x). Try minimizing the applet. You won't see the fancy track and counter graphics, but it might pick things up a bit. You might also try playing CDs with several different applications (such as shareware) to see if other software causes the same problem or just one particular program. Next, the low-level driver that runs a CD will have a profound impact on how it performs with data and audio media. Check with the CD-ROM maker to see if there is an updated driver for the CD-ROM.

Finally, running any drive takes some amount of processing power, even if it's just to play audio CDs. Older 486 systems with limited memory and system resources frequently suffered stalls and poor system performance with CD-ROM drives. Consider upgrading the CPU, and perhaps add some more RAM. Note that a faster CD would *not* resolve the problem because all audio CDs play at the same Red Book data rate of 150KB/s (1X speed).

Peripheral Questions

No PC would be complete without peripherals such as scanners and printers. Still, these common devices can sometimes be difficult to set up and use successfully. This chapter covers a series of questions that frequently arise from peripheral users.

BEGINNER

Scanners

SCANNER FEEDS MULTIPLE SHEETS

Q1006. *Why does my scanner feed multiple sheets through the automatic document feeder? The scans are great when I feed documents manually, but the page counts are all messed up when I use the automatic document feeder.*

A.   Document feeders use an array of sensitive rollers and pads to separate pages. Over time, dust and old age can reduce the contact quality of the document feeder and result in misfeeds. The first step to correcting the problem is to go through the cleaning procedure that was probably outlined in the scanner's user manual. If the problem continues, the scanner's contact pad assembly may be worn and need replacement. In most cases, this is considered a consumable item on the scanner, and requires periodic replacement. The life of the pad assembly will vary depending on the type of documents you are scanning.

Printers

OBTAINING NEW HEWLETT-PACKARD DRIVERS

Q1007. *I've been looking all over for new HP 500C drivers. Can you tell me where I might be able to download new drivers?*

A.   Try the Hewlett-Packard BBS at 208-344-1691. If you have access to the Internet, you might also try the HP Web page that will guide you to the driver at *http://www.hp.com/misc/ peripherals.html*. If you don't have access to the Internet World Wide Web, you can download the drivers from the HP ftp site at *ftp-boi.external.hp.com/pub/*.

GETTING ACCESS TO EPSON

Q1008. I have an old Epson printer but no documentation. Can you tell me how to get in touch with Epson support?

A.   I found three numbers for Epson America. You can try their sales line at 800-922-8911, their tech support line at 213-539-9955, or go on-line with their BBS at 310-782-4531 (9600 bps). If you have access to the Internet, you can find Epson on the World Wide Web at *http://www.epson.com.*

PROPER PRINTER CABLE LENGTH

Q1009. I sure would appreciate it if someone could let me know the maximum length I can use for my printer cable. I have heard that 6 ft is the maximum working length, but I have also heard of people using 15-ft cables with no signal degradation. What's the bottom line?

A.   Traditionally, a Centronics-type parallel printer cable should not exceed 6 ft (10 ft at the most). If you keep to this limit, you can be confident of reliable communications in just about all circumstances. Unfortunately, the actual length possible for a printer varies with the printer and the cable quality. I have heard of a 30-ft cable being used with a TI MicroLaser Pro 600, but the TI MicroMark Color printer does not seem to support any cables over 6 ft. By using high-quality shielded cables, you can reduce signal noise and extend communication up to 20 ft or 25 ft, but there are no guarantees once you exceed 6 ft. If you already have the cables handy, go ahead and experiment (you can't hurt the printer or computer by using an excessively long cable). If you really need reliable, long-distance printing, you can use a printer extender, which is basically a buffer/amplifier which plugs in between your printer and PC.

Using an A/B Switch with Two Printers

Q1010. *Perhaps you can give me some helpful information about connecting two printers to one computer. I want to connect an Epson Stylus 500 jet printer and a Panasonic KX-P2123 24-pin dot-matrix printer using an A/B switch box connected to my 486 computer. I currently have the Epson connected with a bidirectional cable. Can I use an A/B switch box safely with these two printers?*

A.   This shouldn't be a problem. The A/B switch box should work without problems. However, you may want to make sure that the cable between the PC and A/B box will support bidirectional operation (it almost certainly should). If not, you might lose a bit of functionality with the Epson. Also keep in mind that parallel port cables should be as short as possible, so if there must be more than 6 ft in total between the parallel port and Epson, consider using good-quality shielded cables.

Cutting the Costs of Toner

Q1011. *I recently upgraded my old dot matrix printer to a laser printer. Although the print is outstanding, I was distraught to find that a toner cartridge costs up to $110 (sometimes more). What can I do to stretch the toner's life?*

A.   Toner is used to form the images created by electrophotographic printers (laser printers, LED printers, photocopiers, plain paper faxes, and so on). Darker images demand more toner. Keeping image contrast down will result in fainter images but will use less toner. Experiment with the contrast setting to find a good trade-off between image quality and contrast. Keep in mind that you may have to increase contrast slightly as the toner supply is consumed. When printing, select the draft mode or lower-resolution printing, which will also help conserve toner.

As always, you should shop around for the best toner prices. Office supply superstores and warehouse outlets can offer some extremely competitive prices. Another cost-cutting measure to consider is recycled or remanufactured toner cartridges. Although there may be little or no recycled cartridges available for new printers, popular or well-established printers (such as HP5s) usually have a base of recycled cartridges. A toner cartridge provided by a reputable recycler can be just as reliable as an original. When the cartridge is recycled, worn mechanical components are often replaced. More toner is added than was put in originally (so the recycled cartridge often lasts longer). Recycled cartridges are usually less than half the cost of a new cartridge. And of course, the environment benefits from less waste. Use caution when dealing with cartridge recyclers. Not all recycled cartridges are top quality. Table 12.1 offers a brief list of recyclers.

TABLE 12.1 AN ANNOTATED LIST OF TONER CARTRIDGE RECYCLERS

COMPANY	PHONE NUMBER
Advantage Laser Products	800-239-4027
Coastal Laser Products	800-432-1628
Discount Laser Supply	800-786-2270
Laser Quipt	800-777-8444
L.C. Products	800-817-3758
National Toner Recycling	800-676-0749
Willow	800-426-8196

SHELF LIFE OF INK JET CARTRIDGES

Q1012. *I've had some ink jet cartridges in my desk drawer for a while now, but I'm not sure if they're good anymore. How long is the shelf life of the ink?*

A. The actual shelf life of ink depends on several different things such as the quality of the ink, the seal on new ink containers, and the storage temperature. Most ink will remain viable for about 2 yr when stored at normal room temperature. Better-quality inks may last longer. Check the packaging on your ink cartridges for an expiration date. In actual practice, you can probably use ink cartridges up to several years beyond their expiration date, but you may find that they do not produce the same image quality as fresh ink cartridges.

CLEANING A CLOGGED INK JET CARTRIDGE

Q1013. Can you suggest any means to get a dried-up HP print cartridge to work again? I have a Desk Jet 310 and a CMY cartridge which hasn't been used for a few months. I also have one of those small black storage containers for it, too. The cartridge has been kept in there, but when I try to print the test page, I get an occasional streak of color every five or six test runs. It can't possibly be empty since it hasn't been used all that often.

A.   Clogged ink cartridges are probably the single most troublesome aspect of ink jet technology. Because printer ink is not water soluble, moistening the nozzles with steam will have no effect (except perhaps to corrode the cartridge's electrical contacts). Instead, ink is typically alcohol soluble, so try wiping the nozzles with isopropyl alcohol on a clean cotton swab. You may have to repeat the process several times before all the nozzles will clear. If you need to use a more radical technique, try setting the cartridge (nozzles down) in a shallow bath of clean isopropyl alcohol (a bottle cap full should be plenty). Try using 30-min intervals until all the nozzles are clear. Also use some fresh alcohol on a cotton swab to clean the electrical contacts on the cartridge and printer.

Here's something else to keep in mind. A CMY (or three-color) ink cartridge holds far less ink than a standard black cartridge (less than one third as much ink for each color). This means your cartridge will only last for one third as many pages. Even if it doesn't seem that you used the cartridge a lot, it may still be empty. If you cannot unclog the ink cartridge with alcohol, you should simply replace it.

USING PC SIMMS IN PRINTERS

Q1014. Can I use a regular PC SIMM in HP4+ printer?

A.   The answer is Yes. The HP4+ printers use standard SIMMs, so they will work in a PC, or you can take SIMMs from a PC for use in the HP4+. Remember, however, that your SIMMs must be the proper speed (around 70 ns) and should be simple DRAM SIMMs (try to avoid EDO, FPM, or SDRAM SIMMs). Also observe consistent parity with the other SIMMs in the printer.

CHOOSING AND USING PRINTER CABLES

Q1015. *I recently purchased a new printer, and I want to connect it as an additional printer. The new printer is an Epson Stylus 500, and I was told that it will require either a standard bidirectional printer cable ($10) or an IEEE-1284 cable ($30). Does the IEEE cable allow for faster printing?*

A.   The IEEE-1284 standard allows for enhanced parallel ports (EPP) which support faster communication and control of devices, as well as more sophisticated features like controlling multiple devices. In practice, an IEEE-1284 cable is better built and shielded to support higher data transfer rates, but for printers, higher data rates will not dramatically increase printing speed. You would probably be just fine with a regular, good-quality bidirectional printer cable. If you were using a parallel port CD-ROM or other IEEE-1284 device, I would probably suggest using an IEEE-1284 cable.

CAN'T UPDATE A PRINTER DRIVER

Q1016. *I'm installing new drivers for my Canon BJC-4100, and now I get an error message that says "Unable to update driver, driver is currently being used by Windows." How can I get around this error?*

A.   Windows uses the files CTL3D.DLL and CTL3DV2.DLL, which are located in the Windows\System directory. During new driver installation, the printer is trying to use these files as well and therefore causes the error. Exit Windows, rename the files to CTL3D.OLD and CTL3DV2.OLD. Restart Windows and then load the new driver.

LOOSE CABLES STOP PRINTING

Q1017. *The printer refuses to print under DOS or Windows. The cable is connected and the printer is on, but I simply cannot get any response from the printer. I see error messages that indicate that the printer is not ready.*

INTERMEDIATE

A.   In virtually all cases, your cable is not connected properly, or the cable is damaged. Check the cable installation and then try a new printer cable. If problems persist, check to be sure that the proper printer type and driver are selected in your application. Try the printer on another PC. If the printer works, the original LPT port may be defective. If not, the printer itself may be defective.

CLEANING ASCII TRASH FROM PRINTED OUTPUT

Q1018. *I am printing to an HP 1200C using Windows 95, and I keep having problems. When I print graphics or a true-type font, I get extended ASCII characters in the output. They are not every-where—maybe only one or two instances in a given page, but it sure messes up good output. When I print regular text, the output is clean. I just don't understand what's causing it.*

A.   I've seen this kind of problem with the HP 1200C when using a faulty or inexpensive printer cable. Cheap parallel cables may not have all the pins connected or may use only limited electrical noise shielding. The 1200C seems to be particularly sensitive to this problem. I also had the same effect when I tried to use a long 10-ft cable connected to an A/B switch and another 6-ft cable going from the A/B switch to the printer. Try using a short 3-ft high-quality shielded printer cable and see if the ASCII junk disappears. You should always use the latest Windows 95 printer drivers for your HP 1200C.

PRINTER PRINTS GARBAGE OR EXTRA CHARACTERS

Q1019. *I'm resurrecting a used Bubble Jet printer for my cousin. I've got the cables and Windows 3.1x drivers, but when I try to print, all I see are mixed up characters and other garbage ASCII characters. Any ideas?*

A.   In almost all cases, there is a serious communication problem between the PC and printer. The first step is to ensure the drivers are up to date and installed properly and that your printer is selected as the default printer. Make sure that you are using a good-quality printer cable under 6-ft long and then check the

CMOS Setup routine to see that mode your LPT port is set for (i.e., EPP, ECP, or bidirectional). Try setting the LPT mode to bidirectional. Check for print jobs queued up in Print Manager. Delete any pending print jobs and attempt to print again. If the problem persists, disable Print Manager. If you want to use Print Manager, make sure you have enough space left on your hard drive, and see that you have a valid SET TEMP statement in your AUTOEXEC.BAT file to hold your temporary printer files.

CANON MULTIPASS PRINTER PERFORMING POORLY

Q1020. *A friend of mine has a 4-yr-old 486 33-MHz system. It was built by a local computer shop, so I don't know what components are in it. He just recently bought a new Canon CS2500 MultiPass printer. It takes almost 5 min to print one page of simple black and white text. I told him that he should get a new I/O card with a high-speed ECP/EPP LPT port to speed printing. Will this dramatically speed up his printing, or is there something else that I am not thinking about? He is running Windows 3.1 with 16MB of RAM, a permanent swap file, and 32-bit disk access.*

A.   Printers can always be finicky devices, but I would focus on drivers and your system setup before worrying about adding new hardware. First, try a new, good-quality shielded printer cable which is less than 6 ft long. Next, start your CMOS Setup and look for any entries concerning your parallel port. If your system BIOS allows you to select different port modes (i.e., EPP, ECP, bidirectional, or unidirectional), try setting the port to bidirectional (EPP and ECP modes can sometimes cause printer problems). Also try disabling the 32-bit disk access. I doubt that this is your problem, but it's a simple check and easy enough to reenable. If problems persist, I would suspect your printer driver. Download the latest driver for Canon, and make sure that you obtain the driver that is for your exact printer model.

If new drivers do not resolve the problem, there is probably a communication problem between the printer and PC. Try the printer on another PC (preferably running Windows 3.1 with the same driver you're currently using). If the printer performs measurably better on another PC, you can try adding a new LPT port in the original PC.

INTERMEDIATE

LASER PRINTER IMAGES ARE TOO LIGHT

Q1021. *I just got my first laser printer. It's a used Epson Action Laser 1500. I bought a new toner cartridge for it, and the print is still light. Are there some tricks for restoring or cleaning it? I think the printer has not been used for a while.*

A.   There are several factors that affect image darkness. First, check to see what the printer driver settings are. If you are using Windows 95, you can adjust the intensity settings from light to dark and graphics settings from fine to coarse. Mine are set at medium intensity, fine graphics. Next, check the printer for a print intensity control, and set it for a darker image. Also shake the cartridge gently and evenly to distribute the toner (it may have been sitting on the shelf for a long time). Is it a new Epson replacement cartridge or a rebuilt one? A rebuilt one could be giving you problems, so try an original cartridge.

INK CARTRIDGE MOVES, BUT NOTHING PRINTS

Q1022. *I'm using an ink jet printer, and it's been working without problems. The problem is that I just replaced an ink cartridge and now the cartridge moves, but the ink doesn't print?*

A.   All ink jet cartridges ship with a thin strip of tape covering the ink nozzles. Check to see if the orange shipping tape has been removed from the bottom of your ink cartridge. Also check to see that the cartridge is seated properly in its holder. If you remove the tape and the problem persists, you will need to clean the print head with isopropyl alcohol on a clean cotton swab. If the ink cartridge still won't print, it may be defective. Try replacing the ink cartridge (you can always return the defective cartridge if necessary).

CLEANING UP A NO INK MESSAGE

Q1023. *I've got a problem with my Epson Stylus 800+ ink jet printer. Due to a bad refillable ink cartridge, ink has leaked into the printing head and is now dry. As a result, I get the error message that says "no ink." Do you know a good way to solve that?*

A. Start by using isopropyl alcohol on a cotton swab to clean the print head. You might also try setting the print head in a shallow bath of isopropyl alcohol for a time in order to loosen the clogs. Finally, you'll need to purge the printing head with clean isopropyl alcohol. As an absolute last-ditch measure, you may have to replace the ink head outright. Once your ink head is working again, check the printer for the print head's parking cover. Many ink printers rest the idle ink head on a sponge or other surface to keep the print head covered during idle or off times. If your printer has such a cover, make sure that it is clean and working effectively.

PRINTER BEEPS AND PRINT CARTRIDGE STALLS

Q1024. *After I installed a new print cartridge and pressed the self-test button, I heard three beeps and the cartridge stayed in the middle. I don't have any documentation for this printer, so can you help me out?*

A. Audible beeps will sound if the cartridge is seated incorrectly. Remove and reseat the cartridge to fix the problem. You might also try cleaning the electrical contacts in the cartridge and holder with isopropyl alcohol on a clean cotton swab.

PRINTER REFUSES TO PRINT AN ENTIRE DOCUMENT

Q1025. *I'm having problems getting my BJC4100 to print a whole document. It seems like no matter what application I use to print with, the last 25 percent of the last page is* always *missing. I've checked for page settings and they don't do a thing. Any ideas?*

A. This is a known problem with the BJC4100, and you can find a more complete explanation at the Microsoft Web site (*www.microsoft.com*). Basically, you have to slow down the printer port for it to work. If the port is configured for ECP or EPP operation in CMOS Setup, try setting the port to bidirectional or compatibility. Remember to save your changes before exiting the CMOS Setup.

INTERMEDIATE

Laser Printing Problems and Memory

Q1026. *I am working on a Canon LPB4-Lite laser printer. Often it cannot print a complete page properly (especially when heavily formatted text and graphics are printed). It also says "page full" on the LED, but the page is in fact only half full. The printer has 512KB a total of RAM, and when running the self-test, it reports 279KB of free RAM. Could this due to insufficient memory or what? How much RAM is adequate for general use?*

A.   Laser printers don't need much memory for ordinary text in one or two basic fonts, but heavily formatted text and graphics as you describe will demand lots of printer memory. It's hard to predict precisely how much memory you need, but I've seen similar problems with an Epson laser printer. I added 2MB of DRAM, and the problem never returned. Go for a 2MB upgrade. If you can't afford a memory upgrade, reduce the printer resolution. For example, if you're using 600x600 resolution now, reduce it to 300x300. If the printer has a draft printing mode, try using that. Reducing resolution (or otherwise reducing image quality) will reduce the demand on printer memory.

Printing Stops Half Way Through a Page

Q1027. *A client's HP 820 refuses to print an entire page. About halfway through the page (or envelope), the printing stops. An LED begins flashing, he presses the button above that LED, and the page is ejected. However, only half the page printed. What's wrong?*

A.   This is the classic description of a printer data overflow. There isn't enough memory in the printer to accommodate the entire page. This causes an error (indicated by the LED) which requires you to eject the incomplete page manually. There are generally three ways to address such a problem: reduce the printing resolution, simplify the image (i.e., remove fancy fonts or unneeded graphics), or add more memory to the printer.

Printer Refuses to Work Under Windows 95

Q1028. *A client of mine just purchased a P133 with a no-name mother-board using a 430VX chipset. She could not get her Panasonic dot matrix P1123 printer to work in Windows 95. When booting to DOS mode, the printer does work.*

A.   I'm assuming that you installed the proper printer drivers for the Panasonic printer. If so, take a look at your LPT port configuration in CMOS. Many current systems use the EPP mode as a default setting, but older dot matrix printers won't operate in EPP mode. If this is the case, try changing the LPT setting to compatibility mode or bidirectional mode. I think that'll solve the problem.

Not Enough Memory to Print Error

Q1029. *I do not know whether this is a hardware or software problem. Last night when I tried to print, I kept getting the message in Windows 95: "Not enough memory to print," and it would not let me use the printer. I tried several things and then tried to rein-stall the driver with the HP disk, but then this did not work either because Windows 95 was using the driver. Do you know a solution for this? I've got 40MB of RAM in this machine. All has been working since I got this printer over 6 months ago, and nothing was done to the system recently.*

A.   I think there is a very simple explanation for your problem. You're out of hard drive space. Windows 95 prints in terms of graphics, and each page is prepared as a temporary image file on the hard drive before being sent across the parallel port to your printer. If you're running short of hard drive space, there may not be enough room to prepare the printer files. Make sure you've got at least 10MB of drive space available.

INTERMEDIATE

PRINTING CAUSES OUT OF MEMORY ERRORS

Q1030. *I'm using a Canon BJC-4100 printer under Windows 3.1, but I am getting Out of Memory errors when trying to print. What can I do about this?*

A.   Memory errors when printing are a common problem, especially under Windows 3.1. Try the following points to track down the problem:

■   Shut down all other programs running except the one you are printing from.

■   Ensure the BJC-4100 is set as your default printer.

■   Turn off the Print Manager (under Windows 3.1).

■   Verify a proper SET TEMP statement for printer files. The drive that contains the SET TEMP directory may not have enough available space. This can be done from the DOS command prompt by typing SET. Find the TEMP= statement. Examples are TEMP=C:\DOS and TEMP=C:\WINDOWS.

■   Reduce the printer resolution by selecting the standard or draft mode.

■   If printing a multiple page document, print only one or two pages at a time.

■   Lower the video resolution to 680 x 480.

REMOVING AN EXTERNAL DRIVE CAUSES PRINTING PROBLEMS

Q1031. *For several months, my setup has been a Windows 95 Pentium 166-MHz system and an external Ditto tape backup chained together with an auto A/B switch. I could access that one printer from either my 486 system or my Pentium 166. I removed the external tape backup in favor of a larger Ditto 3200 internal drive. While the setup prints from either system correctly, it has a strange glitch. Whenever I reboot, paper feed starts in the printer and then it goes into a reset mode. I must reset the printer, and it's fine from then on until I shut the system down and restart. I have eliminated the problem by using a manual A/B switch, but it's a pain. Why did it work without a hitch until I removed that external tape backup?*

A.   My guess is that when you removed the external drive, you forgot to remove any drivers that were operating the drive. When
the system powers up, the drivers attempt to find the drive, but
only the printer remains, and the printer responds unexpectedly.
Check your CONFIG.SYS and AUTOEXEC.BAT files, and edit
out any references to the old driver(s). If the drive was installed
under Windows 95, run the Add/Remove Hardware applet under
Control Panel to remove any trace of the drive. You may also
need to manually edit the SYSTEM.INI file.

DEALING WITH AN HP 50 ERROR

*Q1032. I'm receiving a Material 50 error message on my HP Laser Jet III
printer. The printer fails its autotest at start-up and displays the
error message. Can you help?*

A.   According to my information, an Error 50 on the Hewlett-
Packard Laser Jet III indicates a fusing problem. Either the fusing
assembly is not getting to the proper temperature within 30 s of
power up, or the fuser drops below the acceptable temperature
range. There are two generally recognized ways to fix this problem. First, try replacing the fuse unit. If this doesn't fix the problem, replace the printer's ac power supply module. Of course,
you could also send the printer out to a shop for repair if you'd
prefer not to handle the problem yourself.

*Always allow at least 15 min for a laser printer to cool before
opening it for examination or any type of service.*

Note

HP 560C PRINTER NEEDS NEW ROLLERS

*Q1033. My HP 560C has been making "spring-popping" noises upon
start-up. All the panel lights randomly flash, and it freezes up.
The printer then has to be manually turned off, and then turned
back on. The problem comes and goes. Any help or suggestions?*

A.   I've seen this kind of problem on a few old HP 560Cs. The roller
material is worn out and needs to be replaced. HP used roller
material that lost its friction properties over time. Combined with

low humidity, low temperature, light use, and excess paper dust, the printer just could not pick up paper. This caused all manor of errors because there was still paper in the tray. You'll need to send the printer back to HP for retrofit. They can replace the rollers and other friction parts with those using newer and better materials. Before sending the printer back, check with HP technical support to see if there are any field upgrade kits now available. If you're really stuck for a solution, try a rubber revitalizer such as you might find in a stationary store. Remember to try the revitalizer first on only a very small edge of a roller in case the chemical is too harsh.

VERTICAL STREAKS ON A LASER JET 4

Q1034. *I have an HP 4 Laser Jet, and it makes streaks, smears, and stray lines on the printouts. The first three to five pages are fine when it first powers up, but any subsequent printouts have vertical streak lines on the left of the page from top to bottom. The cartridge inside the printer is about 4 years old and still has plenty of toner in it. This printer has given me this problem in the past five uses. Any suggestions?*

A.   I doubt that the toner cartridge is at fault because a lack of toner would leave light (or faded) streaks down the page. Anything that is visible on the page is there because the image drum inside the printer has been exposed. This means that either the drum material has failed or the drum is not being charged properly in the first place. I suggest that you replace the printer drum engine or drum cartridge. This is the mechanism that contains the electrophotographic drum and other critical rollers (do not replace the fusing mechanism). You will find that the drum assembly is rather expensive, but they *do* wear out after a while.

COMPAQ PROBLEMS USING LASER PRINTERS

Q1035. *I've connected a laser printer to my Deskpro 4000, but when I print, I only see half a page (sometimes nothing at all). I know it's not the printer because I've used it on other systems without any trouble. What's the deal?*

A.   This is a problem with the LPT.VXD printer driver and usually surfaces when the LPT port is set in the ECP mode. You can clear the problem by reconfiguring the LPT port to bidirectional mode. You can fix the problem on a more permanent basis by updating LPT.VXD. You can download an updated LPT.VXD file from Compaq (*www.compaq.com*).

PRESARIO 7100 PRINTING WITH CANON 4000 SERIES PRINTERS

Q1036. *I can't use my cousin's Canon 4000 printer to print from a Compaq Presario 7100. All I see are a few garbage characters (like [k) at the top of the page.*

A.   In this case, the Canon 4000 printer *requires* an ECP port in order to print, so you need to use an ECP-compliant printer cable and to reconfigure the PC's printer port to ECP mode:

1.   While the system is booting up, enter Setup by pressing the <Del> key.

2.   Select Advanced System Settings.

3.   Select Integrated Peripherals.

4.   Select LPT Extended Mode.

5.   Press the <Space Bar> to select ECP.

6.   Press <F10> and select Yes to Save Changes and EXIT.

PRINTER ONLY PRODUCING ONE LINE PER PAGE

Q1037. *I'm working on a Fujitsu laser printer which is only printing one line per page. This isn't the problem it came in for, so I'm wondering if I'm doing something wrong under Windows 95.*

A.   I'll bet that you're not using a true Fujitsu driver for the printer. You're probably using an HP LaserJet II or LaserJet III driver. If so, make sure the Print TrueType as Graphics option is selected. Right-click on the printer icon and select Properties. Click on the tab labeled Fonts. Click on Print TrueType as Graphics. Click on OK. The ideal solution would be to install the Fujitsu native driver, but this may not be desirable if you're just working on the printer temporarily.

ADVANCED

PRINTED COLOR DOES NOT MATCH THE SCREEN COLOR

Q1038. *I'm setting up a color ink jet printer, but the printed colors don't really match the PC display. Is there anything I can do about this?*

A.   Ordinarily, printed ink colors rarely match screen colors precisely because printed colors are literally mixed from three ink reservoirs. But if the colors are *way* off, there are several things to check for. First make sure that the ink cartridge is full. For example, if you've been printing images with lots of red recently, brown colors may appear too blue. If there's plenty of ink, make sure that the ink head is clean. You should also be using the very latest drivers for your printer (older drivers may have a bug with the color balance). If the printer applet allows for color adjustment, try tweaking the colors manually.

Glossary

The following popular terms and acronyms frequently encountered in e-mail messages, news groups, and mailing lists.

286 — systems and components related to PCs using the Intel 286-vintage microprocessor.

386 — systems and components related to PCs using the Intel 386-vintage microprocessor.

486 — systems and components related to PCs using the Intel 486-vintage microprocessor.

586 — systems and components related to PCs using Pentium or similar microprocessors.

6x86 — a Pentium-equivalent CPU manufactured by Cyrix.

adapter (also called a *board* or *card*) — typically an expansion board (that plugs into a motherboard's bus slot) which provides features or services not already on the motherboard or superior to the motherboard's existing features. An EIDE drive adapter is one example of a popular adapter.

AMD (Advanced Micro Devices) — a major manufacturer of CPUs for use in personal computers.

API (application programming interface) — a set of common software routines that applications can utilize to operate various standard hardware systems.

ASPI (advanced SCSI programming interface) — a specification that defines software drivers and applets used to operate SCSI adapters and devices with SCSI interfaces. For example, a SCSI CD-ROM drive will require an ASPI driver to communicate with the SCSI interface.

AT	a classic term loosely used to denote any modern personal computer. More specifically, it is used to denote the IBM PC/AT personal computers utilizing the Intel 286 CPU.
ATAPI (AT attachment packet interface)	a specification that defines software drivers and applets used to operate IDE devices such as CD-ROM drives. For example, an IDE CD-ROM drive will require an ATAPI driver to communicate with an IDE interface.
benchmark	a program or series of programs used to evaluate the performance of a PC or a specific area of a PC (such as the drive or video system).
BIOS (basic input/ output system)	the firmware located on a motherboard that acts as the interface between an operating system and the motherboard hardware.
CD (compact disc)	a plastic disc 12 cm in diameter which uses optical storage techniques to hold over 600MB of data or audio.
CD-R (compact disc recorder)	an optical drive which can record (or burn) data or audio to blank compact discs.
COM	an abbreviation for *communication*. Used to refer to the serial ports in a PC (i.e., COM 1).
CMOS (complementary metal oxide semiconductor)	the small amount of very low-power static RAM used to store a PC's configuration data such as date, time, drive parameters, wait states, and so on.
CPU	an acronym for central processing unit.
Cyrix	a major manufacturer of CPUs for use in personal computers.
daughterboard (also called a *daughtercard*)	a small module which plugs into full-sized adapter boards. Daughterboards are often made available as add-on devices (usually memory) for devices such as video capture or sound cards.
DIMM (dual in-line memory module)	the new generation of 168-pin high-capacity PC memory devices designed to eventually replace smaller SIMMs.
disc	optical-based media such as a CD or DVD.
disk	magnetic-based media such as a floppy disk or hard disk.
DOS (disk operating system)	the software which allows users to launch application programs and otherwise interact with a PC. Commonly used to mean Microsoft's MS-DOS command-line based operating system.

DMA (direct memory access)	a method of transferring data within a PC without the direct intervention of the CPU. There are eight DMA channels in a typical PC (expressed DMA 0 to DMA 7).
DRAM (dynamic RAM)	the generic name given to standard, high-density memory used in today's PCs.
driver (also called a *device driver*)	small software programs used to identify and interact with various pieces of hardware that are not directly supported by BIOS.
DVD (digital video disc, or digital versatile disc)	the next generation of optical storage which offers from 4.7 to 17GB of storage on a single 12-cm disc. DVD offers enough storage capacity to support full-length movies and sound, as well as massive amounts of data.
DX	nomenclature popularly used with the 386 and 486 CPUs denoting the presence of an on-board math coprocessor (i.e., a 486DX/33 CPU has a built-in math coprocessor, while a 486SX/33 does not).
DX2 (clock doubler)	nomenclature popularly used with the 486 CPUs denoting a clock-doubling CPU. For example, a 486DX2/66 actually used a motherboard clock speed of 33 MHz but ran internally at 66 MHz.
DX4 (clock tripler)	nomenclature popularly used with the 486 CPUs denoting a clock-tripling CPU. For example, a 486DX4/120 actually used a motherboard clock speed of 40 MHz but ran internally at 120 MHz.
EDO (extended data output)	a type of enhanced RAM commonly employed in contemporary PCs.
EIDE (enhanced IDE)	the latest implementation of BIOS-supported hard drive interfaces for the PC. EIDE supports very fast and very large hard drives, as well as ATAPI devices like CD-ROMs, DVD-ROM drives, and tape drives.
EISA (enhanced industry standard architecture)	an older 32-bit bus intended to replace the ISA bus. EISA supported backward compatibility with ISA cards.
EXE	the file extension used to note executable program files under DOS and other popular operating systems.
FAT (file allocation table)	a critical area of every disk which keeps track of the starting cluster of every file.
FDD	an acronym for floppy disk drive; a basic removable storage drive.

FPM (fast page mode)   a type of enhanced RAM commonly employed in contemporary PCs.

GB (gigabyte)   1 billion bytes, or 1 thousand megabytes.

GIF (graphic interchange format)   a common file format used for graphic images often shown on the Internet or other on-line sources.

HDD   an acronym for hard disk drive.

IDC (insulation displacement connector)   the type of long, flat connectors fitted to ribbon cables (often referred to as *ribbon cable connectors*). IDC-type cables are popular with SCSI, EIDE, and FDD drive signal cables.

IDE (integrated drive electronics)   an older form of BIOS-supported hard drive interface for the PC which supported hard drives up to 528MB.

INI   the file extension used for Windows and Windows initialization files. Such files are critical to the proper operation of Windows and its applications (i.e., SYSTEM.INI or WIN.INI).

Intel   the world's leading manufacturer of high-performance CPUs and chipsets for PC applications.

I/O (input/output)   a physical address where hardware can be accessed. Often expressed as a three-character hexadecimal number (i.e., 220h).

IRQ (interrupt request)   a hardware signal line used by some devices to demand the attention of the CPU. There are 16 hardware interrupt lines in a typical PC (expressed IRQ 0 to IRQ 15). Also simply called an *interrupt*.

ISA (industry standard architecture)   a basic, well-established 16-bit bus used with all PCs since the IBM PC/AT. Still a popular interface with relatively low-throughput devices like sound boards and modems.

ISP (internet service provider)   a company which provides full-time or dial-up access to the Internet and is typically used by individuals and small businesses.

jumper   physical connections (often found on motherboards, adapters, and drives) which act like switches and can be used to select various operating parameters for the respective device. Jumpers must be set properly to ensure proper operation of the device and to avoid conflicting with other devices.

K5	a Pentium-equivalent CPU manufactured by AMD.
K6	a Pentium MMX-equivalent CPU manufactured by AMD.
KB (kilobyte)	one thousand bytes.
KBC (keyboard controller)	the controller and BIOS used to interface the keyboard to the motherboard.
L1	a designation used to represent internal cache—cache inside the CPU itself.
L2	a designation used to represent external cache—cache on the motherboard.
LBA (logical block addressing)	an alternative means of addressing clusters on a drive which makes EIDE architecture possible.
M2	a Pentium MMX-equivalent CPU manufactured by Cyrix.
MB (megabyte)	1 million bytes, or 1 thousand kilobytes.
MBR (master boot record)	an area of every bootable disk which holds the information needed to launch an operating system. Loss or corruption of the MBR can prevent a PC from booting.
MCA (micro-channel architecture)	a 32-bit bus popularized in the IBM PS/2 line of computers. The MCA bus offered advanced features like IRQ sharing and bus mastering but never gained broad acceptance in the PC industry.
MHz (megahertz)	millions of cycles (usually clock cycles) per second.
MMX (multimedia extension)	an advancement in Pentium CPU architecture which adds new instructions and other internal enhancements designed to aid in the processing of data-intensive applications (like multimedia).
motherboard (also called a *mainboard* or *mobo*)	the main hardware subassembly in a PC which houses the CPU, chipset, cache, and main memory. Today, the motherboard also offers serial and parallel ports, a USB port, video port, and drive controller ports.
OverDrive	a term coined by Intel used to denote upgrade or enhancement CPUs. For example, it is often possible to upgrade an existing Pentium CPU with a Pentium MMX OverDrive CPU.
PC	an acronym for the personal computer.

PCI (peripheral component interconnect)	a high-performance 32/64-bit bus typically used for drive and video controllers.
Pentium	the generation of Intel microprocessor first released in 1993.
PIO (programmed I/O)	an efficient means of data transfer between two devices but commonly used to denote the PIO mode between a hard drive and controller (i.e., PIO mode 4).
PnP (plug-and-play)	a technique now used commonly in PCs which assigns interrupts and other computing resources automatically each time the PC is powered up rather than assigning resources manually via jumpers. True PnP operation demands PnP-aware devices, BIOS, and operating system in order to be effective.
POST (power-on self-test)	the series of hardware tests performed by the BIOS each time a PC initializes.
RAM (random access memory)	a generic term used to denote any temporary or writeable storage medium.
RISC (reduced instruction set computing)	an alternative computing architecture which trades the versatility of a CPU for processing speed and performance. RISC systems are usually task-specific computers (like the RISC processor used in a laser printer).
ROM (read only memory)	a generic term used to denote any permanent or unchangeable storage medium.
SCSI (small computer system interface)	a bus-level interface used for connecting various different devices to the same signal cable.
SDRAM (synchronous dynamic RAM)	a type of enhanced RAM commonly employed in contemporary PCs.
SIMM (single in-line memory module)	a common memory structure available in 30- and 72-pin versions.
SMP (symmetric multiprocessing)	an advanced computing architecture which supports more than one CPU operating concurrently on the motherboard. This yields little improvement over single-processor designs unless an SMP-aware operating system (such as Windows NT) and SMP-optimized applications are used.
soft boot	restarting the computer using the reset switch or pressing the <Ctrl>+<Alt>+<Del> keys simultaneously. Soft boots provide the fastest restart for a system.

SRAM (Static RAM)	very fast RAM that does not require refresh. Typically it is used for L2 cache.
SX	nomenclature popularly used with the 386 and 486 CPUs denoting the use of a simplified 16-bit data bus.
UART (universal asynchronous receiver/transmitter)	the key component in a serial port or internal modem which is responsible for the conversion of parallel data into serial data for transmittal and conversion of received bits back into parallel form.
UMA (upper memory area)	the 384KB memory space located between 640 and 1024KB inside the first 1MB of RAM. Using memory managers, the UMA can hold drivers and some TSRs, thereby freeing more conventional memory space below 640KB.
UPS (uninterruptable power supply)	a battery-based power source which drives a PC directly and is kept constantly charged by ac from a wall outlet. In the event ac power is lost, there is no interruption switching to battery power because the batteries are supplying power anyway.
USB (universal serial bus)	a relatively new bus architecture designed to simplify the connection of basic peripherals such as mice and keyboards, as well as other devices such as external drives and monitors. USB is widely available but not yet in broad use.
URL (universal resource locator)	the designation used to indicate a Web address. For example, the URL for Dynamic Learning Systems is *http://www.dlspubs.com*. Often, the http:// is omitted for simplicity such as *www.dlspubs.com*.
VESA (video electronics standards association)	an industry group responsible for developing video and display standards, primarily for the PC industry.
VRAM (video RAM)	a form of high-performance memory often used with high-resolution video boards. VRAM uses two different data busses, so it can be written to and read from at the same time.
VLB (Video Local Bus)	a 32-bit bus initially designed to augment video operations but later pressed into service as a general-purpose bus (now largely replaced by the PCI bus).
warm boot	restarting the computer by physically powering down and then turning the PC on again. Warm boots are preferable restart methods when it is necessary to ensure that no drivers or other software remains in memory.

WAV   a file format usually used for digital sound files.

Web   abbreviation for the Internet's World Wide Web.

XT   the designation originally used for IBM PC/XT, later broadened to cover any 8086-based clone computer.

ZIF (zero insertion force)   a type of socket (usually used to hold CPUs) which can be opened or closed using a lever. This simplifies the insertion and removal of high pin count ICs, such as CPUs, and reduces the possibility of accidental damage.

ZIP   a file format used for files that have been compressed with PKWARE's PKZIP utility; also the trade name of Iomega's high-capacity floppy-type Zip drive.

Index

About the Author

Stephen J. Bigelow is the founder and president of Dynamic Learning Systems, a technical writing, research, and publishing company specializing in electronic and PC service topics. Bigelow is the author of 12 feature-length books for TAB/McGraw-Hill, and almost 100 major articles for mainstream electronics magazines such as *Popular Electronics, Electronics NOW, Circuit Cellar INK,* and *Electronic Service & Technology.* Bigelow is also the editor and publisher of *The PC Toolbox,* a premier PC service newsletter for computer enthusiasts and technicians. He is an electrical engineer with a BS EE from Central New England College in Worcester, MA. You can contact the author at:

Dynamic Learning Systems
PO Box 282
Jefferson, MA 01522-0282 USA
Internet: sbigelow@cerfnet.com

Or visit the Dynamic Learning Systems Web site at: *http://www.dlspubs.com*